Handbook of Research on Building Greener Economics and Adopting Digital Tools in the Era of Climate Change

Patricia Ordóñez de Pablos
The University of Oviersity of Oviedo, Spain

A volume in the Advances in Environmental
Engineering and Green Technologies (AEEGT)
Book Series

Published in the United States of America by
    IGI Global
    Engineering Science Reference (an imprint of IGI Global)
    701 E. Chocolate Avenue
    Hershey PA, USA 17033
    Tel: 717-533-8845
    Fax: 717-533-8661
    E-mail: cust@igi-global.com
    Web site: http://www.igi-global.com

Library of Congress Cataloging-in-Publication Data

Names: Ordóñez de Pablos, Patricia, 1975- editor.
Title: Handbook of research on building greener economics and adopting
   digital tools in the era of climate change / Patricia Ordonez de Pablos,
   editor.
Description: Hershey, PA : Engineering Science Reference, [2022] | Includes
   bibliographical references and index. | Summary: "This book offers a
   collection of chapters sharing knowledge and tools to understand global
   challenges like the transition towards a circular, greener, and digital
   economy , proposing actions to advance global agenda toward climate
   friendly businesses and economies"-- Provided by publisher.
Identifiers: LCCN 2022004106 (print) | LCCN 2022004107 (ebook) | ISBN
   9781668446102 (hardcover) | ISBN 9781668446126 (ebook)
Subjects: LCSH: Sustainable development. | Economic policy--Environmental
   aspects. | Technological innovations--Environmental aspects.
Classification: LCC HC79.E5 H328536 2022 (print) | LCC HC79.E5 (ebook) |
   DDC 338.9/27--dc23/eng/20220202
LC record available at https://lccn.loc.gov/2022004106
LC ebook record available at https://lccn.loc.gov/2022004107

This book is published in the IGI Global book series Advances in Environmental Engineering and Green Technologies (AEEGT) (ISSN: 2326-9162; eISSN: 2326-9170)

British Cataloguing in Publication Data
A Cataloguing in Publication record for this book is available from the British Library.

All work contributed to this book is new, previously-unpublished material. The views expressed in this book are those of the authors, but not necessarily of the publisher.

For electronic access to this publication, please contact: eresources@igi-global.com.

Advances in Environmental Engineering and Green Technologies (AEEGT) Book Series

Sang-Bing Tsai
Zhongshan Institute, University of Electronic Science and
Technology of China, China & Wuyi University, China
Ming-Lang Tseng
Lunghwa University of Science and Technology, Taiwan
Yuchi Wang
University of Electronic Science and Technology of China
Zhongshan Institute, China

ISSN:2326-9162
EISSN:2326-9170

MISSION

Growing awareness and an increased focus on environmental issues such as climate change, energy use, and loss of non-renewable resources have brought about a greater need for research that provides potential solutions to these problems. Research in environmental science and engineering continues to play a vital role in uncovering new opportunities for a "green" future.

The **Advances in Environmental Engineering and Green Technologies (AEEGT)** book series is a mouthpiece for research in all aspects of environmental science, earth science, and green initiatives. This series supports the ongoing research in this field through publishing books that discuss topics within environmental engineering or that deal with the interdisciplinary field of green technologies.

COVERAGE

- Waste Management
- Contaminated Site Remediation
- Cleantech
- Green Technology
- Electric Vehicles
- Sustainable Communities
- Air Quality
- Biofilters and Biofiltration
- Industrial Waste Management and Minimization
- Pollution Management

IGI Global is currently accepting manuscripts for publication within this series. To submit a proposal for a volume in this series, please contact our Acquisition Editors at Acquisitions@igi-global.com or visit: http://www.igi-global.com/publish/.

Titles in this Series

For a list of additional titles in this series, please visit: http://www.igi-global.com/book-series/advances-environmental-engineering-green-technologies/73679

Biomass and Bioenergy Solutions for Climate Change Mitigation and Sustainability
Ashok Kumar Rathoure (M/s Akone Services, India) and Shankar Mukundrao Khade (Ajeenkya D Y Patil University, India)
Engineering Science Reference • © 2022 • 340pp • H/C (ISBN: 9781668452691) • US $250.00

Improving Integrated Pest Management for Crop Protection and Food Security
Muhammad Haseeb (Florida A&M University, USA) Lambert H.B. Kanga (Florida A&M University, USA) and Jawwad A. Qureshi (University of Florida, USA)
Engineering Science Reference • © 2022 • 315pp • H/C (ISBN: 9781799841111) • US $215.00

Geoscientific Investigations From the Indian Antarctic Program
Neloy Khare (Ministry of Earth Sciences, India)
Engineering Science Reference • © 2022 • 305pp • H/C (ISBN: 9781668440780) • US $250.00

Handbook of Research on Green Technologies for Sustainable Management of Agricultural Resources
R.S. Sengar (Sardar Vallabhbhai Patel University of Agriculture and Technology, India) Reshu Chaudhary (Sardar Vallabhbhai Patel University of Agriculture and Technology, India) and H.S. Bhadauriya (Jiwaji University, Gwalior, India)
Engineering Science Reference • © 2022 • 637pp • H/C (ISBN: 9781799884347) • US $325.00

Urban Sustainability and Energy Management of Cities for Improved Health and Well-Being
Roberto Alonso González-Lezcano (Universidad CEU San Pablo, Spain)
Engineering Science Reference • © 2022 • 281pp • H/C (ISBN: 9781668440308) • US $250.00

Handbook of Research on Water Sciences and Society
Ashok Vaseashta (International Clean Water Institute, USA & Transylvania University of Brasov, Romania & Academy of Sciences of Moldova, Moldova) Gheorghe Duca (Institute of Chemistry, Moldova State University, Moldova & Academy of Science of Moldova and Romanian Academy, Romania.) and Sergey Travin (Federal Research Center for Chemical Physics and N. N. Semenov of the Russian Academy of Sciences, Russia)
Engineering Science Reference • © 2022 • 728pp • H/C (ISBN: 9781799873563) • US $515.00

701 East Chocolate Avenue, Hershey, PA 17033, USA
Tel: 717-533-8845 x100 • Fax: 717-533-8661
E-Mail: cust@igi-global.com • www.igi-global.com

Editorial Advisory Board

List of Contributors

Table of Contents

Detailed Table of Contents

Chapter 1

Sivasubramanian K., Kristu Jayanti College, India
Madhusudhanan R., Kristu Jayanti College, India
Jaheer Mukthar K. P., Kristu Jayanti College, India
Nirmala M. M., Kristu Jayanti College, India

This chapter highlights the significance of digital policy framework and the practice carried out by the manufacturing industrial sector in India for the sustainable green growth during the digitalization era. The Industry 4.0 has been put forward for an innovative path for industrial rebellion that would support the industry through connectivity, automation, robotics, and machine learning. In this juncture, the industry has to adopt the various technology which brings the comprehensive and sustainable green growth through digitalization in their production process. This chapter follows the descriptive research method through the conceptual framework of the various existing related works done at the national and international levels. A well-defined and comprehensive degree of literature has been collected and structured on the basis of significance of the study. On the whole, the study reveals that the digitalization supports the industries to reduce the emission and maximizes output and profitability of the manufacturing sector with sustainability.

Chapter 2

Bình Nghiêm-Phú, University of Hyogo, Japan
Jillian Rae Suter, Shizuoka University, Japan

From a psychological approach, brands are attached to human personality traits to make them more appealing and facilitate future consumption. Brand personality, however, cannot independently exist. In other words, it must be projected by and transferred through appropriate functional tools and activities. Nevertheless, a precise knowledge of anthropomorphic marketing from a functional approach is missing. In addition, the contribution of artificial intelligence or AI to the implementation of anthropomorphic marketing is unclear. This chapter aims to synthesize the existing literature about these functional practices of anthropomorphic marketing. The outcomes revealed that anthropomorphic marketing was apparent in commercial and social activities. However, the contribution of AI to these marketing practices is limited at present. Based on these observations, this chapter discusses the theoretical and practical implications and the application of anthropomorphic marketing to build a greener economy.

Chapter 3

Asha Thomas, Wroclaw University of Science and Technology, Poland
Rosa Palladino, University of Milan Bicocca, Italy
Chiara Nespoli, University of Bologna "Alma Mater Studiorum", Italy
Maria T. d'agostino, Department of Economics and Law, University of Cassino and
Southern Lazio, Italy
Giuseppe Russo, University of Cassino and Southern Lazio, Italy

Green innovation (GI) refers to an invention that simultaneously benefits the environment and customers. Academics and policymakers have recently focused on GI to understand how innovation and sustainability interact. Indeed, governments and non-governmental organizations pressure businesses to abandon "traditional environmentally harmful products" in favor of green products (GPI) and green process innovations (GPrI). GI research has attracted the attention of many scholars, adopting diverse perspectives, but there has been a lack of publications on the green process and green product innovation (GPI) together. In this way, the current study conducts a literature review and bibliometric analysis to evaluate the "literary corpus" on GI and its various forms. The research provides a comprehensive understanding of GI's various determinants and outcomes. Managers and policymakers can also benefit from the most recent research findings to gain a better understanding of key determinants and outcomes.

Chapter 4

Mohamed Bouteraa, Universiti Utara Malaysia, Malaysia
Raja Rizal Iskandar Raja Hisham, Universiti Utara Malaysia, Malaysia
Zairani Zainol, Universiti Utara Malaysia, Malaysia

Sustainability has become the global need for survival in all scopes due to financial development's side effects that have resulted in environmental destruction. The world leaders have proposed green banking (GB) to reduce carbon footprints from banking operations by promoting paperless financial services based on technology. However, the adoption of GB remains unsatisfactory in the UAE. The study attempts to investigate the determinants of consumers' adoption of GB technology. An exploratory sequential mixed-method approach is employed. The qualitative analysis identified six new challenges facing customers' intention adoption of GB technology: customer awareness, personal innovativeness, bank reputation, security and privacy, system quality, and government support. The preliminary qualitative findings are mostly confirmed by quantitative study whereby customer awareness, personal innovativeness, system quality, and bank reputation significantly impact customers' intention to adopt GB technology. The discussions and implications of these findings are further elaborated.

Chapter 5

Sulayman Al-Qudsi, Kuwaiti Institute for Scientific Research, Kuwait
Husam Arman, Kuwait Institute for Scientific Research, Kuwait
Shaikha Al-Fulaij, Kuwaiti Institute for Scientific Research, Kuwait

Gulf Cooperation Council (GCC) countries, including Kuwait, have been trying to surf the tides of digital transformation to improve their competitiveness and leapfrog into innovation-led economies. The recent turbulence caused by COVID-19 and oil price collapse has accelerated the need for long-term and sustainable strategies. This chapter reviews the desired transformational paths for GCC countries with a special focus on Kuwait. The chapter utilizes original data resulting from empirical work that the authors have recently completed. It will also review existing policies, availability of tech-savvy human resources, and incentive structures that drive firms and institutions to accelerate digitization. Moreover, a comprehensive analysis of the compendium of global indices related to competitiveness, digitization, and innovation will be utilized to trace the journey of GCC countries and the way forward to address urgent global challenges such as the transition towards a digital economy.

Chapter 6

Chandra Sekhar Patro, Department of Management Studies, Gayatri Vidya Parishad College
of Engineering (Autonomous), India

In the digital era, cross-cultural communication in the business environment has become more widespread than ever before. Many organizations have spread their business units overseas not only to strengthen their financial status but also to establish a strong business network worldwide. Cultural awareness shapes the behaviour of business organizations in cross-culturally reflected international markets. Therefore, understanding cultural differences is one of the significant skills for organizations to develop to have a competitive advantage in international business. Digital technologies are changing the business environments through which they interact with their clients. The chapter articulates the changing business environment and the need for cross-cultural communication in the digital environment. The influence of globalization on cross-cultural communication, adoption of various communicative strategies, cultural impacts, issues faced by global managers, overcoming barriers to cultural adaptations, and key areas influencing adoption of digital communication are assessed.

Chapter 7

Nausheen Sodhi, Panjab University, India
Adem Gök, Kırklareli University, Turkey

Renewable energy sources have a minimal detrimental impact on health quality compared to non-renewable energy sources owing to the reduced carbon dioxide emissions that reduce negative externalities of pollution. Health quality can be measured through changes in life expectancy owing to changes in variables directly impacted by renewable energy usage. The chapter analyses the impact of renewable energy on life expectancy through four channels for 23 emerging market economies for the time period 1994-2015 using panel vector auto regression. Four hypotheses were developed for four channels: CO_2 emissions, GDP per capita, technology level, and urbanization. The results conform to all the hypotheses:

increase in renewable energy increases life expectancy by decreasing CO2 emissions and by increasing GDP per capita, technology level, and urbanization. Thus, to increase life expectancy, emerging market economies should increase their renewable energy usage since it reduces per capita CO2 emissions and increases GDP per capita, technological advancement, and urbanization.

Chapter 8

Dr. Supriya Dam, Netaji Subhash Mahavidyalaya, Udaipur, India
Raghunandan Das, Government Degree College, Dharmanagar, India
Sujit Ranjan Das, Government Degree College, Dharmanagar, India

Ever-increasing crude oil prices across the globe coupled with high cost and sustainability concerns attached to hydro power generation led to exploring new avenues for switching to alternate/renewable energy than ever before. The present study sheds light on the prospect of promoting cow dung as an alternative source of energy with respect to tiny mountainous state Tripura and its role on socioeconomic development. Available literature provides the impression that energy from cow dung can be produced from biogas or by burning the dried dung to a power steam engine. The state has been blessed with cow dung across its rural centers, which are primarily used as bio-manures for agriculture and adjoining sectors. Centralized mobilization of these resources for energy generation have already paid rich dividends for states like Tamilnadu, Chattisgarh, Jharkhand, and other parts of India. This study examines the viability and challenges associated with power generation from cow dung for Tripura and presents a case for its adoption.

Chapter 9

Joan Nyika, University of Johannesburg, South Africa & Technical University of Kenya, Kenya
Megersa Olumana Dinka, University of Johannesburg, South Africa

The relevance of sustainability in contemporary society is on a growing trend owing to the predominance of economic development and environmental conservation plans amidst challenges of climate change. Eco-efficiency is a growing tool to qualify economic and environmental sustainability. In this chapter, the trends of eco-efficiency over the last three decades were evaluated in a bibliometric analysis from publications in the Web of Science database. An analysis of the publications, the journals they were published in, keywords used, and citations among other aspects was done using the VOSviewer software. Findings showed that the eco-efficiency concept was predominantly applied in the environmental sciences and technology fields among others. The growth in the concept was exponential, and the majority of publications were from developed countries. The application of the concept is a roadmap to better resource management and sustainable development.

Chapter 10

The Sustainable Development Goals are a bold pledge by leaders of the world to establish a global agenda that encompasses aspects of the economy, environment, and society. India as a UN member has approved the "Agenda 2030" comprising 17 goals and 169 targets. This study intends to measure India's progress toward the SDGs by evaluating the performance of all Indian States/UTs using the NITI Aayog's SDG India Index versions 1.0, 2.0, and 3.0 produced in compliance with international standards. The findings of the study suggest a consistent improvement in the overall score of India from 57 in 2017-18 to 66 in 2020-21. This suggests a considerable improvement in state and UTs performance during the tenure. The study emphasizes that if nations have to adhere to the SDG goals by 2030, robust frameworks and indexes have to be designed and implemented in an effective manner.

Chapter 11

Considering the region is highly vulnerable to climate change, all ASEAN Member States have ratified the Paris Agreement and agreed to the Regional Roadmap for Implementing the 2030 Agenda for Sustainable Development in Asia and the Pacific. To provide the ASEAN taxonomy for sustainable finance, Islamic finance should be considered as a part of it. Therefore, this chapter will provide an Islamic Green Financing Taxonomy to help stakeholders determine which activities qualify as sustainable and which instrument is suitable for the activity. As a leading community in the world that drives the global halal industry, ASEAN also can be a best practice for implementing Islamic Green Financing. Through literature study, this chapter purposes to (1) describe the framework of ASEAN for the circular economy and sustainable energy in tackling the climate change, (2) describe the ASEAN taxonomy, and (3) describe the proposed Islamic Green Financing Taxonomy.

Chapter 12

Digital inclusion in banking services was drafted to provide fast and uninterrupted services to a broad pool of customers with an aim to extend financial services to unprivileged groups. Competitive edge associated made it a vibrant policy for bankers across the state with varying degrees of application to suit the customer needs. The present study explores the extent of digital banking interface help improve the status of rural banking in Tripura on the basis of secondary data. Taking cue from four CRISIL Inclusix in view (i.e., branch penetration, deposit penetration, credit penetration, insurance penetration), results are indicative of Tripura's progress in rural front becoming one of the best performing state among NESs. The study again specifies that proper policy measures, vis-a-vis its implementation could place the state amongst top five digitally inclusive states in India and also promote much desired cashless economy and transparency among others.

Chapter 13

Eda Ustaoglu, Gebze Technical University, Turkey
Arif Cagdas Aydınoglu, Gebze Technical University, Turkey

This chapter focuses on the estimation of marginal and total external costs of road transportation in Turkey in terms of accidents, air pollution, climate change, noise, and traffic congestion. The study estimates marginal external costs for cars, light commercial vehicles (LCVs), heavy duty vehicles (HDVs), busses, and motorcycles, which comprise total vehicle fleet stock of the Turkish road transport sector. The researchers reviewed the literature of both local and international studies for the quantification and monetisation of the specified external costs of road transport. This will provide a base for the future studies on Turkish transport research and transport policy appraisal guidelines. The authors conclude that accidents are the most important externality of road use and that local air pollution and congestion appear to be more important than noise and climate change. This implies that priority should be given to road accidents, air pollution, and congestion alongside noise and global warming.

Chapter 14

Xuan Tran, University of West Florida, USA
Faith Grover, University of West Florida, USA
Kenzie Leeser, University of West Florida, USA
Kiara Bly, University of West Florida, USA
Mitchell Whelan, University of West Florida, USA
Brieana Cassidy, University of West Florida, USA
Nhi Truong, Danang Vocational Tourism College, Vietnam

Although disruptive innovation is a shortcut to increase revenue by technology, it has been applied little in the hotel industry. The purpose of this study is to examine how disruptive innovation has been applied in hotels via adopting a digital tool of linguistic inquiry word count (LIWC) to explore guests' unconscious needs to increase hotel revenue. The study has been based on the Maslow's hierarchy and the McClelland's motivation to examine the relationships between hotel criteria and guests' unconscious needs to increase hotel revenue. The study sample includes 10918 comments from online travel agency websites of hotels in the southeast destinations of the United States from January 2015 to October 2016. Findings from canonical correlation analyses indicate that hotel value and cleanliness would attract guests with a high-power motive whereas hotel service and quality would attract guests with a high affiliation motive. Finally, hotel room and location would attract guests with a high achievement motive. Implications have been discussed.

    Subhanil Banerjee, Department of Economics, School of Humanities, KR Mangalam
        University, Gurgram, India
    Shilpi Gupta, Amity University, Raipur, India
    Souren Koner, Amity University, Raipur, India

The concept of sustainable development has been introduced following the Brundtland Commission's report "Our Common Future." Though significant volume of literature does exist on the various aspects and impacts of the mentioned commission, the actual impact of the commission on the environment for which it was initiated has never been considered by any academicians. The chapter tries to quantify the qualitative aspect of environment through per capita emission of CO_2 over the years. It shows that the concerned commission is successful in bringing down the rate of growth of per capita CO_2 emissions, but it is yet to be negative. The chapter opines that to restore the resilience of the environment and to make ecology and economy synonymous again, further efforts are needed.

    Noor Fareen Abdul Rahim, Universiti Sains Malaysia, Malaysia
    Mohd. Nizam Sarkawi, Universiti Utara Malaysia, Malaysia
    Abdul Rahman Jaaffar, Universiti Utara Malaysia, Malaysia
    Jauriyah Shamsuddin, Universiti Utara Malaysia, Malaysia
    Yashar Salamzadeh, Sunderland University, UK
    Sameh Mohamed Abdelhay, Umm al Quwain University, UAE

Industry 4.0 is revolutionizing the way companies work and integrate enabling technologies, including the internet of things (IoT), cloud computing, analytics, and AI and machine learning, to the production facilities and entire operations or on delivering their services. Advanced sensors, embedded software, and robotics are used in smart factories to collect and analyze data, allowing for better decision-making by more predictive analysis. Furthermore, the COVID-19 pandemic posed challenges to the society to adapt to a new reality. While the rest of the world searches for answers, Industry 4.0 technology has become a vital component of how we survived the pandemic and how we will survive in the post-pandemic future. The main purpose of this chapter is to understand the future and reality of jobs in IR 4.0. There are several ways IR 4.0 will reinvent jobs in the future. For the readers, the authors divided the chapter into the following sections: "How IR 4.0 Reinvents Jobs," "Types of Jobs in IR 4.0," and "Conclusion."

Preface

INTRODUCTION

Cities, economies, and societies around the world need to address some urgent global challenges, like climate change, biodiversity loss or the transition towards a greener and digital economy (Chang, Shih and Peng, 2022; Jiang *et al.*, 2019; Khanra *et al.*, 2022; Nayal et al., 2022). It is important that economies are transformed into resources-efficient, competitive, and resilient ones. In a context of rapid change, transformative technologies like artificial intelligence, blockchain or Internet of Things play a key role in this digital transition (Almunawar, Islam and Ordóñez, 2022; European Commission, 2021; OECD, 2019, 2020; Ordóñez, 2021; Ordóñez *et al.*, 2021, 2022a,b; Zhang et *al.*, 2019) across a wide range of areas (economy, education, healthcare innovation, society). Additionally, new skills will be needed for the new jobs in the Digital Age (Ordóñez *et al.*, 2022c). These challenges are an opportunity to change the economic model and generate new opportunities for innovation and research, create jobs and build a more resilient economy.

OBJECTIVES OF THE BOOK

It is important to understand digital, climate and environmental challenges and turn them into opportunities for companies and societies, creating more resilient and inclusive economies and societies.

This book offers a collection of chapters sharing knowledge and tools to understand global challenges like the transition towards a circular, greener, and digital economy, combat climate change, propose actions to advance the agenda towards climate friendly businesses and economies, foster cooperation among researchers, companies, and policy makers to share national initiatives and disseminate relevant knowledge, anticipate the demand for new skills and jobs in the digital age, actionable recommendations for policy makers and more.

TARGET AUDIENCE

Professors in academia, deans, heads of departments, director of masters, students (undergraduate and postgraduate level), politicians, policy makers, corporate heads of firms, senior general managers, managing directors, information technology directors and managers, libraries, etc.

CONTENTS OF THE BOOK

The book presents a collection of 16 book chapters addressing key topics like circular and digital economy, digital transformation, electronic payment services, the development of a national innovation system, green issues and sustainability and covering different countries like India, Turkey, UAE and USA, ASEAN region, and some emerging economies.

Patricia Ordóñez de Pablos
The University of Oviedo, Spain

REFERENCES

Almunawar, M. N., Islam, Z., & Ordóñez de Pablos, P. (2022). *Digital Transformation Management: Challenges and Futures in the Asian Digital Economy*. Routledge. doi:10.4324/9781003224532

Chang, C.-H., Shih, M.-Y., & Peng, H.-J. (2022). Enhancing entrepreneurial opportunity recognition: Relationships among green innovative capability, green relational capability, and co-innovation behavior. *Business Strategy and the Environment*, *31*(4), 1358–1368. doi:10.1002/bse.2959

European Commission. (2021). *A European Green Deal. Striving to be the first climate neutral continent*. https://ec.europa.eu/info/strategy/priorities-2019-2024/european-green-deal_en

Jiang, S., Zhang, X., Cheng, Y., Xu, D., Ordoñez De Pablos, P., & Wang, X. (2019). Dynamic impact of social network on knowledge contribution loafing in mobile collaboration: A hidden Markov model. *Journal of Knowledge Management*, *23*(9), 1901–1920. doi:10.1108/JKM-10-2018-0641

Khanra, S., Kaur, P., Joseph, R. P., Malik, A., & Dhir, A. (2022). A resource-based view of green innovation as a strategic firm resource: Present status and future directions. *Business Strategy and the Environment*, *31*(4), 1395–1413. doi:10.1002/bse.2961

OECD. (2019). *Measuring the Digital Transformation: A Roadmap for the Future*. OECD Publishing. doi:10.1787/9789264311992-

OECD. (2020). *Roadmap toward a Common Framework for Measuring the Digital Economy*. https://www.oecd.org/sti/roadmap-toward-a-common-framework-for-measuring-the-digital-economy.pdf

Nayal, K., Raut, R. D., Yadav, V. S., Priyadarshinee, P., & Narkhede, B. E. (2022). The impact of sustainable development strategy on sustainable supply chain firm performance in the digital transformation era. *Business Strategy and the Environment*, *31*(3), 845–859. doi:10.1002/bse.2921

Ordóñez de Pablos, P. (2021). *Handbook of Research on Developing Circular, Digital, and Green Economies in Asia*. IGI Global.

Ordóñez de Pablos, P., Zhang, X., Almunawar, M. N., & Gayo Labra, J. E. (2021). *Handbook of Research on Big Data, Green Growth, and Technology Disruption in Asian Companies and Societies*. IGI Global.

Ordóñez de Pablos, P., Zhang, X., & Almunawar, N. (2022a). *Green, Circular, and Digital Economies as Tools for Recovery and Sustainability*. IGI Global.

Ordóñez de Pablos, P., Zhang, X., & Almunawar, M. (2022b). *Handbook of Research on Artificial Intelligence and Knowledge Management in Asia's Digital Economy*. IGI Global.

Ordóñez de Pablos, P., Zhang, X., & Almunawar, M. (2022c). *Education Institutions, Skills and Jobs in the Digital Era: Towards a More Inclusive and Resilient Society*. IGI Global.

Zhang, X., Wang, X., Zhao, H., Ordóñez de Pablos, P., Sun, Y., & Xiong, H. (2019). An effectiveness analysis of altmetrics indices for different levels of artificial intelligence publications. *Scientometrics*, *119*(3), 1311–1344. doi:10.100711192-019-03088-x

Chapter 1

Digitalization Policy and Practice Towards the Comprehensive and Sustainable Green Growth of the Industrial Sector With Special Reference to the Indian Economy

Sivasubramanian K.
ⓘ https://orcid.org/0000-0001-6137-0847
Kristu Jayanti College, India

Jaheer Mukthar K. P.
ⓘ https://orcid.org/0000-0002-7888-0242
Kristu Jayanti College, India

Madhusudhanan R.
Kristu Jayanti College, India

Nirmala M. M.
Kristu Jayanti College, India

ABSTRACT

This chapter highlights the significance of digital policy framework and the practice carried out by the manufacturing industrial sector in India for the sustainable green growth during the digitalization era. The Industry 4.0 has been put forward for an innovative path for industrial rebellion that would support the industry through connectivity, automation, robotics, and machine learning. In this juncture, the industry has to adopt the various technology which brings the comprehensive and sustainable green growth through digitalization in their production process. This chapter follows the descriptive research method through the conceptual framework of the various existing related works done at the national and international levels. A well-defined and comprehensive degree of literature has been collected and structured on the basis of significance of the study. On the whole, the study reveals that the digitalization supports the industries to reduce the emission and maximizes output and profitability of the manufacturing sector with sustainability.

DOI: 10.4018/978-1-6684-4610-2.ch001

INTRODUCTION

Green industrial growth is expected be a key driver for the economic development and formulation environmental policy. Economic growth and development in the era of industrialization has been reached at the cost of severe over utilization non-renewable exhaustive energy sources. The green industrial policy framework could able to support transformation to economic system that equalize environmental sustainability and generate wealth for the sustainable future too. Industrial sector production measures the level of output of various businesses combined in the manufacturing segments of the economy. Industry is the important segment and records 78 percent of the national output. The widest segments within the industries are such as metals, which constitutes 13 percent of the total production, twelve percent from refined petroleum, chemical products consist of 8 percent, food motor vehicle, machinery and pharmaceutical constitutes 5 percent respectively. The green businesses are classified as two categories namely environmental goods considered as renewable energy, green technology and pollution abatement technique. Secondly, creation of green businesses (Khanna, 2020). The mining registered with fourteen percent of the total manufacturing. Industrial sector emerged as one of the major growing sectors among the other segments in India. The year-on-year production of industrial commodities has been increased by 3.2 percent up to October 2021 and it further rose to 3.3 percent at the end of September 2021 (MOSPI, 2021). India is one of the fastest growing industrial and manufacturing hub and playing a key function in the global economy. The concept of make in India scheme is the supporting a lot to enhance the industrial capacity (Pilicherla, et al., 2021). Industrialization is an integral part of the economic growth of a nation and presents a phase where revenue, productivity and increase in employment. Manufacturing industries are the second biggest contributor to the nation's discharge about 25 percent of the total GDP. The manufacturing sector activity is a single biggest consumer of delivered energy, as a result (Biswas, et al., 2019). The monetary market didn't always hold adequate information to precisely assess the hazards tangled in the financing of new business projects, and financial mediators may henceforth fail to clutch profitable openings, making government involvement is compulsory. The markets generally fail to adequately cost the environmental influence of economic activity, and this could lead to economically feasible whereas socially unwanted economic activity. The state has a vital role in flattening the playing arena for green businesses, positioning private revenues more carefully with social returns (Schwarzer, 2013). In this backdrop, the present chapter is constructed reveal the industrial growth, significance of industries, pollution, controlling measures of pollution and green growth policy for the sustainability. This chapter is organized with introduction, reviewing of dimensions of existing studies and analysis with relevant data. Based on the comprehensive study expresses the similarities and dissimilarities of the existing works. Based on the analytical review, the present study concluded with major findings of the study.

This chapter work follows the descriptive research method through the conceptual framework of the various existing related works done at national and international level. A well-defined and comprehensive degree of literature has been collected and structure on the basis of significance of the study. It describes the various dimensions of this chapter such as concepts, meaning, and definitions of various dichotomy used in this chapter. It also moves with the direction of identifying and analyzing the concepts of digital transformation, significance of industry, role of government, industrial pollution, industrial policy, green growth policy, and sustainability. This conceptual method of work is used to bring out the existing practice and suggest suitable area for the development of the existing findings through evaluating the present works. Based on the collection, arrangement and evaluation of various works would bring out the in-depth knowledge of the specific areas such as digitalization, industrialization, pollution, ecological issues, government policy and sustainability. The evaluation of various published research works on this present topic shown to identify the similarity, links and differentiation of results and conclusion of the respective authors. Besides, the conceptual framework, this chapter is also brought out certain empirical evidences through the secondary data sources from published articles and government reposts.

Objectives of this Chapter

To understand the significance of digitalization in industrial sector for green growth in the economy.

To emphasize globalization, industrialization, industrial pollution, and environment.

To review the digital policy, process, practice for the green growth and environmental sustainability.

To suggest extended industrial growth through environmental digital policy framework to conservation of natural resources and atmosphere.

Significance of this Study

The industry 4.0 is identified as the transitional influence for nation's industrial competitiveness. The India's industrial sector required to implement the revolution at the earliest through the digital technology and hike the performance of the sector. (Dutta et al., 2020). This conceptual research work is had been carried out to bring out the in-depth knowledge on various key touch points of the green industrial policy at regional, national and also at international level. This work is becoming important because of the environmental sustainability and green growth. It is also quite important to emphasize the various existing policy measures to follow green growth. Environmental sustainability can be possible to through proper use of digital technology in the industry. In this juncture, this chapter is aims to suggest industrialists and policy makers for innovative green growth policy.

Digitalization Policy and Practice in India

Globalization, Industrialization and Environment

Industrialization takes place to reach the economic progress and it resulted in the global ecological damage. While the effects of industrial sector activity on the environment are a main concern in both developed and developing nations (Park, 1998). The fastest economic growth has been achieved after the globalization by many developing nations, have forced considerable social costs and it has become a main hazard to the sustainable growth. Though, it also extremely significant for developing nations to reach a great level of economic revival to alleviate their social and economic issues. The textile manufacturing sector affects the environmental quality of the study area (Nelliyat, 2007). The environmental degradation and depletion of natural resources are the most concerning concept in the current situation. As the population growth and technological advancement impact negatively on the ecological systems (Gogoi, 2013). The industrialization leads to the growth of assorted areas such as agriculture, industrial segments, automobile, chemicals and mining. This have been surely developed the economic status of India and enhance the standard of the people in the nation. Similarly, it has led to the degrade the quality of environment. The main cause of environmental damage due to the deforestation and the industrialization. The rapid rise of industrial growth resulted in the hike of emission of damaging effluents and pollute the natural resources. It is also responsible for global warming and depletion of ground water (Bhandari & Garg. 2016). The major reason for the environmental depletion is the modern industrialization (Chopra, 2016). Industrial pollution has become the major reason for the depletion of the environmental condition which makes many chain reactions on the globe. It causes for the natural disasters (Gulati, 2009). The globalization has freed the industrial operations from inherent drawbacks of protectionism and determined international platform with a great range of avenues and issues. The local business houses looking into various implications such as technological advancement, research, capacity enhancement and resource allocation to meet the global competition (Roy, 2017).

Industrial Pollution and Environment

Pollution created through the industrialization is become the major issues of developing nations. In India, there is no major reforms on environmental issues has been initiated to control the impact (Khan, 2015).

Industrial Emission Reduction for Sustainable Development

Industrial pollution caused by the emission produced from the industrial activities and those smoke stacks floated into the atmosphere directly from industrial plants. Industrial emissions are the most vulnerable pollutant that affects the quality of the air in many countries (Cricelli, & Strazzullo, 2021). It is recorded as one of the main air pollutants and also waste gasses produced from various economic activities cause a health and environmental crisis to the people and atmosphere respectively. Moreover, because of the industrial emissions, the health and safety of employees working in those industries are also significantly affected. India made a significant voluntary obligation for plummeting the emission strength of gross domestic product for the year 2020 with 20 to 25 percent as compare to the year 2005. The industrial approach in India is based on cost-effective application of resources to reduce the emission level (Shukla., and Dhar, 2016). Increasing inclusive persistence of the fuel-based energy system plays a vital role in the upward move in carbon discharge. Due to the urbanization and transportation, the level of air pollution arises along with the growth of industries (Verma, *et al.*, 2017). According to United Nations Industrial Development Organization (2010), the world is facing challenging times for the organization due to huge use of raw materials from nature.

An international climate agreement should find measures to catalyze deep discharge reduces in the developing nations like India, both in the short and long term. This would not be necessarily required, hence, that the nation bear the economic burden for global warming and climate change mitigation. The global financing mechanisms and other forms of partnership could act an important place in develop the widespread transfer and employment of appropriate low-emissions of industrial technology. This can be possible the close and strong partnership with the highly industrialized nations, especially the European Union. India and the European Union voiced various perspectives on some important challenges related to a futuristic climate change structure. Normally, European Union seems into the futuristic and look into India as an important element of greenhouse gas emission which should be brought to a futuristic international climate agreement through discharge commitments and entire participation in the international carbon markets. In contrast, India seems at the past and argues that grown nations bear entire responsibility to pay for mitigation and adaptation in developing nations, based not only on the accountability of greenhouse gas pollution, it also depends on their enhanced capacity to pay and significantly greater per capita discharge. India is undergoing a tremendous expansion in energy production and power creation and subsequently greenhouse gas discharge is composed to increase enormously. India is normally very supportive in making efforts for the industrialized nations, such as European Union, to reduce the carbon discharge in India, based on the resources are not diverted from the development support and effort themselves for the environmental progress (Atteridge *et al.,* 2009). Modern industrial sector witnessed a countless improvement since the industrial growth during the 18th century. The introduction of industry 4.0 evolves a rapid movement of industrial growth with digital technology (Gadre, Monika., and Deoskar, Aruna, 2020). For a better understanding of industry 4.0, it is a very powerful and revolutionary initiative for the technical advancement, economic growth and demographic situations for the process of sustainable green growth with digitalization (Bhat, T. P, 2020). The circular economy with sustainability in business practice as emerging area of research that focuses on industry 4. 0 for sustainable green growth (Khan, *et al.,* 2021).

Comprehensive and Sustainability Development

Digital transformation provides admittance to a combined network of fallow big data with possible advantages for society and environment. The growth of smart computers connected with the internet of things could create unique avenue to deliberately address challenges associated with UN SDGs to assure an equitable, sustainable atmosphere, healthier society. This ideology enables the opportunities that the digital initiation in industry could provide towards establishing a sustainable globe for the future (Mondejar, *et al.,* 2021). Digital transformation is a key element of sustainable growth and development of the city's economic and social dynamics with the potential to foster climate-friendly urban atmosphere and societies. The industrial revolution 4.0 has evidently seen the enhanced application of digital framework for several fields and at various heights. High-defined digital equipment, and digital platforms have been deployed to enhance higher level of output with sustainability. The digitalization in industry supports more effective and early cautionary and security systems to minimize the climatic hazards (Balogun, et al., 2020 & Ceipek, et al., 2020). It reveals that the digitalization is a key driver for the sustainability in the industrial sector. In the process of development, the digital technology (Gomez, et al, 2021 & Reserve Bank of India, 2021).

Industrial Policy for Green Growth

Industrial policy is posterior on the schedule and the accord is that it should be varied from the past. Redefining the industrial policy becomes the integral part of the environmental sustainability (Aiginger, 2014). The green growth policy is the quest by the respective governments to achieve the nation's economic and environmental excellence in industrial sector for the global competitiveness. It normally differs slightly from traditional industrial policy of the respective government. It shown in private sector industries to enhance the environmental benefit of the society. Green industrial policy is significantly increasing in the usage by many governments in developed and developing nations and it led to enhance the real green growth of the countries in the near future. To achieve this target the alternative way of energy sources to be used for the industrial production. It is reported that Indian environmental and industrial policies for increasing the contribution of renewable energy sources to achieve the social, economic, and the industrial goals. It concludes that green growth is possible based on the green policy initiatives to match the new challenges (Ganesan, *et al.,* 2014 & Government of India, 2015). The industrial policy for the green growth, therefore, has a key role to act in the systematic digital and technological transformation towards for a carbonless future. So, the green industrial policy assures the carbon free industrial growth for economic development without harming the environment (Anzolin, Guendalina., and Lebdioui, Amir (2021).

The Green Industrial Policy

With enhanced indication for the harmful effects of predictable economic movement on the ecological, policy-makers across the world have been observing for traditions to arouse more ecological friendly developmental route for their economies. The green industries are started booming in many developing countries in the recent decades, the policy makers are mainly resorting to greener industrial policies to stand-in their internal development and statuette out a competitive structure for their countries. Hence, the green technology industries are generally the new and start-up industries at the entry level, with all the behavioral characteristic of the conservative newer manufacturing industries and based on same avenues and issues of elevating them. Later, given the non-ability of markets to cost ecological externalities, greener industries are, on a greater extent, determined on the basis of policy framework that help the market by encouragement of both supply and demand. The role of government in encouraging for a greater transformation of green industries. The structure of green manufacturing and market size is purely determined on the basis of appropriate green initiative policy of government. The industrialization promotes economic growth and creation of employment opportunities, the industrial revolution has massive potential to transform the society, increasing living standards and drill-down the difference between the poor and rich peoples in the countries (UNIDO, 2010). Complex nature of the green transition process requires a appropriate policy process could able to respond to these issues. The requirement of such appropriate approach could not be a high impacting now-a-day. The systematic policy formulation, have two important dimensions such as learning from others for a particular period of time and cycles of learning must be put in appropriate time and place (Lutkenhorst, et al., 2014). The green technology approach in developed and developing nations a reveal a green transformation (Hallsworth, 2012, and Kemp, Rene., and Never, Babette (2017). The government of India has to focus more on the use of sustainable, effective and affordable energy resources for the healthy green growth in the industrial sector (Gopinath, 2016).

This piece of conceptual analysis identifies the significance of globalization policy in generating trade advantages and industrial growth of India. It also measures the various waste generated from the industrial output. The industrial process and productivity are based on the usage of the input of various industrial needs. Various related literature has been reviewed on industrial development, industrial pollution and industrial policy for the sustainable green growth in India (Sharma, 2015).

Along with the above stated literature survey, this chapter is also analyzing certain environmental pollutant namely, CO_2 emission of manufacturing industries.

Table 1. Comparative CO_2 emission level

CO2 Emission Level	1868.6
Electricity & Heat Production	944.6
Other Energy for Own use	43.1
Industry & Construction	492.9
Total Transportation	222.3
Road Transport	206.4
Other Sectors	165.7
Residential Use	87.2

Source: IEA CO2 Discharge from fuel burning

The above table expresses the comparative CO_2 emission level of the country with total CO_2 level. The aggregate level of the emission includes all the sectoral emission recorded as 1868.6 parts per million by volume (PPMV). Among the total emission level, 944.6 PPMV, the other energy sources for the own use contributing 43.1 PPMV. The second largest portion of the CO2 emission arises due to the industry and construction sector with 429.9 PPMV next to electricity and heath generation sector. All transportation purposes records 222.3, other sectors with 165.7 and the residential use with 87.2 PPMV. Among the total transportation Co2 emission, the road transport contributes 206.4 PPMV.

Table 2. Energy and emission intensity of selected countries compared to India

Country	Energy Intensity	Emission Intensity
Brazil	0.38	0.68
China	0.3	1.79
European Union	0.16	0.57
India	0.36	2
Japan	0.19	1.03
Korea	0.14	0.59
Russia	0.38	1.09

Source: IEA, World Energy Outlook, 2018.
Note: Energy intensity measured in terms of million tons of steel & Emission intensity measured in terms of MtCO2

Industrial emissions are the most vulnerable pollutant that affects the quality of the air in many countries. It is recorded as one of the main air pollutants and also waste gasses produced from various economic activities cause a health and environmental crisis to the people and atmosphere respectively. Moreover, because of the industrial emissions, the health and safety of employees working in those industries are also significantly affected. Table. 2 emphasizes the energy intensity of various countries such as Brazil, China, European Union, India, Japan, Korea and Russia. India is having comparatively higher energy intensity next to Brazil and Russia with 0.36 as compare to 0.38 $MtCO_2$ But on the other hand, the emission intensity is registered with 2 $MtCO_2$.

Table 3. Global level investment in renewable and fuel capacity in developing and developed nations

Year	India & China	Other Developing Countries	Developed Countries	World Total
2009	35.3	17	94	146.3
2010	43.6	24	145.1	212.7
2011	51.4	26.7	186.5	264.6
2012	61.6	33.9	144.5	240
2013	66.4	26.1	119.3	211.8
2014	91.1	32.4	141.7	265.2
2015	126.9	39.6	133.9	300.4
2016	116	29	135	280
2017	156.3	39.7	119.2	315.2
2018	101.9	50.7	127.5	280.1
2019	92.7	59.5	130	282.2

Source: Global Status Report. Renewables 2020.

Figure 1.

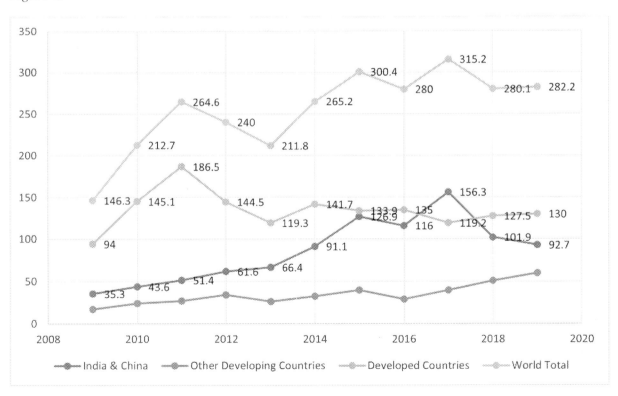

The countries like India and China have started moving ahead on investment for renewable energy use for the industrial purposes. The investment on green growth has consistently increased from 2009 to 2019 time period. Investment level has little declined at the end of 2019, due to global pandemic crisis. The other developing countries had a very progressive way of increase in the investment. It is very evident from the data that it has increased consistently even in the pandemic period. It shows the countries are very keen on transforming into green growth. While, looking into the global scenario, there is no doubt that the investment on renewable energy has grown up considerably and consistently for the sustainable industrial growth.

Sustainable and environmentally friendly production of industrial commodities has initiated by Ministry of Environment. The major aim of this project is to alleviate a number of environmental and climate change problems, particularly with the focus of industrial waste discharge and management. The policy is working towards the reduction of severe ecological issues and promote resource efficiency in production of Industries. The environmental policy initiatives regarded with the following goals such as environment-oriented technological inclusion, establishing conductive status at both national and state levels and initiation for knowledge management and diffusion (Shulka, & Dhar, 2016). The sustainable environmental policy is also aims to reach on conveyance, water treatment, reusing of certain resources, recycling of waste water, and promotion of renewable energies. Based on the policy initiatives and practices from developed countries emphasizes the importance of green industries. The environmental laws and regulatory bodies for the law enforcement control the pollution and regulate the industries to shift for reducing the pollution inputs. Various policy approaches including energy standards, finance opportunities for renewable inputs, tax credits and incentives. By initiating regulatory relief for certain efforts, along with technical support and government recognition, the industries are stated adopting environmentally friendly management provisions, pollution control and prevention methodologies and also other green technologies. The environmental policy formulation is kept to be separated from the process of economic planning and arrangement and there is no connection between economic tools implemented to reach growth, poverty alleviation and environmental protection. Based on the analysis between economic development and ecological issues, it is noticed that the nations have to move towards sustainable practices (Dev, et al 2020).

CONCLUSION

The industrial waste is also on the other side, contributing a major portion of various ecological issues. Similarly, the over use of non-renewable energy resources for the industrial output is too becomes the challenge for the environment. In this juncture, the industry has to adopt the various technology which brings the comprehensive and sustainable green growth through digitalization in their production process. To carry out the present study, various existing related research works reviewed and particular secondary data has been collected for analysis to infer the relationship among the variables. The industrial growth of India has been calculated in both pre-implementations of digitalization and post-digitalization practices. In this backdrop, the present chapter is constructed reveal the industrial growth, significance of industries, pollution, controlling measures of pollution and green growth policy for the sustainability. This chapter is organized with introduction, reviewing of dimensions of existing studies and analysis with relevant data. Based on the comprehensive study expresses the similarities and dissimilarities of the existing works. The industrialization leads to the growth of assorted areas such as agriculture, industrial segments, automobile, chemicals and mining. This have been surely developed the economic status of India and enhance the standard of the people in the nation. Similarly, it has led to the degrade the quality of environment. The main cause of environmental damage due to the deforestation and the industrialization (Prabhat, & Zetterberg, 2009). The rapid rise of industrial growth resulted in the hike of emission of damaging effluents and pollute the natural resources. Industrial emissions are the most vulnerable pollutant that affects the quality of the air in many countries. It is recorded as one of the main air pollutants and also waste gasses produced from various economic activities cause a health and environmental crisis to the people and atmosphere respectively. Moreover, because of the industrial emissions, the health and safety of employees working in those industries are also significantly affected. The green growth policy is the quest by the respective governments to achieve the nation's economic and environmental excellence in industrial sector for the global competitiveness. It normally differs slightly from traditional industrial policy of the respective government. It shown in private sector industries to enhance the environmental benefit of the society. Green industrial policy is significantly increasing in the usage by many governments in developed and developing nations and it led to enhance the real green growth of the countries in the near future. To achieve this target the alternative way of energy sources to be used for the industrial production. The industrialization leads to the growth of assorted areas such as agriculture, industrial segments, automobile, chemicals and mining. This have been surely developed the economic status of India and enhance the standard of the people in the nation. Similarly, it has led to the degrade the quality of environment. The main cause of environmental damage due to the deforestation and the industrialization. The digitalization in industry supports more effective and early cautionary and security systems to minimize the climatic hazards. On the whole, the study reveals that the digitalization supports the industries to reduce the emission and maximizes output and profitability of the manufacturing sector with sustainability. More importantly, the industrial green policy also evidently supports the manufacturing sector for the promotion of digital technology application for the business enhancement.

REFERENCES

Aiginger, K. (2014). *Industrial Policy for a Sustainable Growth Path. Policy Paper No.13.* Welfare Wealth Work for Europe.

Anzolin, G., & Lebdioui, A. (2021). Three Dimensions of Green Industrial Policy in the Context of Climate Change and Sustainable Development. *European Journal of Development Research, 33*(2), 371–405. doi:10.105741287-021-00365-5

Atteridge, A., Axberg, G. N., Goel, N., Kumar, A., Lazarus, M., Ostwald, M., Polycarp, C., Tollefsen, P., Tovanger, A., Upadhyaya, Balogun, D. M., Sharma, R., Shekhar., Balmes, Meheng, D., Arshad, A., & Salehi, P. (2020). Assessing the Potentials of Digitalization as a tool for Climate Change Adaptation and Sustainable Development in Urban Centers. *Sustainable Cities and Society, 53.*

Bhandari, D., & Garg, R. K. (2016). *Effects of Industrialization on Environment (Indian Scenario).* Academic Press.

Bhat, T. P. (2020). *India and Industry 4.0.* Working Paper. Institute for Studies in Industrial Development.

Biswas, T., Genesan, K., & Ghosh, A. (2019). Sustainable Manufacturing for India's Low-carbon Transition. Four Bets for Hard-to-abate Sectors. Issue Brief. Council of Energy, Environment and Water.

Ceipek, R., Hautz, J., & Petruzzelli, A. M., Massis, D. A., & Marzler, K. (2020). A Motivation and Ability Perspective on Engagement in Emerging Digital Technologies: The Case of Internet of Things Solutions. *Long Range Planning*.

Chopra, R. (2016). Environmental Degradation in India: Causes and Consequences. *International Journal of Applied Environmental Sciences, 11*(6), 1593–1601.

Cricelli, L., & Strazzullo, S. (2021). The Economic Aspect of Digital Sustainability: A Systematic Review. Systematic Review. *Sustainability, 13*(8241), 1–15. doi:10.3390u13158241

Dev, N. K., Shankar, R., & Qaiser, F. H. (2020). Industry 4.0 and Circular Economy: Operational Excellence for Sustainable Reverse Supply Chain Performance. *Resources, Conservation and Recycling, 153*.

Dutta, G., Kumar, R., Sindhwani, R., & Singh, R. (2020). Digital Transformation Priorities of India's Discrete Manufacturing SMEs – A Conceptual Study in Perspective of Industry 4.0. *Competitiveness Review. An International Business Journal Incorporating Journal of Global Competitiveness*.

Gadre, M., & Deoskar, A. (2020). Industry 4.0 – Digital Transformation, Challenges and Benefits. *International Journal of Future Generation Communication and Networking., 13*(2), 139–149.

Ganesan, K., Choudhury, P., Palakshappa, R., Jain, R., & Raje, S. (2014). *Assessing Green Industrial Policy: The India Experience*. Academic Press.

Gogoi, L. (2013). Degradation of Natural Resources and its Impact on Environment: A Study in Guwahati City, Assam, India. International Journal of Scientific and Research Publications, 3(12).

Gomez, V., Maria, A., & Gonzalez-Perez, M. A. (2021). *Digital Transformation as a Strategy to Reach Sustainability*. Smart and Sustainable Built Environment.

Gopinath, D. (2016). Why a Clearer Green Industrial Policy Matters for India: t Reconciling Growth, Climate Change and Inequality. *Local Economy: The Journal of the Local Economy Policy Unit, 31*(8), 830-835.

Government of India. (2015). *Green Growth and Sustainable Development in India. Towards the 2030 Development Agenda. Summary for Policymakers*. The Energy and Resource Institute & Global Green Growth Institute.

GulatiM. (2009). Industrial Pollution, Environmental Degradation and Disasters – Leveraging the Industry – Community. SSRN. doi:10.2139/ssrn.1531591

Hallsworth, M. (2012). How Complexity Economic Can Improve Government: Rethinking Policy Actors, Institutions and Structures. In *Complex New World: Translating New Economic Thinking into Public Policy* (pp. 39–49). Institute for Public Policy Research.

Kemp, R., & Never, B. (2017). Green Transition, Industrial Policy and Economic Development. *Oxford Review of Economic Policy, 33*(1), 66–84. doi:10.1093/oxrep/grw037

Khan, I. S., Ahmed, M O., & Majava, J. (2021). *Industry 4.0 and Sustainable Development: A Systematic Mapping of Triple Bottom Line, Circular Economy and Sustainable Business Models Perspectives.* Academic Press.

Khan, M., & Tarique. M. (2015). Industrial Pollution in Indian Industries: A Post Reform Scenario. *Journal of Energy Research and Environmental Technology, 2*(2), 182–187.

Khanna, M. (2020). *Growing Green Business Investments in Asia and the Pacific. Trends and Opportunities.* ADB Sustainable Development Working Paper Series. No.72. Asian Development Bank.

Lutkenhorst, W., Altenburg, T., Pegels, A., & Georgeta, V. (2014). *Green Industrial Policy Managing Transformation under Uncertainty.* Discussion Paper.

Mondejar, M. E., Avtar, R., Diaz, H. L. B., Dubey, R. K., Esteban, J., Morales, A.G., Hallam, B., Mbungu, N. T., Okolo, C. C., Prasad, A. K., She, Q., & Segura, S. G. (2021). Digitalization to achieve Sustainable Development Goals: Steps towards a Smart Green Planet. *Science of the Total Environment, 794*(10).

Nelliyat, P. (2007). *Industrial Growth and Environmental Degradation: A Case Study of Tirupur Textile Cluster.* Development Economics Working Papers. No.22507. East Asian Bureau of Economic Research.

Park, S. H. (1998). *Industrial Development and Environmental Degradation. A Source Book on the Origins of Global Pollution.* Edward Elgar Publishing.

Pilicherla, K. K., Adapa, V., Ghosh, M., & Ingla, P. (2021). Current Efforts on Sustainable Green Growth in the Manufacturing Sector to Complement "Make in India" for Making "Self-Reliant India. *Environmental Research.* PMID:34695432

Prabhat & Zetterberg. (2009). *Reducing Greenhouse Gas Emission in India. Financial Mechanism and Opportunities for EU-India Collaboration.* Report for Swedish, Mistry of Environment. Stockholm Environment Institute. Project Report.

Reserve Bank of India. (2021). *Green Finance in India: Progress and Challenges.* RBI Bulletin.

Roy, T. (2017). The Origins of Import Substituting Industrialization in India. *Journal of Economic History of Developing Regions, 32*(1), 71–95. doi:10.1080/20780389.2017.1292460

Schwarzer, J. (2013). *Industrial Policy for a Green Economy. International Institute for Sustainable Development Report.* Trade Investment & Climate Change.

Sharma, N. K. (2015). Industry Initiatives for Green Marketing in India. *Business and Economics Journal, 7*(1). doi:10.4172/2151-6219.1000192

Shulka, P. R., & Dhar, S. (2016). *India's GHG Emission Reduction and Sustainable Development. Enabling Asia Stabilize the Climate.* Springer.

United Nations Industrial Development Organization. (2010). A Greener Footprint for Industry: Opportunities and Challenges of Sustainable Industrial Development. Author.

Verma, R., Sah, N. K., Sharma, D. K., & Bisen, P. S. (2017). Journal of Energy, Environment & Carbon Credits. Strategies for Reduction of Carbon Emission in India. *Policy Review.*

Chapter 2
The Application of Anthropomorphism in Marketing:
Implications for Green Economy in a digital world

Bình Nghiêm-Phú
University of Hyogo, Japan

Jillian Rae Suter
Shizuoka University, Japan

ABSTRACT

From a psychological approach, brands are attached to human personality traits to make them more appealing and facilitate future consumption. Brand personality, however, cannot independently exist. In other words, it must be projected by and transferred through appropriate functional tools and activities. Nevertheless, a precise knowledge of anthropomorphic marketing from a functional approach is missing. In addition, the contribution of artificial intelligence or AI to the implementation of anthropomorphic marketing is unclear. This chapter aims to synthesize the existing literature about these functional practices of anthropomorphic marketing. The outcomes revealed that anthropomorphic marketing was apparent in commercial and social activities. However, the contribution of AI to these marketing practices is limited at present. Based on these observations, this chapter discusses the theoretical and practical implications and the application of anthropomorphic marketing to build a greener economy.

DOI: 10.4018/978-1-6684-4610-2.ch002

INTRODUCTION

Human beings tend to give nonhuman agents humanlike characteristics and behaviors. On the one hand, this tendency is facilitated by related cues, such as characters, forms, objects, and symbols, among others (Epley et al., 2007; Lloyd and Woodside, 2013; Puzakova et al., 2009). On the other hand, it is motivated by the need to understand and explain the behaviors of the nonhuman agents (effectance motivation) and the desire for social contact and affiliation (sociality motivation) (Epley et al., 2007). Such a motivation is either implicit (totemic or spiritual) or explicit (fetishist or entertaining) (Lloyd and Woodside, 2013; Neal, 1985).

The tendency to humanize unhuman objects is often regarded as an anthropomorphic act. Due to its essential impact on human beings' perceptions and behaviors, anthropomorphism has been employed in many sectors of socioeconomic life, including marketing activities. For example, from a psychological approach, brands are often attached to human personality traits, such as friendly, happy, sincere, and sophisticated, to make them more appealing and to facilitate future consumption (Bairrada et al., 2019; Coelho et al., 2020; Lu and Siao, 2019; Shaari et al., 2019). A more thorough understanding of customers' perception of brand personality, the psychological aspect of anthropomorphism, can be found in the reviews of Eisend and Stokburger-Sauer (2013), Lara-Rodríguez et al. (2019), MacInnis and Folkes (2017), Radler (2018), Saeed et al. (2021), and Yang et al. McGill (2020).

Brand personality, however, cannot independently exist. In other words, it must be projected by and transferred through appropriate tools and activities or anthropomorphic agents (De Gauquier et al., 2019; Grohmann et al., 2013; Hohenberger and Grohs, 2020; Luffarelli et al., 2019; Vinyals-Mirabent et al., 2019). From this point of view, the projection or creation of anthropomorphic agents is a functional process, which is different from the perception of brand personality traits mentioned previously. Nevertheless, precise knowledge about the functional processes of anthropomorphic marketing is mainly missing.

In today's world, the projection and delivery of the psychological brand personality traits can be assisted by an additional force: Artificial Intelligence or AI (Martin, et al., 2020; Yang et al., 2021). However, due to its novelty, customers seem to be reluctant and skeptical regarding the acceptance of AI and AI-related products and services despite the appearance of anthropomorphic agents (Karimova and Goby, 2021; Pelau et al., 2021; Watson, 2019). An intensive understanding of the functional processes of anthropomorphic marketing, combined with state-of-the-art knowledge about AI, will help facilitate these specific marketing initiatives in the future.

This chapter aims to synthesize the existing literature about anthropomorphic marketing to identify the particular functional marketing practices that are creating or employing anthropomorphic agents, together with the conditions and effects of these practices. In addition, it also summarizes relevant research to determine the potential contributions of AIs to the operations of such functional marketing exercises. Furthermore, implications for building a greener economy using knowledge about anthropomorphic marketing are assessed. The outcomes of this review will enrich the literature about anthropomorphic marketing. They will also assist in bettering green anthropomorphic marketing practices in the future.

ANTHROPOMORPHISM AND MARKETING

Anthropomorphism is a phenomenon that "describes the tendency to imbue the real or imagined behavior of nonhuman agents with humanlike characteristics, motivations, intentions, or emotions" (Epley et al.,

2007, p. 864). In other words, this phenomenon is related to humanization or personification (Brown, 2011; Delbaere et al., 2011; Reavey et al., 2018). On the contrary, the human agents may also be dehumanized or animalized for a variety of, probably opposite, purposes such as humiliation and promotion (Karanika and Hogg, 2020). This undertaking is regarded as zoomorphism (Healy and Beverland, 2013; Nanay, 2021).

Anthropomorphism appeared very early in human beings' history, as can be observed through the lens of totemism (Neal, 1985). However, despite its universal existence, the meanings, methods, and intensities of anthropomorphizing, humanizing, or personifying objects and animals differ among individuals, times, and cultures (Epley et al., 2007; Hand, 1998; Knight et al., 2014).

In addition, anthropomorphism can be seen everywhere and in every sector, from sacred religious sites to popular commercial products (Epley et al., 2007; Garnier and Poncin, 2013; Jones, 2017; Lloyd and Woodside, 2013). In marketing in particular (Kotler and Armstrong, 2018), anthropomorphism can help companies create values and satisfaction for their customers through a combination of various marketing processes, such as product design, price and distribution channel determination, and promotional campaign implementation. An anthropomorphic design can create a bond or attachment between customers and products, thus, facilitating the purchase and sustaining the consumption processes (Veer, 2013). Similarly, anthropomorphic agents used in advertising and public relations can help increase customers' engagement with and affection toward the brands or the products (Chen et al., 2015). Such agents can also be employed to promote environmentally friendly behaviors (Hayden and Dills, 2015; Laksmidewi and Soelasih, 2019; Osinski, et al., 2019; Tam et al., 2013; Zhu et al., 2019).

From a narrower perspective, the personification of brands, in particular, has become a phenomenal tendency (Aguirre-Rodriguez, 2014; Chen et al., 2015). The concept of brand personality, thus, has been proposed and adopted in both research and practice (Aaker and Fournier, 1995; Puzakova et al., 2009). Brand personality is usually regarded as the human traits that are given to a brand, including sincerity, excitement, competence, sophistication, and ruggedness (Aaker, 1997). However, due to the differences in contexts (products, brands, and customers), other brand personality dimensions can also be observed elsewhere, such as sympathy, trendiness, traditionalism, success, and happiness (Lara-Rodríguez et al., 2019; Radler 2018). Since brand personality is subjectively perceived through a psychological process, it is affected by perceivers' characteristics, for example, education, personality, attitude, self-confidence, and nationality (Eisend and Stokburger-Sauer, 2013; Saeed et al., 2021). On the other hand, brand personalities' effects are numerous, including brand attitude, brand image, brand relationship strength, brand commitment, and customer behaviors and intentions (Eisend and Stokburger-Sauer, 2013; Saeed et al., 2021). However, brand personality must be projected and carried by other objects through a functional process due to its invisible nature. The functional anthropomorphic agents, fortunately, can happily undertake this task.

SYNTHESIS METHOD

This chapter adopted the PRISMA-P protocol of synthesizing (Shamseer, et al., 2015) to achieve its purpose. Two steps were specifically implemented.

Step 1: The Functional Practices of Anthropomorphic Marketing

The synthesis began with the search for related papers in the existing literature. While previous reviews tend to use intermediaries such as Web of Science database, Scopus database, or Google Scholar search engine, this study used a more organic and cost-free method. Specifically, the search was mainly implemented on the publishers' databases instead of the intermediate platforms to gather the source data. This tactic ensures that researchers who do not have access to the paid databases (e.g., Web of Science and Scopus) can find articles published by journals listed in these databases. For this study, eight famous publishers of reputable academic journals and other products were referred to, including Elsevier or ScienceDirect, Emerald, Inderscience, JSTOR, Sage, Springer, Taylor & Francis, and Wiley. The researchers chose these publishers given their experiences, resources, and the guidance from trustworthy research institutes (California State University, 2020). However, bearing in mind that there were other publishers rather than these eight, Google Scholar was also employed to search for papers published.

The initial search was conducted in late February and early March 2020 by the two researchers of the research group. "Anthropomorphic marketing" was the only keyword used in the search. This combination reflected the content of anthropomorphism within the literature and the marketing approach to using anthropomorphic knowledge. Nonetheless, using a single search keyword might lead to missing specific papers in which anthropomorphism, marketing, and other related terms were not explicitly and consciously used. However, if the researchers of previous studies were not consciously aware that they adopted an anthropomorphic approach, their papers could be considered unsuitable for this review. In addition, given the resources currently available at the affiliated institutes of the researchers, especially the databases, the research group decided to select only full-paper journal articles. Books, book chapters, extended abstracts, papers in conference proceedings, and other publication types were overlooked. As the search outcome demonstrated, the keyword "anthropomorphic marketing" was able to extract research papers concerning both the functional and psychological approaches of anthropomorphic marketing. Therefore, no additional keywords were employed in the original and further searches.

In order to choose the relevant papers from the search outcome, the researchers read all the titles and abstracts generated by the search engines. If a paper addressed an issue concerning the functional aspect of anthropomorphic marketing, it was included in the search list. Otherwise, the paper was excluded. A collection of 160 papers published in 109 journals from 1985 to 2021 was generated due to this process. This sample is comparable with or well exceeds those of other reviews cited in this chapter (Eisend and Stokburger-Sauer, 2013; Garnier and Poncin, 2013; Kaartemo and Helkkula, 2018; Kraak and Story, 2015a; Lara-Rodríguez et al., 2019; MacInnis and Folkes, 2017; Radler, 2018). The papers were kept in separate folders organized according to their publication years.

After that, each researcher read half of the collection and analyzed its contents using the thematic analysis method (Braun and Clarke, 2006; Buetow, 2010) to narrow down the functional approaches applied in anthropomorphic marketing. The analysis was mastered in an Excel file, and the abstract, purpose, findings, and concluding remarks of each paper were mainly referred to. Each researcher initially proposed a compilation of themes resulting from their analysis. After that, the two separate compilations were compared and combined to create a common one which includes six significant themes belonging to two different marketing principles (Figure 1). In this process, the total agreement between the two researchers served as the criterion of reliability (Kassarjian, 1977).

Figure 1. Functional applications of anthropomorphism in marketing
Source. Authors' synthesis

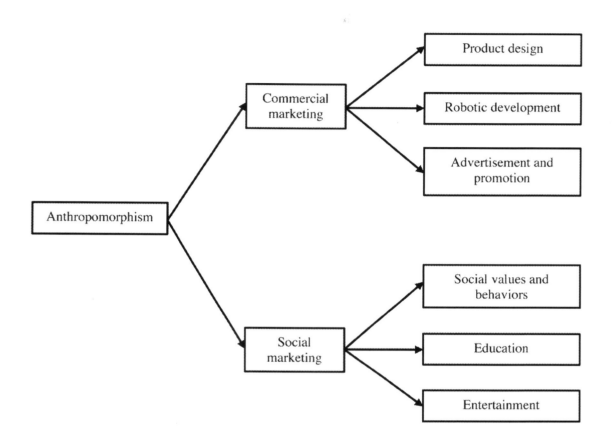

Step 2: Anthropomorphic Marketing and Artificial Intelligence

The second step of this synthesis involved artificial intelligence applications in anthropomorphic marketing. As the first step revealed, AI has hardly been mentioned in anthropomorphic marketing literature, with only a few exceptions (Dirican, 2015; Gursoy et al., 2019; Kaartemo and Helkkula, 2018; Kaplan and Haenlein, 2019). The contribution of AI to these particular marketing practices remained largely unknown.

Therefore, the research group decided to search for additional journal articles to explore the potential role of AI. Given the exploratory nature of this undertaking, a narrow and limited search was implemented in Google Scholars using the combination of "artificial intelligence" and other keywords related to the six themes identified earlier, such as "product design," "website," "robot," "character," and "education." The purpose was to locate the articles that mentioned the use of AI in creating and delivering human-like features of products and services. A small collection of 12 articles published between 2015 and 2021 was compiled and analyzed to illustrate the recent use of AI in virtual assistance, chatbot, and robot services in late 2021.

It should be noted that this undertaking was not exhaustive, given the topic's novelty. The aim was to raise the issue and give some illustrations of the potential of AI in anthropomorphic marketing, given the current situation of AI technologies.

ANTHROPOMORPHISM IN COMMERCIAL MARKETING

Product Design

The principles of anthropomorphism have widely been applied to the *design* of various *physical products*. For example, Steinberg (2010) observed that the most popular designer toys were given unique body forms and distinct faces. The more similar the toys were to the actual human figures, the more memorable they might become (De Bondt et al., 2018). Alternatively, Landwehr et al. (2011), and Miesler et al. (2011) found that the humanlike shapes could also work wonders on car design. Specifically, an upturned grill was seen as a friendly mouth shape, while slanted headlights were related to an aggressive eye shape. Combining these two shapes could generate positive feelings in customers, such as pleasure and arousal. However, this pattern might be more relevant to those customers who preferred the hedonic consumption values rather than those who preferred its utilitarian values (Miesler, 2012; Triantos et al., 2016). In addition, the level of humanization tended to depend on the complexity of the product (Hart, Jones, and Royne, 2013).

In addition, the use of humanlike shapes and promotional characters on *product packaging* was also a widespread practice (Hebden et al., 2011; Kirkpatrick et al., 2019; Triantos et al., 2016). Nevertheless, this design trend might suggest that the involved products, particularly food and beverages, were less healthy than those that did not use such packaging designs (Hebden et al., 2011). Moreover, this practice might facilitate other less healthy consumption behaviors, such as smoking (Kirkpatrick et al., 2019). Nonetheless, using anthropomorphic agents in packaging design on consumers' future behavior might be more relevant with low-involvement or novel products than with high-involvement or familiar products (Choi, 2019).

Furthermore, functional anthropomorphic practices could also be found in the *presentation* and *delivery* of *virtual products*. However, differing from most physical products, both visual and audio anthropomorphic cues could be used for these products. Specifically, André, Rist, and Müller (1998) and Kang and Gratch (2014) observed that the appearance of a virtual agent could help ease the perceived difficulty of using a website and increase the dynamic behaviors of its users. Araujo (2018) and Qiu and Benbasat (2009) added that such an agent could improve the perceived social presence of users, which in turn could affect their perceived trust. Nonetheless, Qiu and Benbasat (2010) noted that the agent's ethnicity should match that of the potential users to maximize its effect. In addition, Mimoun, Poncin, and Garnier (2012) found that an attractive and intelligent agent was undoubtedly more favored than an ugly and unintelligent one.

Robotic Development

Overall, robots have been used in specific industries and life domains for a long time. Humanlike or *humanoid robots*, however, have only been recruited in the service sectors, such as hospitality and health care in recent years (Belanche et al., 2020; Belk, 2016; Dario et al., 2001; Dirican, 2015; Giger et al.,

2019; Kumari et al., 2019; Lu, Cai, and Gursoy, 2019; Murphy, Gretzel, and Pesonen, 2019; Tondu, 2012; Wirtz et al., 2018; Yu, 2020). This development was supported by the anthropomorphic design of the robots, their abilities to express and recognize emotions, and their abilities to imitate human movements and interact with human users (Abe et al., 2017; Appel et al., 2020; Kaartemo and Helkkula, 2018; Rincon et al., 2018; Weber, 2005; Zhao, 2006).

The employment of humanoid robots could have essential impacts on users' perceptions and feelings or attitudes. For example, Kiesler et al. (2008), van Pinxteren et al. (2019), and Xu (2019) observed that users engaged in, trusted more, and disclosed less unfavorable behaviors (such as overeating) when being presented with a human-like robot agent as compared to a robot-like agent. Moreover, Tay, Low, Ko, and Park (2016) noted that users were more tolerable of racist and sexist jokes when a humanoid robot delivered them.

From another perspective, Tung (2016) found that a moderate humanlike robot was more preferred than a very humanlike one in a group of children. However, Cheng, Huang, and Huang (2017) and Yu and Ngan (2019) noted that the preference might differ between users' biological sexes and cultural backgrounds, both children and adults. In other studies, Fan, Wu, Miao, and Mattila (2020) and Goudey and Bonnin (2016) specified that not all users were likely to accept a humanoid robot or be satisfied with the services provided by humanoid robots. Those who had a certain level of technological familiarity might show more favorable evaluations than those who did not.

Advertisement and Promotion

Functional anthropomorphic agents in advertisement and promotion came in different forms. Among them, the most explicit form was the *humanlike avatars and characters* usually found on virtual platforms, such as online gaming and shopping websites (Choi et al., 2001; Jin and Sung, 2010; Moon et al., 2013; Mull et al., 2015; Phillips et al., 2019; Soni and Jain, 2017; Yang, 2006). The roles of an avatar were diverse, including "helper, solving problems and labor-saving," "friendly, sociable, welcoming host," and "personal shopper, recommending agent" (McGoldrick et al., 2008). In addition, the humanization of advertising and promotional agents seemed to be more influential than animals and natural objects (Guido and Peluso, 2015; Gupta and Jain, 2019; Noble et al., 2013; Reavey et al., 2018), but less persuasive than human celebrities (Trivedi, 2018). Moreover, the more human-like the agents were, the more influential the advertisement and promotion could become (Laksmidewi et al., 2017; Reavey et al., 2018). Moreover, male agents are more preferred than female ones (Unal et al., 2018).

The second form of functional anthropomorphic agents in advertisement and promotion was *anthropomorphized animals*. At one level, animals were usually humanized to advertise and promote food and beverages for both humans and pets (Spears, Mowen, & Chakraborty, 1996). At another level, animals could be transformed into mascots to represent a country, an organization, or an event (Hand, 1998; Hornsey, 2018; Hosany et al., 2013; Knight et al., 2014). All mascots had their own cultural, historical, and symbolic meanings. However, the meanings were highly contextual and differed among cultures and settings (Aguirre-Rodriguez, 2014; Bharucha, 2018; Cayla, 2013; Hand, 1998; Miles and Ibrahim, 2013; Patterson et al., 2013).

The third form of functional anthropomorphic agents in advertisement and promotion, and the most implicit one, was *partly anthropomorphized agent* or act. For example, Chérif and Lemoine (2019), Delbaere, McQuarrie, and Phillips (2011), Letheren, Martin, and Jin (2017), and Touré-Tillery and McGill (2015) proposed that a product might be presented as if it was engaging in a human act, or a message was speaking a human tone. In this way, the ad might trigger more positive emotions and brand liking. In addition, Eskine and Locander (2014) suggested that a product might be given a human name. However, if customers mistrusted the company, they might trust a nonhuman-named product instead of a human-named one. In another sense, Barcelos, Dantas, and Sénécal (2019) recommended that a website could be designed with a human voice. The inclusion of this feature made website viewers focus more on a page's cover photos and profile pictures.

Overall, the use of a functional anthropomorphic agent had many significant impacts, such as increasing a sense of social-/tele-presence, improving perceptions, and promoting good behaviors (Gursoy et al., 2019; Muzumdar et al., 2013; Nan et al., 2006; Sivaramakrishnan et al., 2007; Tuškej and Podnar, 2018; Vandana and Kumar, 2018; Veer, 2013). However, the impacts differed when taking into account the amount, type, or level of customization of information provided, the perceived credibility of the website, users' perceived values or needs, and users' characteristics and relationships, among others (Başfirinci and Çilingir, 2015; Bélisle and Bodur, 2010; Hart and Jha, 2015; Hart and Royne, 2017; Hellén and Sääksjärvi, 2013; Lin and Huang, 2018; Nan et al., 2006; Singh et al., 2016). Table 1 provides some examples concerning these points.

Table 1. Examples in the commercial context

Research	Antecedents	Consequences
Chen (2017)	Agent knowledge Alternative knowledge	Ad engagement
Chen, Chen, and Yan (2020)		Sadness reduction Product selection
Chen, Wan, and Levy (2017)	Social inclusion Social exclusion	Brand attitude Purchase intention
Choi, Miracle, and Biocca (2001)		Social presence Telepresence
Fan, Wu, and Mattila (2016)		Switching intention
Guido and Peluso (2015)		Brand personality
Han, Baek, Yoon, and Kim (2019)	Types of appeal	Attitude toward brand
Hellén and Sääksjärvi (2013)	Sex	Product evaluation Willingness to attach
Hudson, Huang, Roth, and Madden (2016)	Cultural background	Brand evaluation
Jin and Bolebruch (2009)		Enjoyment of online-shopping Product involvement Attitude toward the product
Kang and Watt (2013)		Psychological co-presence Interactant satisfaction
Kim and McGill (2018)	Financial status	
Kwak, Puzakova, and Rocereto (2017)	Personality	Price fairness
Lee and Oh (2021)	Advertising appeal Accommodation type	Perceived warmth Visit intention
Mull, Wyss, Moon, and Lee (2015)	Avatar type	Intention to interact

Continued on following page

Table 1. Continued

Research	Antecedents	Consequences
Puzakova, Rocereto, and Kwak (2013)	Customized message	Attitude towards the ad Likelihood to click on the ad Willingness to provide personal information
Rauschnabel and Ahuvia (2014)		Brand love Emotional attachment Willingness to invest Self-brand integration
Severson and Lemm (2016)	Age	
Yang (2006)		Interface evaluation Liking of the ad Recall of product information Feeling of immersion

Source. Authors' synthesis

ANTHROPOMORPHISM IN SOCIAL MARKETING

Social Values and Behaviors

This functional practice is similar to the third one but looks from a noncommercial angle. Specifically, the effect of anthropomorphism in the *relationship between pet owners and their pets* has been observed. For example, Antonacopoulos and Pychyl (2008) found that individuals who perceived low social support tended to engage in anthropomorphic behaviors (e.g., celebrating their pets' birthdays). This behavior, in turn, could help reduce owners' perceived stress. However, female and unmarried owners were more likely to anthropomorphize their pets than male or married ones. In another study, Leighty, et al. (2015) discovered that putting an animal in an anthropomorphic environment (e.g., an office space) could increase its desirability as a pet. Nevertheless, pet-related perceptions and behaviors were also affected by other factors, such as types of pet and the motivation to own a pet (Chartrand et al., 2008; Epley et al., 2008).

In addition, the influence of anthropomorphic presentation on *environmental behaviors* has also been recognized (Hayden and Dills, 2015; Laksmidewi and Soelasih, 2019; Osinski et al., 2019; Tam, Lee, & Chao, 2013). For example, users tended to use fewer paper towels to dry their hands when an ad was linked to a sad tree face (Ketron and Naletelich, 2019). Alternatively, when a river was humanized, people tended to report a stronger intention to protect it (Zhu, Wong, & Huang, 2019).

Moreover, the impact of anthropomorphic presentation on *healthy behaviors* (e.g., eating healthy food) has been noticed (Newton, Newton, & Wong, 2017). For example, companies used anthropomorphic agents to promote healthy products (Hebden et al., 2011; Lieberman, 2004). However, such an approach could generate a reversed effect (e.g., consuming more unhealthy food) (Kraak & Story, 2015a, b; Longacre et al., 2015).

Furthermore, anthropomorphism could also affect users' perception of *social engagement, social inclusion*, and *social influence* (Mourey, Olson, & Yoon, 2017; Sherman & Haidt, 2011; Waytz, Cacioppo, & Epley, 2010). Nonetheless, all perceptions and behaviors were likely to be affected by human beings' characteristics (Mousas, Anastasiou, & Spantidi, 2018; Newton, Newton, & Wong, 2017; Sashittal and Jassawalla, 2019; Severson and Lemm, 2016). Table 2 summarizes the observations mentioned above.

Table 2. Examples in the noncommercial context

Research	Antecedents	Consequences
Antonacopoulos and Pychyl (2008)	Social support Sex Marital status	Stress
Chartrand, Fitzsimons, and Fitzsimons (2008)	Pet types	
Epley, Waytz, Akalis, and Cacioppo (2008)	Motivation	
Ketron and Naletelich (2019)		Sustainable behaviors
Leighty, et al. (2015)		Pet desirability
Mourey, Olson, and Yoon (2017)		Social inclusion Social exclusion
Mousas, Anastasiou, and Spantidi (2018)	Sex	Emotional reaction
Newton, Newton, and Wong (2017)	Sense of power	Food intake
Sashittal and Jassawalla (2019)	Fear of being ignored	Healthy narcissism
Severson and Lemm (2016)	Age	
Sherman and Haidt (2011)		Social engagement
Tam, Lee, and Chao (2013)		Connectedness to nature Environmental support
Zhu, Wong, and Huang (2019)		Sustainable behaviors

Source. Authors' synthesis

Education

According to Badot, et al. (2016), Chae, Lee, and Seo (2016), and Gulz and Haake (2006), the inclusion of a functional anthropomorphic agent could help *motivate learners* to engage in education programs actively. Bennett and Thompson (2016), Griol and Callejas (2013), Jin (2010), and Moore (2003) added that such an agent could make the learning process more enjoyable.

Nevertheless, the anthropomorphizing of scientific contents might reduce the completeness of the knowledge. As Geerdts, Van De Walle, and LoBue (2016) and Wood (2019) observed, the anthropomorphic approach might be biased toward the emotional effect of educational processes rather than the scientific aspect. In addition, the impact might be reduced when the learners get distracted (Moremoholo and de Lange, 2018).

To facilitate a positive contribution, the design of the anthropomorphic agents should carefully take into account several vital elements, including characteristics of the movement, facial expressions, vocal characteristics, dialogue and conversational characteristics, emotional expressions, and personality traits (Gulz and Haake, 2006). In addition, the intractability of the agents should not be ignored (Bennett and Thompson, 2016).

Entertainment

Finally, the functional anthropomorphic agents have also been used in *entertaining objects*. For example, Brabant and Mooney (1989) found in a study in the US that most greeting cards with anthropomorphic agents had a neutral tone and were presented in the present time. Holliday (2016), and Lanier, Rader, and Fowler (2013), when examining animation movies such as Ratatouille and Toy Story, argued that the use of anthropomorphic agents helped explain the relationship between human beings and the outside world. In addition, this approach could evoke empathy and facilitate personal meaning-making in human viewers (Robertson, 2014; van Rooij, 2019).

ANTHROPOMORPHIC MARKETING AND ARTIFICIAL INTELLIGENCE

Generally, artificial intelligence (AI) is a computer system with the "ability to interpret external data correctly, to learn from such data, and to use those learnings to achieve specific goals and tasks through flexible adaptation" (Kaplan & Haenlein, 2019). Generations of AI have been developed and utilized in many industries and sectors.

Specifically, AI has been used to design physical products (Verganti, Vendraminelli, & Iansiti, 2020; Zha, 2005). However, the existence of AI has mainly been observed with virtual products. For example, AI was the fundamental force behind creating virtual artists and virtual assistants (Ameen et al., 2021; Canbek and Mutlu, 2016). The perceived quality of these AI-enabled services had a significant impact on customers' trust in technology and the brand (Ameen et al., 2021).

In addition, AI was also the primary technological reason behind the inclusion of chatbots in certain service websites. The perceived usability and responsiveness of such functional anthropomorphic agents could enhance the values that users expected (Chen, Le, & Florence, 2021; Riikkinen et al., 2018). In addition, the use of chatbots might also strengthen customer-brand relationships and facilitate customer response (e.g., purchasing behavior) (Cheng & Jiang, 2021; Luo, Tong, Fang, & Qu, 2019). However, users also were aware that they had to simplify their languages and lengthen the conversations when communicating with AI agents (Hill, Ford, & Farreras, 2015). Moreover, users might use more offensive words if they perceived a higher degree of the chatbots' human-likeness (Park et al., 2021).

In the robotics domain, AI was employed to give robots the voices of humans and the ability to perform other humanlike acts, such as walk and dancing. AI voice robots, together with chatbots, were expected to assist effectively and even replace human agents in several service sectors, such as education and health care (Edwards & Cheok, 2018; Fiske, Henningsen, & Buyx, 2019). However, older learners preferred older AI voice instructors over younger ones (Edwards et al., 2019). In addition, the voice and the humanlike design of the devices might unwantedly trigger negative feelings of privacy invasion and strain in their users in the home setting (Benlian, Klumpe, & Hinz, 2020).

DISCUSSION

Anthropomorphic marketing is most apparent in commercial advertisement and promotion, where humanized animals (zoomorphism), humanized characters (anthropomorphism), and humanized features are created and employed as the agents. Humanized imaginary creatures (teramorphism) are usually included in the second category of humanized characters, perhaps due to their similarity in visual presentation. Generally, humanized features are regularly adopted in product design (including robotic development) and promotion (including commercial and social marketing activities). Despite their forms, the humanization of characters and features in marketing impacts human beings' thoughts, feelings, and behaviors (or their attitudes). This fact explains why research on anthropomorphism and personification has received much attention for several decades.

The humanized visual, audio, and tactile elements in anthropomorphic marketing demonstrate that this is a functional approach rather than a psychological one. In addition, this operation makes anthropomorphic marketing very close to sensory marketing, which employs marketing cues related to the five senses of human beings (Hultén, 2015; Krishna, 2012). However, similar to sensory marketing, the visual and audio practices seem to dominate the other sensory ones. The tactile elements are limited to 3D characters in virtual environments and social humanoid robots. On the other hand, unlike sensory marketing, anthropomorphic marketing only uses humanlike features to project and deliver its cues and final products. Its effects, therefore, may be less influential since sensory marketing uses all possible (both humanlike and non-humanlike) cues. However, AI can easily participate in creating and delivering these sensory elements from the perspective of anthropomorphic marketing rather than that of sensory marketing.

Practical Implication

In recent years, many researchers have enthusiastically advocated projecting personality traits to brands, products, places, and other entities. However, its practicality is still questionable. According to previous studies (Dickinger and Lalicic, 2016; Oklevik, Supphellen, & Maehle, 2020), the public seemed to be unaware of the academically developed traits or confused between personality traits and affective states. This review has noticed that the projection of the functional anthropomorphic agents seemed to neglect their impacts on perceived brand personality traits (Guido and Peluso, 2015). Thus, a definite link between the functional and psychological aspects is still vastly unrecognized and overlooked. More importantly, with the current practices of anthropomorphic marketing, the projection of multiple personality traits is impossible.

Therefore, practitioners should limit their efforts to the few most prominent personality traits (one or two) in the future. Too many traits will require too many cues, which is problematic for design and production. In addition, too many cues will create unnecessary confusion for customers or viewers, especially when many of them may be distracted during the exposure or encounter with the product or the ad (Moremoholo and de Lange, 2018). In addition, the projection and delivery of the humanized features should carefully consider the cultural aspects of the target settings and the personal characteristics of the customers or viewers. Moreover, the level of humanization should also be considered since each product or marketing practice may require a different approach.

Implications for Green Economy Enhancement

A green economy aims at developing a sustainable economy without sacrificing the environment. Fortunately, anthropomorphic marketing can help with creating and developing a green economy. Examples of specific activities include:

- To educate and change consumers' perceptions of and behaviors toward current environmental issues, mentioned in the Sustainable Development Goals (SDG) 13, 14, and 15,
- To promote a more responsible consumption culture concerning SDG 12,
- To encouraging healthy products consumption, achieving SDGs 2 and 3.

In these processes, AI can help project the most relevant anthropomorphic characters or characteristics and the most persuasive messages. AI's ability to understand customer perception and behavior via analyzing big data about them is an invaluable asset. In addition, AI can act as an anthropomorphic agent to increase the active engagement of the public and prominent economic and environmental issues. AI's ability to learn via actual contact is also a helpful resource. However, in addition to these positive contributions, AI can also exploit nature and the customers further and cause harmful impacts (Dauvergne, 2020; Watson, 2019). Therefore, a change in the mindset of business people, in general, and marketers, in particular, is necessary. AI can harm the green economy rather than help it without a right vision and intention.

CONCLUDING REMARK

Anthropomorphism has been applied in marketing practices for several decades from commercial and social perspectives (Kotler and Armstrong, 2018; Lee and Kotler, 2020; Patsiaouras et al., 2014). The application of anthropomorphism in marketing, thus, is broad.

In addition, anthropomorphic marketing is implemented based on a thorough understanding of human beings' perception of and behavior toward cute and lovely objects (Delgado-Ballester et al., 2017; Shea, 2014). Anthropomorphic agents are the means for potential users or viewers to understand and get used to unfamiliar products and situations. In addition, they provide excuses for users or viewers to connect with their peers and the outside world (Yang, Aggarwal, & McGill, 2020). However, anthropomorphic agents may signify reversed effects, which restrain users or viewers from consuming certain products or engaging in certain activities due to, for example, some ethical reasons (Stevens, Kearney, & Maclaran, 2013; Yang, Aggarwal, & McGill, 2020). This fact can help facilitate the protection of the natural environment and lead to a greener economy. It should be noted that practitioners also understand that the original and reversed impacts of anthropomorphic marketing differ among cultures, products and situations, and users or viewers (Chartrand, Fitzsimons, & Fitzsimons, 2008; Hudson, Huang, Roth, & Madden, 2016; Kwak, Puzakova, & Rocereto, 2017; Lee & Oh, 2021). The application of anthropomorphism in marketing, thus, also has depth.

In the upcoming years, anthropomorphic marketing, with the help of, possibly, sensory marketing, robotic technology, and artificial intelligence technology, may become a practical approach in marketing in general. Since human beings are still driven, in part, by cute and lovely objects, anthropomorphic marketing will be able to demonstrate and maintain its significant impacts.

Limitations

The main limitation of this study, similar to other syntheses, involves the collection of relevant papers. In a sense, using a single search keyword might lead to missing specific papers. However, the number of papers employed (n = 160+12) is comparable with or exceeds those of other reviews cited in this chapter. In another sense, excluding other types of publication rather than journal papers has undoubtedly reduced the number of studies under review. Nonetheless, a complete selection could not be obtained given the researchers' limited resources and finite knowledge.

Future Research Directions

Given these limitations and the practices found in previous studies, several directions for future research can be proposed. First, the suitable level of human-likeness for each product or marketing effort should be investigated. Second, both positive and negative, the dual effect of anthropomorphism and functional anthropomorphic agents should be further examined, taking into account the environmental (e.g., social norms), personal (e.g., characteristics and values), and product/effort-related factors. Third, the suitability and replaceability of living human agents, dead human agents, animal agents, anthropomorphic agents, and dehumanized agents (humans perform as animals) in certain marketing efforts, such as advertisement and promotion, can be explored since current studies tended to inspect these phenomena separately. Fourth, the potential use of the olfactory and gustatory sensory elements in anthropomorphic marketing can also be tested.

Lastly, but not least, the role of AI and the application of anthropomorphic marketing in the creation and development of greener economic activities should be further investigated. At the time of this synthesis, these contents still were somewhat insignificant.

REFERENCES

Aaker, J., & Fournier, S. (1995). A brand as a character, a partner and a person: Three perspectives on the question of brand personality. *Advances in Consumer Research. Association for Consumer Research (U. S.)*, *22*, 391–395.

Aaker, J. L. (1997). Dimensions of brand personality. *JMR, Journal of Marketing Research*, *34*(3), 347–356. doi:10.1177/002224379703400304

Abe, N., Laumond, J.-P., Salaris, P., & Levillain, F. (2017). On the use of dance notation systems to generate movements in humanoid robots: The utility of Laban notation in robotics. *Social Sciences Information. Information Sur les Sciences Sociales*, *56*(2), 328–344. doi:10.1177/0539018417694773

Aguirre-Rodriguez, A. (2014). Cultural factors that impact brand personification strategy effectiveness. *Psychology and Marketing*, *31*(1), 70–83. doi:10.1002/mar.20676

Ameen, N., Tarhini, A., Reppel, A., & Anand, A. (2021). Customer experiences in the age of artificial intelligence. *Computers in Human Behavior*, *114*, 106548. Advance online publication. doi:10.1016/j.chb.2020.106548 PMID:32905175

André, E., Rist, T., & Müller, J. (1998). WebPersona: A lifelike presentation agent for the World-Wide Web. *Knowledge-Based Systems*, *11*(1), 25–36. doi:10.1016/S0950-7051(98)00057-4

Antonacopoulos, N. M.-D., & Pychyl, T. A. (2008). An examination of the relations between social support, anthropomorphism and stress among dog owners. *Anthrozoos*, *21*(2), 139–152. doi:10.2752/175303708X305783

Appel, M., Izydorczyk, D., Weber, S., Mara, M., & Lischetzke, T. (2020). The uncanny of mind in a machine: Humanoid robots as tools, agents, and experiencers. *Computers in Human Behavior*, *102*, 274–286. doi:10.1016/j.chb.2019.07.031

Araujo, T. (2018). Living up to the chatbot hype: The influence of anthropomorphic design cues and communicative agency framing on conversational agent and company perceptions. *Computers in Human Behavior, 85,* 183–189. doi:10.1016/j.chb.2018.03.051

Badot, O., Bree, J., Damay, C., Guichard, N., Lemoine, J. F., & Poulain, M. (2016). The representation of shopping in children's books. *International Journal of Retail & Distribution Management, 44*(10), 976–995. doi:10.1108/IJRDM-08-2015-0134

Bairrada, C. M., Coelho, A., & Lizanets, V. (2019). The impact of brand personality on consumer behavior: The role of brand love. *Journal of Fashion Marketing and Management, 23*(1), 30–47. doi:10.1108/JFMM-07-2018-0091

Barcelos, R. H., Dantas, D. C., & Sénécal, S. (2019). The tone of voice of tourism brands on social media: Does it matter? *Tourism Management, 74,* 173–189. doi:10.1016/j.tourman.2019.03.008

Başfirinci, Ç., & Çilingir, Z. (2015). Anthropomorphism and advertising effectiveness: Moderating roles of product involvement and the type of consumer need. *Journal of Social and Administrative Sciences, 2*(3), 108–131.

Belanche, D., Casaló, L. V., Flavián, C., & Schepers, J. (2020). Service robot implementation: A theoretical framework and research agenda. *Service Industries Journal, 20*(3-4), 203–225. doi:10.1080/02642069.2019.1672666

Bélisle, J.-F., & Bodur, H. O. (2010). Avatars as information: Perception of consumers based on their avatars in virtual worlds. *Psychology and Marketing, 27*(8), 741–765. doi:10.1002/mar.20354

Belk, R. (2016). Understanding the robot: Comments on Goudey and Bonnin (2016). [English Edition]. *Recherche et Applications en Marketing, 31*(4), 83–90. doi:10.1177/2051570716658467

Benlian, A., Klumpe, J., & Hinz, O. (2020). Mitigating the intrusive effects of smart home assistants by using anthropomorphic design features: A multi-method investigation. *Information Systems Journal, 30*(6), 1010–1042. doi:10.1111/isj.12243

Bennett, D. E., & Thompson, P. (2016). Use of anthropomorphic brand mascots for student motivation and engagement: A promotional case study with Pablo the Penguin at the University of Portsmouth Library. *New Review of Academic Librarianship, 22*(2-3), 225–237. doi:10.1080/13614533.2016.1162179

Bharucha, J. (2018). Cutting through the clutter: Mascots in Indian marketing. *International Journal of Economics and Business Research, 16*(4), 534–545. doi:10.1504/IJEBR.2018.095351

Brabant, S., & Mooney, L. A. (1989). When "critters" act like people: Anthropomorphism in greeting cards. *Sociological Spectrum, 9*(4), 477–494. doi:10.1080/02732173.1989.9981906

Braun, V., & Clarke, V. (2006). Using thematic analysis in psychology. *Qualitative Research in Psychology, 3*(2), 77–101. doi:10.1191/1478088706qp063oa

Brown, S. (2011). It's alive inside! A note on the prevalence of personification. *Irish Marketing Review, 21*(1-2), 3–11.

Buetow, S. (2010). Thematic analysis and its reconceptualization as 'saliency analysis'. *Journal of Health Services Research & Policy*, *15*(2), 123–125. doi:10.1258/jhsrp.2009.009081 PMID:19762883

California State University. (2020, December 15). *Academic publishing guide for faculty and researchers*. Retrieved March 25, 2021, from California State University: https://csus.libguides.com/publishing/choosing-a-publisher

Canbek, N. G., & Mutlu, M. E. (2016). On the track of Artificial Intelligence: Learning with Intelligent Personal Assistants. *International Journal of Human Sciences*, *13*(1), 592–601. doi:10.14687/ijhs.v13i1.3549

Cayla, J. (2013). Brand mascots as organisational totems. *Journal of Marketing Management*, *29*(1-2), 86–104. doi:10.1080/0267257X.2012.759991

Chae, S. W., Lee, K. C., & Seo, Y. W. (2016). Exploring the effect of avatar trust on learners' perceived participation intentions in an e-learning environment. *International Journal of Human-Computer Interaction*, *32*(5), 373–393. doi:10.1080/10447318.2016.1150643

Chartrand, T. L., Fitzsimons, G. M., & Fitzsimons, G. J. (2008). Automatic effects of anthropomorphized objects on behavior. *Social Cognition*, *26*(2), 198–209. doi:10.1521oco.2008.26.2.198

Chen, F., Chen, R. P., & Yan, L. (2020). When sadness comes alive, will it be less painful? The effects of anthropomorphic thinking on sadness regulation and consumption. *Journal of Consumer Psychology*, *30*(2), 277–295. doi:10.1002/jcpy.1137

Chen, J.-S., Le, T.-T.-Y., & Florence, D. (2021). Usability and responsiveness of artificial intelligence chatbot on online customer experience in e-retailing. *International Journal of Retail & Distribution Management*, *49*(11), 1512–1531. doi:10.1108/IJRDM-08-2020-0312

Chen, K.-J. (2017). Humanizing brands: An examination of the psychological process of anthropomorphism and its effects on consumer responses. *Journal of Marketing Management*, *5*(2), 75–87. doi:10.15640/jmm.v5n2a7

Chen, K.-J., Lin, J.-S., Choi, J. H., & Hahm, J. M. (2015). Would you be my friend? An examination of global marketers' brand personiðcation strategies in social media. *Journal of Interactive Advertising*, *15*(2), 1–14. doi:10.1080/15252019.2015.1079508

Chen, R. P., Wan, E. W., & Levy, E. (2017). The effect of social exclusion on consumer preference for anthropomorphized brands. *Journal of Consumer Psychology*, *27*(1), 23–34. doi:10.1016/j.jcps.2016.05.004

Cheng, C.-C., Huang, K.-H., & Huang, S.-M. (2017). Exploring young children's images on robots. *Advances in Mechanical Engineering*, *9*(4), 1–7. doi:10.1177/1687814017698663

Cheng, Y., & Jiang, H. (2021). Customer–brand relationship in the era of artificial intelligence: Understanding the role of chatbot marketing efforts. *Journal of Product and Brand Management*. Advance online publication. doi:10.1108/JPBM-05-2020-2907

Chérif, E., & Lemoine, J.-F. (2019). Anthropomorphic virtual assistants and the reactions of Internet users: An experiment on the assistant's voice. *Recherche et Applications en Marketing*, *34*(1), 28–47. doi:10.1177/2051570719829432

Choi, Y. K. (2019). Characters' persuasion effects in advergaming: Role of brand trust, product involvement, and trust propensity. *Internet Research, 29*(2), 367–380. doi:10.1108/IntR-01-2018-0021

Choi, Y. K., Miracle, G. E., & Biocca, F. (2001). The effects of anthropomorphic agents on advertising effectiveness and the mediating role of presence. *Journal of Interactive Advertising, 2*(1), 19–32. doi:10.1080/15252019.2001.10722055

Coelho, F. J.-F., Bairrada, C. M., & de Matos Coelho, A. F. (2020). Functional brand qualities and perceived value: The mediating role of brand experience and brand personality. *Psychology and Marketing, 37*(1), 41–55. doi:10.1002/mar.21279

Dario, P., Guglielmelli, E., & Laschi, C. (2001). Humanoids and personal robots: Design and experiments. *Journal of Robotic Systems, 18*(12), 673–690. doi:10.1002/rob.8106

Dauvergne, P. (2020). Is artificial intelligence greening global supply chains? Exposing the political economy of environmental costs. *Review of International Political Economy.* Advance online publication. doi:10.1080/09692290.2020.1814381

De Bondt, C., Van Kerckhove, A., & Geuens, M. (2018). Look at that body! How anthropomorphic package shapes systematically appeal to consumers. *International Journal of Advertising, 37*(5), 698–717. doi:10.1080/02650487.2018.1470919

De Gauquier, L., Brengman, M., Willems, K., & Kerrebroeck, H. V. (2019). Leveraging advertising to a higher dimension: Experimental research on the impact of virtual reality on brand personality impressions. *Virtual Reality (Waltham Cross), 23*(3), 235–253. doi:10.100710055-018-0344-5

Delbaere, M., McQuarrie, E. F., & Phillips, B. J. (2011). Personification in advertising using a visual metaphor to trigger anthropomorphism. *Journal of Advertising, 40*(1), 121–130. doi:10.2753/JOA0091-3367400108

Delgado-Ballester, E., Palazón, M., & Pelaez-Muñoz, J. (2017). This anthropomorphised brand is so loveable: The role of self-brand integration. *Spanish Journal of Marketing - ESIC, 21*(2), 89-101. doi:10.1016/j.sjme.2017.04.002

Dickinger, A., & Lalicic, L. (2016). An analysis of destination brand personality and emotions: A comparison study. *Information Technology & Tourism, 15*(4), 317–340. doi:10.100740558-015-0044-x

Dirican, C. (2015). The impacts of robotics, artificial intelligence on business and economics. *Procedia: Social and Behavioral Sciences, 195,* 564–573. doi:10.1016/j.sbspro.2015.06.134

Edwards, B. I., & Cheok, A. D. (2018). Why not robot teachers: Artificial intelligence for addressing teacher shortage. *Applied Artificial Intelligence, 32*(4), 345–360. doi:10.1080/08839514.2018.1464286

Edwards, C., Edwards, A., Stoll, B., Lin, X., & Massey, N. (2019). Evaluations of an artificial intelligence instructor's voice: Social Identity Theory in human-robot interactions. *Computers in Human Behavior, 90,* 357–362. doi:10.1016/j.chb.2018.08.027

Eisend, M., & Stokburger-Sauer, N. E. (2013). Brand personality: A meta-analytic review of antecedents and consequences. *Marketing Letters, 24*(3), 205–216. doi:10.100711002-013-9232-7

Epley, N., Waytz, A., Akalis, S., & Cacioppo, J. T. (2008). When we need a human: Motivational determinants of anthropomorphism. *Social Cognition, 26*(2), 143–155. doi:10.1521oco.2008.26.2.143

Epley, N., Waytz, A., & Cacioppo, J. T. (2007). On seeing human: A three-factor theory of anthropomorphism. *Psychological Review, 114*(4), 864–886. doi:10.1037/0033-295X.114.4.864 PMID:17907867

Eskine, K. J., & Locander, W. H. (2014). A name you can trust? Personiðcation effects are inñuenced by beliefs about company values. *Psychology and Marketing, 31*(1), 48–53. doi:10.1002/mar.20674

Fan, A., Wu, L., & Mattila, A. S. (2016). Does anthropomorphism influence customers' switching intentions in the self-service technology failure context? *Journal of Services Marketing, 30*(7), 713–723. doi:10.1108/JSM-07-2015-0225

Fan, A., Wu, L., Miao, L., & Mattila, A. S. (2020). When does technology anthropomorphism help alleviate customer dissatisfaction after a service failure? – The moderating role of consumer technology self-efficacy and interdependent self-construal. *Journal of Hospitality Marketing & Management, 29*(3), 269–290. doi:10.1080/19368623.2019.1639095

Fiske, A., Henningsen, P., & Buyx, A. (2019). Your robot therapist will see you now: Ethical implications of embodied artificial intelligence in psychiatry, psychology, and psychotherapy. *Journal of Medical Internet Research, 21*(5), e13216. Advance online publication. doi:10.2196/13216 PMID:31094356

Garnier, M., & Poncin, I. (2013). The avatar in marketing: Synthesis, integrative framework and perspectives. *Recherche et Applications en Marketing, 28*(1), 85–115. doi:10.1177/2051570713478335

Geerdts, M., Van De Walle, G., & LoBue, V. (2016). Using animals to teach children biology: Exploring the use of biological explanations in children's anthropomorphic storybooks. *Early Education and Development, 27*(8), 1237–1249. doi:10.1080/10409289.2016.1174052

Giger, J.-C., Piçarra, N., Alves-Oliveira, P., Oliveira, R., & Arriaga, P. (2019). Humanization of robots: Is it really such a good idea? *Human Behavior and Emerging Technologies, 1*(2), 111–123. doi:10.1002/hbe2.147

Goudey, A., & Bonnin, G. (2016). Must smart objects look human? Study of the impact of anthropomorphism on the acceptance of companion robots. *Recherche et Applications en Marketing, 31*(2), 1–20. doi:10.1177/2051570716643961

Griol, D., & Callejas, Z. (2013). An architecture to develop multimodal educative applications with Chatbots. *International Journal of Advanced Robotic Systems, 10*(3), 1–15. doi:10.5772/55791

Grohmann, B., Giese, J. L., & Parkman, I. D. (2013). Using type font characteristics to communicate brand personality of new brands. *Journal of Brand Management, 20*(5), 389–403. doi:10.1057/bm.2012.23

Guido, G., & Peluso, A. M. (2015). Brand anthropomorphism: Conceptualization, measurement, and impact on brand personality and loyalty. *Journal of Brand Management, 22*(1), 1–19. doi:10.1057/bm.2014.40

Gulz, A., & Haake, M. (2006). Design of animated pedagogical agents - A look at their look. *International Journal of Human-Computer Studies, 64*(4), 322–339. doi:10.1016/j.ijhcs.2005.08.006

Gupta, R., & Jain, K. (2019). The impact of anthropomorphism on purchase intention of smartphones: A study of young Indian consumers. *Indian Journal of Marketing*, *49*(5), 7–20. doi:10.17010/ijom/2019/v49/i5/144021

Gursoy, D., Chi, O. H., Lu, L., & Nunkoo, R. (2019). Consumers acceptance of artificially intelligent (AI) device use in service delivery. *International Journal of Information Management*, *49*, 157–169. doi:10.1016/j.ijinfomgt.2019.03.008

Han, N. R., Baek, T. H., Yoon, S., & Kim, T. (2019). Is that coffee mug smiling at me? How anthropomorphism impacts the effectiveness of desirability vs. feasibility appeals in sustainability advertising. *Journal of Retailing and Consumer*, *51*, 352–361. doi:10.1016/j.jretconser.2019.06.020

Hand, D. (1998). Footix: The history behind a modern mascot. *French Cultural Studies*, *9*(26), 239–247. doi:10.1177/095715589800902607

Hart, P., & Royne, M. B. (2017). Being human: How anthropomorphic presentations can enhance advertising effectiveness. *Journal of Current Issues and Research in Advertising*, *38*(2), 129–145. doi:10.1080/10641734.2017.1291381

Hart, P. M., & Jha, S. (2015). The variation of consumer anthropomorphism across cultures. *Indian Journal of Marketing*, *45*(11), 7–16. doi:10.17010/ijom/2015/v45/i11/81873

Hart, P. M., Jones, S. R., & Royne, M. B. (2013). The human lens: How anthropomorphic reasoning varies by product complexity and enhances personal value. *Journal of Marketing Management*, *29*(1-2), 105–121. doi:10.1080/0267257X.2012.759993

Hayden, D., & Dills, B. (2015). Smokey the bear should come to the beach: Using mascot to promote marine conservation. *Social Marketing Quarterly*, *21*(1), 3–13. doi:10.1177/1524500414558126 PMID:26877714

Healy, M. J., & Beverland, M. B. (2013). Unleashing the animal within: Exploring consumers' zoomorphic identity motives. *Journal of Marketing Management*, *29*(1-2), 225–248. doi:10.1080/0267257X.2013.766233

Hebden, L., King, L., Kelly, B., Chapman, K., & Innes-Hughes, C. (2011). A menagerie of promotional characters: Promoting food to children through food packaging. *Journal of Nutrition Education and Behavior*, *43*(5), 349–355. doi:10.1016/j.jneb.2010.11.006 PMID:21906547

Hellén, K., & Sääksjärvi, M. (2013). Development of a scale measuring childlike anthropomorphism in products. *Journal of Marketing Management*, *29*(1-2), 141–157. doi:10.1080/0267257X.2012.759989

Hill, J., Ford, W. R., & Farreras, I. G. (2015). Real conversations with artificial intelligence: A comparison between human–human online conversations and human–chatbot conversations. *Computers in Human Behavior*, *49*, 245–250. doi:10.1016/j.chb.2015.02.026

Hohenberger, C., & Grohs, R. (2020). Old and exciting? Sport sponsorship effects on brand age and brand personality. *Sport Management Review*, *23*(3), 469–481. doi:10.1016/j.smr.2019.05.002

Holliday, C. (2016). 'I'm not a real boy, I'm a puppet': Computer-animated films and anthropomorphic subjectivity. *Animation*, *11*(3), 246–262. doi:10.1177/1746847716661456

Hornsey, R. (2018). "The penguins are coming": Brand mascots and utopian mass consumption in interwar Britain. *The Journal of British Studies*, *57*(4), 812–839. doi:10.1017/jbr.2018.116

Hosany, S., Prayag, G., Martin, D., & Lee, W.-Y. (2013). Theory and strategies of anthropomorphic brand characters from Peter Rabbit, Mickey Mouse, and Ronald McDonald, to Hello Kitty. *Journal of Marketing Management*, *29*(1-2), 48–68. doi:10.1080/0267257X.2013.764346

Hudson, S., Huang, L., Roth, M. S., & Madden, T. J. (2016). The influence of social media interactions on consumer–brand relationships: A three-country study of brand perceptions and marketing behaviors. *International Journal of Research in Marketing*, *33*(1), 27–41. doi:10.1016/j.ijresmar.2015.06.004

Hultén, B. (2015). *Sensory Marketing: Theoretical and Empirical Grounds*. Routledge. doi:10.4324/9781315690681

Jin, S.-A. A. (2010). The effects of incorporating a virtual agent in a computer-aided test designed for stress management education: The mediating role of enjoyment. *Computers in Human Behavior*, *26*(3), 443–451. doi:10.1016/j.chb.2009.12.003

Jin, S.-A. A., & Bolebruch, J. (2009). Avatar-based advertising in Second Life - The role of presence and attractiveness of virtual spokespersons. *Journal of Interactive Advertising*, *10*(1), 51–60. doi:10.1080/15252019.2009.10722162

Jin, S.-A. A., & Sung, Y. (2010). The roles of spokes-avatars' personalities in brand communication in 3D virtual environments. *Journal of Brand Management*, *17*(5), 317–327. doi:10.1057/bm.2009.18

Jones, R. A. (2017). What makes a robot 'social'? *Social Studies of Science*, *47*(4), 556–579. doi:10.1177/0306312717704722 PMID:28466752

Kaartemo, V., & Helkkula, A. (2018). A systematic review of artificial intelligence and robots in value co-creation: Current status and future research avenues. *Journal of Creating Values*, *4*(2), 211–228. doi:10.1177/2394964318805625

Kang, S.-H., & Gratch, J. (2014). Exploring users' social responses to computer counseling interviewers' behavior. *Computers in Human Behavior*, *34*, 120–130. doi:10.1016/j.chb.2014.01.006

Kang, S.-K., & Watt, J. H. (2013). The impact of avatar realism and anonymity on effective communication via mobile devices. *Computers in Human Behavior*, *29*(3), 1169–1181. doi:10.1016/j.chb.2012.10.010

Kaplan, A., & Haenlein, M. (2019). Siri, Siri, in my hand: Who's the fairest in the land? On the interpretations, illustrations, and implications of artificial intelligence. *Business Horizons*, *62*(1), 15–25. doi:10.1016/j.bushor.2018.08.004

Karanika, K., & Hogg, M. K. (2020). Self–object relationships in consumers' spontaneous metaphors of anthropomorphism, zoomorphism, and dehumanization. *Journal of Business Research*, *109*, 15–25. doi:10.1016/j.jbusres.2019.10.005

Karimova, G. Z., & Goby, V. P. (2021). The adaptation of anthropomorphism and archetypes for marketing artificial intelligence. *Journal of Consumer Marketing*, *38*(2), 229–238. doi:10.1108/JCM-04-2020-3785

Kassarjian, H. H. (1977). Content analysis in consumer research. *The Journal of Consumer Research, 4*(1), 8–18. doi:10.1086/208674

Ketron, S., & Naletelich, K. (2019). Victim or beggar? Anthropomorphic messengers and the savior effect in consumer sustainability behavior. *Journal of Business Research, 96*, 73–84. doi:10.1016/j.jbusres.2018.11.004

Kiesler, S., Powers, A., Fussell, S. R., & Torrey, C. (2008). Anthropomorphic interactions with a robot and robot-like agent. *Social Cognition, 26*(2), 169–181. doi:10.1521oco.2008.26.2.169

Kim, H.-Y., & McGill, A. L. (2018). Minions for the rich? Financial status changes how consumers see products with anthropomorphic features. *The Journal of Consumer Research, 45*(2), 429–450. doi:10.1093/jcr/ucy006

Kirkpatrick, M. G., Cruz, T. B., Unger, J. B., Herrera, J., Schiff, S., & Allem, J.-P. (2019). Cartoon-based e-cigarette marketing: Associations with susceptibility to use and perceived expectations of use. *Drug and Alcohol Dependence, 201*, 109–114. doi:10.1016/j.drugalcdep.2019.04.018 PMID:31207451

Knight, P., Freeman, I., Stuart, S., Griggs, G., & O'Reilly, N. (2014). Semiotic representations of Olympic mascots revisited: Virtual mascots of the games 2006-2012. *International Journal of Event and Festival Management, 5*(1), 74–92. doi:10.1108/IJEFM-03-2012-0010

Kotler, P., & Armstrong, G. (2018). *Principles of Marketing* (17th ed.). Pearson.

Kraak, V. I., & Story, M. (2015a). Influence of food companies' brand mascots and entertainment companies' cartoon media characters on children's diet and health: A systematic review and research needs. *Obesity Reviews, 16*(2), 107–126. doi:10.1111/obr.12237 PMID:25516352

Kraak, V. I., & Story, M. (2015b). An accountability evaluation for the industry's responsible use of brand mascots and licensed media characters to market a healthy diet to American children. *Obesity Reviews, 16*(6), 433–453. doi:10.1111/obr.12279 PMID:25875469

Krishna, A. (2012). An integrative review of sensory marketing: Engaging the senses to affect perception, judgment and behavior. *Journal of Consumer Psychology, 22*(3), 332–351. doi:10.1016/j.jcps.2011.08.003

Kumari, R., Jeong, J. Y., Lee, B.-H., Choi, K.-N., & Choi, K. (2019). Topic modelling and social network analysis of publications and patents in humanoid robot technology. *Journal of Information Science*. Advance online publication. doi:10.1177/0165551519887878

Kwak, H., Puzakova, M., & Rocereto, J. F. (2017). When brand anthropomorphism alters perceptions of justice: The moderating role of self-construal. *International Journal of Research in Marketing, 34*(4), 851–871. doi:10.1016/j.ijresmar.2017.04.002

Laksmidewi, D., & Soelasih, Y. (2019). Anthropomorphic green advertising: How to enhance consumers' environmental concern. *DLSU Business & Economics Review, 29*(1), 72–84.

Laksmidewi, D., Susianto, H., & Afiff, A. Z. (2017). Anthropomorphism in advertising: The effect of anthropomorphic product demonstration on consumer purchase intention. *Asian Academy of Management Journal, 22*(1), 1–25. doi:10.21315/aamj2017.22.1.1

Landwehr, J. R., McGill, A. L., & Herrmann, A. (2011). It's got the look: The effect of friendly and aggressive "facial" expressions on product liking and sales. *Journal of Marketing, 75*(3), 132–146. doi:10.1509/jmkg.75.3.132

Lanier, C. D. Jr, Rader, C. S., & Fowler, A. R. III. (2013). Anthropomorphism, marketing relationships, and consumption worth in the Toy Story trilogy. *Journal of Marketing Management, 29*(1-2), 26–47. doi:10.1080/0267257X.2013.769020

Lara-Rodríguez, J. S., Rojas-Contreras, C., & Oliva, E. J.-D. (2019). Discovering emerging research topics for brand personality: A bibliometric analysis. *Australasian Marketing Journal, 27*(4), 261–272. doi:10.1016/j.ausmj.2019.06.002

Lee, N. R., & Kotler, P. (2020). *Social Marketing: Behavior Change for Social Good*. SAGE.

Lee, S., & Oh, H. (2021). Anthropomorphism and its implications for advertising hotel brands. *Journal of Business Research, 129*, 455–464. doi:10.1016/j.jbusres.2019.09.053

Leighty, K. A., Valuska, A. J., Grand, A. P., Bettinger, T. L., Mellen, J. D., Ross, S. R., Boyle, P., & Ogden, J. J. (2015). Impact of visual context on public perceptions of non-human primate performers. *PLoS One, 10*(2), 1–6. doi:10.1371/journal.pone.0118487 PMID:25714101

Letheren, K., Martin, B. A., & Jin, H. S. (2017). Effects of personification and anthropomorphic tendency on destination attitude and travel intentions. *Tourism Management, 62*, 65–75. doi:10.1016/j.tourman.2017.03.020

Lieberman, A. (2004). The effect of enforcement of the master settlement agreement on youth exposure to print advertising. *Health Promotion Practice, 5*(3), 66S–74S. doi:10.1177/1524839904265427 PMID:15231099

Lin, C.-H., & Huang, Y. (2018). How self-construals affect responses to anthropomorphic brands, with a focus on the three-factor relationship between the brand, the gift-giver and the recipient. *Frontiers in Psychology, 9*(2070), 1–17. doi:10.3389/fpsyg.2018.02070 PMID:30455652

Lloyd, S., & Woodside, A. G. (2013). Animals, archetypes, and advertising (A3): The theory and the practice of customer brand symbolism. *Journal of Marketing Management, 29*(1-2), 5–25. doi:10.1080/0267257X.2013.765498

Longacre, M. R., Roback, J., Langeloh, G., Drake, K., & Dalton, M. A. (2015). An entertainment-based approach to promote fruits and vegetables to young children. *Journal of Nutrition Education and Behavior, 47*(5), 480–483. doi:10.1016/j.jneb.2015.06.007 PMID:26363938

Lu, J.-L., & Siao, P.-Y. (2019). Determining the antecedents and consequences of the airline brand personality. *Journal of Airline and Airport Management, 9*(1), 1–13. doi:10.3926/jairm.121

Lu, L., Cai, R., & Gursoy, D. (2019). Developing and validating a service robot integration willingness scale. *International Journal of Hospitality Management, 80*, 36–51. doi:10.1016/j.ijhm.2019.01.005

Luffarelli, J., Stamatogiannakis, A., & Yang, H. (2019). The visual asymmetry effect: An interplay of logo design and brand personality on brand equity. *JMR, Journal of Marketing Research, 56*(1), 89–103. doi:10.1177/0022243718820548

Luo, X., Tong, S., Fang, Z., & Qu, Z. (2019). Frontiers: Machines vs. humans: The impact of artificial intelligence chatbot disclosure on customer purchases. *Marketing Science, 38*(6), 913–1084. doi:10.1287/mksc.2019.1192

MacInnis, D. J., & Folkes, V. S. (2017). Humanizing brands: When brands seem to be like me, part of me, and in a relationship with me. *Journal of Consumer Psychology, 27*(3), 355–374. doi:10.1016/j.jcps.2016.12.003

Martin, B. A.-S., Jin, H. S., Wang, D., Nguyen, H., Zhan, K., & Wang, Y. X. (2020). The influence of consumer anthropomorphism on attitudes towards artificial intelligence trip advisors. *Journal of Hospitality and Tourism Management, 44*, 108–111. doi:10.1016/j.jhtm.2020.06.004

McGoldrick, P. J., Keeling, K. A., & Beatty, S. F. (2008). A typology of roles for avatars in online retailing. *Journal of Marketing Management, 23*(3-4), 433–461. doi:10.1362/026725708X306176

Miesler, L. (2012). Product choice and anthropomorphic designs: Do consumption goals shape innate preferences for human-like forms? *The Design Journal, 15*(3), 373–392. doi:10.2752/175630612X13330186684231

Miesler, L., Leder, H., & Herrmann, A. (2011). Isn't it cute: An evolutionary perspective of baby-schema effects in visual product designs. *International Journal of Design, 5*(3), 17–30.

Miles, C., & Ibrahim, Y. (2013). Deconstructing the meerkat: Fabular anthropomorphism, popular culture, and the market. *Journal of Marketing Management, 29*(15-16), 1862–1880. doi:10.1080/0267257X.2013.803142

Mimoun, M. S.-B., Poncin, I., & Garnier, M. (2012). Case study—Embodied virtual agents: An analysis on reasons for failure. *Journal of Retailing and Consumer Services, 19*(6), 605–612. doi:10.1016/j.jretconser.2012.07.006

Moon, J. H., Kim, E., Choi, S. M., & Sung, Y. (2013). Keep the social in social media: The role of social interaction in avatar-based virtual shopping. *Journal of Interactive Advertising, 13*(1), 14–26. doi:10.1080/15252019.2013.768051

Moore, L. J. (2003). 'Billy, the sad sperm with no tail': Representations of sperm in children's books. *Sexualities, 6*(3-4), 277–300. doi:10.1177/136346070363002

Moremoholo, T. P., & de Lange, R. W. (2018). Anthropomorphic graphics: How useful are they as an instructional aid to facilitate learning? *The Independent Journal of Teaching and Learning, 13*(2), 67-81.

Mourey, J. A., Olson, J. G., & Yoon, C. (2017). Products as pals: Engaging with anthropomorphic products mitigates the effects of social exclusion. *The Journal of Consumer Research, 44*(2), 414–431. doi:10.1093/jcr/ucx038

Mousas, C., Anastasiou, D., & Spantidi, O. (2018). The effects of appearance and motion of virtual characters on emotional reactivity. *Computers in Human Behavior, 86*, 99–108. doi:10.1016/j.chb.2018.04.036

Mull, I., Wyss, J., Moon, E., & Lee, S.-E. (2015). An exploratory study of using 3D avatars as online salespeople: The effect of avatar type on credibility, homophily, attractiveness and intention to interact. *Journal of Fashion Marketing and Management, 19*(2), 154–168. doi:10.1108/JFMM-05-2014-0033

Murphy, J., Gretzel, U., & Pesonen, J. (2019). Marketing robot services in hospitality and tourism: The role of anthropomorphism. *Journal of Travel & Tourism Marketing, 36*(7), 784–795. doi:10.1080/105 48408.2019.1571983

Muzumdar, J. M., Schommer, J. C., Hadsall, R. S., & Huh, J. (2013). Effects of anthropomorphic images and narration styles in promotional messages for generic prescription drugs. *Research in Social & Administrative Pharmacy, 9*(1), 60–79. doi:10.1016/j.sapharm.2012.04.001 PMID:22695216

Nan, X., Anghelcev, G., Myers, J. R., Sar, S., & Faber, R. (2006). What if a web site can talk? Exploring the persuasive effects of web-based anthropomorphic agents. *Journalism & Mass Communication Quarterly, 83*(3), 615–631. doi:10.1177/107769900608300309

Nanay, B. (2021). Zoomorphism. *Erkenntnis, 86*(1), 171–186. doi:10.100710670-018-0099-0

Neal, A. G. (1985). Animism and totemism in popular culture. *Journal of Popular Culture, 19*(2), 15–24. doi:10.1111/j.0022-3840.1985.00015.x

Newton, F. J., Newton, J. D., & Wong, J. (2017). This is your stomach speaking: Anthropomorphized health messages reduce portion size preferences among the powerless. *Journal of Business Research, 75*, 229–239. doi:10.1016/j.jbusres.2016.07.020

Noble, C. H., Bing, M. N., & Bogoviyeva, E. (2013). The effects of brand metaphors as design innovation: A test of congruency hypotheses. *Journal of Product Innovation Management, 30*(S1), 126–141. doi:10.1111/jpim.12067

Oklevik, O., Supphellen, M., & Maehle, N. (2020). Time to retire the concept of brand personality? Extending the critique and introducing a new framework. *Journal of Consumer Behaviour, 19*(3), 211–218. doi:10.1002/cb.1805

Osinski, B. L., Getson, J. M., Bentlage, B., Avery, G., Glas, Z., Esman, L. A., Williams, R. N., & Prokopy, L. S. (2019). What's the draw? Illustrating the impacts of cartoons versus photographs on attitudes and behavioral intentions for wildlife conservation. *Human Dimensions of Wildlife, 24*(3), 231–249. doi:10 .1080/10871209.2019.1587649

Park, N., Jang, K., Cho, S., & Choi, J. (2021). Use of offensive language in human-artificial intelligence chatbot interaction: The effects of ethical ideology, social competence, and perceived humanlikeness. *Computers in Human Behavior, 121*, 106795. Advance online publication. doi:10.1016/j.chb.2021.106795

Patsiaouras, G., Fitchett, J., & Saren, M. (2014). Boris Artzybasheff and the art of anthropomorphic marketing in early American consumer culture. *Journal of Marketing Management, 30*(1-2), 117–137. doi:10.1080/0267257X.2013.803141

Patterson, A., Khogeer, Y., & Hodgson, J. (2013). How to create an inñuential anthropomorphic mascot: Literary musings on marketing, make-believe, and meerkats. *Journal of Marketing Management, 29*(1-2), 69–85. doi:10.1080/0267257X.2012.759992

Pelau, C., Dabija, D.-C., & Ene, I. (2021). What makes an AI device human-like? The role of interaction quality, empathy and perceived psychological anthropomorphic characteristics in the acceptance of artificial intelligence in the service industry. *Computers in Human Behavior, 122*, 106855. Advance online publication. doi:10.1016/j.chb.2021.106855

Petty, R. D., & D'Rozario, D. (2009). The use of dead celebrities in advertising and marketing: Balancing interests in the right of publicity. *Journal of Advertising, 38*(4), 37–49. doi:10.2753/JOA0091-3367380403

Phillips, B. J., Sedgewick, J. R., & Slobodzian, A. D. (2019). Spokes-characters in print advertising: An update and extension. *Journal of Current Issues and Research in Advertising, 40*(2), 214–228. doi: 10.1080/10641734.2018.1503110

Puzakova, M., Kwak, H., & Rocereto, J. (2009). Pushing the envelope of brand and personality: Antecedents and moderators of anthropomorphized brands. *Advances in Consumer Research. Association for Consumer Research (U. S.), 36*, 413–420.

Puzakova, M., Rocereto, J. F., & Kwak, H. (2013). Ads are watching me - A view from the interplay between anthropomorphism and customisation. *International Journal of Advertising, 32*(4), 513–538. doi:10.2501/IJA-32-4-513-538

Qiu, L., & Benbasat, I. (2009). Evaluating anthropomorphic product recommendation agents: A social relationship perspective to designing information systems. *Journal of Management Information Systems, 25*(4), 145–182. doi:10.2753/MIS0742-1222250405

Qiu, L., & Benbasat, I. (2010). A study of demographic embodiments of product recommendation agents in electronic commerce. *International Journal of Human-Computer Studies, 68*(10), 669–688. doi:10.1016/j.ijhcs.2010.05.005

Radler, V. M. (2018). 20 Years of brand personality: A bibliometric review and research agenda. *Journal of Brand Management, 25*(4), 370–383. doi:10.105741262-017-0083-z

Rauschnabel, P. A., & Ahuvia, A. C. (2014). You're so lovable: Anthropomorphism and brand love. *Journal of Brand Management, 21*(5), 372–395. doi:10.1057/bm.2014.14

Reavey, B., Puzakova, M., Andras, T. L., & Kwak, H. (2018). The multidimensionality of anthropomorphism in advertising: The moderating roles of cognitive busyness and assertive language. *International Journal of Advertising, 37*(3), 440–462. doi:10.1080/02650487.2018.1438054

Riikkinen, M., Saarijärvi, H., Sarlin, P., & Lähteenmäki, I. (2018). Using artificial intelligence to create value in insurance. *International Journal of Bank Marketing, 36*(6), 1145–1168. doi:10.1108/IJBM-01-2017-0015

Rincon, J. A., Costa, A., Novais, P., Julian, V., & Carrascosa, C. (2018). A new emotional robot assistant that facilitates human interaction and persuasion. *Knowledge and Information Systems, 60*(1), 363–383. doi:10.100710115-018-1231-9

Robertson, V.-L. D. (2014). Of ponies and men: My little pony: Friendship is magic and the brony fandom. *International Journal of Cultural Studies, 17*(1), 21–27. doi:10.1177/1367877912464368

Saeed, M. R., Burki, U., Ali, R., Dahlstrom, R., & Zameer, H. (2021). The antecedents and consequences of brand personality: A systematic review. *EuroMed Journal of Business*. Advance online publication. doi:10.1108/EMJB-12-2020-0136

Sashittal, H., & Jassawalla, A. (2019). Brand entification as a post-anthropomorphic attribution among Twitter-using Millennials. *Marketing Intelligence & Planning*, *37*(7), 741–753. doi:10.1108/MIP-10-2018-0446

Severson, R. L., & Lemm, K. M. (2016). Kids see human too: Adapting an individual differences measure of anthropomorphism for a child sample. *Journal of Cognition and Development*, *17*(1), 122–141. doi:10.1080/15248372.2014.989445

Shaari, H., Salleh, S. M., Yong, P. L., Perumal, S., & Zainol, F. A. (2019). Assessing the effect of university brand personality and attitude towards donation on alumni donor behavioural intention: Malaysian perspective. *International Journal of Management Education*, *13*(4), 377–396. doi:10.1504/IJMIE.2019.102595

Shamseer, L., Moher, D., Clarke, M., Ghersi, D., Liberati, A., Petticrew, M., Shekelle, P., & Stewart, L. A. (2015). Preferred reporting items for systematic review and meta-analysis protocols (PRISMA-P) 2015: Elaboration and explanation. *BMJ, 349*. doi:10.1136/bmj.g7647

Shea, M. (2014). User-friendly: Anthropomorphic devices and mechanical behaviour in Japan. *Advances in Anthropology*, *4*(1), 41–49. doi:10.4236/aa.2014.41006

Sherman, G. D., & Haidt, J. (2011). Cuteness and disgust: The humanizing and dehumanizing effects of emotion. *Emotion Review*, *3*(3), 245–251. doi:10.1177/1754073911402396

Singh, S., Sapre, A., & Kewlani, S. (2016). Differential priming of gender and coupling of affect and cognition in anthropomorphic stimulation. *Metamorphosis*, *15*(2), 91–101. doi:10.1177/0972622516675949

Sivaramakrishnan, S., Wan, F., & Intera, Z. T. (2007). Giving an "e-human touch" to e-tailing: The moderating roles of static information quantity and consumption motive in the effectiveness of an anthropomorphic information agent. *Journal of Interactive Marketing*, *21*(1), 60–75. doi:10.1002/dir.20075

Soni, S., & Jain, S. (2017). Building anthropomorphic brands: Big success of Chhota Bheem. *FIIB Business Review*, *6*(2), 58–66. doi:10.1177/2455265820170209

Spears, N. E., Mowen, J. C., & Chakraborty, G. (1996). Symbolic role of animals in print advertising: Content analysis and conceptual development. *Journal of Business Research*, *37*(2), 87–95. doi:10.1016/0148-2963(96)00060-4

Steinberg, M. (2010). A vinyl platform for dissent: Designer toys and character merchandising. *Journal of Visual Culture*, *9*(2), 209–228. doi:10.1177/1470412910372760

Stevens, L., Kearney, M., & Maclaran, P. (2013). Uddering the other: Androcentrism, ecofeminism, and the dark side of anthropomorphic marketing. *Journal of Marketing Management*, *29*(1-2), 158–174. doi:10.1080/0267257X.2013.764348

Tam, K.-P., Lee, S.-L., & Chao, M. M. (2013). Saving Mr. Nature: Anthropomorphism enhances connectedness to and protectiveness toward nature. *Journal of Experimental Social Psychology, 49*(3), 514–521. doi:10.1016/j.jesp.2013.02.001

Tay, B. T.-C., Low, S. C., Ko, K. H., & Park, T. (2016). Types of humor that robots can play. *Computers in Human Behavior, 60*, 19–28. doi:10.1016/j.chb.2016.01.042

Tondu, B. (2012). Anthropomorphism and service humanoid robots: An ambiguous relationship. *The Industrial Robot, 39*(6), 609–618. doi:10.1108/01439911211268840

Touré-Tillery, M., & McGill, A. L. (2015). Who or what to believe: Trust and the differential persuasiveness of human and anthropomorphized messengers. *Journal of Marketing, 79*(4), 94–110. doi:10.1509/jm.12.0166

Triantos, A., Plakoyiannaki, E., Outra, E., & Petridis, N. (2016). Anthropomorphic packaging: Is there life on "Mars"? *European Journal of Marketing, 50*(1/2), 260–275. doi:10.1108/EJM-12-2012-0692

Trivedi, J. (2018). Measuring the comparative efficacy of endorsements by celebrities vis-à-vis animated mascots. *Journal of Creative Communications, 13*(2), 117–132. doi:10.1177/0973258618761407

Tung, F.-W. (2016). Child perception of humanoid robot appearance and behavior. *International Journal of Human-Computer Interaction, 32*(6), 493–502. doi:10.1080/10447318.2016.1172808

Tuškej, U., & Podnar, K. (2018). Consumers' identification with corporate brands: Brand prestige, anthropomorphism and engagement in social media. *Journal of Product and Brand Management, 27*(1), 3–17. doi:10.1108/JPBM-05-2016-1199

Unal, S., Dalgic, T., & Akar, E. (2018). How avatars help enhancing self-image congruence. *International Journal of Internet Marketing and Advertising, 12*(4), 374–395. doi:10.1504/IJIMA.2018.095400

van Pinxteren, M. M.-E., Wetzels, R. W.-H., Rüger, J., Pluymaekers, M., & Wetzels, M. (2019). Trust in humanoid robots: Implications for services marketing. *Journal of Services Marketing, 33*(4), 507–518. doi:10.1108/JSM-01-2018-0045

van Rooij, M. (2019). Carefully constructed yet curiously real: How major American animation studios generate empathy through a shared style of character design. *Animation, 14*(3), 191–206. doi:10.1177/1746847719875071

Vandana, & Kumar, V. (2018). Mom I want it: Impact of anthropomorphism on pester power among children. *International Journal of Business Innovation and Research, 16*(2), 168-185. doi:10.1504/IJBIR.2018.091912

Veer, E. (2013). Made with real crocodiles: The use of anthropomorphism to promote product kinship in our youngest consumers. *Journal of Marketing Management, 29*(1-2), 195–206. doi:10.1080/0267257X.2012.759990

Verganti, R., Vendraminelli, L., & Iansiti, M. (2020). Innovation and design in the age of artificial intelligence. *Journal of Product Innovation Management, 37*(3), 212–227. doi:10.1111/jpim.12523

Vinyals-Mirabent, S., Kavaratzis, M., & Fernández-Cavia, J. (2019). The role of functional associations in building destination brand personality: When official websites do the talking. *Tourism Management*, *75*, 148–155. doi:10.1016/j.tourman.2019.04.022

Watson, D. (2019). The rhetoric and reality of anthropomorphism in artificial intelligence. *Minds and Machines*, *29*(3), 417–440. doi:10.100711023-019-09506-6

Waytz, A., Cacioppo, J., & Epley, N. (2010). Who sees human?: The stability and importance of individual differences in anthropomorphism. *Perspectives on Psychological Science*, *5*(3), 219–232. doi:10.1177/1745691610369336 PMID:24839457

Weber, J. (2005). Helpless machines and true loving care givers: A feminist critique of recent trends in human-robot interaction. *Journal of Information. Communication and Ethics in Society*, *3*(4), 209–218. doi:10.1108/14779960580000274

Wirtz, J., Patterson, P. G., Kunz, W. H., Gruber, T., Lu, V. N., Paluch, S., & Martins, A. (2018). Brave new world: Service robots in the frontline. *Journal of Service Management*, *29*(5), 907–931. doi:10.1108/JOSM-04-2018-0119

Wood, M. (2019). The potential for anthropomorphism in communicating science: Inspiration from Japan. *Cultura e Scuola*, *2*(1), 23–34. doi:10.1177/209660831900200103

Xu, K. (2019). First encounter with robot Alpha: How individual differences interact with vocal and kinetic cues in users' social responses. *New Media & Society*, *21*(11-12), 2522–2547. doi:10.1177/1461444819851479

Yang, K. C.-C. (2006). The influence of humanlike navigation interface on users' responses to Internet advertising. *Telematics and Informatics*, *23*(1), 38–55. doi:10.1016/j.tele.2005.03.001

Yang, L. W., Aggarwal, P., & McGill, A. L. (2020). The 3 C's of anthropomorphism: Connection, comprehension, and competition. *Counselling Psychology Review*, *3*(1), 3–19. doi:10.1002/arcp.1054

Yang, Y., Liu, Y., Lv, X., Ai, J., & Li, Y. (2021). Anthropomorphism and customers' willingness to use artificial intelligence service agents. *Journal of Hospitality Marketing & Management*. Advance online publication. doi:10.1080/19368623.2021.1926037

Yu, C.-E. (2020). Humanlike robots as employees in the hotel industry: Thematic content analysis of online reviews. *Journal of Hospitality Marketing & Management*, *29*(1), 22-38. doi:10.1080/19368623.2019.1592733

Yu, C.-E., & Ngan, H. F. (2019). The power of head tilts: Gender and cultural differences of perceived human vs human-like robot smile in service. *Tourism Review*, *74*(3), 428–442. doi:10.1108/TR-07-2018-0097

Zha, X. F. (2005). Artificial intelligence and integrated intelligent systems in product design and development. In C. T. Leondes (Ed.), *Intelligent Knowledge-Based Systems* (pp. 1067–1123). Springer. doi:10.1007/978-1-4020-7829-3_32

Zhao, S. (2006). Humanoid social robots as a medium of communication. *New Media & Society*, *8*(3), 401–419. doi:10.1177/1461444806061951

Zhu, H., Wong, N., & Huang, M. (2019). Does relationship matter? How social distance influences perceptions of responsibility on anthropomorphized environmental objects and conservation intentions. *Journal of Business Research*, *95*, 62–70. doi:10.1016/j.jbusres.2018.10.008

ADDITIONAL READING

Ali, F., Dogan, S., Amin, M., Hussain, K., & Ryu, K. (2021). Brand anthropomorphism, love and defense: Does attitude towards social distancing matter? *Service Industries Journal*, *41*(1/2), 58–83. doi: 10.1080/02642069.2020.1867542

Ashforth, B. E., Schinoff, B. S., & Brickson, S. L. (2020). "My company is friendly," "mine's a rebel": Anthropomorphism and shifting organizational identity from "what" to "who". *Academy of Management Review*, *45*(1), 29–57. doi:10.5465/amr.2016.0496

Bresciani, S., Ferraris, A., Santoro, G., & Nilsen, H. R. (2016). Wine sector: Companies' performance and green economy as a means of societal marketing. *Journal of Promotion Management*, *22*(2), 251–267. doi:10.1080/10496491.2016.1121753

Brown, S. (2010). Where the wild brands are: Some thoughts on anthropomorphic marketing. *The Marketing Review*, *10*(3), 209–224. doi:10.1362/146934710X523078

Chung, K. C. (2020). Green marketing orientation: Achieving sustainable development in green hotel management. *Journal of Hospitality Marketing & Management*, *29*(6), 722–738. doi:10.1080/19368623.2020.1693471

Cooremans, K., & Geuens, M. (2019). Same but different: Using anthropomorphism in the battle against food waste. *Journal of Public Policy & Marketing*, *38*(2), 232–245. doi:10.1177/0743915619827941

Hasan, Z., & Ali, N. A. (2015). The impact of green marketing strategy on the firm's performance in Malaysia. *Procedia: Social and Behavioral Sciences*, *172*, 463–470. doi:10.1016/j.sbspro.2015.01.382

Ofori, D. (2021). Opportunities and challenges of green marketing. In C. Mukonza, R. E. Hinson, O. Adeola, I. Adisa, E. Mogaji, & A. C. Kirgiz (Eds.), *Green Marketing in Emerging Markets. Palgrave Studies of Marketing in Emerging Economies* (pp. 251–276). Palgrave Macmillan. doi:10.1007/978-3-030-74065-8_11

Supaat, S. H., Ahamat, A., & Nizam, N. Z. (2020). Green marketing strategies for sustainability development of firm's performance in Malaysia: For green economy. *International Journal of Business Competition and Growth*, *7*(1), 41–67. doi:10.1504/IJBCG.2020.108437

Wang, X., Ming, M., & Zhang, Y. (2020). Are "people" or "animals" more attractive? Anthropomorphic images in green-product advertising. *Journal of Cleaner Production*, *276*, 122719. Advance online publication. doi:10.1016/j.jclepro.2020.122719

KEY TERMS AND DEFINITIONS

Anthropomorphic Marketing (the Functional Approach): The process of projecting or creating anthropomorphic agents.

Anthropomorphism: The tendency to give the nonhuman agents humanlike characteristics, motivations, intentions, and emotions.

Brand Personality: The human traits given to a brand.

Commercial Marketing: Marketing activities for business-related purposes.

Social Marketing: Marketing activities aim at addressing social issues.

Zoomorphism: The dehumanization or animalization of human agents.

Chapter 3
Determinants and Outcomes of Green Innovations:
A Conceptual Model

Asha Thomas
Wroclaw University of Science and Technology, Poland

Rosa Palladino
University of Milan Bicocca, Italy

Chiara Nespoli
University of Bologna "Alma Mater Studiorum", Italy

Maria T. d'agostino
Department of Economics and Law, University of Cassino and Southern Lazio, Italy

Giuseppe Russo
University of Cassino and Southern Lazio, Italy

ABSTRACT

Green innovation (GI) refers to an invention that simultaneously benefits the environment and customers. Academics and policymakers have recently focused on GI to understand how innovation and sustainability interact. Indeed, governments and non-governmental organizations pressure businesses to abandon "traditional environmentally harmful products" in favor of green products (GPI) and green process innovations (GPrI). GI research has attracted the attention of many scholars, adopting diverse perspectives, but there has been a lack of publications on the green process and green product innovation (GPI) together. In this way, the current study conducts a literature review and bibliometric analysis to evaluate the "literary corpus" on GI and its various forms. The research provides a comprehensive understanding of GI's various determinants and outcomes. Managers and policymakers can also benefit from the most recent research findings to gain a better understanding of key determinants and outcomes.

DOI: 10.4018/978-1-6684-4610-2.ch003

INTRODUCTION

In the modern world, firms are mainly concerned with protecting the environment and managing the consequences of energy shortages, as well as with customers' greater understanding of "environmentally friendly products" and environmental pollution (Taoketao et al., 2018; Yin et al., 2018). Any new "practice introduced into an organization, including equipment, products, processes, policies, and projects" is considered innovative. Hence, this context pushes companies toward green innovation (GI) (Du et al., 2018; Wang, 2019). The active participation of firms in GIs reduces negative environmental effects, while increasing production and improving organizational status and corporate performance as well as competitiveness (Chen et al., 2006). GI has gained popularity in academic and political circles in recent years due to the passage of "remedial legislation" in several countries to avoid or mitigate adverse environmental impacts (Boons & Lüdeke-Freund, 2013). Indeed, earlier studies have recognized the importance of GI in growing businesses (Chiou et al., 2011; Lin et al., 2013; Tseng et al., 2013; Gao et al., 2020 Zhao, X., & Bai, X. 2021). Many empirical studies use a single criterion to assess GI, but have not distinguished between green product innovation (GPI) and green process innovation (GPrI) (Chen et al., 2012; Song & Yu, 2018; Sun & Sun, 2021). Many researchers have studied GPI (Andersén, 2021; Awan et al., 2021b; Peters & Buijs, 2022;Song et al., 2020; Serrano-García et al., 2021) and process innovation (Achi et al., 2022; Xie et al., 2022; Zameer et al., 2021l; Khan et al., 2021), in various studies, with some notable exceptions considering both in combination (Armbruster et al., 2008; Awan et al., 2021a; Kivimaa, 2007; Stucki et al., 2018; Wagner, 2008; Wang et al., 2021; Yang & Roh, 2019). Considering that GI has a greater degree of complexity than conventional innovations, because it requires more specialized skills to activate processes of exchange as well as the sharing of knowledge from the outside to overcome the technological and cognitive gap, this study provides a comprehensive overview of GI (Gupta & Thomas, 2019). Although earlier evaluations of the literature have increased the knowledge about the subject, a full examination of the research on the determinants and outcomes of green products and process innovation remains lacking.

Despite the fact that numerous research studies have been conducted on the determinants and consequences of green processes or products, this chapter tries to fill the gap in the literature by providing a comprehensive review of these analyses to improve conceptual clarity. The main objective is to systematize and classify the literature on GI by combining both GPI and GPrI. The following research questions are reviewed in this research:

Research Question One: Which themes have been studied in the GI research that can be observed by performing a conceptual structure map?

Research Question Two: What research contexts have been studied in terms of GIs that can be evaluated by performing a bibliometric analysis (assessing the most productive sources of publications, as well as country and annual scientific production)?

In this way, this chapter tries to identify the main key constructs based on the antecedents and results of GPI and GPrI. Therefore, this study offers a conceptual model as well as practical implications, improving the understanding of how GIs can ultimately impact society and business.

The chapter is structured as follows: first, the literature review defines GI and its different types. The next section explains the methodology. Following that, a bibliometric analysis of previous studies in GI is performed and a conceptual model based on the output is proposed. Finally, the conclusion discusses the primary theoretical and managerial inferences, as well as possible directions for future research.

LITERATURE REVIEW AND THEORETICAL UNDERPINNING

GIs include technological advances that reduce pollution, conserve energy, reprocess and reuse products, generate green products, and improve corporate environmental management (Chen et al., 2006, Tang et al., 2018). GI is defined as "eco-friendly product designs and manufacturing processes" (Zailani et al., 2015).

GIs include the development of new or modified procedures, skills, methods, and products to reduce or avoid environmental issues. GI is defined in the literature as "green," "ecological," "environmental," and "sustainable" (Boons & Lüdeke-Freund, 2013; Carrillo-Hermosilla et al., 2010)

There are two types of GI: GPrI and GPI (Karabulut et al., 2020). GPrI combines green process technologies such as "clean production, pollution control, pollution prevention, environmental efficiency, and recirculation" with new or improved activities that contribute to goods or services from an environmental point of view (Gao et al., 2020; Shahzad et al., 2020). GPrI, like GPI, improves manufacturing and production processes (Yang & Roh, 2019). According to academic literature, GIs are a "subset" of shared innovations that share characteristics (Tang et al, 2018; Wagner, 2008).

GPI makes an organization's goods or services new or significantly better than the rest of the environment. GPI involves the creation of products that "save energy, reduce pollution, recycle trash, and are nontoxic" (Dangelico & Pujari, 2010; Sun & Sun, 2021).

The emphasis on GPrI is new. In fact, manufacturing companies are attempting to reduce pollution and waste in their operations while also increasing the applicability of resources (Dangelico & Pujari, 2010). These efforts are required because, in many situations, strict environmental standards apply to both global and domestic markets, and customers care more about decreasing pollutants than product attributes.

METHODOLOGY

This paper used a qualitative approach to find documents on GI. The articles of the data collection were collected through detailed searches on the ISI Web of Science (WoS) search engine, according to common search procedures (Fink, 2010). The process of extracting the main documents on the subject was based on the following keywords: "green innovation," "green products Innovation" (GPI) and "green process innovation" (GPrI). For each article, the authors checked the relevance of the abstract and keywords in relation to the research objectives. The final sample of articles was subjected to bibliometric analysis, employing "bibliographic data" from online databases. The bibliometric analysis is founded on data that enable scientific investigation and provide a comprehensive field view. The bibliometrics R-package (biblioshiny) (Aria & Cuccurullo, 2017) collects and documents quantitative data on the various publications chosen for this investigation (Thomas & Gupta, 2021a,b; Thomas &Gupta , 2022).

Table 1 summarizes the essential characteristics of the documents recovered by WoS for bibliometric study (Sharma et al, 2021; Thomas et al., 2021a; Thomas et al., 2021). The 886 articles chosen for bibliometric analysis were those that were published in the *Social Science Citation Index* (*SSCI*) journal only to retain the quality associated with bibliometric analysis. Additionally, the authors of this paper conducted a thorough literature study by categorizing papers by whether they concerned GPI or GPrI to identify the important determinants and outcomes.

Table 1. The essential characteristics of the documents for the bibliometric study

Description	Results
MAIN INFORMATION ABOUT DATA	
Timespan	2002:2022
Sources (journals, books, etc.)	214
Documents	886
Average years from publication	3.02
Average citations per document	27.38
Average citations per year per doc	5.884
DOCUMENT TYPES	
Article	761
Article; book chapter	2
Article; early access	75
Article; proceedings paper	4
Book review	19
Correction	2
Editorial material	9
Meeting abstract	2
Review	11
Review; early access	1

BIBLIOMETRIC REVIEW

Conceptual Structure

A conceptual structure map with contextual structure visualization was created for each phrase frequently used in GI research publications. Each word is ordered according to the values of Dim 1 and Dim 2, which is a bibliometric term for a diminutive particle.

The conceptual framework aids multiple correspondence analysis (MCA) and K-means clustering in locating papers that convey similar ideas. MCA is a multivariate exploratory technique for analyzing graphical and numerical data. There are two sections highlighted in red and blue in a word map. Each section depicts words that are linked. The "keyword conceptual framework" of GI papers is depicted in Figure 1.

Figure 1. Conceptual structure map

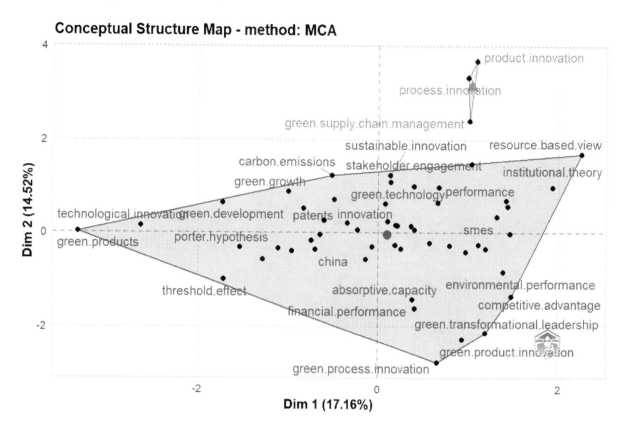

Source of Articles

Figure 2 summarizes the journals that published the publications in the sample. It depicts the papers concerning GI in top international journals with strong impact factors. Most of the articles were published in *Sustainability* (116) and the *Journal of Cleaner Production* (108) (Figure 2).

Figure 2. Journal titles

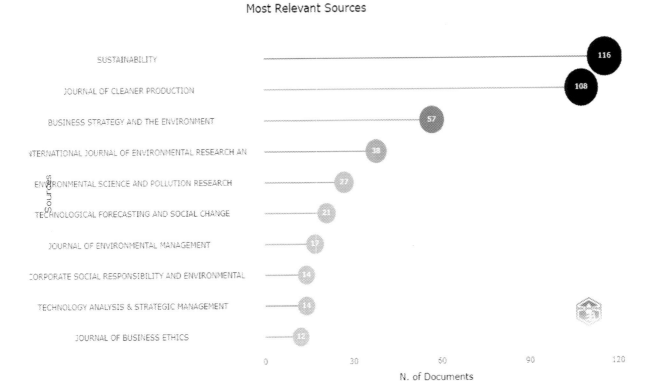

Most Relevant Sources

Country Scientific Production

Figure 3 depicts the countries considering the GI topic. China has the maximum number of articles on GI (1,240), followed by the United States of America (96), the United Kingdom (94), Italy (88), Spain (62), Pakistan (53), Malaysia (49), Germany (41), South Korea (34), and Australia (32). This theme has spread to numerous countries/continents and highlights a growing interest in GI. Figure 3 depicts a notable increase in the GI in various countries (highlighted in blue).

Figure 3. Countries considering the GI theme

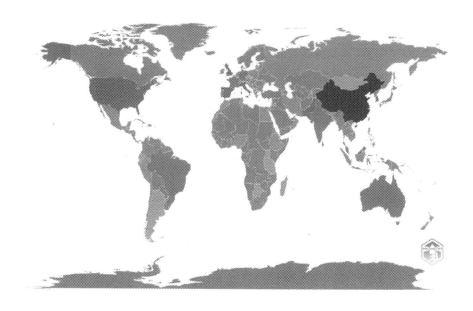

Annual Scientific Production

Figure 4 depicts the distribution of 886 documents published on GI from 2002 to 2022. In the first five years, eight papers on GI were published. Since 2011, the number of GI articles published has increased. Overall, annual GI article publications have risen steadily since 2016, with 252 articles published in the previous year, i.e., 2021.

Figure 4. Distribution of 886 documents published on GI

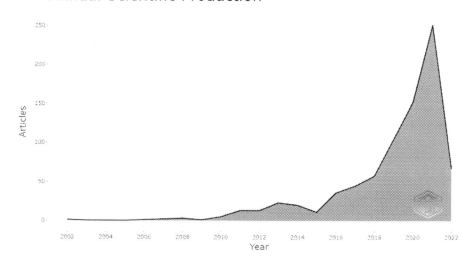

DEVELOPMENT OF CONCEPTUAL FRAMEWORK

Based on detailed studies on GPI and GPrI, an integrated conceptual framework model is proposed (See figure 5). This section will discuss the key determinants and outcomes of GPI and GPrI.

Green Product Innovation

Determinants

Innovators help businesses save money, reduce waste, gain more market share, develop new markets, and achieve first-mover advantages throughout the product life cycle (Porter & van der Linde, 1995). Green product design reduces the use of potentially hazardous substances (Kammerer, 2009). It is impossible to overestimate the significance of the corporate and consumer environments. To remain competitive, organizations must employ adaptable methods and products (Chang & Chiu, 2007). Van Hemel and Cramer (2002) argue that internal rather than external factors influence the development of environmentally friendly products. Eco-design is controlled by various factors, including new market opportunities, innovation, and anticipated improvements in product quality. However, according to Chiou et al. (2011), buyers are becoming more eco-aware, meaning they want products that use less energy and are better for the environment. Formal and social control is also key to improving GPI. Zhang et al. (2021) investigate the extent of the interaction between "formal control" and "social control" in the context of "green supply chain collaboration" and identify the antecedent part of the inter-organizational control mechanism.

Begum et al. (2022) investigates the impact of green transformational leadership and creative process involvement on GPI in four Chinese high-tech manufacturing industries and discovered that these factors had a significant impact on GPI (Begum et al., 2022). Green suppliers, another important driver of GPI, can provide resources, such as environmental knowledge, that help the company differentiate itself (Dangelico et al., 2017). Melander (2018) examines both internal and external capabilities and emphasizes the importance of finding a compatible partner. Collaborators must be concerned about environmental issues and contribute to the organization's cutting-edge information or technology. Firms must integrate relational characteristics such as trust with contractual commitments in collaborative inventions. The findings underscore the value of knowledge management within and between firms (Thomas & Gupta, 2022). According to the results, a collaboration between partners does not take place in a vacuum but rather in a networked environment.

Andersén (2021) demonstrates that green suppliers can provide pivotal factors and resources to assist an organization to effectively reach its GPI potential. According to Lee and Kim (2011), changing relationships with green suppliers from market distance to supply chain collaboration, can make the underlying competencies less imitable and thus the differentiating advantage more sustainable. To run a sustainable business, a company's suppliers must be environmentally friendly (Andersén et al., 2020).

The adoption of new technologies, particularly GPI, is then used to meet market demands and gain a competitive advantage. Customers' benefits and prices are frequently mentioned as determinants of market demand (Kammerer, 2009). According to the empirical findings of Lin et al. (2013), market demand is positively correlated with GPI. Furthermore, the acquisition of skills, collaborative networks, and external knowledge ties are highlighted as critical components of GPI by Dangelico et al. (2017). Companies that value market knowledge from suppliers, consumers, rivals, and external consultants are also more eco-friendly (Segarra-Oña et al., 2014). Firms require information to assist them in their efforts to engage in GI. This type of innovation requires the organization to acquire and transform new knowledge. Because absorptive capacity applies new information to produce significantly improved or novel products, services, or processes, it can be seen as a significant motivator for a firm's intention to adopt GI approaches. According to Albort-Morant et al. (2018), potential absorptive capacity influences the realized absorptive capacity, which affects the performance of both green products.

Businesses, according to Chan et al. (2016), must align their operations with environmental regulations. As a result, a company's ability to create green products and achieve business success will improve. According to environmental management research, GPI serves as a bridge between environmental regulation and operational or economic performance. On the other hand, the government is responsible for enacting and enforcing environmental laws and policies. That is, policymakers set the constraints imposed by such legislation or regulations. Given the existence of a moderating factor (GPI) between such demands and company performance, policymakers should assess the industry's capacity for GPI.

Outcomes

Businesses can gain long-term competitive advantages by developing green products that help them achieve environmental sustainability criteria, extend their present market, and exceed customer expectations (Chang, 2011, 2016). The development of environmentally friendly products is a crucial aspect of improving competitiveness (Chen et al., 2006; Chang, 2011; Skordoulis et al., 2020). On the other hand, non-green product companies have not been studied to see how they preserve their competitive advantage while shifting to green product creation. "Green dynamic capability," as outlined by Qiu et al. (2020), gives GPI in China's manufacturing industry a competitive advantage over traditional method. "Green dynamic capability," "resource integration," "reconfiguration capabilities" and "environmental" understanding are essential for green product creation and competitive advantage (Dangelico, 2016; Dangelico et al., 2017).

Organizations are looking for ways to profit from "waste dumps" by converting them into "commercial goods" (Kammerer, 2009). Branded environmental technologies or service sales can improve brand images and create new sales channels (Chen et al., 2006). Green product development can assist businesses in increasing their efficiency and primary capabilities. Rising start-up costs, overdue accounting practices, and complex construction projects prevent success (Ilg, 2019).

Consumers are concerned about environmental issues and companies will thrive in the global market (Chiou et al., 2011). Many scholars believe that GPI significantly affects firm performance (Ch'ng et al., 2021; Dangelico et al., 2017). Indeed, according to Chan et al. (2015), environmental dynamism influences the link between GI and firm performance. Green product innovators can increase their cost efficiency and profitability in a volatile environment. More specifically, the improvement in cost efficiency rather than firm profitability is demonstrated. This empirical finding suggests that cost efficiency may outweigh profitability in a fast-paced business environment. Although cost efficiency is easier to assess than profitability, it is recommended that managers prioritize cost-cutting activities when the environment is more dynamic. Similarly, Li et al. (2020) demonstrate through empirical research that GPI has a positive influence on the economic and social performance of a country, as well as an organization's financial performance. Environmental performance measures an organization's effectiveness in reducing the amount of carbon dioxide and other harmful gases emitted from its operations, such as production and transference (Dubey et al., 2015). Zhang et al. (2021) note that when the environmental impacts of the resources used in production are reduced, GPI is helpful in improving the organization's ecological functioning.

Green Process Innovation

Determinants

GPrI helps firms improve their environmental sustainability strategies (Chen et al., 2006), making the industrial output more sustainable and eco-efficient (Hart & Ahuja, 1996). International customers are important in organizations that use GPrI strategies, according to Guoyou et al. (2013). The impact is limited to "foreign-invested" organizations accepting GPrI. Stucki et al. (2018) use a unique collection of information in Austria, Germany, and Switzerland to observe the relationship between policy and green product and process innovation. They find that policies have a more significant impact on process innovation than product innovation. GPrI is an important strategy for manufacturing organizations pursuing sustainable development. However, it is unclear how to assist manufacturing organizations in removing roadblocks when GPrI is implemented. Foreign customers help organizations drive green processes and product innovation. The effect is limited to foreign-invested firms adopting GPrI. This also demonstrates that community and regulatory stakeholders have little discernible impact on the green processes and products of a company.

GPrI is promoted by government subsidies, not environmental restrictions, according to Liu et al. (2020). As environmental regulations and government subsidies have a threshold influence on GPrI, restrictions and subsidies should be raised. Xie et al. (2019) use panel data from manufacturing-listed companies in China between 2013 and 2017 to explore the causes, contingent conditions, and outcomes of GPrI. The observe that green subsidies are significantly related to two aspects of GPrI, namely, cleaner production technology and end-of-pipe technology. Both cleaner production technology and end-of-pipe technology are significantly associated with firms' green image.

Wei and Sun (2021) identify the critical role of GPrI and manufacturing digitalization value in acquiring green capabilities in the digitalization era. They also help by revealing contingent components that can influence manufacturing digitalization from the point of data processing. They note that manufacturing digitalization has a significant impact on GPrI and the performance of organizations. Technological capability is defined as the ability to innovate to achieve a competitive advantage (Thomas & Chopra, 2020; Jain et al., 2022). It involves advanced technology, patents and copyrights, research and development (R&D), and specialist employees. Firms with advanced digital competence can improve production process efficiency, lower production costs, and increase competitiveness. Technology-capable firms must invest in both workers and new technologies. While environmental change may present new growth opportunities, it also raises market and technology risk and uncertainty. Zhang et al. (2021) analyze the effects of environmental dynamism on GPrI, focusing on the moderating effects of supply chain collaboration. They identify a positive link between GPrI and technological dynamism in 210 Chinese manufacturing businesses.

To pursue green development, businesses must adopt an internal resource integration strategy and significant external collaboration with stakeholders, also known as "open innovation." Furthermore, open innovation between businesses will make GI more efficient and sustainable (Thomas, 2021). Many studies have found that collaborating with external networks improves innovation activities while lowering costs and risks. This is especially true for high-tech but difficult-to-implement innovations, such as GI, where open innovation provides access to a wide range of external ideas, skills, and resources (Thomas, 2021; Zhang, 2021). According to Yang and Roh (2019), open innovation will be strongly linked to GPrI. Furthermore, collaboration with other organizations increases the likelihood of enterprises overcoming competence lock-in during radical GI (Chadha, 2011). As a result, collaboration is essential to the GPrI.

The influence of leadership on green activity and green creativity (Zhang et al., 2021), environmental performance (Singh et al., 2020), and strategy (Huang et al., 2021) has been studied by several authors. There is a large amount of research focusing on green transformational leadership. Likewise, transformational leadership and creative process engagement have a significant impact on GPrI (Begun et al., 2022).

Outcomes

Environmental responsibility is critical for environmental decisions and a firm's competitiveness. Similarly, it is nearly impossible to implement green manufacturing techniques without an environmental approach. Enhancing environmental performance through GPrI and environmental focus, according to Zameer et al. (2021), can help the manufacturing sector contribute to carbon neutrality.

GPrI, like any new technology, has implications for the firm's financial performance. The existing literature categorizes GPrI into two groups: clean technology and end-of-pipe technologies (Xie et al., 2016). Clean technologies aid in the reduction of waste and pollution during the manufacturing process. Investing in clean technologies is costly, but it lowers environmental compliance costs and improves long-term performance (Chien & Peng, 2012). Furthermore, the use of clean technology improves the firm's performance by lowering costs, speeding up operations, and increasing operational flexibility, all of which improve the firm's financial performance (Klassen & Whybark, 1999). Both cleaner production technology and end-of-pipe technology are significantly associated with firms' green image (Xie et al., 2016).

Figure 5. Conceptual model

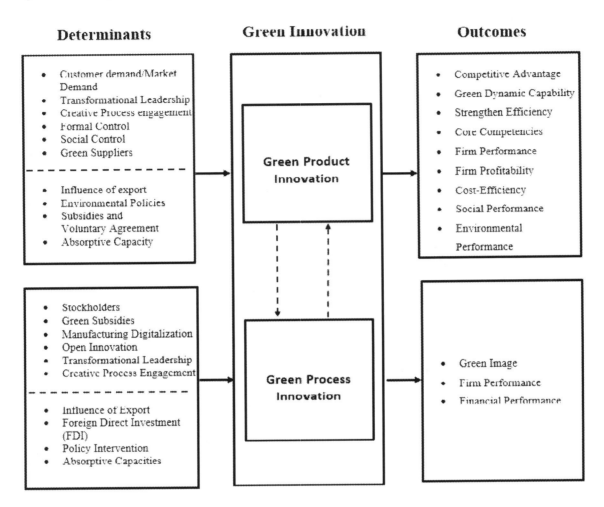

Theoretical and Practical Implications

Our results suggest several practical and theoretical implications. First, the identification of outcomes and determinants of green product and process innovation (see, appendix table 1 for detailed information) accompanies the increase of differentiation strategies inspired by ethical and environmental values. Therefore, organizations should adopt an iterative approach by controlling the action-measure-reaction sequence, responsibly orienting their decisions on the market to achieve better performance. Indeed, GI depends on various external and internal factors. In this regard, building environmental management systems could favor the integration of eco-innovative capabilities of companies and the introduction of structural procedures capable of strengthening an eco-innovative strategy. This virtuous chain can stir the ecological conscience of consumers to achieve sustainability, especially when resources are limited. In fact, the results of this paper suggest that green technological solutions, in both the product and the process, require widespread diffusion, leading to the opening of new market areas, as well as increasing stakeholder confidence and orienting customer preferences.

Therefore, public policies should be oriented towards regulatory transparency for the implementation of reform programs that are capable of supporting companies in the adoption of GI and supporting corporate performance in the long term, in order to achieve a positive benefit for the environment as well as people. In fact, environmental policies can stimulate the adoption of responsible strategies, in the case of both coercive policies and public subsidies to promote research and development functions. Investments in GI imply the conservation of the environment and the realization of social goals, connected to the improvement of the quality of life. Furthermore, organizations involved in the adoption of green technologies should invest in knowledge management programs, aimed at spreading the culture of innovation related to ecological processes and products based on market demand and the prerogatives of national and international legislation. Finally, considering the complexity of GI, this study suggests the importance of activating staff training courses, in order to update and strengthen company skills based on market dynamics.

CONCLUSION AND AVENUES FOR FUTURE RESEARCH

GI is essential for economic progress, environmental sustainability, and improved quality of life. Understanding how innovation and sustainability interact has become a strategic focus for both theory and practice.

GI must be promoted by environmental regulations to achieve rapid green transformation. Because of the improvement of "market mechanisms," firms, and public environmental awareness, voluntary environmental regulations have the most incentivizing linear impact on GI.

GI is classified as "GPrI" and "GPI" in the current research. The determinants and outcomes of these two types of innovation are explored. This helps to bridge the gap and contributes to the literature on GI. The growing importance of the "green" brand or "green" reputation of companies reveals how globalization has contributed to spreading the concept of sustainability on the market. This trend favors the enhancement of GPrI and GPI, making company production responsible and guiding consumers towards the purchase of eco-friendly products. Green products and GPrI are effective differentiation strategies for all organizations and new businesses. Organizations must emphasize "GPrI" as it aids "GPI," especially when resources are limited. Organizations can offer the best green products to their customers while minimizing their environmental impact through GPI. As a result of GPI, organizations can seize green opportunities and steer toward the green upcoming market. Under stern environmental regulations and the well-known consumer environmentalism, business duties cannot be avoided. Product innovation has a significant impact on the environment (Hoffmann, 2007). In the future, poor product design and environmental legislation in countries (namely, during the product's disposal phase) have the potential to exacerbate waste problems (Greenpeace, 2005). As a result, many organizations are implementing "green" features into their product development processes to separate themselves from competitors and gain a competitive advantage (Reinhardt, 1998).

GI tends to improve a company's overall image, which leads to better market performance. The concept of green image is a key motivator for GPrI. Majumdar and Marcus (2001) argue that GI increases a company's market value. Eco-friendly business improvements may open new market doors, increase client loyalty, and support sales efforts. The success of GPI is dependent on both environmental and market performance. Organizations should prioritize the cultivation of a green image. This will increase consumers' willingness to pay for green products. Organizations can increase their market share and financial performance by doing so. A significant challenge is to determine how organizations can incorporate their environmental vision into their organizational strategies rather than focusing solely on the promotion of their green brands (Chen, 2010,Thomas & Paul, 2019; Thomas et al., 2020). Additionally, for a good green image, organizations must promote their environmental practices, such as product recycling, water and energy conservation, avoiding disposable goods, and minimizing the emission of harmful gases into the air, water, and soil.

At the macro-level, government policies can inspire GI through either progressive measures such as "grants and rebates" or punitive ones such as tariffs and quotas. Outside of green subsidies, the government must design efficient tools for motivating and supporting green strategies. It should also investigate why green subsidies are not as effective as expected (Zhang et al., 2021). Organizations that receive green subsidies must be inspected to ensure that the funds are used in the most beneficial ways. Managers should also keep in mind that GPI and firm performance should take into account concerns about the availability of market demand characteristics knowledge (Lin et al., 2013). In the past, cultural characteristics may have limited the generalizability of research. As a result, the findings of future studies should be validated through investigations conducted in various cultural settings. Indeed, future evaluations could include an analysis in the least developed countries in order to consider whether and how macroeconomic factors, as well as physical and social infrastructure, in addition to workers' skills, the institutional environment and policy efficiency can affect GI. This could suggest the advisability of adopting intervention strategies focused on the context, which take into account the variables of incidence on GI processes.

Despite the fact that this study offers some novel implications in the field, it also presents some limitations related to the current analysis. First, the authors of this paper have only included articles from peer-reviewed English-language journals that are available on Web of Science (WoS); as a result, there is a possibility that pertinent studies have been overlooked. Second, WoS undergoes continuous fluctuations due to the constant updating of the database. This involves changing the number of articles pertaining to the field. In the future, bibliometric and systematic reviews may look at other significant databases, such as Scopus, as well as those that are published in languages other than English. In addition, a literature search may be performed using additional academic databases.

REFERENCES

Achi, A., Adeola, O., & Achi, F. C. (2022). CSR and green process innovation as antecedents of micro, small, and medium enterprise performance: Moderating role of perceived environmental volatility. *Journal of Business Research, 139*, 771–781. doi:10.1016/j.jbusres.2021.10.016

Albort-Morant, G., Henseler, J., Cepeda-Carrión, G., & Leal-Rodríguez, A. L. (2018). Potential and realized absorptive capacity as complementary drivers of green product and process innovation performance. *Sustainability, 10*(2), 381.

Andersén, J. (2021). A relational natural-resource-based view on product innovation: The influence of green product innovation and green suppliers on differentiation advantage in small manufacturing firms. *Technovation, 104*, 102254. doi:10.1016/j.technovation.2021.102254

Andersén, J., Jansson, C., & Ljungkvist, T. (2020). Can environmentally oriented CEOs and environmentally friendly suppliers boost the growth of small firms? *Business Strategy and the Environment, 29*(2), 325–334. doi:10.1002/bse.2366

Aria, M., & Cuccurullo, C. (2017). bibliometrix: An R-tool for comprehensive science mapping analysis. *Journal of Informetrics, 11*(4), 959–975. doi:10.1016/j.joi.2017.08.007

Awan, U., Arnold, M. G., & Gölgeci, I. (2021). Enhancing green product and process innovation: Towards an integrative framework of knowledge acquisition and environmental investment. *Business Strategy and the Environment, 30*(2), 1283–1295. doi:10.1002/bse.2684

Awan, U., Nauman, S., & Sroufe, R. (2021). Exploring the effect of buyer engagement on green product innovation: Empirical evidence from manufacturers. *Business Strategy and the Environment, 30*(1), 463–477. doi:10.1002/bse.2631

Begum, S., Ashfaq, M., Xia, E., & Awan, U. (2022). Does green transformational leadership lead to green innovation? The role of green thinking and creative process engagement. *Business Strategy and the Environment, 31*(1), 580–597. doi:10.1002/bse.2911

Boons, F., & Lüdeke-Freund, F. (2013). Business models for sustainable innovation: State-of-the-art and steps towards a research agenda. *Journal of Cleaner Production, 45*, 9–19. doi:10.1016/j.jclepro.2012.07.007

Carrillo-Hermosilla, J., Del Río, P., & Könnölä, T. (2010). Diversity of eco-innovations: Reflections from selected case studies. *Journal of Cleaner Production, 18*(10-11), 1073–1083. doi:10.1016/j.jclepro.2010.02.014

Ch'ng, P. C., Cheah, J., & Amran, A. (2021). Eco-innovation practices and sustainable business performance: The moderating effect of market turbulence in the Malaysian technology industry. *Journal of Cleaner Production, 283*, 124556.

Chadha, A. (2011). Overcoming competence lock-in for the development of radical eco-innovations: The case of biopolymer technology. *Industry and Innovation, 18*(3), 335–350.

Chan, H. K., Yee, R. W., Dai, J., & Lim, M. K. (2016). The moderating effect of environmental dynamism on green product innovation and performance. *International Journal of Production Economics, 181*, 384–391. doi:10.1016/j.ijpe.2015.12.006

Chang, C. H. (2011). The influence of corporate environmental ethics on competitive advantage: The mediation role of green innovation. *Journal of Business Ethics, 104*(3), 361–370. doi:10.100710551-011-0914-x

Chang, C. H. (2016). The determinants of green product innovation performance. *Corporate Social Responsibility and Environmental Management, 23*(2), 65–76. doi:10.1002/csr.1361

Chen, Y., Chang, C., & Wu, F. (2012). Origins of green innovations: The differences between proactive and reactive green innovations. *Management Decision, 50*(3), 368–398. doi:10.1108/00251741211216197

Chen, Y. S., Lai, S. B., & Wen, C. T. (2006). The influence of green innovation performance on corporate advantage in Taiwan. *Journal of Business Ethics, 67*(4), 331–339. doi:10.100710551-006-9025-5

Chien, C. C., & Peng, C. W. (2012). Does going green pay off in the long run? *Journal of Business Research, 65*(11), 1636–1642.

Chiou, T. Y., Chan, H. K., Lettice, F., & Chung, S. H. (2011). The influence of greening the suppliers and green innovation on environmental performance and competitive advantage in Taiwan. *Transportation Research Part E, Logistics and Transportation Review, 47*(6), 822–836. doi:10.1016/j.tre.2011.05.016

Dangelico, R. M. (2016). Green product innovation: Where we are and where we are going. *Business Strategy and the Environment, 25*(8), 560–576. doi:10.1002/bse.1886

Dangelico, R. M., & Pujari, D. (2010). Mainstreaming green product innovation: Why and how companies integrate environmental sustainability. *Journal of Business Ethics, 95*(3), 471–486. doi:10.100710551-010-0434-0

Dangelico, R. M., Pujari, D., & Pontrandolfo, P. (2017). Green product innovation in manufacturing firms: A sustainability-oriented dynamic capability perspective. *Business Strategy and the Environment, 26*(4), 490–506. doi:10.1002/bse.1932

Du, L., Zhang, Z., & Feng, T. (2018). Linking green customer and supplier integration with green innovation performance: The role of internal integration. *Business Strategy and the Environment, 27*(8), 1583–1595. doi:10.1002/bse.2223

Fink, A. (2010). *Conducting research literature reviews*. Sage.

Gao, Y., Tsai, S. B., Xue, X., Ren, T., Du, X., Chen, Q., & Wang, J. (2018). An empirical study on green innovation efficiency in the green institutional environment. *Sustainability, 10*(3), 724. doi:10.3390u10030724

Greenpeace. (2005). *Recycling of Electronic Wastes in China & India: Workplace & Environmental Contamination*. Greenpeace International.

Guoyou, Q., Saixing, Z., Chiming, T., Haitao, Y., & Hailiang, Z. (2013). Stakeholders' influences on corporate green innovation strategy: A case study of manufacturing firms in China. *Corporate Social Responsibility and Environmental Management, 20*(1), 1–14. doi:10.1002/csr.283

Gupta, V., & Thomas, A. (2019). Fostering tacit knowledge sharing and innovative work behaviour: An integrated theoretical view. *International Journal of Managerial and Financial Accounting, 11*(3-4), 320–346. doi:10.1504/IJMFA.2019.104134

Hart, S. L., & Ahuja, G. (1996). Does it pay to be green? An empirical examination of the relationship between emission reduction and firm performance. *Business Strategy and the Environment, 5*(1), 30–37. doi:10.1002/(SICI)1099-0836(199603)5:1<30::AID-BSE38>3.0.CO;2-Q

Hoffmann, E. (2007). Consumer integration in sustainable product development. *Journal of Production Innovation Management, 16*(5), 332-338.

Huang, S. Y., Ting, C. W., & Li, M. W. (2021). The effects of green transformational leadership on adoption of environmentally proactive strategies: The mediating role of green engagement. *Sustainability, 13*(6), 3366. doi:10.3390u13063366

Ilg, P. (2019). How to foster green product innovation in an inert sector. *Journal of Innovation & Knowledge*, *4*(2), 129–138. doi:10.1016/j.jik.2017.12.009

Jain, N., Thomas, A., Gupta, V., Ossorio, M., & Porcheddu, D. (2022). Stimulating CSR learning collaboration by the mentor universities with digital tools and technologies – An empirical study during the COVID-19 pandemic. *Management Decision*. doi:10.1108/MD-12-2021-1679

Kammerer, D. (2009). The effects of customer benefit and regulation on environmental product innovation.: Empirical evidence from appliance manufacturers in Germany. *Ecological Economics*, *68*(8-9), 2285–2295. doi:10.1016/j.ecolecon.2009.02.016

Kammerer, D. (2009). The effects of customer benefit and regulation on environmental product innovation.: Empirical evidence from appliance manufacturers in Germany. *Ecological Economics*, *68*(8-9), 2285–2295. doi:10.1016/j.ecolecon.2009.02.016

Khan, S. J., Kaur, P., Jabeen, F., & Dhir, A. (2021). Green process innovation: Where we are and where we are going. *Business Strategy and the Environment*, *30*(7), 3273–3296. doi:10.1002/bse.2802

Kivimaa, P. (2007). The determinants of environmental innovation: The impacts of environmental policies on the Nordic pulp, paper and packaging industries. *European Environment*, *17*(2), 92–105. doi:10.1002/eet.442

Klassen, R. D., & Whybark, D. C. (1999). The impact of environmental technologies on manufacturing performance. *Academy of Management Journal*, *42*(6), 599–615.

Lee, K. H., & Kim, J. W. (2011). Integrating suppliers into green product innovation development: An empirical case study in the semiconductor industry. *Business Strategy and the Environment*, *20*(8), 527–538. doi:10.1002/bse.714

Lin, R. J., Tan, K. H., & Geng, Y. (2013). Market demand, green product innovation, and firm performance: Evidence from Vietnam motorcycle industry. *Journal of Cleaner Production*, *40*, 101–107. doi:10.1016/j.jclepro.2012.01.001

Liu, J., Zhao, M., & Wang, Y. (2020). Impacts of government subsidies and environmental regulations on green process innovation: A nonlinear approach. *Technology in Society*, *63*, 101417. doi:10.1016/j.techsoc.2020.101417

Majumdar, S. K., & Marcus, A. A. (2001). Rules versus discretion: The productivity consequences of flexible regulation. *Academy of Management Journal*, *44*(1), 170–179.

Melander, L. (2018). Customer and supplier collaboration in green product innovation: External and internal capabilities. *Business Strategy and the Environment*, *27*(6), 677–693. doi:10.1002/bse.2024

Peters, K., & Buijs, P. (2022). Strategic ambidexterity in green product innovation: Obstacles and implications. *Business Strategy and the Environment*, *31*(1), 173–193. doi:10.1002/bse.2881

Porter, M. E., & Van der Linde, C. (1995). Toward a new conception of the environment-competitiveness relationship. *The Journal of Economic Perspectives*, *9*(4), 97–118. doi:10.1257/jep.9.4.97

Qiu, L., Jie, X., Wang, Y., & Zhao, M. (2020). Green product innovation, green dynamic capability, and competitive advantage: Evidence from Chinese manufacturing enterprises. *Corporate Social Responsibility and Environmental Management, 27*(1), 146–165. doi:10.1002/csr.1780

Reinhardt, F.L. (1998). Environmental product differentiation: implications for corporate strategy. *California Management Review, 40*(4), 43-73.

Serrano-García, J., Bikfalvi, A., Llach, J., & Arbeláez-Toro, J. J. (2021). Orchestrating capabilities, organizational dimensions and determinants in the pursuit of green product innovation. *Journal of Cleaner Production, 313*, 127873. doi:10.1016/j.jclepro.2021.127873

Shahzad, M., Qu, Y., Javed, S. A., Zafar, A. U., & Rehman, S. U. (2020). Relation of environment sustainability to CSR and green innovation: A case of Pakistani manufacturing industry. *Journal of Cleaner Production, 253*, 119938. doi:10.1016/j.jclepro.2019.119938

Sharma, G. D., Thomas, A., & Paul, J. (2021). Reviving tourism industry post-COVID-19: A resilience-based framework. *Tourism Management Perspectives, 37*, 100786. doi:10.1016/j.tmp.2020.100786 PMID:33391988

Singh, S. K., Giudice, M. D., Chierici, R., & Graziano, D. (2020). Green innovation and environmental performance: The role of green transformational leadership and green human resource management. *Technological Forecasting and Social Change, 150*, 119762. doi:10.1016/j.techfore.2019.119762

Skordoulis, M., Kyriakopoulos, G., Ntanos, S., Galatsidas, S., Arabatzis, G., Chalikias, M., & Kalantonis, P. (2022). The Mediating Role of Firm Strategy in the Relationship between Green Entrepreneurship, Green Innovation, and Competitive Advantage: The Case of Medium and Large-Sized Firms in Greece. *Sustainability, 14*(6), 3286. doi:10.3390u14063286

Song, M., Wang, S., & Zhang, H. (2020). Could environmental regulation and R&D tax incentives affect green product innovation? *Journal of Cleaner Production, 258*, 120849. doi:10.1016/j.jclepro.2020.120849

Song, W., Wang, G. Z., & Ma, X. (2020). Environmental innovation practices and green product innovation performance: A perspective from organizational climate. *Sustainable Development, 28*(1), 224–234. doi:10.1002d.1990

Song, W., & Yu, H. (2018). Green innovation strategy and green innovation: The roles of green creativity and green organizational identity. *Corporate Social Responsibility and Environmental Management, 25*(2), 135–150. doi:10.1002/csr.1445

Sun, Y., & Sun, H. (2021). Green innovation strategy and ambidextrous green innovation: The mediating effects of green supply chain integration. *Sustainability, 13*(9), 4876. doi:10.3390u13094876

Tang, M., Walsh, G., Lerner, D., Fitza, M. A., & Li, Q. (2018). Green innovation, managerial concern and firm performance: An empirical study. *Business Strategy and the Environment, 27*(1), 39–51. doi:10.1002/bse.1981

Taoketao, E., Feng, T., Song, Y., & Nie, Y. (2018). Does sustainability marketing strategy achieve payback profits? A signaling theory perspective. *Corporate Social Responsibility and Environmental Management, 25*(6), 1039–1049. doi:10.1002/csr.1518

Thomas, A. (2021). Business Beyond COVID-19: Towards Open Innovation. In Globalization, Deglobalization, and New Paradigms in Business (pp. 189-212). Palgrave Macmillan.

Thomas, A., & Chopra, M. (2020). On how big data revolutionizes knowledge management. In *Digital transformation in business and society* (pp. 39–60). Palgrave Macmillan. doi:10.1007/978-3-030-08277-2_3

Thomas, A., Cillo, V., Caggiano, V., & Vrontis, D. (2020). Drivers of social capital in enhancing team knowledge sharing and team performance: Moderator role of manager's cultural intelligence. *International Journal of Managerial and Financial Accounting*, *12*(3-4), 284–303. doi:10.1504/IJMFA.2020.112358

Thomas, A. & Gupta, V. (2021a). Tacit knowledge in organizations: bibliometrics and a framework-based systematic review of antecedents, outcomes, theories, methods and future directions. *Journal of Knowledge Management*. doi:10.1108/JKM-01-2021-0026

Thomas, A., & Gupta, V. (2021b). Social capital theory, social exchange theory, social cognitive theory, financial literacy, and the role of knowledge sharing as a moderator in enhancing financial well-being: From bibliometric analysis to a conceptual framework model. *Frontiers in Psychology*, *12*, 12. doi:10.3389/fpsyg.2021.664638 PMID:34093360

Thomas, A., & Gupta, V. (2022). The role of motivation theories in knowledge sharing: An integrative theoretical reviews and future research agenda. *Kybernetes*, *51*(1), 116–140. doi:10.1108/K-07-2020-0465

Thomas, A., Gupta, V., Riso, T., Briamonte, M. F., Usai, A., & Fiano, F. (2021, November). Enhancing Innovative Behavior at the Workplace: the Moderating Role of Entrepreneurial Orientation and Web 2.0. In *2021 IEEE International Conference on Technology Management, Operations and Decisions (ICTMOD)* (pp. 1-8). IEEE. 10.1109/ICTMOD52902.2021.9739415

Thomas, A., & Paul, J. (2019). Knowledge transfer and innovation through university-industry partnership: An integrated theoretical view. *Knowledge Management Research and Practice*, *17*(4), 436–448. doi:10.1080/14778238.2018.1552485

Tseng, M. L., Wang, R., Chiu, A. S., Geng, Y., & Lin, Y. H. (2013). Improving performance of green innovation practices under uncertainty. *Journal of Cleaner Production*, *40*, 71–82. doi:10.1016/j.jclepro.2011.10.009

Van Hemel, C., & Cramer, J. (2002). Barriers and stimuli for ecodesign in SMEs. *Journal of Cleaner Production*, *10*(5), 439–453. doi:10.1016/S0959-6526(02)00013-6

Wagner, M. (2008). Empirical influence of environmental management on innovation: Evidence from Europe. *Ecological Economics*, *66*(2-3), 392–402. doi:10.1016/j.ecolecon.2007.10.001

Wang, M., Li, Y., Li, J., & Wang, Z. (2021). Green process innovation, green product innovation and its economic performance improvement paths: A survey and structural model. *Journal of Environmental Management*, *297*, 113282. doi:10.1016/j.jenvman.2021.113282 PMID:34314965

Wei, Z., & Sun, L. (2021). How to leverage manufacturing digitalization for green process innovation: An information processing perspective. *Industrial Management & Data Systems*, *121*(5), 1026–1044. doi:10.1108/IMDS-08-2020-0459

Xie, X., Hoang, T. T., & Zhu, Q. (2022). Green process innovation and financial performance: The role of green social capital and customers' tacit green needs. *Journal of Innovation & Knowledge*, *7*(1), 100165. doi:10.1016/j.jik.2022.100165

Xie, X., Huo, J., Qi, G., & Zhu, K. X. (2015). Green process innovation and financial performance in emerging economies: Moderating effects of absorptive capacity and green subsidies. *IEEE Transactions on Engineering Management*, *63*(1), 101–112. doi:10.1109/TEM.2015.2507585

Yang, J. Y., & Roh, T. (2019). Open for green innovation: From the perspective of green process and green consumer innovation. *Sustainability*, *11*(12), 3234. doi:10.3390u11123234

Yin, J., Gong, L., & Wang, S. (2018). Large-scale assessment of global green innovation research trends from 1981 to 2016: A bibliometric study. *Journal of Cleaner Production*, *197*, 827–841. doi:10.1016/j.jclepro.2018.06.169

Zailani, S., Govindan, K., Iranmanesh, M., Shaharudin, M. R., & Chong, Y. S. (2015). Green innovation adoption in automotive supply chain: The Malaysian case. *Journal of Cleaner Production*, *108*, 1115–1122. doi:10.1016/j.jclepro.2015.06.039

Zameer, H., Wang, Y., Vasbieva, D. G., & Abbas, Q. (2021). Exploring a pathway to carbon neutrality via reinforcing environmental performance through green process innovation, environmental orientation and green competitive advantage. *Journal of Environmental Management*, *296*, 113383. doi:10.1016/j.jenvman.2021.113383 PMID:34328865

Zameer, H., Wang, Y., Vasbieva, D. G., & Abbas, Q. (2021). Exploring a pathway to carbon neutrality via reinforcing environmental performance through green process innovation, environmental orientation and green competitive advantage. *Journal of Environmental Management*, *296*.

Zhang, F., Chen, J., & Zhu, L. (2021). How Does Environmental Dynamism Impact Green Process Innovation? A Supply Chain Cooperation Perspective. *IEEE Transactions on Engineering Management*.

APPENDIX

Table 2. Determinants and outcomes of green product and green process innovation

Green Product Innovation	
Determinants	**References**
Customer demand/Market demand Influence of export Transformational leadership Creative process engagement Formal control Social control Green Suppliers Environmental policies Subsidies and (partly) voluntary agreements Absorptive capacities	Guoyou et al., 2013; Zhang et al., 2021; Lin et al., 2013; Singh et al., 2020; Andersén et al., 2020, 2021; Melander, 2018; Chan et al., 2015; Stucki et al., 2018; Song et al., 2020; Albort-Morant et al., 2018; Chiou et al., 2011
Outcomes	**References**
Competitive advantage Green dynamic capability Strengthen efficiency Core competencies Social performance Environmental performance Firm performance Firm profitability Cost efficiency	Ilg, 2017; Qiu et al., 2020; Tang et al., 2018; Chang, 2011, 2016; Lin et al., 2013; Chan et al., 2015
Green Process Innovation	
Determinants	**References**
Influence of export Stockholders Foreign direct investment (FDI) Green subsidies Manufacturing digitalization Open innovation Transformational leadership Creative process engagement Policy intervention Absorptive capacities	Guoyou et al., 2013; Xie et al., 2019; Wei and Sun, 2021; Yang and Roh, 2019; Zhang et al., 2021; Singh et al., 2020; Stucki et al., 2018; Albort-Morant et al., 2018
Outcomes	**References**
Green image Firm performance	Xie et al., 2019; Wei and Sun, 2021; Tang et al., 2017

Chapter 4
Bank Customer Green Banking Technology Adoption:
A Sequential Exploratory
Mixed Methods Study

Mohamed Bouteraa

(iD) https://orcid.org/0000-0003-4834-8973
Universiti Utara Malaysia, Malaysia

Raja Rizal Iskandar Raja Hisham
Universiti Utara Malaysia, Malaysia

Zairani Zainol
Universiti Utara Malaysia, Malaysia

ABSTRACT

Sustainability has become the global need for survival in all scopes due to financial development's side effects that have resulted in environmental destruction. The world leaders have proposed green banking (GB) to reduce carbon footprints from banking operations by promoting paperless financial services based on technology. However, the adoption of GB remains unsatisfactory in the UAE. The study attempts to investigate the determinants of consumers' adoption of GB technology. An exploratory sequential mixed-method approach is employed. The qualitative analysis identified six new challenges facing customers' intention adoption of GB technology: customer awareness, personal innovativeness, bank reputation, security and privacy, system quality, and government support. The preliminary qualitative findings are mostly confirmed by quantitative study whereby customer awareness, personal innovativeness, system quality, and bank reputation significantly impact customers' intention to adopt GB technology. The discussions and implications of these findings are further elaborated.

DOI: 10.4018/978-1-6684-4610-2.ch004

INTRODUCTION

The issues of environmental protection have become very critical for emerging countries, as they are exposed to the pressing challenges of climate change, pollution, deforestation, loss of biodiversity and arable land (Doh et al., 2019). The dependency on natural resources for economic development underpins the necessity for implementing sustainable strategies (Stockholm Environment Institute, 2013). This has resulted in supervisory authorities like United Nations Environment Programme (UNEP) and International Finance Corporation (IFC) initiating a sustainable transformation of the financial system to mitigate the severe problems of environmental emissions (Zhang et al., 2019; United Nations Framework Convention on Climate Change [UNFCCC], 2021). To tackle climate change and its negative impacts, world leaders at the UN Climate Change Conference in Paris reached a breakthrough in December 2015: the historic Paris Agreement that was adopted by 196 countries, which includes commitments to reduce their emissions over time (UNFCCC, 2021). The digitalisation of businesses through various Industry Revolution (IR) 4.0 technologies like the Internet of Things (IoT) and Artificial Intelligence (AI) has been suggested as means to alleviate pressure on the environment and natural resources (UNFCCC, 2021; Bukhari et al., 2022). However, many emerging economies are trailing behind in environmental unsustainability and lack of digitalisation (Bukhari et al., 2022).

Acknowledgement of digitalisation and environmentalism as a worldwide concern exerted pressure on the financial institutions to adopt green agenda, particularly in the banking industry (Julia & Kassim, 2020). The banking sector is considered the driving force behind economic sustainability (Bukhari et al., 2022). It plays a fundamental role in economic growth and key financier to consumers (Ozili & Opene, 2021). Banks may contribute to environmental conservation by incorporating green concepts into their lending and investment practices, diverting customers' attention to environmental management and the deployment of relevant green technology (Masukujjaman & Aktar, 2014). Thus, the country's sustainability is mainly dependent on the greening and digitalising of the banking industry. This led to the development of the concept of Green Banking (GB), a banking ideology that is based on the principles of environmental sustainability by integrating structural technology upgrades to banking operations and promoting paperless based financial services (Bouteraa et al., 2021). In other words, through technological and operational improvements and changing client habits, green banking has gradually made inroads in promoting environment-friendly practices, with a clear vision of future sustainability. This concept is mutually beneficial for banks, customers, and economies not only guarantees greening but also facilitates improvements in banks' assets quality (Naveenan et al., 2021) as well as their financial performance (Finger et al., 2018). However, this innovative ideology is still struggling to be adopted by many developing countries (Bukhari et al., 2022).

The United Arab Emirates (UAE) is considered among the world's highest energy consumers, and with the continuous increase in population has escalated demands for energy production for constant economic growth (Juaidi et al., 2016). As natural reserves are limited, sustainable resources are necessary to be explored. Thus, environment and sustainability have received significant attention from the UAE's government (Dubai Carbon, 2018; UAE-Ministry of Climate Change and Environment [MOCCAE], 2017). The UAE-MOCCAE has highlighted that the idea of GB is essential to the economy by affirming that an investment of only 1-2% of GDP in the green agenda will bring the country a 4-5% increase in GDP by 2030 (Arcadis, 2018). According to Stiftung (2019), "with rapid economic growth remaining predominant, it cannot be said that the UAE is currently on a sustainable path". The UAE has recorded a high pollution level and violent CO_2 emission increase caused by human and business activities at the rate of 236.9% between 2000 (84,540kt) and 2018 (200,300kt) (World Bank Group, 2018). This renders the country the world's number one for having the most extensive environmental footprint for a long stand-up period (WorldWide Fund for Nature [WWFN], 2010; Worldatlas, 2019). Certainly, this is a worrisome situation in this environmentally conscious era.

In this regard, most of the financial institutions in the UAE are seeking sustainability. In October 2016, the UAE officially introduced green initiatives for the financial sector (UAE-MOCCAE, 2017). Following this, it has become mandatory for all financial institutions in the country to adopt a GB framework in a formal manner (UAE-MOCCAE, 2017). Consequently, most banks in the UAE have been extending their services to innovative eco-friendly channels, launching several green initiatives, and investing considerable funds to attain sustainability (UAE-MOCCAE, 2017; KPMG, 2020). However, this issue is still a challenging task for the country (UAE-MOCCAE, 2017), which requires substantial efforts by all concerned stakeholders, especially customers as they are the key stakeholders who are at the forefront of utilising these measures in their banking transactions (Iqbal *et al.*, 2018; Herath & Herath, 2019). GB technology is still at a primary stage in the UAE as the adoption level remains unsatisfactory among customers and private businesses as they face diverse barriers and challenges (UAE-Ministry of Environment and Water [MoEW], 2017a, 2017b). According to the national survey of UAE-MoEW (2017a), less than 38% of customers have adopted GB technology transactions, and only 4% have a green account. The striking finding is that 59% do not have a future intention to adopt GB services (UAE-MoEW, 2017a). These statistics illustrate that the majority of the green services have demonstrated a shallow adoption level. Therefore, this study is motivated to address the challenges of customers' GB technology adoption in the UAE. This is essential because undermining the importance of this issue might lead to numerous sustainability concerns and cost large financial losses.

Overall, limited literature exists on GB adoption (Shaumya & Arulrajah, 2017; Bukhari et al., 2019, 2020; Bouteraa et al., 2020). According to the recent systematic literature review by Bukhari et al. (2022), few publications exist in the ðeld of GB adoption. In particular, customers' adoption of GB is not commonly studied, which requires a comprehensive exploration (Sahoo et al., 2016; Javeria et al., 2019; Bouteraa, 2020; Bouteraa et al., 2021). The existing studies primarily investigate the phenomena of GB adoption from an organisational perspective (e.g., Rifat et al., 2016; Mehedi & Kuddus, 2017; Julia & Kassim, 2019; Nisha et al., 2020; Bukhari et al., 2019, 2020, 2021, 2022) However, few researchers explored challenges facing customers to adopt GB technology (e.g., Iqbal et al., 2018; Iqbal et al., 2019; 2021; Bouteraa et al., 2021; Malik, & Singh, 2022).

Understanding the technology diffusion process is vital for promoting technology services in emerging markets (Olaleye et al., 2019). Prior studies have extensively used the UTAUT and Technology Acceptance Model (TAM) to investigate the adoption of GB technology (e.g., Iqbal et al., 2018; Iqbal et al., 2019; 2021; Malik & Singh, 2022). However, the phenomenon of customer GB adoption has not been adequately studied due to various limitations in the existing studies (Iqbal et al., 2018; Iqbal et al., 2019; 2021; Malik & Singh, 2022). They largely focus on studying the individual features that reflect the personal attributes of the customers. However, they lack in considering individual, technological, organisational, and environmental determinants, which form a solid theoretical foundation for comprehensively understanding customers' behaviour towards technology (Jeyaraj et al., 2006; Bouteraa et al., 2021). Thus, the literature has identified a theoretical need to broadly investigate the challenges of customers' GB adoption. Contextually, the factors inñuencing GB adoption may vary among contexts (Shaumya & Arulrajah, 2017; Bukhari et al., 2022). The existing studies mainly concentrated on identical settings in their experiments like Bangladesh, Pakistan and India. Their results may not be applicable in different Middle Eastern regions like the UAE with unique cultural backgrounds, social infrastructure and economic indicators, which is less considered in the literature on GB, as highlighted by Shaumya and Arulrajah (2017). Hence, the identification of the need to conduct country-specific studies on customers' GB adoption. Regarding their research design, they have mostly adopted a positivist stance by merely conducting cross-sectional surveys to validate an adapted research model. Their determinants were constructed from the syntheses of previous literature and existing theories. Therefore, most models were principally defined as narrow and tactical because they disregarded the exploratory approach and combined the strength of quantitative and qualitative methods within the same study to establish the methodological contributions.

Aiming to address the above research gaps, the study attempts to answer the following research questions (RQs). RQ1: What are the customers' challenges to adopting GB technology in the UAE? RQ2: What is the effect of the individual, technological, organisational and environmental factors on the customers' intention to adopt GB technology? RQ3: Is the UTAUT model relevant to explaining customer adoption of GB technology in the UAE? Overall, the current study is a novel attempt to investigate the challenges of customer GB technology adoption by applying and validating the UTAUT framework through a mixed-method approach.

This study makes multiple contributions to the literature on GB technology in particular. First, this study is one of the first attempts to uncover the various challenges of GB technology adoption in the UAE. Secondly, it applies and empirically validates the UTAUT model to predict GB technology adoption in the UAE. Thirdly, the study adopts a mixed-methods approach by employing both qualitative and quantitative methods. This methodological approach contributes significantly to a finer cognizance of the complex relationships among the factors of GB technology adoption. Finally, the findings from this research will present new insights to researchers as well as assist policymakers and managers in devising effective strategies to raise customers' green and digital consumption behaviour, which would drive the principle of sustainability.

The remaining sections of this paper are organized as follows. Section 2 outlines a review of current literature on the concept of GB technology and its theoretical background. Section 3 focuses on the data collection process and research methods for both phases qualitative and quantitative. Subsequently, Section 4 exhibits the qualitative data analysis findings. The research model and the hypotheses are explained in Section 5. Section 6 presents the numerical quantitative data analysis. Lastly, Section 7 discusses the findings and implications of the research, limitations and future research directions.

LITERATURE REVIEW

Green Banking

Typically, banks' operational activities are not directly associated with the environment; however, their eco-friendly stance has a considerable external effect on the overall environment (Javeria et al., 2019; Rehman et al., 2021). Traditional banks heavily contribute to carbon emission through paper use and electricity consumption through extensive networks of branches, apart from financing intermediaries that have an external impact on the environment (Rehman et al., 2021). However, the promotion of GB technology services and green financing can contribute to minimising the adverse environmental impact to a greater extent (Rehman et al., 2021).

Overall, GB is a banking ideology adopted by the banking sector to inculcate the values of environmental ethics in the daily banking operations and financing portfolio (Bukhari et al., 2022). The operation of GB adoption is context-based, owing to its reliance on the several external aspects existing in the respective countries, the internal capabilities of the banking industry, and other related resources (Shaumya & Arulrajah, 2017). It can be in the form of implementing green management practices, green operations, green buildings, green ðnance, green information technology, green human resource management, promoting green products and services, green marketing, and green disclosure (Bukhari et al., 2019) or the digitalisation of banking services to reduce the usage of resources such as paper (Bukhari et al., 2022).

There are many definitions of GB technology in the literature, although essentially, they do not differ much. It is the provision of innovative products to support activities that are not harmful to the environment; it aims to use bank resources responsibly while prioritising the environment and society (Bukhari et al., 2020). GB technology also refers to an ideology driven by the need for sustainable approaches that facilitate transforming the industry by applying innovative technologies that aid in the efficient and effective delivery of banking services (Ibe-enwo et al., 2019). Javeria et al. (2019) described GB technology as environmentally friendly lending and depository products and services provided by banks to their regular and prospective customers in the form of technology banking services. In the current study, GB technology refers to eco-friendly practices that lower carbon footprints from banking operations by promoting paperless-based technology financial services. These innovative mediums of financial services delivery promote GB since it reduces paper use and achieves environmental sustainability (Iqbal et al., 2018).

The Unified Theory of Acceptance and Use of Technology (UTAUT)

Intention to use and user behaviour have been examined using established theoretical frameworks from various socio-cultural contexts. While existing ones have been and are still being used, validated, modified, or criticised, new ones are evolving to improve the flaws/inadequacies inherent in the existing ones (Izuagbe et al., 2019). Prominent amongst the theories/models for the acquisition of insight into individuals' and organisations' predisposition to accept, adopt and use technology are the TAM and its variants of TAM2 and TAM3, Social Cognitive Theory (SCT), Diffusion of Innovations Theory (IDT), and UTAUT. Out of all these frameworks, TAM-based models and UTAUT have been adjudged as the most preferred (Shachak et al., 2019). While UTAUT has been adjudged as the most powerful model to explain the procedure of adopting technologies due to its high explanatory/predictive constructs (Souiden et al., 2020) derived from the unification of eight powerful existing models and drawing from their most robust root constructs (Venkatesh et al., 2003; Ghalandari, 2012; Tarhini et al., 2019).

Venkatesh et al. (2003) proposed the UTAUT model after consolidating and testing the variables in eight dominant theories and models: Theory of Reasoned Action (TRA), TAM, Motivation Model (MM), Theory of Planned Behaviour (TPB), a combined TBP/TAM, the model of PC utilisation, IDT and SCT. The model identified three constructs: "performance expectancy, effort expectancy, and social influence" that directly influence behavioural intention and two other constructs "behavioural intention and facilitating conditions" that directly affect technology use. Those relationships were moderated by "age, gender, experience and use voluntariness". The UTAUT model was able to explain the variance of 70% in technology acceptance, which outperformed previous models. Since technology forms the basis of GB, it is necessary to understand individual acceptance and use of this sort of technology services under information systems research. Furthermore, the operation of GB technology is very much relevant to the elements of technology and information system. This study relied on the UTAUT model as the underpinning framework to address the issue of customers' intention to adopt GB technology service.

The UTAUT model has been proven to be strong in studying individuals' adoption within different IT domains as per the recent systematic review of Souiden et al. (2020). Yet, the explanatory power of the UTAUT model may be limited while explaining the IT adoption by users in specific customer contexts (Tarhini et al., 2016). In the same vein, Venkatesh et al. (2012) claimed that the addition of new determinants could help expand UTAUT's horizons in a consumer context. Against this backdrop, the principal contribution of this study is not only to replicate the UTAUT model in a new setting but also to extend it with new individual, technological, organisational, and environmental determinants to form a solid foundation to comprehensively explain customers' intention to adopt GB technology within a new emerging economic context like the UAE.

RESEARCH METHODOLOGY

The mixed-method approach proposed by Venkatesh et al. (2013) and Venkatesh et al. (2016) is adopted to design the research methodology. Using a mixed-methods approach combines the strengths of the qualitative and quantitative methods within the same study and minimises both approaches' limitations (Creswell & Creswell, 2018). It permits the researcher to approve, cross-validate and verify findings within a single study from the distinct mechanisms of the research (Creswell & Creswell, 2018; Sekaran & Bougie, 2019). Thus, this study embraced the exploratory sequential mixed methods designs to investigate the challenges affecting bank customers' intention to adopt GB technology in the UAE. The study õrst reviewed the relevant literature to broadly view the subject matter. The study identiðed the likely empirical codes which formed the basis of the research using the data collected during the initial stage of the semi-structured interviews. This helped to explore a core set of factors and place the research in a broader context. Sequentially, the study formulated a hypothesis for each empirical code to produce the study's final model. Lastly, the study tested the proposed hypotheses through a quantitative cross-sectional survey on a larger sample to obtain further empirical support for the theoretical framework.

In view of that, the purposes of the mixed-method approach in this study are development and complementarity. The findings from the preliminary qualitative approach sustain the subsequent quantitative approach through development (Greene et al., 1989). Through complementarity, the study clarified the results from one approach to the findings of another approach. Thus, it also increased the interpretability, relevance and validity of findings by the most out of one-method strengths (Greene et al., 1989).

Venkatesh et al. (2013) and Venkatesh et al. (2016) addressed the significance of meta-inferences following the acquisition of research findings from the mixed research study, where a meta-inference is a theoretical statement or narrative that provides a holistic explanation for an observed phenomenon by combining findings from both qualitative and quantitative studies. Thus, after reviewing qualitative and quantitative investigations sequentially and acquiring research data, this study used the meta-inference analysis to synchronise the findings from these two studies in the last section of the mixed methods research. The following description expands on each phase's research method.

Phase One: Qualitative Study

This study conducted a preliminary qualitative phase using open-ended semi-structured interviews with the various managers of different banks in the UAE to explore the essential factors that affect their customers' perception of GB technology. The inductive approach in this case study is employed to discover and classify the factors from the interview transcripts. Conceptualised interpretations regarding customers' adoption intention of GB technology are developed in a hierarchical structure, with the top-level concepts forming the main factors related to the research objective. Finally, the framework explaining these factors is described in the theoretical narrative.

Focus group interview is the primary procedure for data collection in this research. The main objective of qualitative research is to gather in-depth insight regarding the issue. Therefore, qualitative research typically embraces non-random sampling (Creswell & Poth, 2018). This study used a purposive sampling technique to select the appropriate informants who are experts and able to understand the phenomena under investigation, as recommended by many qualitative scholars (Yin, 2017; Creswell & Poth, 2018; Creswell & Creswell, 2018; Sekaran & Bougie, 2019).

The researchers planned an interview protocol in accordance with the research objective based on the predetermined identified elements "individual, technological, organisational, and environmental determinants". The interview protocol contains three main sections as presented in Appendix -A. The first section is an introduction: the interviewer introduces himself and the purpose of the interview, assures confidentiality, asks permission to record the interview, and gives warm-up questions. The second section consists of the main questions covering the purpose of the interview. This part is developed in a logical order and derived from the research questions with consideration of previous literature. A set of probing questions is prepared for more specific and in-depth information within the main questions. The last section includes the concluding instructions to end the interview and thank the informants.

Regarding the qualitative sampling size, most the recent qualitative scholars have mentioned that the subjective assessment of the researcher determines the sample size when he/she realises that the point of saturation has been reached (Yin, 2017; Creswell & Poth, 2018; Creswell & Creswell, 2018; Sekaran & Bougie, 2019). The point of saturation means that the information has become redundant and no more new themes are being identified, at that point the researcher can end the process (Creswell & Poth, 2018; Sekaran & Bougie, 2019). Correspondingly, ten participants from various positions and sites participated in the semi-structured interview, which was sufficient to reach saturation in this study.

The qualitative software program NVivo 11 Plus was used for the Thematic Content Analysis (TCA) to analyse the data in transcriptions and identify the codes associated with theoretical underpinning, which formed the research bases. The qualitative data analysis involved the steps presented by Braun and Clarke (2006). These steps include interviewing and recording, listening to recorded tapes, transcribing the recordings, getting respondents to confirm the transcripts, coding the confirmed transcripts, naming and organising codes, loading quotations and memos to appropriate codes, analysing and producing outputs, and lastly writing the reports.

Phase Two: Quantitative Study

Based on the results of the semi-structured interviews, a number of potential factors were identified that could contribute to customers' GB technology adoption. A set of hypotheses was formulated to produce the study's proposed final model. Afterwards, a quantitative cross-sectional survey was performed among a larger sample of bank customers in the UAE collected through an online survey to test the proposed hypotheses and validate the results using PLS-SEM in Smart PLS 3.3. Smart PLS tests a model in two stages. The measurement model to verify the reliability and validity of the instrument, while the structural model to test the research hypotheses. PLS-SEM is considered a variance-based approach that depends on the least-squares functions, and it attempts to maximize the explained variance of the dependent variables (Hair et al., 2021). This study used PLS-SEM owing to its fitness in the exploratory stage for theory building and prediction or extension of an existing structural theory and the study's objective is to determine the key target drives construct (Hair et al., 2012).

Concerning the sample size, the study employed power analysis to determine the minimum sample size due to the absence of the sample frame, as suggested by Creswell & Creswell (2018), Sekaran & Bougie (2019) and Hair et al. (2021). Referring to Cohen's (1988) sample size formula to identify the adequate sample size, the study used G*Power as a function of the standardised significance criterion α, the effect size (ES), the statistical power $(1-\beta)$, and the number of indicators. By doing so, using G*Power for two tails, medium ES (0.05), α (0.05), power (0.95), and ten predictors, the results indicated a minimum of 242 respondents required to achieve the statistical power of .95 at the significant level 0.05 (α). Yet, the researcher increased the sample size to 332 to generate more reliable results.

The study employed a convenience sampling technique using an electronic survey to collect data. According to Sekaran and Bougie (2019), convenience sampling is the most often used and efficient technique for experimental research for collecting data. The electronic questionnaire was developed using Google survey platforms and disseminated on social media, e.g., Facebook and WhatsApp owing to its massive usage among the UAE citizens. An online survey of 53 questions, excluding demography, had been categorised into three sections. Section A for describing the purpose of the research. Section B consists of respondents' demographic data, while section C includes measurement items of each variable.

The study developed a survey focusing on the factors affecting customers' intention to adopt GB technology. To the extent possible, it was adapted measurement scales used in prior studies to fit the context of the study and to ensure the validity of all instruments. All the constructs were measured with multiple items on a five-point Likert scale, with anchors ranging from "strongly disagree" (1) to "strongly agree" (5). The survey items together with their source are listed in Appendix -B. Even though the majority of the UAE's population masters the English language. A licensed bilingual translator translated the original instruments into the Arabic language. Then, the Arabic version was edited and translated back into English by a second licensed bilingual translator independently. The equivalence between the back-translated and the source versions has been reviewed regarding their semantic equivalence. Minor discrepancies were found between the source and the back-translated versions. Furthermore, two senior academic experts and one bank practitioner validated the questionnaire to identify any complications with its wording, content, and question ambiguity as a pre-test. The survey was piloted on a small sample of 50 customers at the request of academic experts. Pilot test results were satisfactory, given that the reliability of all buildings exceeded 0.70 (Shmueli et al., 2016, 2019; Hair et al., 2019).

Phase One: Qualitative Data Analysis and Findings

The researcher approached several bank professionals to conduct the semi-structured interviews. Eventually, ten individuals agreed to participate in the study, which was sufficient to reach the saturation point as the report has become redundant and no more new arguments are being found. The participants were denoted as P1, P2…P10 to preserve the anonymity of their personal identities. The informants were chosen based on their professional experience in the banking industry, position and expertise in the field of the research study (Table 1).

Table 1. Business profile of the participants

S/N	Bank Name	Site/ Location	Current Position	Working Experience in the Current Position	Working Experience in the Current Bank	Highest Qualification
P1	Dubai Bank	Branch/ Dubai	Head of Branch	3 years	8 years	MBA Finance
P2	Abu Dhabi Islamic Bank	Branch/ Abu Dhabi	Head of Branch	2 years	7 years	MBA Finance
P3	Abu Dhabi Islamic Bank	Branch/ Ajman	Head of Branch	4 years	10 years	MBA Finance
P4	Noor Bank	Branch/ Fujairah	Head of Branch	2 years	7 years	MSc Finance and Banking
P5	Abu Dhabi Islamic Bank	HQ/ Abu Dhabi	Regional Manager	1 year	12 years	MBA Finance
P6	Emirates Bank	HQ/ Dubai	Head of the Strategic Planning Unit	2 years	8 years	PhD. Business Management
P7	Emirates Bank	HQ/ Dubai	Junior General Manager	2 years	9 years	MSc Business Management
P8	Dubai Bank	HQ/ Dubai	Sales Executive Manager	3 years	16 years	DBA International Business
P9	Sharjah Bank	HQ/ Sharjah	Marketing Manager	2 years	9 years	MSc Business Management
P10	Sharjah Bank	HQ/ Sharjah	Sales Manager	3 years	10 years	MBA Finance

Theoretical Narrative

The qualitative analysis produced six new subthemes consistent with the four predetermined determinants: customer awareness and personal innovativeness represent the individual determinant; bank reputation represents the organisational determinant; security and privacy and system quality form the technological determinant; government support represents the environmental determinant (Table 2). The researchers validated the study by requesting some experts in the ðeld to assess the pattern in the data about the associated themes. The following highlights the findings under each factor based on the direct quotes from the informants during the semi-structured interview, which present how the findings achieve the objective of the first phase.

Table 2. Summary of the qualitative study output

Factors Extracted	Participants										Total participants	Total (%)
	P1	P2	P3	P4	P5	P6	P7	P8	P9	P10		
Customer Awareness	✓	✓	✓	✓	✓	✓	✓	✓	×	×	08	80%
Personal Innovativeness	✓	✓	✓	×	✓	×	✓	✓	✓	×	07	70%
Privacy & Security	✓	✓	✓	✓	✓	×	×	×	×	✓	06	60%
System Quality	✓	✓	✓	✓	✓	✓	×	✓	×	×	07	70%
Bank Reputation	×	✓	✓	×	×	×	✓	✓	✓	×	05	50%
Government Support	✓	×	×	✓	✓	✓	×	✓	×	✓	06	60%

The qualitative data reveals that customer awareness determines the bank customers' intention behaviour. The majority of informants (80%) established that customer awareness is an essential individual factor in determining their adoption of GB technology, whereas the lack of information regarding availability, importance, concept, knowledge, and benefits are the main barrier. Thus, customer awareness is operationalised in this study as the amount of information about GB technology services and the bank customers' levels of consciousness of its existence, concept, purpose, and benefits. Moreover, 70% of the informants stressed that the customers hesitate and are unwilling to try out new GB technology because of the absence of an innovative mindset, lack of openness to taking chances, and preference to be in their comfort zone. Such personality attributes might restrict the customers from trying new products and adopting new technologies, as it will require them to change their usual work routines on top of the risk of failure or loss due to the switch to those new GB technology services. Therefore, this study operationalised personal innovativeness as the bank customers' tendency and willingness to try out the new GB technology services.

The frequent technology contributor to the phenomenon being studied was the worry and concern about the security and privacy of the customers' data, as expressed by 60% of the informants. The customers' perception of less protection and the fear of illegitimate penetration by various cyber-attacks on privacy stands as an obstacle. This barrier makes the adoption of GB technology services an intimidating option for bank customers. In other words, a greater security and privacy concern may serve as a hindering factor to customers' intention to adopt GB technology services. Based on the outcomes of the qualitative field, this study operationalises perceived security and privacy as the degree to which a bank customer believes that the GB technology services will be free of security and privacy threats. In addition, 70% of the informants stressed that customers are very much concerned about the system's comprehensive design, response time speed, trustworthiness and flexibility in performing a range of operations consistently without interruptions. Thus, system quality refers to the degree to which the comprehensive design of the system, response time, system reliability, system availability, functionality, and flexibility influence the perception of the bank customer regarding the adoption of GB technology services.

Additionally, half of the informants (50%) imply that customers rely on the company's status like better bank ranking, larger bank size, and a longer tenure in the banking industry, demonstrating its ability, integrity, and goodwill to deliver efficient, beneficial, and reliable services. Such organisational attributes have a higher chance of attracting customers to adopt GB technology services and are more likely to be committed to adopting its survives or carrying out other actions in its favour. Accordingly, bank reputation is operationalised as the value judgment among the customers about the bank's qualities.

The shortage in government support was highlighted as a central environmental challenge, which is anticipated to affect customers' adoption of GB technology. The informants (60%) stressed that the government is able to create a favourable environment and provide incentives for technology implementation and vice versa. Thus, when adopting financing technology services like GB services, consumers expect to receive assistance from the government concerning policies, incentives, and subsidies. Accordingly, government support can be operationalised as the role of government-related policies that cover a different set of rules and promotion incentives to adopt GB technology services.

RESEARCH FRAMEWORK AND HYPOTHESES DEVELOPMENT

Individual determinant refers to the factors related to the users' attributes and personal merits. Technological determinants, also known as innovation features, refer to the aspects related to the attributes of the innovation itself. Organisational determinants are those internal situational enablers or constraining factors that form an organisation's confidence in its ability to perform or undertake a particular behaviour. Environmental determinants are external factors that reside outside the organisation's control but still affect the IT adoption process (Jeyaraj et al., 2006). Those elements form the basis for exploring all-inclusive variables and developing a framework that may shape the customer's intention to adopt GB technology.

Based on the output of the qualitative data analysis, the final model of the study was formed. Along with four key constructs of the UTAUT model, six additional factors (customer awareness, personal innovativeness, bank reputation, security and privacy, system quality and government support) are grouped under four generic categories (individual, technology, organisation, and environment) to form the conceptual model presented in Figure 1. Thus, it is expected to comprehensively explain the customers' intention to adopt GB technology in the UAE. All variables hypothesised in this study and their likely relationships have been discussed next.

Figure 1. Final Research Framework

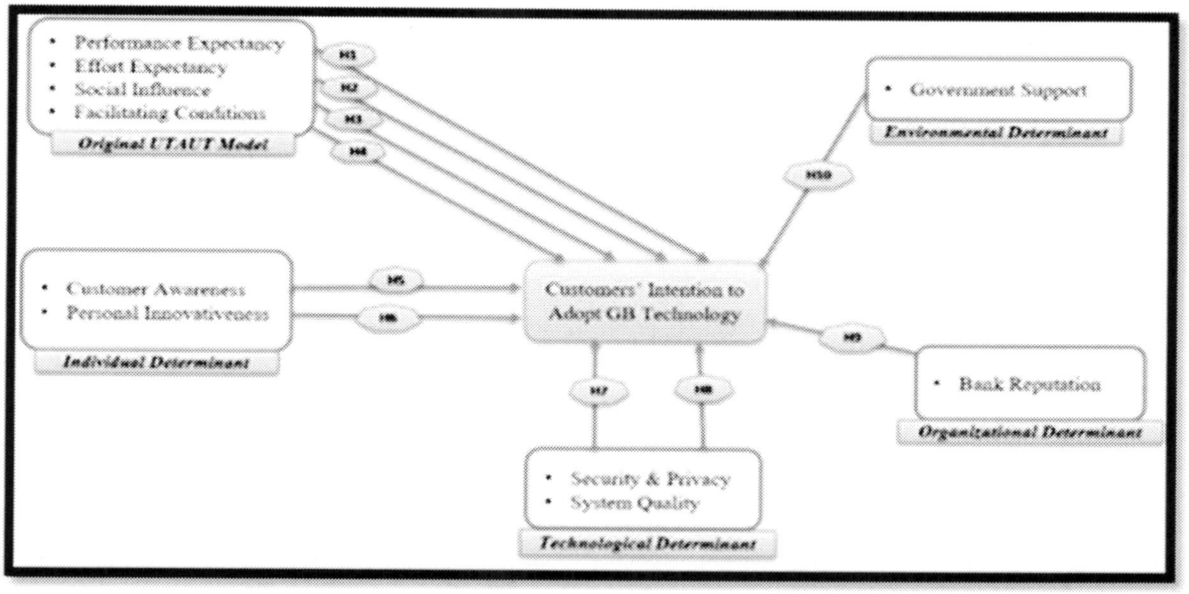

Performance Expectancy

Performance expectancy is a construct in the UTAUT model by Venkatesh et al. (2003) to predict consumers' belief in task implementation improvement through technologies (Venkatesh et al., 2003). In a later revision of the model UTAUT2, Venkatesh et al. (2012) reserved performance expectancy as the strongest predictor of user behavioural intention. Performance expectancy is one of the constructs that has received considerable attention from several researchers (Wiafe et al., 2019; Gupta & Arora, 2019; Do et al., 2020; Bouteraa et al., 2020; Petersen et al., 2020). These studies imply that performance expectancy is a key construct to enhancing information systems' usage. Particularly, the practicality of GB technology can only be captured by the extent to which it can meet the expectations of the clients (Rifat et al., 2016; Iqbal et al., 2018; Iqbal et al., 2019). Thus, if bank customers perceive that GB technology services will contribute meaningfully to enhancing their financial performance, they may be favourably disposed to adopt them. In keeping with the literature on GB technology adoption and the UTAUT model, which asserted that IT-based products or services improve job performance and offer many facilities in the form of efficiency, usefulness, effortless and timeliness transactions, this study anticipates that performance expectancy will describe consumers' intention to adopt GB technology services. This argument led to the first hypothesis:

H1: Performance expectancy significantly affects customers' intention to adopt GB technology.

Effort Expectancy

According to Venkatesh et al. (2003), effort expectancy measures people's level of convenience when using specific information technology. The previous literature documented inconsistent results regarding the output of effort expectancy towards technology behaviour. Many studies reported a significant influence of effort expectancy on consumers' intention (Karjaluoto et al., 2019), Tele-dentistry (Alabdullah et al., 2020). Similar findings in the context of GB technology (Rifat et al., 2016; Iqbal et al., 2018). On the contrary, several empirical studies claimed that effort expectancy is not a critical determinant as such, e-learning systems usage (El-Masri & Tarhini, 2017) and e-voting system adoption (Mensah, 2020). These considerable inconsistent conclusions motivate examining the effect of effort expectancy on the customers' intention to adopt GB technology in developing economies like the UAE. The UTAUT model anticipated that customers might not refrain from using IT-based services that are convenient and useful to conduct financial transactions. This offers a sufficient load of effort expectancy to describe the consumers' intention to adopt GB technology. This study sets up the second hypothesis:

H2: Effort expectancy significantly affects customers' intention to adopt GB technology.

Social Influence

Social psychology theories highlight the importance of social influence in determining behaviour. The Social Learning Theory (SLT) by Bandura and Walters (1977) indicated that people learn from one another through communications with their trusted contacts. Furthermore, the Conflict Elaboration Theory of Social Influence (CETSI) of Mugny et al. (1995) suggested that when an individual decides whether to adopt or reject an innovation, the effect of the decision upon the individual's relationship with others in the group is considered. Based on the Social Influence Theory (SIT) of Kelman (1974), the most rudimentary form of influence is compliance which occurs when people accept influence to create a promising reaction from another person or group; internalization occurs when a user accepts others' belief as evidence of reality, while identification occurs when users adopt a belief to establish or maintain their relationship with the group. Thus, influence could be described as an attitude change produced by external messages (Kelman,1974).

According to numerous theories and models of acceptance and use of technology like TRA, TBP, TAM and UTAUT, social influence is a core determinant of behavioural intention. Social influence refers to the extent to which the individual's technology usage is affected by others' opinions (Venkatesh et al., 2003). The idea behind social influence is that even though a person may not support technology, they intend to use it because of the belief it will raise his/her image among peers (Venkatesh & Davis, 2000). Many empirical IT adoption studies have found that social influence plays a vital role in users' intention behaviour (Al-Saedi et al., 2020; Flavian et al., 2020). However, this later conflicted with other investigations that did not report significant proof (Raza et al., 2019; Handarkho, 2020; Purwanto & Loisa, 2020; Abbasi et al., 2021). Similarly, GB technology adoption literature documented inconsistent conclusions regarding the role of social influence. A study by Rifat et al. (2016) confirmed the positive effect of social influence. Conversely, Iqbal et al. (2018) reported that social influence is not an important variable to explain the customers' intention to adopt GB technology. These inconsistent conclusions imply that social influence is a context-dependent factor thus motivating the examination within the context of this study. Based on the UTAUT model, it can be inferred that technology services that are trendy to use offer a load of the social influence construct to influence the customers'' intention to adopt GB technology services. Hence, the hypothesis is as follow:

H3: Social influence significantly affects customers' intention to adopt GB technology.

Facilitating Condition

Facilitating condition in the UTAUT model refers to the availability of the required technical resources for users to support the implementation of a specific technology (Venkatesh et al., 2003). The UTAUT identifies the facilitating condition as a construct that reflects a person's perception of their control over their behaviour (Venkatesh et al., 2008). Although the original UTAUT did not show a direct association between facilitating condition and behavioural intention, the extended UTAUT2 by Venkatesh et al. (2012) validated this direct effect. The literature stressed the importance of facilitating conditions as a vital predictor of intention to use a wide range of sundry technologies (Wang et al., 2020; Jahanshahi et al., 2020). The synthesis of GB technology studies demonstrated a definite agreement regarding the importance of facilitating conditions in capturing consumer intention behaviour (Iqbal et al., 2018; Iqbal et al., 2019; Nisha et al., 2020). Despite the importance of facilitating conditions in GB technology adoption models, there remains a lack of evidence from customers in the UAE as a Middle Eastern region with unique social and economic structures. The practical notion of facilitating conditions is that when bank customers have sufficient supporting resources such as the knowledge to adopt GB technology, easy access to the internet and required smart devices, being guided and supported by experts or bankers, they may develop a positive perception. Hence, the hypothesis is formulated:

H4: Facilitating condition significantly affects customers' intention to adopt GB technology.

Customer Awareness

Awareness is essential in the innovation adoption process (Guiltinand & Donnelly, 1983). The likelihood of innovation tends to increase by providing additional information on the characteristics of technology (Rogers, 1983). People who are well informed about a particular service will ultimately become more aware of it, and they will be motivated to support it (Lujja et al., 2018). On the other hand, the lack of awareness about the benefits, advantages and disadvantages acts as a barrier to the acceptance of technology (Pai & Alathur, 2019). Various researchers highlighted concern about the ability of awareness to influence customer intention behaviour (Bouteraa, 2019; Chaurasia et al., 2019; Singh & Sinha, 2020; Baabdullah, 2020; Bouteraa & Al-Aidaros, 2020). This implies that providing more information on specific innovation attributes like GB technology might positively affect adopters' decisions. Despite the intensive discussion of awareness construct in the IT adoption literature, a lack of studies addressed this crucial variable in customers' intention to adopt GB technology. Thus, a realistic understanding of customer awareness by experimentation is essential to fill this gap. Considering the belief of the informants in the qualitative study along with the above discussion, it can be predicted that consumers with high awareness are more inclined to adopt these innovative measures. Hence, the hypothesis can be formulated:

H5: Customer awareness significantly affects customers' intention to adopt GB technology.

Personal Innovativeness

Diffusion theory asserts that adopters optimistically anticipate new technologies (Rogers, 1995). Optimistic attitudes on technology acceptance positively control user satisfaction (Khan & Ullah, 2014), promoting innovativeness and enhancing technology usage behaviour (Khan et al., 2019). Agarwal and Prasad (1998) have proposed personal innovativeness specifically for the field of technology which they defined as "the willingness of an individual to try out any new information technology". Even though personal innovativeness was initially introduced as a moderator (Agarwal & Prasad, 1998), it was also proven to be theoretically and empirically a key antecedent in innovation adoption (Thakur et al., 2016). The findings of many empirical IT adoption studies have shown that personal innovativeness is a significant factor in behavioural intention (Cao et al., 2019; Lee, 2019; Bervell et al., 2020; Abbasi et al., 2021). This implies that individuals with high innovativeness are more likely to use various IT-based services. Despite the rigorous investigations on personal innovativeness, limited studies examined the effect of this factor on customers' intention to adopt GB technology. A practical understanding of personal innovativeness in determining customers' intention toward GB technology is essential to fill the identified gap. Based on the anticipation of the informants in the qualitative investigation and the prior literature, the following hypothesis can be formulated:

H6: Personal innovativeness significantly affects customers' intention to adopt GB technology.

Security and Privacy

New technologies' growing capacity for information processing and their integration into consumers' daily lives have made security and privacy an increasingly important matter. Consumers are unwilling to accept that they do not have full control over their behaviours (Pikkarainen et al., 2004) because their insecurity perception increases regarding how their personal data is being gathered and processed (Flavián & Guinalíu, 2006). The quantitative importance of this issue is shown by Yoon et al. (2020), who stressed that security and privacy is a conditional concern of technology adoption. Security and privacy forecast a broad range of behavioural and attitude outcomes. For instance, people with high perceived security and privacy are more likely to use new financial systems (Merhi et al., 2019) exhibit higher levels of e-Satisfaction (Alalwan et al., 2019) and services choice (Deb et al., 2019). Contrary to these studies, Chatterjee (2020) claimed that users in specific contexts may not be concerned regarding the issue of security and privacy while adopting new technology. Although, this construct is rarely examined in the field of customers' intention to adopt GB technology. Thus, the study aims to fill this gap by firmly establishing the relevance of this factor with customers' intention to adopt GB technology. Considering GB technology services necessitate high-security measures to protect users' private data, along with the anticipation of the qualitative phase, it can be concluded that security and privacy will determine customers' intention to adopt GB technology. Consequently, the following hypothesis is proposed:

H7: Security and privacy significantly affects customers' intention to adopt GB technology.

System Quality

System quality is one of the strategic elements in the original IS success model (DeLone & McLean, 1992) and the revised model (Delone & McLean, 2003), which is necessary for the production output of the information processing system. The system's quality focuses on the technical level of success of a system concerning information production (DeLone & McLean, 1992). It is related to the software and data components, and it is used to measure the soundness of the technical aspects of the system (Gorla, 2011). System quality centres on customers' perception of information retrieval and services delivery (Ngoc-Duy & Thi-Dai, 2018). Usability, availability, reliability, adaptability, accessibility, and response time are examples of system qualities demanded by users (Delone & McLean, 2003). The literature stressed the importance of system quality as a vital predictor of intention to use a wide range of various technologies (Zhang et al., 2020; Sensuse et al., 2021; Anggreni et al., 2020; Albashrawi et al., 2020). This suggests the better system quality, the more consumers are inclined to adopt the service. However, the system quality is rarely inspected in the field of GB technology. In essence, studying system quality through experimentation is crucial to fill this gap in explaining the customer's behaviour intention towards GB technology. Consistent with the informants' anticipation in the qualitative study and the above arguments, technology-based services like GB technology necessitate a comprehensive system design, speed response time, and trustworthiness in flexibly performing a range of operations without interruptions, entailing a significant weight of system quality to affect customers' intention to adopt GB technology. Consequently, the following hypothesis is posited:

H8: System quality significantly affects customers' intention to adopt GB technology.

Bank Reputation

Reputation is one of the most imperative intangible assets of a corporation built through its believability and credibility in actions over time (Nguyen & Leblanc, 2001), which predominantly affects customers' behaviour (Helm et al., 2010). Corporate reputation is the overall appeal of an organisation to stakeholders in the past actions and prospects compared to the other leading competitors (Fombrun, 1996). Corporate reputation has always been an important factor in consumer decision-making (Nguyen & Leblanc, 2001). Customers are very much concerned about the company's reputation to form their overall perception, including behavioural intention, satisfaction, loyalty (Ikhsan & Simarmata, 2021; Islam et al., 2021) and customer trust (Stravinskienė et al., 2021). Numerous studies have demonstrated the significant role of reputation in predicting technology acceptance (Chaudhary, 2019; Mijoska et al., 2020; Picoto & Pinto, 2021). This suggests that customers use a company's reputation as an information cue to form behaviour about its products or services. However, less consideration was given to the effect of bank reputation on customers' intention to adopt GB technology. Accordingly, a practical understanding of bank reputation is essential to fill this gap in outlining the customers' intention to adopt GB technology. Consistent with the anticipation of the output of qualitative inquiry and the extant literature, which implies that customers rely on the bank's status, i.e., its ability, integrity, and goodwill to deliver efficient, beneficial, and reliable services, it is reasonable to anticipate that customers are likely to adopt GB technology. Thus, it is hypothesised that:

H9: Bank reputation significantly affects customers' intention to adopt GB technology.

Government Support

The government has a virtuous standing in increasing the credibility and reliability of services by improving the promotion of technology application in financial innovation and investing in infrastructure, making consumers feel more secure in using particular financing services when the government provision is involved (Hu et al., 2019). Empirical conclusions found a significant association between government support and consumers' intention to adopt technologies (Hu et al., 2019; Haleem et al., 2019; Cha et al., 2020). On the contrary, there is overwhelming support for studies that claim that government support is the least important factor (Marakarkandy et al., 2017; Sánchez-Torres et al., 2018; Maryam et al., 2019). This indicates that government support is a country-specific and context-dependent determinant. Nevertheless, out of the considerable number of empirical studies investigating government support in various settings, there is a lack of existing research regarding the relationship between government support and customers' intention to adopt GB technology services in the UAE. The rationale behind government support as a determinant to explain customers' intention to adopt GB technology is that government encouragement, promotions, and provision of guaranteed incentives could help the customers consider the transactional condition of GB technology. The preliminary qualitative field and the above discussion provided a reference for this research to predict that government support will impact consumers' intention to adopt GB technology. Therefore, it hypothesised the following:

H10: Government support significantly affects customers' intention to adopt GB technology.

Phase Two: Quantitative Data Analysis and Results

Sample of Study

The descriptive statistics analysis was applied using IBM-SPSS 26 to discover the missing values. The results showed that there were no missing values. However, as per the standard approach to detect multivariate outliers by computing the squared Mahala-Nobis distance at p <.001 for each case in the data set (Byrne, 2010), out of 338, only 6 cases were reported to be multivariate outliers and should be omitted (Tabachnick & Fidell, 2013). Thus, leaving a final sample size of 332 valid cases for the actual data analysis. The summary of the sample's demographic statistics is displayed in Table 3. The common method bias, which might occur in survey data, is also examined using Harman's single-factor test using IBM-SPSS 26. The results show a value of 37%, which is less than 50%. This indicates that the data does not suffer from common method bias (Podsakoff et al., 2003).

Table 3. Demographic information of sample N=332 (100%)

Variable	Category	Frequency	Percentage
Gender	Male	217	65.4%
	Female	115	34.6%
Age	Young (18 to 39 years old)	209	63%
	Old (40 years old and above)	123	37%
Education level	College Diploma	28	8.4%
	First Degree (Bachelor)	130	39.2%
	Professional certificate	62	18.7%
	Others	5	1.5%
Occupation	Professional e.g., lawyer, Doctor, engineer	148	44.6%
	Manager/ Executive	38	11.4%
	Academician	34	10.2%
	Student	28	8.4%
	Merchant/Businessman	77	23.2%
	Unemployed	4	1.2%
	Others	3	0.9%

Assessment of Measurement Model

The measurement model was performed by evaluating reliability (composite reliability-CR), convergent validity (Factor loadings and average variances extracted - AVE) and discriminant validity (Hetrotrait-Monotrait-HTMT) (Hair et al., 2019). Table 4 findings show that the factor loadings, AVE and CR exceed the suggested values, i.e., 0.70, 0.5 and 0.7, respectively (Shmueli et al., 2016, 2019; Hair et al., 2019; Hair et al., 2021).

Table 4. Summary results of convergent validity, and reliability

Constructs	Indicators	Loadings	CR	AVE
Intention	INT1	0.819	0.966	0.802
	INT2	0.828		
	INT3	0.942		
	INT4	0.932		
	INT5	0.939		
	INT6	0.927		
	INT7	0.872		
Performance Expectancy	PE1	0.830	0.897	0.687
	PE2	0.906		
	PE3	0.817		
	PE4	0.755		
Efforts Expectancy	EE1	0.869	0.884	0.658
	EE2	0.743		
	EE3	0.753		
	EE4	0.871		
Facilitating Condition	FC1	0.742	0.895	0.632
	FC2	0.842		
	FC3	0.833		
	FC4	0.840		
	FC5	0.705		
Social Influence	SI1	0.834	0.900	0.693
	SI2	0.895		
	SI3	0.882		
	SI4	0.705		
Personal Innovativeness	PI1	0.844	0.888	0.665
	PI2	0.734		
	PI3	0.801		
	PI4	0.876		

Continued on following page

Table 4. Continued

Constructs	Indicators	Loadings	CR	AVE
Customer Awareness	AWA1	0.852	0.924	0.710
	AWA2	0.787		
	AWA3	0.896		
	AWA4	0.878		
	AWA5	0.793		
System Quality	SQ1	0.720	0.902	0.609
	SQ2	0.877		
	SQ3	0.802		
	SQ4	0.824		
	SQ5	0.849		
	SQ6	0.568		
Bank Reputation	BR1	0.905	0.934	0.738
	BR2	0.837		
	BR3	0.865		
	BR4	0.812		
	BR5	0.873		
Security and Privacy	SP1	0.884	0.905	0.704
	SP2	0.850		
	SP3	0.828		
	SP4	0.790		
Government Support	GS1	0.857	0.951	0.794
	GS2	0.858		
	GS3	0.924		
	GS4	0.925		
	GS5	0.889		

Note: All factor loadings are significant at p < 0.05

This study also assessed discriminant validity by applying HTMT ratios (Kline, 2016). Results in Table 5 reveal that all the HTMT values of all constructs were lower than 0.85 (Henseler et al., 2015). Accordingly, no issues related to the discriminant validity. This leads to the conclusion of the validation of the measurement model.

Table 5. Heterotrait-Monotrait ratio (HTMT)

	AWA	BR	EE	FC	GS	INT	PE	PI		SI	SQ	SP
AWA												
BR	0.377											
EE	0.505	0.394										
FC	0.551	0.619	0.729									
GS	0.203	0.624	0.323	0.558								
INT	0.680	0.367	0.567	0.651	0.305							
PE	0.578	0.451	0.694	0.652	0.298	0.847						
PI	0.785	0.473	0.385	0.486	0.323	0.600	0.475					
SI	0.352	0.614	0.568	0.753	0.530	0.493	0.524	0.317				
SQ	0.611	0.648	0.641	0.784	0.523	0.678	0.708	0.471		0.651		
SP	0.557	0.574	0.486	0.656	0.372	0.596	0.643	0.419		0.571	0.845	

Notes: Intention = INT, Performance Expectancy = PE, Efforts Expectancy = EE, Social Influence = SI, Facilitating Condition = FC, Awareness = AWA, Personal Innovativeness = PI, System Quality = SQ, Bank Reputation = BR, Security and Privacy = SP, Government Support = GS. All values of HTMT £ 0.85.

Assessment of Structural Model

Even though discriminant validity has been met in the outer model assessment, lateral collinearity issues might lead to statistical instability or/and inaccurate results (Hair et al., 2017; Hair et al., 2018). Therefore, it was decided to be investigated. Variance Inflated Factor (VIF) value of 5 or greater indicates potential collinearity matter (Hair et al., 2011; Shmueli et al., 2016, 2019; Hair et al., 2021). However, the findings of this study presented in Table VI confirm no apprehensions on the multi-collinearity as all the VIF values were lower than 5.

Subsequently, structural model analyses were performed to test the study's formulated hypotheses. Therefore, bootstrapping process with 5000 iterations was employed as per the recommendations of Hair et al. (2021). Table 6 and Figure 2 reveal the results of the hypotheses. Moreover, the model's factors generated $R^2 = 72.2\%$ of the variance toward behaviour intention, which substantially permits the criteria specified by many scholars (Shmueli et al., 2019; Hair et al., 2019; Hair et al., 2021). The effect size (f^2) was also calculated. Findings show that most variables have small to medium effect size according to criteria specified by Cohen (1992). Besides, this study further calculated predictive relevance (Q^2). Results revealed that the Q^2 value for the endogenous construct was greater than zero (Intention: $Q^2 = 0.579$) (Hair et al., 2021).

Figure 2. The PLS results of the Structural Model.
*Notes: NS, not significant. * p< 0.05; ** p< 0.01; *** p< 0.001*

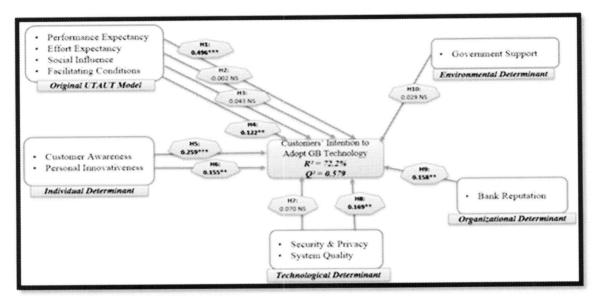

Table 6. Path coefficients, hypotheses testing and effect size.

Relationship	H	Std.β	t- Statistics	P-value	Confidences Interval		Decision	VIF	(f²)
					Lower	Upper			
PE » INT	H1	0.496	12.446	0.000***	.413	.571	Accepted	2.132	0.420
EE » INT	H2	-0.002	0.096	0.923	-.092	.096	Rejected	2.265	0.003
SI » INT	H3	0.043	1.038	0.299	-.033	.116	Rejected	2.000	0000
FC » INT	H4	0.122	2.713	0.007**	.035	.208	Accepted	2.763	0.014
Awa » INT	H5	0.259	5.515	0.000***	.164	.348	Accepted	3.027	0.082
PI » INT	H6	0.155	2.709	0.007**	.037	.263	Accepted	2.077	0.035
SP » INT	H7	0.070	1.433	0.152	-.028	.173	Rejected	2.737	0.003
SQ » INT	H8	0.169	2.685	0.007**	.042	.291	Accepted	3.499	0.028
BR » INT	H9	0.158	3.472	0.001**	.248	.074	Accepted	2.068	0.043
GS » INT	H10	0.029	0.782	0.434	-.052	.102	Rejected	1.690	0000

*Notes: Intention = INT, Performance Expectancy = PE, Efforts Expectancy = EE, Social Influence = SI, Facilitating Condition = FC, Awareness = AWA, Personal Innovativeness = PI, System Quality = SQ, Bank Reputation = BR, Security and Privacy = SP, Government Support = GS. *p < 0.5, ** p < 0.01, *** p < 0.001. Effect size calculated manually using formula of* Cohen *(1988) as f² = (R² included – R² excluded) ¤ (1 – R² included).*

Furthermore, this study assessed PLS Predict to further validate the predictive relevance of the model. PLS predict is a set of procedures proposed by Shmueli et al. (2016) that permitted the study to measure the out-of-sample prediction, which involves estimating the model on an analysis sample and evaluating its predictive performance on data other than the analysis sample (Shmueli et al., 2019). For this study, PLS predict is used to compute the case-level predictions of PLS predict with k = 10 as recommended by Hair et al. (2019) and Shmueli et al. (2019). The findings show that all the Q^2 predict values are larger than zero (Q^2 predict > 0), indicating that all the indicators had outperformed the LM benchmark. This allows for the subsequent comparison of the RMSE values with the naïve LM benchmark. The comparison results between PLS-SEM and LM indicate that a majority of the indicators (4 out of 7) in the PLS-SEM analysis yield smaller prediction errors compared to the LM (PLS-SEM<LM) (Table 7). This means that the study's model has medium predictive power, as set by Shmueli et al. (2019). This statistically implies that the model can accurately predict the responses out of the sample and its ability to generate testable predictions in various technology adoption contexts like e-commerce, smart devices usage, and high-tech innovations adoption since their technical characteristics, design, and benefits are similar to the GB technology.

Table 7. Assessment of Q^2 Predict and the Predictive Performance of the PLS Model Vs. Benchmark LM

Indicators	PLS Predict		LM predict		(PLS-LM)
	RMSE	Q^2 predict	RMSE	Q^2 predict	RMSE
INT7	0.691	0.561	0.653	0.608	**0.038**
INT4	0.511	0.634	0.498	0.653	**0.013**
INT3	0.537	0.613	0.565	0.572	-0.028
INT6	0.543	0.602	0.533	0.617	**0.01**
INT2	0.628	0.417	0.586	0.494	**0.042**
INT1	0.685	0.459	0.720	0.403	-0.035
INT5	0.540	0.635	0.575	0.586	-0.035

Note: Intention = INT; Root Mean Squared Error = RMSE; Linear Model LM.

CONCLUSION

Meta-Inference

To evaluate the study findings, meta-inference is employed in conjunction with the bridge strategy to establish a consensus between qualitative and quantitative findings (Venkatesh et al., 2013; Venkatesh et al., 2016). The qualitative data analysis reveals that customer awareness and personal innovativeness are the vital individual factors that could improve their adoption of GB technology. The qualitative results also indicate that the technology features of GB technology might become barriers, and the most influential factor could be the security and privacy and system quality. The informants also highlighted during the interviews that the value judgment among the customers about the bank's qualities (i.e., reputation) is a constraining factor that from an organisational motivation force or barrier for customers. Furthermore, government-related policies, regulations, and incentives have been identified as crucial environmental barriers influencing customers' intention adoption of GB technology. The preliminary qualitative findings are mostly confirmed by quantitative data analysis whereby customer awareness, personal innovativeness, system quality, and bank reputation significantly impact customers' intention to adopt GB technology. However, the effects of security and privacy and government support are insignificant.

As an inference, the study results show that most qualitative findings can be generalised through quantitative research, implying that the mixed method approach effectively connects the qualitative and quantitative research gap and synchronises the virtues of both research methods. The empirical outcomes in both research approaches can also be cross-referenced to enrich the understanding of the issue under study. Thus, the mixed research method of this study provides a more in-depth insight into customers' GB adoption intention than a single-method approach.

Discussion

This study reveals that the sustainable qualities of GB technology, such as efficiency, saving time, and usefulness in managing finances (i.e., performance expectancy) along with the availability of the required technical resources for users (i.e., facilitating condition), can contribute to increasing the customers' intention adoption of GB technology with significant effect size. These results align with the UTAUT model and previous literature (Iqbal et al., 2018; Iqbal et al., 2019; Wang et al., 2020; Jahanshahi et al., 2020). Contrary to the UTAUT model, effort expectancy is found to be insignificant. This interprets that the customers do not tend to judge the importance of GB technology based on convenience, easiness of learning, interaction, and proficiency. Such behaviour might be related to their lack of innovativeness and hesitation to experience new services. These findings could also be associated with some societal attributes and the values which shape the individuals' perceptions (Venkatesh & Zhang, 2010). Similarly, this study established an insignificant relationship between social influence on customer adoption intention of GB technology. This finding may explain that financial matters are regarded as a solo act and private to users, which rationalises the limited sharing of information with peers and lessens the impact of social pressure. Another possible explanation for this result is generation Y, to which most of the respondents in the sample of this study are young people (18 - 39 years old) who were born and have grown in the age of technologies, and one of the characteristics of this generation is more "self-directed" than previous X generations (Abbasi et al., 2021). Overall, these findings imply that the UTAUT model is partially able to explain the issue under study.

This study also reveals that individual factors like customer awareness significantly affect the customers' GB adoption intention in both investigation phases. This signifies that empowered people are likely to find GB technology meaningful in managing their financial tasks efficiently. Prior knowledge and well-informed interest regarding the existence, moral concept, objectives, and the wide range of benefits of GB technology would positively shape the customer's adoption intention. This result is consistent with the literature (Bouteraa, 2019; Chaurasia et al., 2019; Singh & Sinha, 2020; Baabdullah, 2020). Personal innovativeness is equally a fundamental individual element to be significantly related to customers' intention to adopt GB technology with a considerable predictive relevance and effect size. According to qualitative and quantitative outputs, customers with higher levels of innovativeness are expected to develop more positive beliefs toward GB technology and vice versa. Thus, the personal innovativeness of customers is a substantial enabler to address the issue of low GB technology adoption. This conclusion supports the existing studies (Lee, 2019; Cao et al., 2019; Bervell et al., 2020).

The bank professionals perceived that security and privacy are essential for improving customers' intention to adopt GB technology. However, customers have denied this perception during the quantitative phase as security and privacy are not a significant concern to the UAE's customers. This optimistic perception among customers could be attributed to the high secrecy law and the solid infrastructure of the banking industry in the UAE, which is among the world's top reputable and well-structured. Furthermore, the less anxiety of customers about the imminent security risks and privacy violations could be related to the notion of desensitisation, where society is accustomed to living and working in a compromised environment. On the contrary, customers are very concerned about the system's quality. Thus, it can be understood that customers are attracted by the capabilities and robustness of the system. This is consistent with the literature that indicates when the quality improvement of a particular technology system exists, a weighty impact on the customers' intention will be positively resultant (Zhang et al., 2020; Sensuse et al., 2021; Anggreni et al., 2020).

Bank reputation is also revealed as having a significant impact on customers' intention to adopt GB technology in both study phases. This implies the excellent reputation means the bank is perceived to provide reliable GB technology to be integral and good-willed. Customers' intention would be greater for GB technology services with a higher selection risk. The elevated potential adverse effects resulting from an error in choosing service providers have led customers to rely heavily on the organisation's reputation in the market. Thus, customer intention is primarily motivated by the prestigious and attractive name of the bank in the market. This supports the literature that infers bank reputation as an intangible organisational enabler of consumer technology adoption (Sridhar & Mehta, 2018; Mijoska et al., 2020; Balakrishnan & Foroudi, 2020; Picoto & Pinto, 2021).

Bank professionals during the qualitative perceived that government support as an environmental determinant would increase the customers' intention to adopt GB technology. However, customers did not feel that the involvement of the UAE's had any effect on their intention. The possible explanation is that the policies implemented by the government have been ineffective, or users may consider them irrelevant to their decision to use these services. Another likely interpretation is that the UAE banks are primarily private and have distanced themselves from the customer's government policies. Notably, the UAE's economic freedom score is 76.2, making it the wolrd's18th freest in the 2020 index due to lower government integrity (The Heritage Foundation, 2020).

Theoretical Implication

The empirical findings of this study make notable contributions toward a more nuanced academic understanding of customers' adoption of GB technology. First, exploring six new factors that reflect the challenges of customers to adopt GB technology in the UAE. Second, it extends the applicability and validity of the UTAUT model in explaining GB technology adoption in the UAE as a new emerging economy context. Thirdly, the research outlined the key UTAUT variables that drive GB technology among Emirati bank customers, thereby contributing to an enhanced understanding of user behaviour with GB technology. Moreover, the high variance level explained by the model shows the relevance and potency of the UTAUT framework to this research. Conspicuously, the principal contribution is not only on replicating the UTAUT model in a new setting but also in significantly contributing to the theory by means of undertaking six new key factors as a source of competitive advantage to explain the customers' intention to adopt GB technology. As the broader theoretical contribution, the PLS predict analysis revealed that the study's model has medium predictive power. This means that the model can accurately predict the responses out of the sample and generate testable predictions in various technology adoption.

Methodologically, this work enriches extant literature on GB technology by using two complementary analytical approaches of TCA and PLS-SEM. The TCA contributed incrementally to the findings by proposing six new combinations of challenges to adopting GB technology. Beyond this, the PLS-SEM findings have shown the net effects of the new factors along with the UTAUT variables on GB technology adoption. The ensuing results verified that some of the variables that were insignificant to the PLS-SEM evaluation could promote the adoption of GB technology when integrated with other variables. Overall, our study contributes significantly to the literature by dissecting multiple precursors of customers' intention to adopt an innovation such as GB technology.

Practical Implication

From a practical perspective, the study's findings can be valuable for policymakers, researchers and bank managers in understanding the implications of GB technology in the UAE. Having explored and discussed how various individual, technological, organisational and environmental determinants influence customers' intention towards adopting GB technology, the study can be a viable reference in the development of effective GB policies that seek to maximise the benefits for mass customers, banks, and the economy of the country as well as to attain sustainability. The study suggests a model for practitioners by providing a better description of their customers' actual issues and challenges in adopting GB technology services. Therefore, it gives a solid foundation for policy formulation, planning and coordination of development strategies towards a successful transition to green and digital consumption behaviour, which would drive the principle of sustainability.

Based on the output of the study, bankers in the UAE should pay more attention to the individual features of their customers like awareness and motivational incentives to foster the customers' innovativeness and improve their perception through direct marketing rather than focusing on social influence. Furthermore, bank professionals need to enhance the technological features of the GB system by offering useful, accessible, fast, clear, convenient, functional and flexible services to maintain consistency in quality rather than focusing on security and privacy measures which are the least concern of the UAE's customers. Moreover, the banks need to maintain an excellent reputational identity as it is a crucial intangible asset to attract customers to adopt GB technology rather than seek government backing.

As practical incentives to encourage GB technology adoption, potential customers are subjected to enjoy convenient channels of financial services delivery in the form of virtuous and speedy service quality along with high security and reliability at lower costs. Furthermore, adopting GB technology helps banks in cutting down huge costs of operation and prevent wastage incurred by paper-based banking methods. Other motivations for GB technology adoption include economic benefits, image enhancement, convenience, satisfaction, time-saving, social benefits, hazard avoidance and sustainability attainment. Furthermore, the extensive developments in GB technology within the banking sector would support the green economic growth of the UAE.

Limitations and Future Directions

This study mainly focused on investigating the concept of GB technology services to provide necessary knowledge regarding specific scenarios. However, it did not include other types of GB products like green loans, green credit cards or green bonds due to the issue of heterogeneity among the GB products and services, as one study is incapable of covering all the issues simultaneously. Consequently, this study proposes that future studies might investigate other types of GB products that are equally important to attain sustainability. Furthermore, introducing demographic factors as such gender, age, and experience as moderating variables in the same model will offer a richer understanding of customers' behaviour based on their demographic features. Moreover, the data collected for the survey questionnaire of this study used the non-probability convenience sampling technique, which suffers from the inability to generalise the results to the whole population. Upcoming studies can collect data using probability sampling techniques to produce more generalisable conclusions. The findings of this study can be further validated by testing the proposed model in different industrial sectors such as hospitality, healthcare and education and other contexts like the Gulf Cooperation Council (GCC) and Developing-8 (D-8) countries (i.e., Bangladesh, Egypt, Nigeria, Indonesia, Iran, Malaysia, Pakistan, and Turkey) since their development indicators are similar to the UAE's.

REFERENCES

Abbasi, G. A., Tiew, L. Y., Tang, J., Goh, Y. N., & Thurasamy, R. (2021). The adoption of cryptocurrency as a disruptive force: Deep learning-based dual-stage structural equation modelling and artificial neural network analysis. *PLoS One*, *16*(3), 1–26. doi:10.1371/journal.pone.0247582 PMID:33684120

Agarwal, R., & Prasad, J. (1998). A Conceptual and Operational Definition of Personal Innovativeness in the Domain of Information Technology. *Information Systems Research*, *9*(2), 204–215. doi:10.1287/isre.9.2.204

Al-Saedi, K., Al-Emran, M., Ramayah, T., & Abusham, E. (2020). Developing a general extended UTAUT model for M-payment adoption. *Technology in Society*, *62*, 101293. doi:10.1016/j.techsoc.2020.101293

Alabdullah, J. H., Van Lunen, B. L., Claiborne, D. M., Daniel, S. J., Yen, C. J., & Gustin, T. S. (2020). Application of the unified theory of acceptance and use of technology model to predict dental students' behavioral intention to use teledentistry. *Journal of Dental Education*, *84*(11), 1262–1269. doi:10.1002/jdd.12304 PMID:32705688

Alalwan, A. A., Baabdullah, A. M., Rana, N. P., Dwivedi, Y. K., & Kizgin, H. (2019). Examining the Influence of Mobile Store Features on User E-Satisfaction: Extending UTAUT2 with Personalization, Responsiveness, and Perceived Security and Privacy. In *Conference on e-Business, e-Services and e-Society* (pp. 50-61). Springer. 10.1007/978-3-030-29374-1_5

Albashrawi, M. A., Turner, L., & Balasubramanian, S. (2020). Adoption of Mobile ERP in Educational Environment. *International Journal of Enterprise Information Systems*, *16*(4), 184–200. doi:10.4018/IJEIS.2020100109

Anggreni, N., Ariyanto, D., Suprasto, H., & Dwirandra, A. A. N. B. (2020). Successful adoption of the village's financial system. *Accounting*, *6*(6), 1129–1138. doi:10.5267/j.ac.2020.7.005

Arcadis. (2018). *Sustainable Finance in the UAE*. Author.

Baabdullah, A. M. (2020). Factors influencing adoption of mobile social network games (M-SNGs): The role of awareness. *Information Systems Frontiers*, 2(2), 411–427. doi:10.100710796-018-9868-1

Bandura, A. & Walters, R.H. (1977). *Social learning theory*. Prentice-Hall.

Bervell, B., Umar, I. N., & Kamilin, M. H. (2020). Towards a model for online learning satisfaction (MOLS): Re-considering non-linear relationships among personal innovativeness and modes of online interaction. *Open Learning*, 35(3), 236–259. doi:10.1080/02680513.2019.1662776

Bouteraa, M. (2019). Conceptual study: Barriers of Islamic estate planning. *IBMRD's. Journal of Management Research*, 8(1), 28–34. doi:10.17697/ibmrd/2019/v8i1/142673

Bouteraa, M. (2020). Descriptive Approach of Green Banking in the United Arab Emirates (UAE). *IBMRD's. Journal of Management Research*, 9(1), 1–9. doi:10.17697/ibmrd/2020/v9i1/152324

Bouteraa, M., & Al-Aidaros, A. (2020). The Role of Attitude as Mediator in the Intention to Have Islamic Will. *International Journal of Advanced Research in Economics and Finance*, 2(1), 22–37.

Bouteraa, M., Hisham, R. R. I. R., & Zainol, Z. (2020). Green banking practices from Islamic and Western perspectives. *International Journal of Business. Economics and Law*, 21(5), 1–11.

Bouteraa, M., Hisham, R. R. I. R., & Zainol, Z. (2021). Exploring Determinants of Customers' Intention to Adopt Green Banking: Qualitative Investigation. *Journal of Sustainability Science and Management*, 16(3), 187–203. doi:10.46754/jssm.2021.04.014

Bouteraa, M., Raja Hisham, R. R. I., & Zainol, Z. (2020). Islamic Banks Customers' Intention to Adopt Green Banking: Extension of UTAUT Model. *International Journal of Business and Technology Management*, 2(1), 121–136.

Braun, V., & Clarke, V. (2006). Using thematic analysis in psychology. *Qualitative Research in Psychology*, 3(2), 77–101. doi:10.1191/1478088706qp063oa

Bukhari, S. A. A., Hashim, F., & Amran, A. (2019). Determinants of Green Banking Adoption: A Theoretical Framework. *KnE Social Sciences*, 3(22), 1–14. doi:10.18502/kss.v3i22.5041

Bukhari, S. A. A., Hashim, F., & Amran, A. (2020). Green Banking: A road map for adoption. *International Journal of Ethics and Systems*, 36(3), 371–385. doi:10.1108/IJOES-11-2019-0177

Bukhari, S. A. A., Hashim, F., & Amran, A. (2021). Green banking: A conceptual framework. *International Journal of Green Economics*, 15(1), 59–74. doi:10.1504/IJGE.2021.117682

Bukhari, S.A.A., Hashim, F. & Amran, A. (2022). Pathways towards Green Banking adoption: moderating role of top management commitment. *International Journal of Ethics and Systems*. . doi:10.1108/IJOES-05-2021-0110

Bukhari, S. A. A., Hashim, F., Amran, A. B., & Hyder, K. (2020). Green Banking and Islam: Two sides of the same coin. *Journal of Islamic Marketing*, 11(4), 977–1000. Advance online publication. doi:10.1108/JIMA-09-2018-0154

Cao, J., Shang, Y., Mok, Q., & Lai, I. K. W. (2019). The impact of personal innovativeness on the intention to use cloud classroom: an empirical study in China. In *International conference on technology in education* (pp. 179-188). Springer. 10.1007/978-981-13-9895-7_16

Carbon, D. (2018). *State of Green Economy Report 2018.* World Green Economy Summit.

Chatterjee, S. (2020). Factors Impacting Behavioral Intention of Users to Adopt IoT in India. *International Journal of Information Security and Privacy, 14*(4), 92–112. doi:10.4018/IJISP.2020100106

Chaudhary, R. (2019). Green human resource management and job pursuit intention: Examining the underlying processes. *Corporate Social Responsibility and Environmental Management, 26*(4), 929–937. doi:10.1002/csr.1732

Chaurasia, S. S., Verma, S., & Singh, V. (2019). Exploring the intention to use M-payment in India: Role of extrinsic motivation, intrinsic motivation and perceived demonetization regulation. *Transforming Government: People. Process and Policy, 13*(3/4), 276–305. doi:10.1108/TG-09-2018-0060

Cohen, J. (1988). *Statistical power analysis for the behavioral sciences.* Lawrence Erlbaum Associates.

Cohen, J. (1992). A power Primer. *Psychological Bulletin, 112*(1), 155–159. doi:10.1037/0033-2909.112.1.155 PMID:19565683

Creswell, J., & Creswell, J. D. (2018). *Research Design: Qualitative, Quantitative, and Mixed Methods Approaches* (5th ed.). Sage publications, Inc.

Creswell, J. W., & Poth, C. N. (2018). *Qualitative Inquiry & Research Design Choosing Among Five Approaches* (4th ed.). SAGE Publications, Inc.

Deb, S. K., Deb, N., & Roy, S. (2019). Investigation of Factors Influencing the Choice of Smartphone Banking in Bangladesh. *Evergreen, 6*(3), 230–239. doi:10.5109/2349299

DeLone, W. H., & McLean, E. R. (1992). Information systems success: The quest for the dependent variable. *Information Systems Research, 3*(1), 60–95. doi:10.1287/isre.3.1.60

Delone, W. H., & McLean, E. R. (2003). The DeLone and McLean Model of Information Systems Success: A Ten-Year Update. *Journal of Management Information Systems, 19*(4), 9–30. doi:10.1080/07421222.2003.11045748

Do, N., Tham, J., Azam, S., & Khatibia, A. (2020). Analysis of customer behavioral intentions towards mobile payment: Cambodian consumer's perspective. *Accounting, 6*(7), 1391–1402. doi:10.5267/j.ac.2020.8.010

Doh, J. P., Tashman, P., & Benischke, M. H. (2019). Adapting to grand environmental challenges through collective entrepreneurship. *The Academy of Management Perspectives, 33*(4), 450–468. doi:10.5465/amp.2017.0056

El-Masri, M., & Tarhini, A. (2017). Factors affecting the adoption of e-learning systems in Qatar and USA: Extending the Unified Theory of Acceptance and Use of Technology 2 (UTAUT2). *Educational Technology Research and Development, 65*(3), 743–763. doi:10.100711423-016-9508-8

Finger, M., Gavious, I., & Manos, R. (2018). Environmental risk management and financial performance in the banking industry: A cross-country comparison. *Journal of International Financial Markets, Institutions and Money, 52*(C), 240–261. doi:10.1016/j.intfin.2017.09.019

Flavián, C. & Guinalíu, M. (2006). Consumer trust, perceived security and privacy policy. *Industrial Management & Data Systems, 106*(5), 601–620. . doi:10.1108/02635570610666403

Flavian, C., Guinaliu, M., & Lu, Y. (2020). Mobile payments adoption – introducing mindfulness to better understand consumer behavior. *International Journal of Bank Marketing, 38*(7), 1575–1599. doi:10.1108/IJBM-01-2020-0039

Fombrun, C. J. (1996). *Reputation: Realizing Value from the Corporate Image*. Harvard University Press.

Ghalandari, K. (2012). The Effect of Performance Expectancy, Effort Expectancy, Social Influence and Facilitating Conditions on Acceptance of E-Banking Services in Iran: The Moderating Role of Age and Gender. *Middle East Journal of Scientific Research, 12*(6), 801–807. doi:10.5829/idosi.mejsr.2012.12.6.2536

Gorla, N. (2011). An assessment of information systems service quality using SERVQUAL+. *ACM SIGMIS Database: the DATABASE for Advances in Information Systems, 42*(3), 46–70. doi:10.1145/2038056.2038060

Greene, J. C., Caracelli, V. J., & Graham, W. F. (1989). Toward a Conceptual Framework for Mixed-Method Evaluation Designs. *Educational Evaluation and Policy Analysis, 11*(3), 255–274. doi:10.3102/01623737011003255

Guiltinand, J.P. & Donnelly, J.H. (1983). The use of product portfolio analysis in bank marketing planning. *Management Issues for Financial Institutions*, 50.

Gupta, K., & Arora, N. (2019). Investigating consumer intention to accept mobile payment systems through unified theory of acceptance model. *South Asian Journal of Business Studies, 9*(1), 88–114. doi:10.1108/SAJBS-03-2019-0037

Hair, J. F. Jr, Hult, G. T. M., Ringle, C. M., & Sarstedt, M. (2021). *A primer on partial least squares structural equation modeling (PLS-SEM)* (3rd ed.). SAGE Publications, Inc. doi:10.1007/978-3-030-80519-7

Hair, J. F., Ringle, C. M., & Sarstedt, M. (2011). PLS-SEM: Indeed a Silver Bullet. *Journal of Marketing Theory and Practice, 19*(2), 139–152. doi:10.2753/MTP1069-6679190202

Hair, J. F., Risher, J. J., Sarstedt, M., & Ringle, C. M. (2019). When to use and how to report the results of PLS-SEM. *European Business Review, 31*(1), 2–24. doi:10.1108/EBR-11-2018-0203

Hair, J. F. Jr, Sarstedt, M., Ringle, C. M., & Gudergan, S. P. (2018). *Advanced Issues in Partial Least Squares Structural Equation Modeling*. SAGE Publications, Inc.

Hair, J. F., Sarstedt, M., Ringle, C. M., & Mena, J. A. (2012). An assessment of the use of partial least squares structural equation modeling in marketing research. *Journal of the Academy of Marketing Science, 40*(3), 414–433. doi:10.100711747-011-0261-6

Haleem, A., Khan, M. I., & Khan, S. (2019). Halal certification, the inadequacy of its adoption, modelling and strategising the efforts. *Journal of Islamic Marketing*, *11*(2), 384–404. doi:10.1108/JIMA-05-2017-0062

Handarkho, Y. D. (2020). Impact of social experience on customer purchase decision in the social commerce context. *Journal of Systems and Information Technology*, *22*(1), 47–71. doi:10.1108/JSIT-05-2019-0088

Helm, S., Eggert, A., & Garnefeld, I. (2010). Modeling the Impact of Corporate Reputation on Customer Satisfaction and Loyalty Using Partial Least Squares. In *Handbook of Partial Least Squares* (pp. 515–534). Springer Berlin Heidelberg. doi:10.1007/978-3-540-32827-8_23

Henseler, J., Ringle, C. M., & Sarstedt, M. (2015). A new criterion for assessing discriminant validity in variance-based structural equation modelling. *Journal of the Academy of Marketing Science*, *43*(1), 115–135. doi:10.100711747-014-0403-8

Herath, H. M. A. K., & Herath, H. M. S. P. (2019). Impact of Green Banking Initiatives on Customer Satisfaction: A Conceptual Model of Customer Satisfaction on Green Banking Impact of Green Banking Initiatives on Customer Satisfaction: A Conceptual Model of Customer Satisfaction on Green Banking. *IOSR Journal of Business and Management*, *21*(1), 24–35. doi:10.9790/487X-2101032435

Hu, Z., Ding, S., Li, S., Chen, L., & Yang, S. (2019). Adoption Intention of Fintech Services for Bank Users: An Empirical Examination with an Extended Technology Acceptance Model. *Symmetry*, *11*(3), 340. doi:10.3390ym11030340

Ibe-enwo, G., Igbudu, N., Garanti, Z., & Popoola, T. (2019). Assessing the Relevance of Green Banking Practice on Bank Loyalty: The Mediating Effect of Green Image and Bank Trust. *Sustainability*, *11*(17), 4651. doi:10.3390u11174651

Ikhsan, R. B., & Simarmata, J. (2021). SST-Servqual and customer outcomes in service industry: Mediating the rule of corporate reputation. *Management Science Letters*, *11*, 561–576. doi:10.5267/j.msl.2020.9.010

Iqbal, M., Nisha, N., & Raza, S. A. (2019). Customers' Perceptions of Green Banking: Examining Service Quality Dimensions in Bangladesh. In *Green business: Concepts, methodologies, tools, and applications*. IGI Global. doi:10.4018/978-1-5225-7915-1.ch053

Iqbal, M., Nisha, N., Rifat, A., & Panda, P. (2018). Exploring Client Perceptions and Intentions in Emerging Economies: The Case of Green Banking Technology. *International Journal of Asian Business and Information Management*, *9*(3), 14–34. doi:10.4018/IJABIM.2018070102

Iqbal, M., Rifat, A., & Nisha, N. (2021). Evaluating Attractiveness and Perceived Risks. *International Journal of Asian Business and Information Management*, *12*(1), 1–23. doi:10.4018/IJABIM.20210101.oa1

Islam, M.A., Hossain, K.F., Siddiqui, M.H., & Yousuf, S. (2014). Green-Banking Practices in Bangladesh-A Scope to Make Banking Green. *International Finance and Banking*, *1*(1), 1-38. . doi:10.5296/ifb.v1i1.5161

Islam, T., Islam, R., Pitafi, A. H., Xiaobei, L., Rehmani, M., Irfan, M., & Mubarak, M. S. (2021). The impact of corporate social responsibility on customer loyalty: The mediating role of corporate reputation, customer satisfaction, and trust. *Sustainable Production and Consumption*, *25*, 123–135. doi:10.1016/j.spc.2020.07.019

Izuagbe, R., Ifijeh, G., Izuagbe-Roland, E. I., Olawoyin, O. R., & Ogiamien, L. O. (2019). Determinants of perceived usefulness of social media in university libraries: Subjective norm, image and voluntariness as indicators. *Journal of Academic Librarianship*, *45*(4), 394–405. doi:10.1016/j.acalib.2019.03.006

Jahanshahi, D., Tabibi, Z., & van Wee, B. (2020). Factors influencing the acceptance and use of a bicycle sharing system: Applying an extended Unified Theory of Acceptance and Use of Technology (UTAUT). *Case Studies on Transport Policy*, *8*(4), 1212–1223. doi:10.1016/j.cstp.2020.08.002

Javeria, A., Siddiqui, S. H., Rasheed, R., & Nawaz, M. S. (2019). An Investigation into Role of Leadership Commitment on Implementation of Green Banking: Moderating Influence of Responsible Leadership Characteristics. *Review of Economics and Development Studies*, *5*(2), 245–252. doi:10.26710/reads.v5i2.561

Jeyaraj, A., Rottman, J. W., & Lacity, M. C. (2006). A Review of the Predictors, Linkages, and Biases in IT Innovation Adoption Research. *Journal of Information Technology*, *21*(1), 1–23. doi:10.1057/palgrave.jit.2000056

Juaidi, A., Montoya, F. G., Gázquez, J. A., & Manzano-Agugliaro, F. (2016). An overview of energy balance compared to sustainable energy in United Arab Emirates. *Renewable & Sustainable Energy Reviews*, *55*, 1195–1209. doi:10.1016/j.rser.2015.07.024

Julia, T., & Kassim, S. (2019). Exploring green banking performance of Islamic banks vs conventional banks in Bangladesh based on Maqasid Shariah framework. *Journal of Islamic Marketing*, *11*(3), 729–744. doi:10.1108/JIMA-10-2017-0105

Julia, T., & Kassim, S. (2020). Green Banking. In *Banking and Finance*. IntechOpen. doi:10.5772/intechopen.93294

Karjaluoto, H., Shaikh, A. A., Leppäniemi, M., & Luomala, R. (2019). Examining consumers' usage intention of contactless payment systems. *International Journal of Bank Marketing*, *38*(2), 332–351. doi:10.1108/IJBM-04-2019-0155

Kelman, H.C. (1974). Further Thoughts on the processes of compliance, identification, and internalization. *Perspectives on Social Power*, 125-171.

Khan, A., Masrek, M. N., & Mahmood, K. (2019). The relationship of personal innovativeness, quality of digital resources and generic usability with users' satisfaction. *Digital Library Perspectives*, *35*(1), 15–30. doi:10.1108/DLP-12-2017-0046

Kline, R. (2016). *Mean structures and latent growth models. Principles and Practice of Structural Equation Modeling* (4th ed.). The Guildford Press.

KPMG. (2020). *UAE Banking Perspectives 2020: Adapting for new technologies, regulations and culture*. KPMG.

Lee, M. S. (2019). Effects of personal innovativeness on mobile device adoption by older adults in South Korea: The moderation effect of mobile device use experience. *International Journal of Mobile Communications, 17*(6), 682. doi:10.1504/IJMC.2019.102719

Lujja, S., Mohammed, M. O., & Hassan, R. (2018). Islamic banking: An exploratory study of public perception in Uganda. *Journal of Islamic Accounting and Business Research, 9*(3), 336–352. doi:10.1108/JIABR-01-2015-0001

Malik, G., & Singh, D. (2022). Personality matters: Does an individual's personality affect adoption and continued use of green banking channels? *International Journal of Bank Marketing, 40*(4), 746–772. doi:10.1108/IJBM-04-2021-0133

Marakarkandy, B., Yajnik, N., & Dasgupta, C. (2017). Enabling internet banking adoption. *Journal of Enterprise Information Management, 30*(2), 263–294. doi:10.1108/JEIM-10-2015-0094

Maryam, S. Z., Mehmood, M. S., & Khaliq, C. A. (2019). Factors influencing the community behavioral intention for adoption of Islamic banking. *International Journal of Islamic and Middle Eastern Finance and Management, 12*(4), 586–600. doi:10.1108/IMEFM-07-2017-0179

Masukujjaman, M., & Aktar, S. (2014). Green Banking in Bangladesh: A Commitment towards the Global Initiatives. *Journal of Business and Technology (Dhaka), 8*(1–2), 17–40. doi:10.3329/jbt.v8i1-2.18284

Mehedi, S., & Kuddus, M. A. (2017). Green Banking: A Case Study on Dutch-bangla Bank Ltd. *Academy of Accounting and Financial Studies Journal, 21*(2), 1–20.

Mensah, I. K. (2020). Impact of Performance Expectancy, Effort Expectancy, and Citizen Trust on the Adoption of Electronic Voting System in Ghana. *International Journal of Electronic Government Research, 16*(2), 19–32. doi:10.4018/IJEGR.2020040102

Merhi, M., Hone, K., & Tarhini, A. (2019). A cross-cultural study of the intention to use mobile banking between Lebanese and British consumers: Extending UTAUT2 with security, privacy and trust. *Technology in Society, 59*, 101151. doi:10.1016/j.techsoc.2019.101151

Mijoska, B. M., Trpkova-Nestorovska, M., & Trenevska, B. K. (2020). Predicting Consumer Intention to Use Mobile Banking Services in North Macedonia. *International Journal of Multidisciplinary in Business and Science, 6*(10), 5–12.

Mugny, G., Butera, F., Sanchez-Mazas, M. & Pérez, J.A. (1995). Judgements in conflict: The conflict elaboration theory of social influence. *Perception-Evaluation-Interpretation*, 160-168.

Naveenan, R. V., Madeswaran, A., & Arun, K. R. (2021). Green Banking Practices In India-The Customer's Perspective. *Academy of Entrepreneurship Journal, 27*(4), 1–19.

Ngoc Duy, P. (2018). Repurchase Intention: The Effect of Service Quality, System Quality, Information Quality, and Customer Satisfaction as Mediating Role: A PLS Approach of M-Commerce Ride Hailing Service in Vietnam. *Marketing and Branding Research, 5*(2), 78–91. doi:10.33844/mbr.2018.60463

Nguyen, N., & Leblanc, G. (2001). Corporate image and corporate reputation in customers' retention decisions in services. *Journal of Retailing and Consumer Services, 8*(4), 227–236. doi:10.1016/S0969-6989(00)00029-1

Nisha, N., Iqbal, M., & Rifat, A. (2020). Green Banking Adoption. *International Journal of Technology and Human Interaction, 16*(2), 69–89. doi:10.4018/IJTHI.2020040106

Olaleye, S. A., Ukpabi, D., Karjaluoto, H., & Rizomyliotis, I. (2019). Understanding technology diffusion in emerging markets: The case of Chinese mobile devices in Nigeria. *International Journal of Emerging Markets, 14*(5), 731–751. doi:10.1108/IJOEM-01-2018-0055

Ozili, P. K., & Opene, F. (2021). (Preprint). The role of banks in the circular economy," SSRN. *The Electricity Journal.* Advance online publication. doi:10.2139srn.3778196

Pai, R. R., & Alathur, S. (2019). Determinants of individuals' intention to use mobile health: insights from India. *Transforming Government: People, Process and Policy, 13*(3/4), 306–326. doi:10.1108/TG-04-2019-0027

Picoto, W. N., & Pinto, I. (2021). Cultural impact on mobile banking use – A multi-method approach. *Journal of Business Research, 124*, 620–628. doi:10.1016/j.jbusres.2020.10.024

Pikkarainen, T., Pikkarainen, K., Karjaluoto, H., & Pahnila, S. (2004). Consumer acceptance of online banking: An extension of the technology acceptance model. *Internet Research, 14*(3), 224–235. doi:10.1108/10662240410542652

Podsakoff, P. M., MacKenzie, S. B., Lee, J.-Y., & Podsakoff, N. P. (2003). Common method biases in behavioral research: A critical review of the literature and recommended remedies. *The Journal of Applied Psychology, 88*(5), 879–903. doi:10.1037/0021-9010.88.5.879 PMID:14516251

Purwanto, E., & Loisa, J. (2020). The Intention and Use Behaviour of the Mobile Banking System in Indonesia: UTAUT Model. *Technology Reports of Kansai University, 62*(6), 2757–2767.

Ratanya, F. C. (2017). Institutional repository: Access and use by academic staff at Egerton University, Kenya. *Library Management, 38*(4/5), 276–284. doi:10.1108/LM-02-2017-0018

Raza, S. A., Shah, N., & Ali, M. (2019). Acceptance of mobile banking in Islamic banks: Evidence from modified UTAUT model. *Journal of Islamic Marketing, 10*(1), 357–376. doi:10.1108/JIMA-04-2017-0038

Rehman, A., Ullah, I., Afridi, F. E. A., Ullah, Z., Zeeshan, M., Hussain, A., & Rahman, H. U. (2021). Adoption of green banking practices and environmental performance in Pakistan: A demonstration of structural equation modelling. *Environment, Development and Sustainability, 23*(9), 13200–13220. doi:10.100710668-020-01206-x

Rifat, A., Nisha, N., Iqbal, M., & Suviitawat, A. (2016). The role of commercial banks in green banking adoption: A Bangladesh perspective. *International Journal of Green Economics, 10*(3/4), 226. doi:10.1504/IJGE.2016.081906

Rogers, M. (1983). *Diffusion of Innovation* (3rd ed.). The Free Press.

Rogers, M. (1995). *Diffusion of Innovations* (4th ed.). The Free Press.

Sahoo, B., Singh, A. & Jain, N. (2016). Green Banking In India: Problems And Prospects. *International Journal of Research -Granthaalayah, 4*(8), 92–99. doi:10.5281/zenodo.61169

Sánchez-Torres, J. A., Sandoval, A. V., & Alzate, J.-A. S. (2018). E-banking in Colombia: Factors favouring its acceptance, online trust and government support. *International Journal of Bank Marketing*, *36*(1), 170–183. doi:10.1108/IJBM-10-2016-0145

Sekaran, U., & Bougie, R. J. (2019). *Research methods for business: A skill building approach* (8th ed.). Wiley and Sons.

Sensuse, D. I., Rochman, H. N., Al Hakim, S., & Winarni, W. (2021). Knowledge management system design method with joint application design (JAD) adoption. *VINE Journal of Information and Knowledge Management Systems*, *51*(1), 27–46. doi:10.1108/VJIKMS-10-2018-0083

Shachak, A., Kuziemsky, C., & Petersen, C. (2019). Beyond TAM and UTAUT: Future directions for HIT implementation research. *Journal of Biomedical Informatics*, *100*, 103315. doi:10.1016/j.jbi.2019.103315 PMID:31629923

Shaumya, S., & Arulrajah, A. (2017). The Impact of Green Banking Practices on Banks Environmental Performance: Evidence from Sri Lanka. *Journal of Finance and Bank Management*, *5*(1), 77–90. doi:10.15640/jfbm.v5n1a7

Shmueli, G., Ray, S., Estrada, J. M. V., & Chatla, S. B. (2016). The elephant in the room: Predictive performance of PLS models. *Journal of Business Research*, *69*(10), 4552–4564. doi:10.1016/j.jbusres.2016.03.049

Shmueli, G., Sarstedt, M., Hair, J. F., Cheah, J. H., Ting, H., Vaithilingam, S., & Ringle, C. M. (2019). Predictive model assessment in PLS-SEM: Guidelines for using PLSpredict. *European Journal of Marketing*, *53*(11), 2322–2347. doi:10.1108/EJM-02-2019-0189

Singh, N., & Sinha, N. (2020). How perceived trust mediates merchant's intention to use a mobile wallet technology. *Journal of Retailing and Consumer Services*, *52*, 101894. doi:10.1016/j.jretconser.2019.101894

Souiden, N., Ladhari, R., & Chaouali, W. (2020). Mobile banking adoption: A systematic review. *International Journal of Bank Marketing*, *39*(2), 214–241. doi:10.1108/IJBM-04-2020-0182

Sridhar, M., & Mehta, A. (2018). The Moderating and Mediating Role of Corporate Reputation in the Link Between Service Innovation and Cross-Buying Intention. *Corporate Reputation Review*, *21*(2), 50–70. doi:10.105741299-018-0044-9

Stiftung, B. (2019). *BTI 2018 | United Arab Emirates Country Report, Sustainability*. Available at: https://www.bti-project.org/en/reports/country-reports/detail/itc/ARE/

Stockholm Environment Institute. (2013). *Annual Report 2013*. Stockholm Environment Institute. Available online: https://www.sei.org/wp-content/uploads/2017/12/sei-us-annualreport-2013.pdf

Stravinskienė, J., Matulevičienė, M., & Hopenienė, R. (2021). Impact of Corporate Reputation Dimensions on Consumer Trust. *The Engineering Economist*, *32*(2), 177–192. doi:10.5755/j01.ee.32.2.27548

Tabachnick, B. G., & Fidell, L. S. (2013). *Using multivariate statistics* (6th ed.). Pearson/Allyn & Bacon.

Tarhini, A., Alalwan, A. A., Shammout, A. B., & Al-Badi, A. (2019). An analysis of the factors affecting mobile commerce adoption in developing countries. *Review of International Business and Strategy*, *29*(3), 157–179. doi:10.1108/RIBS-10-2018-0092

Tarhini, A., El-Masri, M., Ali, M., & Serrano, A. (2016). Extending the UTAUT model to understand the customers' acceptance and use of internet banking in Lebanon. *Information Technology & People*, *29*(4), 830–849. doi:10.1108/ITP-02-2014-0034

Thakur, R., Angriawan, A., & Summey, J. H. (2016). Technological opinion leadership: The role of personal innovativeness, gadget love, and technological innovativeness. *Journal of Business Research*, *69*(8), 2764–2773. doi:10.1016/j.jbusres.2015.11.012

The Heritage Foundation. (2020). *United Arab Emirates, economic freedom index 2020.* Available at: https://www.heritage.org/index/country/unitedarabemirates

The World-Wide Fund for Nature. (2010). *UAE has the world's largest environmental footprint, The nation.* Available at: https://www.thenational.ae/uae/environment/uae-has-world-s-largest-environmental-footprint-1.525694

UAE Ministry of Climate Change and Environment (MOCCAE). (2017). *UAE State of Green Economy report 2017.* Author.

UAE Ministry of Environment and Water (MoEW). (2017a). *State of Green Finance in the UAE The first national survey on contributions of financial institutions to Green Economy.* Author.

UAE Ministry of Environment and Water (MoEW). (2017b). *United Arab Emirates State of Green Economy Report.* Author.

United Nations Framework Convention on Climate Change (UNFCCC). (2021). *The Paris Agreement, What is the Paris Agreement?* Available at: https://unfccc.int/process-and-meetings/the-paris-agreement/the-paris-agreement

Venkatesh, V., Brown, S., & Sullivan, Y. (2016). Guidelines for Conducting Mixed-methods Research: An Extension and Illustration. *Journal of the Association for Information Systems*, *17*(7), 435–494. doi:10.17705/1jais.00433

Venkatesh, V., Brown, S. A., & Bala, H. (2013). Bridging the Qualitative-Quantitative Divide: Guidelines for Conducting Mixed Methods Research in Information Systems. *Management Information Systems Quarterly*, *37*(1), 21–54. doi:10.25300/MISQ/2013/37.1.02

Venkatesh, V., Brown, S. A., Maruping, L. M., & Bala, H. (2008). Predicting Different Conceptualizations of System Use: The Competing Roles of Behavioral Intention, Facilitating Conditions, and Behavioral Expectation. *Management Information Systems Quarterly*, *32*(3), 483–502. doi:10.2307/25148853

Venkatesh, V., & Davis, F. D. (2000). A Theoretical Extension of the Technology Acceptance Model: Four Longitudinal Field Studies. *Management Science*, *46*(2), 186–204. doi:10.1287/mnsc.46.2.186.11926

Venkatesh, V., Morris, M. G., Davis, G. B., & Davis, F. D. (2003). User Acceptance of Information Technology: Toward a Unified View. *Management Information Systems Quarterly*, *27*(3), 425–478. doi:10.2307/30036540

Venkatesh, V., Thong, J. Y. L., & Xu, X. (2012). Consumer Acceptance and Use of Information Technology: Extending the Unified Theory of Acceptance and Use of Technology. *MIS Quarter, 36*(1), 157–178. doi:10.2307/41410412

Venkatesh, V., & Zhang, X. (2010). Unified Theory of Acceptance and Use of Technology: U.S. Vs. China. *Journal of Global Information Technology Management, 13*(1), 5–27. doi:10.1080/1097198X.2010.10856507

Wang, H., Tao, D., Yu, N., & Qu, X. (2020). Understanding consumer acceptance of healthcare wearable devices: An integrated model of UTAUT and TTF. *International Journal of Medical Informatics, 139*, 104156. doi:10.1016/j.ijmedinf.2020.104156 PMID:32387819

Wiafe, I., Koranteng, F. N., Tettey, T., Kastriku, F. A., & Abdulai, J. D. (2019). Factors that affect acceptance and use of information systems within the Maritime industry in developing countries. *Journal of Systems and Information Technology, 22*(1), 21–45. doi:10.1108/JSIT-06-2018-0091

World Bank Group. (2018). *CO2 emissions (kt), World Bank group*. Available at: https://data.worldbank.org/indicator/EN.ATM.CO2E.KT?locations=AE

Worldatlas. (2019). *Countries with The Largest Ecological Footprints, world Atlas*. Available at: https://www.worldatlas.com/articles/countries-with-the-largest-ecological-footprints.html

Yin, R. K. (2017). *Case study research and applications: Design and methods* (6th ed.). SAGE Publications, Inc.

Yoon, J., Vonortas, N. S., & Han, S. (2020). Do-It-Yourself laboratories and attitude toward use: The effects of self-efficacy and the perception of security and privacy. *Technological Forecasting and Social Change, 159*, 120192. doi:10.1016/j.techfore.2020.120192

Zhang, D., Zhang, Z., & Managi, S. (2019). A bibliometric analysis on green finance: Current status, development, and future directions. *Finance Research Letters, 29*, 425–430. doi:10.1016/j.frl.2019.02.003

Zhang, Z., Cao, T., Shu, J., & Liu, H. (2020). Identifying key factors affecting college students' adoption of the e-learning system in mandatory blended learning environments. *Interactive Learning Environments*, 1–14. doi:10.1080/10494820.2020.1723113

ADDITIONAL READING

Ahn, T., Ryu, S., & Han, I. (2007). The impact of Web quality and playfulness on user acceptance of online retailing. *Information & Management, 44*(3), 263–275. doi:10.1016/j.im.2006.12.008

Ajzen, I. (1991). The theory of planned behavior. *Organizational Behavior and Human Decision Processes, 50*(2), 179–211. doi:10.1016/0749-5978(91)90020-T

Amin, H., Rahim Abdul Rahman, A., Laison Sondoh, S. Jr, & Magdalene Chooi Hwa, A. (2011). Determinants of customers' intention to use Islamic personal financing. *Journal of Islamic Accounting and Business Research, 2*(1), 22–42. doi:10.1108/17590811111129490

Chan, E. S., Okumus, F., & Chan, W. (2020). What hinders hotels' adoption of environmental technologies: A quantitative study. *International Journal of Hospitality Management*, *84*, 102324. doi:10.1016/j.ijhm.2019.102324

Chawla, D., & Joshi, H. (2019). Scale Development and Validation for Measuring the Adoption of Mobile Banking Services. *Global Business Review*, *20*(2), 434–457. doi:10.1177/0972150918825205

Kim, D. J., Ferrin, D. L., & Rao, H. R. (2008). A trust-based consumer decision-making model in electronic commerce: The role of trust, perceived risk, and their antecedents. *Decision Support Systems*, *44*(2), 544–564. doi:10.1016/j.dss.2007.07.001

Lee, M.-C. (2009). Factors influencing the adoption of internet banking: An integration of TAM and TPB with perceived risk and perceived benefit. *Electronic Commerce Research and Applications*, *8*(3), 130–141. doi:10.1016/j.elerap.2008.11.006

Pariag-Maraye, N., Munusami, N., & Ansaram, K. (2017). A Customer's Perspective of Green Banking: A Case Study of Commercial Banks in Mauritius. *Theoretical Economics Letters*, *7*(7), 1975–1985. doi:10.4236/tel.2017.77134

Saleh, M. A., Quazi, A., Keating, B., & Gaur, S. S. (2017). Quality and image of banking services: A comparative study of conventional and Islamic banks. *International Journal of Bank Marketing*, *35*(6), 878–902. doi:10.1108/IJBM-08-2016-0111

Tan, M., & Teo, T. (2000). Factors Influencing the Adoption of Internet Banking. *Journal of the Association for Information Systems*, *1*(1), 1–44. doi:10.17705/1jais.00005

Zheng, G. W., Siddik, A. B., Masukujjaman, M., Fatema, N., & Alam, S. S. (2021). Green Finance Development in Bangladesh: The Role of Private Commercial Banks (PCBs). *Sustainability*, *13*(2), 795. doi:10.3390u13020795

KEY TERMS AND DEFINITIONS

Bank Reputation: The term "bank reputation" is used for the current study since the case study is in the banking sector. Previous literature had interchangeably used the concepts of corporate reputation (Özkan et al., 2019), company reputation (Ikhsan & Simarmata, 2021) or bank reputation (Osakwe et al., 2020) based on the industry under investigation. Although the vocabularies differ in conceptualising the term of corporate reputation, one can observe the consensus on the essence of the concept as it is a result of the firm's past actions. From a well-adjusted perspective, this study trails the comprehensive focus of Tang (2007), who views reputation as the value judgments among the public about an organisation's qualities. Accordingly, bank reputation is operationalised in the current study as the value judgment among the customers about the bank's qualities.

Customer Awareness: Awareness can be defined as the volume of information that customers receive regarding the product's advantages and disadvantages (Hanafizadeh & Khedmatgozar, 2012), or the degree of users' consciousness of using technology (Selevičienė & Burkšaitienė, 2015). Meanwhile, Ratanya (2017) linked the level of awareness to the existence of technology services. However, the current study's definition scope is broader to cover a more comprehensive concept of awareness. Thus, awareness is operationalised as the amount of information about GB technology services and the bank customers' levels of consciousness of its existence, concept, purpose, and benefits.

Effort Expectancy: Effort expectancy is the level of convenience and usability that people feel when using a specific information system (Venkatesh et al., 2003). The current study operationalises effort expectancy as the convenience and usability that bank customers perceive when using GB technology services.

Facilitating Conditions: According to Venkatesh et al. (2003), facilitating conditions refer to the availability of the required technical resources for the customer to support the implementation of a specific technology. In the current study, facilitating conditions denote the availability of the essential resources for the bank customer to support the adoption of GB technology services.

GB Technology Services: GB technology refers to encouraging environment-friendly practices and reducing carbon footprints from banking operations through the promotion of financial services related to information technology like online banking, mobile banking, e-fund transfer, e-currency, e-payment, e-statement, and other paperless based financial transactions provided by the banks.

Government Support: Government support refers to the role of the government in promoting and encouraging the implementation and usage of technology (Tornatzky & Fleischer, 1990). The central meaning of this concept is that the government is an important external factor that is able to create a favourable environment and provide incentives for technology implementation. Thus, when adopting financing technology services like GB services, consumers expect to receive support from the government concerning policies, incentives, and subsidies to accelerate the rate of acceptance. Accordingly, government support in the context of this study can be operationalised as the role of the government-related policies that cover a different set of rules and promotion incentives to adopt GB technology services.

Intention to Adopt GB Technology Services: Behavioural intention is the dependent variable for the UTAUT model and this study. Behavioural intention is a person's degree of willingness to use innovative high-tech (Venkatesh et al., 2003). In the context of the current study, the intention is a person's degree of willingness to adopt GB technology services.

Performance Expectancy: Performance expectancy is the extent to which an individual believes that using a particular system would be more beneficial to him/her and would improve the performance of the task (Venkatesh et al., 2003). In this context, performance expectancy can be operationalised as the extent to which bank customers perceive that using GB technology services would improve their performance of banking transactions.

Personal Innovativeness: Personal Innovativeness refers to the individual's propensity and willingness to explore and examine new technologies and innovations (Agarwal & Prasad, 1998). This definition measures the innovativeness of an individual on a scale from high to low, thus helping to identify individuals who are likely to adopt IT innovations earlier or later than others. Following Agarwal and Prasad (1998), this study operationalises personal innovativeness as the bank customers' tendency and willingness to try out new GB technology services.

Security and Privacy: The security and privacy construct mainly describes the perceived credibility (Wang et al., 2003), which is defined as the degree of belief and trust in internet-based products and services to transmit sensitive information (Salisbury et al., 2001). In the setting of GB technology, perceived security and privacy is the degree to which a bank customer believes that the GB technology services will be free of security and privacy threats.

Social Influence: Social influence refers to the degree to which the views of the other relevant parties influence the person's actions regarding the usage of innovative technologies (Venkatesh et al., 2003).

In the GB technology context, social influence refers to the extent to which the view of peers, families and relevant parties influence the behavioural intention of the bank customer regarding the adoption of GB technology services.

System Quality: System quality is the degree to which the system is easy to use and complies with functionality, reliability, flexibility, data quality, and integration requirements to accomplish certain tasks (Delone & McLean, 2003). Therefore, the measure of system quality in this study focuses on the features and performance characteristics of GB technology. In keeping with Delone and McLean (2003), system quality in this current study's setting refers to the degree to which the comprehensive design of the system, response time, system reliability, system availability, functionality, and flexibility influence the perception of the bank customer regarding the adoption of GB technology services.

Chapter 5
Digital Transformation Journey of GCC Countries and the Way Forward

Sulayman Al-Qudsi
Kuwaiti Institute for Scientific Research, Kuwait

Husam Arman
Kuwait Institute for Scientific Research, Kuwait

Shaikha Al-Fulaij
Kuwaiti Institute for Scientific Research, Kuwait

ABSTRACT

Gulf Cooperation Council (GCC) countries, including Kuwait, have been trying to surf the tides of digital transformation to improve their competitiveness and leapfrog into innovation-led economies. The recent turbulence caused by COVID-19 and oil price collapse has accelerated the need for long-term and sustainable strategies. This chapter reviews the desired transformational paths for GCC countries with a special focus on Kuwait. The chapter utilizes original data resulting from empirical work that the authors have recently completed. It will also review existing policies, availability of tech-savvy human resources, and incentive structures that drive firms and institutions to accelerate digitization. Moreover, a comprehensive analysis of the compendium of global indices related to competitiveness, digitization, and innovation will be utilized to trace the journey of GCC countries and the way forward to address urgent global challenges such as the transition towards a digital economy.

DOI: 10.4018/978-1-6684-4610-2.ch005

INTRODUCTION

The emergence of the Internet, the information and communication technologies (ICTs), and recently the Internet of things, Artificial Intelligence (AI), and smart devices have revolutionized the digital economy and increased its rapid growth (Marcus et al., 2015). Bukht and Heeks (2017) reviewed many definitions before arriving at a concise and solid digital economy based solely on the economic output derived from digital technologies with a business model based on digital goods or services. Another perspective of the digital economy is its transformational effect. It can sometimes be disruptive and cause radical changes, where digital technologies create disruptions to improve an entity and create new value (Vial, 2019).

Both definitions emphasize the economic aspect of the transformation, which is key to diversification. However, in a recent comprehensive review digital transformation phenomenon, Dąbrowska et al. (2022) proposed a multi-perspective to include individuals, organizations, ecosystems and geopolitical frameworks. Hence, they extended the definition to "a socioeconomic change across individuals, organizations, ecosystems, and societies that are shaped by the adoption and utilization of digital technologies." On the downside too, digital technologies increase the extent of global polarization in incomes, and knowledge-derived wealth, and thereby worsen income and asset distributions given that one-third of humanity are virtually off-line (WEF, 2022).

Although developed countries have led the digitization so far (Afonasova et al., 2018), especially in the private sector, there is considerable potential for emerging and developing countries to participate and utilize digitization to boost their economic growth and access the global markets (Dahlman et al., 2016). This stems from the fact that four characteristics describe the exponential technological growth that underpins digitization: It is volatile and uncertain because business disruptive innovations produce high volatility and uncertainty and is associated with complexities of adoption, together with a measurable amount of ambiguity, or VOCA for short. However, countries with blessed resources and assets like Kuwait can accelerate the digital transformational journey by investing in hard and soft digital infrastructure. These include physical infrastructure and system, and most importantly, people with the right skills to make it happen.

Resource-rich countries aspire to diversify their economies by implementing swift digitization strategies and creating sustainable economic growth. COVID-19 has accelerated the growth of digital-based sectors. For instance, the IT industry has expanded due to increased demand for online digital platforms (Belitski et al., 2021). Moreover, the IT industry has aided other industries by improving their performance in sales and delivery, education, and online business meetings (Soni, 2020). In the pandemic, firms were forced to swiftly make drastic measures such as changing customer demands to digital channels, reconfigured supply chains, additional necessary workforce collaboration capacity and bandwidth, licenses and equipment to support remote work, and other issues requiring immediate scale and resiliency (Lillie et al., 2020). According to McKinsey, such digital transformation usually takes five years, but it was completed in around eight weeks due to the pandemic pressure (Baig et al., 2020).

This chapter aims to describe the progress of the Gulf Cooperation Council (GCC) countries, with great emphasis on Kuwait's drive to foster digitization and capture their potential dividends in terms of innovative export commodity paths and diversified sustainable economic growth trajectories.

To address the aforementioned objective, a straightforward methodology was utilized to constituting two main phases. The first phase included a comparative analysis using secondary data to review GCC progress in digitization and its enabling factors. It has used relevant international indices produced by respected organizations such Word Economic Forum (WEF), World Bank, and IMD World Competitiveness Center. The second phase was the empirical part, which was a field survey conducted in Kuwait targeting 262 firms. Most of these firms (84%) owned by the private sector, 10% by the government sector, and 6% by joint ownership (public-private). In terms of size, nearly 30% of the firms are medium-sized that employ 50-249 workers, large firms employing more than 250 workers represent 37% of the total sample, while small firms constitute 33%. All the major economic sectors are represented in the sample, where 29% of the firms are in the non-finance sector, another 21% are in the manufacturing sector; similarly, 21% are in the finance sector, 20% are in the trade sector, and the remaining 10% are in the construction sector.

The survey collected information on the assessments of business leaders regarding the impact of the 2020 coronavirus recession on the Kuwaiti economy measured in impact on sales, production, liquidity, and employment. Moreover, the role of innovative technology on their company operations and on demand for labor and training needs was also investigated. Finally, questions regarding to the challenges to transforming Kuwait onto the digitized and knowledge-based economy and the roles of the envisioned government in ensuring Kuwait remains firmly gripped on the tracks of sustainable economic growth.

The GCC Economies: Riding the Digitization Transformation Horse to Diverse Into Sustainable Economic Growth Trajectories

The global digital transformation is rendering human capital the most critical and valuable factor of production well ahead of natural, physical, and financial capital. The GCC countries, Bahrain, Kuwait, Oman, Qatar, KSA, and the UAE, with fabulous sets of financial and natural capital, taking advantage of digitization in order to transform their human capital into internationally competitive levels capable of dynamically producing new innovative export products which can transform their economies into diversified paths and ride on sustainable growth trajectories in the post oil era. A recent report highlighted the progress of the GCC economies in catching up with high achievers of the digital transformation stating that the digital age is the age of exponential change instigated by technology firms which tempt individuals and households to acquire in order to discharge their personal, social and job-related chores and tasks more efficiently and expeditiously (Al-Qudsi and Hussain, 2022). For many decades past, Kuwait was considered an overwhelmingly single-based oil resource economy, generating more than 90% of government and export revenues from crude oil and exports. Sharp shocks and economic volatilities and uncertainties frequently shook-up fiscal policy and the budget expenditure processes and the business cycles were profoundly affected by oil market volatilities and dynamics. While digitization is considered as a form of diversification in the post-oil era, the Kuwaiti oil industry itself has been pioneer in applying digital technology in its operations. For instance, seeking to achieve higher efficiency and productivity, Kuwait National Petroleum Company (KNPC) is using digital operator rounds (DOR) which aims to digitalize the operational activities of field operators across KNPC's refineries by relying on a completely digital infrastructure for data collection as part of its digitization strategy. The solution uses handheld devices that the operators utilize to collect structured refinery data, which is synced to dedicated servers for data collection, verification and analysis (Al-Duaij, 2019; KFAS, 2021).

In the current age of exponential change, the rate of adoption of technology by individuals and households is also fast but tends to be slower than that of the exponential growth rate of technology itself. Thirdly, the curve of technology-adoption by business firms tends to be slower than that of technology and individuals\households' adoption of tech products. Finally, the public sector catches up and provides the regulatory framework that govern the new digitized sectors and functions. The benefits of digital transformation go beyond efficiency enhancement. In fact, it can pave the way for countries to embark in the knowledge economy era since digitization and automation have created masses of data that can be utilized to create knowledge that can be applied and converted to all sorts of innovation. Digital firms in the GCC have been impressively active in their businesses to customer, B2C, operations but only recently started to pay more attention to devising digital solutions to cater to emerging business needs, B2B solutions. Kuwait is quite indicative in this domain where initially, 5G services in Kuwait were mainly targeted at residential users and mobile broadband consumers, with the propositions centred around applications such as video streaming. In 2020, the operators have started to develop more business-focused services: for instance, by offering 5G solutions such as dedicated data access and dedicated internet access, as well as on-demand services B2B areas such as CCTV and cloud PBX.

Such transformation was not just for developed countries. Most countries, especially those blessed with financial resources like GCC countries quickly moved to digital platforms. Many businesses digitized part of their operations and will most likely continue their digital transformation and automation journey. In a local survey, 28% of Kuwaiti firms reported that they are pivoting more towards digital facilities during the pandemic, while 11% have already invested in digitization (Bensirri, 2020). In Section 4, we report part of the results from our field survey regarding how much firms will rely on automation in the future.

Governments are also striving to improve their operation and services at the national level through digitization. In the GCC region, three countries have made radical changes quickly. Their global rank is evident in the World Digital Competitiveness Ranking which is produced annually by the IMD World Competitiveness Center since 2017 (Figure 1). United Arab Emirates (UAE) is leading the region and the GCC countries. This can be attributed to the aggressive eGovernment strategies adopted by the government to improve the business environment and public services that would attract foreign investment (Al-Khouri, 2012).

Figure 1. The IMD World Digital Competitiveness Ranking of selected GCC countries (source: IMD, 2021)

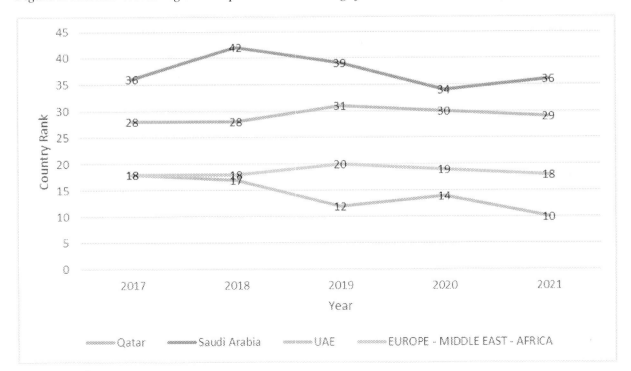

This index measures the capacity and readiness of 64 countries to adopt and explore digital technologies as a key driver for economic transformation in business, government and broader society using a mixture of hard data and surveys. Unfortunately, Kuwait, Bahrain and Oman are not listed in this global index. To compare Kuwait with other GCC countries on a common measure with relent data, we used the ICT adoption sub-index which is part of the Global Competitiveness Index (GCI) that is produced annually by the Word Economic Forum (WEF). In this measure, UAE is leading the region and globally, and Qatar seems to be a fast follower (Figure 2). The rest of the GCC countries, including Kuwait, are in a different consortium, although Saudi Arabia is making visible and consistent progress.

If compared to the Middle East and North Africa (MENA) region, the GCC countries is taking the lead in e-government according to the E-Government Survey 2020 of the United Nations (United Nations, 2020). UAE ranked first (21st globally), followed by Bahrain (38), Saudi Arabia (43), Kuwait (46), Oman (50) and Qatar (66).

Figure 2. ICT adoption according to The Global Competitiveness Index (source WEF (2019, 2018, 2017)

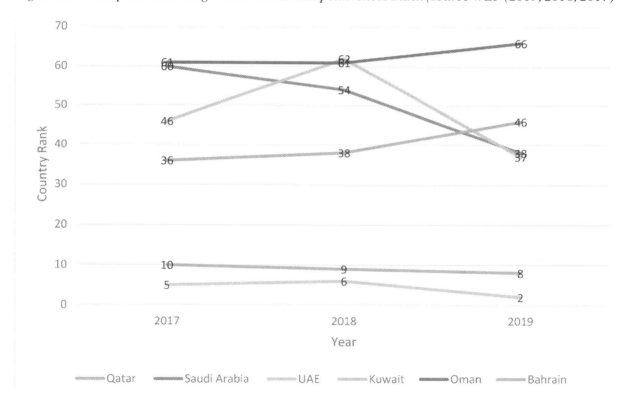

Figure 3 displays the e-government ranking for a set of advanced, emerging, and GCC economies according to three basic components of the index (human capital, telecommunication infrastructure, and online service).

Figure 3. E-Government Index Components: GCC and Comparators

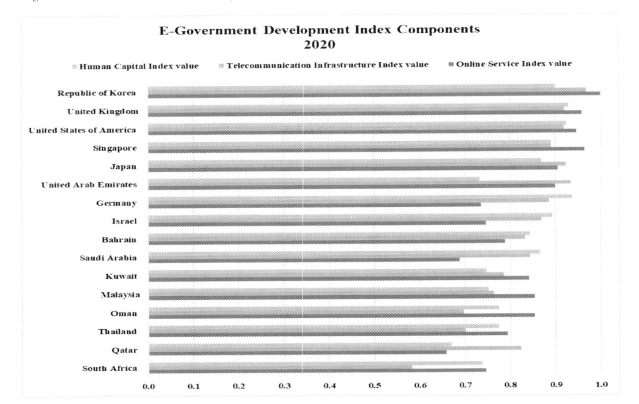

The GCC countries have been enthusiastic of the potential of digital technology, and they have developed ambitious strategic plans such as Smart Dubai, Qatar's Connect 2020 ICT Policy, and Oman's digital strategy (e-Oman). However, the implementation of strategic digital initiatives is not at the same level as some other parts of the world (Bohsali et al., 2016), only 3 percent of GCC executives believe they are at an advanced stage in their digital transformation.

The lack of speed and the quality implementation can be attributed to different challenges. There is a lack of high skills professionals to implement the immense work, and the internal factors at firms such as the culture and processes of an organization (Bohsali et al., 2016). With increased digitalization, one notable concern is cybersecurity and the potential of cyber-attacks. Developing countries and the GCC countries have become more vulnerable to cyber-attacks due to the speed of digitization and sometime lack of robust cybersecurity strategies (PwC, 2019). Another important challenge is data protection and maintaining user privacy, since GCC have weak regulatory frameworks and laws, if any, in this area (GSMA, 2019).

Role of Hi-Tech Human Capital in GCC Countries

One of the stylized facts about the GCC economies is that despite massive investments in education over the past few decades, the size and magnitude of human resources is small. Moreover, the contribution of human resources to the development process has often been modest. A recent study by the World Bank indicates that the culprit is in the quality of education (El-Saharty et al., 2020). That is, the learning intake of the education process tends to be smaller than actual years of schooling completed by cohorts. For example, for graduates of the General Secondary School System, the effective (actual adjusted) learning is smaller than years actually spent in secondary schools. For instance, an 18-year-old graduate after 12 years from Secondary Schooling System in Kuwait has an actual learning of 7.6 years implying that the gap between years spent and actual learning capacity is large, 4,8 which essentially\ goes to waste (Table 1).

Table 1. Learning-adjusted years of school in the Gulf Cooperation Council countries, 2018 (Source: World Bank 2018)

Country	Years	Lays	Gap
Bahrain	13.3	9.6	3.7
Kuwait	12.4	7.6	4.8
Oman	13.1	8.9	4.2
Qatar	12.3	8.5	3.8
Saudi Arabia	12.4	8.1	4.3
united Arab Emirates	13.1	9.5	3.6

The same pattern holds in the case of other GCC countries, although the gap between actual and effective learning is highest in Kuwait. The best performers are Bahrain and the UAE still suffer a loss of 1.5 years (Table 2).

Table 2. Human Capital Index in the Gulf Cooperation Council countries, 2018 (Source: World Bank 2018)

Country	Human Capital Index	Rank
Bahrain	0.67	47
Kuwait	0.58	77
Oman	0.62	54
Qatar	0.61	60
Saudi Arabia	0.58	73
united Arab Emirates	0.66	49

The impact of past policy on human capital in terms of quality, composition (STEM vs literature\ cultural, and quality of education) in the GCC countries including Kuwait is also demonstrable from the small cluster of graduates in scientific competencies and fields, Table 3 indicates the composition of university graduates which clearly tends to cluster in humanities. Inadvertently, the top challenges for digital transformation, as seen by private sector leaders in the GCC and Kuwait, pertains to insufficiency of higher level human capital gauged by requisite STEM competensies and related ICT skills (KFAS, 2021). The downside of these challenges is pervasive and spillover to lower total factor productivity and widespread skill gaps (Al-Qudsi et al., 2021).

Table 3. Percentage of graduates from Science, Technology, Engineering and Mathematics programs in tertiary education, both sexes (%) (Source: World Bank-Education Statistics - All Indicators)

Country Name	2010	2011	2012	2013	2014	2015	2016	2017	2018	2019
Kuwait										
Bahrain						18.92	17.02	15.59	16.15	15.59
Oman	38.94					42.54	44.81	46.27	46.15	44.50
Qatar	24.00	29.81	33.57				29.70	22.93	22.55	24.23
Saudi Arabia	35.79	34.38	29.26			23.92	23.15	21.91	21.14	22.03
United Arab Emirates		25.68	26.21			21.82	21.99	27.73		

Table 4 shows that relative to emerging economies, the GCC countries are at the early stages of producing high tech exports that affect their growth trajectories. The overall competitiveness performance outcome is summarized by the share of high-tech exports in total GCC exports, Table 4. As predicted by Hidalgo and Hausmann, if deviations continue away from the innovative path, future growth and trade is likely to be rather shallow and based on "natural" as opposed to brain-power developed products.

Accordingly, Kuwait and other GCC export products innovation is much below potential and falls short of export product diversification of oil-resource economies and of emerging innovators, like Malaysia, Thailand, and S Korea. contrived. Country experience indicate that digital transformation which Kuwait ascribes to achieve, New Kuwait Vision 2035, hinges on the productivity and quality of human capital. Our findings therefore corroborate recent literature which demonstrated that Kuwait's labor and total factor productivity have been low when contrasted regionally and internationally. Existing welfare-state wage policy are distorting the relationship between efforts and rewards and are inadvertently driving overall wages (especially public sector wages) to grow at rates that are double the rate of productivity growth (Al-Qudsi et.al, 2021). Mounting empirical evidence is therefore overwhelmingly implicating the distortive effect of wages and incentives policy: Unintentionally they inhibited innovations into exports diversification and therefore the government's wage and incentives policy is the main culprit for Kuwait's contrived number and value of innovative exports diversification1.

Table 4. High-technology exports (% of manufactured exports) (source: The World Bank Data)

Country	2010	2011	2012	2013	2014	2015	2016	2017	2018	2019	2020
Kuwait	3.11	2.77		1.66	0.13	0.13	0.15	0.20	4.12	0.90	1.35
Bahrain	0.11	0.15	0.39	0.59	1.50	0.94	1.06	0.62	0.45	4.45	
Oman			3.39	3.44	4.36	3.24	1.52	1.12	1.26		
Qatar		0.01	0.00	0.00	0.05	5.13	0.00	0.01	1.80	0.00	7.10
Saudi Arabia	0.75	0.59	0.66	0.71	0.59	0.79	1.30	0.73	0.54	0.65	0.61
United Arab Emirates			3.77	3.61	10.17	5.30	2.62	2.72	3.05	2.86	5.18
China	32.12	30.48	30.85	31.57	29.70	30.42	30.24	30.91	31.47	30.78	31.27
Israel	19.38	18.40	19.89	19.03	19.41	22.90	21.81	21.07	22.54	23.09	28.20
Japan	19.08	18.35	18.20	17.73	17.75	18.02	17.59	17.57	17.27	17.00	18.60
Korea, Rep.	32.07	28.18	28.22	29.82	30.06	31.21	30.52	32.55	36.39	32.40	35.71
Malaysia	49.30	47.21	47.48	48.45	49.20	48.47	49.05	51.12	53.27	51.84	53.81
Thailand	26.27	22.68	22.83	22.12	22.63	23.91	24.15	25.09	23.70	23.54	27.67
United States	22.61	20.61	20.16	20.18	20.47	21.38	22.41	19.26	18.47	18.67	19.48

The minority Kuwaitis who graduated in science, technology, engineering and mathematics, STEM, were often assigned to admin and supervisory jobs in public sector positions where rank is determined by seniority and which as widely practiced, is also a key criterion for job promotion and mobility. These "rigidities" reinforced Kuwait's segmented and dual labor market, and invariably and inadvertently became bureaucratic forces that inhibit initiative, creativity and innovation. This is reflected in the no ranking of Kuwait on global AI index and the poor ranking of Kuwait on global government AI Readiness index (Table 5).

Table 5. Table Kuwait and country ranks on global AI index and on AI readiness index

Country	AI Country Rank				
	Talent	Research	Government Strategy	Global AI Index	AI Readiness Index
Kuwait					54
SaudiArabia	55	31	3	26	38
Bahrain	52	43	54	51	43
Qatar	62	33	49	47	37
United Arab Emarites	58	42	13	34	16
Oman					48
Singapore	4	4	15	6	6
South Korea	28	12	7	7	7
China	24	2	2	2	19
Japan	26	19	21	16	13
USA	1	1	17	1	1
Germany	11	6	10	9	4
Israel	5	7	45	5	20
Egypt	60	50	27	59	56
Turkey	43	37	29	48	67

Source: AI Global Index and Government AI Readiness Index. Note: Kuwait was not ranked on the AI country rank due to insufficient data on AI related indicators such as talent, and research competencies and product innovations.

Recurring fabulous investments in human capital and in employing successive waves of Kuwaiti citizens in the ranks and files of its public sector yielded little demonstrable effect in terms of the number of high-tech workers who innovate and produce new manufactured goods and services and who can neck-in-neck compete in global markets for new diversified products and whose "supply creates its own demand", similar to that seen in smart phone and related internet products and electronic industry products. In other GCC countries, notably the UAE, there is a rising trend of sharper income and wealth fostered in part by the cluster of millionaire class which is expected to grow by 60% during 2019 and 2030. Rising inequality will invariably foster the development and provision of highly personalized innovative products of goods and services that cater to demands and preferences of this specific socio-demographic income clustering and polarizing cohorts. The trend will also reinforce demand for high quality human capital formation along with the acquisition of outside digital talent and accelerate upskilling of segments of the labor force in the region (Keller, 2000).

GCC Digitization Resolve and Incentive Structure

According to a recent report by Strategy& (El-Darwiche et al, 2022), the GCC investments in digital transformation, including physical infrastructure, as well as training and upskilling of human capital is promising to lead to new era of digital human-capital driven development. Again, there is a big push to l GCC execs' biggest priority in 2022 is digital transformation. Large companies in GCC countries are using data and machine learning analytics to track consumer behavior, monitor website traffic, forecast demand, adjust pricing, and much more. By gathering data from IoT-connected devices, payment systems, augmented reality applications, and more, companies can optimize product positioning, the consumer experience, and, ultimately, the bottom line. Furthermore, the GCC countries are fast adopting AI and machine learning, particularly in the UAE and Saudi Arabia. To illustrate, in recent years KSA has invested over $135 billion in AI (Dienes R Abat M. and Haddd, 2021), the objective is to use automation in the workplace in order to replace routine tasks with AI and machine learning.

In particular, KSA, the UAE, Qatar, and Bahrain investing substantial sums on digital technology including 5G, broadband, and our analysis shows that, once controlling for other patenting activities, AI patent applications generate an extra-positive effect on companies' labor productivity. The effect concentrates on SMEs and services industries, suggesting that the ability to quickly readjust and introduce AI-based applications in the production process is an important determinant of the impact of AI observed to date. particular talent, innovation, and local production. Kuwait with had mobile penetration of 157% of its population in 2020, has been one of the phenomenal countries in the introduction of 5G services: All three operators and government giving 5G a central role in the digital transformation strategies fast revenue growth of internet providers, estimated at CAGR of 42% and revenue growth of 5G enabled services including IoT applications, mobile broadband and fixed will reach almost $1.1 billion by 2025 accounting for 43% of total revenue from services using cellular technologies. This is promoting the three internet providers in the country to invest, along with foreign MNOs several billions of dollars in developing infrastructural facilities requisite for the expansion of 5G related services (Gabriel et al., 2021).

GCC countries continue to invest heavily in order to upgrade the size and quality of their STEM and digital human resources. To illustrate, according to Strategy & the STEM gap between the GCC countries and their advanced counterparts is clear. For example, the GCC has an average of 2,964 science, technology, engineering and math (STEM) graduates per million people, compared to 4,225 in the OECD. The impact of this shortfall is felt in many areas. The average proportion of artificial intelligence (AI) specialists in GCC countries is 1.7 per cent of the total workforce, significantly lower than the 5.4 per cent in European Union countries and 6.9 per cent in Singapore.

GCC countries also need to increase research and development (R&D) and financial resources to support digital innovation. Although the regional startup scene is growing fast, this is from a low level. Our analysis of Crunchbase data reveals that startup concentration in the region ranges from one startup per million people in Qatar to around 15 per million in the United Arab Emirates, compared to 150 and 173 per million in Estonia and Singapore respectively (El-Darwiche et al, 2022).

Kuwait Businesses on the Path of Digitization: A Tale from a Field Survey

The initial findings from the literature showed that COVID-19 has accelerated automation deployment, and it will continue after the pandemic (Loewen and Lee-Whiting, 2021). There is evidence that CO-

VID-19 might facilitate digital transformation introduced as part of their future visions for developing countries, including GCC countries.

In our field survey of a representative sample of 262 firms, only 6% of CEOs think they will not use automation in the future (the year 2024), and another 6% think they will use it less than 5%. A relative cluster of CEOs (36%) indicate they will use automation between 20% and 60%, and 23% of Kuwait CEOs indicate they will use automation steadily more intensely (more than 60%) (Figure 4). When asked about the automation driver, most CEOs responded that it will reduce their expenses and improve productivity and quality. Most of the CEOs (85%) think using technology will positively impact the Kuwaiti economy. The remaining 15% thinks the effect of using technology is neutral, and none think that using technology will have a negative impact on the Kuwaiti economy.

Figure 4. CEOs view on the future reliance on automation

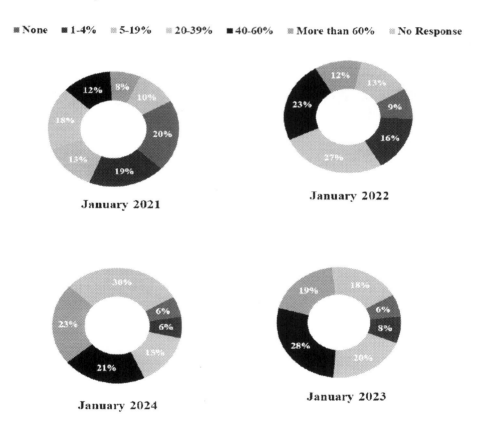

According to Egaña-delSol et al (2021), COVID-19 might facilitate digital transformation in developing economies. These countries have many deficiencies where automation and digitization can make leapfrogs in improving public and private sector efficiency. At the same time, employment will be affected. For instance, our CEOs survey responded informatively to the post coronavirus's impact of likely technology penetration on hiring (Kuwaitis and non-Kuwaitis). According to 55% of CEOs, technology penetration during the post coronavirus era will have a neutral impact on hiring Kuwaiti workers in their companies. Only 18% stated that post coronavirus will have led to decreased hiring of Kuwaiti workers, with 31% of those estimating the extent of the diminished hiring of Kuwaiti workers to be greater than 20%. Specifically, 9% indicated that hiring Kuwaitis will diminish by 40% or more, whereas 28% put the reduction in hiring Kuwaiti workers in the range of 20% to 40%. In response to the likely impact of technology penetration on investment in the post-coronavirus era, a sizeable majority (62%) of Kuwaiti CEOs indicate that company investment will decline, 50% expected to decline at 20% or more, where 26% believe the decline will range between 10% -19%. This is consistent with the survey conducted on 500 firms in 10 emerging markets which showed that COVID-19 encouraged firms to reduce investment (Beck et al., 2020).

Figure 5. The expected change in employment due to technology Penetration

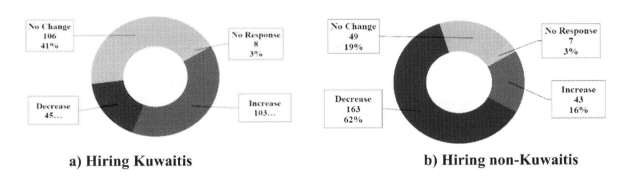

a) Hiring Kuwaitis　　　　**b) Hiring non-Kuwaitis**

CEOs response to the question of evaluating the training programs needed to enhance the productivity of Kuwaiti workers is illustrated in Figure 6. The majority (79%) indicate that ICT is the most crucial training program Kuwaiti workers need to enhance future productivity. Another 64% believe that "training on online working and communications" would fill a critical need. However, 58% believe that upskills and productivity-enhancing programs are essential, followed by training programs on artificial intelligence and machine learning with 54% and 50% for creative and talent programs and 37% for training on using and dealing with robots. Interestingly, the majority (more than 85%) of well-established firms (more than 20 years old) indicated that demand for AI is medium and above, which shows that mature firms are aware of future changes. Still, it will be noteworthy to check startups view one this, but unfortunately, our sample didn't include them in the survey, which opens the door for future studies focusing on startups.

Figure 6. The training programs needed to enhance the productivity of Kuwaiti workers in the future digital future

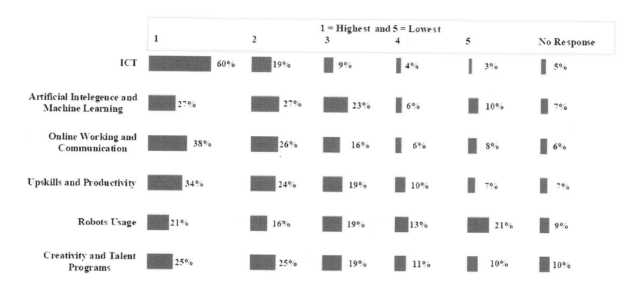

KISR conducted two innovation surveys in collaboration with Kuwait Direct Investment Promotion Authority (KDIPA) and Kuwait Central Statistical Bureau (CSB). The results showed that innovative Kuwaiti firms generally have high utilization of Information and Communication Technology (ICT) in their operations as enabling technology (Salih et al., 2018). In the survey that was conducted in 2015, about 89% of the innovative firms applied ICT in more than 20% of their operations (Figure 7), but 80% for the all surveyed firms. In the 2018 survey, although the innovative firms increased in numbers, the percentage of firms using ICT more than 20% decreased to 84%, and for the all surveyed firms it ended up at 69%. This shows that although there has been improvement in innovation activities in businesses in Kuwait, it is not with the same progress when compared to ICT usage. Such empirical findings beg for decision-makers to increase ICT policies at the national level to make sure that the businesses in Kuwait are able to catch-up with digitization as quickly as possible.

Figure 7. Use of ICT in innovative enterprises (N = 234 for 2015, N= 289 for 2018).

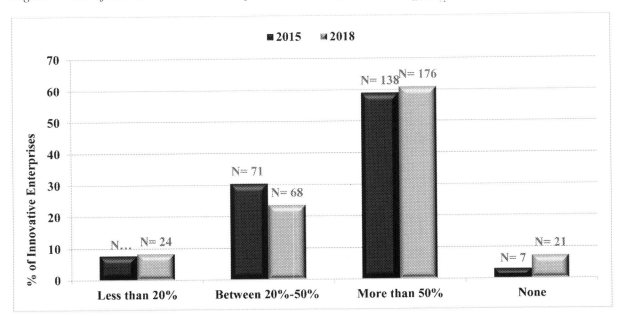

In a recent survey conducted in Kuwait mid 2021of a sample of exporting and importing manufacturing sector firms, findings indicated that over the past three years, most companies engaged in tech-innovations (product, process, marketing or admin regulations), and their distribution across exporters and importers is shown in Table 6.

Table 6. innovation by export-import companies

Has the Company Made any Innovations During the Last Three Years as Follows (Possible More Than One Choice)?	Count	%
Product	85	55%
Process	73	47%
Markting	69	45%
Administrative regulation	50	32%
No Response	20	13%
Total Firms	154	

CONCLUSION

Powerful socio-economic forces are contributing to the uptrend in digital transformation in the GCC countries. These include the drive of households and business sectors to provide and utilize e-trade and e-commerce especially during the curfews and lockdowns which were triggered by the pandemic and continued unabated in the aftermath of the COVID-19. Rising inequality clusters are also putting pressures on the demand for innovative and creative products and services in the region and through preservers on high-end labor demand businesses and workers are tuning to upskilling of their labor force. Demand for digital products including high-end smart phones, palmtops, laptops and other household and personal electronics is thriving in the region. The government are also anxious to ride the high tide of digital transformation in order to rid their economies of recurrent volatilities and dependence on a single source of fiscal revenue and oil export products. This is demonstrable in improvements in the ranks of GCC on the index of E-Government. In the business sector, ICT- and electronic firms are increasingly moving towards the provision of B2B applications after virtually saturating the market of B2 consumer applications. This will enhance business sector efficiency and produce discernible automation penetration and change the composition of workforce most obviously through its effects on labor demand of mostly foreign workers. However, there is fly in the ointment: existing dual labor market structures where highly educated Kuwaitis crowd in Government offices, attracted by the welfare-state's highly paid wages and benefits, side by side with "masses of low-educated and low paid foreign workers" who occupy 95% of private sector jobs has been acting to de-facto trap innovation potential" in government offices and prevent its flow to the sector that needs it most, the private sector. Elsewhere in many country settings, it is private sector corporations and firms that are responsible for most innovations and patents which lead to diversification paths into new products by slicing larger shares in export markets and for generate firm revenue for the companies and for the economies that host them. These policies have lately been blamed for the stagnation and volatile growth that the GCC economies realized historically and change is increasing pressed for.

CEOs are cognizant of the automation impact on their operations and workers but may be less concerned about the nation-wide impact, including the macro dimensions such as unemployment or wasted investment in educating workers in areas and technologies that might be obsolete in the future. Firms need to invest in new programs to address the future challenges due to rapid technological changes, especially after the COVID-19 shock. The impact of automation is high in replacing many low skilled imported labor. Hence, the digitation and automaton will promote importing high skilled human capital and train indigenous labor to upgrade their skills. CEOs think highly of AI, and they are willing to invest in training to match the future demand on productivity and creativity. The large business firms in Kuwait are the powerhouse of Kuwait's economy, and they have been forward-looking. Therefore, these firms will remain the lever to advance any digital transformation in Kuwait and encourage the SMEs and the government to be more proactive to keep up the pace of global technological development and innovation. In the human capital side, Kuwaiti workers need to be equipped urgently with the essential skills to deal with the penetration of Industry 4.0 and its associated technologies such as AI, which will become imperatively needed to deal with automation and for the successful and smooth transformation to the digital economy. In the long-term, the education system needs to be revamped to produce new graduates that are ahead of the state-of-the-art of Industry 4.0 technologies.

Practcial Implication and Limitations

The findings that emerged from the analysis have some practical implications. This study provides a general picture of digitization in GCC countries and shows their progress so far. It contributes to advancing our understanding of the role of digitization in the future for these countries and how they can take advantage of such transformation. The empirical findings are of great importance to the decision-makers in GCC and Kuwait in particular. It highlights the importance of transforming the current natural assets to building hi-tech human capital that is capable not just to meet the challenge of the future disruptive technologies, but be part of creating them.

Despite the rigorous analysis of blending secondary data and empirical findings in this study, some limitations must be acknowledged. First, the empirical part only included Kuwait, and it would be ideal for matching the GCC analysis with cross-country surveys. Second, a more extensive survey sample could have increased the overage of sub-sectors. Third and related to the second point, the analysis was only descriptive and no inferential analysis was conducted. The aforementioned analysis and discussion are subject to important cavets. That is, Kuwait;s drive to foster digital transformation will lead to increased inequalityies in digital access for productive, economic purposes. Past inequalities in the access to math, sciences, engineering and technology education as shown Section 3 will be exacerbated by digital transformation as corroborated by a recent empirical study of Kuwait's digital inequalities (Al-Sumait et al., 2022).

REFERENCES

Afonasova, M.A., Panfilova, E.E., & Galichkina, M.A. (2018). *Social and economic background of digital economy: Conditions for transition.* Academic Press.

Al-Duaij, A. (2019). The digitization of refinery data collection at KNPC Process. *KNPC-Tech,* (4).

Al-Khouri, A.M. (2012). eGovernment strategies the case of the United Arab Emirates (UAE). *European Journal of ePractice, 17*(September), 126-150.

Al-Qudsi. (2021). *The 2020 Coronavirus Outbreak and Global Growth and Trade Collapse: Impact on Kuwait's overall Economy and Society, its Sectors and Business Firms and Vital Fiscal Recovery Plan.* Kuwait Institute for Scientific Research.

Al-Qudsi, S., & Hussain, A. (2022). *Abdullah Al-Salem University (ASU) and Digital Transformation.* Kuwait Institute for Scientific Research.

Al-Sumait, F., Helsper, E. J., Navarro, C., Al-Saif, N., & Raut, N. (2022). *Kuwait's Digital Inequalities Report. from Digital Skills to Tangible Outcomes Project Report. From Digital Skills to Tangible Outcomes Project Report.* LSE.

Baig, A., Hall, B., Jenkins, P., Lamarre, E., & McCarthy, B. (2020). The COVID-19 recovery will be digital: A plan for the first 90 days. *McKinsey Digital,* 14.

Beck, T., Flynn, B., & Homanen, M. (2020). Covid-19 in emerging markets: Firmsurvey evidence. *Covid Economics,* (38).

Belitski, M., Kalyuzhnova, Y., & Khlystova, O. (2021). The Impact of the COVID-19 Pandemic on the Creative Industries: A Literature Review and Future Research Agenda. *Journal of Business Research.*

Bensirri. (2020). *COVID-19 Kuwait Business Impact Survey.* Academic Press.

Bohsali, S., Abdel Samad, R., Papazian, S., Eid, O., Schroeder, B., & Hatz, K. (2016). *Preparing for the Digital Era: The State of Digitalization in GCC Businesses.* PWC.

Bukht, R., & Heeks, R. (2017). *Defining, conceptualising and measuring the digital economy.* Development Informatics Working Paper (68).

Dąbrowska, J., Almpanopoulou, A., Brem, A., Chesbrough, H., Cucino, V., Di Minin, A., Giones, F., Hakala, H., Marullo, C., Mention, A.-L., Mortara, L., Nørskov, S., Nylund, P. A., Oddo, C. M., Radziwon, A., & Ritala, P. (2022). Digital transformation, for better or worse: A critical multi-level research agenda. *R & D Management*, radm.12531. doi:10.1111/radm.12531

Dahlman, C., Mealy, S., & Wermelinger, M. (2016). *Harnessing the digital economy for developing countries.* Academic Press.

Dienes, R., Abat, M., & Haddd, J. (2021). *GCC Digital Trends for 2021.* Oliver Wyman.

El-Darwiche. (2022). *Energizing the Digital Economy in the Gulf Countries.* Strategy.

El-Saharty, S., Kheyfets, I., Herbst, C. H., & Ajwad, M. I. (2020). *The GCC countries' responses to COVID-19.* Anonymous. doi:10.1596/978-1-4648-1582-9_ch4

GSMA. (2019). *Data Privacy Frameworks in MENA: Emerging Approaches and Common Principles.* GSMA.

Keller, W. (2000). Do trade patterns and technology flows affect productivity growth? *The World Bank Economic Review*, *14*(1), 17–47. doi:10.1093/wber/14.1.17

KFAS. (2021). *Kuwait Corporate Readiness for 4th Industrial Revolution.* Kuwait Foundation for the Advancement of Sciences.

Lillie, M., Kark, K., Mossburg, E., & Tweardy, J. (2020). *COVID-19: shaping the future through digital business.* Deloitte Global.

Loewen, P., & Lee-Whiting, B. (2021). *Automation, AI and COVID-19.* Public Policy Forum, Ottawa, Ontario.

Marcus, A., Weinelt, B., & Goutrobe, A. (2015). *Expanding Participation and Boosting Growth: The Infrastructure Needs of the Digital Economy.* Academic Press.

PwC. (2019). *Data Privacy Landscape.* Author.

Salih, S., Arman, H., & Al-Qudsi, S. (2018). *An Action Plan for Improving Kuwait's Global Competitiveness Path: An Engine for Transformation into Knowledge Innovation Economy.* Kuwait Institute for Scientific Research.

Soni, V. D. (2020). Information technologies: Shaping the World under the pandemic COVID-19. *Journal of Engineering Sciences*, *11*(6).

United Nations. (2020). *E-Government Survey 2020. Digital Government in the decade of action for Sustainable Development. With addendum on COVID-19 Response*. Author.

Vial, G. (2019). Understanding digital transformation: A review and a research agenda. *The Journal of Strategic Information Systems*, 28(2), 118–144. doi:10.1016/j.jsis.2019.01.003

WEF. (2022). *More than A Third of the World's Population is Still Offline*. Available at: https://www.weforum.org/videos/more-than-a-third-of-the-world-s-population-is-still-offline

ENDNOTE

[1]   The Atlas of Economic Complexity. 2021, Harvard. https://atlas.cid.harvard.edu/countries/122/new-products

Chapter 6
Cross–Cultural Communication in the Digital Business Environment

Chandra Sekhar Patro

(iD) https://orcid.org/0000-0002-8950-9289

Department of Management Studies, Gayatri Vidya Parishad College of Engineering (Autonomous), India

ABSTRACT

In the digital era, cross-cultural communication in the business environment has become more widespread than ever before. Many organizations have spread their business units overseas not only to strengthen their financial status but also to establish a strong business network worldwide. Cultural awareness shapes the behaviour of business organizations in cross-culturally reflected international markets. Therefore, understanding cultural differences is one of the significant skills for organizations to develop to have a competitive advantage in international business. Digital technologies are changing the business environments through which they interact with their clients. The chapter articulates the changing business environment and the need for cross-cultural communication in the digital environment. The influence of globalization on cross-cultural communication, adoption of various communicative strategies, cultural impacts, issues faced by global managers, overcoming barriers to cultural adaptations, and key areas influencing adoption of digital communication are assessed.

INTRODUCTION

The management of cross-cultural communication expresses the working conditions of employees and clients from different cultures in an organization. Organizational culture refers to norms, shared values, and expectations that regulate an organization. It states an individual's approach and communication at the work (Lewis, 2014). It is deceptive that culture contributes significantly to organizational effectiveness, if not it may signal the need for either internal or external deviations for an organization. The internal

DOI: 10.4018/978-1-6684-4610-2.ch006

sources may include a change in managers, employees or infrastructural aspects, while the external sources may be of political, economic, or technological aspects (Onyusheva, et al., 2020).

With the increased importance of international business and the growing number of multinational organizations, the issue of cross-cultural communication has become critical as it impacts many managerial processes including planning and organizing activities, decision making, and public relations (Kesari, et al., 2014). Within the global business environment, the ability to communicate effectively can be a challenge. Even when both parties speak the same language there can still be misunderstandings due to ethnic and cultural differences. Understanding the impact of globalization on cross-culture communication is imperative for organizations seeking to create a competitive advantage in the global market. As society becomes more globally connected, the ability to communicate across cultural boundaries has gained increasing prominence. Global businesses must understand how to communicate with employees and customers from different cultures to fulfil the organization's mission and build value for stakeholders (Okoro, 2013).

New technologies, globalization and changing organizational cultures affect cross-cultural communication. Communication is one of the most important functions to master for any business to be successful in today's increasingly competitive markets, particularly for organizations doing business internationally. The role of cross-cultural communications has been significantly contributing to the success of business operations. (Bauman & Shcherbina, 2018). The use of technology has a profound impact on how businesses communicate globally and market their products and services across the globe. Cultural factors have long been known to influence the communication and success potential of competition. Cultural awareness shapes how business organizations behave in cross-culturally reflected international markets. It is broadly recognized that cultural factors act as invisible barriers in international business communications (Guang & Trotter, 2012).

Digital technologies and digital media are changing the environments through which business organizations interact with their clients. The evolution of digital organizational forms, customer technology use, and the nature of customer journeys differ significantly across global markets. The explosive growth of innovative digital technologies over the past two decades has revolutionized the way customers browse for information, compare products and services, make purchases, and engage with organizations and other customers. Customers today interact with the organizations and other customers through multiple online touchpoints in multiple channels and media. Although the basic technologies underlying digital innovations are much the same all over the world, the nature of customers' interactions with different touchpoints in a digital environment differs significantly across global markets (Nam & Kannan, 2020).

Cross-cultural business communication demands that organizations be aware of and sensitive to cultural differences. To respect the right to culture by consumers in various cultures and marketplaces, marketers should understand that their customers have a right to their cultures. If the marketers want success in cross-cultural marketing, they must work in a way to respect the consumer's values and the right to their culture. Therefore, to match marketing with consumer preferences, purchasing behaviour, and product-use patterns, marketers benefit from understanding the market's cultural environment. Organizations should not focus on cultural differences only to adjust business communication programs to make them acceptable to consumers. It requires that organizations discover if markets are viable by including the study of the culture in which the company is going to do business in its business and marketing planning. To do this the organizations should identify cultural factors that can be employed to support business communication in proposed markets.

The chapter articulates changing business environment and the need for cross-cultural communication in the digital environment. The chapter assesses the influence of globalization on cross-cultural communication, the adoption of various communicative strategies in cross-cultural business communication, framing in cross-cultural communication, and cross-cultural negotiation. Further, the chapter examines the cultural impacts, issues faced by global managers in cross-cultural business communication, and overcoming barriers to cultural adaptations.

THEORETICAL BACKGROUND

Recent political changes in the countries around the world, economic cooperation and interdependencies, and information and communication technologies increased the degree of globalization as well as changed both labor markets and work environments (Thompson et al., 2013). Many organizations have transformed from domestic into multicultural as they operate in the international, multinational, global or transnational environment (Anand, 2014). These changes increase the role of communication in the overall success of the business and emphasize the need for employees with cross-cultural communication skills (Safina & Valeev, 2015).

According to Barker et al. (2017), sensitivity to diversity now demands a strategic understanding of the importance of cross-cultural communication competence in every action in organizations, communities, and nations throughout the world. Glover and Friedman (2015) stated that functioning successfully within different cultures can be a struggle for many professionals. As the world changes, it becomes clear that dealing with other cultures, both domestic and international, requires competence in both identifying and transcending cultural boundaries. Language barriers, differences in values and standards of behaviour, lack of experience, lack of trust, and inadequate knowledge about other cultures or stereotypical thinking are among the most widespread obstacles for cross-cultural communication (Liðntsev & Canavilhas, 2017).

Hofstede, et al. (2010) provide an in-depth analysis of national cultures' dimensions, which represent independent preferences for one state of affairs over another that distinguish countries from each other. The Hofstede model of national culture consists of six dimensions including power distance, individualism/collectivism, masculinity/femininity, uncertainty avoidance, long term/short term orientation, indulgence/restraint (Minkov, 2018). Colbert, et al. (2016) emphasize that digitalization reduces authenticity in terms of less face-to-face communication and interactions characterized by less fully present participants. Liðntsev and Wellbrock (2019) identified that new generations (Millennials and Generation Z) are highly interested in cross-cultural communication and believe that digitalization signiðcantly simpliðes cross-cultural communication processes including facilitating language barriers problems.

Global business communication is a process that crosses national boundaries for business purposes. Communication among individuals from the same culture is often difficult. Therefore, communication between individuals from different cultures from the point of view of language, values, beliefs, customers and ways of thinking, will be far more difficult, a degree of miscommunication being almost inevitable (Ferraro, 2021). Cross-cultural communication is the interaction between culturally diverse people with different value orientations and varied communication codes within a community of work and socialization (Abugre, 2018). Successful cross-cultural interaction between multinational staff has now been accepted as the most critical management issue in international business both at the individual and group levels of analysis (Barner-Rasmussen, et al., 2014), as it can impact positively on expatriates' work outcomes in Multinational Corporations (MNCs).

Tung (2008) proposes that there is the need to balance cross-national and cross-cultural investigations to truly understand the globalization of the cultural phenomena. The differences in cultures, multicultural team members working together in MNCs vary in their communicative behaviours, and this can pose a challenge to effectively understand each other. Thus, prescriptions for effective communication in cross-cultural encounters often suggest adapting one's behaviour to that of the other culture by learning to understand the value systems and communicative behaviours of the local or indigenous people (Abugre & Debrah, 2019). This is why communicating parties would normally attribute cultural meanings to their experiences and actions which are shaped by the social and political relationship in which they are embedded (Lauring and Klitmøller, 2015). Harzing and Feely (2008) argue that failure to communicate effectively leads to uncertainty, anxiety, and mistrust, which produces misattribution, conflict and cognitive distortion of expatriates in subsidiary locations. Thus, an important role of expatriates or global managers is to effectively communicate across cultures to produce a well-managed team comprising both expatriates and local or indigenous staff.

INFLUENCE OF GLOBALIZATION ON CROSS-CULTURAL COMMUNICATION

In today's world of globalization and the internationalization of businesses, the marketing relationship is becoming increasingly important as a means to meet the marketing needs of sales organizations. However, when it comes to establishing specific business relationships in a particular culture, business people can resort to their cultural values and communication strategies, which may go beyond the area of marketing to include broader social dimensions (Zhu, et al., 2006).

Because of globalization and the rapid development of economics, multinational organizations are more and more prevalent. Organizations that extend their business abroad have to face the challenge of cross-cultural communication. Communication is the only approach by which group members can cooperate toward the goal of the organization. Especially for multi-culture business organizations with some subsidiaries in other countries, managers must have frequent communication and a sufficient understanding of the organizational goal. Technical developments have removed most of the physical barriers to communication. However, managers still encounter some cultural barriers. To achieve success, managers working in global environments must be proficient in cross-cultural communication (Erez, 1992). By contrast, the differences in management style, staff behaviours and communication systems between different cultures the barriers of cross-cultural communication in multi-nation organizations can be found (He & Liu, 2010).

Globalization of markets or the flow of products, resources, and culture requires professionals to find ways to communicate effectively and efficiently. As organizations become global and outsource manufacturing, assembly, and delivery of products to international partners, they rely on the communication technologies that allow cross-cultural teams to work together across time zones and geographical distances (Holtbrügge, et al., 2013). Although communication devices such as phones and fax have existed for decades, the Internet and especially the introduction of Web 2.0 in 2004 made a breakthrough with interactive tools. Web 2.0 describes a set of technologies allowing people to create content on the Internet rather than on their desktops (O'Reilly, 2005). The most significant changes in the workplace are caused by technological tools, such as blogging and wikis, video and audio conferencing, which employees use to virtually work together either synchronously (at the same time) or asynchronously (with the delay in response time) as their schedules allow (Deal, et al., 2010). This transformation of communication was noted as one of the most significant changes in the work environment.

An organization's profitability is in part determined by its business communication strategies and skills. However, top managers in organizations working globally sometimes neglect the significance of the invisible barriers that create cultural differences in business communication. Cultural factors play an important role in functioning as invisible barriers. Even as the world is becoming globalized, many economies have increasingly voiced their claim to a right to culture in international businesses. It is predicted that national culture will be a critical factor affecting economic development, demographic behaviour, and general business policies around the world. Such claims at the macro level will be important for making trade policy, protecting intellectual property rights, and creating resources for national benefits. At the micro-level, these claims could be invisible barriers for organizations working in or wanting to enter international markets (Lillis & Tian, 2010).

If globalization is an inevitable process, then cross-culture will also be inevitable. On the one hand, the world is becoming more homogeneous, and distinctions between national markets are fading and, for some products, disappearing altogether. This means that business communication is now a world-encompassing discipline (Guang & Trotter, 2012). Consequently, the cultural differences between nations, regions and ethnic groups, far from being extinguished, are becoming stronger (Lillis & Tian, 2010). This means that global business communication, a cross-cultural process, requires managers to be well informed about cultural differences nationally, locally, and ethnically to win in global markets. Cross-cultural solutions to international business, therefore, are increasingly being suggested as a valid and necessary method in enhancing communication and interaction in and between business partners, between organizations and customers, and between coworkers.

TYPES OF COMMUNICATIVE STRATEGIES

In cross-cultural business environments, communication plays an imperative role. Every reasonable business person in the international professional community understands and values communication. However, a proper understanding of its significance cannot stand for successful business and closed business deals. This is where communication strategies come in handy and take the lead. Communication strategies forge and help maintain connections, communication strategies when properly applied help build up international teams and develop cross-border business effectively, communication strategies stand at attention to translate the message smoothly to reach the desired communicative goal. Thus, the frequently used communicative strategies in the global business environment include (Chaika, 2020).

1. **Nomination:** Nomination refers to a communicative strategy by employing which, the speaker/ sender of the information wants to open a topic with some people an individual is talking to or demonstrating an object. This strategy allows for collaboration and productivity at the same time. When an individual employs nomination, the speaker/ encoder presents a particular topic in a clear, distinct and truthful way. The key aspect with nomination is to say only what is relevant. It is also important to mention that the encoder may use nomination not only for introducing an idea or object but also in the course of their interaction. In such a situation, nomination deliverables are associated with ways of continuing communication. Thus, with the nomination as a communicative strategy

an individual can consider certain criteria attributable to the interaction. These criteria include the introduction of an idea, object, etc. as well as the continuance of communication, presentation of the information clearly and understandably to the recipient/decoder, and relevance of the topic presented.

2. **Restriction:** Restriction refers to a communicative strategy employed with limitations of any kind, which may arise with the speaker/sender of the relevant information. In certain contexts, the speaker/sender of the information faces several constraints. Such constraints may include constrained response/reaction within a set of categories, and restricted response (fully or partially) of the other communicant/decoder involved in the communication act. The decoder, i.e. the listener/observer has to respond only within that set of categories, which is made by the encoder/speaker.

3. **Turn-Taking:** Turn-taking as a communicative strategy pertains to the process by which speakers, both the encoder and the decoder, decide who takes the conversational floor. It is worth mentioning that across cultures people may keep to some accepted behaviours that may envelop into social attributes and thought patterns. However, the underlying part is to establish and move along a productive conversation and the key to success is with the idea of giving all communicators a chance to speak and share their understanding, agree or disagree on the mentioned information. Yet, it is not the only criterion to establish the strategy. The two others inter alia are, timing and ways of communication, and stepping in at the appropriate moment. The former relates to recognizing the proper moment to speak in a certain environment as well as how to speak or start speaking when their turn comes. The latter requires that everyone among the speakers – encoders and decoders, respects all the communicants and attributes the encoding role, a role of the speaker, only when it is their turn in the course of interaction.

4. **Topic control:** Topic control is another communicative strategy employed to cover the ways of procedural formality and informality influencing the development of the topic once the speaker/encoder of the message introduces it and takes it further into a conversation. As the matter concerns it is important to develop the topic collectively once it is initiated. This helps the communicants to avoid interruptions and untimely questions as well as topic shifts. Topic control rests on the question and answers formula that helps to move the discussion forward and keeps the interaction live and ongoing using asking questions and listening to replies. Altogether, the strategy enables the communicants to take turns, share their ideas or argue points, and develop the discussion.

5. **Topic Shifting:** Topic shifting is another communicative strategy that involves a change in the topic, i.e. gradual or unexpected movement from one topic to another. The strategy anticipates two stages. Stage one foresees the end of one topic in a conversation or part of the conversation. Stage two envelopes the introduction of the new topic to be followed by its continuation among the communicants, or introduction of another adjacent topic. Topic shifting as a strategy in communication works best with a follow-through. It means that it is critical for strategy employment that the newly introduced topic develops into further discussion. There are a lot of introductory phrases and parentheses, which open the message, among the other signs, in the beginning, middle or end of the message.

6. **Repair:** Repair is a communicative strategy that refers to how the speaker/the encoder of the message addresses some difficulties or lack of experience in speaking, listening, and understanding the message, which the speaker/encoder/decoder may encounter in a conversation. Repair aims to overcome interaction breakdown to send more understandable messages that the recipient/the decoder may find easier to decode and translate.

7. **Termination:** Termination as a communicative strategy anticipates closing/winding up a conversation. Thus, termination can be described via the following means attributable to this communicative strategy.
   a. Close-initiating phrases, expressions, set clusters that end the topic in a conversation,
   b. Use of verbal and non-verbal signs to mean the end of the interaction,
   c. Verbal and non-verbal messages that end communication are sent by the speaker/encoder of the message and the listener/decoder of the message to each other.

Termination may be quick and short or it may last longer to make room for clarifications, further questions and answers. Sometimes the topic may continue into further discussion, however, the language including body language speaks of approaching the end and this is an interaction point just about to end communication.

FRAMING IN CROSS-CULTURAL COMMUNICATION

The field of business communication is a specific division of social intercourse, where the constant pressure of framing is further enhanced by such stakes as professional prestige, position in the organization hierarchy. Here, the role acting is even stricter than in regular social interaction, since the rules are proportionately more rigid and the people involved are more aware and hunting for weak spots to exploit to their organization's benefit. Transferred to the level of multinational communication, this issue gains new dimensions not only in terms of extension but also as a result of the wide range of systems of values involved. In the age of globalization, where geographic borders have gradually lost their traditional separating rigidity, gaining an integrative rather than a separating meaning, cross-cultural communication abilities have become crucial for the survival and development of any company.

Therefore, communicating across cultures involves a good command of a complex network of cultural frames that yields a heterogeneous business environment, where people bring along their individual culturally and ethnically determining values, beliefs, and perceptions. Under these circumstances, awareness of different framing systems endows the business person with the flexibility of thinking and behaviour, as well as with the ability to adjust and react efficiently when in contact with other cultural backgrounds. According to Goman (1994), cultural differences go as deep as to the medium of communication, whose variations delineate three basic oppositions: high-context/low-context, sequential/synchronic, and affective/neutral cultures.

1. **High-context and Low-context Cultures:** In high-context cultures, communication relies more on the context, extracting meaning from such non-verbal cues as body language, silence, and pauses, rather than from the spoken or written message. In such cultures, personal relations and informal agreements are more bindings than any formal contract. Low-context cultures value explicit and specific messages the precision of the spoken or written words underlying interpersonal relations being considered of utmost importance. The major business challenge for people in a low-context culture is to realize the importance of building and maintaining personal relationships when dealing with high-context cultures.

2. **Sequential and Synchronic Cultures:** These culture types display different ways of perceiving time and the associate concepts of timing, dealing with deadlines and scheduling. Sequential cultures

appropriate temporality as a sequence, according to which time becomes a linear commodity to spend, save or waste. Synchronic cultures perceive temporality as a constant, circular flow that can be experienced only fragmentarily. This divergent perception has a determining impact on building business relations, as it establishes the meaning of being on time and implicitly the approach to such concepts as deadlines, strategic thinking, investments, and long-term planning. These elements can cause misunderstandings between people from a sequential culture, who view being late as a sign of bad planning or disrespect, and people from a synchronic culture, who consider the insistence on timeliness as a sign of immature impatience. In sequential cultures, business people give full attention to one agenda item after another, whereas professionals in other parts of the world do several things at the same time regularly.

3. **Effective and Neutral Cultures:** This distinction is established according to the proportion of reason and emotion involved in business interactions and delineates two categories of cultural framing. The effective type, in which people show their feelings plainly, and the neutral type, is characterized by carefully controlled and subdued emotions. Cultural framing is a matter of actively using our cultural background, determining our way of thinking and acting and, more importantly, providing the set of criteria by which an individual perceive and appreciate others. That is why experts in intercultural communication recommend that productive business relations should be built on the awareness that cultures are not right or wrong, better or worse; they are just different. Therefore, in the contemporary global business community, what is proper in one culture may be ineffective, or even offensive in another, and therefore, the key to cross-cultural success is the understanding of and respect for diversity.

CROSS-CULTURAL NEGOTIATION

Cross-cultural negotiation is a specialized area within the field of cross-cultural communication that provides a theoretical framework for the training of negotiators and sales personnel so that they should have a solid knowledge of the culture, values, beliefs, etiquette and approaches to business, meetings and negotiations in the target countries to maximize the potential of a positive outcome (Storti, 2011a). Training in cross-cultural negotiation involves a series of factors that can influence the proceedings of a business interaction (Dumbravă, 2010). These include:

1. **Eye contact**. In certain organizations, strong direct eye contact conveys confidence and sincerity and trustworthiness, whereas, prolonged eye contact is considered rude and is generally avoided in other organizations.

2. **Personal space and touch:** In business, people usually leave a certain amount of distance between themselves when interacting, as touching is permitted only between friends and family members. However, in some business organizations, people are tactile and, therefore, personal space shrinks significantly. These non-verbal cues require special attention since they are known to have a much greater impact and higher reliability than the spoken word, due to an individual's capacity to interpret symbols and cues recognizable on the level of collective memory (Dumbravă & Koronka, 2009).

3. **Time:** In some businesses, people are clock conscious and punctuality is crucial as being late is taken as an insult, whereas in certain organizations, being on time for a meeting does not carry the same sense of urgency.

4. **Meeting and greeting:** Although most international business people meet with a handshake, in some countries, this is not appropriate for genders. At the same time, some cultures view a weak handshake as a sign of weakness, whereas others perceive an organization's handshake as aggressive. Other useful details are related to addressing people by first name, surname or title, and the suitability of small talk.

5. **Gift giving:** Some organizations have the protocol of gift-giving as an integral part of business protocol, in some organizations it has negative connotations. The major details to be considered are related to where gifts should be exchanged, colours that should be avoided, and whether they should be lavish, wrapped or reciprocated (Storti, 2011b).

Cross-cultural negotiation training starts from the premise that cultural blunders can have disastrous consequences in business and relies on the understanding of etiquettes and approaches to business abroad before focusing on cross-cultural negotiation styles and techniques. Therefore, specialists in this field have detected three interconnected aspects that need to be considered before entering into cross-cultural negotiation:

- **Basis of Relationship:** The basis of the relationship has to do with the affective-neutral divergence in terms of cultural framing. For instance, where personal relationships are seen as unhealthy and dangerous to objectivity, business is mostly contractual. On the contrary, for some organizations, business is personal, and partnerships will be made only between people who know, trust and feel comfortable with one another. Therefore, in this type of culture, it is necessary to invest in relationship building before conducting business.

- **Information:** Some business cultures emphasize presented and rationally argued business proposals using statistics and facts, while others, are more visual and oral, preferring information presented through speech or using maps, graphs and charts.

- **Negotiation:** Negotiation styles also differ significantly across cultures. The organizations approach in different manners. The organizations can make the decisions using various approaches like talking simultaneously rather than sequentially, negotiating and making decisions as a team, by the senior figure, by making detailed analysis, and deals are closed under the pressure of deadlines.

These are the main factors that need to be considered when approaching cross-cultural negotiation, to be able to prepare effective presentations and adjust our behaviour following a particular global business environment.

CULTURAL IMPACTS ON CROSS-CULTURAL COMMUNICATION

The globalization of the world economies had made it important for marketing managers to understand how to do business in different cultures. The ability of marketers and consumers to communicate cross-culturally is critical for success. Business communication is two-way interactive communication. Marketers deliver information to the market, and they gather and collect, interpret, and put the information they gather from the markets to use. Failure to do either may lead to a loss of business (Tian, 2000).

A business' understanding of cultural boundedness is imperative for successful international business communication and marketing to ethnic populations domestically (Reese, 1998). Griffith (1998) states that cultural overtones in marketing operations derive, to some extent from customer preferences. They suggest that the cultural characteristics of a target market will be responsive to certain culturally bound channel structures, such as local stores, or bazaars. It will be difficult for marketers to understand the market system in developing countries. Unless perceived and understood, profound differences in attitudes, expectations and unworded messages will frustrate the organization's effort to do business with huge and developing markets, and elsewhere in tradition-based cultures (Emery & Tian, 2003).

Cross-cultural business communication among consumers or customers whose culture differs from that of the marketer's own culture in at least one fundamental aspect of cultures such as language, religion, social norms and values, education and living style. Cross-cultural business communication demands that organizations be aware of and sensitive to cultural differences. To respect the right to culture by consumers in various cultures and marketplaces, marketers should understand that their customers have a right to their cultures. If the marketers want success in cross-cultural marketing they must work in a way to respect the consumer's values and the right to their culture. Business communication is not an independent behaviour but related to all other business or market behaviours (Guang & Trotter, 2012).

Therefore, to match marketing with consumer preferences, purchasing behaviour, and product-use patterns, marketers benefit from understanding the market's cultural environment. Business organizations should not focus on cultural differences only to adjust business communication programs to make them acceptable to consumers. It is to suggest that the organizations should also identify cultural similarities, identify opportunities and plan standard marketing strategies based on business communication theory-informed with cultural information. To skillfully work with these cultural similarities and differences in the worldwide marketplace is an important marketing task for businesses.

CULTURAL ISSUES AND BARRIERS FACED BY GLOBAL MANAGERS

Global managers are often confronted with many issues in managing the global workforce. This is because employees across borders have their own cultures that may affect the business operation and performance. Some of the known cultural issues and barriers that hinder cultural adaptation are mentioned as follows (Jain & Pareek, 2019):

1. **Narrow-mindedness:** Individuals might think that organizations from the country where they originate operate with the same scope of responsibilities and processes as the global businesses that they are newly engaging with. But the reality is, that global business activities have wider scope and responsibilities than domestic organizations and the social system is different from the former organization. So, the employees tend to be narrow-minded and they fail to realize the differences between their own culture and other cultures and remain to behave with their own culture over the new culture brought by internationalization. They also perceive the triviality of their culture and the new culture resulting in non-recognition of the new culture.

2. **Uniqueness:** Several employees become distinctive rather than collective. So, the idea of teamwork seems difficult to attain because the employees do not aspire to be team builders but the attitude is

more inclined to self-interest and self-gratification. Hence, they are steered by the motto of 'self-first before others'.

3. **Ethnocentrism:** Another barrier to cultural acceptance is the idea of ethnocentrism. This holds the fact that employees from their homeland tend to smear their own culture to the global environment and workplace. They always believed that the culture, conditions, and working environment in their country are far better than the new environment which hinders them to adopt the new culture. Moreover, their judgment and perception are based on self-criterion that eventually affects negatively their productivity and performance. So, there is a need to understand other cultures and temporarily forget the native homeland's culture.

4. **Cultural Detachment:** Cultural detachment plays an imperative part in assessing the quantity of cultural adaptation that employees can achieve in moving from one's homeland to another country. Cultural distance impacts the feedback and responses of employees in the business. The difficulty of employees to distinguish the homeland's culture from the new culture signifies the higher degree of cultural distance that might result in being ethnocentric. So, managing this problem is important to remove cultural barriers.

5. **Culture shock:** Culture shock can be described as a condition that employees experience by having difficulty to adapt the new culture because of insecurities and disorientations facing different cultures. Employees might not know how to react or respond to the conditions. They lose self-confidence and may emotionally be upset. Although it is a universal condition, many people are struggling much that may result in others isolating themselves or even planning to go back home because they have not overcome their fears and insecurities. Some of the reasons for cultural shock are different management philosophies; language, food, dress, driving patterns, attitude towards work and productivity, and separation from friends and colleagues.

OVERCOMING BARRIERS TO CULTURAL ADAPTATIONS

There are several steps that the organization can undertake to prevent cultural shock and reduce the impact of the other barriers listed above. Some of them are given below:

1. **Vigilant selection:** Employees can be selected based on the attitude of low ethnocentrism and other possibly troublesome features. The desire to experience other cultures and live in another nation and learning the attitude of employees' spouses towards the assignment may also be an important prerequisite attitude worth assessing.

2. **Like-minded preps:** The adjustment to a new country becomes easy for the employees especially on their first international assignment if they are sent to countries that are similar to their homeland.

3. **Pre-departure training:** Many organizations try to accelerate fine-tuning to a host nation by encouraging employees to learn the local language. They offer training before giving the assignments. It often includes orientation to the geography, customs, culture and political environment in which the employees will be living.

4. **Orientation and support:** In the new country, adjustment is further encouraged after arrival if there is a special effort made to help the employee and family get settled, this may include assistance with housing, transportation and sopping. It is especially helpful if a mentor can be assigned to ease the transition.

5. **Incentives and assurances:** Another problem that can arise when employees transfer to another culture is that their need satisfactions are not as great as those of comparable employees who remain at home. Although a move to another nation may be an exciting opportunity that provides new challenges, responsibilities, and recognition, an international job assignment may bring about financial difficulties, inconveniences, insecurities, and separation from relatives and friends. To motivate such employees to accept such assignments in other nations, organizations frequently should give them extra pay and fringe benefits to compensate for the problems they may experience. They should also be assured of a better position in the organization upon their return to their home country, which could help them to relieve their job insecurities.

6. **Preparation for reentry:** Employees returning to their home country after foreign assignment tends to suffer some cultural shock in their own country. This is sometimes called cross-cultural reentry and may cause reverse cultural shock. After adjusting to the culture of another nation and enjoying its uniqueness, it is difficult for employees to readjust to the surroundings of the home country. This situation is made more difficult by the multitude of changes that have occurred since they departed.

DIGITAL TRANSFORMATION OF BUSINESS

Digital transformation is concerned with the changes digital technologies can bring about in a company's business model, products or organizational structures' and is perhaps the most pervasive managerial challenge for incumbent business units of the last and coming decades (Hess, et al., 2020). Digital transformation is an organizational change triggered by digital technologies, and stated that there are two perspectives of digital transformation within organizations must be captured: a technology-centric and an actor-centric perspective. However, digital possibilities need to come together with skilled employees and executives in order to reveal its transformative power. Digital technologies are considered a major asset for leveraging organizational transformation, given their disruptive nature and cross-organizational and systemic effects (Besson & Rowe, 2012). In order to achieve successful digital transformation, changes must occur at various levels within the organization, including an adaptation of the core business (Karimi & Walter, 2015), the exchange of resources and capabilities (Yeow, et al., 2018), the reconfiguration of processes and structures (Resca, et al., 2013), adjustments in leadership, and the implementation of a vivid digital culture (Singh & Hess 2020). Therefore, the scope of our review revolves around digital transformation at the organizational level only.

Digital transformation and resultant business model innovation have fundamentally altered consumers' expectations and behaviors, pressured traditional firms, and disrupted numerous markets. Consumers have access to dozens of media channels, actively and effortlessly communicate with firms and other consumers, and pass through rapidly increasing number of touch points in their customer journey, many of which are digital (Lemon & Verhoef, 2016). At the company level, many traditional firms have been surpassed by innovative fast-growing digital entrants, and suffered as a result of this. Digital transformation affects the whole company and its ways of doing business (Amit & Zott, 2001) and goes beyond digitalization — the changing of simple organizational processes and tasks. It rearranges the processes to change the business logic of a firm (Li et al., 2018) or its value creation process (Gölzer & Fritzsche, 2017). The use of IT is transformative and leads to fundamental changes to existing business processes, routines and capabilities, and allows healthcare providers to enter new or exit current markets. Moreover, digital transformation utilizes digital technologies to enable interactions across borders with suppliers, customers and competitors (Singh & Hess, 2017). Hence, digital technologies can help to attain a competitive advantage by transforming the organization to leverage existing core competences or develop new ones (Liu, et al., 2011). Therefore, digital transformation is inherently linked to strategic changes in the business model as a result of the implementation of digital technologies (Sebastian, et al., 2020). In sum, digital transformation is a company-wide phenomenon with broad organizational implications in which, most notably, the core business model of the firm is subject to change through the use of digital technology (Iansiti & Lakhani, 2014).

EFFECT OF DIGITAL COMMUNICATION TOOLS ON BUSINESS ACTIVITY

Communication is the process of sending information to others and receiving information back from them. Digital communication involves sending and receiving such information electronically. There are a number of digital tools that are commonly used in business to communicate, both internally and externally, including:

- **Email:** Electronic mail enables written messages to be sent instantly to others, and files can be shared as attachments.
- **Mobile phones:** Mobile phones enable verbal conversations to be conducted anywhere. They also allow short written messages to be sent (see instant messaging).
- **Mobile applications:** Applications (apps) are designed to run on smart phones and tablets. They can be used to create documents, capture images and enable banking transactions.
- **Websites:** A page or group of pages containing written and visual information using various media.
- **Social media:** A variety of web platforms that enable users to share ideas, content, information and messages.
- **Web conferencing:** A meeting that uses communications software to stream images and/or voices over the internet between participants in different locations.
- **Cloud services:** Software, such as online document editing and data storage, that is run from a remote location but that can be accessed from anywhere as long as a connection to the internet is maintained.
- **Instant messaging:** Software that enables users to send instant messages, usually in the form of text, to each other.

These tools have affected business activity in several ways (BBC, 2022):

1. **Improved speed and accuracy of information** - electronic tools allow easy editing and checking of written communication, helping to reduce grammatical and spelling errors. Messages can be communicated at a much faster pace, which can help to keep external stakeholders up to date while giving internal stakeholders information quickly to aid decision-making.
2. **Better customer service** - the use of digital communication has enabled businesses to improve the service they provide to their customers by offering a wider range of options for getting in touch. Customers are now able to contact businesses at a time that is convenient to them.

3. **Improved productivity** - digital communication makes it possible to solve many problems with production machinery remotely, for example, screen sharing to address computer issues. This reduces costs and lessens the impact of equipment breakdowns.

4. **Access to a wider audience** - businesses can now access a wider audience much more easily. This can be beneficial when targeting customers with marketing materials. However, the human resources function may also find this useful, as they may want to attract a wide pool of applicants for a job vacancy.

KEY AREAS INFLUENCING ADOPTION OF DIGITAL COMMUNICATION

A key feature of the organizational landscape has been the surging river of technology that has become a torrent in recent years. Its impact has been evident in every aspect of organizational life. The implementation of new technology must not be viewed as a solution that will in and of itself solve problems. Relatively, it must fit into an already existing communication strategy. However, technology alone does not lead to progress. It merely offers new opportunities that need to be properly harnessed if benefits are to be reaped (O'Kane, et al., 2004).

The use of technology in the communication process has been forming a vital part of the communicative infrastructure of organizations. Traditional media, such as written messages, phone calls and face-to-face contact, are now often replaced by e-mail as the preferred channel in the business world, while glossy brochures and organization-wide memos find their importance diminishing with the increasing use of the Internet and intranet applications. These changes have influenced organizational communication, both internally and externally.

To maximize the impact of technology as a communication method, organizations must be aware of the possible benefits and associated problems to create both the process and atmosphere necessary for effective communication (Foreman, 1997). Flanagin (2000) proposed three key areas that influence the adoption of digital communication in organizations:

1. **Organizational features** such as age, size and culture. Organizations with higher levels of technology tend to implement innovations earlier. This does not restrict adoption to these organizations, rather it indicates that some may need to take into consideration other factors such as ensuring that employees are introduced gradually to the technology and are provided with sufficient support to master it.

2. **Perceived benefits** of increased communication and information flow, and the organizational advantage. An organization needs to assess these possibilities before introducing technology to ensure that their expectations are met when it is introduced. At the individual level, the media substitution theory senses that people already carrying out a particular job function, such as sending regular memos or carrying out research, will be more likely to start using new technologies if they facilitate these particular functions.

3. **Social pressures** such as self-image and the face an organization present to its customers, competitors and suppliers can encourage it to adopt digital communication.

CONCLUSION

The organizations notice that current business trends of globalization, diverse workforce, team-based organizations, advances in technology, and flatter organizational structure impact communication trends in the workplace. Moreover, technology is brought down to the level of the individual and the physical location of an employee often does not matter as employees become a part of the global network. Between globalization and technology 'modern business communication has become a diverse, dynamic field that has increased its relevance and significance than ever before.

Organizations' ability to attract, retain, and motivate people from diverse cultural backgrounds, may lead to competitive advantages in cost structures and through maintaining the highest quality human resources. Further capitalizing on the potential benefits of cultural diversity in workgroups, organizations may gain a competitive advantage in creativity, problem-solving, and flexible adaptation to change. A multi-cultural workforce is becoming the custom. To achieve organizational goals and avoid potential risks, the managers should be culturally sensitive and promote creativity and motivation through flexible leadership.

MANAGERIAL IMPLICATIONS

Although every culture is unique, certain basic guidelines are appropriate for consistent cross-cultural success. Successful managers acquire a base of knowledge about the values, attitudes, and lifestyles of the cultures with which they interact. Managers need to be aware of the political and economic background of target countries, their history, current national affairs, and perceptions about other cultures. Such knowledge facilitates understanding of the partner's mindset, organization, and objectives. Decisions and events become substantially easier to interpret. Higher levels of language proficiency pave the way for acquiring competitive advantages. In the long run, managers knowing multiple languages are more likely to negotiate successfully and have positive business interactions than managers who speak only one language.

Conceivably the principal cause of culture-related problems is the ethnocentric assumptions managers may unconsciously hold. Problems arise when managers assume that foreigners think and behave just like the people back home. They misrepresent communications with foreigners. They may perceive the other's behaviour as odd and possibly inappropriate. Such situations may affect the manager's ability to interact effectively with the foreigner, even leading to communication interruption. In this way, cultural bias can be a significant barrier to successful interpersonal communication. Most people view their own culture as the norm as everything else may seem eccentric. Understanding the self-reference criterion is a critical first step to avoiding cultural bias and ethnocentric reactions. Working effectively with counterparts from other cultures requires an investment in professional development. Each culture has its ways of carrying out business transactions, negotiations, and dispute resolution.

REFERENCES

Abugre, J. B. (2018). Cross-cultural communication imperatives: Critical lessons for western expatriates in multinational organizations (MNCs) in Sub-Saharan Africa. *Critical Perspectives on International Business, 14*(2/3), 170–187. doi:10.1108/cpoib-01-2017-0005

Abugre, J. B., & Debrah, Y. A. (2019). Assessing the impact of cross-cultural communication competence on expatriate business operations in multinational corporations of a Sub-Saharan African context. *International Journal of Cross Cultural Management, 19*(1), 85–104. doi:10.1177/1470595819839739

Amit, R., & Zott, C. (2001). Value creation in e-business. *Strategic Management Journal, 22*(6-7), 493–520. doi:10.1002mj.187

Anand, P. K. K. (2014). Cross cultural diversity in today's globalized era. *Journal of Human Resource Management, 2*(6-1), 12-16.

Barker, K., Day, C. R., Day, D. L., Kujava, E. R., Otwori, J., Ruscitto, R. A., Smith, A., & Xu, T. (2017). Global Communication and Cross-Cultural Competence: Twenty-First Century Micro-Case Studies. *Global Advances in Business Communication, 6*(1), 5.

Barner-Rasmussen, W., Ehrnrooth, M., Koveshnikov, A., & Mäkelä, K. (2014). Cultural and language skills as resources for boundary spanning within the MNC. *Journal of International Business Studies, 45*(7), 886–905. doi:10.1057/jibs.2014.7

Bauman, A. A., & Shcherbina, N. V. (2018). Millennials, technology, and cross-cultural communication. *Journal of Higher Education Theory and Practice, 18*(3), 75–85.

BBC. (2022). *The influence of digital communication on business activity.* Retrieved from https://www.bbc.co.uk/bitesize/guides/zjdwd6f/revision/3

Besson, P., & Rowe, F. (2012). Strategizing information systems-enabled organizational transformation: A transdisciplinary review and new directions. *The Journal of Strategic Information Systems, 21*(2), 103–124. doi:10.1016/j.jsis.2012.05.001

Colbert, A., Yee, N., & George, G. (2016). The digital workforce and the workplace of the future. *Academy of Management Journal, 59*(3), 731–739. doi:10.5465/amj.2016.4003

Deal, J. J., Altman, D. G., & Rogelberg, S. G. (2010). Millennials at work: What we know and what we need to do (if anything). *Journal of Business and Psychology, 25*(2), 191–199. doi:10.100710869-010-9177-2

Dumbravă, G. (2010). The concept of framing in cross-cultural business communication. *Annals of the University of Petrosani. Economics, 10*(Part I), 83–90.

Dumbravă, G., & Koronka, A. (2009). "Actions Speak Louder than Words" – Body Language in Business Communication. *Annals of the University of Petrosani. Economics, 9*(3), 249–254.

Emery, C. R., & Tian, R. G. (2003). The effect of cultural differences on the effectiveness of advertising appeals: A comparison between China and the US. *Transformations in Business & Economics, 2*(3), 48–59.

Erez, M. (1992). Interpersonal communication systems in organisations, and their relationships to cultural values, productivity and innovation: The case of Japanese corporations. *Applied Psychology*, *41*(1), 43–64. doi:10.1111/j.1464-0597.1992.tb00685.x

Ferraro, G. P. (2021). *The cultural dimension of international business*. Prentice-Hall.

Flanagin, A. J. (2000). Social pressures on organizational website adoption. *Human Communication Research*, *26*(4), 618–646. doi:10.1111/j.1468-2958.2000.tb00771.x

Foreman, S. (1997). IC and the healthy organization. In E. Scholes (Ed.), *Gower Handbook of Internal Communication*. Gower.

Glover, J., & Friedman, H. L. (2015). *Transcultural competence: Navigating cultural differences in the global community*. American Psychological Association. doi:10.1037/14596-000

Gölzer, P., & Fritzsche, A. (2017). Data-driven operations management: Organisational implications of the digital transformation in industrial practice. *Production Planning and Control*, *28*(16), 1332–1343. doi:10.1080/09537287.2017.1375148

Goman, C. K. (1994). *Managing in a global organization: Keys to success in a changing world*. Thomson Crisp Learning.

Griffith, D. A. (1998). Cultural meaning of retail institutions: A tradition-based culture examination. *Journal of Global Marketing*, *12*(1), 47–59. doi:10.1300/J042v12n01_04

Guang, T., & Trotter, D. (2012). Key issues in cross-cultural business communication: Anthropological approaches to international business. *African Journal of Business Management*, *6*(22), 6456–6464.

Harzing, A. W., & Feely, A. J. (2008). The language barrier and its implications for HQ-subsidiary relationships. *Cross Cultural Management*, *15*(1), 49–61. doi:10.1108/13527600810848827

He, R., & Liu, J. (2010). Barriers of cross cultural communication in multinational organizations: A case study of Swedish company and its subsidiary in China. Halmstad School of Business and Engineering, 1-32.

Hess, T., Matt, C., Benlian, A., & Wiesböck, F. (2020). Options for formulating a digital transformation strategy. In *Strategic Information Management* (pp. 151–173). Routledge. doi:10.4324/9780429286797-7

Hofstede, G., Hofstede, G. J., & Minkov, M. (2010). *Cultures and organizations: Software of the mind. Revised and Expanded* (3rd ed.). McGraw-Hill.

Holtbrügge, D., Weldon, A., & Rogers, H. (2013). Cultural determinants of email communication styles. *International Journal of Cross Cultural Management*, *13*(1), 89–110. doi:10.1177/1470595812452638

Iansiti, M., & Lakhani, K. R. (2014). Digital ubiquity: How connections, sensors, and data are revolutionizing business. *Harvard Business Review*, *92*(11), 19.

Jain, T., & Pareek, C. (2019). Managing Cross-Cultural Diversity: Issues and Challenges. *Global Management Review*, *13*(2), 23–32.

Karimi, J., & Walter, Z. (2015). The role of dynamic capabilities in responding to digital disruption: A factor-based study of the newspaper industry. *Journal of Management Information Systems, 32*(1), 39–81. doi:10.1080/07421222.2015.1029380

Kesari, B., Soni, R., & Khanuja, R. S. (2014). A review on the need of cross cultural management in multinational corporations. *International Journal of Advanced Research in Management and Social Sciences, 3*(8), 120–127.

Lauring, J., & Klitmøller, A. (2015). Corporate language-based communication avoidance in MNCs: A multi-sited ethnography approach. *Journal of World Business, 50*(1), 46–55. doi:10.1016/j.jwb.2014.01.005

Lemon, K. N., & Verhoef, P. C. (2016). Understanding customer experience throughout the customer journey. *Journal of Marketing, 80*(6), 69–96. doi:10.1509/jm.15.0420

Lewis, R. (2014). How different cultures understand time. *Business Insider, 1.*

Li, L., Su, F., Zhang, W., & Mao, J. Y. (2018). Digital transformation by SME entrepreneurs: A capability perspective. *Information Systems Journal, 28*(6), 1129–1157. doi:10.1111/isj.12153

Lifintsev, D., & Wellbrock, W. (2019). Cross-cultural communication in the digital age. *Estudos em Comunicação, 1*(28), 93–104.

Lifintsev, D. S., & Canhavilhas, J. (2017). Cross-cultural management: Obstacles to effective cooperation in a multicultural environment. *Scientific Bulletin of Polissya, 2*(2 (10)), 195–202. doi:10.25140/2410-9576-2017-2-2(10)-195-202

Lillis, M., & Tian, R. (2010). Cultural issues in the business world: An anthropological perspective. *Journal of Social Sciences, 6*(1), 99–112. doi:10.3844/jssp.2010.99.112

Liu, D. Y., Chen, S. W., & Chou, T. C. (2011). Resource fit in digital transformation: Lessons learned from the CBC Bank global e-banking project. *Management Decision, 49*(10), 1728–1742. doi:10.1108/00251741111183852

Minkov, M. (2018). A revision of Hofstede's model of national culture: Old evidence and new data from 56 countries. *Cross Cultural & Strategic Management, 25*(2), 231–256. doi:10.1108/CCSM-03-2017-0033

Nam, H., & Kannan, P. K. (2020). Digital environment in global markets: Cross-cultural implications for evolving customer journeys. *Journal of International Marketing, 28*(1), 28–47. doi:10.1177/1069031X19898767

O'Kane, P., Hargie, O., & Tourish, D. (2004). Communication without frontiers: The impact of technology upon organizations. In D. Tourish & O. Hargie (Eds.), *Key Issues in Organizational Communication* (pp. 74–95). Routledge.

O'Reilly, T. (2005). *What is Web 2.0: Design patterns and business models for the next generation of software.* Retrieved from http://www. oreillynet. com/pub/a/oreilly/tim/news/2005/09/3 0/what-is-web-20. html

Okoro, E. (2013). International Organizations and Operations: An Analysis of Cross-Cultural Communication Effectiveness and Management Orientation. *Journal of Business and Management, 1*(1), 1–13.

Onyusheva, I., Thammashote, L., & Thongaim, J. (2020). Urban Business Environment: Managing Cross-Cultural Problems. *The EUrASEANs: Journal on Global Socio-Economic Dynamics*, *1*(20), 30–43. doi:10.35678/2539-5645.1(20).2020.30-43

Reese, S. (1998). Culture Shock. *Marketing Tools.*, (May), 44–49.

Resca, A., Za, S., & Spagnoletti, P. (2013). Digital platforms as sources for organizational and strategic transformation: A case study of the Midblue project. *Journal of Theoretical and Applied Electronic Commerce Research*, *8*(2), 71–84. doi:10.4067/S0718-18762013000200006

Safina, M. S., & Valeev, A. A. (2015). Study of humanitarian high school student's readiness for intercultural communication formation. *Review of European Studies*, *7*(5), 52–60. doi:10.5539/res.v7n5p52

Sebastian, I. M., Ross, J. W., Beath, C., Mocker, M., Moloney, K. G., & Fonstad, N. O. (2020). How big old companies navigate digital transformation. In *Strategic information management* (pp. 133–150). Routledge. doi:10.4324/9780429286797-6

Singh, A., & Hess, T. (2020). How chief digital officers promote the digital transformation of their companies. In *Strategic Information Management* (pp. 202–220). Routledge. doi:10.4324/9780429286797-9

Storti, C. (2011a). Figuring foreigners out: A practical guide. Academic Press.

Storti, C. (2011b). The Art of Crossing Cultures. Academic Press.

Thompson, A., Peteraf, M., Gamble, J., Strickland, A. J. III, & Jain, A. K. (2013). *Crafting & executing strategy 19/e: The quest for competitive advantage: Concepts and cases*. McGraw-Hill Education.

Tian, R. G. (2000). The implications of rights to culture in trans-national marketing: An anthropological perspective. *High Plains Applied Anthropologist*, *20*(2), 135–145.

Tung, R. L. (2008). The cross-cultural research imperative: The need to balance cross-national and intra-national diversity. *Journal of International Business Studies*, *39*(1), 41–46. doi:10.1057/palgrave. jibs.8400331

Yeow, A., Soh, C., & Hansen, R. (2018). Aligning with new digital strategy: A dynamic capabilities approach. *The Journal of Strategic Information Systems*, *27*(1), 43–58. doi:10.1016/j.jsis.2017.09.001

Zhu, Y., Nel, P., & Bhat, R. (2006). A cross-cultural study of communication strategies for building business relationships. *International Journal of Cross Cultural Management*, *6*(3), 319–341. doi:10.1177/1470595806070638

KEY TERMS AND DEFINITIONS

Collaboration: Collaboration refers to the working condition whereby individuals work together for a common purpose to achieve the business objectives.

Communication: Communication refers to the exchanging of information by speaking, writing, phone, computer or using some other medium.

Cross-Culture: Cross culture is a concept that recognizes the differences among business people of different nations, backgrounds, and ethnicities, and the importance of bridging them.

Digitization: Digitization refers to creating a digital representation of physical objects or attributes i.e., converting something non-digital into a digital representation.

Globalization: Globalization is a term used to describe how trade and technology have made the world a more connected and interdependent place.

Organizational Culture: Organizational culture refers to the collection of values, expectations, and practices that guide and inform the actions of all team members.

Synchronic Communication: Synchronic communication occurs when the interactants share common cultural norms and whose psychological orientation toward each other is one of harmony and cooperation.

Technology: Technology refers to methods, systems, and devices that are the result of scientific knowledge being used for practical purposes.

Chapter 7
Spillovers From Renewable Energy to Life Expectancy in Emerging Market Economies:
Panel Vector Auto Regression Analysis

Nausheen Sodhi
(iD) https://orcid.org/0000-0002-2492-1491
Panjab University, India

Adem Gök
Kırklareli University, Turkey

ABSTRACT

Renewable energy sources have a minimal detrimental impact on health quality compared to non-renewable energy sources owing to the reduced carbon dioxide emissions that reduce negative externalities of pollution. Health quality can be measured through changes in life expectancy owing to changes in variables directly impacted by renewable energy usage. The chapter analyses the impact of renewable energy on life expectancy through four channels for 23 emerging market economies for the time period 1994-2015 using panel vector auto regression. Four hypotheses were developed for four channels: CO2 emissions, GDP per capita, technology level, and urbanization. The results conform to all the hypotheses: increase in renewable energy increases life expectancy by decreasing CO2 emissions and by increasing GDP per capita, technology level, and urbanization. Thus, to increase life expectancy, emerging market economies should increase their renewable energy usage since it reduces per capita CO2 emissions and increases GDP per capita, technological advancement, and urbanization.

DOI: 10.4018/978-1-6684-4610-2.ch007

INTRODUCTION

Life expectancy is a basic measure of health quality which tells the average expected life span of population. Till the end of nineteenth century, life expectancy remained below 40 years for all the nations. In the early 1900s, it started increasing in the industrialized nations and the following years were characterized by inequality between rich and poor nations. Over the recent years, the gap has reduced to an extent that even the nation with least life expectancy now has a value more than the highest life expectancy in the 1800s (Roser et al., 2013). Average life expectancy has more than doubled globally since 1900s but the gap between nations in terms of lowest and highest values remains at 30 years in 2019. In a recent study by Pyrkov et al. (2019), life expectancy has been found to be as high as 120-150 years if various stresses can be checked. This brings out the need to investigate the link that various factors have with rising life expectancy. The idea of life expectancy and its significance has surfaced time and again in forums of discussion on varying socio-economic and political aspects of growth and development. It has been included in numerous indices to measure health quality in general and longevity or mortality in particular. Improvement in life expectancy since early 1900s can be linked to the technical advancements in countries, which in turn have lead to higher usage of renewable energy sources. Numerous studies show that increased usage of renewable energy leads to higher life expectancy (Caruso et al., 2020; Steinberger et al., 2020). Renewable energy sources are sustainable in the sense that their supply is not depleted by higher usage. For example, the solar energy that reaches our planet in an hour exceeds the total annual energy demand. The health impacts of renewable energy are similar to nuclear generated electricity owing to lower carbon emissions. Several studies confirm that higher usage of renewable energy leads to lesser carbon emissions (Caruso et al., 2020; Silva et al., 2012). Rising usage of fossil fuels in the past has led to higher carbon emissions, thus increasing the pace of climate change and global warming. This in turn, has had detrimental impact on human health quality and life expectancy. The growing demands to correct this environmental and health impact extends to making it duty of the government to protect the future generations for the same. In this regard, a group of eight teenagers in Australia filed a court case seeking to make government responsible to protect them from climate change (Burton and Wong, 2021). This was in response to Vickery Extension Project to construct an open-cut coal mine. Such instances of growing expectations for sustainable policies put pressure on governments to balance conflicting interests. In that backdrop, renewable energy has increased considerably since 2011 and in 2019, its installed power capacity has grown more than 200 gigawatts (Ranalder, 2020). Apart from the health benefits owing to no or low emission of greenhouse gases and air pollutants, renewable energy is cost effective, employment oriented (generating 11million jobs globally in 2018), accessible and secure supply-wise. Increased usage of renewable energy adds to the economic growth of nations, along with technical advancements and urbanization trend.

The present study analyses the impact that renewable energy has on life expectancy of 23 emerging market economies (listed in Appendix-B) for the years 1994 to 2015. The average life expectancy in these countries rose from 69.54 years in 1996 to 74.48 years in 2015, while the percentage of their average renewable energy consumption to total energy consumption fell from 21.41 in 1996 to 18.52 in 2015. Life expectancy was lowest at 60.60 years in South Africa and highest at 77.69 years in Greece in 1996. In 2015, life expectancy was lowest at 62.65 years in South Africa and highest at 82.02 years in Korea Republic. Renewable energy consumption as a percentage of total energy consumption was lowest at 0.01 in Saudi Arabia and highest at 53.77 in India a in 1996. In 2015, renewable energy was lowest at 0.01 in Saudi Arabia and highest at 46.48 in Pakistan. The present study identifies four channels that link life expectancy to renewable energy and the impact is analyzed through these channels. These include carbon dioxide emissions, per capita incomes, technological advancements and urbanization. Each of these channels and their role in linking renewable energy to life expectancy has been explained and hypothesized in the theoretical perspective section of this chapter.

The chapter has several contributions to the relevant literature. First, it sheds light on a new subject: the positive spillovers (indirect effects) of renewable energy on life expectancy for emerging market economies. Second, the chapter develops hypothesis for each identified channel mainly based on the literature review. Third, the chapter conforms all four hypotheses that are developed in order to assess the impact of renewable energy on life expectancy. Finally, the chapter gives policy recommendations for emerging market economies to sustain higher life expectancy for each indirect channel.

The structure of the chapter is as follows: Section 1 briefly gives an introduction, Section 2 presents theoretical perspective, Section 3 presents empirical analysis and last section concludes.

THEORETICAL PERSPECTIVE

High consumption of renewable energy sources improves life expectancy, while high consumption of non-renewable energy sources significantly reduces life expectancy (Gohlke et al., 2011). If managed well, the renewable energy usage can minimize health risks (Smith et. al., 2013). Caruso, Colantonio and Gattone (2020) found a two-way linkage between life expectancy and renewable energy. Life expectancy significantly impacts renewable energy, which in turn positively impacts life expectancy. Thus, demand for renewable energy sources could go up with improvements in living conditions and public awareness, which further help in improvement of public health. But improvement in life expectancy of some nations in the past has not been on account of renewable energy usage. Steinberger, Lamb & Sakai (2020) find only a quarter of life expectancy improvement in the past owing to renewable energy usage. This suggests that increased fossil fuel use is not a key determinant of increased life expectancy, i.e. growing consumption of renewable energy sources did not play a significant role in increasing life expectancy across countries (University of Leeds, 2020). Instead, level of carbon emissions, economic growth, technical progress and urbanization are strongly dynamically coupled to improvements in life expectancy. The present study establishes this linkage between renewable energy and life expectancy via four identified channels viz. CO2 emissions, GDP per capita, technology level and urbanization. Each of these has been explained in the subsequent sub-sections.

The Indirect Effect of Renewable Energy on Life Expectancy Through the Channel of CO2 Emissions

The impact that renewable energy has on CO2 emissions is spilled over to life expectancy as well. Increased use of non-renewable energy increases CO2 emissions which further reduces life expectancy (Martins et. al., 2019; Wang et. al., 2019, 2020). But with higher renewable energy usage which produce lesser CO2 emissions, life expectancy increases. For example, burning natural gas for electricity releases between 0.6 and 2 pounds of CO2 per kilowatt-hour (CO2E/kWh), while coal emits between 1.4 and 3.6 pounds of CO2E/kWh. Wind releases only 0.02 to 0.04 pounds of CO2E/kWh on a life-cycle basis; solar 0.07 to 0.2; geothermal 0.1 to 0.2; and hydroelectric between 0.1 and 0.5 (Union of Concerned Scientists, 2017). Higher renewable energy seems to be linked to lower levels of CO2 (Caruso, Colantonio and Gattone, 2020) or the other way round (Ahmed & Shimada, 2019). Boosting the renewable energy source implementation is necessary to decrease the CO2 emissions (Bilan et al., 2019). For countries with different levels of economic development but similar investment in renewable energy, increasing renewable energy share had an evident decrease of CO2 emissions per capita (Silva, Soares & Pinho, 2012). Bilgili, Koçak & Bulut (2016) support the EKC hypothesis and the negative relationship between renewable energy consumption and CO2 emissions. The study shows that if nations focus on increasing renewable energy supply, they can help reduce global warming along with increasing their GDPs. Increased carbon emissions are associated with environmental degradation (Bekhet et al., 2017; Wang et al., 2018; Zakaria & Bibi, 2019), which deteriorated health quality (Wang et al., 2019 ; Zaidi and Saidi, 2018). Decrease in CO2 emissions further increase life expectancy owing to the positive externalities of reduced pollution. This leads to reduced risks of asthma, respiratory problems, cancer and other damages to the immune system, endocrine and reproductive systems (The World Counts, 2021). Osabohien et al., 2020 showed that carbon emissions can reduce life expectancy by 0.35% and recommends governments to generate alternative sources of energy to reduce carbon emissions for sustainable development. Balan (2016) shows that carbon dioxide emissions in terms of consumption of coal, natural gas and petroleum is related to the causes of education and the quality of human life in these countries. Consumption of fossil fuel significantly affects mortality and it is due to variability in CO2 that highest variability of mortality could be explained (Rasoulinezhad et al., 2020).

From the above discussion, the first hypothesis to be tested in this study is mentioned below:

Hypothesis 1: An increase in renewable energy increases life expectancy by decreasing CO2 emissions.

The Indirect Effect of Renewable Energy on Life Expectancy Through the Channel of Income Per Capita

An increase in renewable energy increases GDP per capita which in turn improves life expectancy. Increased renewable energy consumption helps attain (sustainable) growth owing to its cost effectiveness. This is because of reduced need for budgetary allocations towards correcting air pollution. Policy tradeoffs between reducing air pollution, improving energy efficiency and increasing economic activity can be dealt with by following sustainable growth strategies. Across 58 percent of 38 renewable-energy-consuming countries, renewable energy consumption positively impacted economic growth (Shahbaz et al., 2020). Ahmed & Shimada (2019) find that nations with renewable energy consumption still underway, economic growth is led by non-renewable energy sources. Marinaş, Dinu, Socol & Socol (2018) show that in the short run, higher consumption of renewable energy adds to the economic growth in Hungary, Lithuania and Slovenia. Whereas, in the long run, there exists a two-way causality between renewable energy consumption and economic growth for the countries. These results allow proposing public policies to achieve Europe 2020 goals regarding the increase of energy efficiency. But increasing expenditure on renewable energy sources can have economic costs in terms of GDP per capita (Silva, Soares & Pinho, 2012). If nations can provide for improved and easy access to the renewable sources of energy, they can contribute to their GDPs (Bilgili, Koçak & Bulut, 2016). Further, increase in GDP per capita increases life expectancy (Mahyar, 2016; Miladinov, 2020). Economic growth provides a conducive environment for advancements in medicine and health infrastructure, which further improves health quality and life expectancy. For populations with a moderate income, achieving low carbon emissions on one hand along with high life expectancy on the other is possible. But it is not so for populations with the highest per capita GDP values, where there seems to be a trade-off between the two goals. But prioritizing economic growth over climate stability seems less defensible, especially for countries with same life expectancies (Steinberger et al., 2016).

The second hypothesis based on the above linkage to be tested in this study is mentioned below:

Hypothesis 2: An increase in renewable energy increases life expectancy by increasing GDP per capita.

The Indirect Effect of Renewable Energy on Life Expectancy Through the Channel of Technological Advancement

An increased use of renewable energy leads to technological advancement via additional renewable energy installation and infrastructure. Increasing targets for renewable electricity result in additional renewable energy capacity building and reduction in cumulative CO_2 emissions (Qi, Zhang & Karplus, 2014). Various policies on renewable energy subsequently impact R&D, innovation initiatives and patent penetration in the renewable energy sector, which are proxies for technological advancements. You and Okunade (2017) identified share of elderly (for life expectancy) as a proxy for technological advancement since "changes in fertility rates and life expectancy (and consequently the share of the aged) might be influenced by technologies for improving longevity or delaying fertility". Further, technological advancement increases life expectancy by providing better access to medical information, improved food safety and sanitation standards, advancements in cost-effective medical equipments, vaccines and other health services. Higher IT investments in information integration, workflow coordination, and collaborative planning at the country level are positively associated with higher life expectancy (Mithas, Khuntia & Agarwal, 2009). Fonseca et al., 2021 find that technological progress is responsible for half of the increase in life expectancy in the United States over the period 1965–2005. Technological progress is also a main driver of health expenditure growth and increases in life expectancy are partly explained by new technologies that improve health outcomes (Smith, Newhouse & Freeland, 2009). Hence, the third hypothesis to be tested in this study is as below:

Hypothesis 3: An increase in renewable energy increases life expectancy by increasing technology level.

The Indirect Effect of Renewable Energy on Life Expectancy Through the Channel of Urbanization

An increase in renewable energy encourages urbanization as availability of cost-effective, clean and green energy helps in sustainable GDP growth, thereby creating employment avenues and improved standard of living, which encourages migration from rural to urban areas. It provides favorable conditions for populations in developing countries to grow, adding further to urbanization (Avtar, Tripathi, Aggarwal & Kumar, 2019). Upon examining the relationship between energy consumption and urban development, Saryazdi, Homaei & Arjmand (2018) showed that high budget allocation without growing green space and vice versa does not affect urban development. Hence, sustainable practices of urban development add further to urbanization. In turn, urbanization increases life expectancy (Bible, 2013). It provides for easy access to healthcare infrastructure and connectivity across urban areas. Provision of better education facilities and ease of access to social and public services in urban areas create a suitable environment for increased awareness among people. This in turn increases the demand for better healthcare and willingness on the part of public to pay for the same. But increasing demand adds pressure to the healthcare system which can also impact life expectancy negatively. Torres et al. (2019) and Sudharsanan & Ho (2020) show that rural life expectancy is higher than urban life expectancy. The present study tests for a positive relation between urbanization and life expectancy and the final hypothesis based on the above discussion is as under:

Hypothesis 4: An increase in renewable energy increases life expectancy by increasing urbanization.

EMPIRICAL ANALYSIS

Data and Variables

The study analyzes 23 emerging market economies for the period 1994-2015 due to data availability. See Appendix A for the list of variables and their source. See Appendix B for the list of emerging market economies that are analyzed. Table 1 presents descriptive statistics for the actual variables at level for this period. Since one of the variables needed differencing twice to be stationary, panel VAR analysis is conducted for the period 1996-2015.

Table 1. Descriptive statistics

Variables	Obs	Mean	Std. Dev.	Min	Max
renew	506	19.81	15.49	0.01	55.56
co2	506	5.23	4.09	0.68	20.4
gdppc	506	8717.35	6477.99	639.27	30054.89
tech	506	24658.82	91259.11	300	1101864
urban	506	63.71	18.02	26.40	91.50
life	506	71.62	5.24	53.44	82.02

Cross section dependency test in Table 2 indicates that all variables have cross section dependency. Hence, second generation unit root test of Pesaran (2007) has been applied.

Table 2. Cross section dependency test

Variables	CD-Test	p-value
renew	10.914	0.000
co2	21.306	0.000
gdppc	64.722	0.000
tech	19.547	0.000
urban	37.491	0.000
life	65.401	0.000

According to the results of the unit root tests in Table 3, it is found that renew, co2, gdppc, urban are I(1), and life is I(2).

Table 3. Pesaran unit root tests

Variable	Level		First-Difference		Second-Difference	
	Cons.	Cons.&Tr.	Cons.	Cons.&Tr.	Cons.	Cons.&Tr.
renew	-1.841	-2.194	-4.167***	-4.318***		
co2	-2.315***	-2.309	-4.435***	-4.608***		
gdppc	-1.041	-0.982	-2.556***	-3.009***		
tech	-1.624	-1.965	-3.488***	-3.747***		
urban	-0.639	-0.803	-1.471	-3.620***		
life	-2.027	-1.833	-2.057	-2.126	-3.311***	-3.634***

Notes: Null hypothesis is the presence of unit root. CIPS values are reported for Pesaran [32]. ***, ** and * denote significance levels at % 1, % 5 and % 10 respectively. The variables of co2 and urban have trend.

Panel VAR Methodology

All six variables in Panel Vector Auto Regression (Panel VAR) are taken as endogenous to allow for unobserved individual heterogeneity (Love and Zicchino, 2006). According to Granger causality tests, there exist bivariate causal relationships between all of the variables i.e. they are endogenous. Hence, panel VAR was used by building a system of six simultaneous equations. Since the optimal lag-length for the panel VAR model is found one, a first order panel VAR model was applied. The same is stated below:

$$y_{it} = \Gamma_0 + \Gamma_1 y_{it-1} + f_i + d_{c,t} + e_t \tag{1}$$

where y_{it} is a vector of six-variables comprising renewable energy, CO2 emissions, income per capita, technology level, urbanization and life expectancy.

Further, in order to allow for individual heterogeneity and to capture aggregate, country-specific macro shocks, the study introduced fixed effects, f_i, and country-specific time dummies, $d_{c,t}$ (Love and Zicchino, 2006). To eliminate fixed effects, forward mean- differencing (Helmert procedure) was used instead of mean-differencing procedure, as the latter creates biased coefficients (Love and Zicchino, 2006; Abrigo and Love, 2016). Also, Helmert procedure helps preserve the orthogonality between transformed variables and lagged regressors. This allows to use lagged regressors to estimate the coefficients by system GMM, which requires small *T*, large *N* (Love and Zicchino, 2006; Abrigo and Love, 2016).

Panel VAR utilizes five different tools comprising stability test, Granger causality test, panel vector auto-regression, impulse response functions, and forecast-error variance decomposition. The first test of stability condition is satisfied when all the eigenvalues lie inside the unit circle. The second test of causality i.e. Granger causality test is used to identify bilateral causal relationship between variables and to justify treating them as endogenous variables, in case bilateral causal relationship exists between them. Since first-order panel VAR has been used, it presents the effects of first lag of each independent variable on each of the five-variable dependent vector. The impulse-response functions show the reaction of a variable to shocks given to another variable, keeping all other shocks in the system equal to zero. Further, confidence intervals are generated using Monte Carlo simulations to calculate the standard errors of the impulse-response functions. The difference between Panel VAR estimation results and impulse response function is that the former indicates the direct effect that each variable has on other variables, but the latter indicates the overall effect that each variable has on other variables. That is, impulse response function includes both direct and indirect effects. Hence, Panel VAR estimation results have been used for showing the indirect effects of renewable energy on life expectancy for each channel. Indirect effect takes together the two relationships (between renewable energy and the channel and between the channel and life expectancy), if both are significant. To determine the overall effect of renewable energy on life expectancy, impulse response function has been used. Also, variance decompositions showing the magnitude of the total effect have been presented. They show variability in one variable as explained by shocks to another variable, accumulated over time. Lastly, the total effect accumulated over 10 years has been reported with the help of variance decomposition (Love and Zicchino, 2006).

For the Panel VAR analysis, the STATA package, which is developed by Abrigo and Love (2016) has been used.

Results and Discussion

Since all the eigenvalues lie inside the unit circle, Panel VAR satisfies stability condition, according to the results in Table 4.

Table 4. Panel VAR stability test

Eigenvalue		Modulus
Real	**Imaginary**	**Modulus**
0.822	-0.237	0.855
0.822	0.237	0.855
0.365	-0.602	0.705
0.365	0.602	0.705
-0.525	0	0.525
-0.245	0	0.245

According to the results in Table 5, it is only urbanization that does not Granger cause technology and renewable energy consumption that does not Granger cause life expectancy. Hence there are at least four bi-directional causal relationship between the variables indicating that the variables are endogenous, which justify using panel VAR technique.

Table 5. Granger causality test

	d_renew	**d_co2**	**d_gdppc**	**d_tech**	**d_urban**	**d2_life**
d_renew		0.000	0.000	0.000	0.001	0.876
d_co2	0.000		0.000	0.000	0.000	0.000
d_gdppc	0.000	0.000		0.000	0.000	0.003
d_tech	0.000	0.000	0.000		0.000	0.000
d_urban	0.000	0.000	0.000	0.269		0.000
d2_life	0.050	0.000	0.000	0.002	0.000	

Notes: The numbers are the Prob > chi2 values. Null hypothesis is that the row variables do not Granger-cause column variables.

According to the results in Table 6, renewable energy has no significant direct effect on life expectancy. But it has significant indirect effects through the channels of CO2 emissions, GDP per capita, technology level and urbanization.

For the case of first channel, renewable energy has a negative significant effect on CO2 emissions supporting Caruso et al. (2020), Ahmed & Shimada (2019), Bilan et al. (2019), Silva et al. (2012) and Bilgili et al. (2016), and CO2 emissions has negative significant effect on life expectancy supporting Balan (2016) and Rasoulinezhad et al. (2020). Taking together both effects as they are both significant, renewable energy has positive spillover (positive significant indirect effect) on life expectancy through the channel of CO2 emissions confirming Hypothesis 1.

For the case of second channel, renewable energy has positive significant effect on GDP per capita supporting Shahbaz et al. (2020), Marinaș et al. (2018) and Bilgili et al. (2016), and GDP per capita has positive significant effect on life expectancy supporting Mahyar (2016) and Miladinov (2020). Taking together both effects since they are both significant, renewable energy has positive spillover (positive significant indirect effect) on life expectancy through the channel of GDP per capita confirming Hypothesis 2.

For the case of third channel, renewable energy has a significant and positive impact on technology and technology has a significant and positive impact on life expectancy supporting You & Okunade (2017), Fonseca et al. (2021) and Smith et al. (2009). Taking together both effects since they are both significant, renewable energy has positive spillover (positive significant indirect effect) on life expectancy through the channel of technology level confirming Hypothesis 3.

For the case of last channel; renewable energy has positive significant effect on urbanization supporting Avtar et al. (2019) and urbanization has positive significant effect on life expectancy supporting Bible (2013). Taking together both effects since they are both significant, renewable energy has positive spillover (positive significant indirect effect) on life expectancy through the channel of urbanization confirming Hypothesis 4.

Table 6. Panel VAR estimation results

	d_renew	d_co2	d_gdppc	d_tech	d_urban	d2_life
d_renew	0.549***	-0.056***	73.680***	66915.310***	7.40e-03***	8.46e-04
	(0.037)	(0.013)	(10.460)	(2940.080)	(2.22e-03)	(5.41e-03)
d_co2	0.810***	-0.167***	-391.984***	60733.280***	0.023***	-0.062***
	(0.035)	(0.017)	(20.041)	(3355.846)	(0.003)	(0.006)
d_gdppc	-3.46e-04***	7.65e-04***	0.924***	57.941***	-9.52e-05***	4.10e-05***
	(6.25e-05)	(3.33e-05)	(0.034)	(4.214)	(4.85e-06)	(1.38e-05)
d_tech	1.04e-05***	-8.89e-06***	-3.16e-03***	-0.150*	-3.37e-07***	2.18e-06***
	(1.96e-06)	(6.76e-07)	(8.12e-04)	(0.083)	(5.75e-08)	(3.81e-07)
d_urban	-1.252***	0.429***	1137.704***	-25896.100	0.829***	0.936***
	(0.288)	(0.115)	(101.660)	(23451.550)	(0.025)	(0.068)
d2_life	0.242**	-0.386***	433.066***	19593.330***	-0.056***	-0.380***
	(0.123)	(0.045)	(56.275)	(6363.295)	(0.011)	(0.025)

Notes: Six variable VAR model is estimated by GMM; country-time and fixed effects are removed prior to estimation. Column variables indicate dependent variables while row variables indicate independent variables. Reported numbers show the coefficients of regressing the column variables on lags of the row variables. Heteroskedasticity adjusted z-statistics are in parentheses. ***, ** and * denote significance levels at % 1, % 5 and % 10 respectively.

According to the results in Figure 1, a shock of one standard deviation given to renewable energy gives a positive significant effect on life expectancy. Hence, there is a significant and positive overall effect of renewable energy on life expectancy. Despite other channels that could not be included in the analysis, the overall effect of renewable energy on life expectancy remains positive and significant by including all possible channels.

Figure 1. Impulse Response Functions

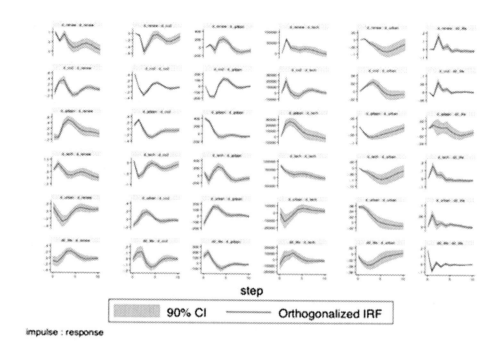

According to variance decomposition at a horizon of ten years in Table 7, forecast error variance of life expectancy is third most attributed to renewable energy by more than 26%. Hence increasing renewable energy is a powerful strategy to increase life expectancy.

With respect to the four channels discussed earlier, forecast error variance of life expectancy is second most attributed to technological advancement by more than 28%. The sum of all other channels is less than 10%. Hence the positive spillovers form renewable energy to life expectancy is mostly through the channel of technological advancement.

Table 7. Variance decomposition

	d_renew	**d_co2**	**d_gdppc**	**d_tech**	**d_urban**	**d2_life**
d_renew	0.398	0.251	0.162	0.356	0.284	0.263
d_co2	0.041	0.143	0.105	0.026	0.015	0.045
d_gdppc	0.098	0.127	0.342	0.099	0.188	0.011
d_tech	0.419	0.404	0.220	0.488	0.376	0.289
d_urban	0.025	0.045	0.082	0.016	0.092	0.037
d2_life	0.019	0.030	0.089	0.015	0.045	0.355

Notes: Percent of variation in the column variable (10 periods ahead) is explained by row variable.

CONCLUSION AND POLICY IMPLICATIONS

Renewable energy usage promotes green energy with least detrimental effect on health quality. An important determinant of health quality is life expectancy. The impact that renewable energy usage has on life expectancy can be looked at directly, via the significance of relationship between the two, or indirectly, via the significance of relationship through the channels that link the two. Although it seems that renewable energy has no direct effect on life expectancy, it affects life expectancy indirectly via the four channels of CO_2 emissions, GDP per capita, technology level and urbanization in emerging market economies. That is, renewable energy usage impacts the level of CO_2 emissions, GDP per capita, technology level and urbanization, which further impact life expectancy. The present study analyzed the impact of renewable energy on life expectancy through these four channels for 23 emerging market economies for the period 1994-2015.

It is found that renewable energy usage leads to higher life expectancy, since higher renewable energy usage leads to decreased CO_2 emissions, which further improve life expectancy in emerging market economies i.e. the first channel. This conforms to our first hypothesis of CO_2 emission channel that links renewable energy and life expectancy. Based on these results, emerging market economies are recommended to have policies to boost their renewable energy source implementations to increase their renewable energy share so as to reach higher life expectancy, less mortality, good health and well-being. This is because increase in renewable energy use leads to lower per capita CO_2 emissions compared to fossil fuel use and lower CO_2 emissions are less harmful to human health since it decreases the risks of asthma and other respiratory problems, cancer and other damages to the immune system, endocrine and reproductive systems. This requires a shift in policy approach for energy usage to be inclined towards encouraging higher share of renewable sources and reducing CO_2 emissions, and aligning these policies to the healthcare policies.

The study also finds that renewable energy usage leads to higher life expectancy, since higher renewable energy usage leads to higher GDP per capita, which further improve life expectancy in emerging market economies i.e. the second channel. This conforms to the second hypothesis of GDP per capita channel that links renewable energy and life expectancy. Based on this, emerging market economies are recommended to increase their share of renewable energy use since it generates higher income per capita levels and economic growth that is sustainable. The increase in income per capita comes from efficient usage of energy that adds to cost effectiveness by reducing the need for budgetary allocation towards energy consumption. This reduces opportunity cost of energy consumed and increases levels of per capita income. Higher level of per capita income further increases life expectancy by allowing higher disposal of finances for gaining access to better healthcare services and sanitation facilities. Increase in income per capita also raises the demand for health insurance, thereby creating an environment conducive for advancements in medicine and health infrastructure. This requires aligning economic policies to policies of energy consumption and healthcare, such that competing objectives can be eliminated. For example, the growth strategy in emerging market economies should include additional energy capacity building via renewable sources and the long term expected savings from the same should be channelized towards (a) employment policies that increase income per capita and (b) healthcare services.

Further, the study has found evidence that renewable energy usage leads to higher life expectancy, since higher renewable energy usage leads to advancing technology, which further improves life expectancy in emerging market economies i.e. the third channel. This conforms to the third hypothesis of technological advancement channel which links renewable energy and life expectancy. Hence, emerging market economies are recommended to boost their renewable energy capacity by additional renewable energy installation and infrastructure expansion since it subsequently impacts R&D, innovation initiatives and patent penetration not only in the renewable energy sector, but spills over to other sectors as well, adding further to technological advancement. Technological advancement increases life expectancy via advancement in medical knowledge, better access to medical information, improved food safety and sanitation standards, advancements in cost-effective medical equipments, vaccines and other health services ultimately increasing life expectancy. This requires re-defining policies for technological advancements in both energy and medical sectors. Renewable source oriented energy consumption goes hand in hand with technical advancements in energy usage that has a spillover effect on the medical technologies as well. Hence, a unified approach is needed while framing policies for expanding renewable energy and technology.

Lastly, the study finds that renewable energy leads to higher life expectancy, since higher renewable energy usage leads to increasing urbanization, which further improves life expectancy in emerging market economies i.e. the fourth channel. This conforms to the fourth hypothesis of urbanization channel which links renewable energy and life expectancy. Thus, it is recommended that emerging market economies should encourage usage of renewable energy because it makes available cost-effective, clean and green energy and helps in sustainable GDP growth. This further creates employment avenues and improves standard of living, which increases migration from rural to urban areas leading to higher urbanization. In turn, higher urbanization leads to higher life expectancy because of the provision of better education and health facilities. With urbanization, there is ease of access to social and public services that creates a suitable environment for better healthcare. Apart from that, higher earnings in urban areas increase the capacity and willingness on the part of public to pay for such services. This makes budgetary priorities of urban government bodies incline towards improving the quality of social and health services. Policy requisites for the same would include a well chalked out urban sector plan that encompasses energy demand from renewable sources, along with appropriate prioritization of the healthcare sector.

REFERENCES

Abrigo, M. R., & Love, I. (2016). Estimation of panel vector autoregression in Stata. *The Stata Journal*, *16*(3), 778–804. doi:10.1177/1536867X1601600314

Ahmed, M. M., & Shimada, K. (2019). The effect of renewable energy consumption on sustainable economic development: Evidence from emerging and developing economies. *Energies*, *12*(15), 2954. doi:10.3390/en12152954

Avtar, R., Tripathi, S., Aggarwal, A. K., & Kumar, P. (2019). Population–urbanization–energy Nexus: A review. *Resources*, *8*(3), 136. doi:10.3390/resources8030136

Balan, F. (2016). Environmental quality and its human health effects: A causal analysis for the EU- 25. *International Journal of Applied Economics*, *13*(1), 57–71.

Bekhet, H. A., Matar, A., & Yasmin, T. (2017). CO2 emissions, energy consumption, economic growth, and financial development in GCC countries: Dynamic simultaneous equation models. *Renewable & Sustainable Energy Reviews*, *70*, 117–132. doi:10.1016/j.rser.2016.11.089

Bible, M. (2013). The impacts of Côte d'Ivoire's urbanization on its economy and populace. *Global Majority E-Journal*, *4*(2), 94–105.

Bilgili, F., Koçak, E., & Bulut, Ü. (2016). The dynamic impact of renewable energy consumption on CO2 emissions: A revisited Environmental Kuznets Curve approach. *Renewable & Sustainable Energy Reviews*, *54*, 838–845. doi:10.1016/j.rser.2015.10.080

Bilan, Y., Streimikiene, D., Vasylieva, T., Lyulyov, O., Pimonenko, T., & Pavlyk, A. (2019). Linking between renewable energy, CO2 emissions, and economic growth: Challenges for candidates and potential candidates for the EU membership. *Sustainability*, *11*(6), 1528. doi:10.3390u11061528

Burton, M., & Wong, J. (2021). *Australian teens lead class action against Whitehaven's coal mine expansion*. Thompson Reuters Foundation News. https://news.trust.org/item/20210301061639-sel6u

Caruso, G., Colantonio, E., & Gattone, S. A. (2020). Relationships between renewable energy consumption, social factors, and health: A panel vector auto regression analysis of a cluster of 12 EU countries. *Sustainability*, *12*(7), 2915. doi:10.3390u12072915

Fonseca, R., Michaud, P. C., Galama, T., & Kapteyn, A. (2021). Accounting for the rise of health spending and longevity. *Journal of the European Economic Association*, *19*(1), 536–579. doi:10.1093/jeea/jvaa003 PMID:33679266

Gohlke, J. M., Thomas, R., Woodward, A., Campbell-Lendrum, D., Prüss-Üstün, A., Hales, S., & Portier, C. J. (2011). Estimating the global public health implications of electricity and coal consumption. *Environmental Health Perspectives*, *119*(6), 821–826. doi:10.1289/ehp.1002241 PMID:21339091

Love, I., & Zicchino, L. (2006). Financial development and dynamic investment behavior: Evidence from panel VAR. *The Quarterly Review of Economics and Finance*, *46*(2), 190–210. doi:10.1016/j.qref.2005.11.007

Mahyar, H. (2016). Economic growth and life expectancy: The case of Iran. *Studies in Business and Economics*, *11*(1), 80–87. doi:10.1515be-2016-0007

Miladinov, G. (2020). Socioeconomic development and life expectancy relationship: Evidence from the EU accession candidate countries. *Genus*, *76*(1), 1–20. doi:10.118641118-019-0071-0

Mithas, S., Khuntia, J., & Agarwal, R. (2009). Information technology and life expectancy: A country-level analysis. *ICIS 2009 Proceedings*, 146.

Marinaş, M. C., Dinu, M., Socol, A. G., & Socol, C. (2018). Renewable energy consumption and economic growth. Causality relationship in Central and Eastern European countries. *PLoS One*, *13*(10), e0202951. doi:10.1371/journal.pone.0202951 PMID:30296307

Martins, F., Felgueiras, C., Smitkova, M., & Caetano, N. (2019). Analysis of fossil fuel energy consumption and environmental impacts in European countries. *Energies*, *12*(6), 964. doi:10.3390/en12060964

Osabohien, R., Aderemi, T., Akindele, D. B., & Okoh, J. I. (2020). *Carbon Emissions and Life Expectancy in Nigeria*. Academic Press.

Pesaran, M. H. (2007). A simple panel unit root test in the presence of cross-section dependence. *Journal of Applied Econometrics*, 22(2), 265–312. doi:10.1002/jae.951

Pyrkov, T. V., Avchaciov, K., Tarkhov, A. E., Menshikov, L. I., Gudkov, A. V., & Fedichev, P. O. (2019). Longitudinal analysis of blood markers reveals progressive loss of resilience and predicts ultimate limit of human lifespan. *bioRxiv, 618876*. Advance online publication. doi:10.1101/618876

Qi, T., Zhang, X., & Karplus, V. J. (2014). The energy and CO_2 emissions impact of renewable energy development in China. *Energy Policy*, 68, 60–69. doi:10.1016/j.enpol.2013.12.035

Rasoulinezhad, E., Taghizadeh-Hesary, F., & Taghizadeh-Hesary, F. (2020). How is mortality affected by fossil fuel consumption, CO_2 emissions and economic factors in CIS region? *Energies*, 13(9), 2255. doi:10.3390/en13092255

Ranalder, L., Busch, H., Hansen, T., Brommer, M., Couture, T., Gibb, D., & Sverrisson, F. (2020). *Renewables in Cities 2021 Global Status Report*. Academic Press.

Roser, M., Ortiz-Ospina, E., & Ritchie, H. (2013). *Life Expectancy*. Retrieved from: https://ourworldindata.org/life-expectancy

Shahbaz, M., Raghutla, C., Chittedi, K. R., Jiao, Z., & Vo, X. V. (2020). The effect of renewable energy consumption on economic growth: Evidence from the renewable energy country attractive index. *Energy*, 207, 118162. doi:10.1016/j.energy.2020.118162

Shen, L., & Zhou, J. (2014). Examining the effectiveness of indicators for guiding sustainable urbanization in China. *Habitat International*, 44, 111–120. doi:10.1016/j.habitatint.2014.05.009

Silva, S., Soares, I., & Pinho, C. (2012). *The impact of renewable energy sources on economic growth and CO_2 emissions: A SVAR approach*. Academic Press.

Smith, S., Newhouse, J. P., & Freeland, M. S. (2009). Income, insurance, and technology: Why does health spending outpace economic growth? *Health Affairs*, 28(5), 1276–1284. doi:10.1377/hlthaff.28.5.1276 PMID:19738242

Smith, K. R., Frumkin, H., Balakrishnan, K., Butler, C. D., Chafe, Z. A., Fairlie, I., ... Schneider, M. (2013). Energy and human health. *Annual Review of Public Health*, 34. PMID:23330697

Steinberger, J. K., Lamb, W. F., & Sakai, M. (2020). Your money or your life? The carbon-development paradox. *Environmental Research Letters*, 15(4), 044016. doi:10.1088/1748-9326/ab7461

Steinberger, J. K., Roberts, J. T., Peters, G. P., & Baiocchi, G. (2016). Pathways of Human Development and Carbon Emissions Embodied in Trade (2012). *The Globalization and Environment Reader*, 396.

Sudharsanan, N., & Ho, J. Y. (2020). Rural–Urban Differences in Adult Life Expectancy in Indonesia: A Parametric g-formula–based Decomposition Approach. *Epidemiology (Cambridge, Mass.)*, 31(3), 393–401. doi:10.1097/EDE.0000000000001172 PMID:32267655

The World Counts. (2021). *How Does Pollution Affect Humans?* https://www.theworldcounts.com/stories/how-does-pollution-affect-humans

Torres, C., Canudas-Romo, V., & Oeppen, J. (2019). The contribution of urbanization to changes in life expectancy in Scotland, 1861–1910. *Population Studies*, *73*(3), 387–404. doi:10.1080/00324728.2018 .1549746 PMID:30702026

Union of Concerned Scientists. (2017). *Benefits of Renewable Energy Use*. https://www.ucsusa.org/ resources/benefits-renewable-energy-use

University of Leeds. (2020, March 26). Longer lives not dependent on increased energy use. *ScienceDaily*. Retrieved May 21, 2021 from www.sciencedaily.com/releases/2020/03/200326193906.htm

Wang, B., & Wang, Z. (2018). Imported technology and CO2 emission in China: Collecting evidence through bound testing and VECM approach. *Renewable & Sustainable Energy Reviews*, *82*, 4204–4214. doi:10.1016/j.rser.2017.11.002

Wang, Z., Asghar, M. M., Zaidi, S. A. H., & Wang, B. (2019). Dynamic linkages among CO2 emissions, health expenditures, and economic growth: Empirical evidence from Pakistan. *Environmental Science and Pollution Research International*, *26*(15), 15285–15299. doi:10.100711356-019-04876-x PMID:30929174

Wang, Z., Asghar, M. M., Zaidi, S. A. H., Nawaz, K., Wang, B., Zhao, W., & Xu, F. (2020). The dynamic relationship between economic growth and life expectancy: Contradictory role of energy consumption and financial development in Pakistan. *Structural Change and Economic Dynamics*, *53*, 257–266. doi:10.1016/j.strueco.2020.03.004

WDI. (2021). *World development indicators*. The World Bank. https://databank.worldbank.org/source/ world-development-indicators

You, X., & Okunade, A. A. (2017). Income and technology as drivers of Australian healthcare expenditures. *Health Economics*, *26*(7), 853–862. doi:10.1002/hec.3403 PMID:27683015

Zaidi, S., & Saidi, K. (2018). Environmental pollution, health expenditure and economic growth in the Sub-Saharan Africa countries: Panel ARDL approach. *Sustainable Cities and Society*, *41*, 833–840. doi:10.1016/j.scs.2018.04.034

Zakaria, M., & Bibi, S. (2019). Financial development and environment in South Asia: The role of institutional quality. *Environmental Science and Pollution Research International*, *26*(8), 7926–7937. doi:10.100711356-019-04284-1 PMID:30684185

ADDITIONAL READING

Okunade, A. A., & Murthy, V. N. (2002). Technology as a 'major driver' of health care costs: A cointegration analysis of the Newhouse conjecture. *Journal of Health Economics*, *21*(1), 147–159. doi:10.1016/ S0167-6296(01)00122-9 PMID:11852912

APPENDIX A.

Table 8. Variables

Code	Description	Source
d_renew	Renewable energy consumption (% of total final energy consumption)	[35]
d_co2	CO_2 emissions (metric tons per capita)	[35]
d_gdppc	GDP per capita (constant 2010 US$)	[35]
d_tech	Patent applications, residents	[35]
	Patent applications, nonresidents	[35]
d_urban	Urban population (% of total population)	[35]
d2_life	Life expectancy at birth, total (years)	[35]

APPENDIX B.

Table 9. List of Emerging Market Economies included in analysis

Argentina	Hungary	Philippines
Brazil	India	Poland
Chile	Indonesia	Russian Federation
China	Korea, Rep.	Saudi Arabia
Colombia	Malaysia	South Africa
Czech Republic	Mexico	Thailand
Egypt, Arab Rep.	Pakistan	Turkey
Greece	Peru	

Chapter 8
Prospect of Cow Dung as a Source of Renewable Energy in Tripura, India:
Viability and Challenges

Dr. Supriya Dam
Netaji Subhash Mahavidyalaya, Udaipur, India

Raghunandan Das
Government Degree College, Dharmanagar, India

Sujit Ranjan Das
Government Degree College, Dharmanagar, India

ABSTRACT

Ever-increasing crude oil prices across the globe coupled with high cost and sustainability concerns attached to hydro power generation led to exploring new avenues for switching to alternate/renewable energy than ever before. The present study sheds light on the prospect of promoting cow dung as an alternative source of energy with respect to tiny mountainous state Tripura and its role on socioeconomic development. Available literature provides the impression that energy from cow dung can be produced from biogas or by burning the dried dung to a power steam engine. The state has been blessed with cow dung across its rural centers, which are primarily used as bio-manures for agriculture and adjoining sectors. Centralized mobilization of these resources for energy generation have already paid rich dividends for states like Tamilnadu, Chattisgarh, Jharkhand, and other parts of India. This study examines the viability and challenges associated with power generation from cow dung for Tripura and presents a case for its adoption.

DOI: 10.4018/978-1-6684-4610-2.ch008

INTRODUCTION

Use of replenishable source of energy got prominence in recent decades due to scarcity of conventional source of power to meet ever increasing demands. Conventional source of energy like hydroelectricity, crude oils, gas turbine etc. are subject to high costs and non-renewable in nature (except hydro power) along with scarcity of storage capacity made it a one shot affair since its inception. Obviously, impending energy crisis in multiple fronts along with green environment considerations calls for carbon neutral efficient source of power (Mahapatra et al, 2014); with a propensity to renew it in accordance with ever-increasing demand. Escalating growth of population across India led to spurt in demand for energy (both as fuel and power) necessitates policy makers' attention to non-exhaustible source of energy than ever before. In this regard, Kumar and Majid (2020) stressed that an opportune economic situation coupled with strong government backing propelled India towards one of the top producers of renewable energy across the world. This in turn calls for a clear delineation between exhaustible and non-exhaustible sources of energy, dominated recent academic discourses, keeping in mind sustainability considerations.

Renewable energy is inexhaustible form of energy primarily obtained from wind power, solar power, geothermal energy, tidal power, hydroelectric power, biogas among others. Conventional non-renewable energy primarily generated from fossil fuel such as coal, oil, gas and nuclear energy likely to deplete with ever increasing consumption. As per estimates, close to 74 per cent of the energy resources are met from costliest coal and oil (as cited in Kumar and Majid, 2020, p1) and recent soaring of oil prices badly impacted the economies of third world countries. Again, amongst the renewable sources of energy, hydroelectric power considered as costliest form of inexhaustible form of energy and likely to have environmental hazards as well. In fact, Hudek et al (2020) amply remonstrates that hydroelectric power plants in protected areas cause severe impact on biodiversity and environment. In addition, greenhouse gas emission from hydroelectric reservoirs posing serious threat to environmental sustainability (Deemer et al, 2016) as well.

Recent literature demonstrate that cow dung has emerged as alternative renewable energy for biogas production for a country like India in which dairy farming widely practiced across the country. Gupta et al (2016) opined that microflora generated from bio-resources like cow dung have the texture to significantly contribute towards sustainable agriculture and energy needs not fully utilized as yet. Kumar et al (2020) argued that number of cattle and family size are integral for biogas production while its improper knowledge and cattle ratio lead to less than proportionate growth of biogas as a source of energy. Conversely, developing productive enterprise from locally available resources for production of sustainable energy will strengthen rural folklore, increasing economic opportunities and much needed employment for skilled workforce (Patnaik et al, 2020) hitherto underutilized segments.

As of now, the state depends on two sources of power generation, namely, hydro and thermal, for meeting the demands of consumers both inside and outside Tripura. Of which, thermal power generated from Baramura Gas Thermal Projects (BGTP) and Rokhia Gas Thermal Projects (RGTP) over and above of Gomti Hydro Electric Projects (GHEP) with combined installed capacity of 152 megawatts (MWs). RGTP has seven operating units followed by GHEP (three operating units) while BGTP (two operating units) in descending order. In addition, Oil and Natural Gas Commission (ONGC) Tripura Power Company's gas turbine project at Palatana (situated at Gomti district) has been catering to needs of people of the state over the years. Of these, thermal power accounts for 77 per cent of the total power generation of the state while the rest are met from hydro power. Obviously, number of powers generating stations, as mentioned above, failed to meet the peak demand consistently over a period of time causing frequent power cuts, fluctuating voltage, uneven distribution of power, lower productivity, low quality of life and environmental degradation (Bhattacharjee et al, 2008) among others.

Figure 1. Study area

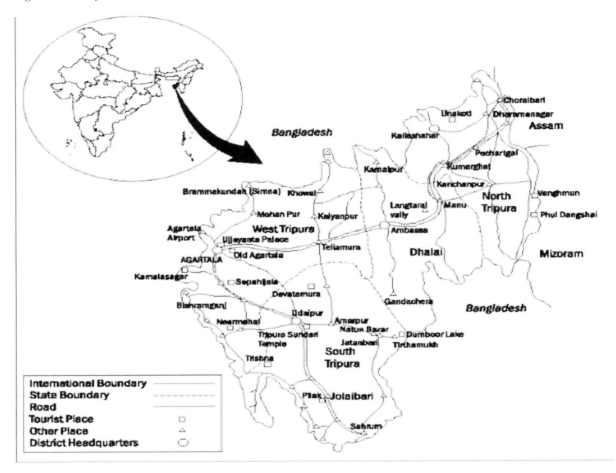

Again, Northeast Electric Power Corporation (NEEPCO) sponsored solar power plant at Monarchok, Tripura tapping non-conventional source of energy has been feeding to the grid of Tripura State Electricity Corporation Ltd. (TSECL) since its inception in 2015. In spite of these developments, the state found wanting in peak demand period resulting frequent power cuts largely because of productivity, capacity building and so on.

Present paper attempts to explore the possibilities of cow dung as a source of renewable energy with respect to Tripura considering its viability and challenges posed. Preliminary study has given us impression that, although cow dung as a source of renewable energy has not been explored as yet, easy availability of environment friendly cow dung along with energy friendly policy framework can replenish inadequate power scenario while reducing excessive dependency upon exhaustible gas turbine project in the state. Obviously, availability of undigested residue of plant matter excreted by bovine animal species provides the realistic opportunity to venture upon biogas plant. Again, locally generated power for meeting local needs on a small scale could reduce power loss of transmission over a long distance. As this segment forms integral part of priority sector lending schemes of Reserve Bank of India (RBI), financing for biogas plant can be extended upto 50 lakhs INR (5 million INR) especially for community based projects. In addition, recent reports suggests (Gupta et al, 2016, p4) cow dung as promising untapped source of biological waste can be converted into an electrode materials for other energy storage and conversion system as well. Given the propensity of usages, a thrust on cow dung based energy projects destined to address energy woes for the state in particular while providing employment opportunities for the locals within a given sustainability parameters.

OBJECTIVES AND METHODOLOGY

- To make an overview of process of power generation from cow dung;
- To shed light on cattle population and power scenario of the state over the years; and
- To provide a level playing field for promotion of power generation from cow dung for sustainable socio-economic development of Tripura.

The nature of this chapter calls for collection of secondary data from relevant sources engaged in this field of study. Information from central and state departments, reports, livestock population census considered integral for realistic analysis of the study. Similarly, international publications, journal articles as well as books and periodicals devoted to this are taken into account for cross reference. The information so compiled will be processed and analyzed by using suitable statistical tools as per need of the chapter. As the findings of the study rest upon secondary source alone, limitations associated with the same would apply.

This chapter comprised of five sections. Section I presents the thematic perception followed by objectives and methodology in Section II. In order to better understand the prospects, next section throws light on livestock population along with energy scenario of the state for the last two decades. Section IV dealt with process of generation of energy from cow dung followed by discussion on the issues cropped up (Section V) and conclusion of the chapter (Section VI).

Livestock Population and Energy Scenario in Tripura

This section throws light on livestock population and status of energy consumption for the state in recent times. Table 1 depicts comparative status of livestock population of Tripura vis-à-vis India during 2019. Ratio of respective species to population for both Tripura and country as a whole are taken as yardstick for assessing growth of livestock population during 2019. It's evident from the table that the state exhibits better ratio in cattle population (i.e. 0.179) in comparison to India's (0.142) for the period provides best comparative advantage for the state to embark upon. With respect to other species, state also have better pig-population ratio (of 0.049) as 20th Livestock Population Census 2019 depicted.

Table 1. Comparative status of livestock population during 2019

Major Species	India		Tripura	
	Nos	Ratio as per population (1366.4 million)	Nos	Ratio as per population (4.129 million)
Cattle	194362871	0.142	739031	0.179
Buffalo	109851678	0.080	7131	0.002
Sheep	7460615	0.006	5460	0.001
Goat	148884786	0.109	360204	0.087
Pig	9055488	0.007	206035	0.049
Horse & Ponies	342226	0.003	17	0.000
Mule & Donkey	207848	0.000	12	0.000
Camel	252956	0.000	02	0.000
Total	536317468		1317892	

Source: 20th Livestock Population Census 2019, Govt. of India.

Rest of the species does not offer reasonable comparative advantage for the state for the period under review.

Following table 2 highlights the demand, targets, and achievement of milk production from cattle population in Tripura during 2011-12 till 2019-20. This assumes great significance due to involvement of both government and community in catering these services in open markets pave the way for collaborative efforts in dairy farming of cattle population.

Table 2. Year-wise milk production in Tripura (000 Tonne)

Year	Demand	Target	Achieved	Annual Growth (%)	Consumption per day
2011-12	161.81	115.99	110.30	4.81	81 gm/ day
2012-13	168.56	116.00	118.04	7.01	84 gm/ day
2013-14	176.68	121.26	129.70	9.88	94.01 gm/day
2014-15	185.20	141.37	141.43	8.89	101.00 gm/ day
2015-16	194.13	167.97	152.23	7.79	106.87 gm/ day
2016-17	203.48	167.97	158.72	4.83	113.03 gm/ day
2017-18	213.29	178.74	174.26	9.14	123.00 gm/ day
2018-19	223.57	197.13	183.51	5.31	129.00 gm/day
2019-20	234.35	214.01	197.27	7.50	136.29 gm/ day
CAGR	4.20%	7.04%	6.67%		5.95%

Source: www.ardd.tripura.gov.in

It's quite evident that the demand for and supply of milk production have gone up significantly during the course of nine years. The compound annual growth rate (CAGR) of demand, target and achievement of milk production stood at 4.20 per cent, 7.04 per cent and 6.67 per cent respectively for the period.

There are notable surge in milk consumption per day as it was 81 gram per day during 2011-12 gone up to 136.29 grams per day in 2019-20 registering CAGR of 5.95 per cent for the period.

Table 3. District-wide spread of cattle population in Tripura during 2020

Districts	Cattle Population	%age
West District	89499	12.11
Sipahijala District	125849	17.03
Khowai District	67060	9.07
Gomti District	101284	13.71
South District	125692	17.01
Unakoti District	61690	8.35
North District	77278	10.46
Dholai District	90679	12.27
Total	739031	100.00

Source: www.ardd.tripura.gov.in

District-wise spread of cattle population (table 3) in Tripura shows wide dispersal across its geographical territory. Sipahijala (17.03%) and South district (17.01%) accounted for highest percentage of cattle population followed by Gomti (13.71%), Dholai (12.27%), West (12.11%) and North (10.46%) districts in descending order. Khowai (9.07%) and Unakoti (8.35%) recorded least cattle population during 2020.

Table 4. Electricity usage as a source of lighting

Locations	Year		Difference (%) (2011-2001)
	2001 (%)	2011(%)	
Total	41.8	68.4	26.6
Rural Areas (R)	31.8	59.5	27.7
Urban Areas (U)	86.4	91.6	5.2
Difference (R-U)	-54.6	-32.1	

Source: Census 2011.

Table 4 provides a good account of electrical usages as a source of lighting during the last census in 2011. It goes to show that total coverage and rural-urban divide has been narrowing during 2001-11 in Tripura but still a sizeable portion of rural households yet to be electrified in comparison to urban segment.

Table 5. Usages of fuel for cooking during 2001-2011

Source of Fuel	Year		Difference (%) (2011-2001)
	2001 (%)	2011 (%)	
Firewood	82.4	80.47	-1.93
Crop Residue	2.14	0.78	-1.36
Cow Dung Cake	0.1	0.14	0.04
Coal, Lignite, Charcoal	0.08	0.08	0
Kerosene	1.62	0.63	-0.99
LPG/PNG	12.91	17.64	4.73
Electricity	0.12	0.04	-0.08
Biogas	0.03	0.07	0.04
Others	0.19	0.08	-0.11
No Cooking	0.42	0.08	-0.34

Source: Census 2011

Usages of fuel for cooking (table 5) dominated by firewood especially in rural segments slowly but surely replaced by Liquefied Petroleum Gas (LPG)/ Piped Natural Gas (PNG) in urban segments across the state. Use of cow dung cake as fuel as well as biogas registered marginal increase during 2001-11. Usages of kerosene, crop residue, electricity as fuel recorded marginal decrease for the period.

Table 6. Generated and consumption of electricity in Tripura

Year	Installed Capacity (MW)	Power Generated (G) (MW)	Electricity Purchased (MW)	Power Consumption (C) (MW)	Generation to Consumption (GC Ratio) (%)	Rural Electrification (%age of villages)
(1)	(2)	(3)	(4)	(5)	(6)	(7)
1999-2000	85.35	314.18	259.15	366.34	85.76	79.80
2000-01	85.35	318.38	268.00	388.00	82.06	80.05
2001-02	85.35	283.73	332.00	350.69	80.91	80.36
2002-03	127.35	337.38	344.28	354.28	95.23	80.58
2003-04	105.00	501.48	178.08	423.38	118.45	95.91
2004-05	105.00	536.78	78.56	440.49	121.86	95.91
2005-06	110.00	487.95	623.81	438.76	111.21	95.92
2006-07	110.00	557.79	537.74	389.85	143.08	96.00
2007-08	110.00	620.22	511.51	397.81	155.91	96.00
2008-09	110.00	658.62	495.30	450.86	146.08	96.00
2009-10	110.00	658.38	421.00	465.00	141.59	96.00
2010-11	131.00	722.14	484.06	817.76	88.31	86.25
2011-12	131.00	816.58	435.68	888.25	91.93	92.07
2012-13	132.00	800.74	429.69	998.39	80.20	92.07
2013-14	153.00	763.70	729.31	1043.20	73.21	97.11
2014-15	116.00	756.94	1169.21	786.12	96.29	97.11
2015-16	116.00	723.64	1669.83	813.06	89.00	98.22
2016-17	115.00	87.00	270.00	284.00	30.63	100.00
2017-18	115.00	87.00	270.00	284.00	30.63	100.00
Mean	113.28	528.03	500.38	546.33	98.02	

Source: Tripura State Electricity Corporation Ltd (TSECL), Agartala.

Table 6 illustrates generated and consumption pattern of electricity in Tripura during 1999-2000 to 2017-18. Installed capacity, power generated, and power consumption registered incremental increase over the period of time recording mean growth of 113.28 mw, 528.03 mw and 546.33 mw respectively for nineteen years. State often resorts to purchase of electricity from relevant sources for meeting domestic demand reached alarming proportions during 2014-15 and 2015-16. The reasons for this attributable to consistent pilferage of power, unproductive uses as well as sale of power to adjoining locations for economic reasons. The generation to consumption (GC) ratio establishes relationship between power generated and power consumed indicative state's fluctuating pattern of growth during the period. Since 2003-04, the state gained momentum in self-sustaining growth in power front for seven years in succession which drastically came down to 30.63 per cent in terms of GC ratio during 2016-17 and 2017-18. The mean score of GC ratio stands at 98.02 per cent for the period. In a bid to electrify all the 901 villages, Tripura could achieve cent percent electrification drive in rural front during the course of nineteen years.

Table 7. Peak load and power scenario in Tripura during 2010-11 to 2020-21

Year/ parameters	2010-11	2011-12	2012-13	2013-14	2014-15	2015-16	2016-17	2017-18	2018-19	2019-20	2020-21
Peak Load	250 MW	282 MW	309 MW	331 MW	355 MW	374 MW	367 MW	396 MW	405 MW	414 MW	423 MW
Own Generation (effective)	79.5 MW	79.5 MW	172 MW	172 MW	172 MW	172 MW	172 MW	130 MW	130 MW	126 MW	126 MW
Central Sector (Share)	99 MW	149 MW	149 MW	149 MW	149 MW	149 MW	149 MW	149 MW	149 MW	149 MW	149 MW
Central Sector (effective drawal)	45 MW	45 MW	50 MW	50 MW	50 MW	50 MW	50 MW	50 MW	50 MW	50 MW	50 MW
Palatana & Monarchok share	100 MW	200 MW	200 MW	200 MW	200 MW	200 MW	200 MW	200 MW	200 MW	200 MW	200 MW
Shortfall/ surplus	-25.5 MW	42.5 MW	113 MW	91 MW	67 MW	48 MW	55 MW	-16 MW	-25 MW	-38 MW	-76 MW

Source: Tripura State Electricity Corporation Ltd. (TSECL), 2022.

Table 7 shed light on power scenario of the state during peak load period during 2010-11 to 2020-21. It can be noticed that, barring 2011-12 to 2016-17, Tripura failed to sustain energy needs of peak load period resulting frequent shortfalls in power segment. Situation has been quite pronounced since 2017-18 recording ever-increasing shortfalls in four years in succession despite power sharing deal with central agencies for the same. The reasons for such shortfalls during peak load period given rise to alternative arrangements for power generation keeping in mind locally available resources and its technology base from renewable sources of energy.

PROCESS OF GENERATION OF ENERGY FROM COW DUNG

Since the time immemorial, it's well-known fact that cows produce a lot of manure for use in agriculture. There are a whopping 1.4 billion cattle in the world that, along with other grazers, produce 40% of the world's methane totals. With respect to energy production, cows don't actually generate methane of their own rather they break down tough grasses with the help of microbes that reside in their stomachs. These microbes that produce methane as a waste product, formed while they are inside the cow and get excreted as bio-manure conducive for environment. Non-bio manures contain phosphorus and nitrogen in good proportions. These are useful elements in fertilizer but can get washed away as runoff to contaminate nearby bodies of water and generate more toxic substances.

Cow manure is now being used to generate electricity. This is just one of the ways farms can prevent harmful methane gas from being released into the atmosphere.

Firstly, the cow manure and other waste liquids are dumped into a digester. The shapes and sizes of digesters vary from location to location. The digester is an artificial container that functions much like a supersized cow stomach. This one, however, does not let waste gasses to escape. Instead, it captures the gasses for later use.

The facilities are kept at temperatures ranging between 100°F and 104°F, optimal conditions for the microbes. Inside of the digesters, bacteria break manure and other organic material down into smaller components (GE, 2010). Among the products are the gases, CO_2 (carbon dioxide), H_2S (hydrogen sulphide), and CH_4 (methane). The digesters then capture these gasses (sometimes referred to as biogas) for use in a power generator.

Figure 2. Process of Energy Production from Cow Dung

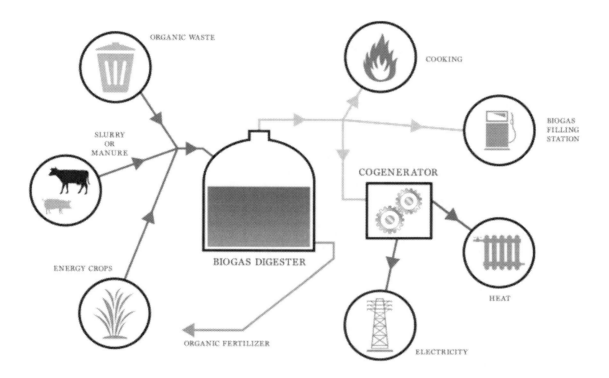

Most of us are familiar with the term, "natural gas." The natural gas that gets pumped from underground wells is primarily composed of methane (plus a few other trace gasses) that was generated by decomposing plant matter and which has been trapped underground for millions of years (GE, 2009). The bacteria that created ancient gas performed much the same job as the modern bugs found in cow guts. It is not such a surprise that methane produced from manure digesters is quite similar to natural gas, and either type can be used in the same burners and power generators.

There is a hitch to burning the resultant biogas, though, especially when it's done in bulk. The dangerous and foul-smelling hydrogen sulfide first needs to be removed or at least brought down to safe levels. When combusted, H_2S is converted into sulfur dioxide (SO_2). There are several methods to remove H_2S. With the more dangerous constituents removed, the methane biogas is ready for use.

With some exceptions, the methane from a digester is converted into electricity on site; the output is typically not enough to make transportation of the gas itself very economical. Instead, it is burned to boil the water in an onsite generator, and the steam turns turbines to produce electricity. The overall size and output of the generator, of course, depends on the output of the digester. Larger generators are more efficient, but some farmers don't capture enough gas to justify investing in a large machine. Farms can use the power on site or sell it to the power company as an additional source of revenue.

Bio-digester Design

Bio digester vessel was made from a 120 liters plastic drum of diameter 505 mm and 970 mm of height. The lid of the vessel was drilled in two places with a hot soldering iron, one at the right side for a 12.7 mm PVC pipe biogas outlet ducts and the other at the left side for a gas pressure gauge. On the sides of the digester vessel, the substrate inlet duct was created using a 50.8mm PVC pipe and ball valve while the slurry outlet ducts were created using a 38.1mm PVC pipe and ball valve. All perforations were properly sealed with rubber tubes and adhesives to make the whole bio-digester system airtight

It's worth noting that once a digester is prepared for creating methane, a number of products still remain. The leftover manure solids can still be used as fertilizer providing its usages in multiple fronts. These are typically drier than they were at the beginning, making them much easier to transport as well. The overall process can be described by the following reaction:

$$C_6H_{12}O_6 \rightarrow 3\ CO_2 + 3\ CH_4$$

Digesters capture the methane, preventing it from escaping into the atmosphere. Burning the methane releases thermal energy, which turns a turbine and powers a generator.

$$CH_4 + 2\ O_2 \rightarrow CO_2 + 2\ H_2O + Energy$$

The farmers use the electricity generated from burning methane to power their farms, heat their homes, and surpluses, if any, sell it back to the power company engaged for the same.

DISCUSSION

The state has been blessed with a number of power generation plants encapsulating thermal gas turbine, hydroelectric and solar plants across the territory. In spite of surplus power generation in multiple fronts, Tripura failed to address peak load period scarcity of power over the years resulting frequent power cuts, voltage fluctuations, low productivity etc during that point of time. Scenarios of this sort calls for a relook at the power distribution system across the state than ever before.

As the state make use of conventional thermal and gas turbine-based power generation for meeting 77 per cent of its energy requirements; these non-renewable sources of energy are bound to exhaust at certain point of time propelled policy makers to bank on renewable energy like hydro power, solar and wind power generation to compensate future possible uncertainties. Moreover, fossil fuel-based energy are extremely sensitive to the global changes, most often than not, results in increase in operating costs. These again raise the issue of capital and operating costs associated and the related sustainability considerations. In addition, the state lack quality water resources to back its hydroelectric power generation and the sole hydro electricity generation project situated alongside Gomti river is not in a position to meet entire future energy requirements of Tripura. Obviously, NEEPCO solar power plant through central initiatives is the only viable alternative in power front for the state unless new avenues are explored.

Table 8. Comparative analysis of capital and operating costs of different technology based power plants

Technology	Capital Cost (USD/kw)	Operating Cost (USD/kw)
Coal-fired combustion turbine	500-1000 USD/kw	0.02-0.04
Natural gas combustion turbine	400-800 USD/kw	0.04-0.10
Coal gasification combine cycle	1000-1500 USD/kw	0.04-0.08
Natural gas combined cycle	600-1200 USD/kw	0.04-0.10
Wind turbines	1200-5000 USD/kw	Less than 0.01
Nuclear	1200-5000 USD/kw	0.02-0.05
Photovoltaic Solar	4500 USD/kw and above	Less than 0.01
Hydroelectric	1200-5000 USD/kw	Less than 0.01
Biogas plant	400-500 USD/kw	0.0022-0.0039

Source: http://www.e-education.psu.edu./eme801/node/530.

Table 8 depicts comparative analysis of capital and operating costs of different technology-based power plants do not include subsidies, incentives or any other social costs associated. It can be noticed that wind turbines, photovoltaic solar and hydroelectric technology accounts for less than 0.01 USD per kw operating costs forms the core of renewable energy. However, capital costs associated with these technology-based power plants quite higher than fossil fuel based projects as well. Conventional fossil fuel-based combustion turbines and combined cycles have relatively low capital costs USD per kw along with high operating costs runs the prospect of diminishing returns once the resource exhausted. Biogas plant has the luxury of least capital cost as well as low operating cost amongst the technology options provided and best suited for landlocked Tripura.

CONCLUSION

Threadbare discussion along the preceding sections presents the viable environment for cow dung-based power generation to take off. Addressing peak time load of energy segment emerged as a major bone of contention for policy makers along with excessive dependence of power generated from exhaustible fossil fuel-based projects to date. Again, high capital costs associated with wind turbines, photovoltaic solar and hydroelectric technology based renewable energy hinders the growth of new avenues power generation. In addition, scarcity of notable water resources limits large scale power generation from hydroelectric sources along the geographical territory of Tripura.

Power generation from community-based cow dung projects with available low cost technology provides the possible energy generation opportunities to embark upon. As both capital costs as well as operating costs are in lower side, suitable policy framework on this front can see these projects light of the day. This, in turn, provides optimum use of locally available resources coupled with opportunities for employment generation for rural populace augurs well for economic development of the state. Again, losses of power in distribution and transmission (T & D) can be reduced to a greater extent from locally generated power on a small scale (ET, 2021) and its distribution thereto in the vicinity. State of Tripura poised to leap forward on this front with conducive technology and financial back up on the part of central government along the lines of successful Bharat Biogas Energy Limited, Umreth, Gujarat; in which 700 families got direct benefit under the scheme.

REFERENCES

Bhattacharjee, S., Ghosh, B., & Chakraborty, N. (2008). Renewable Energy Assessment of Tripura for Power Generation. *Journal of Resources, Energy and Development, 5*(2).

Deemer, R. B., Harrison, A. D., Siyue, I., Beaulieu, J. J., Delsontro, T., & Barrows, N. (2016). Greenhouse Gas Emission from Reservoir Water Surface: A New Global Synthesis. *Bioscience, 66*, 1–16.

Economic Times (ET). (2021). *Economic Survey flags high T & D Losses in Power Sector*. Retrieved on 25th February, 2022 from: https://m.economictimes.com/industry/energy/power/economic-survey-flags-high-td-losses-in-power-sector/articleshow/80585965.cms

General Electric (GE). (2009). *Co Jen – GE Energy - Jenbacher Gas Engines*. https://www.gepower.com/prod_serv/products/recip_engines/en/cojen_issue_2009_en/GE_CoJen.pdf

General Electric (GE). (2010). *Now You Can Have It All – More Innovation, Power & Efficiency – J920*. Author.

Gupta, K. K., Aneja, K. R., & Rana, D. (2016). Current Status of Cow Dung as a Bioresource for Sustainable Development. *Bioresources and Bioprocessing, 3*(1), 1–12. doi:10.118640643-016-0105-9

Hudek, H., Zganec, K., & Pusch, M. T. (2020). A Review of Hydro-power Dams in South-East Europe-Distribution, Trends and Availability of Monitoring Data using the example of a Multinational Danube Catchment Subarea. *Renewable & Sustainable Energy Reviews, 117*, 1–11. doi:10.1016/j.rser.2019.109434

Kumar, J. C. R., & Majid, M. A. (2020). Renewable Energy for Sustainable Development in India: Current Status, Future Prospects, Challenges, Employment and Investment Opportunities. *Energy, Sustainability and Society, 10*(2), 1–36. doi:10.118613705-019-0232-1

Kumar, K. A., Pinto, P., Hawaldar, I. T., & Kumar, B. R. P. (2016). Biogas from Cattle Dung as a Source of Sustainable Energy: A Feasibility Study. *International Journal of Energy Economics and Policy, 10*(6), 370–375. doi:10.32479/ijeep.10135

Mahapatra, R. N., Swain, R., & Pradhan, R. R. (2014). A Synergetic Effect of Vegetative Waste and Cow Dung on Biogas Production. *International Journal of Emerging Technology and Advanced Engineering, 4*(11), 184–190.

Patnaik, S., Sen, S., & Mahmoud, M. S. (Eds.). (2020). Smart Village Technology: Concepts and Developments. Springer. doi:10.1007/978-3-030-37794-6

Chapter 9
A Bibliometric Analysis on Efficient Use of Environmental Resources

Joan Nyika

 https://orcid.org/0000-0001-8300-6990

University of Johannesburg, South Africa & Technical University of Kenya, Kenya

Megersa Olumana Dinka

 https://orcid.org/0000-0003-3032-7672

University of Johannesburg, South Africa

ABSTRACT

The relevance of sustainability in contemporary society is on a growing trend owing to the predominance of economic development and environmental conservation plans amidst challenges of climate change. Eco-efficiency is a growing tool to qualify economic and environmental sustainability. In this chapter, the trends of eco-efficiency over the last three decades were evaluated in a bibliometric analysis from publications in the Web of Science database. An analysis of the publications, the journals they were published in, keywords used, and citations among other aspects was done using the VOSviewer software. Findings showed that the eco-efficiency concept was predominantly applied in the environmental sciences and technology fields among others. The growth in the concept was exponential, and the majority of publications were from developed countries. The application of the concept is a roadmap to better resource management and sustainable development.

INTRODUCTION

Over the last ten years, concerns regarding sustainability have increased in academic forums and in scientific fields as Caiado et al. (2017) pointed out. For instance, a publication by the United Nations titled, "The future we want" and an outcome of the Rio global conference on sustainable development in 2012 has laid bare these concerns (Leal Filho et al. 2015). The aim of these concerns is to develop a

DOI: 10.4018/978-1-6684-4610-2.ch009

pathway in which the quality of life will be improved for the current and future generations. With respect to greening and environmental sustainability, most organizations are proactively seeking for solutions and production processes that embrace eco-efficiency (Caiado et al. 2017). Eco-efficiency links economic performance (production and consumption) to environmental sustainability and is therefore, a valuable metric of sustainable development (Zielinska-Chmielewska et al., 2021).

Efficient use of environmental resources commonly known as eco-efficiency is an essential tool for sustainable industrial activities. The relatively new concept involves control of environmental effects of manufacturing and production activities and misuse or overuse of resources during the life cycle of products to prevent the earth from exceeding its consumption limits (Wursthon et al., 2011). According to Gomez et al. (2018), eco-efficiency is a transformational tool towards enhanced environmental value, economic costs and production processes with minimal negative environmental effects. The processes involved in this concept ensure multi-sectoral diversity in production processes using lower input quantities that ultimately result to reduced carbon emissions (Koskela & Vehmas, 2012; Li et al., 2012; Yin et al., 2014). Adoption of effective eco-efficiency entails both economic and environmental re-considerations of production processes using techniques such as indexes system method, stochastic frontier analysis, data envelopment analysis and life cycle analysis (Ji, 2013; Barath & Ferto, 2015). By value addition using fewer inputs for environmental sustainability, eco-efficiency has been widely applied in many fields of business economics, science and engineering among other anthropogenic and industrial activities.

With advances in eco-efficiency, productive approaches are moving away from short-term and adopting long-term profit strategies to provide clients with durable products. Evenly, clients are increasingly aware of environmental benefits of consuming newly designed greener products. Consequently, sustainable production approaches have become a competitive advantage for manufacturing firms (Czaplicka-Kolarz et al. 2013). Although there are benefits associated with eco-efficiency, some authors question if it represents overall sustainability change considering that it measures the environmental pressure associated with productive activities (Bonfiglio et al. 2017). To support this suggestion Czyzewski and Matuszczak (2017) were of the viewpoint that eco-efficiency is a measure of absolute environmental pressure levels. To demystify the actual trends in eco-efficiency and understand its actual output, an extensive analysis of research on the topic is essential.

An extensive assay of the current trends and data on eco-efficiency is therefore effective to track and monitor its application in various institutions and fields as the environmental sustainability debate advances. Bibliometric analysis is one of the suitable methods to track the concepts, technologies and emergent topics in eco-efficiency. Li and Zhao (2015) lauded the technique as effective in quantitative and statistical analysis of any specified research interest. This book chapter aimed at applying bibliometric analysis to assay the research trends on eco-efficiency application and provide insight in the area as well as advice on the future prospects in the field towards environmental sustainability. The research will promote the adoption of eco-efficiency in future production and consumption activities and make recommendations on how to promote research in the subject globally. Eco-efficiency trends in the last three decades (1990 – 2020) were assayed based on the growth in publication predispositions, journals, institutions, countries, citations and keywords using the VOSviewer software.

MATERIALS AND METHODS

The study approach used in this research involved scientometric analysis, which is assessing, assaying and measuring scholarly literature. In this case, scholarly literature on eco-efficiency was analysed and measured from the Web of Science (WoS) databases. Some of the databases included in the search were the science citation index-expanded, the social sciences citation, emerging sources citation, conference proceedings citation and the arts and human citation indices. The data collection was done in October 2020 from the Web of Science, University of Johannesburg, South Africa. The author used the keywords "Eco-efficiency" or "Ecoefficient*" or "Eco-efficient" on a "topic" basis. After completing the search, details of article journals including their full record (affiliation, publisher, date of publication, authors, abstract and full title) were downloaded. Using a filtering method, 2466 articles were obtained and downloaded alongside their cited references. The articles were used as the primary sources of the data for these bibliometric analyses. The exclusive use of articles was targeted to get the scientometric information from empirical findings (Nyika et al. 2021; Nyika & Dinka, 2022). Search years were not limited.

The VOSviewer software, which generates interrelationships of various bibliometric analysis aspects was used in processing the downloaded data (Van Eck & Waltman, 2010). Using the software, networks of citations, countries, journals, keywords and organizations were generated. The software uses circles and curved lines. Curved lines measure the relationship strength of various research aspects while circles represent specific items whose relationship is being quantified. Larger circles and thicker lines indicate highly ranked items and stronger interrelationships, respectively. Using the software, a bibliometric mapping of the article sources, subjects of searched articles, keywords, countries, institutions and authors' analyses was done. XLSTAT tools were also used in the growth trend analysis of the searched topic. The 2466 materials used in this study were not mutually exclusive since the total document types were 2681. The distribution of the material using both percentage and numbers were: retracted publications (0.04%, 1), reprints (0.04%, 1), corrections (0.08%, 2), book chapters (0.11%, 3), letters (0.15%, 4), news items (0.19%, 5), meeting abstracts (0.19%, 5), book reviews (0.4%, 11), editorial materials (1.5%, 40), early access (1.7%, 46), proceedings papers (2.5%, 67), reviews (5.5%, 147) and articles (92%, 2466).

RESULTS AND DISCUSSION

Categories and Journal Analysis

Category Analysis

Categorical analyses occurred using two approaches: 1) the Web of Science categories and 2) the research area. The former was based on the grouping of the database using its subfields and specification of subjects while the latter constituted of broad and general fields of study such as agriculture, business economics and engineering just to mention a few. The identified Web of Science categories were 137 and out of this total, 58 had at least 10 publications. The twenty highest categories are shown in Table 1.

Table 1. Top 20 Web of Science categories identified

Rank	Web of Science Categories	Records	Percentage (%)
1	Environmental sciences	1,177	43.9
2	Green sustainable science technology	791	29.5
3	Engineering environmental	700	26.1
4	Environmental studies	329	12.3
5	Energy fuels	180	6.7
6	Materials science multidisciplinary	171	6.4
7	Economics	170	6.3
8	Management	166	6.2
9	Construction building technology	142	5.3
10	Engineering chemical	137	5.1
11	Engineering civil	127	4.7
12	Chemistry multidisciplinary	109	4.1
13	Operations research management science	104	3.9
14	Ecology	84	3.1
15	Business	80	3.0
16	Engineering manufacturing	67	2.5
17	Engineering industrial	56	2.1
18	Chemistry physical	49	1.8
19	Water resources	48	1.8
20	Biotechnology applied microbiology	43	1.6

Overall, 78 research categories were identified and out of the total, 36 had more than 10 publications. Twenty of the highest categories identified are shown in Table 2. The two categories confirmed that most of the studies related to eco-efficiency are carried out in environmental sciences and engineering fields. Science technology studies on greening and sustainability as well as business economics also had a larger share of the publications. Although these categories dominated in the number of published articles, it was evident from the high number of research (78) and Web of Science (137) categories that eco-efficiency research spans across many disciplines.

Table 2. Top 20 research categories identified

Rank	Research Categories	Records	Percentage (%)
1	Environmental sciences ecology	1324	49.4
2	Engineering	1066	39.8
3	Science technology other topics	826	30.8
4	Business economics	374	14.0
5	Material science	213	7.9
6	Chemistry	182	6.8
7	Energy fuels	180	6.7
8	Construction building technology	142	5.3
9	Operations research management science	104	3.9
10	Agriculture	103	3.8
11	Water resources	48	1.8
12	Biotechnology applied microbiology	43	1.6
13	Public administration	43	1.6
14	Computer science	41	1.5
15	Transportation	36	1.3
16	Biodiversity conservation	32	1.2
17	Social sciences other topics	32	1.2
18	Food science technology	31	1.2
19	Thermodynamics	31	1.2
20	Physics	25	0.9

Journal Analysis

Web of Science search resulted to 2466 articles that had information on eco-efficiency in a period of 30 years. Of this total, only 33 journals had 10 or more articles records. Table 3 shows 20 journals with the highest number of publications. The Journal of Cleaner Production, which publishes information related to environmental sustainability and cleaner production practices, recorded the highest number of archived articles. Total articles retrieved from the journal were 409 representing 16.6% of the total. The Sustainability journal that publicizes issues to do with social, economic, cultural and environmental wellbeing of humans had a record high number of articles at 110 representing 4.5% of the total. It was second from the Journal of Cleaner Production. Other journals with high number of articles were related to the energy, ecology, engineering, environment, science and technology fields.

Table 3. Identified journals related to eco-efficiency

Rank	Source Title	Records	Percentage (%)
1	Journal of cleaner production	409	16.6
2	Sustainability	110	4.5
3	Journal of industrial ecology	61	2.5
4	International journal of life cycle assessment	47	1.9
5	Journal of environmental management	47	1.9
6	Ecological economics	46	1.9
7	Environmental science and pollution research	44	1.8
8	Constructions and building materials	42	1.7
9	Science of the total environment	38	1.5
10	Resources conservation and recycling	34	1.4
11	Ecological indicators	28	1.1
12	Energy	22	0.9
13	Energy policy	22	0.9
14	Clean technologies and environmental policy	20	0.8
15	Environmental engineering and management journal	20	0.8
16	Energies	17	0.7
17	European journal of operational research	16	0.6
18	International journal of environmental research and public health	15	0.6
19	Production planning control	15	0.6
20	Waste management	15	0.6

The bibliographic coupling of the journals was represented using Figure 1. In this map analyses the minimal number of journals was 5. In the presentation, a circle represents a journal, which is connected to another using a curved line. The curve also describes the collaborative relationship of journals that met the threshold. The thickness of the curve signifies the strength of the link between journals while the size of the circle is associated to the number of publications.

Figure 1. Bibliographic coupling between journals

Growth Trend Analysis

A trend analysis of the publications, their growth during the review period and the total citations excluding self-citations is presented in Table 4 and Figure 2. From the analyses, a steady increase in the number of articles documented since 1997 to 2020 was evident. However, a record increase in publications on eco-efficiency was predominant in the last 8 years since 2012. The lowest publications occurred in the 1990s. A similar trend was evident for the cited articles whose growth was steady and predominant in the last decade. The observed trend of increased publications and citations on the topic could be attributable to the relevance of the subject, the increasing global awareness on the need for sustainability and efficient resource management in the wake of environmental degradation and climate change (Nyika, 2020).

Table 4. Trend in publication growth, total citing of articles excluding self-citations, total citations and citation report frequency

Year	Publication	%	Citation report	Total citing articles	%	Total citing without self-citations	%
2020	344	14.0	9261	5835	17.9	5558	18.0
2019	336	13.6	9755	6065	18.6	5796	18.7
2018	295	12.0	7468	4540	14.0	4320	14.0
2017	236	9.6	5942	3505	10.8	3340	10.8
2016	195	7.9	4719	2822	8.7	2680	8.7
2015	177	7.2	3826	2364	7.3	2240	7.2
2014	142	5.8	3006	1899	5.8	1813	5.9
2013	139	5.6	2204	1514	4.6	1446	4.7
2012	105	4.3	1688	1103	3.4	1042	3.4
2011	78	3.2	1358	854	2.6	806	2.6
2010	71	2.9	968	652	2.0	606	2.0
2009	73	3.0	781	506	1.6	464	1.5
2008	53	2.1	489	356	1.1	331	1.1
2007	49	2.0	346	245	0.8	226	0.7
2006	36	1.5	191	126	0.4	111	0.4
2005	45	1.8	131	77	0.2	62	0.2
2004	24	1.0	66	52	0.2	47	0.2
2003	23	0.9	36	29	0.1	26	0.1
2002	13	0.5	11	11	0.03	9	0.03
2001	14	0.6	5	3	0.00	2	0.00
2000	5	0.2	4	3	0.00	1	0.00
1999	7	0.3	1	1	0.00	1	0.00
1998	1	0.04	2	1	0.00	1	0.00
1997	3	0.1	1	2	0.00	2	0.00
1996	1	0.04	0	-	-	-	-
1992	1	0.04	0	-	-	-	-

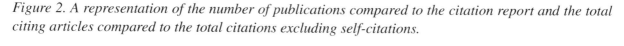

Figure 2. A representation of the number of publications compared to the citation report and the total citing articles compared to the total citations excluding self-citations.

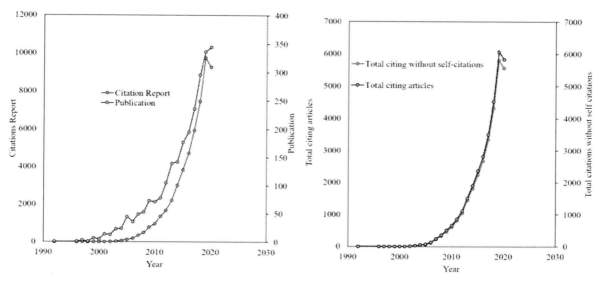

Details of the top 20 cited articles including the authors, title of article, the date of publication and the journal among other aspects are presented in Table 5. A review article by Mohanty et al. (2002) on the advantages and challenges in using bio-composites made from renewable materials has the highest citations at 1268. This is an indication of the high demand for cleaner and greener production towards sustainability in the contemporary world and at the same time being cautious of the challenges and opportunities ahead. An article by Armand et al. (2009), which focused on the use of two organic salts with conjugated carboxylate groups to make renewable organic electrodes, was ranked second with 606 citations. The two studies emphasize on the need to shift from non-renewables to renewables for sustainable development, which is the underpinning of this study. Overall, a high number of articles focus on eco-efficiency application in the fields of ecology, environmental science and technology, life cycle analysis and engineering. This trend is attributable to the close association in the consumption of resources, entrepreneurship, environmental management, industrialization and the need for sustainable development.

Keyword Analysis

Keywords are also important aspects of bibliometric analyses and have been used in trend analyses, as is the case in a study by Zhang et al. (2017) in a bibliometric analysis on water footprint. This study identified 9568 keywords in the VOSviewer analysis and 708 conformed to the threshold. All keywords were 9568 while author keywords were 6495 and those used in the study were 3973. The co-occurrence links of keywords and the strength of their linkages is as shown in Figure 3. This study focused on the keywords with significant strength and were clustered using different colours in the generated map.

Table 5. Title, date, journal, research area, institution and citations of the most cited articles on eco-efficiency

Rank	Title	Author/Year	Journal	Research Area	Country/Institute	Citations
1	Sustainable bio-composites from renewable resources: opportunities and challenges in the green materials world.	Mohanty et al., 2002	Journal of polymers and the environment	Polymer science, Engineering	Michigan State University, USA	1268
2.	Conjugated dicarboxylate anodes for Li-ion batteries	Armand et al., 2009	Nature materials	Physics, Chemistry, Material science	Centre National de la Recherche Scientifique Univ Picardie, France	606
3	Stakeholder influences on sustainability practice in the Canadian forest products industry	Sharma & Henriques, 2005	Strategic management journal	Business and economics	Wilfrid Laurier University, Waterloo, Canada	555
4	Life cycle assessment of building materials: Comparative analysis of energy and environmental impacts and evaluation of the eco-efficiency improvement potential.	Bribian et al., 2011	Building and environment	Engineering, Construction and building technology	University of Zaragoza Univ Zaragoza, Spain	486
5	Product-services as a research field: past, present and future. Reflections from a decade of research.	Tukker & Tischner, 2006	Journal of cleaner production	Environmental sciences and ecology, engineering, Science and technology	Netherlands organization of applied science research, Netherlands	434
6	Life cycle sustainability assessment of products.	Kloepffer, 2008	International journal of life cycle assessment	Environmental sciences and ecology, engineering	LCA Consult and Review, Frankfurt, Germany	381
7	Life cycle assessment of various cropping systems utilized for producing biofuels: bioethanol and biodiesel.	Kim & Dale, 2005	Biomass and bioenergy	Energy and fuels, biotechnology and applied microbiology, agriculture	Michigan State University, USA	353
8	Eco-efficiency analysis of power plants: an extension of data envelopment analysis.	Korhonen & Luptacik, 2004	European journal of operational research	Operations research and management science, business and economics	Aalto University Helsinki, Finland	344
9	Circular economy: The concept and its limitations.	Korhonen et al., 2018	Ecological economics	Business and economics, Environmental science and ecology	Royal Institute of Technology, Sweden	331
10	The E factor 25 years on: the rise of green chemistry and sustainability	Sheldon, 2017	Green chemistry	Science and technology, chemistry	University of Witwatersrand, South Africa	311

Continued on following page

Table 5. Continued

Rank	Title	Author/Year	Journal	Research Area	Country/Institute	Citations
11	Cradle-to-cradle design: creating healthy emissions-a strategy for eco-effective product and system design.	Braungart et al., 2007	Journal of cleaner production	Environmental sciences and ecology, engineering, science and technology	Braungart consulting, Germany	311
12	The eco-efficiency premium puzzle.	Derwall et al., 2005	Financial analysts journal	Business and economics	Erasmus University Rotterdam, Netherlands	295
13	Recent developments in eco-efficient bio-based adhesives for wood bonding: opportunities and issues.	Pizzi, 2006	Journal of adhesion science and technology	Mechanics, material science, engineering	University de Lorraine Univ Nancy 1, France	290
14	Towards a national circular economy indicator system in China: an evaluation and critical analysis.	Geng et al., 2012	Journal of cleaner production	Environmental science and technology, engineering	Chinese Academy of Sciences, Shenyang, China	276
15	Eco-efficiency analysis of industrial system in China: a data development analysis approach	Zhang et al., 2008	Ecological economics	Business and economics, environmental sciences and ecology	Nanjing University, China	269
16	Measuring eco-efficiency of production with data envelopment analysis.	Kuosmanen & Kortelainen, 2005	Journal of industrial ecology	Environmental sciences and ecology, Engineering	Wageningen University, Netherlands	267
17	Consumption and the rebound effect- an industrial ecology perspective.	Hertwich, 2005	Journal of industrial ecology	Environmental sciences and ecology, engineering	Norwegian University of Science and Technology	265
18	Corporate sustainability and innovation in SMEs: evidence of themes and activities in practice	Bos-Brouwers & Hilke, 2010	Business strategy and the environment	Environmental sciences and ecology, business and economics	Vrije Universiteit, Amsterdam, Netherlands	258
19	Sustainable value added- measuring corporate contributions to sustainability beyond eco-efficiency.	Figge & Hahn, 2004	Ecological economics	Business and economics, Environmental sciences and ecology	University of Leeds, England	253
20	The link between green and economic success: environmental management as the crucial trigger between environmental and economic performance.	Schaltegger & Synnestvedt, 2002	Journal of environmental management	Environmental sciences and ecology	Leuphana University, Luneburg, Germany	248

Figure 3. Keyword analyses and their clustering

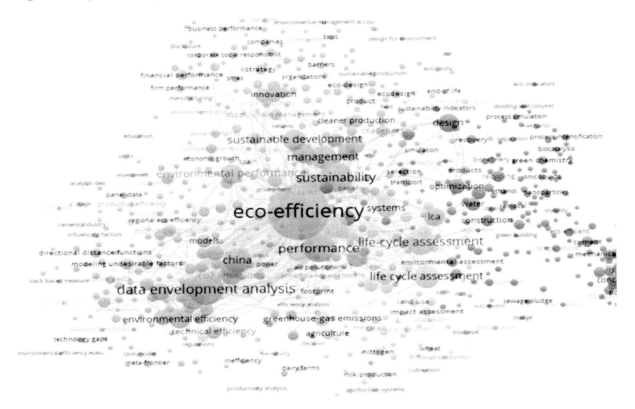

Four clusters differentiated using red, yellow, green and blue colours were evident. Keywords were represented using circles while curved lines represented co-occurrence relationships. The green cluster included words associated with eco-efficiency. This is a management technique of doing more with little. It involves creating more goods and services using fewer raw materials and concurrently minimizing wastes and pollution (Caiado et al., 2017). The second cluster that was yellow focused on life cycle assessment, which is a technique that assays the environmental effects associated with manufacturing of a given product throughout the production cycle while considering aspects of cradle-to-cradle and cradle-to-grave for environmental sustainability (Burnley et al., 2019). In this aspect, the motive is to produce more with less and with great caution on environmental conservation. The third cluster in blue grouped keywords related to data envelopment analysis, which is a linear programming based decision support tool that compares the operational efficiency of a variety of decision sets based on inputs and outputs (Xu et al., 2020). In eco-efficiency research, data envelopment analysis computes the weights of production inputs and outputs to rate the efficiency levels or otherwise (Mardani et al., 2018). The last cluster in yellow consisted of keywords related to life cycle assessment such as system performance, environmental assessment, impact assessment and greenhouse gas emissions among others. Life cycle assessment in eco-efficiency is a measure of how competitive and environmental friendly products or production processes are (Baum & Bienkowski, 2020).

Countries and Institutional Analyses

Countries Analysis

The first 20 countries with majority publications are shown in Table 6. From the 2466 records from Web of Science database, 102 countries were involved in research on eco-efficiency. China had the highest number of publications at 22.1% followed by Spain, Germany and USA with 9.1, 7.1 and 7.1% of publications, respectively. The top ten countries contributed to 77.1% of the total records identified. Most of these countries are from developed, industrialized nations and the uptake of environmental regulations is more stringent in the regions. The countries share a common challenge of sustainability and as such, eco-efficiency is a potential solution to better resource management amidst looming shortage especially for natural resources of finite nature (Li et al., 2020). Industrialization for instance in China has grown exponentially within the review period as noted by Wang et al. (2018) and therefore its ranking as first was probable. On the contrary, developing countries have not prioritized on the eco-efficiency incentive evident from the limited number of publications from those regions. A related bibliometric analyses on natural resource accounting by Zhong et al. (2016) made a similar observation citing the limited capacity for research in those countries compared to developed ones.

Table 6. Top 20 regions and institutions publishing on eco-efficiency in the last three decades (1990-2020)

Rank	Countries/Region	Records	Rank	Institution	Records
1	China	545	1	Chinese Academy of Sciences	111
2	Spain	225	2	Consejo Superior De Investigaciones Cientificas	44
3	Germany	175	3	Central National De La Rechrche Scientifique	41
4	USA	175	4	Delft University of Technology	33
5	Brazil	160	5	University of Chinese Academy of Sciences	33
6	England	155	6	Tsinghua University	30
7	Italy	141	7	Universidade De Sao Paulo	29
8	Australia	117	8	University of Science Technology of China	29
9	France	110	9	Polytechnic University of Milan	28
10	Netherlands	98	10	ETH Zurich	25
11	Countries/Region	Records	11	Universidade De Lisboa	24
12	Canada	88	12	University of Valencia	24
13	Portugal	87	13	Autonomous University of Barcelona	23
14	Finland	70	14	BASF	22
15	Japan	70	15	Institute of Geographic Sciences Natural Resources Research	22
16	India	66	16	Universidade De Aveiro	22
17	Switzerland	65	17	Aalto University	21
18	Taiwan	64	18	CSIC Institute De Ciencias De La Construccion Eduardo Torroja IETCC	21
19	South Korea	60	19	Islamic Azad University	21
20	Iran	51	20	Wageningen University Research	21

Figure 4 shows a bibliographic coupling map of countries with publications of eco-efficiency. The circles represent individual countries, and their sizes correspond to their publication activity. The curved lines represent the link between the countries. Countries with analogous colours are likely to have common citations in the various publications. Thicker lines signify greater strength between the countries.

Figure 4. Bibliometric coupling of countries with publications on eco-efficiency

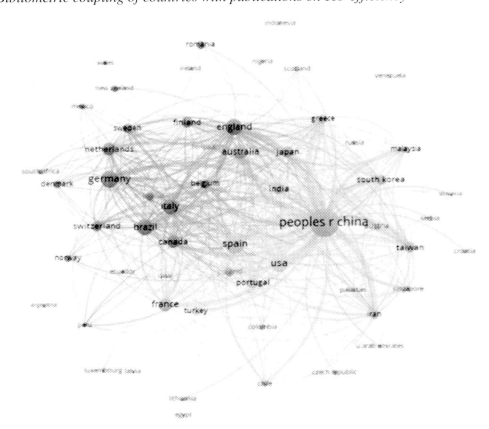

Institutional Analysis

About 2381 institutions were involved in eco-efficiency related publications and of this total, 204 met the threshold of the 5 publications. Table 6 shows the first 20 institutions with majority of publications during the review period. The Chinese Academy of Sciences, which is a national institution offering education and research opportunities on natural sciences, had the highest number of publications at 4.5%. The Spanish National Research Council (Consejo Superior De Investigaciones Cientificas) was the second highest publishing institution with 44 articles. Majority of the top publishing institutions were from developed and fast-developing countries such as Netherlands, China, England, Brazil, USA among others. The trend is affiliated to the high attention given to sustainability in such regions as Wang et al. (2018) noted. In the countries, eco-efficiency is a trade-off between increased economic output and resultant environmental consequences of involved processes (Caiado et al., 2017).

Figure 5. Bibliographic coupling between various publishing institutions

The bibliographic coupling of various institutions was as shown in Figure 5. For the VOSviewer analysis, the minimum documents set for each organization was 5. Research institutions of analogous colour signify joint collaborations for particular research works. A circle represented an institution and the curved lines showed the interrelationships among institutions. In this case, the Chinese Academy of Science that had the highest publications and the most interrelationships, which are conspicuous.

Author Analysis

Some of the top 20 productive authors are listed in Table 7 and all have at least ten publications on eco-efficiency. This author analyses depicts the extent of work in the topic of review. From the database Web of Science, 6415 authors were identified and 22 of these had ten or more publications. Geng Yong was the highest publisher with19 publications. He has conducted extensive research on environmental science and technology (Geng et al., 2008), supply chain management (Zhu et al., 2005; Geng & Doberstein, 2008), industrial ecology and management (Geng et al., 2014). His research focusing on the state and challenges of green procurement in China and in the category of data envelopment analysis has the highest citations that are more than 1400.

Table 7. Top 20 authors with the most publications during the evaluation period

Rank	Authors	Records	Rank	Authors	Records
1	Geng Y	19	11	Gheewala SH	11
2	Frias M	18	12	Kisss AA	11
3	Moreira MT	17	13	Kucukvar M	11
4	Feijoo G	16	14	Li Y	11
5	De Rojas Mis	13	15	Liang L	11
6	Oicazo-Tadeo AJ	13	16	Medina C	11
7	Iribarren D	12	17	Prata DM	11
8	Vazquez-Rowe 1	12	18	Tarascon JM	11
9	Egilmez G	11	19	Yu YT	11
10	Emrouzne Jad A	11	20	Burchart- Korol D	10

The interrelationships between citations of the various authors is as shown in Figure 6. For the VOS-viewer analysis smallest number of citations was assumed to be 5 and from this precondition, a record of 6958 authors were found and out of these, 103 met the set threshold. Authors were represented using circles and their relationships with others using curved lines. Similar colours in this context represent joint citations of a given publication according to Ertz and Leblanc-Proulx (2018). There was evidence of academic development from the various collaborations among different authors shown through their interlinkages.

Figure 6. Citation analysis among authors

FUTURE PROSPECTS OF ECO-EFFICIENCY RESEARCH AND DEVELOPMENT

Eco-efficiency in this context is a viable solution to economic development and environmental conservation concurrently. In fact, some authors such as Li et al. applaud eco-efficiency as, "…a representational index that reflects the coordinated development of regional social development, economic growth and ecological environment" (2020, p.2). Therefore, its inclusion in resource management and accounting of production inputs and outputs is a key component of sustainable development planning. It is from these prospects that this analysis shows that eco-efficiency publications share a lot of features with sustainability and in particular the component of environmental sustainability. Although environmental stewardship is essential and must be precedence, the reviewed publications point to the focus beyond eco-labelling and strict regulations on environmental management. This is because if given practices conform to and with the conditions of promoting economic growth and environmental conservation in the eco-efficiency analysis then their desire to enhance sustainability is beyond doubt. Therefore, providing metrics and indices to quantify the economic and environmental viability during production processes could influence sustainability positively. Inclusion of sector-specific aspects to cater for their particular objectives and quality standards is imperative. Such a measure ensures that in the improvement of environmental performance during production quality improvement and valorisation is not compromised.

To assess the sustainability levels and available options, eco-efficiency has the capacity to integrate tools such as life cycle assessment and data envelopment analysis evident from the keyword analysis. However, the focus of most publications is the environmental effects of the processes rather than the environmental and socio-economic gains of the suggested eco-efficient options. The future could therefore offers environmental, technical and economic efficiencies of suggested choices if eco-efficiency is adopted and decision support tools are implemented in choosing the most suitable production processes.

This review showed that eco-efficiency research is predominant in engineering and science fields although there is evidence of its application in non-engineering and non-science fields. This observation shows that the application of eco-efficiency spans widely and has huge potential in other fields in the road to sustainability. Aspects of local tourism and provision of localized accommodation services and eateries could promote use of local resources for instance. These prospects are viable and applicable using simple eco-efficiency models.

Most of the research on eco-efficiency is from developed and fast-developing nations. This is a wakeup call for developing countries to join in research related to this topic since existent evidence shows that majority of the regions in poor countries bare grave consequences of environmental degradation despite being less polluters. Additionally, the countries are exposed to endemic socio-economic challenges of increased solid waste, limited natural resources, starvation and hunger and are in urgent need for best practices towards better resources management and economic development especially in the climate change era. A considerable portion of their population dwells in rural areas and as such, global sustainability success depends on the state of the rural dwellers of developing countries mainly faced with dire challenges of poverty and climate change (Nyika, 2020).

The practicality of eco-efficiency from a broader viewpoint is imperative in achieving positive change in today's and the future economies. Majority of eco-efficiency publications evaluated are in academic institutions and a few in government agencies and industries. The future will need the participation of the private sector and non-governmental organizations and their partnerships with government agencies in research on sustainability aspects such as eco-efficiencies. Although, it is noteworthy that the Web of Scopus database will not capture government policy documents on eco-efficiency, there is need for a paradigm shift to engage in research on eco-efficiency using models beyond those generated by academia in the near future.

CONCLUSION

This research presented a bibliometric analysis on eco-efficiency research and provided an in-depth analysis of various articles, the journals they were published in, authors, countries, institutions, keywords and citations associated with them for the last three decades (1990-2020). The findings of this analysis showed that research on eco-efficiency has grown exponentially during the evaluation period. It was also evident that most of the publications evaluated in the topic were affiliated to business economics, engineering, environmental science and technology fields although the concept was also applied in other fields extensively. Developing countries were also shown to rarely conduct research associated with the topic owing to the little awareness regarding its importance, limited human and technological capacity to promote sustainable practices compared to fast-developing and developed nations. Most of the evaluated studies focused on environmental sustainability using data envelopment analysis and life cycle assessment. Rarely was the socio-economic aspect of sustainability focused on. Overall, the opportunity to optimize the benefits of eco-efficiency in many fields extensively is presented in this analysis but with caution to use simplified models not only from academia but also government and private sectors. Additionally, the models should be sensitive to situation-specific indicators and parameters.

REFERENCES

Armand, M., Grugeon, S., Vezin, H., Laruelle, S., Ribiere, P., Poizot, P., & Tarascon, J.-M. (2009). Conjugated dicarboxylate anodes for Li-ion batteries. *Nature Materials*, *8*(2), 120–125. doi:10.1038/nmat2372 PMID:19151701

Barath, L., & Ferto, I. (2015). Heterogeneous technology, scale of land use and technical efficiency: The case of Hungarian crop farms. *Land Use Policy*, *42*, 141–150. doi:10.1016/j.landusepol.2014.07.015

Baum, R., & Bienkowski, J. (2020). Eco-efficiency in measuring the sustainable production of agricultural crops. *Sustainability*, *12*(4), 1418. doi:10.3390u12041418

Bonfiglio, A., Arzeni, A., & Bodini, A. (2017). Assessing eco-efficiency of arable farms in rural areas. *Agricultural Systems*, *151*, 114–125. doi:10.1016/j.agsy.2016.11.008

Bos-Brouwers, B., & Hilke, J. (2010). Corporate sustainability and innovation in SMEs: Evidence of themes and activities in practice. *Business Strategy and the Environment*, *19*(7), 417–435.

Braungart, M., McDonough, M., & Bollinger, A. (2007). Cradle to cradle design: Creating health emissions-a strategy for eco-effective product and system design. *Journal of Cleaner Production*, *15*(13-14), 1337–1348. doi:10.1016/j.jclepro.2006.08.003

Bribian, Z., Capilla, V., & Uson, A. (2011). Life cycle assessment of building materials: Comparative analysis of energy and environmental impacts and evaluation of the eco-efficiency improvement potential. *Building and Environment*, *46*(5), 1133–1140. doi:10.1016/j.buildenv.2010.12.002

Burnley, S., Wagland, S., & Longhurst, P. (2019). Using life cycle assessment in environmental engineering education. *Higher Education Pedagogies*, *4*(1), 64–79. doi:10.1080/23752696.2019.1627672

Caiado, R., Dias, R., Mattos, L., Quelhas, L., & Filho, W. (2017). Towards sustainable development through the perspective of eco-efficiency- a systematic literature review. *Journal of Cleaner Production*, *165*, 890–904. doi:10.1016/j.jclepro.2017.07.166

Czaplicka-Kolarz, K., Kruczek, M., & Burchart-Korol, D. (2013). The concept of eco-efficiency in sustainable production management. *Zesz. Naukowe Ser. Organ. Zarz.*, *63*, 59–71.

Czyzewski, B., & Matuszczak, A. (2018). Towards measuring political rents in agriculture: Case studies of different agrarian structures in the EU. *Agricultural Economics*, *64*, 101–114.

Derwall, J., Guenster, N., Bauer, R., & Koedijk, K. (2005). The eco-efficiency premium puzzle. *Financial Analysts Journal, 61*(2), 51–63. doi:10.2469/faj.v61.n2.2716

Ertz, M., & Leblanc-Proulx, S. (2018). Sustainability in the collaborative economy: A bibliometric analysis reveals emerging interest. *Journal of Cleaner Production, 196*, 1073–1085. doi:10.1016/j.jclepro.2018.06.095

Figge, F., & Hahn, T. (2004). Sustainable value added-measuring corporate contributions to sustainability beyond eco-efficiency. *Ecological Economics, 48*(2), 173–187. doi:10.1016/j.ecolecon.2003.08.005

Geng, Y., & Doberstein, B. (2008). Developing the circular economy in China: Challenges and opportunities for achieving leapfrog development. *International Journal of Sustainable Development and World Ecology, 15*(3), 231–239. doi:10.3843/SusDev.15.3:6

Geng, Y., Fu, J., Sarkis, J., & Xue, B. (2012). Towards a national circular economy indicator system in China: An evaluation and critical analysis. *Journal of Cleaner Production, 23*(1), 216–224. doi:10.1016/j.jclepro.2011.07.005

Geng, Y., Xue, Z., Dong, H., Fujita, T., & Chiu, A. (2014). Emergy-based assessment on industrial symbiosis: A case of Shenyang economic and technological development zone. *Environmental Science and Pollution Research International, 21*(23), 13572–13587. doi:10.100711356-014-3287-8 PMID:25023655

Geng, Y., Zhang, P., Cote, P., & Qi, Y. (2008). Evaluating the applicability of the Chinese eco-industrial park standard in two industrial zones. *International Journal of Sustainable Development and World Ecology, 15*(6), 543–552. doi:10.1080/13504500809469850

Gomez, T., Gemar, G., Molinos-Senante, M., Sala-Garrido, R., & Caballero, R. (2018). Measuring the eco-efficiency of wastewater treatment plants under data uncertainty. *Journal of Environmental Management, 226*, 484–492. doi:10.1016/j.jenvman.2018.08.067 PMID:30145504

Hertwich, E. (2005). Consumption and the rebound effect-An industrial ecology perspective. *Journal of Industrial Ecology, 9*(1-2), 85–98. doi:10.1162/1088198054084635

Ji, D. (2013). Evaluation on China's regional eco-efficiency-based on ecological footprint methodology. *Contemporary Economics and Management, 35*, 57–62.

Kim, S., & Dale, B. (2005). Life cycle assessment of various cropping systems utilized for producing biofuels: Bioethanol and biodiesel. *Biomass and Bioenergy, 29*(6), 426–439. doi:10.1016/j.biombioe.2005.06.004

Kloepffer, W. (2008). Life cycles sustainability assessment of products. *The International Journal of Life Cycle Assessment, 13*(2), 89–94. doi:10.1065/lca2008.02.376

Korhonen, J., Honkasalo, A., & Seppala, J. (2018). Circular economy: The concepts and limitations. *Ecological Economics, 143*, 37–46. doi:10.1016/j.ecolecon.2017.06.041

Korhonen, P., & Luptacik, M. (2004). Eco-efficiency analysis of power plants: An extension of data envelopment analysis. *European Journal of Operational Research, 154*(2), 437–446. doi:10.1016/S0377-2217(03)00180-2

Koskela, M., & Vehmas, J. (2012). Defining eco-efficiency: A case study on the Finnish forest industry. *Business Strategy and the Environment, 21*(8), 546–566. doi:10.1002/bse.741

Kuosmanen, T., & Kortelainen, M. (2005). Measuring eco-efficiency of production with data envelopment analysis. *Journal of Industrial Ecology, 9*(4), 59–72. doi:10.1162/108819805775247846

Leal Filho, W., Manolas, E., & Pace, P. (2015). The future we want. *International Journal of Sustainability in Higher Education, 16*(1), 112–129. doi:10.1108/IJSHE-03-2014-0036

Li, J., Cai, C., & Zhang, F. (2020). Assessment of ecological efficiency and environmental sustainability of the Minjiang source in China. *Sustainability, 12*(11), 4783. doi:10.3390u12114783

Li, W., Winter, M., Kara, S., & Herrmann, C. (2012). Eco-efficiency of manufacturing processes: A grinding case. *CIRP Annals Manufacturing Technology, 61*(1), 59–62. doi:10.1016/j.cirp.2012.03.029

Li, W., & Zhao, Y. (2015). Bibliometric analysis of global environmental assessment research in a 20-year period. *Environmental Impact Assessment Review, 50*, 158–166. doi:10.1016/j.eiar.2014.09.012

Mardani, A., Streimikiene, D., Balezentis, T., Saman, M., Nor, K., & Khoshnava, M. (2018). Data envelopment analysis in energy and environmental economics; an overview of the state-of-the-art and recent development trends. *Energies, 11*(8), 1–21. doi:10.3390/en11082002

Mohanty, A., Misra, M., & Drzal, L. (2002). Sustainable bio-composites from renewable resources: Opportunities and challenges in the green materials world. *Journal of Polymers and the Environment, 10*(1-2), 19–26. doi:10.1023/A:1021013921916

Nyika, J. (2020). Climate change situation in Kenya and measures towards adaptive management in the water sector. *International Journal of Environmental Sustainability and Green Technologies, 11*(2), 34–47. doi:10.4018/IJESGT.2020070103

Nyika, J., & Dinka, M. (2022). A scientometric study on quantitative microbial risk assessment in water quality analysis across 6 years (2016-2021). *Journal of Water and Health, 20*(2), 329–343. doi:10.2166/wh.2022.228

Nyika, J., Mwema, F., Mahamood, R., Akinlabi, E. & Jen, T. (2021). A five-year scientometric analysis of the environmental effects of 3D printing. *Advances in Materials and Processing Technologies*, 1-10.

Pizzi, S. (2006). Recent developments in eco-efficient bio-based adhesives for wood bonding: Opportunities and issues. *Journal of Adhesion Science and Technology, 20*(8), 829–846. doi:10.1163/156856106777638635

Schaltegger, S., & Synnestvedt, T. (2002). The link between green and economic success: Environmental management as the crucial trigger between environmental and economic performance. *Journal of Environmental Management, 65*(4), 339–346. PMID:12369398

Sharma, S., & Henriques, I. (2005). Stakeholder influences on sustainability practices in the Canadian forest products industry. *Strategic Management Journal, 26*(2), 159–180. doi:10.1002mj.439

Sheldon, R. (2017). The E factor 25 years on: The rise of green chemistry and sustainability. *Green Chemistry, 19*(1), 18–43. doi:10.1039/C6GC02157C

Tukker, A., & Tischner, U. (2006). Product services as a research field: Past, present and future. Reflections from a decade of research. *Journal of Cleaner Production, 14*(17), 1552–1556. doi:10.1016/j.jclepro.2006.01.022

Van Eck, N., & Waltman, L. (2010). Software survey: VOSviewer, a computer program for bibliometric mapping. *Scientometrics, 84*(2), 532–538. doi:10.100711192-009-0146-3 PMID:20585380

Wang, Z., Zhao, Y., & Wang, B. (2018). A bibliometric analysis of climate change adaptation based on massive research literature data. *Journal of Cleaner Production, 199*, 1072–1082. doi:10.1016/j.jclepro.2018.06.183

Wursthon, S., Poganietz, W., & Schebek, L. (2011). Economic -environmental monitoring indicators for European countries: A disaggregated sector-based approach for monitoring eco-efficiency. *Ecological Economics, 70*(3), 487–496. doi:10.1016/j.ecolecon.2010.09.033

Xu, T., You, J., Li, H., & Shao, L. (2020). Energy efficiency evaluation based on data envelopment analysis: A literature review. *Energies, 12*(14), 3548. doi:10.3390/en13143548

Yin, K., Wang, R., An, Q., Yao, L., & Liang, J. (2014). Using eco-efficiency as an indicator for sustainable urban development: A case study of Chinese provincial capital cities. *Ecological Indicators, 36*, 665–671. doi:10.1016/j.ecolind.2013.09.003

Zhang, B., Bi, J., Fan, Z., Yuan, Z., & Ge, J. (2008). Eco-efficiency analysis of industrial system in China: A data envelopment analysis approach. *Ecological Economics, 68*(1-2), 306–316. doi:10.1016/j.ecolecon.2008.03.009

Zhang, Y., Huang, K., Yajuan, Y., & Yang, B. (2017). Mapping of water footprint research: A bibliometric analysis during 2006-2015. *Journal of Cleaner Production, 149*, 70–79. doi:10.1016/j.jclepro.2017.02.067

Zhong, S., Geng, Y., Liu, W., Gao, C., & Chen, W. (2016). A bibliometric review on natural resource accounting during 1995-2014. *Journal of Cleaner Production, 139*, 122–132. doi:10.1016/j.jclepro.2016.08.039

Zhu, Q., Sarkis, J., & Geng, Y. (2005). Green supply chain management in China: Pressures, practices and performance. *International Journal of Operations & Production Management, 25*(5), 449–468. doi:10.1108/01443570510593148

Zielinska-Chmielewska, A., Olszanska, A., Kazmierczyk, J., & Andrianova, E. (2021). Advantages and constraints of eco-efficiency measures: The case of the Polish food industry. *Agronomy (Basel), 11*(2), 299. doi:10.3390/agronomy11020299

Chapter 10
India's March Forward:
Progress on the Index for the Sustainable Development Goals

Shweta Sharma

Malaviya National Institute of Technology Jaipur, India

Unnati Tripathi

Malaviya National Institute of Technology Jaipur, India

ABSTRACT

The Sustainable Development Goals are a bold pledge by leaders of the world to establish a global agenda that encompasses aspects of the economy, environment, and society. India as a UN member has approved the "Agenda 2030" comprising 17 goals and 169 targets. This study intends to measure India's progress toward the SDGs by evaluating the performance of all Indian States/UTs using the NITI Aayog's SDG India Index versions 1.0, 2.0, and 3.0 produced in compliance with international standards. The findings of the study suggest a consistent improvement in the overall score of India from 57 in 2017-18 to 66 in 2020-21. This suggests a considerable improvement in state and UTs performance during the tenure. The study emphasizes that if nations have to adhere to the SDG goals by 2030, robust frameworks and indexes have to be designed and implemented in an effective manner.

1. INTRODUCTION

The United Nations member states created and accepted the 2030 Sustainable Development Goals (SDGs) in 2015. The Sustainable Development Goals (SDGs) originated from the Millennium Development Goals (MDGs) address the objectives left unmet by the MDGs and are envisioned as the conclusion of a long history of efforts by member countries and UN ministries (Nair et al., 2021). Since the Millennium Development Goals were adopted in 2000, the world has seen tremendous political and economic developments. The gains of growth were not dispersed fairly in many nations. Resulting in a decrease in economic welfare in response to the depletion of natural resources and other material inputs due to a rise in energy consumption. As a result, in 2015, the Sustainable Development Targets (SDGs) were created

DOI: 10.4018/978-1-6684-4610-2.ch010

to address these issues with greater ambitious, inclusive, and comprehensive goals than the MDGs (N. I. T. I. Aayog, 2018). SDGs have a greater reach than MDGs and apply to both developed and developing countries. Three pillars of sustainable development, are economic development, social development, and environmental protection. These characteristics set the Sustainable Development Goals apart from the Millennium Development Goals.

1.1 India and the SDGs

As the global economy shifts southwards, the countries like China and India are gaining economic heft and weight, and policy decisions made by these countries on sustainability will be heavily scrutinized. Therefore, these countries are already pursuing a progressive sustainable development agenda and are keen to lead and influence the future of sustainable development and global governance concepts (Chaturvedi et al., 2019). The world's progress toward achieving the SDGs is primarily dependent on India's success. India is a major contributor to the development of the SDGs, at the same time SDGs reflect much of India's National Development Agenda. SDGs' holistic approach is consistent with the Indian tradition, which emphasizes the harmony between living and non-living life forms, as embodied by the Vedic dictum *Vasudhaiva kutumbakam* meaning, that is, everything on the planet is related to each other. India couples its development process with the SDGs as well as emphasizes quality. (Chaturvedi et al., 2019). The Indian government is firmly committed to Agenda 2030, especially toward the Sustainable Development Goals. The Government of India has strongly pledged its commitment to Agenda 2030 and SDGs on various national and international platforms. Further, they have emphasized the significance of the SDGs on a worldwide scale, such as at G-20 meetings. The Indian parliament has made outstanding efforts to advance the SDG agenda by organizing a briefing session on the SDGs for members of parliament and bringing together legislators from South Africa and other BRICS countries to work together to achieve these goals. In recent years, India has accelerated several of its development initiatives, without misusing the environment and as a result, the economy and society are progressing well. India is confronted with several distinct issues. It is a vast country with population and language diversity across the continent. It also has a lot of geographical variation, including deserts, evergreen woods, and snow-capped mountains, as well as a lot of ecological diversity. As a result, India will have to face several challenges in achieving the Sustainable Development Goals by the deadline. In the last several years, however, there have been numerous successful projects and interventions aimed at achieving inclusive development.

India's Think Tank, the National Institution for Transforming India (NITI Aayog), is responsible for the supervision of the country's progress towards the implementation of the 2030 Agenda for Sustainable Development. Governmental support for the SDG goals drove the NITI Aayog to develop an index that could be used as an advocacy tool to encourage state-level initiatives. SDGs have benefited greatly from the efforts of the NITI Aayog, which has made a substantial contribution by sensitising various stakeholders, assessing progress, providing technical assistance, and encouraging collaborative learning among States/UTs. NITI Aayog has made substantial efforts to generalize the concept of SDGs in India. It has also successfully mapped the government programs at both the national and state level to SDG goals for tracing India's progress towards SDG. Apart from effective execution of policies, it is also important to assess the impact of the policies related to SDGs. Therefore, to keep a track of the progress the nodal agency appointed by the GOI is The Ministry of Statistics and Programme Implementation (MoSPI). The national indicator framework was created by the MoSPI in collaboration with ministries at various levels and in agreement with States and UTs. It has successfully linked the government programs at both the national and state level to SDG goals for tracing India's progress towards SDG. MoSPI has also been at the forefront of debates at the global level over the indicator framework for the SDGs.

1.2 Key Decision Makers: To Register Progress on the SDGs

Since 2016, the Indian government has selected and enabled its entities and institutions to register progress on the SDGs. India is a Union of States, with functional duties being delineated between the Union and States through the Schedule VII of the Constitution embedded in three lists namely (Union List, State List, and Concurrent List). As a result, coordination of efforts by the federal and state governments is critical for meeting the goals outlined in Agenda 2030. Since the policies are developed at the national level but State and local governments are responsible for planning, implementing, and monitoring the majority of the policies connected to the Sustainable Development Goals. (N. I. T. I. Aayog, 2019). Therefore, it is crucial to develop a genuine coalition between various governmental and private bodies working at the Central, State, and District levels to localise SDGs as illustrated in figure 1 in order to leave no one vague.

Figure 1. Institutions responsible for the execution of SDGs at the Central, State, and Local levels.
Source: The National Institution for Transforming India (NITI Aayog)

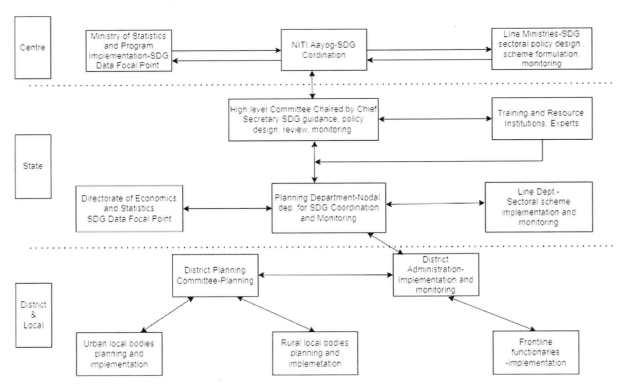

1.3 Introducing the SDG India Index- A Tool for Tracing Progress

Governmental support for the SDG goals drove the NITI Aayog to develop an index that could be used as an advocacy tool to encourage state-level initiatives (Chaturvedi et al., 2019). The SDG India Index is constructed on indicator-based assessment. Indicators are becoming an increasingly significant tool for tracking and evaluating sustainable development. The process of interpreting data from indicators to provide unambiguous policy recommendations is known as indicator-based evaluation (Salem et al., 2020). The SDG India Index is the first subnational government-led evaluation of SDG development in the world. This index serves a dual purpose: it tracks progress on the national development agenda as it relates to the Sustainable Development Goals (SDGs) and it compares the success of subnational administrations as well (Chaturvedi et al., 2019). The goal of the SDG India Index is to construct, popularise, and implement a quick and cross-cutting tool for evaluating subnational success in accomplishing the SDGs individually and cumulatively.

Using the SDG India Index, sub-national governments can compare their development to that of others and can identify the priority areas while promoting fierce competition on a route toward 2030. The SDG India Index aims to present a comprehensive picture of the country's social, economic, and environmental situation, concerning the States and UTs. Figure. 2. depicts the stages involved in the construction of the SDG India Index. The first edition of the index was launched in December 2018, followed by the second edition on December 30, 2019, and the third edition in June 2021. Goal-by-goal ratings of all 16 SDGs are compiled for each State and Union Territory (UT) to estimate the final performance in relation to SD. States and Union Territories are then ranked on a scale of 0 to 100 and a score of 100 indicates that the 2030 agenda has been achieved by a State or UT. The greater the distance to the objective reached by a State/UT, the greater the rating is. Based on their SDG India Index score, States/UTs are classed into four performance categories aspirants, performers, front runners, and achievers.

Figure 2. Levels involved in developing The SDG India Index

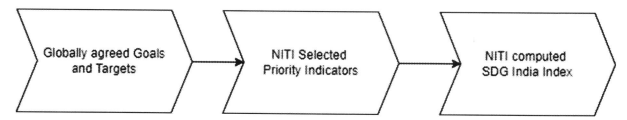

1.3.1. SDG India Index 1.0

The first version of the SDG India Index was created by the NITI Aayog which incorporated 13 out of 17 SDGs (leaving behind 12, 13,14, and 17) and was introduced in December 2018 through the SDG India Index Baseline Report. Using 62 Priority Indicators, the Index assesses each state and union territory's development in light of the policies and plans of the Indian government. In 2018 overall score of India was 57 (N. I. T. I. Aayog, 2018).

Technically sound quantitative indicators that met the following criteria were chosen to establish eligible metrics for the Index:

(I) Relevant to the Sustainable Development Goals

(II) In accordance with the National Indicator Framework (NIF)

(III) Data from official statistical systems should be available at the national level for states and UTs.

(IV) Prior approval from associated ministries/departments.

(V) Accountability of the ministries for the data sourced by them.

(VI) There should be enough data available in order to ensure that at least half of the states and territories are accessible.

1.3.2. SDG India Index 2.0

In line, with the first version of the SDG India Index, the second iteration was constructed and was released in December 2019. It is built using 100 indicators and covers 54 targets throughout 16 goals, except Goal 17, which is largely concerned with partnerships where National Indicators are not available (N. I. T. I. Aayog, 2020). For the reason of data availability across all States/UTs, 68 out of 100 indicators were obtained directly from the National Indicator Framework, while 20 NIF indicators were updated or improved. In discussions with line ministries, 12 indicators that were not included in the NIF were identified. SDG India Index 2.0 attempts to cover the first 16 objectives (indicators for Goal 17 have yet to be found in the NIF).

1.3.3. SDG India Index 3.0

With a larger coverage of targets, the third and current version (Index 3.0) is developed by making enhancements in the 2019-20 edition. This Index gave a comprehensive look at the social, economic, and environmental conditions of the nation and pronounced the progress achieved by States and UTs toward the Sustainable Development Goals (Tripathi & Reddy, 2020). The Index has been constructed in such a way that- policymakers, civil society, businesses, and the general public can put this to use effectively. Index 3.0 is founded on 17 Sustainable Development Goals and 169 goals. The values pertaining to the Index are calculated using data from indicators for the first 16 goals, with a qualitative assessment for Goal 17. It is made up of 115 indicators that span 70 targets from 16 different goals. While the majority of the indicators are derived straight from the NIF, due to data availability across all States/UTs, certain NIF indicators have been adjusted (N. I. T. I. Aayog, 2021). Among the 115 indicators in the SDG India Index 3.0, 75 are shared with Index 2.0. For 57 of these indicators, updated values were considered in comparison to 2019. 76 out of the 115 indicators are in line with NIF, 31 are drawn from NIF, and 8 are built in cooperation with line ministries. To calculate the Index, 109 indicators were employed; 5 indicators under SDG 14 were excluded since they only related to the 9 coastal states, and one indicator under Goal 10 was excluded owing to a lack of comparability. The 3.0 version SDG India Index is more comprehensive than the former version, with a larger range of objectives and metrics that are more closely aligned with the NIF.

The following are the aims of Index 3.0:

(I) All the states and territories were rated based on their performance in the 16 goals to measure how well each state or territory has performed with respect to a variety of goals and objectives.

(II) To encourage healthy competition among the states and UTs as they strive to achieve global goals.

(III) Assist states and territories in the identification of high-priority regions that need further attention.

(IV) To encourage the States/UTs to learn from the critical success factors of their peers.

(V) To draw attention to data gaps in the state/territorial statistics systems and identify areas

where more robust and frequent data collection is required.

A synopsis of all three editions of the SDG India Index is elucidated in Table 1.

Table 1. Summary of all the three versions of the SDG India Index.

Version 1.0	Version 2.0 (2019-20)	Version 3.0 (2020-21)
13 Goals	16 Goals + (Qualitative analysis on goal 17)	16 Goals + (Qualitative analysis on goal 17)
39 Targets	54 Targets	70 Targets
62 Indicators	100 Indicators	115 Indicators
Goal-wise ranking on States/UTs	Goal-wise ranking on States/UTs + State/UT profiles	Goal-wise ranking on States/UTs + State/UT profiles
Preceded National Indicator Framework (NIF)	Aligned with NIF: 68 Indicators completely aligned, 20 refined, 12 new to cover goals 12, 13 and, 14.	Aligned with NIF: 76 Indicators completely aligned, 31 refined, 8 in consultation with line ministries.
(I) Goal-wise ranking of States/UTs. (II) Promotes competition among the States/UTs in line with NITI Aayog's approach of competitive federalism. (III) Enable States/UTs to learn from peers. (IV) Supports States and UTs in identifying priority areas. (V) Highlights gaps in statistical systems.		

2. METHODOLOGY

The methodology for the development of the index was initiated in 2019 under the supervision of the Ministry of Statistics and Programme Implementation (MoSPI) in accordance with the Data and Methodology Committee. The methodology so developed is in line with the methodology of Sustainable Development Solutions Network. Figure. 3. illustrates the different phases involved in the creation of the SDG India Index.

Figure 3. Summary of Methodology adopted for formulating SDG India Index.

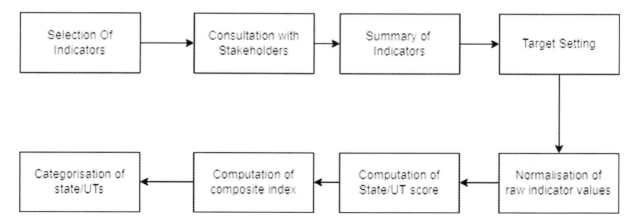

Following are the stages involved in developing the Methodology adopted for formulating SDG India Index:

2.1. Selection of indicators

At first, appropriate indicators from the National Indicator Framework (NIF) were spotted and mapped with the targets. In accordance with the NIF, NITI Aayog has developed a list of 115 indicators based on thorough consultations with Union ministries as well as departments and with all the States and UTs. The inclusion criteria for the indicators to develop a robust index are as follows:

(I)   The indicator should be relevant to the SDG goals.
(II)   The indicator should be in accordance with the National Indicator Framework.
(III) Official data at the national level for States and UTs should be available.
(IV)   Indicators having prior approval of concerned ministries or departments are considered.
(V)   Ownership of the data provided is assigned to the line ministries.
(VI)   Indicators concerning which data is available with the majority of States and UTs are considered.

2.2. Consultation with stakeholders

Stakeholders in the preceding context are the states and UTs. The list of indicators finalised in the prior step was then circulated among the stakeholders and their key decision-makers such as Chief Secretaries, Planning Secretaries, and Head of Departments to receive comments regarding the appropriateness of the indicators concerning conditions prevailing in each State and UTs.

2.3. Summary of indicators

The current and recent versions of the SDG India Index gave a comprehensive picture of social, economic, and environmental conditions pertaining to the nation. SDG India Index 3.0 is based on 15 out of 17 SDGs excluding (SDG 14 and SDG 17) for which data was not available from the majority of States and UTs. It is made up of 115 indicators which constitute 70 targets from different goals. Again, out of 115 indicators upgraded values have been used for 57 indicators with the reference to the 2019 version of the index. To assess the progress of States and UTs against the SDG India Index, a "null" value is assigned to indicators that do not have data from all States/UTs.

2.4. Target setting

A national benchmark for each indicator has been set for 2030 to be fulfilled by all the States/UTs. The indicators and set targets are distributed as follows:

(I)   The UN's global targets are adopted about 74 indicators.
(II)   Targets set by GOI are adopted in relation to the rest of the 28 indicators.
(III) Targets for nine indicators are in accordance with the international standards.
(IV)   Average of the top three scoring states is taken for indicators that cannot be determined in quantitative terms.

2.5. Normalising

For making data comparative across indicators, state-level data points for every single Priority Indicator are resized to their raw form starting from 0 to 100, with 0 designating the worst performance and 100 denoting achievements of the aim.

In the case of indicators where a higher value indicates improved performance (for example, forest area coverage), the outcome was calculated as follows:

$$x' = \frac{x - min(x)}{T(x) - min(x)} \times 100$$

where, x = raw data value, min(x) = minimum observed value of the indicator, T(x) = national target value of the indicator, x' = normalized value after rescaling. Scores were determined as follows for metrics where the greater value indicates lower performance (for example, poverty rate).

$$1 - (x - T(x))/(max() - T(x) X10$$

Here, x = raw data value, max(x) = maximum observed value of the indicator, T(x) = national target value of the indicator, x' = normalized value after rescaling the target values for indicators under goal 14 were not employed in the computation of the normalized score since the ideal value for the majority of them does not have a set value but rather lies within a range. As a result, the raw data for this target was normalized as follows:

When it comes to indicators where a higher value indicates greater performance, such as the Water Quality Index

$$\frac{x - min(x)}{max(x) - min(x)} X100$$

Here, x = raw data value min(x) = minimum observed value of the indicator, max(x) = maximum observed value of the indicator x' = normalized score after rescaling. An Index score of 100 has been set for States and Union Territories (UTs) if they exceeded the goal.

2.6. Computation of State/UT Scores

SDG India Index Scores were determined for every state or union territory except for Goals 12, 13, 14, and 17. After that, all of the Priority Indicators within a Goal's scope were normalized, by taking the arithmetic mean of those values. For the average, each metric was given an equal weighting, and the average score was rounded to the nearest whole number (Nigam & Pant, 2020). The goal scores for each state are calculated using the following formula:

$$I_{ij}(N_{ij}, I_{ijk}) = \sum_{k=1}^{N_{ij}} \frac{1}{N_{ij}} I_{ijk}$$

Where, Iij = Goal score for State I under SDG j, Nij = Number of non-null indicators for State I under SDG j, Iijk = Normalised value for State I of indicator k under SDG j.

States and union territories were classified into four categories for the SDG India Index, one for each of the 17 Sustainable Development Goals (except Goals 12, 13, 14, and 17), as follows:

(I) Achiever – If the score of States/UTs on the SDG India Index is equal to 100.

(II) Front Runner – If the score of States/UTs on the SDG India Index is between 99-65.

(III) Performer – If the score of States/UTs on the SDG India Index is between 64-50.

(IV) Aspirant – If the score of States/UTs on the SDG India Index is between 0-50.

2.7. Composite SDG India Index Score

The composite scores for each state in the SDG India Index and territory are eventually calculated to assess the overall progress made by the states and territories toward the SDGs. To compute this, 13 of the 17 goal scores were averaged to evaluate the arithmetic mean. To do this, each Goal score was given equal weight, and then the arithmetic mean was round to the next full integer (Nigam & Pant, 2020).

$$I_{i}(N_{i}, N_{ij}, I_{ijk}) = \frac{1}{N_{i}} \sum_{j=1}^{N_{i}} I_{ij}(N_{ij}, I_{ijk})$$

Where, Ii = Composite SDG index score of State I, Ni = Number of Goal scores for which State I has nonnull data, Iij = Goal score for State I under SDG j.

To get the composite SDG India Index score, the average score of all the targets related to each state and union territory is calculated and then rounded off to the nearest whole integer. In addition to this, the States/UTs are further broken down into four subcategories as discussed above i.e.: Achievers, Front Runners, Performers, and Aspirants.

2.8. Categorisation of State/UTs

The reach of SDGs across a multitude of social, political, and economic domains of life, as well as the depth of each Goal through the multitude of varying targets and the complex inter-relation and interdependencies between each Goal. Hence, it was decided to use a straightforward categorization technique. This was determined by comparing the scores of each state across all 16 Sustainable Development Goals. According to how far away the states were from the aim, they were divided into four groups. Accordingly, any state with a score of 100 would be referred to as an Achiever, since the state would have met all of the objectives set in the Sustainable Development Goals. Any state making 65 percent or greater progress would be considered a Front Runner, indicating that the state is getting closer to the objective than the other states. States with a population of more than 50 are considered performers. Aspirants are states that have not yet completed even half of the distance to the destination (N. I. T. I. Aayog, 2020).

3. NATIONAL REVIEW: TRACKING PROGRESS TOWARD THE SUSTAINABLE DEVELOPMENT GOALS

Globally, nations are demonstrating consistent support for the SDGs by creating SDG plans and monitoring its progress. Since 2015, over 140 nations have submitted a voluntary national review to the UN (Brown, 2019). The Voluntary National Reviews (VNRs), which are presented yearly to the High-Level Political Forum (HLPF) on Sustainable Development and are considered an essential component of the national review process (Allen et al., 2020). The Voluntary National Review (VNR) is a mechanism through which member states assess and publish their progress in implementing the 2030 Agenda, including the gain around the 17 Sustainable Development Goals and a commitment toward holistic development of the nation. VNRs are meant to examine how the country is progressing toward the Sustainable Development Goals by highlighting the gaps in accelerating the progress and by drawing out the best practice available for integrating the efforts made by states and UTs (OHCHR, Voluntary National Reviews).

Every July at the United Nations headquarters in New York, political leaders belonging to UN member states meet at HLPF to monitor and review progress on Agenda 21 (Chaturvedi et al., 2019). VNR act as the epicentre of the meet. The reviews are state-led and optional, to enable the exchange of experiences, such as achievements, problems, and lessons learned. The process of preparing a country's VNR provides a platform for collaborations, which can include participation from a variety of key parties.

However, these official government evaluations are usually narrative, focused on institutional procedures, discussions, and obstacles rather than offering a quantitative assessment of national progress concerning SDG objectives and indicators based on evidence-based quantitative assessments (Venkatesh., 2021). Quantitative evaluations of progress on the SDGs and goals have evolved as a new supplementary mechanism inside the SDGs' review framework. In recent years, a variety of evaluation techniques has been generated at (international, national, sub-national, and regional levels) by a diverse range of players on a variety of topics. This contains the UN Statistics Division's yearly worldwide evaluation of progress on the Sustainable Development Goals (SDGs). National indicator-based evaluations of progress toward SDG targets have also emerged as a substitute to the VNRs as a means of reporting progress toward SDG targets. In addition to this many sectorial growth assessment techniques have been released, which gave rankings to the states and UTs and drew comparisons among cities and provinces as well as throughout the country. (N. I. T. I. Aayog, 2018.)

Though early evaluations of progress may identify objectives and indicators where a nation is presently off course, aid in the prioritization of targets and the allocation of resources, and allow continuing adaptive management of the country's development.

3.1. India National Review: Tracking Progress Using the SDG India Index

Four of the world's main faiths have their origins in India. Cultural and linguistic traditions are distinct in each of the 37 subnational groupings. With a mixed bag of groups in the society, India is still rapidly developing on a path that promotes wealth and well-being for all people of all cultures and languages, leaving no one behind. This is the point at which India's development ideology and the SDG framework's key concepts collide (N. I. T. I. Aayog, 2020b).

In 2017, the NITI Aayog produced and delivered India's first VNR. Then, in 2020, at the United Nations High-Level Political Forum on Sustainable Development, NITI Aayog submitted India's second Voluntary National Review (VNR). In its second VNR, India has adopted a "whole-of-society" approach, including sub-national and local governments, civil society groups, local communities, vulnerable persons, and the commercial sector to form a partnership (INDIA, Voluntary National Review 2020). The process involved in the preparation of a VNR report is elucidated in figure 4.

Figure 4. Steps involved in VNR Report Preparation

In all, seven primary aspects were engaged in the report preparation process, which is described in full below.

3.1.1. The VNR Forum

The Confederation of Indian Industry (CII) and the WNTA – a civil society network have formed a forum to facilitate consultations with members belonging to NITI Aayog, the Ministry of External Affairs, the Ministry of Finance, and the Ministry of Statistics and Programme Implementation.

3.1.2. The SDG Taskforce

In addition to providing technical views on the Sustainable Development Goals (SDGs), the committee, which was already in existence, made comments on several revisions of the report before its finalization.

3.1.3. Stakeholder Engagement

One of the initial tasks was compiling a comprehensive database that included all of the important players from the civil society, non-governmental organizations, and big players from the commercial sector. This was done by November 2019. Fourteen demographic task forces were constituted, including individuals from specific areas. As a consequence, their problems, expectations, and commitments were documented. Which authenticated the creditability of the VNR report gains as it resulted from the observations and contributions of grassroots organizations.

3.1.4. Government Consultations

National, subnational, and municipal governments played an important role in the development of the VNR report. As they actively took part in the conclave conducted by NITI Aayog in 2020 on SDG together with various stakeholders including academia technical experts and industry personnel to construct strategies for various regions forming part of the SDG framework which later has to be executed by the State Government, Central Ministries, and NITI Aayog.

3.1.5. Communications

In November 2019, communication and outreach strategies was developed for VNR. The core elements of the VNR communication strategy constitute media outreach, short films, and the role of social media in educating the general public regarding SDGs via media campaigns. This media campaign was jointly driven by the UN and NITI Aayog.

3.1.6. Financing the SDGs

For the Sustainable Development Goals (SDGs) to be accomplished by 2030, it is vital that they are adequately funded. To estimate the funding requirement NITI Aayog, The Ministry of Finance and The International Monetary Fund (IMF) conducted collaborative research to estimate the cost of achieving the SDGs by 2030, which resulted in a yearly expenditure of 6.2% of GDP. That now has given a better idea regarding the monetary support required to achieve SDG goals by 2030.

3.1.7. Drafting the VNR Report

The contribution of various stakeholders including CSOs, the commercial sector, central government, state government, and UTs were compiled by the end of April 2020. Government papers, trustworthy research materials, and official records were considered to deliver the VNR report, subject to feedback and comments from states/union territories and other stakeholders.

4. RESULTS AND FINDINGS

4.1. Performance of States/UTs on SDG India Index, 2018

The findings of our study show that Kerala and Himachal Pradesh are the top-scoring states in the SDG India Index, 2018 both earning a score of 69. Kerala's success is attributed to its efforts in providing good health, eliminating hunger, attaining gender egalitarianism, and delivering quality education, while Himachal Pradesh is doing an admirable job of delivering clean water and sanitation, eliminating inequities, and maintaining the alpine habitat. Chandigarh is topping the charts among all the UTs with a score of 68 attributable to its outstanding achievement in delivering clean water, sanitation, and good employment opportunities with sustainable economic growth to its residents. Chandigarh further made excellent progress toward developing a reliable source of economical and alternative source of energy, which is in high demand due to the harsh climate conditions that exist around the world. The combined score of all Indian States and UTs persists between 42 to 69 and 57 to 68 respectively on the SDG India Index for SD as illustrated in figure 5. India's overall score for the year 2018 is 57.

Figure 5. Composite score of States and UTs on SDG India Index, 2018

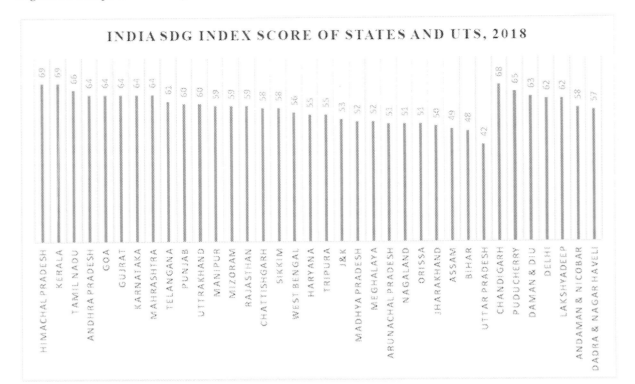

4.2. Performance of States/UTs on SDG India Index, 2019

Our analysis revealed that Kerala is able to defend its position as the top-ranking state by delivering high on SDGs (1, 3, 9, 11, 16) in 2019 and scored 70 points, a 1-point increase over the previous year. Among the UTs, Chandigarh has made tremendous improvement on SDII 2.0, by securing first place with a score of 70, which is two points higher than the preceding year. As elucidated in figure 6, Himachal Pradesh secured the second spot with third place being shared by Andhra Pradesh, Tamil Nadu, and Telangana respectively. The highest gainer of the year 2019 is Uttar Pradesh with a score of 55, 13 points higher than the previous year. Among the SDGs, goal 7 has shown a significant improvement, leapfrogging the previous year by 40 points. India's combined score increased from 57 in 2018 to 60 in 2019.

4.3. Performance of States/UTs on SDG India Index, 2020

Our analysis revealed that the score for the states spans between 52 to 75, whereas it falls between 62 to 79 for the UTs on the SDGII 3.0. As per figure 7, it can be concluded that with a total of 75 points, Kerela is able to maintain its position as the highest-scoring state, showing an increase of 5 points over the SDGII 2.0. With a score of 79, Chandigarh retained its top rank among the UTs. Tamil Nadu and Himachal Pradesh hold the second place on the chart, while Andhra Pradesh, Goa, Karnataka, and Uttarakhand shared the fourth position. The overall ranking of India rose from 60 in 2019-20 to 66 in 2020-21. All states have shown a significant improvement in the scores by one point or more, ranging

Figure 6. Composite score of States and UTs on SDG India Index, 2019.

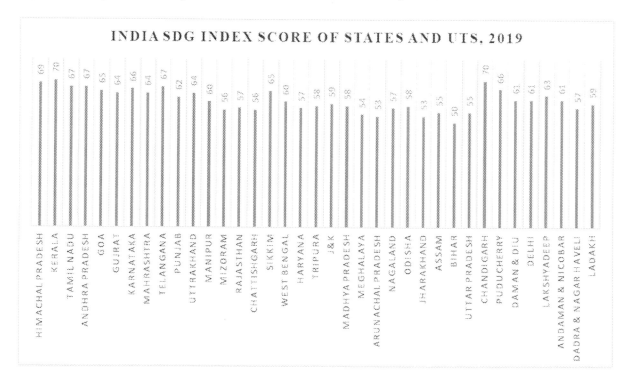

from one to twelve. Based on point gains over the previous year Haryana, Mizoram and Uttarakhand are the top gainers of 2020-21, with an increment of 10, 12, and 8 points respectively. In 2020-21, 12 more States/UTs joined the club of front runners which was earlier occupied by the 10 States/UTs as per SDGII 2.0. Talking about the progress made by States/UTs on SDGs, 25 states emerged as Front Runners in providing clean water and sanitation (Goal 6), while 14 states emerged as aspirants in attaining Gender Equality (Goal 5) and Industry Innovation and Infrastructure (Goal 9). With respect to the SDGs (3, 10, 11, and 12) the country's score has been upgraded from Performer to Front Runner. Figure 8 shows an upward trend in the following seven SDGs- 3 (good health and well-being), 7 (affordable and clean energy), 10 (reduced inequalities), 11 (sustainable cities and communities), 12 (responsible consumption and production), 15 (life on land), and 16 (peace, justice, and strong institutions), where India scored between 65-99. Two SDGs- 2 (zero hunger) and 5 (gender equality) demand additional efforts, as the total nation score is less than 50 in both situations.

5. CONCLUSION

Assessing progress toward all 17 SDGs by analyzing national and subnational efforts made toward achieving these ambitious goals poses a major challenge in the emerging global context in terms of searching for an efficient instrument that integrates efforts made at the central, state, and district levels in order to achieve the goals within the original deadlines set by Agenda 2030. As our analysis is based on The SDG India Index which indicates, that India has shown a significant improvement in terms of composite

Figure 7. Composite score of States and UTs on SDG India Index, 2020.

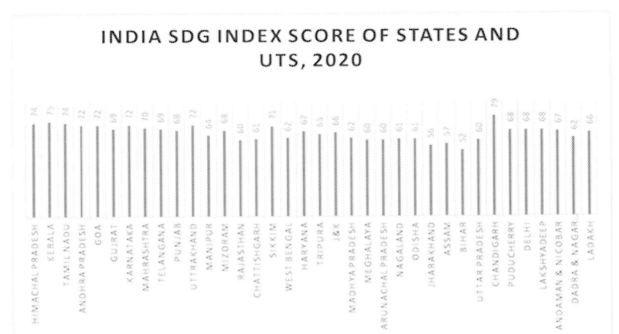

Figure 8. Goal-wise analysis for the years, 2019–20 and 2020-21.

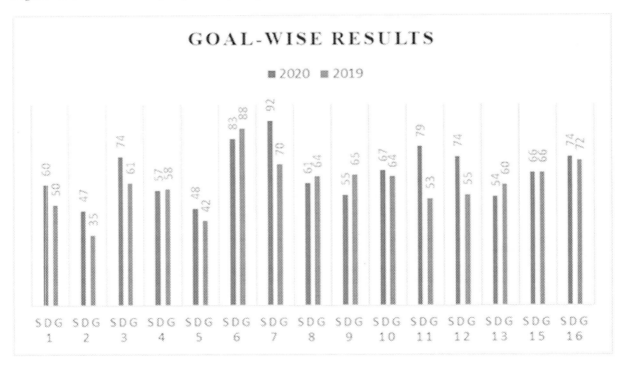

scores from 60 in 2019-20 to 66 in 2020-21. Kerela maintains its position as the highest-scoring state, and Chandigarh is the highest-scoring Union Territory, with scores of 75 and 79 respectively for 2020-21. Talking about the composite efforts made by the States and Union Territories, the following seven SDGs- 3 (good health and well-being), 7 (affordable and clean energy), 10 (reduced inequalities), 11 (sustainable cities and communities), 12 (responsible consumption and production), 15 (life on land), and 16 (peace, justice, and strong institutions), showed an upward trend in the year 2020 as compared to the preceding year. Two SDGs- 2 (zero hunger) and 5 (gender equality) on the counterpart demand additional efforts, as the total nation score is less than 50 in both situations.

The SDG India Index is based on indicator-based assessments of sustainable development, and it is crucial that the method, process, and result of such assessments should be published and evaluated to synthesize the country's progress toward sustainable development to earmark the best practices in the field. It is a unique attempt to review the progress made by subnational governments. This index serves a dual purpose: it tracks progress on the national development agenda such as (Sashakt Bharat, Swachh Bharat, Samagra Bharat, Satat Bharat, and Sampana Bharat) as it is aligned with the Sustainable Development Goals (SDGs) and it compares the success of subnational administrations in implementing policies to improve the performance of relevant State/UT. The inaugural edition of the index was published in December 2018, followed by the second edition on December 30, 2019, and the third edition in June 2021. Based on the above versions of The SDG India Index, States/UTs are classified into four categories: aspirants, performers, front runners, and achievers. Aspirants have the lowest score, while achievers have the highest, indicating that the concerned State/UT is successful in implementing policies related to SDG implementation. The most recent version of the SDG India Index encompasses 115 indicators, with a qualitative assessment for Goal 17. The NITI Aayog is in charge of monitoring the country's progress toward implementing the 2030 Agenda for Sustainable Development, it has made a significant contribution by bringing together various stakeholders, assessing progress, providing technical assistance, and encouraging healthy competition among States/UTs. To evaluate performance and monitor progress periodically countries deliver the Voluntary National Reviews (VNRs) before the High-Level Political Forum (HLPF) on Sustainable Development. The NITI Aayog created and delivered India's first VNR, in 2017. Then, in 2020, before the High-Level Political Forum, India presented its second Voluntary National Review based upon the theme "whole-of-society."

Our research has shown that the outcomes of such evaluations are quite sensitive to both the indicators used and the methodologies employed. Therefore, a holistic SDG framework with a transparent and expert-driven consultative process has to be constructed and acknowledged to develop an instrument for measuring success attained against each goal defined in "Agenda 2030". The key gap which exists is the need for a more precise methodology for indicator selection, target setting, and distribution of composite scores among various categories. Furthermore, as these indexes have policy consequences, there is an urgent need for strengthening India's statistical systems to provide data that can be effectively used to monitor SDGs at the national and state levels in real-time. Moreover, in a world where the issues of public policy and governance are constantly changing, resolving data gaps related to these populations will be critical if the policy is to be evidence-based. To move the sustainable development agenda ahead, inclusive partnerships at all levels - global, national, sub-national, and local - must be established based on a common vision and values. Subsequently, the efforts of each stakeholder, including the government, civil society, and the business sector, should be carefully integrated in order to accelerate the process of attaining success by the year 2030. Even though great progress has been made, there are still obstacles ahead. As India has joined the rest of the world in the "Decade of Action." With less than ten years to meet the Global Goals, countries need to accelerate the process of developing innovative solutions and implementing them to address the world's most pressing issues, such as poverty, climate change, and gender inequality. Technology in this regard should make sure that no one is left behind in the race to reap the benefits of progress.

This study intends to measure India's progress toward the SDGs by evaluating the performance of all Indian states/UTs using the NITI Aayog's SDG India Index version (1.0, 2.0, and 3.0). It has been constructed in such a way that- policymakers, civil society, businesses, and the general public can put this to use effectively. Since our study is based only on the SDG India Index developed by NITI Aayog, future research could consider our study as a base for constructing a new index to register progress at national and sub-national levels against Sustainable Development Goals. Meeting the limitations of the SDG India Index.

REFERENCES

Allen, C., Reid, M., Thwaites, J., Glover, R., & Kestin, T. (2020). Assessing national progress and priorities for the Sustainable Development Goals (SDGs): Experience from Australia. *Sustainability Science*, *15*(2), 521–538. doi:10.100711625-019-00711-x

Brown, K. (2019 December 19). *How 2020 can be a springboard year for the sustainable development goals*. https://unfoundation.org/blog/post/how-2020-can-be-a-springboard-year-for-the-sustainable-development-goals/

Chaturvedi, S., James, T. C., Saha, S., & Shaw, P. (2019). *2030 agenda and India: moving from quantity to quality*. Springer Singapore. doi:10.1007/978-981-32-9091-4

India Voluntary National Review. (2020). *Sustainable Development Goals Knowledge Platform*. Retrieved April 14, 2022, from https://sustainabledevelopment.un.org/memberstates/india

Nair, R., Viswanathan, P. K., & Bastian, B. L. (2021). Reprioritising Sustainable Development Goals in the Post-COVID-19 Global Context: Will a Mandatory Corporate Social Responsibility Regime Help? *Administrative Sciences*, *11*(4), 150. doi:10.3390/admsci11040150

Nigam, A. K., & Pant, M. K. (2020). *Weighted Sustainable Development Goal Index*. Academic Press.

N. I. T. I. Aayog. (2018). *SDG India Index, Baseline Report, 2018*. Author.

N. I. T. I. Aayog. (2019). *Localising SDG's Early Lessons from India 2019*. Author.

N. I. T. I. Aayog. (2020a). *SDG India index & dashboard 2019-20*. Author.

N. I. T. I. Aayog. (2020b). *India VNR 2020 Decade of Action taking SDGs from Global to Local of NITI Aayog*. Author.

N. I. T. I. Aayog. (2021). *SDG India index and dashboard 2020-21 partnerships in the decade of action. NITI Aayog, GoI, 1-202. OHCHR, Voluntary National Reviews, OHCHR and the 2030 Agenda for Sustainable Development*. Retrieved April 13, 2022, from https://www.ohchr.org/en/sdgs/voluntary-national-reviews

Salem, M., Tsurusaki, N., Divigalpitiya, P., Osman, T., Hamdy, O., & Kenawy, E. (2020). Assessing progress towards sustainable development in the urban periphery: A case of greater Cairo, Egypt. *International Journal of Sustainable Development and Planning, 15*(7), 971–982. doi:10.18280/ijsdp.150701

Tripathi, S. N., & Reddy, C. S. (2020). IIPA Inputs to the 19th Session of the Committee of Experts on Public Administration (CEPA). *The Indian Journal of Public Administration, 66*(3), 404–417. doi:10.1177/0019556120963319

Venkatesh, G. (2021). Sustainable Development Goals–Quo Vadis, Cities of the World? *Problemy Ekorozwoju, 16*(1).

KEY TERMS AND DEFINITIONS

Indicator-Based Assessment: Indicators are becoming an increasingly significant tool for tracking and evaluating SD. The process of interpreting data from indicators to provide unambiguous policy recommendations is known as indicator-based evaluation

SDG India Index: The SDG India Index is the first subnational government-led evaluation of SDG development in the world. It is constructed to popularise and implement a quick and cross-cutting tool for evaluating subnational success in accomplishing the SDGs individually and cumulatively.

Sustainable Development (SD): Sustainable development is the concept of meeting societal wants and aspirations while protecting the ability of the natural system to produce fundamental resources in a sustainable way for future generations on which the nation's economy is built.

Sustainable Development Goals (SDGs): The Sustainable Development Goals (SDGs) are a series of 17 ambitious goals approved by the 193 UN member states in order to eradicate poverty, protect the environment, and offer equal growth opportunities for all by 2030 so that no one is left in the vague.

Voluntary National Review (VNR): The Voluntary National Review (VNR) is a mechanism through which member states assess and publish their progress in implementing the 2030 Agenda, including the gain around the 17 Sustainable Development Goals. VNRs are meant to examine how the country is progressing toward the Sustainable Development Goals.

Chapter 11

ASEAN Toward Circular Economy and Sustainable Energy in Tackling Climate Change:
Islamic Green Financing Taxonomy for Sustainable Finance

Khairunnisa Musari

(iD) https://orcid.org/0000-0003-0525-9903

Kiai Haji Achmad Siddiq State Islamic University, Indonesia

ABSTRACT

Considering the region is highly vulnerable to climate change, all ASEAN Member States have ratified the Paris Agreement and agreed to the Regional Roadmap for Implementing the 2030 Agenda for Sustainable Development in Asia and the Pacific. To provide the ASEAN taxonomy for sustainable finance, Islamic finance should be considered as a part of it. Therefore, this chapter will provide an Islamic Green Financing Taxonomy to help stakeholders determine which activities qualify as sustainable and which instrument is suitable for the activity. As a leading community in the world that drives the global halal industry, ASEAN also can be a best practice for implementing Islamic Green Financing. Through literature study, this chapter purposes to (1) describe the framework of ASEAN for the circular economy and sustainable energy in tackling the climate change, (2) describe the ASEAN taxonomy, and (3) describe the proposed Islamic Green Financing Taxonomy.

DOI: 10.4018/978-1-6684-4610-2.ch011

BACKGROUND

All the Association of Southeast Asian Nations (ASEAN) Member States have ratified the Paris Agreement. The ASEAN Heads of State and Government applied the Declaration on Institutionalising the Resilience of ASEAN and Its Communities and Peoples to Disasters and Climate Change where the ASEAN Member States committed to hammering out a more resilient future by conforming to a changing climate, deterring the new risks, and minimizing the existent climate-related risks and disasters through the implementation of social, economic, physical, environmental, and cultural initiatives. All ASEAN Member States have signed to the United Nations Sustainable Development Goals (SDGs) and have approved the Regional Roadmap for Implementing the 2030 Agenda for Sustainable Development in Asia and the Pacific.

ASEAN Centre for Energy (ACE, 2021) reported that five ASEAN Member States in 2020 have proposed or renewed their Nationally Determined Contributions (NDCs), while the other five completed the NDCs in 2021. The newest NDCs of the ASEAN Member States perform more assertive commitments as a representation in the mitigation targets, the conditionality of NDCs, and wider coverage of greenhouse gases (GHG) and sectors. The fairness and ambition of the newest NDCs are assigned based on each national situation. Table 1 shows the some newest ASEAN member countries' commitments to emission reduction.

Table 1. The ASEAN Member Countries' Emission Reduction Commitments in 2030

Emission Reduction ($MtCO_2e$)	Unconditional		Conditional	
	Previous NDCs	Newest NDCs	Previous NDCs	Newest NDCs
Indonesia	832.01	No change	1,176.29	No change
Malaysia	0.531 tCO_2e/thousand Malaysian Ringgit			
Singapore	0.113 $kgCO_2e$/SD and peaking at 65 $MtCO_2e$			
Brunei Darussalam	n.a	5.90	n.a	n.a
Philippines	n.a	90.52	n.a	2,414.70
Thailand	111.00	No change	138.75	No change
Cambodia	n.a	n.a	3.1	64.5
Vietnam	62.99	83.51	196.85	250.53
Myanmar	n.a	244.52	n.a	414.75
Lao PDR	n.a	62.40	n.a	n.a

Source: ACE (2021)

In order to tackle climate change, Ellen MacArthur Foundation (2019, 2021), Musari and Sayah (2021), Musari and Zaroni (2021), Musari (2021c), Van Veldhoven and Schmidt (2021), Kaye (2021) convinced that circular economy has a critical role to decrease GHG. It can mitigate carbon dioxide emissions that emerge from extractive industries, transportation, construction, manufacturing, and other sectors. In the building sector alone, Englund and André (2021) claimed that circular economy actions can reduce emissions by up to 61%. Musari (2021c) also claimed that circular economy paradigm for plastics as a requirement for ASEAN halal industry can be a comparative advantage and leads radically in reducing plastic pollution in halal market and influence this circular economy best practice to Asia.

In order to tackle climate change, ASEAN is also in a struggle to save a sustainable energy future. International Renewable Energy Agency (IRENA) and ACE (2016) and Liu, Sheng, and Azhgaliyeva (2019) predicted that the ASEAN population will enlarge from around 615 million in 2014 to 715 million in 2025. This region is also projected to become the fourth-largest economy in the world by 2030 with a population of more than 10% of 690 million by 2020. It is certain that the total demand for energy will increase rapidly and ASEAN becomes a prominent turning point for the global energy scenery. Therefore, ASEAN has decided on the aspirational goal of securing 23% of its primary energy from modern, sustainable renewable sources by 2025. This purpose implies a two-and-a-half-fold rise in the modern renewable energy share compared to 2014. At the same time, power generation will be twofold by 2025, and on the whole demand for energy will spring up by almost 50%.

Absolutely, as Liu, Sheng, and Azhgaliyeva (2019) mentioned, investments in infrastructure and power generation will be required to meet ASEAN's energy demand which has grown by 60% over the past 15 years, and is estimated that investments will keep on growing by another two thirds by 2040. Shofa (2021) reported that ASEAN needs a severe sum of investments and requires international financing schemes. Each member state can do deal with the financial institutions. Some recommendations suggest the investment scheme must be long-term, simple, and inclusive with extensive access to devise fair contests between private sectors. However, Liu and Noor (2020) noted some of the ASEAN countries, such as Indonesia, Singapore, Thailand, Malaysia, and Viet Nam, have been able to develop more advanced financial schemes, frameworks, and instruments to finance energy efficiency and conservation.

Furthermore, Stewart & Mok (2022) mentioned that many countries today are searching for innovative financial instruments to face the triple crisis of unprecedented climate change, debt levels, and nature loss. Sovereign bonds, representing almost 40% of the $100 trillion global bond market, are the biggest asset class in the portfolio of many institutional investors. One tool to relate sustainable sovereign financing with environmental commitments and national climate could be sustainability-linked bonds (SLBs), which are now being considered by sovereign issuers and arising rapidly in the corporate debt market.

Thus, to provide the taxonomy for ASEAN sustainable finance, Islamic finance should be considered as a part of it. Whitehead (2021) mentioned that input from Islamic finance will smooth the path to the taxonomy development for financial services in this region. Musari (2021b), Musari and Sayah (2021), Musari and Hidayat (2021) also affirmed that Islamic finance has various instruments which can be developed as Islamic green financing. As a leading community in the world that drives the global halal industry (Hidayat and Musari, 2022; Musari and Zaroni, 2021), ASEAN also can be a best practice for implementing Islamic green financing. Therefore, through literature study, this chapter purposes to: (1) Describe the framework of ASEAN for the circular economy and sustainable energy in tackling the climate change; (2) Describe the ASEAN Taxonomy; (3) Describe the proposed Islamic Green Financing Taxonomy.

THE FRAMEWORK OF ASEAN

ASEAN adopted the Framework for Circular Economy for the ASEAN Economic Community (AEC) at the 20th AEC Council Meeting held on 18 October 2021 as shown by Figure 1. ASEAN Secretariat (2021a), ASEAN Secretariat and the Economic Research Institute for ASEAN and East Asia (ERIA)

(2021) explained that this Framework objective is to head ASEAN in reaching its long-term targets of resilient economy, resource efficiency, and sustainable growth. The Framework also embeds a pretentious long-term sight for the circular economy, identifies prime concern areas for action along with enablers, constructs on the strengths of available initiatives to embody circular economy in ASEAN.

Figure 1. The framework for circular economy for the AEC
Source: ASEAN Secretariat and ERIA (2021)

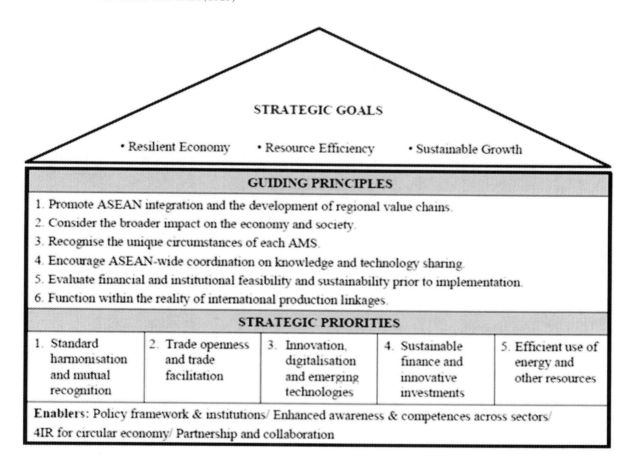

Regarding the strategic goals of the Framework for Circular Economy for the AEC, ASEAN Secretariat and ERIA (2021) clarified that ASEAN fights to achieve harmony between three interdependent goals:

First, ASEAN can leapfrog resource-intensive development paths – which tend to be vulnerable to shocks – by adopting circular economy alternatives. Shaping a circular economy that is resilient to climate change and resource constraints will minimize costs and risks over the long-term, ultimately benefiting ASEAN.

Second, ASEAN's commitment to circular economy-based policies and innovations to attain resource efficiency will boost industries' competitiveness in domestic and foreign markets, both regional and global. A strong regional ecosystem for eco-innovation is very important, to strengthen and support pioneering entrepreneurs and startups, not to mention investors and big corporates.

Third, Environmental, Social and Governance (ESG) criteria is part of the growing international trend towards investment portfolios where profit goes hand in hand with sustainability.

In organizing to be a resilient and designated region, ASEAN is committed to constructing a more circular economy by changing the pattern of consumption and production of its community to reduce waste. The Framework serves six leading principles for circular economy initiatives in the region:

First, promote ASEAN integration and the development of regional value chains. It means, ASEAN aspires to be a highly integrated and cohesive economy. Circular economy initiatives will be trade-enabling and promote new market and investment opportunities.

Second, recognise the unique circumstances of each AMS. It means, AEC's circular economy initiatives should take the diversity of AMS circumstances and socioeconomic development priorities into consideration, while engaging in the collective pursuit of the region's long-term growth prospects.

Third, consider the broader impact on the economy and society. It means, AEC circular economy initiatives shall take into account wider economic and societal dimensions, such as the impact on prices, small businesses, employment, livelihoods, and well-being.

Fourth, encourage ASEAN-wide coordination on knowledge and technology sharing. It means, close cross-sectoral and cross-pillar coordination is required – a Community-wide collaborative approach and cooperation mechanism shall be encouraged to advance circular economy.

Fifth, evaluate financial and institutional feasibility and sustainability prior to implementation. It means, to have long-lasting impact, initiatives shall be pursued with financial and institutional feasibility and sustainability in mind, ensuring they continue to perform and deliver benefits beyond the period of implementation.

Sixth, function within the reality of international production linkages. It means, the continued importance of global value chains means that ASEAN specific circular economy strategies need to recognise global best practices and policies adopted by key ASEAN economic partners.

Then, ASEAN's transition towards circular economy hinges on five strategic priorities:

First, standard harmonisation and mutual recognition of circular products and services. Harmonisation of standards and mutual recognition are required to facilitate circularity of trade in products and services as well as promoting greater transparency, facilitating integration between value chains, and multiplying circularity.

Second, trade openness and trade facilitation in circular goods and services. Circular economy tends to be fragmented and focused on specific products or materials that are located in separate jurisdictions or product clusters. Keeping trade barriers, including non-tariff ones, at their minimum levels, will allow seamless movement of products or services, and facilitate optimal resource allocation at both country and regional levels.

Third, enhanced role of innovation, digitalisation, and emerging/green technologies. Circularity can enhance value chain efficiency, trackability, and resilience through technological innovations that leverage digital platforms, mobile devices, big data and analytics, blockchain, and artificial intelligence. The new frontier of the Fourth Industrial Revolution can further unlock the potential of the circular economy, and, eventually, restore nature's cycles.

Fourth, competitive sustainable finance and innovative ESG investments. Supporting sustainable investment, mainstreaming circular economy in AEC related projects, encouraging public or private financial institutions to fund sustainable projects, and promoting the financing of new business models that support circular economy.

Fifth, efficient use of energy and other resources. The circular economy moves towards efficient use of resources and materials by reducing waste and pollution through recovery and better design. The sustainable use of energy underlies all economic activities in a circular economy. Therefore, focusing on reducing energy use and the adoption of renewable sources of energy is key to promoting circular economy.

Furthermore, the circular economy actually brings the message of sustainability. The circular economy indeed demands resource efficiency, not only raw material resources, but also energy and financial resources. Thus, circular economy and sustainability are two sides of a coin that cannot be separated. Likewise circular economy and sustainable energy as well as circular economy and sustainable finance. People are required to meet the current needs without reducing the rights of future generations to meet their own needs.

In addition, referring to Musari (2020c, 2021b), Musari and Hidayat (2021), Musari and Zaroni (2021), all efforts to restore the quality of environment are in line with Islamic teachings. The existence of Islamic green financing instrument must address *maqasid al-shari'a* as the main objective to achieve. The allocation and impact of this instrument must be the manifestation of the *maqasid al-shari'a.* When people save the environment *(hifdzul al-bi'ah* or *riayatu al-bi'ah),* actually people save *an-nafs, al-aql, an-nasl, al-mal,* and *ad 'din* also. No doubt, Islamic financial instruments automatically should lead to efforts to save the environment. Hence, the environmental preserve in Islamic economics and finance should reduce environmental risks and increase environmental benefits.

THE ASEAN TAXONOMY

The ASEAN Member States, also within individual member states, are diverse in religions, histories, peoples, cultures, languages, including in financial systems and phases of economic structure and development. Table 2 shows the rate of economic growth in each ASEAN Member States during 2011-2020. The Lao People's Democratic Republic (PDR), Myanmar, Cambodia, and Viet Nam were the country with the highest average annual growth and reached 6% during the period. 2012 was the year with the highest average economic growth and 2020 during the pandemic was the year with the lowest average growth for ASEAN. In 2020, when ASEAN's average growth penetrated -3.3%, ASEAN Member Countries that experienced the highest growth decline were the Philippines -9.6%, Thailand -6.1%, Malaysia -5.6%, and Singapore - 5.4%. Interestingly, Laos, Myanmar, Vietnam, and Brunei were countries that still have positive economic growth.

Table 2. Rate of economic growth in ASEAN (%), 2011-2020

Country	2011	2012	2013	2014	2015	2016	2017	2018	2019	2020	Average annual growth 2011-2020
Brunei Darussalam	3.7	0.9	-2.1	-2.5	-0.4	-2.5	1.3	0.1	3.9	1.1	0.4
Cambodia	7.1	7.3	7.5	7.1	9.0	6.9	7.0	7.5	7.1	-3.1	6.3
Indonesia	6.5	6.3	5.6	5.0	4.9	5.0	5.1	5.2	5.0	-2.1	4.6
Lao PDR	8.0	7.9	8.0	7.6	7.3	7.0	6.9	6.3	5.5	3.3	6.8
Malaysia	5.3	5.5	4.7	6.0	5.0	4.4	5.8	4.7	4.6	-5.6	4.0
Myanmar	5.6	7.3	8.4	8.0	7.0	5.9	6.8	6.8	6.2	3.2	6.5
Philippines	3.9	6.9	6.8	6.3	6.3	7.1	6.9	6.3	6.1	-9.6	4.7
Singapore	6.4	4.1	5.1	3.9	2.2	3.3	4.5	3.5	1.7	-5.4	2.9
Thailand	0.8	7.2	2.7	1.0	3.1	3.4	4.2	4.3	2.3	-6.1	2.3
Viet Nam	6.2	5.2	5.4	6.0	6.7	6.2	6.8	7.1	7.0	2.9	6.0
ASEAN	**5.1**	**6.2**	**5.1**	**4.7**	**4.9**	**5.0**	**5.4**	**5.3**	**4.7**	**-3.3**	**4.4**

Source: ASEAN Secretariat (2021b)

As economies grow, Nishimura (2019) reminded that individuals become rich and consume and discard more. ASEAN's 600 million people account for 4% of the world population but produce 9% of rubbish and are expected to double in 2050. Anbumozhi and Kimura (Eds.) (2018) mentioned that the linear approach of growth 'take-make-use-dispose' has been the trend for most countries in ASEAN. As resources become scarcer and more expensive in the future, there is an urgent need to transition to a circular economy in ASEAN.

ASEAN Taxonomy Board (2021), The Fiscal Policy Agency (BKF, 2021) highlighted that financing is key in allowing ASEAN to move forward with its sustainability agenda. The existence of sustainable finance was admitted by the ASEAN Finance Ministers' and Central Bank Governors' Meeting in 2019. Having a similar understanding of what is necessary for sustainability is needed if ASEAN is going to fascinate and direct the capital towards sustainable investments. That is why a reliable regional sustainable finance taxonomy is required, which is compatible with other regional and international taxonomies.

Figure 2. Overview of taxonomy classifications
Source: ASEAN Taxonomy Board (2021)

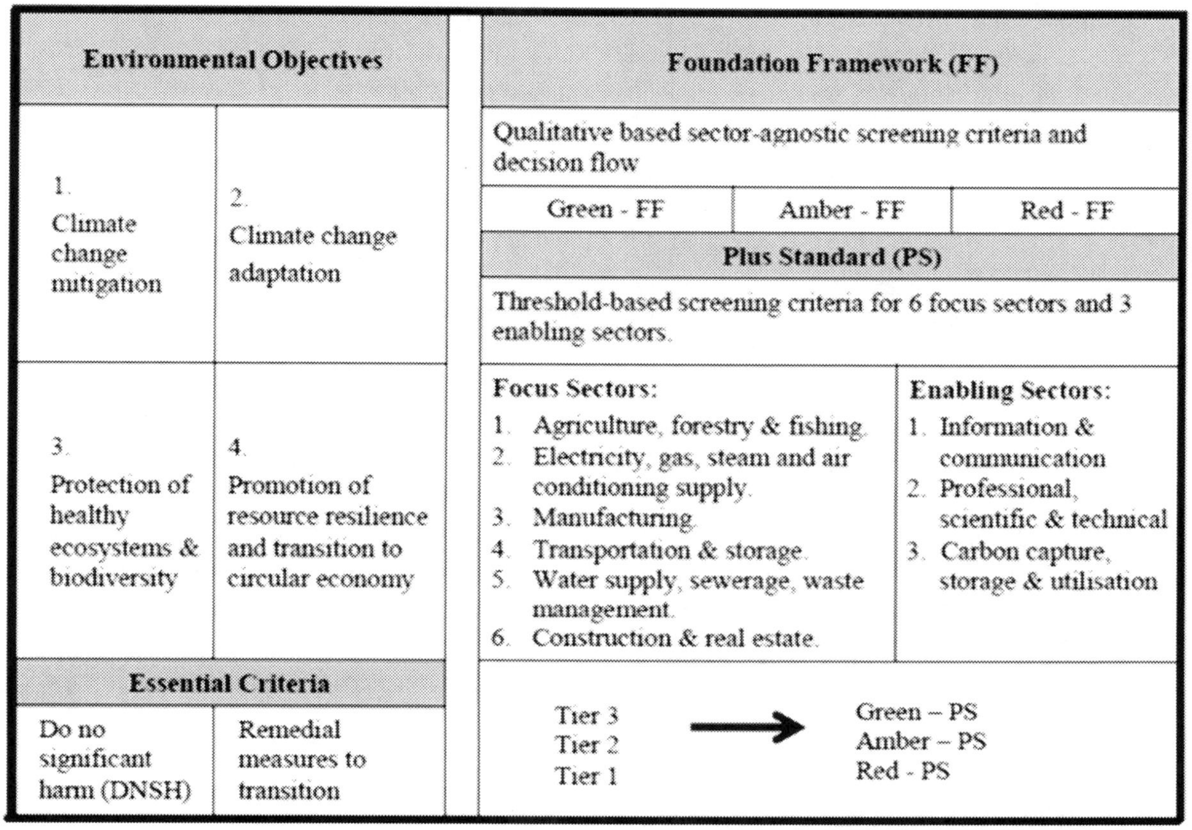

Environmental Objectives		Foundation Framework (FF)		
1. Climate change mitigation	2. Climate change adaptation	Qualitative based sector-agnostic screening criteria and decision flow		
		Green - FF	Amber - FF	Red - FF
		Plus Standard (PS)		
		Threshold-based screening criteria for 6 focus sectors and 3 enabling sectors.		
3. Protection of healthy ecosystems & biodiversity	4. Promotion of resource resilience and transition to circular economy	**Focus Sectors:** 1. Agriculture, forestry & fishing. 2. Electricity, gas, steam and air conditioning supply. 3. Manufacturing. 4. Transportation & storage. 5. Water supply, sewerage, waste management. 6. Construction & real estate.		**Enabling Sectors:** 1. Information & communication 2. Professional, scientific & technical 3. Carbon capture, storage & utilisation
Essential Criteria		Tier 3 → Green – PS Tier 2 → Amber – PS Tier 1 → Red - PS		
Do no significant harm (DNSH)	Remedial measures to transition			

Furthermore, as a collaborative initiative of the sectoral bodies, ASEAN Taxonomy Board has a goal to present a framework for the work of private and public sectors. The ASEAN Taxonomy reflects the collective commitment of ASEAN Member States in changing towards a sustainable region. It is created to be an inclusive and acceptable classification system for sustainable activities and will be one of the key building blocks in attracting investments and financial flows into sustainable projects in the region. The ASEAN Taxonomy serves as a map to assist guide capital towards activities into the real economy for a more sustainable footing. Figure 2 describes how the various sections are appropriate together as a unified overall classification framework.

Furthermore, this Taxonomy-driven capacity building may also help compensate for a perceived lack of standards in the market both globally and regionally as well as help coordinate and guide regulatory frameworks, national taxonomies, and financial market policies for climate change mitigation, adaptation, and resilience investment and solutions. Considering the above, a 'one-size-fits-all' Taxonomy is not regarded as the best solution for ASEAN. For this reason, the ASEAN Taxonomy has been conceived according to a multi-tiered concept; namely a 'Foundation Framework (FF)' and a 'Plus Standard (PS)' with activities which are assessed and classified into green, amber, or red, based on its contribution to the environmental objectives of the Taxonomy. Among the environmental objectives set out earlier in this document, climate change mitigation is the main objective that governs how an activity is classified. Later on, the other environmental objectives can be scoped into the process.

Anbumozhi and Kim (Eds.) (2016) mentioned that current government guarantee systems enable the banking sector to finance innovative waste-to-energy projects that are relevant for circular economy. Expanding the spectrum and creation of innovative financing mechanisms for enhanced social impact would allow the emergence of a broader range of projects under community–corporate partnerships. Climate Bond Initiatives (2020) recorded that ASEAN green, social and sustainability (GSS) issuance has grown strongly. The ASEAN issuance of GSS bonds and loans reached a record high of USD12.8 billion in 2020, up slightly from the USD11.5 billion issued in 2019. The cumulative issuance in ASEAN now stands at USD29.4 billion.

Kapoor, Teo, Azhgaliyeva, and Liu (2020) reported that green bonds issuance in ASEAN is growing fast with a relatively higher rate for green building projects as compared to the rest of the world. One of the factors driving demand is that building design has a more sizeable impact on energy efficiency since Southeast Asia is in the equatorial belt, whereas many countries in the rest of the world are located in temperate zones. Moreover, there are also special forms of green bonds that have been introduced in the market. The type of this instrument is gaining popularity in Indonesia and Malaysia, i.e green sukuk.

Musari (2021b), Musari and Sayah (2021), Musari and Hidayat (2021) mentioned that green sukuk initiative in Indonesia has paved the way for the flow of sustainable financing through Islamic green financing. Indonesia as the world's first green sukuk issuer can be an early model for the development of another Islamic green financing. Therefore, in order to continue finding innovative instruments and to diversify investors and distribute risks, the next section in this chapter try to map the Islamic Green Financing Taxonomy.

THE ISLAMIC GREEN FINANCING TAXONOMY

Climate Bond Initiatives (2020) noted the ASEAN sustainable finance market has been dominated by green debt, but the share of other subjects has risen in fame in recent years both in terms of the number of issuers and the amount issued. GSS bonds were already gaining appeal before COVID-19, and are now an even more important financial instrument for countries to mobilize funds for green and sustainable recoveries and resilience to future systemic shocks.

It is undeniable that debt and the issuance of securities are currently the choices of most countries due to fiscal deficits. Table 3 shows the budget deficit of ASEAN Member States during 2011-2020. All member countries have experienced budget deficits, no exception Singapore, Brunei Darussalam, and Malaysia. However, Singapore, Brunei Darussalam, Malaysia, and Cambodia also experienced a budget surplus at the period. Only in 2015 and 2020 while pandemic indicated that budget deficits occurred in all ASEAN Member States without exception.

Table 3. Government budget deficit in ASEAN (A percentage of GDP), 2011-2020

Country	2011	2012	2013	2014	2015	2016	2017	2018	2019	2020
Brunei Darussalam	25.6	15.5	7.6	-1.0	-14.0	-21.7	-10.4	-3.6	-7.1	-17.1
Cambodia	3.8	-	-	-4.9	-4.7	-4.2	0.0	-5.1	5.3	-2.6
Indonesia	-1.1	-1.9	-2.2	-2.1	-1.8	-2.2	-2.7	-2.1	-1.9	-6.2
Lao PDR	-1.9	-1.3	-4.3	-3.6	-5.9	-5.2	-5.6	-4.6	-5.0	-5.3
Malaysia	0.3	-4.5	-3.9	0.1	-3.2	-3.1	-2.9	-3.7	-3.4	-3.5
Myanmar	-	-	-	-	-	-	-	-	-5.0	-4.9
Philippines	-2.0	-2.3	-1.4	-0.6	-0.9	-2.4	-2.2	-3.2	-3.5	-7.6
Singapore	1.1	1.6	1.3	0.1	-1.0	1.2	2.1	0.4	-0.7	-6.3
Thailand	-4.1	-4.2	-1.9	-2.9	-2.9	-2.3	0.0	-2.5	-0.8	-6.1
Viet Nam	-1.8	-	-	-	-	-	-	-	-3.4	-5.8

Source: ASEAN Secretariat (2021b)

Marimuthu, Khan, and Bangash (2021) mentioned that ASEAN has faced a persistent fiscal deficit for the last three decades. By using annual financial data for the years 1990 to 2019 of ten member countries of ASEAN, they found the fiscal deficit of ASEAN could generate inflation while relying on outstanding debt. They concluded that the fiscal deficit of ASEAN is alarming based on the behavior of government revenues, interest rate dynamics, political stability, and outstanding debt in deficit financing.

A study by Lau and Yip (2019) provided new evidence on the nexus between fiscal deficits and economic growth among ASEAN countries in the pre-Global Financial Crisis (GFC) and post-GFC periods. Using annual data from 2001 to 2015, three results stand out. *First,* fiscal deficits are found to be growth-deteriorating in the pre-Crisis period and growth-enhancing in the post-Crisis period. *Second,* the impact of fiscal deficits on growth in pre- and post-GFC are robust to different measures of economic growth. *Third,* inflation is important in influencing economic growth in the pre-Crisis period while exchange rate and inflow of foreign direct investment have a positive impact on growth in the post-Crisis period.

Study by Habibullah, Cheah, and Baharom (2011) to determine the long-run relationship between budget deficits and inflation in 13 Asian developing countries, namely: Indonesia, Malaysia, the Philippines, Myanmar, Singapore, Thailand, India, South Korea, Pakistan, Sri Lanka, Taiwan, Nepal and Bangladesh by using annual data for the period 1950-1999 concluded that budget deficits are inflationary in the selected Asian developing countries.

For this reason, Fatemi and Fooladi (2013) emphasized that the state budget as the main instrument of fiscal policy needs to be encouraged to be healthier, both in the short, medium and long term perspectives. A healthy state budget is reflected in a relatively low deficit, but still productive for accelerated growth, a positive primary balance and a debt ratio that remains under control within safe limits. The most strategy counts on issuance of government bonds on domestic and foreign markets.

Therefore, this section maps a classification Islamic green financing instrument to help financial players, industries, particularly governments, determine which one is appropriate to finance green projects or programs. Whitehead (2021) highlighted that Islamic finance principles avoid highly toxic, highly speculative, and dangerous financial products such as certain derivatives that can drive pricing volatility. This is purposed to increase the alignment of the financial services sector with the real economy and boost stability.

So far, the Islamic financial instrument that is currently being developed for green financing is the green sukuk. Lesson learned about green sukuk can be obtained from France, Malaysia, Pakistan, and Indonesia. In France, the green sukuk type that is developed is the corporate sukuk. Alam, Duygun, and Ariss (2016) introduced Orasis Sukuk as the first green sukuk issued in France in August 2012 by an investment company specializing in solar energy and real estate investment, ie Legendre Patrimoine, and an Islamic financial institution consulting firm offering financial consulting, brokerage, project management, and training services, ie Anouar Hassoune Conseil. The renewable energy assets served Orasis' underlying. Orasis became the milestone for Islamic financial instruments that opened for investment to private individuals nor institutional investors in that country.

In Malaysia, World Bank (2020) and Brodsky (2020) mentioned the initial green sukuk was released in July 2017 by Malaysia's Tadau Energy. The issuance raised USD58 million to finance its 50 megawatt solar photovoltaic power plant. In Pakistan, Global Islamic Finance and Impact Investing Platform (GIFIIP) (2019) reported that green sukuk initiative arranges a pre-feasibility study at the federal government level, particularly on the Punjab Provincial Government, to map the public and private sector as stakeholders and to verify the occasions and challenges for issuing green sukuk. Then the region and national stakeholders will validate the pre-feasibility study to formulate the next steps.

In Indonesia, green sukuk becomes the gateway to the flow of sustainable financing through Islamic green financing. As the first global and retail Sovereign Green Sukuk issuer in the world, Musari (2020a, 2020d, 2021d, 2021e, 2022a, 2022b), Musari and Sayah (2021) claimed that Indonesia can be a best practice for Islamic green financing to fight the climate change. Then, as the first blended Islamic finance for the fiscal instrument in Indonesia, Cash *Waqf* Linked Sukuk (CWLS) can be integrated with Green Sukuk as a socially responsible investment (SRI) for tackling climate change toward Green CWLS. It provides exponential benefits for investor to participate in resolving the climate change, especially during a pandemic. Then, by adopting the *esham* concept within the blended Green Sukuk and CWLS, Perpetual Green CWLS has a potency to be the next Islamic green financing alternative.

In addition, Buana and Musari (2020) also promoted Blue Sukuk and White Sukuk as other SRI instruments that can be explored to address greenhouse gas emissions and climate change. The study of Hariyanto (2020) proved that Blue Sukuk is worthy of being a source of financing innovation, especially in the context of realizing the SDGs by 2030. In line with Green and Blue Sukuk, Musari (2020a) stated that White Sukuk also has prospects for being developed by making airspace as underlying assets or programs to strengthen the air sector and related industries in addressing greenhouse gas emissions and climate change. Moreover, there is also *esham*. Çizakça (2011, 2013), Musari (2019, 2020b, 2021d, 2022b) recommended *esham* to be developed with cash *waqf* as an alternative to sukuk.

Table 3 illustrates the proposed Islamic Green Financing Taxonomy. There are several eligibility categories for the ASEAN Green Project that contributes to addressing climate change with several Islamic green financing instruments and contracts that can be adopted. Referring to the ASEAN Capital Markets Forum (ACMF) (2018), there are 10 Eligible Green Sectors for ASEAN Green Projects. According to IRENA and ACE (2016), action areas for enabling ASEAN's renewable energy potential can be classified into four areas. Then, all the sectors and areas are mapped into three main categories, namely Public Borrowing, Charity, and Joint-Venture. Public borrowing in the proposed Islamic Green Financing Taxonomy is categorized as an enabler, which are instrumental in enabling other activities to make a substantial contribution to climate change mitigation, e.g., manufacture of very-low-emission technologies. Charity is categorized as transitional, which are still part of GHG-emissive systems, but are important for and contribute to the transition towards a climate-neutral economy, e.g., energy efficiency improvement in manufacturing that directly or indirectly uses fossil fuels. Joint-Venture is categorized as negative or very low and negative emission, which result in negative, zero or very low greenhouse gas emissions and are fully consistent with the long-term temperature goal of the Paris Agreement, e.g., carbon sequestration in land use or some forms of renewable energy.

Table 4. Islamic green financing taxonomy

Eligible Green Sectors	Enabler			Transitional	Negative or very low emissions	Eligible Renewable Energy Action
	PUBLIC BORROWING			CHARITY	JOINT-VENTURE	
	Debt	Debt/Equity	Equity	*Shadaqa*	*Shirkah*	
Renewable Energy	*Qardhul hassan*	1. Green Sukuk 2. Blue Sukuk 3. White Sukuk 4. Catastrophe Sukuk 5. Temporary Green *Waqf* 6. Temporary Green CWLS	1. Perpetual Green Sukuk 2. Perpetual Blue Sukuk 3. Perpetual White Sukuk 4. Perpetual Green CWLS 5. Stock *waqf/ Waqf-shares* 6. Green *Esham* 7. Green *Esham* Linked *Waqf*	1. *Waqf-* Crowdfunding 2. Perpetual Green *Waqf* 3. *Hiba* 4. *Infaq*	1. *Mudharaba* 2. *Musharaka* 3. *Musharaka mutanaqisah (MMQ)* 4. Public Private Partnership (PPP) 5. Venture *Waqf*	Increase power system flexibility in the ASEAN region while using renewables to provide modern energy access for all.
Energy Efficiency						
Environmentally sustainable management of living natural resources and land use						
Pollution prevention and control						Expand efforts for renewable energy uptake in power but also importantly in the heating, cooking and transport sectors.
Terrestrial and aquatic biodiversity conservation						
Clean transportation						
Sustainable water and waste water management						Create a sustainable, affordable and reliable regional bioenergy market
Climate change adaptation						
Eco-efficient and/or circular economy adapted products, production technologies and processes						
Green buildings which meet regional, national or internationally recognised standards or certifications						Address the information challenge by increasing the availability of up-to-date renewable energy data and the sharing of best practice for renewable energy technologies

Source: Developed by Author from ACMF (2018), IRENA and ACE (2016), Khan (2019), IsDB (2021), Musari (2020a, 2020b, 2020c, 2021b, 2022a, 2022b), Buana and Musari (2020).

Regarding the instruments in this Taxonomy, then it can be explained as follows. In the group of **Public Borrowing,** there is *qardhul hassan* which also written as *qard hasan* or *qard-ul-hassan*. It is often referred to as interest-free loan, voluntary loan, zero-return loan, charitable loan, beautiful loan, benevolent loan, or soft loan. This loan extended without any payment or benefit or return or charge or profit-sharing or any other compensation from the borrower (ISRA, 2010; Iqbal and Mirakhor, 2011; Obaidullah and Khan, 2008; Chapra and Khan, 2008).

In this group there are also Green Sukuk, Blue Sukuk, White Sukuk, and Catastrophe Sukuk. They are thematic sukuk with the underlying assets from green, blue (sea), white (air, sky) resources to finance and/or refinance the green, blue, white projects/programs, such as the environmental conservation projects/program, solar power plant, natural disaster mitigation and recovery projects/program (Buana and Musari, 2020; Musari, 2020a, 2020b, 2021d, 2021e, 2022a, 2022b).

Then, there are Temporary and Perpetual Green *Waqf*. Temporary Green *Waqf* is a cash *waqf* to finance eligible green assets which at a certain time, the *waqf* fund will be returned to *waqif*. Meanwhile Perpetual Green *Waqf* is a cash *waqf* to finance eligible green assets without a maturity date. Because of that, Perpetual Green *Waqf* is categorized in a Charity group in this Taxonomy.

Likewise Temporary Green CWLS which integrate Green Sukuk and CWLS for financing the eligible green sectors, which at a certain time, the *waqf* fund will be returned to *waqif*. Meanwhile Perpetual Green CWLS, which at a certain time, the *waqf* fund will be returned to *nazhir* to manage it or becomes the revolving fund to finance the next green projects/programs (Musari, 2022b; Musari and Sayah, 2021).

In the group of Public Borrowing, there is also Green *Esham*. *Esham* actually the origin of sukuk and became the first Islamic securitization. *Esham* was used as fiscal instrument in the Ottoman period. In the modern age, *esham* has the opportunity to be modernized so that it can trigger financial inclusion and sustainable economic growth. The practice of *esham* today is closer to perpetual sukuk (Çizakça, 2013, 2014, 2018; Musari, 2021d, 2022a, 2022b). Regarding the green financing, *esham* can collaborate to *waqf* also toward Green *Esham* Linked *Waqf*. In Perpetual Green CWLS, actually *esham* concept also exists within the integration of Green Sukuk and CWLS. By adopting *esham,* Perpetual Green CWLS is expected to improve the weaknesses of temporary CWLS which have to redeem the principal fund at the maturity date

Stock *waqf* or *waqf*-shares is a movable *waqf* that has been established with liquidity. For creating stock *waqf*, any institutions may issue stock *waqf* with different value so that the founders can purchase its shares adjusting to their budget. The collected money from selling the shares then will be distributed to the beneficiaries (Mohsin, 2012). In this instrument, not only the green stock *waqf* themselves can be *waqf*-ed. The capital gains or dividend from an Islamic stock can be *waqf*-ed. The funds from stock *waqf* or *waqf*-shares and various derivative products will be managed by *nazhir* and the profits from the investment in this instrument will be distributed to the beneficiaries through programs owned by *nazhir*.

In the group of **Charity,** there are *Waqf*-Crowdfunding, Perpetual Green *Waqf, Hiba,* and *Infaq* can be alternatives. *Waqf* crowdfunding is fundraising the waqf through crowfunding which today becomes an attractive instrument in Islamic social finance. The impact of *waqf* on people in need could be greater with crowdfunding, where *waqif* is not limited by geographical barriers. *Waqf* crowdfunding becomes a marketplace platform to increase financial inclusion through collaboration between Islamic social finance and technology. Crowdfunding offers a solution also to the capital problem in developing *waqf* assets by using the concept of raising funds through social media and internet users (Fauzia and Musari, 2021).

Then, *hiba* is the transfer of a determinate property, gift, without any material consideration. The objective is to spread love and cooperation among people. Literally, *hiba* is to give something to another without compensation, whether the thing is wealth or not. Technically, transfer possession without compensation (Khan, 2007; ISRA, 2010, 2015). Meanwhile *infaq* is a type of charity in Islam that is given without any expectation of reward or return.

In the group of **Joint-Venture**, *mudharaba* is a contract between a capital provider and an asset manager, with the profits and losses shared according to the contractual agreement (Askari, Iqbal, and Mirakhor, 2009, 2015). While *musharaka,* according to AAOIFI (2017) and Mawdudi (2013), is an agreement between two or more parties to combine their assets, labour, liabilities, or equity participation for the purpose of making profits on a profit-and-loss-sharing basis.

Musharaka mutanaqisah (MMQ) is a derivative product of the *musharaka* contract, often mentioned as a diminishing partnership. It is a cooperation contract between two or more parties for the ownership of an asset. In this contract, the ownership rights of one party will be diminished and another will be escalated. The transfer of ownership takes place through a payment mechanism for other ownership rights. While Public-Private Partnership (PPP) is a partnership between the public sector and private sector with the intention of presenting projects/programs traditionally provided by the public sector.

Regarding venture *waqf* organization, Khan (2019) explained that is a proposed new incorporated entity for changing the business paradigm from linear to circular. Through an incorporated institutional framework for venture *waqf* is purposed to make impactful small businesses successful and designing a financial contract to loan in favor of responsible businesses that convert to equity stake for the *waqf* in case of default (EaD) replacing collateral and foreclosure requirements. The venture *waqf* would ensure the achievement of this vision by: reorganizing and strengthening all the Islamic institutions; blending profit with compassion; financing through different Islamic instruments, especially an EaD; assuming a more controlling and enabling role in case of distress; capacity building, advising, coaching and mentoring; and playing a social venture role.

It is undeniable that global economic dynamics, although showing a trend of recovery due to the Covid-19 pandemic, is still fraught with the risk of uncertainty, including the threat of the next wave of pandemics. On the fiscal management side to deliver the realization of the SDGs targets, including in meeting the targets in the Paris Agreement, there are still various challenges that need to be responded to with appropriate and effective policy innovation. Efforts to overcome climate change cannot be postponed because the impact will be more dangerous than the Covid-19 pandemic. ASEAN as part of the global economic ecosystem realizes that the volatility of the global economy will affect the performance of the domestic and regional economy.

As home to 25% of the world's Muslims and more than 42% of Southeast Asian Muslims, ASEAN can promote the alternative financing source as sustainable finance to the circular economy and sustainable energy in tackling climate change in Asia. Then, Asia can play its role in influencing countries in the world, at least in the Muslim world or emerging countries, because Asia is home to 65% of the world's Muslims and most of the Muslim countries in the world are emerging countries. As a leading community in the world that drives the global halal industry, ASEAN also can be a best practice for implementing Islamic Green Financing.

CONCLUSION

Climate change nowadays has become a priority on the development agenda as its impact from time to time increasingly requires real efforts to overcome. The impacts of climate change will not only burden low-income and vulnerable communities in developing countries, but will pose a far greater threat to all of humanity than the pandemic Covid-19. In line with the SDGs, the financing gap deters the implementation of climate change mitigation efforts. As part of a responsible global community committed to realizing a low-carbon and climate-resilient future, ASEAN has an opportunity to lead this global shift by becoming a hub for circular economy and sustainable energy innovations as well as mobilizing funds towards circular and energy efficiency investments.

The existence of the Framework for Circular Economy for the AEC provides a pretentious long-term sight for the circular economy, identifies prime concern areas for action along with enablers, constructs on the strengths of available initiatives to embody circular economy in ASEAN. The ASEAN Taxonomy reflects the collective commitment of ASEAN Member States in changing towards a sustainable region. To provide the ASEAN taxonomy for sustainable finance, Islamic finance should be considered as a part of it. As a leading community in the world that drives the global halal industry, ASEAN also can be a best practice for implementing Islamic Green Financing. Through Islamic Green Financing Taxonomy, it helps stakeholders determine which activities qualify as sustainable and which instrument is suitable for the activity. Islamic Green Financing Taxonomy represents some categories of eligibility ASEAN Eligible Green Sectors and Eligible Renewable Energy Action toward a circular economy and sustainable energy in tackling climate change with several Islamic green financing instruments which can be adopted in order to reach sustainable finance.

REFERENCES

AAOIFI. (2015). The accounting and auditing organization for islamic financial institutions shari'ah standards. Manama: Accounting and Auditing Organization for Islamic Financial Institutions (AAOIFI).

ACMF. (2018). *ASEAN green bond standards.* ASEAN Capital Markets Forum (ACMF).

Alam, N., Duygun, M., & Ariss, R. T. (2016). Green sukuk: An innovation in Islamic capital markets. In A. B. Dorsman, Ö. Arslan-Ayaydin, & M. B. Karan (Eds.), *Energy and finance* (pp. 167–186). Springer International Publishing. doi:10.1007/978-3-319-32268-1_10

Anbumozhi, V., & Kim, J. (Eds.). (2016). Towards a circular economy: Corporate management and policy pathways. Jakarta: Economic Research Institute for ASEAN and East Asia (ERIA).

Anbumozhi, V., & Kimura, F. (Eds.). (2018). Industry 4.0: Empowering ASEAN for the circular economy. Jakarta: Economic Research Institute for ASEAN and East Asia (ERIA).

ASEAN Secretariat, . (2015). *ASEAN 2025: Forging ahead together.* ASEAN Secretariat.

ASEAN Secretariat & ERIA. (2021). *Framework for circular economy for the ASEAN economic community.* Jakarta: The ASEAN Secretariat & the Economic Research Institute for ASEAN and East Asia (ERIA).

ASEAN Secretariat. (2021a, October 21). *ASEAN adopts framework for circular economy.* ASEAN. retrieved from https://asean.org/asean-adopts-framework-for-circular-economy/

ASEAN Secretariat, . (2021b). *ASEAN statistical yearbook 2021.* ASEAN Secretariat.

ASEAN Taxonomy Board. (2021). *ASEAN taxonomy for sustainable finance*. The ASEAN Secretariat.

Askari, H., Iqbal, Z., & Mirakhor, A. (2009). New issues in Islamic finance & economics, progress & challenges. Singapore: John Wiley & Sons (Asia).

Askari, H., Iqbal, Z., & Mirakhor, A. (2015). Introduction to islamic economics: Theory and application. Singapore: John Wiley & Sons (Asia).

Aslam, M., & Jaafar, R. (2020). Budget deficit and the federal government debt in Malaysia. In R. M. Yonk & V. Bobek (Eds.), *Perspectives on economic development: public policy, culture, and economic development*. IntechOpen. doi:10.5772/intechopen.91457

BKF. (2021, November 10). ASEAN taxonomy for sustainable finance sebagai komitmen ASEAN dalam menghadapi dampak perubahan iklim. *The Fiscal Policy Agency (BKF)*. Retrieved from https://fiskal.kemenkeu.go.id/baca/2021/11/10/4319-asean-taxonomy-for-sustainable-finance-sebagai-komitmen-asean-dalam-menghadapi-dampak-perubahan-iklim

Brodsky, S. (2020, March 4). What are green sukuk? *Impactivate*. Retrieved from https://www.theimpactivate.com/what-are-green-sukuk/

Buana, G. K., & Musari, K. (2020). *A new sphere of sukuk: linking pandemic to Paris agreement. The World Financial Review*.

Chapra, M. U., & Khan, T. (2008). *Regulation and supervision for sharia bank*. Bumi Aksara.

Çizakça, M. (2011). *Islamic capitalism and finance: Origins, evolution, and the future*. Edward Elgar Publishing. doi:10.4337/9780857931481

Çizakça, M. (2013). Proposal for innovation in the capital markets: Esham. *Global Islamic Finance Report*, 91-93.

Çizakça, M. (2014). *Can there be innovation in Islamic finance? Case study: Esham*. Paper was presented at the 11th IFSB Summit, Knowledge Sharing Partner Session: "New Markets and Frontiers for Islamic Finance: Innovation and the Regulatory Perimeter".

Çizakça, M. (2018). Modernizing a historical instrument (esham) for growth and financial inclusion. In Z. Iqbal, A. Omar, T. A. A. Manap, & A. A. Alawode (Eds.), Islamic finance: A catalyst for shared prosperity? (pp. 236-246) Jeddah: Islamic Development Bank (IsDB).

Dinard Standard. (2020). *State of the global islamic economy report 2020/2021*. Dinar Standard, Dubai Islamic Economic Development Center, and Salam Gateway.

Eisner, R. (1989, Spring). Budget deficits: Rhetoric and reality. *The Journal of Economic Perspectives*, *3*(2), 73–93. doi:10.1257/jep.3.2.73

Ellen MacArthur Foundation. (2012). *Towards the circular economy vol. 1: An economic and business rationale for an accelerated transition*. Retrieved from https://www.ellenmacarthurfoundation.org/publications/towards-the-circular-economy-vol-1-an-economic-and-business-rationale-for-an-accelerated-transition

Ellen MacArthur Foundation. (2013). *Towards the circular economy vol. 1: Opportunities for the consumer goods sector.* Retrieved from https://www.ellenmacarthurfoundation.org/assets/ downloads/ publications/TCE_Report-2013.pdf

Ellen MacArthur Foundation. (2019). *Completing the picture how the circular economy tackles climate change.* Retrieved from https://circulareconomy.europa.eu/platform/sites/default/files/emf_completing_the_picture.pdf

Ellen MacArthur Foundation. (2020). *Financing the circular economy, capturing the opportunity.* Retrieved from https://ellenmacarthurfoundation.org/financing-the-circular-economy-capturing-the-opportunity

Ellen MacArthur Foundation. (2021). *Completing the picture: How the circular economy tackles climate change.* Retrieved from https://ellenmacarthurfoundation.org/completing-the-picture

Englund, M., & André, K. (2021, October 29). *A circular economy: a tool to bridge climate mitigation and adaptation?* Stockholm Environment Institute (SEI). Retrieved from https://www.sei.org/featured/ circular-economy-mitigation-and-adaptation/

ERIA. (2021). *Framework for circular economy for the ASEAN economic community.* Brochure, The Economic Research Institute for ASEAN and East Asia (ERIA).

Fatemi, A. M., & Fooladi, I. J. (2013). Sustainable finance: A new paradigm. *Global Finance Journal, 24*(2), 101–113. doi:10.1016/j.gfj.2013.07.006

Fauzia, I. Y., & Musari, K. (2021). Waqf crowdfunding for financing the MSMEs: Evidence from ASEAN-3. In P. Ordoñez de Pablos, X. Zhang, & M. N. Almunawar (Eds.), *Handbook of research on disruptive innovation and digital transformation in Asia* (pp. 37–49). IGI Global., doi:10.4018/978-1-7998-6477-6.ch003

Govindaraju, C. (2020). Measuring and benchmarking of policy factors influencing I4R: A reality check for ASEAN. In V. Anbumozhi, K. Ramanathan, & H. Wyes (Eds.), Assessing the readiness for industry 4.0 and the circular economy (pp. 108-147). Jakarta: Economic Research Institute for ASEAN and East Asia (ERIA).

Habibullah, M. S., Cheah, C. K., & Baharom, A. H. (2011). Budget deficits and inflation in thirteen asian developing countries. *International Journal of Business and Social Science, 2*(9), 192-204.

Hariyanto, E. (2020). Potensi dan strategi penerbitan blue sukuk. *Indonesian Treasury Review: Jurnal Perbendaharaan, Keuangan Negara dan Kebijakan Publik, 5*(2), 151-170.

Hidayat, S. E., & Musari, K. (2022). ASEAN towards a global halal logistics through the digitally-enabled community. *International Journal of Asian Business and Information Management, 13*(2), 1–15. doi:10.4018/IJABIM.20220701.oa1

Iqbal, Z., & Mirakhor, A. (2011). An introduction to Islamic finance: Theory and practice (2nd ed.). Singapore: John Wiley & Sons (Asia). doi:10.1002/9781118390474

IRENA & ACE. (2016). Renewable energy outlook for ASEAN: a REmap analysis. International Renewable Energy Agency (IRENA) Dhabi and ASEAN Centre for Energy (ACE).

IsDB. (2021). *Common principles for climate mitigation finance tracking.* Islamic Development Bank (IsDB).

ISRA. (2010). ISRA conpendium: For islamic finance terms, arabic-english. Kuala Lumpur: International Shari'ah Research Academy for Islamic Finance (ISRA).

ISRA. (2015). *Sistem keuangan Islam: Prinsip & operasi.* Rajawali Pers.

Kapoor, A., Teo, E. Q., Azhgaliyeva, D., & Liu, Y. (2020). *The viability of green bonds as a financing mechanism for green buildings in ASEAN.* Asian Development Bank Institute (ADBI) Working Paper Series No. 1186.

Karim, Z. A., Asri, N. M., & Abdullah, A. H., Antoni, & Yusoff, Z. Z. M. (2006). The relationship between federal government revenue and spending: Empirical evidence from ASEAN-5 countries. *Jurnal Ekonomi Pembangunan, 11*(2), 91–113.

Kaye, L. (2021, December 6). The circular economy has a critical role in driving climate action. *Triple Pundit.* retrieved from https://www.triplepundit.com/story/2021/circular-economy-climate-action/732521

Khan, M. A. (2007). *Islamic economics and finance: A glossary.* Routledge International Studies in Money and Banking.

Khan, T. (2019). Venture waqf in a circular economy. *ISRA International Journal of Islamic Finance, 11*(2), 187–205. doi:10.1108/IJIF-12-2018-0138

Lau, W. Y., & Yip, T. M. (2019). The nexus between fiscal deficits and economic growth in ASEAN. *Journal of Southeast Asian Economies, 36*(1). *Special Issue: ASEAN: Towards Economic Convergence, 36*(April), 25–36. doi:10.1355/ae36-1d

Liu, Y., & Noor, R. (2020). *Energy efficiency in ASEAN: Trends and financing schemes.* Asian Development Bank Institute (ADBI) Working Paper Series No. 1196.

Liu, Y., Sheng, Z., & Azhgaliyeva, D. (2019). *Toward energy security in ASEAN: Impacts of regional integration, renewables, and energy efficiency.* Asian Development Bank Institute (ADBI) Working Paper Series No. 1041.

Marimuthu, M., Khan, H., & Bangash, R. (2021). Is the fiscal deficit of ASEAN alarming? Evidence from fiscal deficit consequences and contribution towards sustainable economic growth. *Sustainability, 13*(18), 10045. doi:10.3390u131810045

Mohsin, M. I. A. (2012). Waqf-shares: New product to finance old waqf properties. *Banks and Bank Systems, 7*(2), 72–78.

Musari, K. (2020a, January 7). Measuring the opportunities of white sukuk for SDGs. *Bisnis Indonesia,* 2.

Musari, K. (2020b, April 14). Pandemic and catastrophe sukuk. *Bisnis Indonesia,* 2.

Musari, K. (2020c). *Cash waqf linked sukuk, a new blended finance of fiscal instrument for sustainable socio-economic development: Lesson learned from Indonesia*. A paper was presented at 12th International Conference on Islamic Economics and Finance (ICIEF) "Sustainable Development for Real Economy" with hosted by Istanbul Sabahattin Zaim University (IZU) and jointly organized by Islamic Research and Training Institute (IRTI) - Islamic Development Bank (IDB) and International Association of Islamic Economics (IAIE) with the collaboration of Statistical, Economic and Social Research and Training Centre for Islamic Countries (SESRIC) and Hamad Bin Khalifa University, Istanbul, Turkey.

Musari, K., & Zaroni. (2021). Reverse logistics in the age of digital transformation for circular economy and halal logistics through the leadership of Asia. In *Handbook of research on disruptive innovation and digital transformation in Asia* (pp. 83-103). Hershey, PA: IGI Global. . doi:10.4018/978-1-7998-6477-6.ch006

Musari, K. (2021a). Esham, the origin of sukuk for facing the crisis: Historical experience. *Iqtishoduna: Jurnal Ekonomi Islam, 10*(1), 45–58. doi:10.36835/iqtishoduna.v10i1.945

Musari, K. (2021b). Green sukuk, Islamic green financing: A lesson learned from Indonesia. In O. M. Olarewaju & I. O. Ganiyu (Eds.), *Climate change and the sustainable financial sector* (pp. 1–16). IGI Global. doi:10.4018/978-1-7998-7967-1.ch001

Musari, K. (2021c). Circular economy for plastics and digitally-enabled community towards ASEAN halal hub in Asia. In P. Ordóñez de Pablos (Ed.), *Handbook of research on developing circular, digital, and green economies in Asia* (pp. 1–12). IGI Global. doi:10.4018/978-1-7998-8678-5.ch001

Musari, K. (2021d). *Between esham and cash waqf linked sukuk to fiscal and development sustainability: Comparative analysis*. A paper was presented at Research Center for Islamic Economics (IKAM)'s 9th Islamic Economics Workshop under the theme "Economic Growth and Development in Low Income Countries" in collaboration with Scientific Studies Association (ILEM), Turkish Entrepreneurship and Business Ethics Association (IGIAD), and Istanbul Commerce University.

Musari, K. (2021e). Mencari skema pembiayaan syariah inovatif untuk pembangunan. *Kempalan News*. Retrieved from https://kempalan.com/2021/11/27/mencari-skema-pembiayaan-syariah-inovatif-untuk-pembangunan/

Musari, K. (2021f). *The journey of research to find the taxonomy of domestic/public borrowing in history of Islamic public finance: From sakk, esham, to sukuk*. A presentation material in Sharing Session for Capacity Building of Employee in the Environment of Directorate of Islamic Financing (DPS) Directorate General of Budget Financing and Risk Management (DJPPR) Ministry of Finance (MoF) Republic of Indonesia, Jember-Jakarta. doi:10.13140/RG.2.2.25530.31683

Musari, K. (2022a). A comparative study of Islamic fiscal instrument securitization in history to modern ages: Esham, sukuk, cash waqf linked sukuk (CWLS). In Ş. Akkaya & B. Ergüder (Eds.), *Handbook of research on challenges in public economics in the era of globalization* (pp. 397–418). IGI Global. doi:10.4018/978-1-7998-9083-6.ch021

Musari, K. (2022b). *Integrating green sukuk and cash waqf linked sukuk, the blended islamic finance of fiscal instrument in Indonesia: A proposed model for fighting climate change*. International Journal of Islamic Khazanah, 12(2), 133-144. doi: 10.15575/ijik.v12i2.1775010.15575/ijik.v12i2.17750

Musari, K., & Hidayat, S. E. (2021). *The role of green sukuk in maqasid al-shari'a and SDGs: Evidence from Indonesia.* A paper was presented at International Conference on Islamic Finance 2021 – "Sustainability & The Fourth Industrial Revolution, Implications for Islamic Finance and Economy in Post Pandemic Era" held by the Center for Islamic Economics and Finance (CIEF) in the College of Islamic Studies (CIS) at Hamad Bin Khalifa University with the support of the Qatar Financial Centre (QFC) Authority.

Musari, K., & Sayah, F. (2021). *Green financing through green sukuk in the fight against climate change: Lessons from Indonesia.* A paper was presented at the 1st Virtual International Scientific Forum "The Green Economy as A New Development Model to Support the Dimensions of Sustainable Development in Algeria - A Study of Experiences" organized by Université Lounici Ali de Blida 2.

Nishimura, H. (2019). *Challenges and good practices for the 3R and circular economy in ASEAN and East Asia region.* A material presentation at the 9th Regional 3R Forum on Asia and the Pacific 2019.

Obaidullah, M., & Khan, T. (2008). Islamic microfinance development: Challenges and initiatives. Policy Dialogue Paper No. 2. Jeddah: Islamic Research and Training Institute (IRTI) Islamic Development Bank (IDB).

Rado, G., & Filkova, M. (2019). *ASEAN green financial instruments guide.* Climate Bonds Initiative, ClimateWorks Foundation.

Shofa, J. N. (2021, October 14). ASEAN on a mission towards a sustainable energy future. *Jakarta Globe.* Retrieved from https://jakartaglobe.id/news/asean-on-a-mission-towards-a-sustainable-energy-future

Stewart, F., & Mok, R. (2022, January 6). Striking the right note: Key performance indicators for sovereign sustainability-linked bonds. *World Bank Blogs.* Retrieved from https://blogs.worldbank.org/psd/striking-right-note-key-performance-indicators-sovereign-sustainability-linked-bonds

Van Veldhoven, S., & Schmidt, C. (2021, November 5). How the circular economy can help nations achieve their climate goals. *World Resources Institute.* Retrieved from https://www.wri.org/insights/how-circular-economy-can-help-nations-achieve-their-climate-goals

Whitehead, R. (2021, April 27). Planned ASEAN taxonomy for sustainable finance would benefit from Islamic input, say international experts. *Salaam Gateway.* Retrieved from https://www.salaamgateway.com/story/planned-asean-taxonomy-for-sustainable-finance-would-benefit-from-islamic-input-say-international-ex

World Bank. (2020). *Pioneering the green sukuk: Three years on. Knowledge & Research The Malaysia Development Experience Series.* International Bank for Reconstruction and Development/The World Bank.

ADDITIONAL READING

Anoruo, E., & Ramchander, S. (1998). Current account and fiscal deficits: Evidence from five developing economies of Asia. *Journal of Asian Economics, 9*(3), 487–501. doi:10.1016/S1049-0078(99)80099-2

Lai, K. (2022, January 7). Primer: ASEAN Taxonomy for Sustainable Finance – Version 1. *International Financial Law Review*. Retrieved from https://www.iflr.com/article/b1w6rt1bbkbwr8/primer-asean-taxonomy-for-sustainable-finance-version-1

Saleh, A. S., & Harvie, C. (2005). The budget deficit and economic performance: A survey. *The Singapore Economic Review*, *50*(2), 211–243. doi:10.1142/S0217590805001986

KEY TERMS AND DEFINITIONS

Nazhir: Some call it with *qayyim, mutawalli*, trustee, or fund manager who is responsible for generating profits from the *waqf* that are subsequently used to support socioeconomic development; Individual, organization, or under law institution, which is given the responsibility to manage, administrate, and preserve the *waqf* assets from the *waqif*. They have obligation for making sure the sustainability of *waqf* assets to achieve continuous benefit for the beneficiaries.

Waqf: Assets that are donated, bequeathed, or purchased for being held in perpetual trust for general or specific charitable causes that are socially beneficial; an endowment made by a Muslim under Islamic Law to a *nazhir*; an endowment fund but is strongly encouraged in Islam as a contribution to society; an inalienable charitable endowment under Islamic law.

Waqif: Some call it with *al-muḥabbis* or founder of *waqf;* the person who constitutes the *waqf* of his properties; the *waqf* donor.

Chapter 12
Digital Inclusion as a Tool to Rejuvenate the Rural Banking Sector in Tripura, India:
A Descriptive Analysis

Supriya Dam
Netaji Subhash Mahavidyalaya, Udaipur, India

ABSTRACT

Digital inclusion in banking services was drafted to provide fast and uninterrupted services to a broad pool of customers with an aim to extend financial services to unprivileged groups. Competitive edge associated made it a vibrant policy for bankers across the state with varying degrees of application to suit the customer needs. The present study explores the extent of digital banking interface help improve the status of rural banking in Tripura on the basis of secondary data. Taking cue from four CRISIL Inclusix in view (i.e., branch penetration, deposit penetration, credit penetration, insurance penetration), results are indicative of Tripura's progress in rural front becoming one of the best performing state among NESs. The study again specifies that proper policy measures, vis-a-vis its implementation could place the state amongst top five digitally inclusive states in India and also promote much desired cashless economy and transparency among others.

I. INTRODUCTION

Digital financial inclusion or digital inclusion provides unbanked/under banked people to avail financial services to their needs and requirements, allow disadvantaged to withstand financial shocks (Peric, 2015) than ever before. It allows low income earners, poor, women and those underprivileged to join the bandwagon of financial market (Mhlanga, 2020) that otherwise overlooked. Digital inclusion, therefore, "involves cost saving digital means to reach financially excluded with a range of formal financial services suited to their needs" (WB: 2014). In other words, digital financial services has been a cost effective

DOI: 10.4018/978-1-6684-4610-2.ch012

mechanism to usher in speed, security and transparency of transactions suitably tailored to suit financial needs of disadvantaged groups through well designed policy measures.

The advent of 'Digital India initiative' brought about paradigm operational shift from the traditional offerings to technology based banking services across India; North Eastern Region (NER) is no exception. It primarily makes provision for broadband highways to cover 250,000 villages in rural areas, universal access to mobile connectivity in terms of network penetration and coverage, public internet access program for all villages, e-education, electronic delivery of services etc.(GoI, 2015) with a view to bring about digital empowerment of citizens. Extending financial services to downtrodden, who otherwise opt out of normal banking services for want of financial solvency, at cheaper rates to usher in an era of cashless economy across the country. Such a practice of promoting digitalized financial transactions primarily perceived as a tool to reduce operational cost in the one hand and also to promote financial accountability on the other. In doing so, new technology has evolved and is still evolving to provide a well pronged network of financial services at affordable cost. This has given rise to the concept of digital inclusion, a recent catchword, which challenged conventional concept of banking, a systematic approach towards digitalization of all banking transactions for providing low cost services to the disadvantaged, who otherwise kept outside the purview of costly financial services.

Again, success of such a program calls for well-connected Information and Communication Technology (ICT) network across the nation coupled with consumers 'access to smart phone, a basic necessity to promote digital inclusion. In doing so, cyber security of the Information Technology (IT) system of banking sector came up for scanner as the role of chief information security officer assumes greater significance than ever before. Nonetheless, digitalization of banking transactions is considered as first step to create ripe environment for digital inclusion program pursued by the Government of India.

Digital inclusion encapsulates a well-connected network aimed at reducing cost per transactions. It converges online banking services, telecom networks and smart phone service providers, post offices to inter-connective web network so as to provide best possible services. In short, it is built on the premise that improved mobile phone penetration to locales adjunct with feasible ATM access and other online banking facilities will reduce operational costs which will offer better and fast service to the customers in unbanked locations as well. Building upon these premises, greater use of electronic medium and mobile penetration would further support the realization of a number of government objectives, including the vision set out in India's Twelfth Five Year Plan (2012-2017) and the digital India program followed. Accordingly, schematics of digital banking are framed along the similar lines depicted in the figure below.

Figure 1. Schematics of Digital Inclusion
Source: Adapted from CRISIL INCLUSIX, 2018

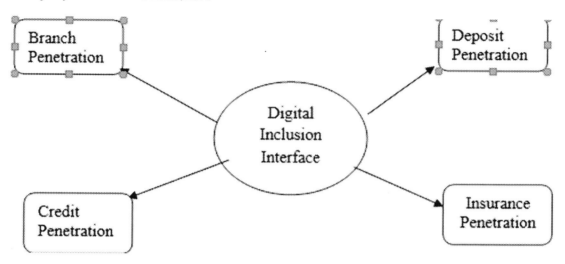

Figure 1 depicts schematics of digital inclusion drawn from CRISIL INCLUSIX 2018, considered as indicators for measuring the same in the form of index (CRISIL, 2018). Obviously, development of this sort of yardstick needs to be compared against a common measuring rod which applies to all States' in general and North Eastern Region (NER) of India in particular. In addition, traditionally, branch, deposit and credit penetration have been regarded as vital elements in expansion of digital inclusion; however, insurance penetration has been included in INCLUSIX 2016 edition to make it comprehensive than ever before. In short, inclusix incorporates inclusive data from three institutions, namely, banks, micro-finance institutions and insurance in single platform with a view to provide standard measuring rod in that front.

India's Telecom Policy 2012 envisioned for secure, reliable, affordable and high quality converged telecommunication services anytime, anywhere for an accelerated inclusive socio-economic development. Its objectives include increase in rural tele-density from around 39 to 70 by the year 2017 and to 100 by 2020. Providing high speed and high quality broadband access to all village panchayets through a combination of technology by the year 2014 and progressively to all villages and inhabitants by 2020. It further defines the role of public sector units under the Department of Telecom, Government of India to identify and exploit strategic synergies so that they play a significant role in service provision, infrastructure creation and manufacturing, pointing directly towards role played by state owned telecom sector towards digital inclusion. The policy also recognizes the predominant role of private sector and the consequent policy imperative of ensuring continued viability of service in a competitive environment among others.

So, at this juncture, present study attempts to explore the role played by digital inclusion upon the rural banking sector in Tripura since 2016 in promoting cashless economy in one hand while ensuring low cost digital banking access to disadvantaged groups on the other. Obviously, rural banking in the State has so far been neglected segment completely overlooked by private sector banking units over the years'. Digital inclusion, along the specified lines, pose challenges with respect to branch penetration, deposit penetration, credit penetration and insurance penetration in rural segment calls for an overall assessment of the same. In doing so, problems specific to the region needs to be captured in detail along with extent of penetration with respect to Tripura. Keeping in mind those imperatives, the specific objectives of this study are framed.

II. OBJECTIVES AND METHODOLOGY

The objectives of the study are:

- To make an overview of Inclusix parameters amongst the North Eastern States (NESs);
- To present a threadbare analysis of digital inclusion in Tripura on the basis of Inclusix; and
- To suggest priority areas of action, if any, for enhancing financial inclusion in the State.

The nature of study calls for collection of secondary data from relevant sources engaged in this field of study. These includes National Family Health Survey (NFHS) 5, Economic Review of Tripura, Reserve Bank of India (RBI) Bulletins, State Level Banker's Committee (SLBC) Reports as well as related publications available in electronic medium including research articles. The information so compiled is analyzed by means of simple statistical techniques for arriving at conclusion of this study.

Again, Credit Ratings and information Services of India Ltd's (CRISIL's) Inclusix forms the basis of this piece of work primarily drawn to make the digital inclusion comparable across India. The study followed the same methodology as it was followed by the CRISIL for arriving at Inclusix. It's segment-wise geographic parameters comprise of branch penetration, deposit penetration, credit penetration and insurance penetration forms the core of this study. This obviously attempts to assess the extent of digital inclusion in Tripura in comparison to rest of NESs of India during the period under review. In doing so, parameters like branch expansion- bank branches per square kilo meter area and automated teller machine (ATM) per square kilo meter area, deposit expansion, credit expansion and insurance expansion are taken into confidence. Information so compiled are analyzed by means of statistical tools like mean, X^2 test for arriving at conclusions. Present study's purely based on secondary source of information; obviously limitations associated with this method of data collection would apply here as well.

This chapter comprises of seven sections. Section I introduce the concept of digital inclusion and establish its linkages with CRISIL's Inclusix. This follows the objectives and methodologies followed and review of literature in Section II and III respectively. Section IV shed light on conditions considered essential for promotion of digital inclusion in the region. In order to better understand the Inclusix, Section V dealt with an in-depth quantitative analysis on the same with respect to Tripura along with its comparison amongst NESs. Last two sections shed light on discussion on the issues cropped up and conclusion of the study.

III. REVIEW OF LITERATURE

Digital inclusion drive has drawn much needed attention across the globe in recent times for its inherent objective to provide organized financial accessibility to downtrodden, who otherwise reluctant to operate digitally. Obviously, digital financial inclusion usually helps those households who otherwise opt for informal financial services due cumbersome procedure of documentation requirements, costs as well as literacy issues (David-West, 2015). Physical access to financial services are, most often than not, inadequate to meet the needs of the target groups (Bora, 2020), led the groups resort to informal financial services than warranted. Studies argued that tools used in digital financial inclusion are, mostly, unreliable, expensive and hard to use on the part of disadvantageous groups (Anon, 2015), considered as prime reason for below par accessibility. In this regard, Kostav et al (2015) argued that aspirations and financial literacy are important ingredients of financial inclusion.

Srouji (2020) envisaged a better understanding of socioeconomic, technological and policy paradigms pave the way to reduce reliance on cash in favor of digitalization. Selvaraj and Ragesh (2019) called for attitudinal changes in banking personnel for attaining cashless economy across the region. Meitei and Singh (2020) study observed that socioeconomic, demographic, and households living below the poverty line (BPL) with bank accounts played a significant role in opting for health insurance schemes.

Traditionally, bankers strategize to tap each rewarding segment by following appropriate approach for it. Obviously, appropriate strategies needs to be adopted for unbanked regions for extending banking infrastructure in those locations can bring desired outcomes (Shylaja, 2020). Singh and Tandon (2013) stressed that commercial banks need to overhaul their policies towards low income groups while treating it both as social obligation and opportunity while raising financial conditions and living standards of the underprivileged for ensuring sustainable economic growth (Lal, 2018). Findings indicate that fewer females are utilizing formal financial services in comparison to males, so attention should be given to women empowerment by extending such services to them (Trivedi, 2016).

Cross country regression findings points to a barrier in inclusiveness due to presence of macroeconomic variables for calculation of systematic risk assessment by regulators (Sayed and Shusha, 2019). However, its wide range of acceptability across the globe made it obligatory on the part of regulators to adopt similar approach for assessment of digital inclusion. In this regard, Sharma (2008) put forward financial inclusion index (FII) for measuring financial inclusion by means of three parameters- penetration of the banking system, the availability as well as the use of financial services while maintaining the same weight for each components. On the contrary, Amidzic et al (2014) developed a composite index for measuring financial inclusion with differential weights for each component. CRISIL's Inclusix considered being an improvement over FII's and could improve management, governance, operational practices and governance through responsible financial initiatives (Rao et al, 2020).

Obviously, inclusix has evolved and still evolving by providing a comprehensive methodology for measuring digital inclusion. CRISIL's inclusix adopted similar methodology followed by the United Nations Development Program's (UNDP's) Human Development Index with due focus on 'number of people' rather than 'amount deposited' presents a comprehensive approach for measuring financial inclusion (Shah and Dubhashi, 2015). Such an index at the national, state and district level across the geographical area prevents disproportionate representation of few large transactions (Singh, 2018) and facilitates comparison, both within or outside the region.

Nautiyal and Ismail (2019) observed that credit and branch penetration, most often, confined to large cities and urban centres should be extended to rural segments as well. Singh et al (2014) argued in favor of self-sustaining solution for easing the intricacies associated with cashless options. Present study is an attempt to assess the status of digital financial inclusion in rural segments of Tripura based on inclusix and provide a basis for its comparative growth.

IV. INDICATORS OF DIGITAL INCLUSION

The geographical segmentation of bank branches is drawn as per Master Office File (MOF) of Reserve Bank of India (RBI) from time to time. Accordingly, population assigned to each segments are categorized as rural, semi-urban, urban as well as metropolitan segments. Rural branches and semi-urban segments comprise of serving population of less than 10000 and 10000 to less than 100000 population per branch respectively. Similarly, urban segment consists of serving population of 100000 to less than 1 million whereas population ranging beyond 1 million or more categorized as metropolitan centers. The following figure depicts the share of rural and semi-urban population of eight NESs during 2016-17.

Figure 2. Rural and Semi-urban Distribution of Households of NESs during 2016-17
Source: NABARD.

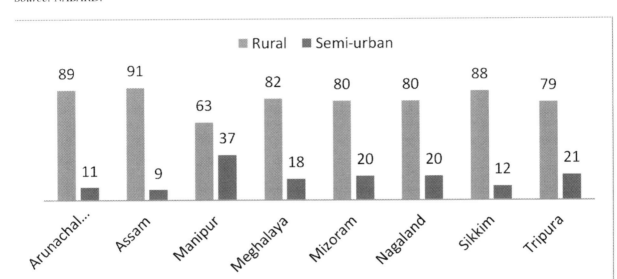

Figure 2 depicts rural-urban distribution of households from the states of NE India during 2016-17. Mean distribution of households of NESs in rural segment stood at 18.5 per cent for the period, quite poor considering the landscape of the region. Manipur (37%) leads the way in holding its rural population from migrating to urban segment through development measures followed by Tripura (21%), Mizoram (20%), Nagaland (20%) down the order. States like Sikkim (12%), Arunachal Pradesh (11%) and Assam (9%) failed to hold its population from migrating to urban segment till 2016-17, having lower rural population than mean distribution of households in the region.

Grant Thornton (GT, 2020, p11) spells out major reasons for digital exclusion with respect to India. These include inadequate money, lack of financial literacy, cost/bank charges/minimum balance requirements of banks, inadequate infrastructure led to unbanked adult population among others. In such a scenario, extension of urban centric operation to rural segment does not bring desired result in digital inclusion front than otherwise. The financial institutions actively engaged in digital inclusion in India encompasses scheduled commercial banks, regional rural banks, payment banks, micro-finance institutions, business correspondents' (bank mitras) and small finance banks among others (GT, 2020). These institutions provide financial services to target population for promotion of digital inclusion.

Figure 3. Mechanism for Digital Inclusion
Source: Adapted from Grant Thornton (GT), 2020

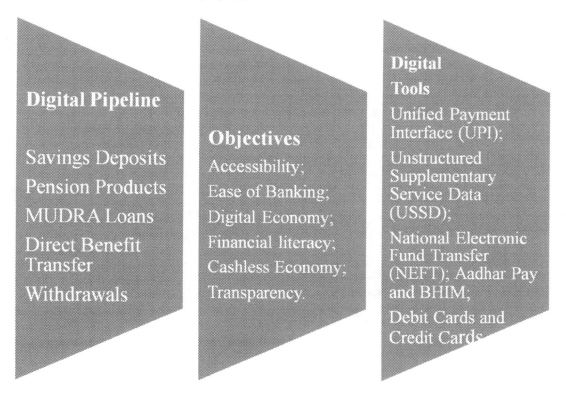

Figure 3 represents the mechanism for digital inclusion categorized into three sets, namely, digital pipeline, objectives aimed at and digital tools. Digital pipeline includes savings deposits accounts of banking institutions, pension products of both departments and specialized institutions, Micro Units Development and Refinance Agency (MUDRA) loans, direct benefit transfer (DBT), as well as withdrawal facilities extended by financial institutions. The prime objectives behind digital inclusion is to provide easy accessibility to clients, ease of doing banking transactions, encouragement of digital economy, financial literacy of customers', promotion of cashless economy and transparency among others. Digital payment tools available to achieve the objectives enshrined encompasses unified payment interface (UPI), unstructured supplementary service data (USSD), immediate payment service (IMPS), real time gross settlements (RTGS), national electronic fund transfer (NEFT), Aadhar Pay and Bharat Interface for Money (BHIM) and debit and credit cards. The other measures include Pradhan Mantri Jan-Dhan Yojana (PMJDY), considered the prime tool behind adoption of digital inclusion initiatives dealt in separate section in the chapter.

Table 1. Number of Households having Computer and Internet Facilities amongst the North Eastern States (NES)'

NE States'	Households	Area in Sq km	Computers	%age	With Internet	%age	Without Internet	%age	Col. 4 / Col. 3
(1)	(2)	(3)	(4)	(5)	(6)	(7)	(8)	(9)	(10)
Arunachal Pradesh	261614	83746	21542	8.2	5232	2.0	16220	6.2	0.26
Assam	6367295	78348	592158	9.3	101877	1.6	490282	7.7	7.56
Manipur	507152	22327	45664	9.0	10650	2.1	34993	6.9	2.05
Meghalaya	538299	22429	40911	7.6	8074	1.5	32836	6.1	1.82
Mizoram	221077	21081	33604	15.2	5527	2.5	28077	12.7	1.59
Nagaland	399965	16579	35597	8.9	6799	1.7	28797	7.2	2.15
Sikkim	128131	7096	14735	11.5	4228	3.3	10507	8.2	2.08
Tripura	842781	10846	60680	7.2	8428	1.0	53095	6.3	5.60
North East	**1158289**		**105611**	**9.6**	**18852**	**1.96**	**86851**	**7.7**	**2.89**
India	246692667		23189111	9.4	7647473	3.1	15541638	6.3	

Source: Census of India, 2011.

Table 1 shows comparative computer usage statistics of households' residing in NESs along with/ without internet facility as per 2011 census. It can be observed that, barring Mizoram and Sikkim, majority of the households in NESs having computer facility lower than both NE and national average. With respect to computer with internet facility, average of the same for NESs (i.e. 1.96) far lower than national average of 3.1. For computer with internet, majority of the NESs, with the exception of Arunachal Pradesh and Meghalaya, possess better rate than the all India average during the period. Column 10 shows the ratio of computer usage per square kilo meter area of each NESs, an indication of computer literacy across the region. In this regard, state of Assam and Tripura holding first and second respectively amongst the eight NESs having better ratio than the other.

Table 2. Households having Landline and Mobile Connectivity amongst NESs

NE States'	Households (Nos)	%age	Landline (Nos)	%age	Mobile (Nos)	%age	Population	Col. 6 / Col. 8 (%)
(1)	(2)	(3)	(4)	(5)	(6)	(7)	(8)	(9)
Arunachal Pradesh	261614	48.3	7587	2.9	104122	39.8	1,383,727	7.53
Assam	6367295	47.9	140080	2.2	2763406	43.4	31,205,576	8.86
Manipur	507152	57.5	15215	3.0	263240	52.3	2,570,390	10.24
Meghalaya	538299	48.1	17698	2.1	229854	42.7	2,966,889	7.75
Mizoram	221077	72.8	3758	1.7	141268	63.9	1,097,206	12.88
Nagaland	399965	53.1	5200	1.3	194383	48.6	1,978,502	9.83
Sikkim	128131	73.0	2306	1.8	86745	67.7	610,577	14.21
Tripura	842781	48.1	17698	2.1	359867	42.7	3,673,917	9.80
North East	**1158289**	**56.1**	**26192.75**	**2.1**	**517861**	**50.14**	**5748348**	**9.99**
India	**246692667**	**63.2**	**9867707**	**4.0**	**131240499**	**53.2**	**1,210,193,422**	**10.85**

Source: Census of India, 2011.

Table 2 depicts households holding landline and mobile connectivity amongst NESs of India as per 2011 census indicating averages of NE States were lower than national level for all the four counts. Barring Sikkim, Nagaland and Mizoram, rest the NESs was either equal to or higher than the NE average for landline connectivity. Similarly, average mobile connectivity of the region stands at 50.14 per cent as per 2011 census in which only three states (namely Sikkim, Mizoram and Manipur) had better mobile connectivity rate than the regional average. The ratio of mobile facilities with respect to population presents a better picture about the same during the period. With the exception of larger states like Arunachal Pradesh, Assam and Meghalaya, the rest five NE states' had better mobile connectivity to population ratio at the regional level fractionally lower than the national standard.

Till December, 2018, total of 8621 villages of eight NESs yet to be covered by mobile connectivity- of which 2805 villages situated at Arunachal Pradesh, 2503 villages in Assam, 2374 in Meghalaya, 528 in Manipur, 252 in Mizoram, 134 in Nagaland, 23 in Sikkim and two in Tripura (Kalita: 2018). Although Tripura achieved total internet and mobile connectivity across all villages by July, 2020, rest of the NESs yet to achieve that feet till early 2021.

Table 3. Internet Users of NESs in the Age Group of 15-49 during 2019-20 (%)

NE States'	Women			Men			Rank
	Urban	Rural	Total	Urban	Rural	Total	
Assam	49.0	24.4	28.2	67.4	37.8	42.3	VI
Manipur	50.8	44.8	44.8	81.5	68.2	73.9	III
Meghalaya	57.8	28.0	34.7	59.2	38.5	42.1	V
Mizoram	83.8	48.0	67.6	92.7	63.9	79.7	II
Nagaland	66.5	40.3	49.9	81.0	55.2	64.6	IV
Sikkim	90.0	68.1	76.7	94.2	69.5	78.2	I
Tripura	36.6	17.7	22.9	47.0	45.2	45.7	VII
NE Average	**62.1**	**38.8**	**46.4**	**74.7**	**50.0**	**60.9**	

Source: National Family Health Survey-5, 2019-20

Table 3 depicts internet users of NESs for the age group of 15-49 during the period of 2019-20 with the exception of Arunachal Pradesh. State of Sikkim ranked first in both urban and rural locations having almost equal percentage of internet users of both men and women for the period. This follows Mizoram, Manipur, and Nagaland etc. in descending order. Barring Sikkim and Mizoram, the urban-rural divide is quite pronounced in terms of internet users for the rest of the NESs in the same age bracket. State of Tripura was the least performer in the 15-49 age groups primarily due to inadequate internet users from womenfolk of the state during the period. Tripura fails to touch 50 per cent mark in all the four counts goes to show lopsided growth of the same inside the state during the period under review. However, in terms of Internet Readiness Index (IRI), Tripura ranked third behind Nagaland and Manipur in which none other NESs could qualify in that category in NE India during 2017 (IAMAI: 2017).

Since 2014, Jan Dhan Yojana (JDY) scheme introduced by Government of India primarily meant for under-privileged groups for lateral entry into banking services. The JDY scheme alone account for 30 crore (300 million) savings deposit accounts under zero balance option immediately after its launching in August, 2014, a drive that brought maximum household under JDY's fold. A brief account of the same is given below.

Table 4. Progress of JDY across NESs

North Eastern States	Total Households (Nos)	Households Coverage (%)	Beneficiaries at rural/semi urban bank branches	Balance in beneficiaries A/C (INR Cr)	Balance per household (INR) (Col. 5/2)	Balance per beneficiary A/C (INR) (Col.5/4)
(1)	(2)	(3)	(4)	(5)	(6)	(7)
Arunachal Pradesh	197861	100.00	243280	219.34	10832.86	8810.42
Assam	5013404	99.96	15970314	4748.92	9472.45	2973.59
Manipur	514604	99.76	624133	217.39	4224.41	3939.35
Meghalaya	477812	100.00	551834	359.38	7521.37	6512.47
Mizoram	181946	99.92	184204	148.05	8137.03	8037.29
Nagaland	334034	99.92	154574	95.58	2861.39	6183.45
Sikkim	131086	100.00	58043	45.37	3461.09	7816.62
Tripura	755041	100.00	673169	426.94	5654.53	6342.24

Source: https://pmjdy.gov.in/statewise-statistics

Table 4 shed light on progress of JDY across NESs till March, 2022. The scheme has outstanding household coverage across the region along with beneficiaries at rural/semi urban bank branches over the years. A realistic assessment of bank balance per households and bank balance per beneficiary gives us impression that, in spite of making inroads, picture has not been encouraging. Highest bank balance per household held by Arunachal Pradesh followed by Assam, Mizoram, Meghalaya, Tripura in descending orders. Arunachal Pradesh, again, holds onto its position in highest bank balance per beneficiary as well. This follows Mizoram, Sikkim, Meghalaya, and Tripura down the order on the same count.

Table 5. Loan disbursed through Self Help Groups (SHGs) of NESs till March, 2021 (Amount in Million)

NE States	Commercial Banks		RRBs		Cooperative Banks		Total		Col 8/ Col 7
	SHGs (nos)	Loan disbursed	SHGs (nos)	Loan disbursed	SHGs (nos)	Loan disbursed	SHGs (nos)	Loan disbursed	
	(1)	(2)	(3)	(4)	(5)	(6)	(7)	(8)	(9)
Arunachal Pradesh	198	18.454	144	15.472	NA	NA	342	33.926	0.099
Assam	41924	3596.231	26761	4945.647	NA	NA	68685	8541.878	0.124
Manipur	301	31.333	332	51.433	144	20.04	777	102.806	0.132
Meghalaya	241	26.68	2520	482.733	324	22.48	3085	531.893	0.172
Mizoram	122	21.483	1969	327.671	140	16.87	2231	366.024	0.164
Nagaland	383	46.094	NA	NA	NA	NA	383	46.094	0.120
Sikkim	955	148.597	NA	NA	22	3.48	977	152.077	0.156
Tripura	2201	162.478	5238	765.983	1107	148.095	8546	1076.556	0.126

Source: NABARD
RRB: Regional Rural Banks, NA: Not Available

Table 5 illustrates the loan disbursed through SHGs among eight NESs till March, 2021. In terms of aggregate number of SHGs and total loan disbursed, state of Assam tops the list followed by Tripura, Meghalaya, Mizoram and Sikkim in descending order; whereas Nagaland and Arunachal Pradesh lies at the bottom. However, in terms of ratio of loan disbursed to number of SHGs, Meghalaya precedes others. This follows Mizoram, Sikkim, Manipur, Tripura in that order.

V. The INCLUSIX: The following table (table 4) shows a comparative statistics of rural reporting offices, aggregate deposits and bank credit (loans and advances) of public sector banks in NER during 2018-19 to 2020-21. Obviously, credit-deposit ratio (relationships of deposits mobilized to credit given) has been the widely accepted criteria for adjudging status of banking institution in consonance with growth of reporting offices.

Table 6. Number of Rural Reporting Offices, Aggregate Deposits and Bank Credit of Public Sector Banks in NER

NE States'	2018-19 Q1				2019-20 Q1				2020-21Q1			
	RO*	Deposit (INR Crore)	Credit (INR Crore	CDR	RO *	Deposit (INR Crore)	Credit (INR Crore)	CDR	RO *	Deposit (INR Crore)	Credit (INR Crore)	CDR
Arunachal Pradesh	73	3674	792	21.56	73	4308	871	20.22	77	4918	1050	21.35
Assam	1063	27079	14612	53.96	1312	30646	17500	57.10	1407	36177	19120	52.85
Manipur	77	1780	1125	63.20	91	2196	1495	68.07	91	2576	1626	63.12
Meghalaya	167	5235	2237	42.73	169	5673	2460	43.36	175	6006	2613	43.51
Mizoram	66	818	359	43.89	67	992	434	43.75	66	1502	566	37.68
Nagaland	51	1082	586	54.16	53	1119	737	65.86	54	1319	871	66.04
Sikkim	70	2117	622	29.38	74	2434	767	31.51	82	2826	859	39.40
Tripura	200	5991	2440	40.73	243	5456	2999	54.97	255	7782	3634	46.70
NER				47.67				51.61				48.08

*RO: Reporting Offices (Nos). CDR: Credit-Deposit Ratio (%).

Source: www.rbi.org.in

Point to point analysis suggests all the North Eastern States' (NESs) registered incremental increase in rural reporting offices, deposits mobilized as well as loan disbursed during the course of three years in succession. Addition to rural reporting offices in Assam gone up by 1.32 times followed by Tripura (1.28 times), Manipur (1.18 times), Sikkim 1.17 times etc in descending orders. Mizoram (1.84 times) recorded highest spurt in aggregate deposit mobilization during the period. This follows Manipur (1.45 times), Arunachal Pradesh, Assam and Sikkim (1.34 times each), Tripura (1.30 times), Nagaland (1.22 times) and Meghalaya (1.15 times) on that count. Similarly, in terms of loan disbursement, Mizoram (1.58 times) topped the list followed by Tripura and Meghalaya (1.49 times each), Manipur (1.45 times), Sikkim (1.38 times) etc in that order. These figures are indicative of disproportionate loan disbursement rate for NESs like Assam, Meghalaya, Arunachal Pradesh in particular in comparison to rest of states' of the region. In this regard bank branches per lakh (one-tenth of a million) of population provide a meaningful index of assessing branch penetration in across locations. In this criterion, Sikkim leads the way with 0.017 bank branches per lakh of population followed by Mizoram (0.015), Tripura (0.010), Arunachal Pradesh (0.009) in that order. States of Assam, Manipur and Nagaland have the least bank branches per lakh of population during the period.

Table 7. Branch and ATM Penetration in North East India during 2020

NE States	Bank Branches per sq km area	Bank branches per 100000 adult population	ATM per sq km area	ATM per 100000 adult Population	Deposit & Credit per 100000 Adult Population	Cumulative Total	Rank
(1)	(2)	(3)	(4)	(5)	(6)	(7)	(8)
Arunachal Pradesh	0.0018	0.16838	0.0030	0.27878	0.01681	0.09375	IV
Assam	0.0294	0.10916	0.0483	0.17922	0.02083	0.07738	VI
Manipur	0.0071	0.08981	0.0147	0.18528	0.01499	0.06238	VIII
Meghalaya	0.0151	0.17846	0.0178	0.21120	0.01526	0.08756	V
Mizoram	0.0088	0.25619	0.0077	0.22451	0.01935	0.10331	II
Nagaland	0.0095	0.09658	0.0189	0.19317	0.00912	0.06545	VII
Sikkim	0.0185	0.29645	0.0264	0.42317	0.02338	0.15758	I
Tripura	0.0422	0.16914	0.0466	0.19031	0.02568	0.09479	III
Mean	**0.0166**	**0.17052**	**0.0229**	**0.23571**	**0.01818**		

Source: Calculated from respective State Level Banker Committee (SLBC) reports.

Table 7 shed light on branch and Automated Teller Machine (ATM) penetration during the year 2020. Due to paucity of rural specific data, the information covered incorporates both urban and rural segments of each NESs. It can be observed that Tripura has been second to none among the NESs with respect to three parameters, namely, bank branches per square kilo meter area, ATM per square kilo meter area as well as deposit mobilized and credit given per 100000 of adult population during 2020. With respect to other two parameters', i.e. bank branches per 100000 adult population and ATM per 100000 adult Population, the state falls short of regional average for 2020. Due to this, Tripura ranked third amongst eight NESs on given counts. On the whole, Sikkim ranked first in the NER followed by Mizoram, Tripura, Arunachal Pradesh down the order whereas Assam, Nagaland and Manipur stood at bottom three ranks on the basis of performance of given five parameters.

In view of covid ridden environment, health insurance seems to provide realistic picture about insurance penetration of NESs. National Family Health Survey 5 provides a good account of this with respect to each of NESs for 2019-20. An account of this is given in table 6 below.

Table 8. Health Insurance Penetration of NESs during 2019-20.

NESs	Urban (%)	Rural (%)	Total (%)	Rank
Arunachal Pradesh	33.6	28.5	29.3	V
Assam	50.1	61.9	60.0	II
Manipur	12.3	15.3	14.2	VIII
Meghalaya	52.8	66.5	63.5	I
Mizoram	41.2	52.8	46.4	III
Nagaland	15.0	23.1	20.5	VII
Sikkim	31.2	21.6	25.7	VI
Tripura	24.9	36.5	33.0	IV
India	**38.1**	**42.4**	**41.0**	

Source: National Family Health Survey (NFHS) 5. http://rchiips.org/nfhs/factsheet_NFHS-5.shtml

Health insurance penetration of NESs has not been encouraging in which only three among eight states' could achieve the national average as per NFHS 5 for 2019-20. Meghalaya, Assam and Mizoram ranked first, second and third respectively among eight NESs, performed better than national aggregates, in both urban and rural segments for the period. Of the rest, Tripura ranked fourth falls short of national aggregates by 13.2 per cent and 5.9 per cent for urban and rural segments correspondingly; followed by Arunachal Pradesh, Sikkim, Nagaland and Manipur down the order. Barring Sikkim, rest of the NESs has better insurance penetration in rural segment than its urban counterparts for 2019-20.

The following table 9 shed light on respective inclusix of eight NESs during the year 2020. The mean inclusix for each has been arrived at after due consideration to branch expansion, deposit mobilization, dispersal of credit as well as insurance penetration as mentioned in methodology for the same. Geographic variables like area in square kilo meter and size of NESs suitably utilized for calculation of inclusix facilitates comparison amongst rest of Indian states for the period.

Table 9. Calculation of Inclusix of NESs for 2020

North Eastern States (per sq km area)	Branch Expansion		Deposit Expansion	Credit Expansion	Insurance Expansion	Inclusix (Mean)
	Bank Branches per sq km area X 100	ATM per sq km area X 100	per sq km area X 100	per sq km area X 100	per sq km area X 100	
(1)	(2)	(3)	(4)	(5)	(6)	(7)
Arunachal Pradesh (83743)	0.18	0.3	5.14	1.04	21.81	5.694
Assam (78438)	2.94	4.83	39.07	22.31	38.39	21.508
Manipur (22327)	0.71	1.47	9.83	6.69	35.29	10.798
Meghalaya (22720)	1.51	1.78	24.97	10.82	44.67	15.75
Mizoram (21081)	0.88	0.77	4.71	2.06	34.42	8.568
Nagaland (16579)	0.95	1.89	6.75	4.45	6.079	4.024
Sikkim (7096)	1.85	2.64	34.3	10.81	49.55	19.83
Tripura (10492)	4.22	4.66	52	28.58	68.71	31.634
X^2 value	50.5887			P value		0.00556

Source: 1. https://necouncil.gov.in/

2. & 3. Same as table 7

4. & 5. Computed from table 6.

Tripura (31.634) ranked first (table 9) amongst the eight NESs in inclusix parameters followed by Assam (21.580), Sikkim (19.83), Meghalaya (15.750) etc down the order. Manipur (10.798), Mizoram (8.568) and Nagaland (4.024) are least performing states in terms of inclusix indicative of inadequate growth of digital inclusion for the period under review. However, irrespective of Tripura's rank on that front, a inclusix score of less than 35 considered as low penetration as per CRISIL methodology and suggests areas for improvement on this front.

Let us hypothesize that let us hypothesize that

H_0: Inclusix variables have statistically significant association.

H_1: Inclusix variables do not have statistically significant association. Applying X^2 test at 5 per cent level of significance.

Table 9 again shows X^2 value of 50.5887 and P value of 0.00556 for five parameter of inclusix. It can be noticed that calculated p value of 0. 00556 lower than tabulated value at 0.05 (i.e. 0. 00556‹0.05) at 5 per cent level of significance. Thus, null hypothesis hold true and it can be inferred that there is significant association between five parameters of inclusix arrived at for the period.

V. DISCUSSION

Inclusix has emerged as tool for assessing digital/financial inclusion since 2013-14 across India to assess the extent of digital inclusion with a prospect of facilitating comparison. Its recognition of inclusive variables, over the years, along with adaptation justifies the unified reporting mechanism followed throughout India. It essentially points to the outreach of digital inclusion destined to encapsulate hitherto under-privileged groups normally desist from digital transactions. However, non-inclusion of factors like education status, income inconsistencies as well as affordability of end users among others can weaken its status across the country.

Although, successful government initiatives, over the years, saw large scale addition to new account holders courtesy Jan Dhan Yojana (JDY), Pradhan Mantri Jeevan Jyoti Bima Yojana (PMJJBY), Pradhan Mantri Suraksha Bima Yojana (PMSBY), Atal Pension Yojana (APY) and host of others. The present status of JDY (table 4) gives us impression that there are good numbers of inoperative accounts under JDY across the region and less number of beneficiaries contributing for scaling up of total deposit mobilization of the banks. In the given scenario, the prime objective of launching JDY gets affected.

Again, Credit-Deposit Ratio (CDR) in rural segment of NESs in general and Tripura in particular has not been encouraging and far below the national level average of 64.6 per cent. Similarly, loan disbursed through SHGs, insurance penetration etc. although seemingly impressive from Tripura's point of view, especially when compared with rest of NESs; but still a lot of stake to catch hold of in comparison to national standard.

VI. CONCLUSION

Ongoing discussion exemplifies the status of digital inclusion of NESs in general and Tripura in particular based on geographical coverage as enshrined in methodology followed for Inclusix. The given set of information points to incremental rise of digitally inclusive growth for Tripura in comparison to the other states of North East India during 2019-20. This is indeed an achievement of sort for the landlocked state to bring back economically disadvantaged groups in banking fold in a self sustained manner backed by policy initiatives from concerned governments over the years. Such an inclusive growth destined to address shyness nature of downtrodden for availing the benefits offered. Consequentially, it eradicates role played by middlemen in financial transactions, pave the way for scaling down of corrupt practices followed for years. Digital inclusion effectively promotes universal payment system (UPS) inside Tripura since its adoption and reinforcement from late 2016. In addition, promotion of cashless economy along with transparency has been one of the reasons for switching to digital inclusion can see light of the day.

Recent thrust on insurance coverage along with credit coverage significantly contributed to the growth of digital banking in rural segment across the region. However, in comparison to rest of India, NES's in general and Tripura in particular yet to match the score of inclusix to mainstream states. In fact, inclusix score of less than 0.35 or 35 considered as poor, as evinced by NESs, during the course of study. Commercial banks, with thrust on valued customers, essentially overlook the perspective of disadvantaged groups especially in rural segments. Instead, much of its activities directed at meeting targets set by the Reserve of Bank India (RBI) as a part of priority sector lending. Again, for successful implementation of digital inclusion program, merely providing banking access to downtrodden will not produce desired results, unless educating the disadvantaged groups for reaping the benefit of the schemes for common good is also equally important. Tripura has been better prepared to take up the challenge of surging ahead on this front by resorting to worthwhile policy measures along with governance in the given direction in the years to come.

REFERENCES

Amidzic, G., Massara, A., & Mialou, A. (2014). *Assessing Countries Financial Inclusion Standing- A New Composite Index*. IMF Working Paper WP/14/36, International Monetary Fund.

Anonymous. (2015). Digital Financial Inclusion. *Journal of Payment Strategy and System, 9*(3), 212–214.

Bora, N. M. (2020). Financial Inclusion in India: A Case Study of North Eastern States. *International Journal of Scientific and Technology Research, 9*(2), 1319–1323.

David-West, O. (2015). The Path to Digital Financial Inclusion in Nigeria: Experience of Firstmonie. *Journal of Payment Strategy and Systems, 9*, 256–273.

Government of India (GoI). (2015). *India's Trillion Dollar Digital Opportunity*. Ministry of Electronic and Information Technology. Retrieved on 25th November, 2021 from: https://www.digitalindia.gov.in/ebook/MeitY_TrillionDollarDigitalEconomy.pdf

Grant Thorton (GT). (2020). *Financial Inclusion in Rural India: Banking and ATM Sector in India*. Retrieved on 11th March, 2022 from: https://www.grantthorton.in/insights/articles

IAMAI. (2017). *Index of Internet Readiness of Indian States*. Retrieved from: https://cms.iamai.in/Content/ResearchPapers/59923bed-ad4f-439b-b6d9-487fbbc16103.pdf

Kalita, P. (2018). *North East States lag behind in internet and mobile connectivity*. Retrieved from: https://timesofindia.indiatimes.com/city/guwahati/northeast-states-lag-behind-in-internet-mobile-connectivity/articleshow/67168080.cms

Kostav, P., Arun, T., & Annim, S. (2015). Access to Financial Services: The Case of the Mzansi Account of South Africa. *Review of Development Finance, 5*(1), 34–42. doi:10.1016/j.rdf.2015.04.001

Lal, T. (2018). Impact of Financial Inclusion on Poverty Alleviation through Cooperative Banks. *International Journal of Social Economics, 45*(5), 808–828. doi:10.1108/IJSE-05-2017-0194

Meitei, M.H. & Singh, H.B. (2020). Coverage and Correlates of Health Insurance in the North Eastern States of India. *Journal of Health Research*. . doi:10.1108/JHR-07-2020-0282

Mhlanga, D. (2020). Industry 4.0 in Finance: The Impact of Artificial Intelligence (AI) on Digital Financial Inclusion. *International Journal of Financial Studies, 8*(3), 1–14. doi:10.3390/ijfs8030045

Nautiyal, T., & Ismail, S. (2019). Financial Inclusion and Economic Growth in India: An Empirical Analysis of Feedback Mechanism. *International Journal of Social Science and Economic Research, 4*(6), 4078–4093.

Peric, K. (2015). Editorial: Digital Financial Inclusion. *Journal of Payment Strategy and Systems, 9*(3), 212–214.

Rao, M. S., Podile, V., & Navvula, D. (2020). Financial Inclusion Index: An Indian Experience. *High Technology Letters*, *26*(9), 816–825.

RBI. (2014). *Financial Inclusion in India-An Assessment*. Retrieved on 25th November, 2021 from: https://rbidocs.rbi.org.in/rdocs/Speeches/PDFs/MFI101213FS.pdf

Sayed, M. N., & Shusha, A. (2019). Determinants of Financial Inclusion in Egypt. *Asian Economic and Financial Review*, *9*(12), 1383–1404. doi:10.18488/journal.aefr.2019.912.1383.1404

Selvaraj, P., & Ragesh, T. V. (2019). Innovative Approach of Regional Rural Bank in Adopting Technology Banking and Improving Service Quality Leading to Better Digital Banking. *Vinimaya*, *39*(1), 22–32.

Shah, P., & Dubhashi, M. (2015). Review Paper on Financial Inclusion- The Means of Inclusive Growth. *Chanakya International Journal of Business Research*, *1*(1), 37–48. doi:10.15410/cijbr/2015/v1i1/61403

Sharma, M. (2008). *Index of Financial Inclusion*. Indian Council for Research on International Relations, Working Paper No. 2015. Retrieved on 25th February, 2022 from: http://icrier.org/pdf/Working_Paper_215.pdf

Shylaja, H. N. (2020). Financial Inclusion with reference to Access to Banking Services. *International Journal of Scientific and Technology Research*, *9*(1), 3749–3755.

Singh, A., & Tandon, P. (2013). Financial Inclusion in India: An Analysis. *International Journal of Marketing. Financial Services and Management Research*, *1*(6), 41–54.

Singh, C., Mittal, A., Goenka, A., Goud, C. R. P., Ram, K., Suresh, R. V., Chandrakar, R., Garg, R., & Kumar, U. (2014). Financial Inclusion in India: Select Issues. *IIMB-WP*, (474), 1–43.

Singh, M. (2018). Study of CRISIL-INCLUSIX as an Index of Financial Inclusion. *International Journal of Management Humanities and Social Science*, *3*(1), 36–49.

Srouji, J. (2020). Digital Payments, Cashless Economy and Financial Inclusion in the United Arab Emirates: Why is everyone still transacting in Cash? *Journal of Risk and Financial Management*, *13*(11), 2–10. doi:10.3390/jrfm13110260

Trivedi, A. S. (2016). Reality of Financial Inclusion: India. *International Journal of Research and Analytical Reviews*, *3*(3), 87–92.

World Bank (WB). (2014). *Digital Financial Inclusion*. Retrieved on 25th November, 2021 from: https://www.worldbank.org/en/topic/financialinclusion/publication/digital-financial-inclusion

Chapter 13
The External Costs of Road Transport:
A Case Study of Turkey

Eda Ustaoglu
Gebze Technical University, Turkey

Arif Cagdas Aydınoglu
Gebze Technical University, Turkey

ABSTRACT

This chapter focuses on the estimation of marginal and total external costs of road transportation in Turkey in terms of accidents, air pollution, climate change, noise, and traffic congestion. The study estimates marginal external costs for cars, light commercial vehicles (LCVs), heavy duty vehicles (HDVs), busses, and motorcycles, which comprise total vehicle fleet stock of the Turkish road transport sector. The researchers reviewed the literature of both local and international studies for the quantification and monetisation of the specified external costs of road transport. This will provide a base for the future studies on Turkish transport research and transport policy appraisal guidelines. The authors conclude that accidents are the most important externality of road use and that local air pollution and congestion appear to be more important than noise and climate change. This implies that priority should be given to road accidents, air pollution, and congestion alongside noise and global warming.

INTRODUCTION

Although transportation sector has a significant share in the national income accounts, it generates side effects, through its negative impacts on public health and on the environmental resources. These effects are known as external effects, such as congestion, road crashes, air pollution, noise, impacts on climate change and water resources; and the costs associated with these are called 'external costs'. Externalities are effects arising from a purchase or use decision by one set of parties that fall on people other than the purchaser or the user (Verhoef, 1994; Boundreaux and Meiners, 2019). Therefore, users are not aware

DOI: 10.4018/978-1-6684-4610-2.ch013

of the impacts of their activities on the society and do not channel this into their purchasing patterns or behavioral decisions. According to the welfare theory, internalisation of external costs through the use of market-based instruments may result in a more efficient use of transport infrastructure, reduce the negative impacts of transport activity on the society and environment, and enhance equity between transport users.

There is abundant literature on the subject, in which negative externalities have drawn the most attention (Mayeres et al., 1996; Griffiths et al., 2019). Regarding road transport externalities, Newbery (1994) pointed to travel delays stemming from road congestion, road damage and accidents as the most relevant externalities covered by the literature. The bulk of literature focusing on travel delays has examined road congestion mainly from economic point of view. Among the studies that focused on models of road pricing in relation to congestion, we can refer to Stopher (2004), Small and Verhoef (2007), Croci (2016), and de Dios Ortuzar et al. (2021). A comprehensive review on road congestion theory and practice can be found in Emmerink et al. (1995), Levinson (2010), Beaudoin et al. (2015) and Gu et al. (2018). Differently, Vitaliano and Held (1990), and Hau (1995) examined road damage externalities through developing theoretical models and searching for policy implications. However, there are more studies researching on accident externalities and relevant policy tools needed to control of externalities. Some examples include: Edlin and Karaca-Mandic (2006), Saito et al. (2010), Dementyeva et al. (2015) and Muehlenbachs et al. (2021).

Other externalities of road transportation include air and noise pollution, climate change, aesthetic impact and barrier effects, among others. Most importantly, there is overwhelming body of evidence that air pollution has significant impacts on the environment and health worldwide (Bel and Holst, 2018; Liu et al., 2020). It has been accepted that road transport is one of the key contributors to the rising levels of greenhouse gases and air pollutants contributing to worsening air quality (Commission of the European Communities, 1990; Duffy et al., 2017). In order to assess potential exposure and estimate long-term impacts on the public health, transport and population exposure models need to be explored. Transport models, in a standard way, predict traffic flows and average speed on the road network can be used to estimate vehicle emissions of air pollutants and noise (Rizzi and De La Maza, 2017). Population exposure can be modelled in several ways from using simple measures (Buzzelli and Jerrett, 2003; Carrier et al., 2014), regression models (Liu et al, 2016) and spatial analysis (Shekarrizfard et al., 2016) to more complex models of atmospheric dispersion (Namdeo et al., 2019), integrated emission (Tang et al., 2018) and hybrid models (Michanowicz, 2016). Though significant, community severance, also known as the barrier effect, has been relatively neglected by the researchers and transport planners. The barrier effects refer to the impact of transport infrastructure or road traffic levels or speeds as a physical or physiological barrier separating people from facilities, services and social networks within a community (Anciaes et al., 2014). Similarly, the studies on aesthetic impact valuation are scarce as the subject impacts have been generally ignored or underestimated in planning and policy making (Kapper, 2004). Examples of studies that included barrier effects and aesthetic impact valuation are INFRAS/IWW (2004); Jiang and Kang (2016); and Evangelinos and Tscharaktschiew (2021).

In economic analysis, it is important to know the monetary values of the transport-related health and environmental impacts born by the society in order to assess the efficacy of both new and existing transport network. These effects of air and noise pollution, congestion, and accidents have been quantified by various studies where a monetary value has been assigned to assess the policy measures planned or implemented. Considering that market prices for the experienced damages are generally unavailable, non-market valuation methods are used to value the external costs (EC, 2019). This is in contrast to market values, which applies to goods and services that are traded in a competitive market. Non-market costs can be difficult to quantify and may require valuation techniques such as contingent valuation (CV) or stated preference (SP) techniques, which are used for estimating the value that a person places on an externality (Pearce et al., 2006; Mouter, 2020). However, critics on these methods argue that 'the CV/SP may not be a good measure for informed policy making or accurate impact assessment (Hausman, 2012) or money appears to be a poor scale for summarising environmental values since evaluating how people perceive the impacts of transport involve more that can be developed from non-market valuation models' (OECD, 2013). It appears that some local externalities such as traffic congestion, noise, risk of accidents fall into this category since these externalities impact on the social welfare on a daily basis (Nash, 1997). The valuation of climate change impacts is a more difficult task given that the impacts are less clear and may not be perceived at all; and therefore people are not able to express consistent preferences for their trade-off (Nash, 2015). Nevertheless, the attempts to estimate social costs of carbon have been increasing in the recent decades (Tol, 2009).

There are different examples of studies that evaluated the transport externalities worldwide. One strand of literature has addressed the assessment of individual (Prud'homme et al., 2012; Bravo-Moncayo et al., 2017) or multiple externalities (Link et al, 2016; Cavallaro, 2018) either in local or national/regional context. Another strand has either focused on theoretical developments on the subject (Baarsma and Lambooy, 2005; Bravo et al., 2010; Pereira et al., 2016) or provided a review on transport externality studies or the evaluation techniques for transport policies (Santos, 2017; Sovacool et al., 2021). Within this body of literature, there are studies that have provided estimates for externalities for the developed countries such as EU (Link et al., 2016), US (Melo and Graham, 2018), and Japan (Komikado et al., 2021). In addition, studies from places other than these countries have estimated external costs: Deng (2006) in China, Jakob et al. (2006) in Auckland, New Zeland, Sen et al. (2010) in India, Cravioto et al. (2013) in Mexico, Dyr et al. (2019) in Poland, Euchi and Kallel (2021) in Tunisia. Despite the emerging literature on estimates of externalities in developing countries, there are still obstacles to get accurate estimates. A critical issue is the quality and quantity of data and applicability of some of the available standard models (Cravioto et al., 2013).

Turkey is an example of a country where road activity has grown steadily, which creates externalities and inefficiency within the sector. It is noted in OECD (2019: 25) that Turkey has faced with the highest greenhouse gas (GHG) emission growth among the OECD member countries (around 500 Mt CO_2 in 2016) and that transportation sector is one of the main contributors to the GHG emissions. Turkey's cities are shown to be one of the worst cases indicating high levels of air pollution observed in Europe (OECD, 2019). The rail network (by 14.5%) grew faster than the road network (by 12.8%) in 2005-2016 but road network largely dominate the transport system in Turkey (OECD, 2019). It is expected that roads will account for 25% of future infrastructure investment, followed by railways at 9% (Garanti and PwC, 2017). This will lead to increasing external costs, particularly in the biggest cities of Turkey. Despite the growing impacts of road transport on the society and environment, the assessment of externalities of the Turkish road transport is still lacking.

Based on the review of literature, the road transportation externalities that are highly influential on transport policies and investments can be listed as: traffic congestion, accidents, climate change, air pollution, and noise (Sen et al., 2010; Mizutani et al., 2011; Cravioto et al., 2013). The quantification and monetization of these externalities are useful in terms of measuring socio-environmental impacts of transport projects, policies and programmes as required by the Article 10 of Environmental Law No. 2872 on Environmental Impact Assessment (EIA), which entered into force in 1993 in Turkey. The

Environmental Law is aimed at alleviating the environmental impacts of projects within the scope of EIA. Unlike most EU countries and other developed countries such as US, Australia, Canada, there is no comprehensive assessment framework for energy and environmental savings from different sectors (e.g. transport) achieved from various government measures or infrastructure investments. '...*The assessment of the gap between policy targets and actions taken is missing and the government has not developed methodologies and indicators to measure the progress...*' (IEA, 2016). The current study will shed light on the external impacts of road transport in Turkey where the quantification and valuation of the selected externalities of road transportation will serve additional purposes. From the review of international literature and local studies, the monetary values of key transport impacts were developed and adopted to the Turkish case, which can be considered as a base for the future studies of transport planning and appraisal guidelines. The study provides estimates of the marginal external costs of traffic congestion, accidents, air and noise pollution of road transport, which are essential in computing the marginal social cost. Given the negative impacts of road transportation, it is necessary to provide efficient transport services and inform policy makers about the negative externalities created by the transport sector. Therefore, cost estimates that are caused by an additional transport user that is not borne by the user but by other people than the user would serve to this aim. Unlike previous studies that focused on a narrow range of road transport vehicles (Sen et al., 2010; Cravioto et al., 2013; Jochem et al., 2016) or limited number of transport externalities evaluated in the country-specific cases (Ko et al., 2011; Hagedorn and Sieg, 2019), this study considered all the road vehicle types that coincides with the complete vehicle fleet structure of Turkey, and included key transport externalities that are associated with the highest contributions to the total external costs of transportation.

BACKGROUND

The issue of environmental management in Turkey has gained a legal stand in 1983 with the Environmental Law No. 2872. The Environmental Impact Assessment (EIA) was first introduced under Article 10 of Environmental Law No. 2872, which entered into force in 1993 in Turkey. The Environmental Law is aimed at alleviating the environmental impacts of projects within the scope of EIA. The EIA Directive that entered into force in 1993 has been amended several times in 1997, 2002, 2003, 2008, 2013, 2014 and 2016. Since 2011, Ministry of Environment and Urbanisation is the responsible body that has been involved in environmental management and Environment Impact Assessments regarding government and private projects and key infrastructure investments. The system that enables the assessment of the environment has become valid in the EU with the Directive No. 85/337/EEC in 1985. The Directive is amended by Council Directives released in 1997 (no. 97/11/EC) and 2003 (no. 2003/35/EC). With the Directive, it is aimed at preventing environmental pollution and its impacts, and it was enforced to the EU member countries to adjust their national laws accordingly. There are continuing arrangements on the environmental legislation as part of Turkey's EU accession negotiations, and Turkey has developed strategies and adopted a range of laws in different environmental sectors such as air quality, climate change and biodiversity.

Since 1992, environmental and sustainable development considerations have been integrated into National Development Plans (NDPs) that is used to provide overall strategic growth and development direction in the Country. In 2008, a Regulation on Ambient Air Quality Assessment and Management was introduced in Turkey and has been implemented through local Clean Air Action Plans (CAAPs).

The CAAPs focus on air pollution related to industry, residential heating and road transport. There are measures for the road transport including development of city rail networks, bicycle lanes, smart traffic control systems and others. In the OECD (2019) Report, it is acknowledged that implementation of CAAPs is limited due to high municipal staff turnover, frequent amendments to the subject legislation and limited technical and human resource capacity at both provincial and municipality levels, particularly in less developed regions. In an attempt to comply with the European Union's regulatory standards, Turkey has adopted a regulation on strategic environmental assessment (SEA) of plans and programmes in 2017. Its implementation has been phased in 2023 covering new plans and programmes, but these will not cover the local plans. There are only plot projects where SEA has been applied. Although there are development plans at all administrative levels in the Country, environmental issues have been addressed at a limited extent due to the absence of SEA applied in the current planning process. This implies that there is still need to aligning the Country's legislation with best international practices.

MAIN FOCUS OF THE CHAPTER

Data and Methodology

In this chapter, external costs of road private vehicles and busses are compared to identify the differences of external costs between different vehicle classes in Turkey. The authors reviewed national studies to specify local cost factors and also focused on European studies considering that they provided comprehensive cost estimates that can be transferred across the countries using the value transfer method. Based on the review of literature and availability of local data, five main categories were specified for the impact assessment of road transport externalities in Turkey. The year 2018 was selected for computing transport externality costs because transport-related data i.e. total vehicle kilometers on the road network and structure of road vehicles were available for the subject year. The external transport costs that are examined in the study were therefore originally computed for the year 2018 and then inflated to 2022 values by using the Consumer Price Index (CPI) for the related period. The average CPI values for Turkey were used to inflate to 2022 values and then these were converted to EURO using the 2022 exchange rates between TL (Turkish Lira) and EURO.

-*Road accidents:* The risks of road accidents were valued by human costs, medical and administrative costs, physical damage and production loss according to the degree of severity.

-*Air pollution:* The impact assessment of the air pollution is based on carbon monoxide (CO), particulate matters (e.g. $PM_{2.5}$), volatile organic compounds (NMVOCs), and nitrogen oxide (NO_x).

-*Climate change:* The assessment is based on greenhouse gases (GHGs) expressed in CO_2 equivalents.

-*Noise pollution:* The noise exposure is distinguished by day and night across urban, sub-urban and rural areas estimated for each vehicle category.

-*Congestion:* The impacts of congestion was estimated for the rural areas and large, medium/small size urban areas for both passenger cars and good vehicles.

Other impacts such as costs of energy consumption and dependency, soil degradation and groundwater pollution, negative impacts on nature and landscape and their ecosystem services as well as economic costs on the households resulting from construction and maintenance works of the transport infrastructure were not included in the study due to their minor importance in the overall external cost value and data availability issues were also influential. In the study, the authors separated cost estimates with respect to fuel type (e.g. diesel, petrol, LPG); vehicle size (e.g. High Duty Vehicles (HDVs) vs. motorcycles) and emission location. The former sub-division is based on the vehicle stock data in Turkey comprising petrol and diesel vehicles with shares of more than 75% of the total vehicle stock. Around 20% of the vehicle stock comprises Liquefied Petroleum Gas (LPG) vehicles, which are mostly used as passenger cars. The emission location factor refers to the impacts of local pollutants such as air and noise pollution on the density of population in different regions (e.g. urban, sub-urban, rural). Pollution cost estimates cannot be distinguished according to the time of the day (e.g. peak and off-peak periods) because there is no data on the traffic flows of the road network for different time periods of the day.

Road Accidents

Information about costs of traffic accidents is required for any transport policy impact assessment that are used to estimate the social return of investments in transport infrastructure and help prioritising transport-related measures. The value of statistical life (VSL)-a non-monetised impact of accidents due to utility losses of the victim and suffering and grief of relatives and friends-constitutes the largest share in external costs of the road transport (ECMT, 1998; UNITE, 2003). The external costs of accidents can be measured following two different approaches: The first one is to estimate the number of accidents related to vehicular traffic and evaluation of the resulting damage (ECMT, 1998; UNITE, 2003; INFRASS/IWW, 2004); and the second one is to calculate the monetary value of damage resulting from accidents (Mayeres et al., 1996; Beuthe et al., 2002). In the current study, the first approach was conducted based on the direct use of accident numbers from the national statistical data on number of fatalities, numbers of serious and minor injuries resulting from road accidents in Turkey.

In the literature, SP has been accepted as the most appropriate and scientifically sound approach to estimate the statistical value of life in the context of road safety (Wijnen et al., 2017; EC, 2019). The studies in the US have mainly focused on Revealed Preference (RP) methods in terms of wage risk studies whereas the studies in Europe rather consider SP values for the assessment of accident risks (Lindhjem et al., 2010). The other examples of studies in Canada and Australia mostly rely on SP methods (OECD, 2012). The most recent study conducted at the European scale, also covering some non-EU countries (e.g. Norway, Switzerland, Canada, US, Japan), is the European Commission's Handbook on the External Costs of Transport (EC, 2019). The Study reported accident costs of 2016 including human costs, production loss, medical costs and administrative costs for each of the EU and non-EU countries covered in the study. In Turkey, the literature on the valuation of road safety is limited as there are few attempts to estimate the external costs of road accidents in the last decades. Among few studies that have focused on road accident costs, it is noteworthy to highlight SWEROAD (2001), Gürses et al. (2003), Naci and Baker (2008), Karadana et al. (2013) and Özen et al. (2014) (Table 1). It can be noted from Table 1 that medical costs of accidents in Turkey are relatively lower than those of the EU average. This is due to the higher ratio of medical insurance coverage in the Turkish healthcare system compared to its European counterparts.

Table 1. Estimates of road accident costs in Turkey

Type of accident cost	Estimated average cost for year of study									
	Karadana et al. (2013)		Gürses et al. (2003)		Özen et al. (2014)		SWEROAD (2001)		Naci and Baker (2008)	
	2009 (TL)	2018[1] (€)	2003 ($)	2018[1] (€)	2013 (TL)	2018[1] (€)	1999[2] (million TL)	2018[1] (€)	2000 ($)	2018[1] (€)
Human costs (fatality)	-	-	-	-	-	-	198,944	575,531	-	-
Human costs (injury)	-	-	-	-	-	-	8,149	23,571	-	-
Medical and administrative (MA) costs (fatality)	1,782[M]	672[M]	496[M]	577[M]			732	2,647	-	-
MA costs (serious injury)	5,347[M]	2,018[M]	929[M]	1,083[M]			1,804	6,524	-	-
MA costs (slight injury)	16[M]	6[M]	341[M]	397[M]	15	4	84	303	-	-
Damage-vehicles (slight injury)	-	-	-	-	1,153	327	-	-	-	-
Material damage (slight injury)	-	-	-	-	3,659	1,039	230	831	-	-
Material damage (serious injury)	-	-	-	-	-	-	2,212	7,930	-	-
Material damage (fatality)	-	-	-	-	-	-	4,764	16,987	-	-
Production loss (slight injury)	-	-	-	-	1,229	349	106	383	-	-
Production loss (serious injury)	-	-	-	-	-	-	2,117	7,656	-	-
Production loss (fatality)	-	-	-	-	-	-	8,685	31,236	325,000	405,063

[1]The Consumer Price Index (CPI) covering the relevant period was used to calculate 2018 price equivalents.

[2]These values represent the average value of corresponding cost items that were originally given for the urban and rural areas. Regarding material costs, it was assumed that 58% of the costs were internalised through the insurance payments as demonstrated inÖzen et al. (2014).

[M]Values represent only medical costs.

To our knowledge, in Turkey, there is no research focused on determining the human costs of traffic accidents based on the Willingness to Pay (WTP) model. Therefore, unit value transfer approach was applied that is aimed at transferring information from the already studied cases to other location where the information is missing. This is based on income adjustments recommended by OECD (2012) and EC (2019). According to this approach, unit values are multiplied by the ratio of income in the policy country to income in study country that is given as (see EC, 2019):

$$WTP_{ps} = WTP_{ss} \left(\frac{I_{os}}{I_{ss}} \right) \quad (1)$$

where WTP_{ps} is the WTP value transferred to the study site, WTP_{ss} is the WTP at the study site, I_{os} and I_{ss} are the income at other and study sites and epsilon is the income elasticity of the WTP. Regarding income elasticity, EC (2019) recommended the value of 0.8; and therefore this value was used in the current study. Alternatively, human cost values estimated for OECD countries (OECD, 2012) were also transferred to Turkey using the value transfer method based on price inflation and PPP adjustment.

Following review of the literature summarised in Table 1, the lower, average and upper cost values were computed for the year 2018. Using the total cost values, marginal external accident costs were calculated by dividing the total costs of accidents of each vehicle type by the relevant vehicle kilometer and the prices were inflated to 2022 using the relevant CPI values (Table 2).

Table 2. Marginal accident costs per kilometer in Turkey (2022 EURcent/km)

	Car	Bus	Motorcycle	LCV	HGV
Fatality	**4.98** (2.01-7.94)	**0.18** (0.07-0.29)	**0.55** (0.22-0.87)	**0.77** (0.31-1.24)	**0.37** (0.15-0.59)
Serious injury	**31.38** (4.85-57.91)	**1.16** (0.18-2.15)	**3.45** (0.53-6.37)	**4.86** (0.75-8.98)	**2.33** (0.36-4.30)
Slight injury	**7.65** (1.18-14.11)	**0.28** (0.04-0.52)	**0.84** (0.13-1.55)	**1.19** (0.18-2.19)	**0.57** (0.09-1.05)

Note: In parenthesis are the upper and lower value estimates, and bold are central estimates

The external costs of accidents (EC_A) were calculated using the following equation:

$$EC_A = F \times V_F + I \times V_I + C_0 - P \tag{2}$$

Where F is the number of fatalities, V_F is the value of human life, I is the number of injuries, V_I is the cost of injuries, C_0 is the other costs including administrative costs, production losses, material damages, and P is the insurance premiums.

Human costs were calculated based on the WTP value of VSL and is based on OECD (2012) and EC (2019). To calculate human costs, consumption loss was deducted from the VSL. The consumption loss is based on annual market consumption and life years lost through the accident. Production losses were estimated using the human capital approach and are based on the values estimated in OECD (2012) and Naci and Baker (2008). It was assumed that 50% of production loss is external (see EC, 2019). Medical costs are based on the values presented in Gürses et al. (2003), Karadana et al. (2013), and Özen et al. (2014). Administrative costs are based on the values presented in SWEROAD (2001). For the calculation of material damage, the values given in SWEROAD (2001) and Özen et al. (2014) were used. It was assumed that 58% of the costs were internalised based on the findings in Özen et al. (2014).

Air Pollution

Local air pollutants including carbon monoxide (CO), particulate matters (e.g. $PM_{2.5}$, PM_{10}), volatile organic compounds (VOCs), sulfuroxide (SO_x) and nitrogen oxide (NO_x) have adverse impacts on the environment and human health (Van Fan et al., 2018). Exposure to road traffic is associated with an increasing risk of all-cause mortality as well as asthma, diminished lung function, adverse birth effects and childhood cancer (Boothe and Shendell, 2008). Other air pollution costs consist of building/material damages, crop losses and costs for further damages for the ecosystem (biosphere, soil, water) and biodiversity (UNITE, 2003). The dramatic increase in the private vehicle ownership, which is also encouraged by the provision of large-scale urban motorways, has led to transport-related pollution, and increasing amounts of transport-related energy consumption in Turkey. In Turkey, road transportation contributed about 40% of the national NO_x and %13 of the NMVOC emissions (EU-RTR Project, 2012). As specified by EEA (2014; 2019), other sources of local air pollution in the Country are CO, NH_3, PM_{10} and $PM_{2.5}$.

For the estimation of social costs of a marginal increase in the emissions of air pollutants by road transport sector in Turkey, the overall cost evaluation methodology provided by CE Delft, INFRAS & Fraunhofer ISI (2011) was adopted. Accordingly, emission factors and transport characteristics for each vehicle category are required as input data. Using this data, the first step is to calculate transport-related emissions resulting from additional vehicle kilometers. Next, concentrations of each type of pollutant due to vehicle emissions are calculated. The last step is to assign a monetary value to different sources of air pollution and allocate total external costs to each vehicle category. EEA (2019) gives the emission factors for passenger cars (PCs), light commercial vehicles (LCVs), heavy-duty vehicles (HDVs), motorcycles, and busses for different fuel types for a variety of air pollutants. Another input required for the calculation of emissions per vehicle category is the vehicle fleet structure. This is provided in EU-RTR (2012) and TurkStat (2020) representing different classes for each vehicle category.

Apart from the explained methodology, an alternative method is to estimate the marginal social costs of air pollution in a given area using the information on the relationship between the degree of air pollution and the traffic volume in the local study area (WHO, 1999). Although the first approach (i.e. CE Delft, INFRAS & Fraunhofer ISI, 2011) is practical to estimate social costs, the conditions of the case study area may be different from those considered in previous studies; therefore estimates reliability may decrease (Mizutani et al., 2011). By contrast, the second approach (WHO, 1999) is more case specific and would provide more reliable estimates of social costs but the approach is based on more detailed information about population, traffic and road conditions and other local data (Mizutani et al., 2011). The latter approach has been utilised in a variety of European studies such as UNITE(2003); ExternE (2005); NEEDS (2006); and HEATCO (2006). Because there is no information on population and traffic conditions at the regional or city level, the authors focused on the first approach and left the second approach for future considerations.

The literature on the estimation of air pollution costs is limited for Turkey. The authors could find only one research that published this information (see EU-RTR, 2012). Therefore, air pollution cost factors were transferred from other studies using the value transfer method. This information is provided in Table 3, which presents the value of air pollution costs from different studies. Among these, EC (2019) is the most recent study that computed the cost factors of air pollutants for all EU countries. In the subject study, the cost factors consisting of health effects, crop losses, biodiversity loss and material damage have been calculated based on NEEDS approach as well as the findings of other studies were also considered (e.g. OECD, 2014). It included up-to-date data on concentration response functions and valuation of damage differentiated per country on population size, density and background concentration (EC, 2019). The cost factors of NMVOC, NO_x and $PM_{2.5}$ were transferred from the EC (2019) Report whereas CO was transferred from HEATCO (2006) estimates using eq. (1).

Table 3. Estimates of air pollution costs from different studies

Pollutants	EU-RTR (2012) Turkey* 2010 prices (€)	EC-DG MOVE (2014) EU-average 2010 prices (€/tonne)	EC (2019) EU-average 2016 prices (€/tonne)	Poland 2016 prices (€/tonne)	Turkey** 2018 prices (€/tonne)	HEATCO (2006) Finland 2000 prices (€/tonne)	Turkey*** 2018 prices (€/tonne)
CO	-	-	-	-	-	120.5	100.63
NMVOC	10	1,566	1,200	700	852	-	-
NO$_x$	2,278	10,640	17,000	11,500	13,987	-	-
NH$_3$	5,443	-	-	-	-	-	-
PM$_{2.5}$ (Urb)	-	270,178	381,000	282,000	342,999	-	-
PM$_{2.5}$ (Sub-Ur)	-	70,258	123,000	91,000	110,682	-	-
PM$_{2.5}$ (Rural)	-	28,108	70,000	52,000	63,247	-	-

*Marginal abatement costs

**Estimated through benefit transfer method where Poland 2016 values were transferred to the Turkish case and then inflated to 2018 using CPI for the 2016-2018 period reported for Turkey in TurkStat (2020).

***Estimated through benefit transfer method where Finland 2000 values were transferred to the Turkish case and then inflated to 2018 using CPI for the 2000-2018 period reported for Turkey in TurkStat (2020).

Based on the vehicle fleet characteristics and emission factors for different vehicle classes, the average pollutant concentrations in tonnes for each vehicle type were estimated. The authors quantified the emissions released per vehicle kilometer (vkm) for the vehicle classes including PRE-ECE, EURO3, EURO4, EURO5 and EURO6 for both diesel and petrol vehicles for each vehicle type on the road. The specified vehicle classes are compatible with the road vehicle fleet structure of Turkey. In Turkey, more than 40% of private vehicles are classified as PRE-ECE, 17% of EURO3 and EURO6, and the rest are EURO4 and EURO5 (see Table 4). It is important to note that the latest vehicle classes (i.e. EURO4-5-6) emit less pollutant compared to earlier classes (i.e. PRE-ECE and EURO3) considering that new vehicle types are more fuel-efficient. For the calculation of total average vehicle kilometers for the year 2018, the number of vehicles was multiplied by an average of 3,817km for motorcycles; 13,107km for passenger cars; 28,172km for LCVs; 50,114 km for HDVs; and 50,141km for busses (see URL1). These figures are based on TurkStat (2020) statistics representing the 2017 values. Since there is no operational transport model covering the ground transportation network at the country level in Turkey, the aforementioned average vehicle kilometres from national statistics were used for the calculation of annual road vehicle kilometres for different road vehicles. In order to estimate air pollution costs for each vehicle category, the information in Table 3 was combined with average pollution concentrations computed for each vehicle category.

Table 4. Vehicle fleet structure in Turkey (2018)

Class	Petrol PC	Diesel PC	LPG PC	Petrol LCV	Diesel LCV	Petrol HDV	Diesel HDV	Bus	Motorcycle
PRE-ECE	1,487,411	0	1,140,881	58,489	106,286	1,283,691	1,003,073	93,965	-
EURO3	588,046	1,744,332	451,046	23,123	42,020	0	396,564	37,149	-
EURO4	311,319	1,241,462	238,789	12,242	22,246	0	209,946	19,667	-
EURO5	484,273	1,555,756	371,450	19,043	34,605	0	326,582	30,593	-
EURO6	588,046	1,744,332	451,046	23,123	42,020	0	396,564	37,149	-
Total	3,459,095	6,285,882	2,653,213	136,020	247,176	1,283,691	2,332,728	218,523	3,211,328

Source: EU-RTR (2012); TurkStat (2020)

Note: PC: passenger car; LPG: Liquefied Petroleum Gas; LCV: light commercial vehicle; HDV: heavy-duty vehicle. The classifications of Petrol PC and Diesel PC were obtained from EU-RTR Project (2012).

Finally, Table 5 presents the marginal external air pollution costs for different vehicle classes per vehicle kilometer in Turkey. From the Table, the variation of marginal air pollution costs across diesel and petrol vehicles is sound. In general, the findings confirmed that diesel vehicles are more fuel-efficient than petrol counterparts.

Table 5. Estimated marginal air pollution costs (in 2022 EURcent/km) in Turkey

Category	CO	NMVOC	NO$_x$	NH$_3$	PM$_{2.5}$
Petrol Car	1.51	0.10	1.57	0.006	0.02
Diesel Car	0.01	0.01	0.01	0.001	0.18
LPG Car	0.00	0.02	0.88	0.004	1.27
Petrol LCV	1.13	0.12	0.12	0.006	0.02
Diesel LCV	0.06	0.01	1.42	0.001	1.72
Petrol HDV	5.41	0.41	8.39	0.001	0.01
Diesel HDV	0.10	0.03	6.98	0.006	1.94
Bus	0.27	0.07	12.37	0.003	4.40
Motorcycle	0.65	0.07	0.40	0.002	0.14

Climate Change

Greenhouse gases (GHG) such as carbon dioxide (CO_2), nitrous oxide (NO_2) and methane (CH_4) are known to contribute to climate change. Carbon dioxide (CO_2) accounts for most GHG emissions mainly generated in fuel combustion (81%), followed by methane mainly produced in agriculture. The emission standard of the vehicles does not influence the GHG emissions directly. However, fuel efficiency of vehicles may contribute to the decrease of GHGs considerably. The release of GHG has adverse impacts on the environment and society. Among these, we can refer to sea level rise, agricultural loss, water supply, pollution and health effects from temperature change (Scheffran and Battaglini, 2010).

To estimate the marginal external costs of GHGs, road transport-related emissions (e.g. CO_2) and the cost factor of CO_2 emissions are required. Road transport emissions can be obtained from previous studies that focused on estimation of the volume of CO_2 emitted by road vehicles (UNITE, 2003; INFRAS/IWW, 2004). An alternative method is to use the volume of CO_2 per traffic volume considering the vehicle types and road conditions (Mayeres et al., 1996). The authors used the transport-related CO_2 emissions from the country estimates of the OECD database (2020), which provided national statistics for Turkey.

The social costs of carbon (SCC) aim at putting a value on the damage that the emission of an extra tonne of GHG emissions will do over time and hence the society should be prepared to pay today to avoid this future damage (Tol and Lyons, 2008). For instance, Tol (2005) found a median estimate of €4 and a mean of €25 per tonne of carbon emitted. However, in HEATCO-an EU the 6th Framework Programme-it is noted that these estimates are conservative due to the fact that only damage, which can be estimated with a reasonable certainty, is included in the analysis and impacts such as extended floods and frequent hurricanes with higher energy density are excluded (HEATCO D5: 2006). The World Bank Report (2017) pointed to a more recent study by International Energy Agency (IEA) that delivered a sub 2°C world scenario as defined by the Paris agreement. IEA (2012) developed detailed scenarios for nine World regions and strategies to reduce dependency on imported fossil fuels, decarbonise electricity, enhance energy efficiency and reduce emissions in the industry, transport and building sectors. Instead of assuming explicit carbon prices, the Energy Technology Perspectives (ETP) scenarios use the marginal abatement cost of various technology options that enhances energy security to construct least-cost scenarios. The 2°C scenario sets the target of cutting energy-related CO_2 emissions by more than half in 2050 (compared to 2009) and ensuring that they continue to fall thereafter. The details of the scenarios can be seen in IEA (2012).

Table 6 indicates global marginal abatement costs of CO_2 emissions from IEA (2012). These values were adopted in the current study to calculate the costs of CO_2 emissions. These values were adjusted to 2018 World prices by using the averages of general CPI statistics for the OECD and non-OECD countries. The external costs of greenhouse gases (EC_G) were estimated using road transport-related CO_2 equivalent emissions (E_G) and the cost factor of the emissions (CF_G):

$$EC_G=E_G \times CF_G \qquad (3)$$

In Turkey, transport-related CO_2 emissions amount to 84.6 million tonnes for the year 2017 (OECD, 2020) where road transport vehicles are associated with 79.0 million tonnes. For the distribution of CO_2 emissions to road vehicle category, the percentage share distribution of CO_2 lube in total vehicle emissions was used. Based on the estimates of CO_2 emissions, total vehicle kilometres and shadow prices of carbon, the marginal external values of CO_2 emissions are given in Table 7.

Table 6. Global marginal abetment costs under the IEA 2°C scenario (2012 prices)

Year of Emission	Values, $/tCO_2
2010-2020	30-50
2020-2030	80-100
2030-2040	110-130
2040-2050	130-160

Source: IEA (2012) as cited by Hood (2017)

Table 7. Marginal social costs of carbon (in 2022 EURcent/km) in Turkey

Category	Low values	Central values	High values
Petrol Car	0.81	1.08	1.35
Diesel Car	0.65	0.86	1.07
LPG Car	0.64	0.91	1.21
Petrol LCV	0.75	1.01	1.25
Diesel LCV	0.75	1.01	1.25
Petrol HDV	1.21	1.61	2.02
Diesel HDV	0.30	0.39	0.49
Bus	1.69	2.25	2.82
Motorcycle	0.94	1.25	1.57

Noise

Noise, or unwanted sound, is one of the most common environmental exposures that causes physical harm or physiological harm to humans. As high urbanisation and increase in traffic volumes result in higher noise levels, the urbanisation has led to more individuals being exposed to traffic noise. There are various sources for environmental noise in urban areas. These are: airports, industries, construction works, railway and roads (Zannin et al., 2003). Chronic environmental noise causes a variety of health effects including sleep disturbance, noise-induced hearing loss, cardiovascular disease (hearth and blood circulation), increased incidence of diabetes, hormonal changes and nervous stress (Hammer et al., 2014). The literature has pointed to environmental noise with larger than the level of 55 dB(A) as it causes serious annoyance in residential areas (Dekkers et al., 2009). The nightime noise greater than 40 dB(A) has been suggested to cause sleep disturbance (WHO, 2009).

For the assessment of average noise costs for various modes of transport, bottom-up and top-down approaches can be distinguished. The authors followed the top-down approach that is based on the willingness-to-pay or willingness-to-accept for more silence and health, and multiplies the unit values with the national data or data from other studies on noise exposure for different noise classes. The top-down approach uses the total noise exposure (differentiated for different noise classes) and allocates it to different modes to get average values. Alternatively, a bottom-up approach can establish a model describing the relationship between traffic and noise using the local data on traffic volume, vehicle speed, city conditions such as the distribution of population density and the noise exposure. UNITE (2003), WHO (2008) and CE Delft (2018) provide estimates of marginal noise costs by using a bottom-up approach. The top-down approach may be more convenient in estimating social costs but the affected areas vary across different studies and it might be difficult to find similar studies to capture the present conditions (Mizutani et al., 2011). By contrast, the latter approach results in more precise estimations compared to the first approach; however, the second approach requires extensive data on transportation and noise exposure which often do not exist.

Based on the data on noise maps, different noise classes can be distinguished for calculation of total noise costs (CE Delft, 2008). For noise levels less than 55 dB(A), it is assumed that there are no adverse effects on annoyance and health. The effects can be multiplied by the noise costs per person exposed for the calculation of total noise costs. Due to the logarithmic nature of the relationship between noise and traffic volume, marginal noise costs are sensitive to existing traffic flows or background noise. Marginal noise costs are defined as the additional costs of noise caused by adding one vehicle to the existing traffic flow. Different methods can be used for the impact valuation of transport noise. In some cases market prices can be used, for instance to value the cost of illnesses stemming from transport noise. However, in others, no market prices exist, WTP values should be considered. For the average noise costs per person per dB(A) per year, HEATCO project recommended state-of-the-art values for the EU countries. Another study i.e. INFRAS/IWW (2004) is representing EU average values for marginal costs of noise and it is suggested that these can be generalised to all route segments throughout Europe (IMPACT, 2008). These values are based on state-of-the-art noise exposure formula, input values and level of differentiation according to different traffic situations, local conditions and time of the day (IMPACT, 2008). In the current study, the cost factors provided as EU-28 average values (EC, 2019) were used through applying the value transfer method. The marginal cost values for Turkey are given in Table 8.

Table 8. Unit values for marginal costs of noise for different network types, Turkey (2022 EURcent/vkm)

	Time of day	Urban	Sub-urban	Rural
Car	Day	**0.55** (0.55-1.34)	**0.09** (0.03-0.09)	**0.01** (0.01-0.011)
	Night	**1.00** (1.00-2.43)	**0.16** (0.06-0.16)	**0.02** (0.01-0.02)
Motorcycle	Day	**1.10** (1.10-2.67)	**0.17** (0.06-0.17)	**0.02** (0.01-0.02)
	Night	**2.01** (2.01-4.87)	**0.32** (0.12-0.32)	**0.04** (0.01-0.04)
Bus	Day	**2.75** (2.75-6.68)	**0.43** (0.15-0.43)	**0.05** (0.02-0.05)
	Night	**5.02** (5.02-12.16)	**0.79** (0.28-0.79)	**0.09** (0.04-0.09)
LCV	Day	**2.75** (2.75-6.68)	**0.43** (0.15-0.43)	**0.05** (0.02-0.05)
	Night	**5.02** (5.02-12.16)	**0.79** (0.28-0.79)	**0.09** (0.04-0.09)
HDV	Day	**5.06** (5.06-12.28)	**0.79** (0.28-0.79)	**0.09** (0.04-0.09)
	Night	**9.23** (9.23-22.37)	**1.44** (0.52-1.44)	**0.17** (0.08-0.17)

Note: In bold are the central values, in brackets are the ranges. The lower limit in the brackets is based on dense traffic situations, while the upper limit is based on thin traffic situations. Central values are chosen based on the predominant traffic situation in the respective regional cluster: urban: dense; sub-urban/rural: thin.

In this study, urban, sub-urban and rural regions were considered separately; making use of case studies from Turkish literature that reported percentage of noise exposure across different noise levels. There are low and high estimates of population exposure where the range of low and high values were adopted from EC (2019) Report. The total external costs of noise were estimated using the following equation (Koyama and Kishimoto, 2001):

$$EC_N = C_N \sum_{j=1}^{n} N_j \times (L_j - L^*)$$

(4)

where C_N is the cost factor, N_j is the population exposed to noise, L^* is the noise threshold value and L_i is the observed noise level.

For the calculation of noise costs, two data inputs are needed: the number of people exposed to noise from road transportation and the noise costs per person exposed. The threshold for disturbance can range from 50 dB to 55 dB (Mayeres et al., 1996; INFRAS/IWW, 2004; EC, 2019). In this study, L^* was set at 55 dB following INFRAS/IWW (2004). Because there is no noise exposure map for Turkey comprising all the cities of the country, the authors generalised the findings of Ece et al. (2018) that modelled the traffic-induced noise in the city of Antalya, southern Turkey. In the subject study, the number of people and dwellings exposed to different noise levels for the road transportation in an urban area were provided. For estimating the number of people subject to noise pollution in an urban area, the percentage population exposure to different noise levels under the conditions of Scenario 1 was considered that is explained in Table 9 (see Ece et al., 2018). Regarding sub-urban and rural areas, scenarios 2 and 3 were adopted (Table 9) (Ece et al., 2018). To obtain the cost factor for noise annoyance and health impacts, the values reported in EC(2019) were used (Table 10). The values are based on the most recent estimates provided by Bristow et al. (2015) for annoyance costs and DEFRA (2014) for the health costs. For the calculation of the average noise costs by allocating the total noise costs to the different transport modes, the weighting factors that were applied (to take differences in noise characteristics between modes into account) are provided in CE/INFRAS/ISI (2011).

Table 9. Parameters for noise estimation

L(dB)	%Population_urban		%Population_sub-urban		%Population_rural	
	Day	**Night**	**Day**	**Night**	**Day**	**Night**
<55	6.49	3.25	2.59	1.30	37.54	18.77
55-65	67.01	33.51	69.13	34.57	46.85	23.43
65-75	22.63	11.32	23.93	11.97	14.21	7.11
75-	3.87	1.94	4.35	2.18	1.40	0.70

Source: Adapted from: Ece et al. (2018)

Note: [1] Scenario 1: Results were obtained from the model scenarios where Heavy Vehicle (HV) speed: 50 km/h; Light Vehicle (LV) speed: 50 km/h; types of road surface: smooth

[2] Scenario 2: Results were obtained from the model scenarios where HV speed: 70 km/h; LV speed: 110 km/h; types of road surface: smooth

[3] Scenario 3: Results were obtained from the model scenarios where HV speed: 50 km/h; LV speed: 50 km/h; types of road surface: porous; 80% of heavy vehicles were redirected to use alternative routes

Table 10. Environmental price of road transport noise for Turkey; 2018EUR/dB/person/year

L (dB)	Annoyance	Health	Total
50-54	9.8	2.1	11.9
55-59	19.6	2.1	21.7
60-64	19.6	4.2	23.8
65-69	37.8	6.3	44.1
70-74	37.8	9.1	46.9
>74	37.8	12.6	50.4

Source: Adopted from EC(2019)

Since there is no traffic modelling work covering traffic day and night flows on the road network covering the whole country of Turkey, traffic flows for all day were computed based on the relative traffic distributions calculated from average distributions of three countries used by ARTEMIS (2007) i.e. Belgium, Switzerland and USA. Using the day traffic distribution values and total vehicle kilometers on the road network, the daily road vehicle kilometres were computed (see Table 11). The day traffic comprises the flows observed between 07:00-19:00 and the rest were considered as night traffic flows.

The total road network of Turkey in 2018 is approximately 247,500 km including all types of roads (highways, arterial roads, provincial roads, residential roads, rural roads etc.) (Turkstat, 2020). There are a total of approximately 42,000 km state highways and motorways; 34,000 km of provincial roads 179,500 km of rural roads. There is no information on the road vehicle traffic flows distributed to urban, sub-urban and rural roads. Therefore, the authors used the information on the ratios of distribution of population to urban, sub-urban and rural regions in Turkey as specified by Ustaoglu and Aydınoglu (2019). Based on Eurostat's (2015) classification of urban-rural typologies, predominantly urban regions have less than 20% rural population, intermediate (peri-urban) regions between 20% and 50%, and predominantly rural regions more than 50%. It is presumed that there was positive correlation with the population and road vehicle flows concerning the urban and rural regions of Turkey and that only 33% and 36.4% of total vehicle flows were concentrated on urban and peri-urban areas whereas the rest was concentrated in rural areas (see Ustaoglu and Aydınoglu, 2019).

Table 11. The distribution of vehicle kilometers (thousand km) on the road network for urban, sub-urban and rural areas, Turkey (2018)

Category	Urban	Sub-urban	Rural	Total
Car				
Day	36,705,667	40,487,463	34,036,164	111,229,293
Night	5,444,381	6,005,317	5,048,426	16,498,125
LCV				
Day	3,102,329	3,421,963	2,876,705	9,400,998
Night	460,154	507,564	426,688	1,394,406
HDV				
Day	52,081,897	57,447,911	48,294,123	157,823,931
Night	7,725,066	8,520,982	7,163,243	23,409,291
Bus				
Day	3,148,757	3,473,174	2,919,756	9,541,688
Night	467,040	515,160	433,074	1,415,274
Motorcycle				
Day	3,522,539	3,885,467	3,266,354	10,674,361
Night	522,482	576,313	484,483	1,583,278

Congestion

The marginal external congestion costs express the change in total external costs for all transport users when an additional user enters to the transport network that reduces the speed of other transport users in the network. The basics of external costs of congestion were formulated by Pigou (1920) expressed as 'Pigou Problem' of traffic assignment on two routes between origin and destination. Transport users experience congestion through increases in travel time, travel time unreliability and operation costs. Therefore, costs related to congestion mainly consist of additional travel time plus some 10% for speed-dependent vehicle operations (CE Delft, 2008). Due to their lesser quantitative importance, other costs such as environmental costs, and fuel congestion costs are negligible (Qingyu et al., 2007).

The marginal external time costs can be measured as the difference in journey time caused by an extra vehicle on the road network multiplied by an estimate of the travel time. Regarding the value of travel time (VOT), local values should be used if possible. In Turkey, there is limited research that focused on the valuation of travel time savings. The study of SWEROAD (2001) suggested use of salary per hour for the VOT-business car trips that should be corrected multiplying by 1.2 and 1.17 to include the employer's additional costs and tax factor, respectively. The car-based trips of other purpose were valued 25% of the salary per hour. A more recent study by Tuydes Yaman and Dalkıç (2019) focused on VOT savings from the trips of high-speed rail in Turkey. They developed different models using the logistic modeling approach and computed value of travel time €15.3 and €25 per hour (2018 prices) from these models. Wardman et al. (2012) applied international meta-analysis for the estimation of VOT in different countries including Turkey. VOT was estimated for 36 countries in Europe and internationally in 2010 prices with regards to the distance bands of 5, 25, 100 and 250 kilometers for cars, busses and trains (see Wardman et al., 2012) (Table 12). These values developed in Wardman et al.'s (2012) study were adopted for the Turkish case (Table 12).

Table 12. Value of travel time for passenger cars and busses in Turkey (€cent per hour)

	Value of time (€cent per hour)					
	Busses			Passenger cars		
References	**Bus commuter**	**Bus business**	**Bus other**	**Car commuter**	**Car business**	**Car other**
Wardman et al. (2012)						
Distance-5 km	1.29	3.51	1.10	2.29	6.28	1.97
Distance-25 km	1.73	4.75	1.5	2.87	7.87	2.48
Distance-100 km	2.25	6.17	1.94	3.49	9.56	3.00
Distance-250 km	2.67	7.32	2.30	3.97	10.86	3.41

Note: 2018 prices were calculated using the annual percentage growth rate of GDP per capita for the period 2010-2018. GDP per capita growth rate: 2011: 6.1%; 2012: 3.4%; 2013: 7.7%; 2014: -2.9%; 2015: -9%; 2016: -1.2%; 2017: -2.4%; 2018: -8.7% (TurkStat, 2019).

Following Cravioto et al. (2013), congestion in an urban area can be quantified using the time delays t_D given as:

$$t_D = n_{CT} \cdot o \cdot \left(\frac{n_{CD}}{365}\right) \cdot \left(\frac{(v_u - v_c) \cdot d}{v_u \cdot v_c}\right) \qquad (5)$$

where n_{CT} is the total number of congested trips per day; o is the average vehicle occupancy; n_{CD} is the number of congested days per year; v_u is the (average) uncongested vehicle speed; and v_c is the congested vehicle speed. In Turkey, Istanbul is in the first place that has been experiencing serious traffic congestion, particularly in the main transport corridors during the peak hours. In the IBB (2016) Report, average number of congested trips of the road vehicles per day is reported as: 1,875,000. This number represents average number of vehicle flows on the main road network where congestion is a critical issue between 7am-8pm in the weekdays, 11:30am-8pm in the weekends. Vehicle occupancy rate is 1.57 for private cars, 30.4 for busses (IBB, 2011). Concerning the main arteries of Istanbul, the average speed in the congested time period is reported as 37km/h in 2017 (Istanbul'un Oto Ritmi, 2017) and it was assumed that average free flow speed on the main road network is 60 km/h. Average trip distance was estimated to be 14.5 km for both busses and private cars (IBB, 2011). t_D was estimated as 5,009 billion hours. Congestion costs (MECC) in Istanbul was modelled by using time delays t_D multiplied by a cost factor i.e. VOT given as:

$$MECC_{ij} = t_D \cdot VOT_{ij} \qquad (6)$$

where i represents the time period and j is the travel mode. The value of travel time for Turkey is updated to 2018 using the estimates of Wardman et al. (2012) (Table 12). It is noted that business trips account for 32%, commuter trips 21%, and leisure and other trips 47% (IBB, 2011). Using these ratios, the total time delays were distributed according to trip purpose and multiplied with the corresponding value of time in Table 12. Because average trip distance was 14.5 km for both busses and private cars, VOT estimates for the distance band of 25 km were used. The authors estimated congestion costs of lower and upper values equal to €11.850 million and €21.475 million, respectively with a central value of €16.360 million.

For the other cities, the authors used the estimated coefficients from an exponential regression indicating the relationship between population and congestion costs from other European regions as reported in EC(2019). The following equation represents the estimated model (with an R² of 0.95):

$$MCC_{oi} = 2.771 \cdot \left(e^{0.00003 \cdot pop_i}\right) \tag{7}$$

where MCC_{oi} is the marginal external cost of congestion in other regions of i and pop refers for the population (in thousands) of that region. The authors estimated an average of €8,278 million of the congestion costs for the other cities in Turkey. The inter-urban congestion costs were ignored as there is no input data to compute these costs but these could be included in the future research based on the availability of the data.

The estimated external costs of congestion by road class and type of area can be seen in Table 13. As it can be observed from the Table, the values are higher in urban areas than rural areas and higher for good vehicles than passenger cars.

Table 13. Marginal external costs of congestion by road class and type of area for Turkey (2022 EUR-cent/vkm)

Area and road type	Passenger cars			Good vehicles			HDV	Bus
	Min.	Central	Max.	Min.	Central	Max.	PCU	PCU
Urban areas (>2,000,000)								
Urban motorways	0.27	0.45	0.82	0.95	1.59	2.85	2.22	1.82
Urban collectors	0.18	0.45	1.09	0.45	1.14	2.73	1.58	1.82
Local streets centre	1.36	1.81	2.73	2.73	3.63	5.44	1.26	1.82
Local streets cordon	0.45	0.68	0.91	0.91	1.36	1.81	1.26	1.82
Inter-urban areas (<2,000,000)								
Urban motorways	0.09	0.23	0.36	0.32	0.80	1.27	2.22	1.82
Urban collectors	0.05	0.27	0.45	0.12	0.68	1.14	1.58	1.82
Local streets cordon	0.09	0.27	0.45	0.18	0.55	0.91	1.26	1.82
Rural areas								
Motorways	0.00	0.09	0.18	0.00	0.32	0.64	2.22	1.82
Trunk roads	0.00	0.05	0.14	0.00	0.12	0.21	1.58	1.82

Note: vkm: vehicle kilometres, HDV: Heavy duty vehicles, PCU: passenger car unit. The distribution of marginal congestion costs across urban, inter-urban and rural areas was based on urban, sub-urban and rural classification explained under the noise costs category. The distributions across motorways and other roads were based on the corresponding ratios obtained from: CE Delft (2008).

RESEARCH FINDINGS

Road Accidents

The total external costs of accidents ranged from €43,412.00 (central estimate) million to €108.00 million (central estimate); the former was obtained for passenger cars while the latter was for busses (Table 14). The costs for the HDVs and motorcycles were similar (more than €1,200 million) and were significantly lower than those for the passenger cars (Figure 1). The cost for LCVs was around €343 million which was also lower than the costs of passenger cars.

Table 14. Distribution of social external costs of road transport in Turkey (2022)

Cost category	Transport mode	Low estimates (million €)	Central estimates (million €)	High estimates (million €)
Accident	Car	7834	43412	77925
	Bus	19	108	207
	LCV	52	343	601
	HDV	323	1794	3221
	Motorcycle	227	1258	2258
Climate change	Car	898	1198	1498
	Bus	185	247	309
	LCV	115	154	192
	HDV	1123	1497	1872
	Motorcycle	82	108	135
Noise	Car	259	304	672
	Bus	117	131	287
	LCV	115	129	283
	HDV	3582	3981	8788
	Motorcycle	53	58	128
Congestion	Car	274	504	843
	Bus	46	86	144
	LCV	53	102	171
	HDV	683	1277	2145
	Motorcycle	0	0	0
Air pollution	Car	1819	2272	2727
	Bus	1717	2146	2576
	LCV	325	406	488
	HDV	16780	20974	25169
	Motorcycle	132	164	198

Figure 1. Distribution of average accident costs per casualty across different road vehicles, Turkey

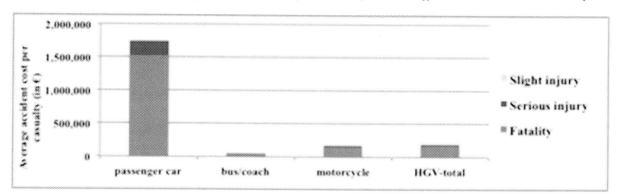

Air Pollution

Regarding CO, NMVOC, NO_x and $PM_{2.5}$, the largest category was HDVs; and regarding NH_3, it was the passenger cars (Table 14). Total air pollution costs for the busses were very close to those of the passenger cars. Motorcycles and LCVs were associated with relatively lower costs compared to other vehicle classes (Table 14). It is noted that petrol vehicles are emitting more pollutants compared to diesel vehicles concerning all vehicle categories (Figure 2). Among these, petrol HDVs have the highest share in total CO, NMVOC and NO_x emissions followed by petrol cars and diesel HDVs. Regarding all vehicle classes, NO_x was associated with the highest cost of air pollution that was followed by $PM_{2.5}$ and CO. For busses, total external costs of $PM_{2.5}$ emissions were higher than passenger cars but the reverse applied for NO_x emissions. The high cost of $PM_{2.5}$ for busses was due to the high cost factors assigned to the subject pollutant. The busses emit more $PM_{2.5}$ per vehicle kilometer compared to those of passenger cars may be another explanation.

Figure 2. Air pollutant emissions for different road vehicles, Turkey

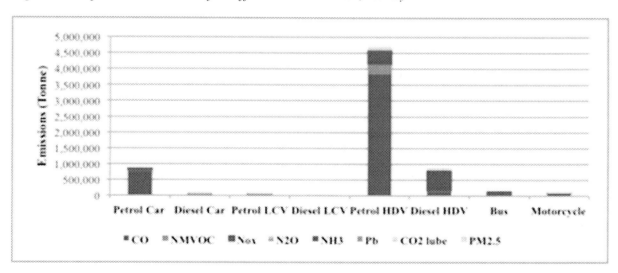

Climate Change

It is noted that petrol HDV emission costs were the highest, which was followed by costs of passenger cars (diesel and petrol), diesel HDVs and busses, respectively (Figure 3, Table 14). These cost estimates for the busses were more than twice those of motorcycles and LCVs. As means of public transportation, busses were associated with lower carbon costs compared to passenger cars of both petrol and diesel types.

Figure 3. Climate change costs across different road vehicles, Turkey

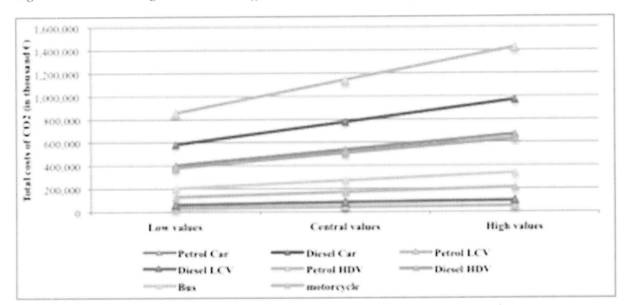

Noise Pollution

Noise costs were highly sensitive to noise level increments in urban and rural areas. The highest cost of noise pollution in urban and sub-urban areas was the HDVs. Passenger cars and motorcycles had similar contribution to the total noise costs, which were significantly lower than those of HDVs. LCVs were associated with the lowest cost for the noise pollution in both urban and rural areas.

Congestion

As expected, congestion costs were sound for urban areas followed by sub-urban and rural areas. The congestion costs were higher for passenger cars compared to light and heavy goods vehicles. Because congestion is not an issue for motorcycles, these were not included in the cost estimations.

Total External Costs of Road Transport

The total external costs of road transport in Turkey ranges from €36.81 to €132.83 billion with a central estimate of €82.65 billion. Accidents have the highest share in total costs followed by air pollution, congestion, noise and climate change. Figure 4 presents the distribution of total costs per category where the cost estimates represent the central cost estimates. Figure 5 shows the distribution of total external costs (central estimates) across different road vehicles where cars and HDVs are associated with the highest shares and LCVs, motorcycles and busses have the lowest share.

Figure 4. Total external costs of road transport in Turkey (in million 2022€)
Note: Cost estimates are based on average cost factors

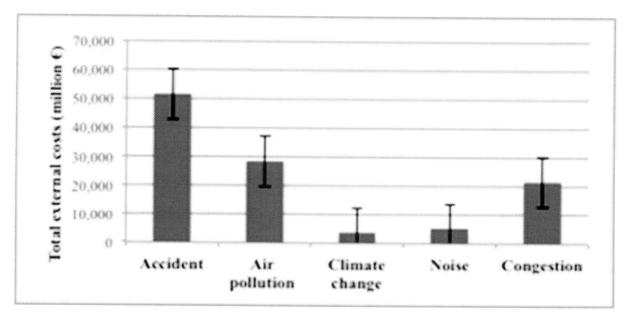

Figure 5. Percentage distribution of total external costs across different road vehicles in Turkey

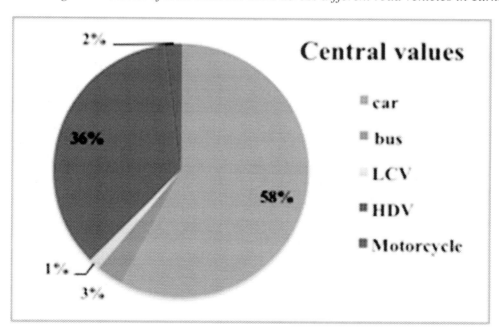

FUTURE RESEARCH DIRECTIONS

Because road vehicles in Turkey impose large external costs both on the users and society, it is of significance for optimal pricing of road transportation based on the principles of marginal social costing. The road transport sector in Turkey faces with the highest tax rates compared to other sectors that consume energy (OECD, 2018). In 2018 prices, the tax rate per tonne of CO_2 emission is 1,100 Turkish Lira (TL) for gasoline, 600 TL for diesel, and 520 TL for biofuels, natural gases and LPG. Though road transport has relatively higher taxes, OECD Report (2019) argued that they do not reflect the climate costs associated with their use. The taxation of road transport vehicles in Turkey has provided environmental incentives; however, the taxation system pushes consumers to get older, second hand vehicles that emit more pollutants (OECD, 2019). To discourage the use of old vehicles, the government brought new measures in 2018 in relation to the taxation system. Accordingly, new vehicles, hybrid and electric vehicles are encouraged with lower tax rates. However, there is no differentiation on the type of the fuel use contributing to increasing demand for diesel vehicles. The share of diesel cars has considerably increased in the past decades in Turkey, from 6.8% to 37% between 2005 and 2018 (OECD, 2019). A relevant measure is therefore required to meet the government's environmental objectives in relation to the type of the fuel use.

Emissions of GHGs have become a global environmental concern, and governments in different countries have developed various policy measures to curb the adverse impacts related to transport emissions. For instance, European Union (Ambient Air Quality Directives) and World Health Organisation have introduced exposure limits regarding different types of air pollutants (see CE Delft, 2018). EU countries and the USA set GHG emission targets compatible with the Kyoto Protocol. Instead, Turkey has not submitted a GHG emission reduction target under the Kyoto Protocol, but it has yet to ratified the Paris agreement within the United Nations Framework Convention on Climate Change. The agreement aims at holding the global average temperature below 2°C above pre-industrial levels and to pursue efforts to limit the temperature increase 1.5°C above pre-industrial levels. In this context, Turkey announced that it would reduce GHG emissions by up to 21% for the 'business-as-usual' level by 2030. This implies that the emissions will be more than doubled between 2015 and 2030 (OECD, 2016): from 411 Mt CO_2e in 2015 to 928 Mt CO_2e in 2030 (Republic of Turkey, 2015). Although there is progress achieved with the reduction of transport-related emissions in the post-2000 (OECD, 2020), there is a continuous trend of increasing GHGs between 1990-2017 period. Therefore, it is essential for Turkey to evaluate and monetise the costs of carbon to inform policy makers about the progress. Given that Turkey is a fast growing economy that is closely linked with the rest of the world, attention should be paid on the contribution of Turkey to global warming and the mitigation measures to be taken to relieve the impacts of climate change on Turkey. Turkey has adopted its National Climate Change Strategy and Action Plan (NCCS in 2010; NCCAP in 2011), which have provided a ground for action with short-term and long-term objectives and a set of actions for mitigating GHG emissions and for adapting to climate change (OECD, 2019). The 2008 transport legislation was amended to establish low emission zones that would be managed at the local level. Besides, the Government has developed a strategy to stimulate domestic demand through investments in infrastructure and incentives for low energy vehicle use (OECD, 2019). These attempts will have important consequences to achieve the socio-economic and environmental benefits from transport emissions.

Besides the use of market mechanisms such as high fuel taxes and other road pricing policies, it is important to encourage a modal shift in favor of public transport, particularly rail-based transport systems, to alleviate the negative impacts of road transportation. The modal shift from road transportation (e.g. cars) to rail based systems is beneficial to the society through savings in energy consumption, reduction in transport-related air pollutants, congestion and accident risks. However, the most important factors according to our findings are accident risks, air pollution and congestion. This is similar to the findings of Delucchi and McCubbin (2011) which found that road accident and congestion are the largest marginal external costs followed by air pollution. Differently, Rizzi and de la Maza (2017) concluded that congestion is the most costly externality followed by local air pollution. The reason for large accident costs in Turkey is that fatalities and serious injuries from road traffic accidents in the Country are considerably higher than the accident rates in European countries. This is because both freight and passenger transportation are concentrated on the road network and the share of rail transportation in total is only minor. Therefore, the most important measure to reduce the risk of accidents is to invest more on rail-based transportation for the goods and people. Nevertheless, to encourage a modal shift from road transport to rail systems would be a long-term goal while in the short-term new measures on the enforcement of traffic laws and road safety, road maintenance and infrastructure policies in relation to transport safety would be efficient.

The authors estimated the costs of traffic congestion in Turkey to be around €20 billion/per year (central estimates) or 2.8% of GDP. It can be noted that some cities of Turkey are ranked at the top places being the most congested cities in the world (OECD, 2019). This implies that congestion is common in large cities of Turkey and it imposes a significant burden in lost time, uncertainty and aggravation of goods and passenger transportation. Among these, Istanbul is placed at the top which is the largest and the most congested city of Turkey. Given the high congestion costs, a new congestion-pricing scheme can be introduced particularly in Istanbul. There is evidence that the cities that introduced congestion pricing (e.g. London, Stockholm, and Singapore) have benefited from reduction in traffic volume, improved air pollution and increase in government revenues (Small et al., 2006; Eliasson, 2009) that can be directed to finance other transport infrastructure and public transit investments (OECD, 2019). Congestion pricing is advantageous over other transport management policies in that it encourages passengers to adjust their travel plans including number of trips, destination, mode of travel, travel route etc. and their long-term decisions on the place of their residence, work and set up business (de Palma and Lindsey, 2011). However, to set the Pigouvian toll, the knowledge on the demand curve for trips is required given that the equilibrium value of link flows depends on the toll. Because traffic flows vary significantly by time of the day, day of the weak or season, formulating a dynamic system optimum on a road network, deriving the tolls that supports the optimum, and solving the system equations have remained a challenge (Friesz et al., 2008; de Palma and Lindsey, 2011). This is also questionable in Turkey due to data availability issues on the required parameters by location, vehicle type, and time of the day as well as speed and real time driving data from network models are hardly available. This indicates that marginal costs and the optimum taxation levels are difficult to derive. It is suggested by OECD (2019) that congestion pricing could be introduced gradually with district pilot projects in the most congested cities of Turkey. However, the congestion pricing schemes should be efficient and acceptable by the public; otherwise it would be a challenge for the enforcement of such a scheme. For instance, a 2017 survey of people in Taksim district of Istanbul concluded that majority of people did not believe that congestion pricing would be efficient (Özgenel and Günay, 2017). The international experience on congestion pricing has shown that public support depends on whether the pricing scheme reduces congestion and pollution significantly, and whether the revenue is used for highly valued transport infrastructure investments. The Turkish Ministry of Transport and Infrastructure has been coordinating a regulation on principles and procedures for energy efficiency in transportation. As part of this process, Istanbul Metropolitan Municipality has considered different options such as congestion pricing at peak hours and restrictions for HDVs (see OECD, 2019). It is also recommended to introduce other measures such as cordon pricing and increased parking fees to lessen congestion and to address local air pollution.

From noise maps, the number of people affected by road traffic, rail traffic or aviation noise can be estimated (see EEA, 2020). Regarding EU member states, noise maps are required to be delivered to the European Commission by each EU member country according to the Directive 2002/49/EC. In the year 2010, Regulation on Assessment and Management of Environmental Noise was delivered by the Turkish Ministry of Urbanisation and Environment. Both regulations have imposed obligations on the delivery of noise mapping and the analysis of the number of people affected by noise. In Turkey, noise maps were developed covering only 18 provinces and the maps for the rest of provinces are currently under development. There are case studies in Turkey where different noise maps were developed for a number of selected study areas; however these are not comprehensive and cannot be generalised for the calculation of the total number of people exposed to noise pollution in Turkey. It is important to develop the noise maps at the country level as this is of great significance in terms of the comparison of costs of actions related to the prevention of noise.

The estimation of marginal social costs has raised the problem that location-specific data and models are required. The estimation process for a specific case study is costly in terms of time and budget and is therefore not a practical option for planners and policy makers. This is the case in the Turkish literature where local marginal cost estimates are limited, and therefore the authors applied the generic knowledge from available case studies for the types of road traffic and vehicle classes of which marginal cost estimates are unavailable. To our knowledge, such a generalised approach for the road transportation sector in Turkey has not been developed and implemented previously.

It can be noted that there are a number of challenges in the evaluation of road transport externalities in Turkey. More detailed data is required for the estimation of the most important parameters. Among these, data on transport characteristics (e.g. vehicle flow data in the peak and off-peak periods, average vehicle speed and travel time) of the road network, spatial distribution of population, risk of accidents, and the emissions from different road vehicles should be specified. Further research should aim at developing such information both at the local and national levels, investigating local cost factors (e.g. noise, congestion and air pollution valuation), and evaluating the impacts of measures taken to reduce the impacts of externalities. It can be argued that marginal external costs estimated in the current study might be under estimated due to the variability of road vehicles, road classes and vehicle kilometres, and the assumptions being made for the calculation of the specified external costs were also effective. The unavailability of data and the research on local estimates of cost factors has limited the study to get fine-scale estimates of external costs. An in-debt analysis on the externality impact assessments at the local/regional scale and development of disaggregated data for the inputs that were used in the model would therefore refine our estimates of external costs.

CONCLUSION

Though important to the economy in connecting all businesses and industries, road transportation activities certainly create adverse impacts. These impacts are referred to as external costs because they are born by those who generate them and fall on people other than the producer or the consumer. Externalities are a common problem associated with our interaction with the environment. The price one pays for the use or consumption of the product does not include the environmental costs to create the product. Therefore, placing a value on external damage arising from the activity is vital to internalizing them; requiring those who generate negative costs to compensate society in an amount equal to the external costs. Governments need to intervene into the market through combining appropriate standards with market-based regulation to price goods and services accurately, taking into account negative externalities. This will shed light on the actual full cost of an activity so that consumption decisions can be made accordingly based on this information on the cost. Regarding road-based transportation services, internalization of external costs will lead to some reduction of transport activities such as the relocation of industrial and commercial activities closer to markets. A further impact may be the shift to a competing mode that is less costly, once external costs are accounted. In this context, updated estimates of transport-related externalities are necessary to inform decision makers obliged to reducing these impacts at the national and local grounds.

The analysis has focused on road vehicles operating in inter-city and intra-city transportation in Turkey. Road based travelling accounts for a very large share of the total miles of all transport activities in the Country. This has constructed a base for the current study that aimed to estimate the external costs of road transportation in Turkey. The analysis were restricted to five different externalities of road transportation because of significant contribution of these externalities to the total social cost and the rapid changes underway in the determinants of these externalities across the country and regions. Instead of evaluating the transportation sector as a whole, the authors focused on the external costs attributable to different road vehicle categories such as petrol and diesel road vehicles including passenger cars, LCVs, HDVs, busses and motorcycles. It was estimated that external costs of accidents from road transport sector were responsible for 47%, followed by air pollution and congestion costs each accounting for 26% and 20% of the total social external costs of road transportation in Turkey. In relation to the distribution of total costs, cars and HDVs represented the largest shares whereas busses were the largest in relation to some specific cost categories.

The conclusion is that although some external costs might be underestimated due to data quality and availability issues, the resulting estimates are sizable enough to attract the attention of policy makers and authorities. External costs affect the welfare of the society and therefore should be fully included in the decision making process to specify the amount of service that is to be consumed by each transportation mode. To the knowledge of the authors, the current research is the first one that provided estimates of external costs of road transport vehicles in Turkey. These estimates can guide to public and private sector decision making in the use of alternative transport modes.

ACKNOWLEDGMENT

The study presented here was funded by The Scientific and Technological Research Council of Turkey (TUBİTAK) linked to BIDEB-2232 Programme, Project No. 118C002.

REFERENCES

Anciaes, P. R., Jones, P., & Mindell, J. S. (2014). *The value of the barrier effects of roads and railways: A literature review*. Street Mobility and Network Accessibility Series, Working Paper 03. University College London.

ARTEMIS (Assessment and Reliability of Transport Emission Models and Inventory Systems). (2007). Emission factor modelling and database for light vehicles. Deliverable 3, Report No: LTE0523. Funded by EU's 5th Framework Programme. INRETS.

Baarsma, B. E., & Lambooy, J. G. (2005). Valuation of externalities through neo-classical methods by including institutional variables. *Transportation Research Part D, Transport and Environment, 10*(6), 459–475. doi:10.1016/j.trd.2005.06.001

Beaudoin, J., Farzin, H. Y., & Lin Lawell, C. C.-Y. (2015). Public transit investment and sustainable transportation: A review of studies of transit's impact on traffic congestion and air quality. *Research in Transportation Economics, 52*, 15–22. doi:10.1016/j.retrec.2015.10.004

Bel, G., & Holst, M. (2018). Evaluation of the impact of Bus Rapid Transit on air pollution in Mexico city. *Transport Policy, 63*, 209–220. doi:10.1016/j.tranpol.2018.01.001

Beuthe, M., Degrandsart, F., Greerts, J.-F., & Jourquin, B. (2002). External costs of the Belgian interurban freight traffic: A network analysis of their internalization. *Transportation Research, 7*(4), 285–301.

Boothe, V. L., & Shendell, D. G. (2008). Potential health effects associated with residential proximity to freeways and primary roads: Review of scientific literature 1999-2006. *Journal of Environmental Health, 70*(8), 33–41. PMID:18468221

Boundreaux, D. J., & Meiners, R. (2019). Externality: Origins and classifications. *Natural Resources Journal, 59*(1), 1–33.

Bravo, M., Briceno, L., Cominetti, R., Cortes, E. C., & Martinez, F. (2010). An integrated behavioural model of the land-use and transport systems with network congestion and location externalities. *Transportation Research Part B: Methodological, 44*(4), 584–596. doi:10.1016/j.trb.2009.08.002

Bravo-Moncayo, L., Naranjo, J. L., Garcia, I. P., & Mosquera, R. (2017). Neural based contingent valuation of road traffic noise. *Transportation Research Part D, Transport and Environment, 50*, 26–39. doi:10.1016/j.trd.2016.10.020

Bristow, A. L., Wardman, M., & Chintakayala, V. P. K. (2015). International meta-analysis of stated preference studies of transportation noise nuisance. *Transportation, 42*(1), 71–100. doi:10.100711116-014-9527-4

Buzzelli, M., & Jerrett, M. (2003). Comparing proximity measures of exposure to geostatistical estimates in environmental justice research. *Global Environment Change B, 5*(1), 13–21. doi:10.1016/j.hazards.2003.11.001

Carrier, M., Apparicio, P., Seguin, A.-M., & Crouse, D. (2014). The application of three methods to measure the statistical association between different social groups and the concentration of air pollutants in Montreal: A case of environmental equity. *Transportation Research Part D, Transport and Environment*, *30*, 38–52. doi:10.1016/j.trd.2014.05.001

Cavallaro, F. (2018). Policy implications from the economic valuation of freight transport externalities along the Brenner corridor. *Case Studies on Transport Policy*, *6*(1), 133–146. doi:10.1016/j.cstp.2017.11.008

CE Delft. (2018). *Health impacts and costs of diesel emissions in the EU*. CE Delft. https://epha.org/wp-content/uploads/2018/11/embargoed-until-27-november-00-01-am-cet-time-ce-delft-4r30-health-impacts-costs-diesel-emissions-eu-def.pdf

Commission of the European Communities. (1990). *Green paper on the urban environment*. European Commission.

Cravioto, J., Yamasue, E., Okumura, H., & Ishihara, K. N. (2013). Road transport externalities in Mexico: Estimates and international comparisons. *Transport Policy*, *30*, 63–76. doi:10.1016/j.tranpol.2013.08.004

Croci, E. (2016). Urban road pricing: A comparative study on the experiences of London, Stockholm and Milan. *Transportation Research Procedia*, *14*, 253–262. doi:10.1016/j.trpro.2016.05.062

De Dios Ortuzar, J., Bascunan, R., Rizzi, L. I., & Salata, A. (2021). Assessing the potential acceptability of road pricing in Santiago. *Transportation Research Part A, Policy and Practice*, *144*, 153–169. doi:10.1016/j.tra.2020.12.007

De Palma, A., & Lindsey, R. (2011). Traffic congestion pricing methodologies and technologies. *Transportation Research Part C, Emerging Technologies*, *19*(6), 1377–1399. doi:10.1016/j.trc.2011.02.010

DEFRA. (2014). *Environmental noise: valuing impacts on: sleep disturbance, annoyance, hypertension, productivity and quite*. DEFRA.

Dekkers, J. E. C., & van der Straaten, W. (2009). Monetary valuation of aircraft noise: A hedonic analysis around Amsterdam airport. *Ecological Economics*, *68*(11), 2850–2858. doi:10.1016/j.ecolecon.2009.06.002

Delft, C. E. (2008). *Health impacts of costs of diesel emissions in the EU*.

Delft, C. E. INFRAS & Fraunhofer ISI. (2011). External costs of transport in Europe. CE Delft.

Dementyeva, M., Koster, P. R., & Verhoef, E. T. (2015). Regulation of road accident externalities when insurance companies have market power. *Journal of Urban Economics*, *86*, 1–8. doi:10.1016/j.jue.2014.11.001

Deng, X. (2006). Economic costs of motor vehicle emissions in China: A case study. *Transportation Research Part D, Transport and Environment*, *11*(3), 216–226. doi:10.1016/j.trd.2006.02.004

Duffy, P., Black, K., O'Brian, P., Hyde, B., Ryan, A. M., Ponzi, J., & Alam, M. S. (2017). *National inventory report 2017*. EPA.

Dyr, T., Misiurski, P., & Ziolkowska, K. (2019). Costs and benefits of using busses fuelled by natural gas in public transport. *Journal of Cleaner Production*, *225*, 1134–1146. doi:10.1016/j.jclepro.2019.03.317

EC. (2019). *Handbook on the external costs of transport*. Publications Office of the European Union.

Ece, M., Tosun, I., Ekinci, K., & Yalçındağ, N. S. (2018). Modeling of road traffic noise and traffic flow measures to reduce noise exposure in Antalya metropolitan municipality. *Journal of Environmental Health Science & Engineering*, *16*(1), 1–10. doi:10.100740201-018-0288-4 PMID:30258637

ECMT (European Conference of Ministers of Transport). (1998). *Efficient transport for Europe*. OECD.

Edlin, A. S., & Karaca-Mandic, P. (2006). The accident externality from driving. *Journal of Political Economy*, *114*(5), 931–955. doi:10.1086/508030

EEA. (2014). *Air pollution fact sheet 2014 Turkey*. EEA.

EEA. (2019). *EMEP/EEA Air pollutant emission inventory guidebook 2019*. EEA.

EEA. (2020). *Environmental noise in Europe-2020*. EEA.

Eliasson, J., Hultkrantz, L., Nerhagen, L., & Smidfelt Rosqvist, L. (2009). The Stockholm congestion-charging trial 2006: Overview of effects. *Transportation Research Part A, Policy and Practice*, *43*(3), 240–250. doi:10.1016/j.tra.2008.09.007

Emmerink, R. H. M., Nijkamp, P., & Rietveld, P. (1995). Is congestion pricing a first-best strategy in transport policy? A critical review of arguments. *Environment & Planning B*, *22*(4), 581–602. doi:10.1068/b220581

EU-RTR. (2012). *Technical assistance for improving emissions control*. Final Report-Part II: Main Technical Results. PM Project number: 300424. Project co-financed by European Union and Republic of Turkey.

Euchi, J., & Kallel, A. (2021). Internalization of external congestion and CO_2 emissions costs related to road transport: The case of Tunisia. *Renewable & Sustainable Energy Reviews*, *142*, 110858. doi:10.1016/j.rser.2021.110858

EUROSTAT. (2015). *Urban-rural typology update*. https://ec.europa.eu/eurostat/statisticsexplained/index.php?title=Archive:Urbanrural_typology_update&oldid=262364

Evangelinos, C., & Tscharaktschiew, S. (2021). The valuation of aesthetic preferences and consequences for urban transport infrastructures. *Sustainability*, *13*(9), 4977. doi:10.3390u13094977

Extern, E. (2005). Externalities of Energy: Methodology 2005 update. EC.

Friesz, T., Kwon, C., & Bernstein, D. (2008). Analytical dynamic traffic assignment models. In D. A. Hensher & K. J. Button (Eds.), *Handbook of transport modelling* (Vol. 1). Elsevier Science.

Garanti & PwC. (2017). Capital projects and infrastructure spending in Turkey. Garanti BBVA Group and PwC.

Griffiths, M. A., Perera, B. Y., & Albinsson, P. A. (2019). Contrived surplus and negative externalities in the sharing economy. *Journal of Marketing Theory and Practice*, *27*(4), 445–463. doi:10.1080/10696679.2019.1644957

Gu, Z., Liu, Z., Cheng, Q., & Saberi, M. (n.d.). Congestion pricing practices and public acceptance: a review of evidence. *Case Studies on Transport Policy, 6*(1), 94-101.

Gürses, D., Sarıoglu-Buke, A., Baskan, M., & Kılıc, I. (2003). Cost factors in pediatric trauma. *Canadian Journal of Surgery, 46*(6), 441–445. PMID:14680351

Hagedorn, T., & Sieg, G. (2019). Emissions and external environmental costs from the perspective of differing travel purposes. *Sustainability, 11*(24), 7233. doi:10.3390u11247233

Hammer, M. S., Swinburn, T. K., & Neitzel, R. L. (2014). Environmental noise pollution in the United States: Developing an effective public health response. *Environmental Health Perspectives, 122*(2), 115–119. doi:10.1289/ehp.1307272 PMID:24311120

Hau, T. D. (1995). A conceptual framework for pricing congestion and road damage. In B. Johansson & L. G. Mattsson (Eds.), *Road pricing: Theory, empirical assessment and policy. Transportation research, economics and policy*. Springer. doi:10.1007/978-94-011-0980-2_4

Hausman, J. (2012). Contingent valuation: From dubious to hopeless. *The Journal of Economic Perspectives, 26*(4), 43–56. doi:10.1257/jep.26.4.43

HEATCO (Developing Harmonised European Approaches for Transport Costing and Project Assessment). (2004-2006). *Deliverable 5*. Funded by 6th Framework Programme IER. Available from: http://heatco.ier.uni-stuttgart.de/

Hood, C. (2017). *Input to the high-level commission on carbon prices. Background paper for the Commission*. EC.

IBB. (2011). *İstanbul Metropoliten Alanı kentsel ulaşım ana planı (IUAP) (Istanbul Metropolitan Region urban transportation plan)*. IBB Ulaşım Daire Başkanlığı-Ulaşım Planlama Mudurlugu.

IBB-Istanbul Buyuksehir Belediyesi. (2016). *İstanbul ulaşım ver hareketlilik raporu (Istanbul transporation and mobility report)*. IBB Ulaşım Daire Başkanlığı.

IEA. (2012). *Energy technology perspectives 2012 (ETP 2012)*. Available at: http://www.iea.org/ etp/ publications/etp2012/

IMPACT. (2008). *Handbook on estimation of external costs in the transport sector-Produced within the study Internalisation Measures and Policies for all external Cost of Transport*. IMPACT.

INFRAS/IWW. (2004). *External costs of transport: Accident, environmental and congestion costs of transport in Western Europe*. INFRAS and IWW.

Istanbul'un Oto Ritmi. (2017). *Online report*. https://www.aa.com.tr/tr/ sirkethaberleri/egitim/istanbul-trafik-otoritmi-raporu-aciklandi/660063

Jakob, A., Craig, J. L., & Fisher, G. (2006). Transport cost analysis: A case study of the total costs of private and public transport in Auckland. *Environmental Science & Policy, 9*(1), 55–66. doi:10.1016/j.envsci.2005.09.001

Jiang, L., & Kang, J. (2016). Combined acoustical and visual performance of noise barriers in mitigating the environmental impact of motorways. *The Science of the Total Environment, 543,* 52–60. doi:10.1016/j.scitotenv.2015.11.010 PMID:26584069

Jochem, P., Doll, C., & Fichtner, W. (2016). External costs of electric vehicles. *Transportation Research Part D, Transport and Environment, 42,* 60–76. doi:10.1016/j.trd.2015.09.022

Kapper, T. (2004). Bringing beauty to account in the environmental impact statement: The contingent valuation of landscape aesthetics. *Environmental Practice, 6*(4), 296–305. doi:10.1017/S146604660400047X

Karadana, A. G., Metin Aksu, N., Akkaş, M., Akman, C., Üzümcügül, A., & Özmen, M. M. (2013). The epidemiology and costs analysis of patients presented to Emergency Department following traffic accidents. *Medical Science Monitor, 19,* 1125–1130. doi:10.12659/MSM.889539 PMID:24316815

Ko, H. J., Il Chang, S., & Lee, B. C. (2011). Noise impact assessment by utilising noise map and GIS: A case study in the city of Chungju, Republic of Korea. *Applied Acoustics, 72*(8), 544–550. doi:10.1016/j.apacoust.2010.09.002

Komikado, H., Morikawa, S., Bhatt, A., & Kato, H. (2021). High-speed rail, inter-regional accessibility, and regional innovation: Evidence from Japan. *Technological Forecasting and Social Change, 167,* 120697. doi:10.1016/j.techfore.2021.120697

Levinson, D. (2010). Equity effects of road pricing: A review. *Transport Reviews, 30*(1), 33–57. doi:10.1080/01441640903189304

Lindhjem, H., Navrud, S., & Braathen, N. A. (2010). *Valuing lives saved from environmental, transport and health policies: A meta-analysis of stated preference studies.* OECD.

Link, H., Nash, C., Ricci, A., & Shires, J. (2016). A generalised approach for measuring the marginal social costs of road transport in Europe. *International Journal of Sustainable Transportation, 10*(2), 105–119. doi:10.1080/15568318.2013.861044

Liu, C., Henderson, B. H., Wang, D., Yang, X., & Peng, Z.-R. (2016). A land use regression application into assessing spatial variation of intra-urban fine particulate matter ($PM_{2.5}$) and nitrogen dioxide (NO_2) concentrations in city of Shanghai, China. *The Science of the Total Environment, 565,* 607–615. doi:10.1016/j.scitotenv.2016.03.189 PMID:27203521

Liu, S., Xing, J., Wang, S., Ding, D., Chen, L., & Hao, J. (2020). Revealing the impacts of transboundary pollution on $PM_{2.5}$-related deaths in China. *Environment International, 134,* 105323. doi:10.1016/j.envint.2019.105323 PMID:31759275

Mayeres, I., Ochelen, S., & Proost, S. (1996). The marginal external costs of urban transport. *Transportation Research Part D, Transport and Environment, 1*(2), 111–130. doi:10.1016/S1361-9209(96)00006-5

Melo, P. C., & Graham, D. J. (2018). Transport-induced agglomeration effects: Evidence for US metropolitan areas. *Regional Science Policy & Practice, 10*(1), 37–47. doi:10.1111/rsp3.12116

Michanowicz, D. R., Shmool, J. L. C., Tunno, B. J., Tripathy, S., Gillooly, S., Kinnee, E., & Clougherty, J. (2016). A hybrid land use regression/AERMOD model for predicting intra-urban variation in $PM_{2.5}$. *Atmospheric Environment, 131,* 307–315. doi:10.1016/j.atmosenv.2016.01.045

Mizutani, F., Suzuki, Y., & Sakai, H. (2011). Estimation of social costs of transport in Japan. *Urban Studies (Edinburgh, Scotland), 48*(16), 3537–3559. doi:10.1177/0042098011399597

Mouter, N. (Ed.). (2020). *Standard transport appraisal methods.* Elsevier.

Muehlenbachs, L., Staubli, S., & Chu, Z. (2021). The accident externality from trucking: Evidence from shale gas development. *Regional Science and Urban Economics, 88,* 103630. doi:10.1016/j.regsciurbeco.2020.103630

Naci, H., & Baker, T. D. (2008). Productivity losses from road traffic deaths in Turkey. *International Journal of Injury Control and Safety Promotion, 15*(1), 19–24. doi:10.1080/17457300701847648 PMID:18344092

Namdeo, A., Goodman, P., Mitchell, G., Hargreaves, A., & Echenique, M. (2019). Land-use, transport and vehicle technology futures: Air pollution assessment of policy combinations for the Cambridge Sub-Region of the UK. *Cities (London, England), 89,* 296–307. doi:10.1016/j.cities.2019.03.004

Nash, C. (1997). Transport externalities: Does monetary valuation make sense? In G. de Rus & C. Nash (Eds.), *Recent developments in transport economics.* Asgate Press.

Nash, C. (Ed.). (2015). *Handbook on research methods and applications in transport economics and policy.* Edward Elgar Publishing. doi:10.4337/9780857937933

NEEDS. (2006). New Energy Externalities Development for Sustainability (NEEDS). Deliverable D4.2: Assessment of biodiversity losses: Econcept AG and ESU-services Zurich.

Newbery, D. (1994). The case for a public road authority. *Journal of Transport Economics and Policy, 28*(3), 235–253.

OECD. (2012). *Mortality risk valuation in environment, health and transport policies.* OECD.

OECD. (2013). *The port and its environment: Methodological approach for economic appraisal.* OECD Publishing.

OECD. (2014). *The costs of air pollution: Health impact of road transport.* OECD.

OECD. (2016). *OECD economic surveys: Turkey 2016.* OECD.

OECD. (2018). *OECD economic surveys: Turkey.* OECD.

OECD. (2019). *OECD environmental performance reviews: Turkey 2019.* OECD.

OECD. (2020). Air and climate: Greenhouse gas emissions from source. OECD Environment Statistics Database.

Özen, E., Genç, E., & Kaya, Z. (2014). Estimation of the costs of traffic accidents in Turkey: An evaluation in terms of the insurance and financial system. *Journal of Yaşar University, 9*(33), 5649–5673. doi:10.19168/jyu.94397

Özgenel, M., & Günay, G. (2017). Congestion pricing implementation in Taksim zone: A stated preference study. *Transportation Research Procedia, 27,* 905–912. doi:10.1016/j.trpro.2017.12.065

Pearce, D., Atkinson, G., & Maurato, S. (2006). *Cost-benefit Analysis and the environment: Recent developments*. OECD.

Pereira, R. H. M., Schwanen, T., & Banister, D. (2016). Distributive justice and equity in transportation. *Transport Reviews, 37*(2), 170–191. doi:10.1080/01441647.2016.1257660

Pigou, A. C. (1920). *The economics of welfare*. MacMillan and Co.

Prud'homme, R., Koning, M., Lenormand, L., & Fehr, A. (2012). Public transport congestion costs: The case of the Paris subway. *Transport Policy, 21*, 101–109. doi:10.1016/j.tranpol.2011.11.002

Qingyu, L., Zhicai, J., Baofeng, S., & Hongfei, J. (2007). Method research on measuring the external costs of urban traffic congestion. *Journal of Transportation Systems Engineering and Information Technology, 7*(5), 9–12. doi:10.1016/S1570-6672(07)60035-X

Republic of Turkey. (2015). *Intended Nationally Determined Contribution (INDC)*. https://www4.unfccc.int/sites/submissions/INDC/Published%20Documents/Turkey/1/The_INDC_of_TURKEY_v.15.19.30.pdf

Rizzi, I. L., & De La Maza, C. (2017). The external costs of private versus public road transport in the Metropolitan Area of Santiago, Chile. *Transportation Research Part A, Policy and Practice, 98*, 123–140. doi:10.1016/j.tra.2017.02.002

Saito, K., Kato, T., & Shimane, T. (2010). Traffic congestion and accident externality: A Japan-US comparison. *The B.E. Journal of Economic Analysis & Policy, 10*(1), 1–31. doi:10.2202/1935-1682.2057

Santos, G. (2017). Road fuel taxes in Europe: Do they internalize road transport externalities? *Transport Policy, 53*, 120–134. doi:10.1016/j.tranpol.2016.09.009

Savacool, B. K., Kim, J., & Yang, M. (2021). The hidden costs of energy and mobility: A global meta-analysis and research synthesis of electricity and transport externalities. *Energy Research & Social Science, 72*, 101885. doi:10.1016/j.erss.2020.101885

Scheffran, J., & Battaglini, A. (2010). Climate and conflicts: The security risks of global warming. *Regional Environmental Change, 11*(S1), 27–39. doi:10.100710113-010-0175-8

Sen, K. A., Tiwari, G., & Upadhyay, V. (2010). Estimating marginal external costs of transport in Delhi. *Transport Policy, 17*(1), 27–37. doi:10.1016/j.tranpol.2009.09.003

Shekarrizfard, M., Faghih-Imani, A., Crouse, D. L., Goldberg, M., Ross, N., Eluru, N., & Hatzopoulou, M. (2016). Individual exposure to traffic related air pollution across land-use clusters. *Transportation Research Part D, Transport and Environment, 46*, 339–350. doi:10.1016/j.trd.2016.04.010

Small, K. A., & Verhoef, E. T. (2007). *The economics of urban transportation*. Routledge. doi:10.4324/9780203642306

Small, K. A., Winston, C., & Yan, J. (2006). Differentiated road pricing, express lanes, and carpools: Exploiting heterogeneous preferences in policy design. *Brookings-Wharton Papers for Urban Affairs, 53*, 96.

Stopher, P. R. (2004). Reducing road congestion: A reality check. *Transport Policy, 11*(2), 117–131. doi:10.1016/j.tranpol.2003.09.002

SWEROAD. (2001). *Methods and values for appraisal of traffic safety improvements. Traffic safety project.* General Directorate of Highways.

Tang, R., Tian, L., Thach, T.-Q., Tsui, T. H., Brauer, M., Lee, M., Allen, R., Yuchi, W., Lai, P.-C., Wong, P., & Barratt, B. (2018). Integrating travel behavior with land use regression to estimate dynamic air pollution exposure in Hong Kong. *Environment International, 113*, 100–108. doi:10.1016/j.envint.2018.01.009 PMID:29421398

Tol, R. (2009). The economic effects of climate change. *The Journal of Economic Perspectives, 23*(2), 29–51. doi:10.1257/jep.23.2.29

Tol, R. S. J. (2005). The marginal damage costs of carbon dioxide emissions: An assessment of the uncertainties. *Energy Policy, 33*(16), 2064–2074. doi:10.1016/j.enpol.2004.04.002

Tol, R. S. J., & Lyons, S. (2008). *Incorporating GHG emission costs in the economic appraisal of projects supported by state development agencies.* Working Paper 247. ESRI.

TurkStat. (2020). *Road vehicle statistics.* https://www.tuik.gov.tr/

Turkstat. (2019). *Economic statistics.* https://www.tuik.gov.tr/

Tuydes Yaman, H., & Dalkıç, G. (2019). Evaluation of the pricing preferences and value of time for High Speed Rail (HSR) users in Turkey. *Journal of the Faculty of Engineering and Architecture of Gazi University, 34*(1), 255–273.

UNITE. (2003). *Unification of accounts and marginal costs for transport efficiency: Final report for publication.* University of Leeds.

Ustaoglu, E., & Aydınoglu, A. C. (2019). Regional variations of land-use development and land-use/cover change dynamics: A case study of Turkey. *Remote Sensing, 11*(7), 885. doi:10.3390/rs11070885

Van Fan, Y., Perry, S., Klemes, J. J., & Lee, C. T. (2018). A review on air emissions assessment: Transportation. *Journal of Cleaner Production, 194*, 673–684. doi:10.1016/j.jclepro.2018.05.151

Verhoef, E. (1994). External effects and social costs of road transport. *Transportation Research Part A, Policy and Practice, 28*(4), 273–287. doi:10.1016/0965-8564(94)90003-5

Vitaliano, D. F., & Held, J. (1990). Marginal cost road damage user charges. *The Quarterly Review of Economics and Business, 30*(2), 32.

Wardman, M., Chintakayala, P., de Jong, G., & Ferrer, D. (2012). *European wide meta-analysis of values of travel time: Final report to the European Investment Bank.* University of Leeds.

WHO. (1999). *Guidelines for community noise.* WHO.

WHO. (2009). *Night noise guidelines for Europe.* WHO Regional Office for Europe.

Wijnen, W., Weijermars, W., & van den Berghe, W. (2017). *Crash cost estimates for European countries: Deliverable 3.2 of the H2020 project SafetyCube.* Loughborough University.

World Bank. (2017). *Report of the high-level commission of carbon prices.* The World Bank.

Zannin, P. H. T., Calixto, A., Diniz, F. B., & Ferreira, J. A. C. (2003). A survey of urban noise annoyance in a large Brazilian city: The importance of a subjective analysis in conjunction with an objective analysis. *Environmental Impact Assessment Review, 23*(2), 245–255. doi:10.1016/S0195-9255(02)00092-6

Chapter 14
Impact of Digital Tools on the Hotel Industry in the USA

Xuan Tran
https://orcid.org/0000-0001-9521-5722
University of West Florida, USA

Faith Grover
University of West Florida, USA

Kenzie Leeser
University of West Florida, USA

Kiara Bly
University of West Florida, USA

Mitchell Whelan
University of West Florida, USA

Brieana Cassidy
University of West Florida, USA

Nhi Truong
Danang Vocational Tourism College, Vietnam

ABSTRACT

Although disruptive innovation is a shortcut to increase revenue by technology, it has been applied little in the hotel industry. The purpose of this study is to examine how disruptive innovation has been applied in hotels via adopting a digital tool of linguistic inquiry word count (LIWC) to explore guests' unconscious needs to increase hotel revenue. The study has been based on the Maslow's hierarchy and the McClelland's motivation to examine the relationships between hotel criteria and guests' unconscious needs to increase hotel revenue. The study sample includes 10918 comments from online travel agency websites of hotels in the southeast destinations of the United States from January 2015 to October 2016. Findings from canonical correlation analyses indicate that hotel value and cleanliness would attract guests with a high-power motive whereas hotel service and quality would attract guests with a high affiliation motive. Finally, hotel room and location would attract guests with a high achievement motive. Implications have been discussed.

DOI: 10.4018/978-1-6684-4610-2.ch014

INTRODUCTION

Failure to examine the underlying motives in the guest comments for hotels has created critical issues in hotel marketing and management. Guest comments in social media have been a great asset for hoteliers to improve their services based on what customers need in hotels after COVID-19. These texts contain conscious and unconscious motives (Winter, 1993) that direct human behavior in their consumption. The conscious motives are often changing but the unconscious ones are not. As a result, the unconscious motives become a reliable independent factor in forecasting (McClelland, 1985). Little research has focused on the unconscious motives of hotel guests even though the travel spending declined by 42 percent in 2020 (nearly $500 billion) from 2019, with international travel and business travel suffering the sharpest declines. International travel spending fell 76% (compared to 34% for domestic travel) while business travel spending reduced 70% (compared to 27% for leisure travel) (U.S. Travel Association, 2020).

In addition, the American Hotel Lodging Association (AHLA, 2021) report that the first phase of recovery was an increase in domestic leisure travel when the leisure occupancy on Saturdays improved faster than Wednesdays from May 2020 to November 2020. In quarter 2 of 2021, the AHLA also showed there were small and medium events in quarter 2 of 2021 in the second phase of recovery. To succeed in these phases through increasing hotel rating, hoteliers are struggling to find whom and when they will target on price changing to increase hotel revenue.

To know who the target market is and when the guests really need, the hoteliers must know their primary needs or unconscious motives (McClelland, 1985). The needs for hotel lodging are related to the theory of Maslow (1954) and the needs for unconscious motives are regarding the motivation theory of McClelland (1985). The previous studies have had difficulties in measuring the unconscious motives objectively and evaluating the priority of lodging needs accurately due to a lack of technology (Tran, 2006, 2017, 2018).

This study has attempted to use a digital tool called Linguistic Inquiry and Word Count (LIWC) to measure the 3 unconscious motives of hotel guests (achievement, affiliation, and power) from their comments and web 3.0 of social media website to gather the frequency of the 6 most common words from hotel guests' feedback (service, location, quality, room, cleanliness, and value). The priority of lodging needs can be obtained from the above two theories supported by canonical correlation analyses.

The remaining of the paper would be arranged as follows. The digital tool LWIC, the two theories of Maslow (1943) and McClelland (1985) would indicate human lodging needs and unconscious motives in the literature ending by three hypotheses. Then canonical correlation analyses would be conducted in the sample of 10,918 comments to support the hypotheses in the methodology. Finally, the discussion and concluding remarks would be presented.

LITERATURE

The theoretical background of the study includes Linguistic Inquiry Word Count (LWIC, 2022) and the relationships of hotel assessment criteria and guest unconscious motives are based on the most popular concepts from Maslow's human needs and McClelland's (1985) three motives. Linguistic Inquiry Word Count-22 Linguistic Inquiry Word Count in 2022 (LIWC-22) is a digital tool in technology to change web 2.0 with "read and write" to web 3.0 with "read, write, and feel" because of the LIWC-22 can analyze multiple text files and change them into graphs of emotions. The digital tool can analyze over 100 dimensions of text which have been validated by respected research around the world. Over 20,000 scientific articles have used LIWC because it can integrate with other programming languages like Python and R.

The tool can identify the key words which describe a certain emotion type and categorize the emotions in spreadsheets and graphs. *Maslow's (1943) hierarchy* According to Maslow (1943), there are multiple independent motivational systems and these motives form a hierarchy in which some motives have priority over others. Kendrick, Griskevicius, Neuberg, and Schaller (2010) have revisited Maslow's human motives and suggested to consider the order of Maslow's three critical motives: physiological dwelling, safety, and esteem as the human life history from ultimate evolutionary function and developmental sequencing to cognitive priority. They wrote, "Most important, we believe it useful to examine basic human motives at three different levels of analysis often conflated in Maslow's work: (a) their ultimate evolutionary function, (b) their developmental sequencing, and (c) their cognitive priority as triggered by proximate inputs" (p.2). In this study, the three above orders of dwelling, developing, and consolidating of hotel guests have been supported by the electronic word-of-mouth (eWOM) on web 3.0 in social media. The three orders have been translated into (1) location and value from dwelling order, (2) service and quality from developing order, and (3) room and cleanliness for consolidating order. Hoteliers might not succeed in hotel business when their rating online decreases (Blodgett, Wakefield, Barnes, 1995; Vasquez, 2011; Jeacle & Carter, 2011). According to Zeithaml, Bitner, and Gremler (2018), the eWOM theory develops into three stages. In the organic stage called dwelling, the passive and voicers would talk to another about their hotel location and value. Customers have increasingly used internet for their reference before purchasing (Hlee, Lee, & Koo, 2018). In the linear stage called developing, the irates would switch providers if the hoteliers did not improve service and quality in the hotel. Rhee, Yang, and Kim (2016) has proved that owners can employ the online comments to enhance the quality service. Finally, in the network stage called consolidating, the activists would complain all dimensions. The hotel rating online is the evaluation summary of customers about the hotel room and cleanliness though internet (Sparks and Browning, 2011) On the other side of the lodging exchange, Giachanou and Crestani (2016) report that the social media has revealed essential information of business owners via brand stimuli to the motives of potential hotel guests. Zhao, Ye, & Zhu (2016) state that the online user-generated content of quality and service in the linear stage has great impact on hotel online bookings in the organic stage. At the last stage, Lee, Shih, & Chung (2008) report hotel guests would summarize their experiences in a clean room. *McClelland's (1985) motivation* According to Murray (1938), a need is an internal state that is less than satisfactory or lacking in some way. A motive is also an internal state that drives individuals to meet needs and reduce dissatisfaction. McClelland defines a motive as "the reintegration by a cue of a change in an affective situation" (McClelland, 1985, p. 28). The word "reintegration" means previously learning. Therefore, all motives are learned. A motive is, consequently, an affect or emotion occurred when aroused by a stimulus (Tran & Ralston, 2006). Motives are unconscious since they are not apparent without any stimuli. According to McClelland's (1990) motivation theory, there are three types of stimuli: "(1) small variations, (2) threats, interference with having impact, and (3) touching, hearing, or seeing another person" (McClelland, 1990, p.137). The three stimuli create three emotions "(1) interest-surprise, (2) Anger-excitement, and (3) sexual excitement, feeling loved, loving, joy" (McClelland, 1990, p.137). Therefore, there are three types of stimuli of hotels: (1) Novelty and cleanliness in a magnificent safe hotel could attract such a competence and jealousy of a potential guest to reserve a room at the hotel among other guests. It would create a power motive in the reservation. (2) Hotel external striking appearance and service would stimulate guests' physical affect through touching, seeing, and hearing. It would create affiliation motive in the registration. Finally, (3) environment variations including convenient location and hotel room design would make individual guest interest or surprise, which leads to achievement motive in the occupation.

Therefore, the three above stimuli create three unconscious motives during the hotel life cycle: the power motive at the first stage, the affiliation motive at the second stage, and the achievement motive at the last stage before departure. Barbuto and Scholl (1998) reported that these motives are like Maslow's (1954) needs for safety, love, and esteem. For the safety need, the power motive is learned from interference with having impact. The potential guest that decides to make reservation at the safe hotel would be the same scenario that a child learns how to avoid "being punished" by controlling other people. For the love need, the affiliation motive is defined as a concern for establishing, maintaining, or restoring positive friendship or love relationships with other persons (Chusmir, 1989). The hotel guest who has experienced the reliable service and consistent quality of the hotel would love the hotel during the registration. For the esteem need, the achievement motive is the human need for excellence, long-term consistency, and uniqueness (Chusmir, 1989). McClelland (1985) states that high achievement motive persons are competitive and strive to do better than others or better than they did before. Therefore, hotel guests with a high achievement motive would be expected to have a loyalty program from the hotel for them to come back in the future.

Zaman, Botti, and Thanh (2016) have reported service becomes most critical for guests with a high affiliation in France. Chen, Severt, Shin, Knowlden, and Hilliard (2018) have reported higher hotel class with large clean rooms is the most critical for business guests with a high achievement motive in the U.S. Loo and Leung (2016) have reported location and valuable amenities are the most important for luxury hotels for businesspeople with a high power motive in Taiwan. Chang, Ku, & Chen (2017) report the most precise factor affecting hotel rating for hotel guests with a high affiliation motive is service. In sum, the digital tool LIWC has contributed to hotel revenue maximization by providing hoteliers with guests' unconscious needs based on social media. Without comments on the web 3.0 of social media, hoteliers would not be able to maximize hotel revenue. The following would indicate one of the most popular social media in hotels: TripAdvisor and describe its six hotel criteria: location, value, quality, service, room, and cleanliness.

TripAdvisor in Social Media

The role of social media is narrowing the gap between hoteliers and hotel guests. TripAdvisor is the most influencing travel site that communicates with more than 30 million visitors per month and Gretzel and Yoo (2008) report that the TripAdvisor has influenced 97.7 percent of users in changing their purchase decision and among them, 77.9 percent use the customer comments to choose the best place to stay. O'Connor (2010) has recognized Trip Advisor as the most well-known stand-alone user-generated comments website in the hotel sector. In addition, TripAdvisor attracts more than 97 percent of reviewers to revisit the site to plan their next trip. In 2018, TripAdvisor was selected as the largest travel site in the world. How can TripAdvisor create a big impact on hotels? TripAdvisor has offered reviews in texts and ratings of hotel guests' experiences in 6 criteria: location and value in the reservation, quality and service in the registration, and room and cleanliness in the occupancy. *Location, Value, Quality, Service, Room, and Cleanliness* Location, value, quality, service, room and value are the key products of hotels. In the pre-arrival stage, guests would ask where they can stay for safe. Location and value become the key concern in the comments of hotel guests. According to Maslow's hierarchy, the safety need is the second priority to individuals who have home as the first need. When the individuals travel, the safety becomes the first need to find a hotel location. Therefore, a safe location is the first. Room rate, with relating to hospitality, can be monetary or non-monetary (Bojanic, 2009). Non-monetary prices include things like gas, miles, time, etc. guests have spent to approach the hotel, while monetary would be the fees and rates. These are both considerations that can add or detract from the perceived value for the consumer. During the reservation, location and value are optimal when supply and demand are balanced (Zeithaml, Bitner, & Cramle, 2018). In the registration, quality and service become the primary need for guests with a high affiliation. Designs and architecture of services in hotel rooms are from suppliers (Amin, Yahya, Ismayatim, Nasharuddin, & Kassim, 2013). The environment surrounding by physical evidence shows the style and design appearance to impress hotel guests during the check-in process (Tran, Nguyen, & Nguyen, 2015; Tran, Dewi, Jenkins, Tran, & Vo, 2016; Miles, Miles, & Canon, 2012). However, service is intangible, inseparable, heterogeneous, and perishable (Parasuraman, Zeithaml, & Berry, 1988, 1991). Therefore, the well-designed process for hotel rooms includes service availability, consistent quality, ease and convenient to the customers (Zeithaml, Bitner, Gremler, 2018; Cenni & Goethals, 2017, Purcarea, Gheorghe, & Petrescu, 2013). In marketing, there is an integration between intangible and tangible component (Gronroos, 1987). In the occupancy, rooms become customers' experiences when customers are integral parts of the suppliers' operations (Gronroos, 1983, 1987, 2011). Room is the proxy of the quality (Shanker, 2002). Rooms and cleanliness are, however, significantly associated. The architecture or design of a clean room or technology in the hotel reflects the wealthy of the business and owners' concepts to serve customers (Fukey, Issac, Balasubramanian, & Jaykumar, 2014).

The above analyses of the six criteria of TripAdvisor to evaluate hotels have concluded the following potential relationship between unconscious motives in the texts and self-report criteria of hotel guests. Therefore, there would be three following hypotheses regarding motivations of hotel guests. *Hypothesis 1*: In the reservation, room rate and magnificent safe hotel appearance would be the most important to attract potential guests with a high power motive. *Hypothesis 2*: In the registration, service and quality would be the most important to attract guests with a high affiliation motive. *Hypothesis 3*: In the occupation, room and cleanliness would be the most important to attract guests with a high achievement motive.

METHODOLOGY

Sample

The sample of the present study was 10918 comments from online travel agency websites of hotels in southeast destinations of the United States from January 2015 to October 2016. There are two variates to compare. One variate called criteria includes six variables: location, value, quality, service, room, and value. The other variate called motives includes three variables: achievement motive, affiliation motive, and power motive. Canonical correlation analyses were conducted to examine the relationships between criteria and motives to identify which variable in the criteria would be significantly associated with the variable in the motives, respectively.

Discriminant and Convergent Validity

The internal consistency and reliability of the measurements are assessed through Cronbach's and composite reliability. The values for both indicators are above 0.8. The results convergent and discriminant validity of the latent model variables. For the reflective constructs, the square roots of the AVEs (average variance extracted) are higher than the correlations among constructs so that they support discriminant validity for the model (Fornell and Larcker, 1981).

Table 1. Validity of the 6 measurements

Experiential component	α	CR	AVE	1	2	3	4	5	6
1.Location	0.83	0.72	0.65	*0.81*					
2.Value	0.9	0.90	0.76	0.5	*0.87*				
3.SleepQuality	0.81	0.8	0.81	0.40	0.3	*0.9*			
4.Service	0.91	0.93	0.67	0.3	0.5	0.6	*0.82*		
5.Room	0.8	0.78	0.91	0.4	0.2	0.3	0.7	*0.95*	
6.Cleanliness	0.93	0.9	0.76	0.3	0.3	0.7	0.6	0.3	*0.87*

Table 2. Set 1 Canonical Loadings

Variable	1	2	3
Room	-.890	-.152	-.266
Cleanliness	-.812	-0.42	.139
Location	-.584	.696	-.034
Service	-.919	.114	-.332
Quality	-.619	.262	-.449
Value	-.558	-.073	-.310

Table 3. Set 2 Canonical Loadings

Variable	1	2	3
Affiliation	-.891	-.453	-.020
Achievement	.531	-.819	-.220
Power	-.090	-.419	.903

Results

The first canonical correlation function relating two sets of variables (criteria and motives) was calculated and explained 55.5% of the variance in the criteria variables. Wilks' Lamda was significant for the combined function (Λ=.83, p<.01). The first canonical correlation function that indicates how well the three motives could predict each of the criteria variables would be selected to identify pairs of variables between criteria and motives as follows.

The structure matrix with least correlations between set 1 (-.090) and set 2 (-0.584 and -0.588) reveals that power motive is predictive of location and value.

The structure matrix with average correlations between set 1 (.531) and set 2 (-.890 and -.812) reveals that power motive is predictive of location and value.

The structure matrix with max correlations between set 1 (-.891) and set 2 (-.919 and -.619) reveals that power motive is predictive of location and value.

As a result, there are three conclusions for the test of the three research hypotheses as follows.

1. The power motive was correlated positively with the location and value. The research hypothesis H_1 read that a significant relationship would exist between the need for power and the choice for a hotel location and value was not rejected. The need for power was significantly associated with the hotel location and value. People who possess a high need for power tend to choose location and value in the reservation.

2. The affiliation motive was correlated positively with the quality and service. The research hypothesis H_2 read that a significant relationship would exist between the need for affiliation and the choice for a hotel service and quality was not rejected. The need for affiliation was significantly associated with the hotel service and quality. People who possess a high need for affiliation tend to choose service and quality in the registration.

3. The achievement motive was correlated positively with the room and cleanliness. The research hypothesis H_3 read that a significant relationship would exist between the need for achievement and the choice for a hotel room and cleanliness was not rejected. The need for achievement was significantly associated with the hotel room and cleanliness. People who possess a high need for achievement tend to choose room and cleanliness in the occupancy.

DISCUSSION

The digital tool of LWIC has been used to increase hotel revenue by indicating what the hotel guests need for hoteliers to improve their service.

The study findings have contributed to the optimal hotel revenue when it indicates that (1) hotel value and cleanliness would attract guests in the reservation, (2) hotel service and quality would attract guests in the registration. Finally, (3) hotel room and location would attract guests in the occupancy.

If a hotel's exterior is clean including the parking lots, walkways, sidewalks, windows, doors, and walls are clean, this is a sign that the hotel is clean on the inside as well, thus heightening a customer's expectations of service. Regarding the guest rooms, there can be a wide variety of expectations to be met. For example, one customer with a high affiliation motive may only focus on appearance and aesthetic, whereas another customer with a high achievement motive is specific of their expectations regarding cleanliness and room experience. Regarding the value, the differentiation between what a hotel advertises, (including the price, offerings, services, amenities, and quality) and its service performance promises needs to be connected. If services or product offerings are not congruent with advertising and formed perceptions and expectations, it is important that the staff be quick in their response time to fix an issue and to please the customer with a high power within the best of their ability.

The study of the relationships between hoteliers and guest satisfaction has provided helpful strategies for hoteliers. Consumers with a high affiliation, hoteliers should focus on narrowing the gaps of design, performance, and communication. For example, to narrow the gap between service and guest satisfaction in 10%, employees should respond to requests as soon as possible. If a guest requests more towels brought up, they should not have to wait longer than ten minutes. If it is something more specific than a longer time frame may be required. Any major problems a guest encounters should be addressed right away, and steps should be taken to make certain that the solution makes the guest happy. In the study, when checking in the guest, employees' smiles would increase guest satisfaction over 10%. This is the first impression and encounter that a guest will have when arriving, so it is wise to start out with a happy guest.

The gap will simply disappear the moment service improves. That goes for each hotel and is the same for every other gap. If there is a gap in location it is hard to get rid of since you just cannot just move your hotel to a different location. But if it is something like sleep then the hotel can invest in better beds. If it is cleanliness, then the hotel can do a better job of cleaning the property and guest rooms. Service is an easy one to fix. It just takes a little bit of time and a collective effort from all the employees.

Leisure and business travel was at a pause because safety was a priority for most companies and families. For the hotel and resort industry, it made each company relook and update all of their safety policies and protocols. Tripadvisor has been a main website where travelers post positive or negative things about their stays at hotels and resorts. When writing a review, travelers are asked to give an overall rate of their stay based on location, room, cleanliness, service, value, and sleep quality. These six categories are what make up the three guests' motives: achievement, power, and affiliation.

All guests should be treated with respect and greeted with smiles, making their stay more enjoyable and memorable. For performance, some examples would be opening the door for a guest, guiding them out to the pool deck, or simply asking how their stay is going and if there is anything we can do to make it better. For communication, this would be making sure you are keeping contact, actively listening, and speaking positively towards each guest. Everyone working in hospitality should have good customer service, but it is especially important for the front of the house employees. Front of the house employees are the employees that guests see on a regular basis and the ones they go to for any concerns or just talk to in general. Some of these job titles include the front desk, concierge, housekeeping, and servers. Everything in front of guests should be respectful and how you would want to be treated. If a guest were to see bad behavior or hear negative comments from an employee, this could be a deciding factor for them to not want to stay at that hotel or resort. Overall, service is sometimes overlooked, but can end up being one of the biggest factors that makes our hotel or resort stand out from the rest.

Within the hospitality industry, value is described in four different meanings: ''Value is low price, (2) value is whatever one wants in a product, (3) value is the quality that the consumer receives for the price paid, and (4) value is what the consumer gets for what they give'' (Nasution, 2008).

The first thing that guests look at when they are looking for somewhere to stay is the price. Price will determine whether a guest will stay at your hotel or resort.. Most resorts are more expensive than hotels because they have amenities such as spas and tennis courts that hotels do not provide. Guests with a high power motive will first decide where they can afford and go from there. Ways of making the guests want to stay at your location could be discounting and odd pricing. Also, if a customer calls and asks questions about their stay and pricing, making the conversation very personal will make the person want to stay at your place. The second thing the guests look at that is related to value is what one provides at their place. These are the guests that are willing to pay the higher prices for all the amenities, and normally do not need much convincing to stay at a more high-end place.

The third meaning of value is the quality that the customer receives for the price paid. Most people, when they see a high price for a hotel or resort, they think that it is very nice and provides a lot of amenities. When the price is low, people think that it is just a cheap place to stay even though it may not be the nicest or have as many amenities. All guests of course want more than what they are paying for, but these guests are more understanding of receiving what you paid for.

Overall, the hotel service quality has drastically changed over the past two years due to the COVID-19 pandemic. The pandemic took a toll on everyone in many different ways whether it was being cut off from friends and family or losing loved ones, but it also affected different business industry but specifically the hospitality industry. COVID-19 has made the hotel and resort industry relook all the procedures it had set in place in a different way and had them make changes to it cleanliness and safety procedures to ensure that each guest would be safe and healthy for when traveling became normal again after quarantine. Travelers have been eager to get out of their houses and hometowns, therefore travelers now have been traveling not only to see friends and families again, but to experience leisure vacations again and to replace the memories of the lock down procedures with new memories that bring everyone back together. The ratings of hotels on TripAdvisor have been steady with overall ratings of 4 or 5 due to the fact that travelers are excited to be able to enjoy their time in different locations. Resorts and hotels have changed their procedures and have lived up to guest expectations when it comes to keeping everyone safe and while also providing a memorable experience for guests who are traveling.

LIMITATION

The limitation of the current study is the time of the sample used from January 2015 to October 2016 before COVID-19 and the area of study is southeast US hotels. However, due to the consistent unconscious motives of hotel guests, the study findings from the large sample with 10918 comments would be generalized in the United States. Further research could be conducted to expand the time to cover hotels in the US and worldwide.

CONCLUSION

Disruptive innovation has been applied in the hotel industry via adopting a digital tool of Linguistic Inquiry Word Count (LIWC) to build efficient green hotels from social media guest comments. Social media becomes more essential for business because it connects the consumer with the provider. This study has added a digital tool to strengthen the power of hoteliers over social media. The study has contributed models for the provider to measure the attitudes of consumers. To date, no model has been proved to be appropriate. This study has formulated the Trip Advisor categories to measure the guest motives to maximize hotel revenue. Using these findings, hoteliers can find the improvement for each of the hotel life cycle to fit to different guests' motives.

REFERENCES

AH&LA. (2021). *American Hotel Lodging Association.* Available online at www.ahla.com/faq

Amin, M., Yahya, Z., Ismayatim, W., Nasharuddin, S., & Kassim, E. (2013). Service Quality Dimension and Customer Satisfaction: An Empirical Study in the Malaysian Hotel Industry. *Services Marketing Quarterly, 34*(2), 115–125.

Barbuto, J., & Scholl, R. (1998). Motivation Sources Inventory: Development and Validation of New Scales to Measure an Integrative Taxonomy of Motivation. *Psychological Reports, 82,* 1011–1022.

Blodgett, J. G., Wakefield, K. L., & Barnes, J. H. (1995). The effects of customer service on consumer complaining behavior. *Journal of Services Marketing, 9*(4), 31–42.

Bojanic, D. (2009). Hospitality marketing mix and service marketing principles. In *Handbook of Hospitality Marketing Management* (pp. 81–106). Routledge. Retrieved from https://www.routledgehandbooks. com/doi/10.4324/9780080569437.ch3

Cenni, I., & Goethals, P. (2017). Negative hotel reviews on TripAdvisor: A cross-linguistic analysis, *Discourse. Context & Media, 16,* 22–30.

Chang, Y., Ku, C., & Chen, C. (2017) Social media analytics: Extracting and visualizing Hilton hotel ratings and reviews from TripAdvisor. *International Journal of Information Management,* 14. doi:10.1016/j. ijinfomgt.2017.11.001

Chen, S., Severt, K., Shin, Y., Knowlden, A., & Hilliard, T. (2018). How'd you sleep? measuring business travelers' sleep quality and satisfaction in hotels. *Journal of Hospitality and Tourism Insights, 1*(3), 188-202.

Chusmir, L. (1989). Behavior: A measure of motivation needs. *Psychology: A Journal of Human Behavior, 26*(2-3), 1–10.

Fukey, L., Issac, S., Balasubramanian, K., & Jaykumar, V. (2014). Service Delivery Quality Improvement Models: A Review. *Procedia. Social and Behavioral Sciences, 144,* 343–359.

Giachanou, A., & Crestani, F. (2016). Like it or not: A survey of twitter sentiment analysis methods. *ACM Computing Surveys, 49*(28), 21–41.

Gretzel, U., Yoo, K. H., & Purifoy, M. (2007). Online travel reviews study: Role and impact of online travel reviews. *A&M University, Texas: Laboratory for Intelligent Systems in Tourism.* Retrieved April 2, 2015 from http://195.130.87.21:8080/dspace/bitstream/123456789/877/1/Online%20travel%20review%20 study%20role%20and%20impact%20of%20online%20.pdf

Gronroos, C. (1983). *The internal marketing function, strategic management and marketing in the service sector.* Marketing Science Institutes, Cambridge Report, 83-104.

Gronroos, C. (1987). Developing the service offering: a source of competitive advantage. In C. Susprenant (Ed.), *Add Value to Your Services* (p. 83). American Marketing Association.

Gronroos, C. (2011). Value Co-creation in Service Logic: A Critical Analysis. *Marketing Theory*, *11*(3), 279–301.

Hlee, S., Lee, J., Yang, S. B., & Koo, C. (2016). An Empirical Examination of Online Restaurant Reviews (Yelp. com): Moderating Roles of Restaurant Type and Self-image Disclosure. In *Information and Communication Technologies in Tourism* (pp. 339–353). Springer.

Jeacle, I., & Carter, C. (2011). In TripAdvisor we trust: Rankings, calculative regimes and abstract systems. *Accounting, Organizations and Society*, *36*(4), 293–309.

Kenrick, D., Griskevicius, V., Neuberg, S., & Schaller, M. (2010). Renovating the pyramid of needs: Contemporary extensions built upon ancient foundations. *Perspectives on Psychological Science*, *5*(3), 292–314. doi:10.1177/1745691610369469

Lee, W. I., Shih, B., & Chung, Y. (2008). The exploration of consumers' behavior in choosing hospital by the application of neural network. *Expert Systems with Applications*, *34*(2), 806–816.

Linguistic Inquiry Word Count. (2022). Available online at https://www.liwc.app/

Loo, P., & Leung, R. (2016). A service failure framework of hotels in Taiwan: Adaptation of 7Ps marketing mix elements. *Journal of Vacation Marketing*, *24*(1), 79–100. https://doi.org/10.1177/1356766716682555

Maslow, A. H. (1954). *Motivation and Personality*. Harper and Row.

McClelland, D. (1985). *Human Motivation*. Scott, Foresman and Company.

Miles, P., Miles, G., & Cannon, A. (2012). Linking servicescape to customer satisfaction: Exploring the role of competitive strategy. *International Journal of Operations & Production Management*, *32*(7), 772–795.

Murray, H. A. (1938). *Explorations in Personality*. Oxford University Press.

O'Connor, B., Balasubramanyan, R., Routledge, B., & Smith, N. (2010). From tweets to polls: Linking text sentiment to public opinion time series. *Fourth international AAAI conference on weblogs and social media*, 122-129.

Parasuraman, A., Zeithaml, V., & Berry, L. (1988). SERVQUAL: A Multiple-Item Scale for Measuring Consumer Perceptions of Service Quality. *Journal of Retailing*, *64*(Spring), 12–40.

Parasuraman, A., Zeithaml, V., & Berry, L. (1991, Winter). Refinement and reassessment of the SERVQUAL scale. *Journal of Retailing*, *67*(4), 420–450.

Purcarea, V., Gheorghe, I., & Petrescu, C. (2013). The Assessment of Perceived Service Quality of Public Health Care Services in Romania Using the SERVQUAL Scale. *Procedia Economics and Finance*, *6*(2), 573–585.

Rhee, H. T., Yang, S.-B., & Kim, K. (2016). Exploring the comparative salience of restaurant attributes: A conjoint analysis approach. *International Journal of Information Management*, *36*, 1360–1370.

Shanker, R. (2002). *Services Marketing, The Indian Perspective*. Excel Books.

Sparks, B., & Browning, V. (2011). The impact of online reviews on hotel booking intentions and perception of trust. *Tourism Management, 32*(6), 1310–1323.

Tran, X., Dewi, N., Jenkins, Z., Tran, D., & Vo, N. (2016). Applying game theory and time series in Smith Travel Accommodation Resort (STAR). *Advances in Hospitality and Tourism Research, 4*(2), 140–161.

Tran, X., Nguyen, B., & Nguyen, M. (2015). *Effects of the Big Five Personality Traits on Recreation Types – The Case of Vietnam Tourism.* University of Massachusetts Amherst, Travel of Tourism Research Association: Advancing Tourism Research Globally.

Tran, X. V., & Ralston, L. (2006). Travel Preferences: The Influence of Unconscious Motives. *Annals of Tourism Research, 33*(2), 424–441. doi:10.1016/j.annals.2005.10.014

Tran, X. V., Tran, H., & Tran, T. (2018). Information Communications Technology (ICT) and Tourism Experience: Can Serotonin become a measurement for tourism experience*? Ereview of Tourism Research, 9*, 20–24.

Tran, X. V., Williams, J., Carter, K., Joosten, V., & Mitre, B. (2017). Learning Styles, Motivation, and Career Choice: Insights for International Business students from Linguistic Inquiry. *Journal of Teaching in International Business, 28*(3-4), 142–156.

U.S. Travel Association. (2020). Accessed from https://www.ustravel.org

Vasquez, C. (2011). Complaints online: The case of TripAdvisor. *Journal of Pragmatics, Postcolonial Pragmatics, 43*(6), 1707–1717.

Winter, D. G. (1993). Power, affiliation and war: Three tests of a motivational model. *Journal of Personality and Social Psychology, 65*, 532–545.

Zaman, M., Botti, L., & Thanh, T. (2016). Does managerial efficiency relate to customer satisfaction? The case of Parisian boutique hotels. *International Journal of Culture, Tourism and Hospitality Research, 10*(4), 455–470. https://doi.org/10.1108/IJCTHR-08-2015-0095

Zeithaml, V., Bitner, M., & Gremle. (2018). *Services Marketing: Integrating Customer Focus Across the Firm* (7th ed.). McGraw-Hill Education.

Zhao, D., Ye, Q., & Zhu, K. (2016). The influence of consumers' information search behavior on purchase decisions for experience goods: Empirical evidence from hotel industry. *WHICEB 2016 Proceedings*, 297–302.

Chapter 15
Impact of the Brundtland Commission on Select Climate Changing Variables:
An Empirical Analysis

Subhanil Banerjee
ⓘ https://orcid.org/0000-0001-7485-9967
Department of Economics, School of Humanities, KR Mangalam University, Gurgram, India

Shilpi Gupta
ⓘ https://orcid.org/0000-0003-4382-3616
Amity University, Raipur, India

Souren Koner
Amity University, Raipur, India

ABSTRACT

The concept of sustainable development has been introduced following the Brundtland Commission's report "Our Common Future." Though significant volume of literature does exist on the various aspects and impacts of the mentioned commission, the actual impact of the commission on the environment for which it was initiated has never been considered by any academicians. The chapter tries to quantify the qualitative aspect of environment through per capita emission of CO_2 over the years. It shows that the concerned commission is successful in bringing down the rate of growth of per capita CO_2 emissions, but it is yet to be negative. The chapter opines that to restore the resilience of the environment and to make ecology and economy synonymous again, further efforts are needed.

DOI: 10.4018/978-1-6684-4610-2.ch015

INTRODUCTION

At the beginning of the earth, nature was nurtured by nature. All the natural maladies such as extremely high or low temperatures, flash floods, draught came in a cycle and every time has taken care by the nature towards a more sustainable environment that can support complex life forms. The natural order received its first brunt with the mastery of fire by our forefathers (Dartnell, 2019; Harari 2014, 2016). That accidental event left no clue to Mother Nature that how she can supersede the anthropogenic supremacy over all other life and non-life form. The prey and predator balance were dismantled and a less quick, less powerful animal without any natural gifts like sharp teeth, and claw; became the determining agent of all other life forms. A minor animal starting its life at the bottom of the food pyramid, promoting them to the middle of the food pyramid through the invention of minor hunting tools all of a sudden reached the top of the food pyramid owing to the biased blessings of the fire (Dartnell, 2019; Harari 2014, 2016).

As our forefathers mastered farming and settled from hunter gatherers, the unequal geographical distribution of population became prompter and that meant increased biomass pressure on some particular points at the cost of others. These anthropogenic choices and behavioural aspects put Mother Nature in a dismal state. Population pressure slowly laid its eyes on the woods and there was deforestation initially at a bearable level and then at an unprecedented level. However, the anthropogenic atrocities were at a manageable level by Mother Nature. It is worth noticing that the last few lines portray centuries even thousands of years, it was not as quick as it has been portrayed in these few lines.

However, the most brutal attack on nature was yet to come. Following the Industrial Revolution in England in 1750 and the American Industrial Revolution in 1820 mother earth had been ravaged by its most intelligent inhabitant the human being for more than 200 years. Industrialization was urban centric and witnessed huge rural to urban migration that broke all the hell on nature. It has been estimated that the Carbon-Di-Oxide gas content in the atmosphere was increased by many times before and after the industrial revolution (Sumner, 2015).

The Anthropocene era that started from 1950 introduced Plastic and Atomic garbage to the environment (Bostock & Lowe, 2018). These pollutants are non-biodegradable. The global environment was approaching a chocking point. However, from the early 70s of the last millennium following the Stockholm Convention of 1972 certain environmental concerns among the people developed. This concern took shape into the formation of the Brundtland Commission in 1983 and dissolved in 1987 after the publication of their report *Our Common Future* (Brundtland, 1987; Keeble, 1988). This report brought path-breaking changes in our approach to growth and development. The concerned report refuted the conventional growth and development theories and introduced a new concept of sustainable development that is benefitting the present without sacrificing the future. Eventually, sustainable development gained so much momentum that it became a part of the Millennium Development Goals of the United Nations. However, there is a flaw, as we may check that the existing literature on Brundtland commission emphasized this sustainability or sustainable development but somewhere ignored the building block of sustainability i.e., environment. In other words, the existing literature on the Brundtland commission is silent on one aspect what is the actual impact of the Brundtland Commission on the environment? In the 25th year of the emergence of the report (Brundtland, 1987; Keeble, 1988) of the Brundtland commission delving into this aspect becomes quite necessary.

In this background, the present chapter is dedicated towards the evaluation of the impact of the mentioned commission on certain climate changing variables. The chapter considers time series data on these select variables and eventually comments on the impact of the Brundtland Commission on them, which is so far the primary attempt to give back the environment its resilience and bring back the environment from the brink of collapse to its original form or at least stop its further erosion.

The chapter has been designed in a way that after starting with the introduction that ends with the objective of the present chapter, it takes a brief critical review of current literature and then moves to methodology before carrying out the necessary empirical operations apt for the objective of the chapter. Finally, it ends with a conclusion.

BRIEF CRITICAL REVIEW OF CURRENT LITERATURE

Hauschild (2015) considered the Brundtland commission and their off ecological sustainability issue from the industrial perspective. He criticised the commission for mostly resorting to widely flexible definitions and an ordinal approach. He further suggested that the time is apt enough to fix our focus from relative efficiency to absolute efficiency. He also emphasized the determination of measurable aspects of the environment and related them with the mentioned commission. The issue with the author is that environment is dynamic and the aspects or variables that determine the quality of the environment are subject to population and other factors. In this background, the ordinal approach provides better flexibility to adjust to the changes than the cardinal approach.

Pryn, Cornet and Sailing (2015) have focused on the transportation sector and conceptualized a SUSTAIN Decision Support System (DSS) model based on the basic assumptions of the Brundtland Commission. The model valued long-term environmental gain over short-term economic gain. In the background of Denmark, they have successfully determined a benchmark for society, environment, and economy trade-off. However, the article focuses absolutely on the transportation sector and ignores the others that remain a major gap in their research.

Sarabhai (2015) illustrated the genesis of sustainable development as it stands today. He opined that even the developed countries now have to comply with the rules laid by the Millennium Development Goals, unlike the previous sustainable development goals that were meant mainly for developing countries. He has also praised the Brundtland commission and successive discussion rounds that have happened from time to time over the years towards the formation of millennium development goals. The author sounds positive and optimistic about the prospects of sustainability. Most of the countries of the world have set a tie to reach the constructs of the millennium development goals. Sadly most of them are falling behind that timeline. In this circumstance, too much optimism toward the success of the mentioned goal might not be rational. Moreover, the author resorts to descriptive analysis and ignores any sort of statistics or quantitative back up these remain the lacunas of the concerned article.

Emas (2015) similar to Hauschild (2015) criticised the Brundtland commission as somewhat vague. Moreover, mentioned that environmental concern is not solely the contribution of the Brundtland commission rather in the early twentieth century Pigou introduced it with his concept of externalities and that latter took shape in the Pigouvian tax. Emas (2015) suffers from the same shortcomings as Hauschild (2015). Without understanding the dynamism and subjectivity of environmental quality he has emphasized on cardinal approach over the ordinal one.

Choy (2015) has praised the mentioned commission for generating a worldwide environmental concern but also criticised it on the ground of a lack of a common platform as well as action specific ethical guidelines that may have better articulated the idea worldwide with parity. As per Choy the ordinal nature of the commission might make it fall short of the promise that it made. Similar to Hauschild (2015) and

Emas (2015) the concerned article suffers from the same cardinal and ordinal controversy that has been highlighted before in the literature review section as gaps.

Şener, Varoğlu, & Karapolatgil, (2016) in their search for stakeholders to sustainability delved into content analysis of 78 large-scale companies and opined that the nature of commitment towards sustainability for the firms of developed countries can be understood but that of developing countries cannot. Further, they have reckoned the government as one of the prime stakeholders. Considering only 78 large-scale companies and commenting on the difference between the developed and developing nations might be considered an ambitious attempt by the authors. The analysis is somewhat biased and that is a major research gap in the article.

DesJardins (2016) questions the meaningfulness of the Brundtland Commission in the present scenario and manifests his disliking regarding the sustainability concept it promoted. He further moves ahead to lay ahead an alternative sustainability approach that would be apt for the time and for the industries. His criticism regarding the commission was owing to its relevancy regarding time and promoting a more apt time alternative. The author unlike others understands the dynamism of the environment and that is a giant leap. However, when a benchmark is set after considerable research and devotion of time then that benchmark should be met at first before thinking of some alternative or futuristic approach, hence DesJardins (2016) concerns are not baseless but they are ahead of their time.

Lousley (2017) raised the critical question of sustainable consumption and how it might be met with the finite resources of the earth. He further highlighted the clash between the developed and developing countries on sustainability, resource consumption, and what might be done with respect to sustainable development as defined by the Brundtland Commission. His North-South argument is especially engaging. However, when renewable energy and gradual replacement of fossil fuel is a part of the sustainable development as well as consumption approach then Lousley's (2017) concern on finite resources seems to be over-emphasized and a major gap in the basic assumptions of his research.

Efefiong and Sunday (2017) raised a similar question like Lousley (2017). They have emphasized on North-South Debate and criticised the usual blame game that goes on between countries of the north and south. They recommended that putting their discontent aside everyone should sign the *Paris Climate Agreement*. As per the authors, the ultimate achievement of the Brundtland commission is embedded in *Paris Climate Agreement* (Glanemann, Willner, & Levermann, 2020). Over the years lots of agreements have been signed regarding restoring the environment but the actions that followed contradict those agreements. In this circumstance holistic acceptance of a particular agreement will lead to the fulfillment of long-awaited goals of the Brundtland Commission sounds very ambitious and a major business of the concerned research.

Fletcher (2017) opined that committing toward a greener planet following the locus of the Brundtland commission might be hard but it is worth the pain considering the future environmental and sustainable benefits. He further opined those short-term economic achievements will become meaningless unless they can be assured in the long run. Towards this end, the mentioned commission acts as a lighthouse. The issue with his research is the concept of the short-run and the long-run are relative. Further, it is very different for the developed countries and the developing as well as the less developed countries. The short-run economic gains are the life source for developing and less developed countries and they cannot ignore that considering some long-run benefits. There can be no future if there is no present. These kinds of lack of understanding of the ground-level scenario is the major lacuna of Fletcher (2017).

Frecè & Harder (2018) criticised the paradigm of the Brundtland Commission as well as the present concept of corporate social responsibility and opined instead of benefitting the present without sacrificing the future, the motto should be a better future. Their argument is especially important following the fact that it is always better to drive for a better future than to maintain what we already have at the present. Our future generation should have a better life amidst a better environment and plenty of resources. The authors avoid providing any solution that how from today's finite resources we might have more resources with a higher population. Their analysis remains very superficial than realistic exposing the gaps in their research.

Mondini (2019) raised the question of the inability of the Brundtland Commission to curb environmental pollution and also the synthesis of the journey of the Brundtland commission to sustainable development goals. However, his argument lacks adequate empirical backup and that is a major lacuna of his work.

Byrne and Lund (2019) stated "A nearly 16-fold increase in per capita GDP in barely a century counts by most measures as success. But, as the Brundtland report detailed, there are two serious flaws in the model: first, modernization along the lines fashioned in the last 120 years globally is environmentally hazardous on a scale unexperienced by the web of life; second, the model has maintained a global economic structure that is deeply unequal in its distribution of social security and self-governance, allowing endemic poverty amid historically unmatched prosperity. Both flaws have made and will continue to make our future unsustainable unless a significant change in course is undertaken" (Byrne and Lund, pp. 1-2, 2019). The concerns raised by the authors are meaningful and important to consider. However, whether the Brundtland Commission has brought any meaningful change to the scenario described by the authors is not clear from their research and that remains a major research gap.

Isaksson and Rosvall (2020) opined that even in the pioneer country Sweden there is no clear idea about how to ensure sustainability at the industry level. They proposed a zero-carbon footprint should be maintained. However, it is arguable whether zero carbon footprint is at all possible. The authors remain silent regarding how to achieve zero-carbon footprints and raising a problem without delving into the way out of that problem remains a major lacuna of their work.

The above literature review makes it apparent that research regarding the Brundtland commission has been very sporadic in recent years without any commonality among them and none of the literature focuses on an important issue what is the impact of Brundtland Commissions on the environment at least in a measurable sense. This is their research gap and definitely a neglected aspect of the academic world. This dearth of literature on the mentioned aspect courts three important questions does the Brundtland Commission make the environment any better or it has remained the same or even worsen? Considering the fact that the environment is the building block of sustainability and it is the inability of the growth theories till the 1970s to incorporate the environment in their model that ultimately laid the founding stone of the mentioned commission, empirical validation of the impact of Brundtland commission on the environment becomes an interesting and novel aspect to explore. It is hard to quantify the environment but not impossible. Certain environmental indicators can always be used to quantify the environmental quality and turn it from ordinal to cardinal. In this background, the present chapter moves into the methodology section with great caution to avoid any sort of academic ambiguity. On the other hand, avoiding any complex econometrics approach the present chapter limited its methodology to simple arithmetical analysis that is enough to illustrate the impact of the Brundtland Commission on the environment.

Methodology

As mentioned earlier, the first job is to quantify the environmental quality. The present chapter has considered the per capita emission of Carbon-di-Oxide (CO_2) gas as the quantitative indicator of the environment that eventually turns an ordinal concept of environmental quality into a cardinal one. Total 54 years of data starting from 1960 to 2014 have been considered and the data has been divided into two equal parts of 27 years 1960-1987 and 1987-2014. The growth rate of the per capita CO_2 emission has been considered for the two mentioned periods and compared against each other. 1960-1987 time periods refer to pre-Brundtland Commission and 1987-2014 refers to post-Brundtland Commission. The two-time frame bears an equal number of years so they are comparable. Further per capita emission of CO_2 is an important environmental indicator that is already quantified hence it's an apt indicator to compare between pre and post-Brundtland commission environmental quality and therefore capable of commenting on the impact of the mentioned commission on the environment. The starting point of the data has been fixed in 1960 as it is the oldest data available in World Development Indicator. 1987 has been chosen as a benchmark as it stands for the dissolvement of the Brundtland Commission and the emergence of the report *Our Common Future* (Brundtland, 1987; Keeble, 1988). All the data has been collected from World Development Indicator. Some of the other environmental quality indicators like greenhouse gas have been ignored owing to their less coverage in terms of years.

Data and analysis

As mentioned in the methodology part instead of a complex econometric method the present analysis resorts to a simple growth rate as depicted in Table 1.

Table 1. Comparison between pre and post Brundtland commission per capita growth in CO2 emission

Pre Brundtland-Commission growth of emission of per capita CO_2 (1960-1987) in %	Post Brundtland-Commission growth of emission of per capita CO_2 (1987-2014) in %
42.96	2.11

Source: Computed from World Development Indicator

It is apparent from Table 1 that the per capita growth of CO_2 emission over the 24 years preceding the Brundtland Commission was almost 20 times higher than that of succeeding the commission. It is obvious that the Brundtland Commission has managed to tame the onrush of per capita CO_2 emission, which is an important environmental indicator. Hence it might be said that the mentioned commission has led to the betterment of the environment. However, even small but still there is a growth of per capita CO_2 emission instead of a decline in per capita CO_2 emission portrayed by a negative growth rate and that might be considered as one of the failures of the Brundtland Commission.

CONCLUSION

At the beginning of the earth, ecology and economy were mirror images they were more complimentary than substitutes. The economic aspects like demand, supply, scarcity, and all are quite visible in the world beyond the presence of the human agent in the ecology. The introduction of hominids and their evolution from demand by the need to demand by greed has changed the relationship between ecology and economy. From complimentary, they have become substitutes and this transition was always appreciated by our forefathers. From the accidental mastery over the fire to farming and from them to the industrial revolution each epoch left its footprints on Mother Nature. Till, before the industrial revolution Mother Nature had her resilience, and little change was evidenced. The two industrial revolutions one happening in Great Britain and the other in America first put to test the resilience of Mother Nature. The degradation of the environment following the two industrial revolutions can be easily visualized. For various reasons deforestation became synonymous with industrial development and once the mother specie plants received a brunt from the human genome then Pandora's box of environmental maladies opened. Finally in the twentieth century with the introduction of atomic and plastic garbage, which are non-biodegradable, and the domestication of chicken the human being cuts a slice from the Holocene geographical eon for themselves, and the time from 1950 till date is called the Anthropocene era. When the initial growth models by Hicks, Harrod, and Solow and models of development like Lewis, Harris-Todaro, Prebisch-Singer (Thirlwal, 1989) failed to incorporate the environment into their model. Then following the Stockholm Convention (1972) the environmental aspects got highlighted. It was realized that in the name of economic growth and development for the last 200 plus years humans are exploiting Mother Nature which now stands on the brink of collapse. Such concern led to the establishment of the Brundtland Commission *in 1983 and dissolved in 1987 with the report Our Common Future* (Brundtland, 1987; Keeble, 1988) a new term sustainable development that meant benefitting the present without compromising the future came into existence. The concerned report was focused on the environmental replenishment of the earth and dedicated to restoring the environment in its previous form. As depicted in the present chapter that there was a dearth of literature that actually measured the impact of the mentioned commission on the environment. But quantification of this qualitative aspect of the environment is extremely necessary. From that point of view, the present chapter successfully establishes that the Brundtland Commission has done a great deal of good to our ecology and environment. However, it has also laid a note of caution that the growth of per capita CO_2 emission is still positive and our effort should be dedicated to turning it negative in near future to give back to Mother Nature her resilience and restore her to better health where economy and ecology would be complimentary again from the present state of substitutes.

REFERENCES

Bostock, H. C., & Lowe, D. J. (2018). Update on the formalisation of the Anthropocene. *Quaternary Australasia, 35*(1), 14–16.

Brundtland, G. H. (1987). Our common future—Call for action. *Environmental Conservation, 14*(4), 291–294. doi:10.1017/S0376892900016805

Byrne, J., & Lund, P. D. (2019). Sustaining our common future: Transformative, timely, commons-based change is needed. *Wiley Interdisciplinary Reviews. Energy and Environment, 8*(1), 1–6. doi:10.1002/wene.334

Choy, Y. K. (2015). 28 years into "Our Common Future": Sustainable development in the post-Brundtland world. *WIT Transactions on the Built Environment, 168*, 1197–1211. doi:10.2495/SD151032

Dartnell, L. (2019). *Origins : how Earth's history shaped human history.* Basic Books.

DesJardins, J. (2016). Is it time to jump off the sustainability bandwagon? *Business Ethics Quarterly*, *26*(1), 117–135. doi:10.1017/beq.2016.12

Efefiong, A. E., & Sunday, E. (2017). Environmental degradation, North-South debate and sustainable development. *Socialscientia: Journal of Social Sciences and Humanities*, *2*(4), 12–17.

Emas, R. (2015). The concept of sustainable development: Definition and defining principles. *Brief for GSDR*, *2015*, 1–3.

Fletcher, R. (2015). Focus On Festivals: Contemporary European case studies and perspectives. Goodfellow.

Frecè, J. T., & Harder, D. L. (2018). Organisations beyond Brundtland: A definition of corporate sustainability based on corporate values. *Journal of Sustainable Development*, *11*(5), 184–193. doi:10.5539/jsd.v11n5p184

Glanemann, N., Willner, S. N., & Levermann, A. (2020). Paris Climate Agreement passes the cost-benefit test. *Nature Communications*, *11*(1), 1–11. doi:10.103841467-019-13961-1 PMID:31988294

Harari, Y. N. (2014). *Sapiens : a brief history of humankind*. Random House.

Harari, Y. N. (2016). *Homo Deus: A brief history of tomorrow*. Random House.

Hauschild, M. Z. (2015). Better–but is it good enough? On the need to consider both eco-efficiency and eco-effectiveness to gauge industrial sustainability. *Procedia CIRP*, *29*, 1–7. doi:10.1016/j.procir.2015.02.126

Isaksson, R., & Rosvall, M. (2020). Understanding building sustainability–the case of Sweden. *Total Quality Management & Business Excellence*, 1–15. doi:10.1080/14783363.2020.1853520

Keeble, B. R. (1988). The Brundtland report: 'Our common future'. *Medicine and War*, *4*(1), 17–25. doi:10.1080/07488008808408783

Lousley, C. (2015). Narrating a global future: Our common future and the public hearings of the World Commission on Environment and Development. In *Global Ecologies and the Environmental Humanities* (pp. 263–285). Routledge.

Mondini, G. (2019). Sustainability assessment: From brundtland report to sustainable development goals. *Valori e Valutazioni*, (23).

Pryn, M. R., Cornet, Y., & Salling, K. B. (2015). Applying sustainability theory to transport infrastructure assessment using a multiplicative AHP decision support model. *Transport*, *30*(3), 330–341. doi:10.3846/16484142.2015.1081281

Sarabhai, K. V. (2015). ESD for sustainable development goals (SDGs). *Journal of Education for Sustainable Development*, *9*(2), 121–123. doi:10.1177/0973408215600601

Şener, İ., Varoğlu, A., & Karapolatgil, A. A. (2016). Sustainability reports disclosures: Who are the most salient stakeholders? *Procedia: Social and Behavioral Sciences*, *235*, 84–92. doi:10.1016/j.sbspro.2016.11.028

Sumner Thomas. (2015). *Carbon dioxide levels rise fast and high*. Science News for Students. https://www.sciencenewsforstudents.org/article/carbon-dioxide-levels-rise-fast-and-high

Thirlwall, A. P. (1989). *Growth and development: with special reference to developing economies.* Springer. doi:10.1007/978-1-349-19837-5

Chapter 16
Future of Jobs in IR4.0 Era:
The Essential Technologies and Skills of the Future Jobs

Noor Fareen Abdul Rahim
Universiti Sains Malaysia, Malaysia

Mohd. Nizam Sarkawi
Universiti Utara Malaysia, Malaysia

Abdul Rahman Jaaffar
Universiti Utara Malaysia, Malaysia

Jauriyah Shamsuddin
Universiti Utara Malaysia, Malaysia

Yashar Salamzadeh
https://orcid.org/0000-0002-6917-2754
Sunderland University, UK

Sameh Mohamed Abdelhay
Umm al Quwain University, UAE

ABSTRACT

Industry 4.0 is revolutionizing the way companies work and integrate enabling technologies, including the internet of things (IoT), cloud computing, analytics, and AI and machine learning, to the production facilities and entire operations or on delivering their services. Advanced sensors, embedded software, and robotics are used in smart factories to collect and analyze data, allowing for better decision-making by more predictive analysis. Furthermore, the COVID-19 pandemic posed challenges to the society to adapt to a new reality. While the rest of the world searches for answers, Industry 4.0 technology has become a vital component of how we survived the pandemic and how we will survive in the post-pandemic future. The main purpose of this chapter is to understand the future and reality of jobs in IR 4.0. There are several ways IR 4.0 will reinvent jobs in the future. For the readers, the authors divided the chapter into the following sections: "How IR 4.0 Reinvents Jobs," "Types of Jobs in IR 4.0," and "Conclusion."

DOI: 10.4018/978-1-6684-4610-2.ch016

INTRODUCTION

Industry 4.0 is a digital transformation reflected by the automation and the implementation of smart factories (i-SCOOP, 2021). Industry 4.0 is revolutionising the way companies manufacture, improve and distribute their products. Manufacturers integrate enabling technologies, including the Internet of Things (IoT), cloud computing and analytics, and AI and machine learning, to the production facilities and entire operations. Advanced sensors, embedded software, and robotics are used in smart factories to collect and analyse data, allowing for better decision-making. (IBM, n.d.).

The world has already witnessed three industrial revolutions (IRs), having significant impacts (Dogaru 2020). The 1st IR dealt with mechanical processes using water and steam for the mass production of textiles and metals. The 2nd IR dealt with the concept of industries, and here, the use of electricity, oil, and gas took place; the steel and synthetic industries became established with new communication and transport systems. The 3rd IR dealt with new nuclear energy and automation (Dogaru 2020). However, most of these revolutions had enormous consequences on the environment. They caused much damage and harm to the planet and human lives. Hence, the IR 4.0 is a viable, sustainable, and environmentally friendly approach to manufacturing, using renewable resources and recyclable bio-based materials (Carvalho et al. 2018; Dogaru 2020). This key argument that the adoption of new technology has to be accompanied by systemic changes, applies both to the company as well as the societal level. Any novel solutions being developed must take into account the complexity of the interdependencies between different types of actors with various backgrounds, overall market dynamics, as well as the need for knowledge development and institutional reforms. In fact, the need for systemic changes may be particularly relevant in the case of green technologies, such as zero-carbon processes in the energy-intensive industries (Söderholm, 2020).

The 4th Industrial Revolution is driven by four specific technological developments: high-speed mobile Internet, AI and automation, big data analytics, and cloud technology. Out of these technologies, AI and automation are expected to have the most significant impact on employment figures within the global workforce (Recruitment, C, n.d). In today's labour marketplaces, transformations and upheavals are commonplace. Images and documents are kept in the cloud, emails remind us to follow up, and light bulbs can be turned on with a simple voice command. The worldwide labour market is progressively adopting new technology. Due to new technology, businesses are finding it more straightforward to automate routine jobs, disturbing the balance between human-driven tasks and those handled by computers and algorithms. Businesses must consider implementing the most up-to-date technology into their workforce as innovative technology becomes more ubiquitous (Recruitment, C, n.d). Furthermore, the COVID-19 pandemic posed challenges to the society to adapt to a new reality. While the rest of the world searches for answers, Industry 4.0 technology has become a vital component of how we survived the pandemic and how we will survive in the post-pandemic future (Marr, 2019).

The main purpose of this chapter is to understand the future and reality of jobs in IR 4.0 towards building greener economics in the era of climate change. There are several ways on how IR 4.0 will reinvent jobs in the future for the greener economic and sustainability. For the readers understanding, we divided the chapter in the following sections: *Building Greener Economics in the Era of Climate Change, How IR 4.0 Reinvent Jobs In Greener Economics, Types of Job in IR 4.0, and Conclusion.*

BUILDING GREENER ECONOMICS IN THE ERA OF CLIMATE CHANGE

In 2008–2009, financial, socio-economic and environmental problems converged into a triple crisis. There were immediate problems with the banking system, private and sovereign debt. There were also medium-term problems with global markets, high unemployment and growing inequality. Finally, there were long-term problems relating to climate change, biodiversity loss, air and chemical pollution, fresh-water water and land use (UNITED NATIONS, 2021). The United Nations Secretary-General, António Guterres, described the 2021 Intergovernmental Panel on Climate Change (IPCC) Working Group 1 report on climate change as a "code red for humanity". The report underscores the urgency of limiting warming to 1.5°C above pre-industrial levels, which is the threshold required to avoid the most damaging impacts of climate change. The overwhelming evidence is that existing efforts are falling a long way short of what is required to limit warming to 1.5°C, and that continuing the current trajectory will impose tremendous costs on the global economy and individual wellbeing for generations to come (PwC, 2021).

Furthermore, in 2015, countries world-wide adopted the so-called 2030 Agenda for Sustainable Development and its 17 Sustainable Development Goals. These goals recognize that ending world poverty must go hand-in-hand with strategies that build economic growth but also address a range of various social needs including education, health, social protection, and job creation, while at the same time tackling environmental pollution and climate change. The sustainable development goals thus also establish a real link between the ecological system and the economic system. They also reinforce the need for a transition to a green economy, i.e., a fundamental transformation towards more sustainable modes of production and consumption (Soderholm, 2020).

Attempts by governments to turn green growth into competition over jobs translated into trade disputes in the WTO concerning goods used in conjunction with renewable energy sources. This trend accelerated in 2012–2013 among key producers of renewable energy. More than 41 cases on antidumping and countervailing duties have been initiated against biofuel, solar energy and wind products (UNCTAD, 2014a). These cases represented the next generation of trade and environment conflicts, prompted by the rise of green industrial policy (Wu & Salzman, 2014).

HOW IR 4.0 REINVENT JOBS IN GREENER ECONOMICS?

Industry 4.0 and green economics are interlinked. The concept of sustainability in the manufacturing is one of the element in industry 4.0. Thus, it is important to promote green processes in production, such as energy efficiency, the reduction of carbon emissions, and efficient use of resources (https://www.esa-automation.com/en/industry-4-0-and-green-economy-solutions/). Combination of green jobs and industry 4.0 issues are aiming to integrate social, environmental and ethical issues when making environmental decisions in the aspect of the green economy. Such an economy means "admittedly an idealistic concept, but it is vigorously taken in practice, which aims to ensure the growth of well-being and quality of life as well as social equality while stopping the depletion of natural resources and reducing ecological threats" (Górka & Łuszczyk, 2014).

A sustainable mindset builds a constructive feedback loop that will lead to more and more individuals and organisations. A general change in attitudes would probably reflect the relaxation of regulations and current legislation to promote sustainable growth. Industry 4.0 connects machines, sensors, and other appliances to people responsible for monitoring the process for production and efficiency through wireless networking technologies and IoT capabilities. These technologies openness gives operators extensive knowledge necessary for appropriate decisions. It improves connectivity, enabling operators in any part of the production chain to gather big data and expertise to as sist development and recognise crucial areas for creativity and change (Chaim, Muschard, Cazarini & Rosenfeld, 2018; Braccini & Margherita, 2018; Maresova, Soukal, Svobodova, Hedvicakova, Javanmardi, Selamat & Krejcar, 2018).

Technologies enable many changes in the way businesses are organised, business models are developed, and individuals operate, as well as in the professions and skills required to accomplish jobs (Mesquita, Oliviera & Sequira, 2019). IR 4.0 technologies have the potential to increase productivity and efficiency. For raw materials and completed goods production, as well as inventory management, they provide real-time supply chain tracking. To tailor output, artificial intelligence and machine learning can be utilised to gather insights into consumer behaviour. Robotic process automation can save up time for higher-order procedures by automating laborious and repetitive labour-intensive tasks. Workers can use augmented reality and virtual reality training to learn new skills they hadn't before encountered. IR 4.0 technology can help developing countries shift their products and services up the value chain. Automation and artificial intelligence can aid all workers if workers' abilities are developed quickly (Petropoulos, 2021).

Green Jobs

A category of jobs which is and will be a main focus in IR 4.0 era is the "green jobs". Many of the jobs mentioned in green economies including more digital technologies can be both an IR 4.0 job and a green job. In fact, in definition of green jobs despite long years of using it in real business world, there is almost no globally accepted definition (Sulich et al., 2020) and this is the reason in many statistics we have inconsistencies around the world. Green jobs, according to the International Labor Organization (ILO), are "decent jobs that contribute to the preservation or restoration of the environment, be they in traditional sectors like manufacturing and construction or in new, emerging green sectors like renewable energy and energy efficiency."(ILO, 2022)

It can be said that majority of green jobs need to have some links of different strength with sustainable development goals and it is clear that many of those goals can be touched by digital transformation of businesses and jobs. Therefore, the link between green jobs and IR 4.0 gets more and more vivid.

According to OECD report (2021), on "new skills for jobs indicators", there is a long list of skills needed for green jobs which some main ones are shared here as critical thinking, active learning, social skills, social perceptiveness, coordination, persuasion, negotiation, instructing, complex problem-solving skills, technical skills, time management, resource management, system analysis and system evaluation. (Garcia Vaquero et al., 2021).

Some of the ways IR 4.0 reinvent jobs in greener economics include:

Autonomous Robots

Robots are crucial for increasing production. To present, the majority of robot adoption has occurred in the manufacturing industry, where they perform a wide range of manual jobs faster and more consistently than people. However, as technology advances, robots are being used in various industries, including agriculture, logistics, and hospitality. Artificial intelligence is allowing robots to become less expensive, more versatile, more independent. Some robots work in place of humans, while others, such as collaborative robots or "cobots," work alongside them. As long as this trend continues, robot adoption will most certainly be a fundamental factor of productivity increase, reshaping global supply chains in the process (Atkinson, 2019).

Augmented Reality

Microsoft sees augmented reality in the workplace to help organisations and their employees execute tasks faster, safer, and more efficiently than ever before. The company wants to use the HoloLens mixed reality headsets to assist in optimising crucial workflows among "first-line" workers, which are anticipated to number in the billions. On the front lines of enterprises worldwide, they are the first to engage with customers, products, and services. Microsoft continues to believe that augmented and mixed reality will play a significant role in helping usher in a new era of workplace productivity, from allowing field service workers to easily communicate with remote experts when solving problems to training employees on new products, processes, and equipment. (LaPierre, 2019).

Big Data and Analytics

Big data assist HR departments in motivating people, better understanding them, planning, and resource allocation. Organisations now have a wealth of HR-related data, including skills, educational background, previous roles, tenure, and so on. This information can better analyse current performance, risk, and composition to improve staff development, services, and products. HR procedures such as overall organisational performance, staff retention, development, and acquisition may be evaluated and improved using big data applications. This entails combining and analysing internal analytics, social media data, and external benchmarks to provide more educated answers to your company's business concerns (Ravindra, 2019).

According to Corfe (2018), using big data and data analytics has a variety of productivity benefits, including:

i. Cost savings: Using data to discover wastage in supply chains, such as underutilised labour, ineffective investments, and energy and water leakages.
ii. Time savings can be realised by analysing real-time data rather than waiting for it to be compiled. This could include real-time barcode scanner data analysis to determine demand trends and potential supply shortages for various retail products.
iii. Data is used to inform product design and improvement in new product development.
iv. Understanding market conditions entails predicting prospective product demand upticks and downticks and adapting business practices accordingly.
v. Instead of one-size-fits-all solutions, it can give more personalised, tailored products for individuals.

Internet of Things

Like most disruptive technologies, IoT will inherently make some jobs obsolete but will likely create more jobs in aggregate. With insights derived from IoT, workers can execute tasks that produce strategic results making work more meaningful. For example, a company experiencing production slowdowns will want to examine their manufacturing process to measure and free up bottlenecks. Before, this kind of analysis required time-consuming data entry and calculations. With IoT devices embedded into factories, companies can measure production throughput at every node in the chain pinpointing the exact problem areas. With actionable, data-driven insights, professionals will better understand the direct impact of their efforts (Roemer, 2018).

Cloud Computing

COVID-19 has forced the majority of the workers to work from home. As a result, businesses have benefited from cloud computing in their day-to-day operations. Because to cloud computing, businesses were able to continue working as usual. Cloud computing allows businesses to scale up and down their IT infrastructure at a low cost, which was critical as needs changed during the crisis and will continue to be important as the new reality emerges. Now that more firms have experienced the flexibility of cloud computing, they can be more creative in how they use it and improve their methods to develop best practises (Marr, 2020).

Remote Working

Because of the more excellent connectivity as the Internet of Things (IoT) grows, remote working, a growing trend in many firms, is now a more viable choice. Workers can do anything they would in the office, but from anywhere and on any device. This means they can go to clients' offices or job sites without interrupting their work. As a result, employees are less willing to work extra hours to make up for time spent away from the office (Wilkins, 2018). Human-machine interface (HMI) technology is a form of technology that allows personnel to connect with intelligent equipment remotely. Only sensors, software, and hardware, such as programming logic controllers, can be used with HMI (PLC). PLCs are industrial-grade minicomputers that can be used as a component of equipment or integrated into fixed assets. Users can get real-time equipment information by using PLCs and HMI tools. In addition, user-machine interactions can be confined to monitoring equipment attributes like temperature or pressure. Human involvement is only used in rare circumstances, such as when equipment or persons are in danger. As a result, HMI is more beneficial for debugging than carrying out industrial tasks (Gheorghiu, 2020). The new norm of work remotely and in virtual team is significant to Penang MNC. MIDA insights had reported that Penang is among Malaysia's top investment destinations. Manufacturing Sector Approved Investments reached RM137.9 billion, 1980 - March 2019. 70% of the investment are from manufacturing sector. Big MNC company like Intel, AMD, Lumileds, Keysight, Western Digital, Jabil, Plexus, Flextronics, Micron are part of the big player in the FDI. Majority of the MNC company are head quartered in US or home country but set up factory in Penang. With the current situation and trend towards virtual communication at workplace, this would change the landscape of traditional face to face working to leaner towards virtual teams (Soon & Salamzadeh, 2021).

Artificial Intelligence

In the workplace, artificial intelligence increases people's skillsets and, as a result, their compensation in a variety of fields, from healthcare to clerical work. In the workplace, artificial intelligence (AI) can help to improve working conditions. According to an article in the Economist, AI will aid in the elimination of unconscious and conscious biases in employee hiring and remuneration. It also discusses how AI in the workplace will benefit employees in various ways, such as ensuring that staff are wearing the proper safety equipment through intelligent scanning devices. HR is also utilising chatbots to aid with training operations. This is based on the success of several chatbots as in-house advisors to call centre employees in situations where high staff turnover could influence the regularity of responses and capacity to reply to inquiries quickly. The progress of AI also brings up new possibilities in other growing technology fields closely tied to it, such as augmented reality and the internet of things (IoT). According to a recent Accenture worldwide research, 61% of company leaders expect a growth in the number of tasks requiring AI cooperation in the next three years. 54% of respondents view human-machine unions as crucial in achieving their strategic objectives (Rodriquez, 2021).

Most importantly, Industry 4.0 technologies detect the symptoms of COVID-19, which helps to avoid any confusion regarding this disease and can also predict the chances of acquiring the infection. It helps track potential health problems and expected chances of recovery (Javaid, Haleem, Vaishya, Bahl, Suman & Vaish, 2020). For example, AI-based video surveillance has a high capability to reduce the workload of doctors and hospital managers during this crisis. This is useful to observe the activities of the patient affected by this virus. Industry 4.0 technologies improve the working efficiency of a healthcare professional and provide a better solution.

Digital Workforce

A digital workforce is a group of software robots who work alongside human employees to automate routine chores so that humans can focus on higher-value tasks. A digital workforce might be large or small, but it should scale up or down in response to business needs. As defined by Deloitte as "the inevitable evolution of the workplace," a digital workforce is made up of all the technology that employees utilise to complete tasks in today's workplace. HR and core business software, emails, instant messaging, enterprise social media, and social meeting tools are all examples of technology. 2020 (Galea-Pace). According to Deloitte (2017), managing the digital workforce will be a less complex proposition in the long run than managing the traditional workforce, with the capacity to scale quickly, eliminate training for automated activities, and enable 24x7 operations without the need for shift allowances. In their interactions with technology, the digital worker has gained several skills that can be applied at work.

TYPES OF JOBS IN IR 4.0 ERA

According to World Economic Forum (2020), by the year 2025, new jobs will emerge, and there will be a shift in the division of labour between humans and machines. Figure 1 depicts the growing job demands by 2025. It can be seen that most of the jobs involved with the latest technology.

Figure 1. Future of Jobs. Source: World Economic Forum (2020)

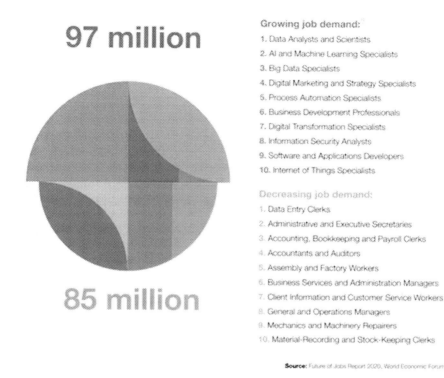

97 million

85 million

Growing job demand:
1. Data Analysts and Scientists
2. AI and Machine Learning Specialists
3. Big Data Specialists
4. Digital Marketing and Strategy Specialists
5. Process Automation Specialists
6. Business Development Professionals
7. Digital Transformation Specialists
8. Information Security Analysts
9. Software and Applications Developers
10. Internet of Things Specialists

Decreasing job demand:
1. Data Entry Clerks
2. Administrative and Executive Secretaries
3. Accounting, Bookkeeping and Payroll Clerks
4. Accountants and Auditors
5. Assembly and Factory Workers
6. Business Services and Administration Managers
7. Client Information and Customer Service Workers
8. General and Operations Managers
9. Mechanics and Machinery Repairers
10. Material-Recording and Stock-Keeping Clerks

Source: Future of Jobs Report 2020, World Economic Forum.

Furthermore, in about 60 per cent of occupations, at least one-third of the constituent activities could be automated, implying substantial workplace transformations and changes for all workers. While the technical feasibility of automation is essential, it is not the only factor influencing the pace and extent of automation adoption. Other factors include the cost of developing and deploying automation solutions for specific uses in the workplace, the labour-market dynamics (including quality and quantity of labour and associated wages), the benefits of automation beyond labour substitution, and regulatory and social acceptance (Manvika, Lund, Chui, Bughin, Woetzel, Batra, Ko, & Sanghvi, 2017). Figure 2 illustrate how automation could impact the workforce.

Figure 2. Impact of Automation on Workforce. Source: McKinsey Global Institute analysis

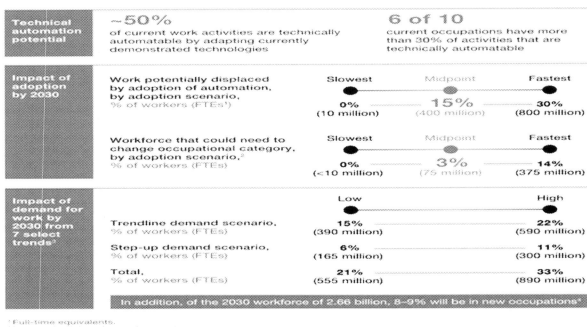

The formal sector is progressively absorbing gig workers as IR 4.0 takes hold. Many people who work in the gig economy also have full-time jobs. Gig labour allows people to supplement their income while also allowing them to learn or practise new talents. Skills obtained in the workplace can be utilised and honed, resulting in a bidirectional signalling process. Consultants, for example, can upload their resumes, which detail their previous job and educational accomplishments, and therefore their formal economy work serves as a signal for gig work. Other types of gig labour, such as selling artwork online or working on a construction site, can, on the other hand, be immediately leveraged into full-time employment, allowing workers to demonstrate talents before committing to a contract. The gig economy can provide adolescents with alternate opportunities to gain or demonstrate skills, redefining what a career looks like and creating new avenues to achieve job goals as the importance of gig work grows (Deloitte, 2018).

SKILLS NEEDED FOR JOBS IN IR 4.0

Virtual Reality (VR), Artificial Intelligence (AI), and cloud technology are all part of Industry 4.0, and they all automatically cause problems. One of the challenges of modern technology is that personnel must learn new skills to operate equipment, code new procedures, and repair new devices. Across the board, skills need to develop among employees (Industry Europe, 2019). While preparing the workforce for 4IR, it is crucial to address skills shortages and lack of preparation for the workplace; despite close engagement with industry, significant mismatches in skills preparation separate employers and training institutions. For example, in Indonesia, 96% of training institutions in Indonesia believed that their graduates were well prepared for work. However, only 33% of employers in F&B manufacturing agreed, along with only 30% in automotive manufacturing. In Cambodia, almost 90% of employers reported that graduates were inadequately educated and/or trained before being hired. Large shares of employers in other countries similarly said they did not find graduates adequately prepared for entry-level positions (Petropoulos, 2021).

Thus, companies can use several different approaches to address skill gaps. They can look outside the organisation, hiring new staff with the right skills. They can build skills internally, retraining their existing workforces to prepare people for new roles. Or they can take a hybrid approach, including using a skilled contract workforce to fulfil short-term needs while developing the necessary skills internally. Some of the skills needed for jobs in IR 4.0 include:

Soft Skills

Adapting to changes, connecting with many groups, and working with people from various backgrounds are examples of soft skills,' which are sometimes referred to as 'generic abilities' (Dixon et al., 2010; Perreault, 2004). As a result, a broad spectrum of soft skills, such as communication, analytical, problem-solving, critical-thinking, visual, oral, and aural skills, have been discovered (Asonitou & Hassall, 2019; Mohamed & Lashine, 2003). Robots cannot duplicate soft talents have grown increasingly vital as more and more job functions become mechanised. Deloitte also predicted in 2017 that "soft skill-intensive occupations will account for two-thirds of all jobs by 2030" and that "hiring people with stronger soft skills may enhance revenue by over $90,000." (Lau, 2021). Soft talents are a collection of characteristics that represent a person's social graces in a specific situation (Haeffner & Panuwatwanich, 2017). These popular abilities are sometimes known as social qualities or non-cognitive abilities (Urciuoli, 2008). These skills are essential because they allow people to better manage their interactions with others by being more adaptive, transdisciplinary, and open to continual learning (Laker & Powell, 2011). (Sackey & Bester, 2016). This competency cluster's value is based primarily on self-monitoring performance (Robles, 2012). Companies dealing with frequent changes, extensive customisation, and R&D involving suppliers and customers, particularly value cooperation, a specific competence in this classification (Bikfalvi, 2011).

Creativity

To fully realise the benefits of all the new things for the future—new goods, ways of working, and technologies—future employees will need to be creative. At the moment, robots cannot compete with humans in terms of originality. New modes of thinking will be required in the future workplace, and human creativity will be essential (Marr, 2019). Organisational leaders consider creativity (i.e., a novel and valuable concept, product, service, etc.) and creative thinking to be among the most valuable abilities for employees to possess (Woodman, Sawyer, & Griffin, 1993). (Accenture, 2013; Forrester Consulting, 2014; IBM, 2010). Employees are inspired to collaborate when they are given the opportunity to be creative. When they have fresh ideas, they seek feedback from their co-workers. By design, the creative process stimulates cooperation and provides an environment conducive to inventive thought (Duverge, 2021).

According to Wahl (n.d), creativity and its importance in business points to four main creative strengths that can be taught:

i. Fluency: generating multiple ideas related to the same topic or theme. Simple exercises encouraging employees to come up with several uses for a single common object are an excellent method to enhance this talent.

ii. Flexibility: generating various ideas on a variety of topics and themes, some of which may or may not be related. This can assist staff in connecting potential ideas.

iii. Elaboration: The ability to add more details, points of view, and perspectives to current data. Examine whether employees can describe a situation using all of their senses.

iv. Creativity: The ability to come up with innovative and out-of-the-box ideas. Hold semi-regular brainstorming sessions with staff, encouraging them to write down all of their ideas, not just the ones they know will succeed.

Digital Leadership Skill

The ultimate goals of organisations are to increase of productivity, efficiency, and profitability through the integration of new technology to connect devices and machines, digital tools such as platforms and digitalized distribution channels. Thereafter, they realize that it is not only the machines and methods to be adapt to the changes resulting from digitalization, but also the ways of leadership within the company and its culture. This means that the communication, working methods and standards must be set. Adequate leadership is essential to react to the changing customer demands and determines the success of a company (Maruthuvellu, Salamzadeh & Richardson, 2022).

A leader's digital mentality is their attitude toward digital technology in general and its use in the workplace. A general willingness to learn about new (digital) technologies is required. Established managers or investors are frequently inaccurate in judging the potential of new technologies and exaggerate their digital talents, therefore digital natives appear to be better qualified for this. To address this issue, they should internalise the concept of lifelong learning and become more familiar with new technologies and their business implications through targeted training and education. They must also have a strong desire to change; a digital leader should question the status quo on a frequent basis and aim for continual improvement in order to stay up with changes in today's dynamic world. Although having the correct mindset is a prerequisite, a digital leader must also possess a digital competence, which is described as the ability to comprehend digital technologies, handle them as smoothly as possible, and use them wisely. Leaders, in particular, must recognise and assess the risks connected with digitalisation, a skill intimately tied to a digital mindset that may be thought of as an iterative learning process (Hensellek, 2020).

According to Dimitrov (2018), leadership effectiveness will be judged by the ability of virtual presence and support to be mirrored in real life and lead to active activities when needed, as well as vice versa. There will be two sorts of leadership. One will place a premium on virtual presence, aiming for effect on a scale that has an impact on real systems—the name leader. Personal encounters in the real world will be an exception. As a human improved and redesigned entity with variable identity, the other leadership type will balance the robust virtual presence with an equally strong effect in the physical world. In other cases, the leader will take on a virtual identity and the physical "I" will become an avatar, and vice versa—creating a cyborg avatar leader. A third, minor type of leadership will rely solely on the internet as a source of knowledge while maintaining traditional leadership principles.

A digital leader must successfully and efficiently incorporate digital technologies into their and their workers' daily job. This is because, on the one hand, they allow for more innovative forms of work with greater autonomy and flexibility, but on the other hand, users today are frequently overwhelmed by the daily flood of email and the pressure to be always available due to, for example, a lack of appropriate behavioural mechanisms to deal with these stressors and reduce potential stress (Mazmanian, 2013).

Technical Competencies

Technical skills are the abilities and knowledge needed to perform specific tasks. They are practical and often relate to mechanical, information technology, mathematical, or scientific tasks. Some examples include programming languages, design programs, mechanical equipment, or tools (Doyle, 2021). With rapid technological advances, including artificial intelligence (AI), the Internet of Things (IoT), data-driven decision-making, increased virtual reality and robotics, it is apparent that the potential workforce needs to be technologically capable. It is expected that robots will take over routine tasks like supervision, in whole or in part (Khan, Khan, Tan & Loon, 2021). Rußmann et al. (2015) point out that nine key technologies are driving and transforming Industry 4.0. These are autonomous robots, simulation, big data and analytics, augmented reality, cloud computing, the (Industrial) Internet of Things; horizontal and vertical system integration; additive manufacturing; and cybersecurity. Zoe (2019) listed five other essential technical competencies for the future workplace. It includes project planning, quality assurance, extensive data analysis, technical writing and subject matter expert skills. It is important to note that a subject matter expert provides reliable answers and resolves problems that may arise unexpectedly. Highly specialised technical knowledge is often the only way to deliver high-quality products or to offer superb services.

Resilience, Stress Tolerance and Flexibility

After setbacks, adversity, or unexpected change, resiliency is defined as the ability to recover positively toward oneself and others—to rebound. More resilient people can sustain (or restore) functionality and vitality in the face of adversity. They have a good balance of strength and adaptability. Natural self-assurance and a positive attitude enable them to see difficulties as opportunities and failure as a learning experience. They don't get caught in disappointment because they believe their personal best is still to come. Instead, they think about all of the wonderful things that will come from achieving their objectives. Stress Tolerance is the ability to withstand pressure or uncertainty without turning hostile toward oneself or others (e.g. hopeless, bitter, or aggressive). Stress-tolerant people can cope with and even flourish in high-pressure conditions. They rise to the challenge of resolving problems and handle unexpected situations with ease, such as when a deadline is pushed back. They cope with their fears and have space for people's varying emotions, and they are often productive and assured despite ambiguity. Others may seek them out for their courage and rely on them in difficult times (Simpson, 2021).

Flexibility in the job, on the other hand, entails quickly adapting to new conditions. A flexible employee can alter their strategy to avoid or overcome unexpected challenges. This is especially true in fast-paced, dynamic businesses, where the capacity to respond quickly to unforeseen events and changing expectations is a valued asset for both employers and employees (Hogarty, 2021).

Apprenticeships

Apprenticeships are likewise supposed to serve many purposes, and the functions of systems in different nations are inextricably linked by their differences. Apprenticeships serve a variety of tasks, according to

Smith (2010), including (but not limited to) a pathway to adulthood for young people, a method of industry and national skill building, and a means of developing occupational identity in a trade (Smith, 2010).

Brown (2019) claims that the engineering and industrial sector's skills deficit is not a new issue. 71 percent of manufacturers believe apprenticeships will soon become a natural alternative to university education, according to the Manufacturer poll. The highly talented and experienced individuals who are currently on the team can and should teach incoming talent. Companies can encourage people to start a career in the industry early in order to train and develop them as specialists – and, more importantly, to evolve them with new technology on the horizon. Using apprenticeships and work placement programmes to engage teenagers and young people and integrate them into organisations has several benefits, especially in the context of Industry 4.0.

CONCLUSION

As previously said, IR 4.0 has altered the global employment landscape. In IR 4.0, skills shortages are expected to worsen across all industries. Artificial intelligence (AI), robotics, and other emerging technologies are growing at a quicker rate than ever before, altering the type of jobs to be done - and the abilities required to perform them (Milano, 2019). Upskilling, or acquiring new skills to assist with current tasks, and reskilling, or learning new skills to take on different or altogether new roles, are two types of changes that will be necessary in the future of work (Ellingrud, Gupta, & Salguero, 2020). As a result, businesses must take responsibility for reskilling their own workforces in order to ensure that they have access to the particular industry- and occupation-specific competencies they require as IR4.0 evolves. Technical skill competence will undoubtedly continue to be significant. However, as more businesses resort to new technology and automation to increase productivity, save costs, and gain a competitive advantage, global experts predict an interesting shift in the skills required of employees in the IR 4.0.

This chapter provides the insight on how future employees and employers can prepare themselves to face the future in greener economics. This chapter highlighted some of the important skills that needs to be reskilled and upskilled. Most importantly, there will be new jobs creation and jobs that will be obsolete in the future. The technological advances has become the accelerator for IR 4.0 and eventually IR 5.0. Proper strategic planning by incorporating human capital management will leads to a dynamic workforce force that can sustain through the test of times. Thus, leaders should focus on building the agility of the workforce. Future research should be conducted on the impact of IR 5.0 on workforce agility in the future. It is hope that the future research will shed some lights on the skills and tools needed to create agile workforce.

REFERENCES

Accenture. (2014). *2013 skills and employment trends survey: Perspectives on training.* Available from https://www.accenture.com/us-en/Pages/insight-accenture-2013-skills-employmenttrends-survey-perspectives-on-training.aspx

Asonitou, S., & Hassall, T. (2019, October 15). Which skills and competencies to develop in accountants in a country in crisis? *International Journal of Management Education, 17*(3), 100308. doi:10.1016/j.ijme.2019.100308

Atkinson, R. D. (2019, October 15). *Robotics and the Future of Production and Work.* https://itif.org/publications/2019/10/15/robotics-and-future-production-and-work

Bikfalvi, A. (2011). Teamwork in production: Implementation, its determinants, and estimates for German manufacturing. *Human Factors and Ergonomics in Manufacturing & Service Industries, 21*(3), 244–259. doi:10.1002/hfm.20230

Braccini, A. M., & Margherita, E. G. (2018). Exploring organizational sustainability of industry 4.0 under the triple bottom line: The case of a manufacturing company. *Sustainability, 11*(1), 36. doi:10.3390u11010036

Brow, M. (2019, May 28). *How industry 4.0 is affecting jobs.* Retrieved October 10, 2021, from https://industryeurope.com/how-industry-4-0-is-affecting-jobs/

Carvalho, N., Chaim, O., Cazarini, E., & Gerolamo, M. (2018). Manufacturing in the fourth industrial revolution: A positive prospect in sustainable manufacturing. *Procedia Manufacturing, 21*, 671–678. doi:10.1016/j.promfg.2018.02.170

Chaim, O., Muschard, B., Cazarini, E., & Rozenfeld, H. (2018). Insertion of sustainability performance indicators in an industry 4.0 virtual learning environment. *Procedia Manufacturing, 21*, 446–453. doi:10.1016/j.promfg.2018.02.143

Dimitrov, A. (2018). The digital age leadership: A transhumanistic perspective. *The Journal of Leadership Studies, 12*(3), 79–81.

Dixon, J., Belnap, C., Albrecht, C., & Lee, K. (2010). The importance of soft skills. *Corporate Finance Review, 14*(6), 35–38.

Dogaru, L. (2020). The main goals of the fourth industrial revolution. renewable energy perspectives. *Procedia Manufacturing, 46*, 397–401. doi:10.1016/j.promfg.2020.03.058

Doyle, A. (2021, September 15). *Important Technical Skills With Examples.* https://www.thebalancecareers.com/technical-skills-list-2063775

Duverge, G. (2021, August 20). *The Manager's Guide to Fostering Creativity in the Workplace.* Touro University WorldWide. Retrieved October 21, 2021, from https://www.tuw.edu/business/creativity-in-the-workplace/

Ellingrud, K., Gupta, R., & Salguero, J. (2021, February 26). *Building the vital skills for the future of work in operations.* McKinsey & Company. Retrieved September 22, 2021, from https://www.mckinsey.com/business-functions/operations/our-insights/building-the-vital-skills-for-the-future-of-work-in-operations

Forrester Consulting. (2014, August). *The creative dividend: How creativity impacts business results.* https://landing.adobe.com/dam/downloads/whitepapers/55563.en.creative-dividends.pdf

Galea-Pace, S. (2020, July 6). *What is a Digital Workforce?* Manufacturing Global. Retrieved September 30, 2021, from https://manufacturingglobal.com/technology/what-digital-workforce

García Vaquero, M., Sánchez-Bayón, A., & Lominchar, J. (2021). European Green Deal and Recovery Plan: Green Jobs, Skills and Wellbeing Economics in Spain. *Energies*, *14*(14), 4145. doi:10.3390/en14144145

Gheorghiu, G. (2020, May 15). *How will the Fourth Industrial Revolution Impact Remote Work?* https://www.g2.com/articles/fourth-industrial-revolution-impact-on-remote-work

Górka, K., & Łuszczyk, M. (2014). "Green economy" and the knowledge-based economy and sustainable development. *Optimum. Economic Studies*, *3*(69), 22–31.

Haeffner, M., & Panuwatwanich, K. (2017). Perceived impacts of industry 4.0 on manufacturing industry and its workforce: the case of Germany. In *International Conference on Engineering, Project, and Product Management*. Springer International Publishing. 10.1007/978-3-319-74123-9_21

Hensellek, S. (2020). Digital Leadership: A Framework for Successful Leadership in the Digital Age. *Journal of Media Management and Entrepreneurship*, *2*(1), 55–69. doi:10.4018/JMME.2020010104

Hogarty, S. (2021, September 7). *What is flexibility in the workplace?* Ideas. Retrieved October 25, 2021, from https://www.wework.com/ideas/professional-development/management-leadership/flexibility-in-the-workplace

IBM 2010 Global CEO Study: Creativity Selected as Most Crucial Factor for Future Success. (2010, May 18). *IBM Newsroom*. Retrieved October 21, 2021, from https://newsroom.ibm.com/2010-05-18-IBM-2010-Global-CEO-Study-Creativity-Selected-as-Most-Crucial-Factor-for-Future-Success

International Labour Organization (ILO). (n.d.). *What Is a Green Job?* Available online: https://www.ilo.org/global/topics/greenjobs/news/WCMS_220248/lang--en/index.htm

Industry Europe. (2019, May 28). *How industry 4.0 is affecting jobs*. Retrieved October 10, 2021, from https://industryeurope.com/how-industry-4-0-is-affecting-jobs/

Industry 4.0 and Green Economy: Solutions. (2021b, December 21). *Industry 4.0 and Green Economy: Solutions*. Retrieved July 18, 2022, from https://www.esa-automation.com/en/industry-4-0-and-green-economy-solutions/

i-SCOOP. (2021, November 5). *Industry 4.0 and the fourth industrial revolution explained*. Retrieved November 6, 2021, from https://www.i-scoop.eu/industry-4-0/

Javaid, M., Haleem, A., Vaishya, R., Bahl, S., Suman, R., & Vaish, A. (2020). Industry 4.0 technologies and their applications in fighting COVID-19 pandemic. *Diabetes & Metabolic Syndrome*, *14*(4), 419–422.

Khan, N., Khan, S., Tan, B. C., & Loon, C. H. (2021, February). Driving Digital Competency Model Towards IR 4.0 In Malaysia. *Journal of Physics: Conference Series*, *1793*(1), 012049.

Laker, D.R., & Powell, J.L. (2011). The differences between hard and soft skills and their relative impact on training transfer. *Human Resource Development Quarterly, 22*(1), 111-122. doi:10.1002/hrdq.20063

LaPierre, J. (2019, November 14). *Augmented Reality in the Workplace*. Filament Games. Retrieved October 11, 2021, from https://www.filamentgames.com/blog/augmented-reality-in-the-workplace/

Lau, Y. (2021, January 19). Soft Skills Are Essential To The Future Of Work. *Forbes*. Retrieved October 19, 2021, from https://www.forbes.com/sites/forbeshumanresourcescouncil/2021/01/20/soft-skills-are-essential-to-the-future-of-work/?sh=b19567e13416

Manyika, J., Lund, S., Chui, M., Bughin, J., Woetzel, J., Batra, P., Ko, R., & Sanghvi, S. (2021, July 2). *Jobs lost, jobs gained: What the future of work will mean for jobs, skills, and wages*. McKinsey & Company. Retrieved October 10, 2021, from https://www.mckinsey.com/featured-insights/future-of-work/jobs-lost-jobs-gained-what-the-future-of-work-will-mean-for-jobs-skills-and-wages

Maresova, P., Soukal, I., Svobodova, L., Hedvicakova, M., Javanmardi, E., Selamat, A., & Krejcar, O. (2018). Consequences of industry 4.0 in business and economics. *Economies, 6*(3), 46.

Marr, B. (2019, April 29). The 10 Vital Skills You Will Need For The Future Of Work. *Forbes*. Retrieved October 20, 2021, from https://www.forbes.com/sites/bernardmarr/2019/04/29/the-10-vital-skills-you-will-need-for-the-future-of-work/?sh=38d50aa33f5b

Marr, B. (2020, December 21). What's Been The Impact Of Covid-19 On The 4th Industrial Revolution? *Forbes*. Retrieved October 21, 2021, from https://www.forbes.com/sites/bernardmarr/2020/12/21/whats-been-the-impact-of-covid-19-on-the-4th-industrial-revolution/?sh=5870b60e5c0d

Maruthuvellu, S. G., Salamzadeh, Y., & Richardson, C. (2022). Digital Leadership Competencies in the Malaysian Context: A Study in Manager Levels. In P. Ordóñez de Pablos (Ed.), *Handbook of Research on Developing Circular, Digital, and Green Economies in Asia* (pp. 13–41). IGI Global. doi:10.4018/978-1-7998-8678-5.ch002

Mazmanian, M. (2013). Avoiding the trap of constant connectivity: When congruent frames allow for heterogeneous practices. *Academy of Management Journal, 56*(5), 1225–1250.

Mesquita, A., Oliveira, L., & Sequeira, A. (2019, April). The future of the digital workforce: current and future challenges for executive and administrative assistants. In *World Conference on Information Systems and Technologies* (pp. 25-38). Springer.

Milano, M. (2019). *The digital skills gap is widening fast. Here's how to bridge it*. Https://Www.Weforum.Org/Agenda/2019/03/the-Digital-Skills-Gap-Is-Widening-Fast-Hereshow-to-Bridge-It/

Mohamed, E., & Lashine, S. (2003). Accounting knowledge and skills and challenges in a global business environment. *Managerial Finance, 29*(6), 3–16.

Perreault, H. (2004). Business educators can take a leadership role in character education. *Business Education Forum, 59*(1), 23–24.

Petropoulos, G. (2021). *Automation, COVID-19, and Labor Markets. ADBI Working Paper 1229*. Asian Development Bank Institute. Available https://www.adb.org/publications/automation-covid-19-and-labor-markets

PricewaterhouseCoopers. (2021, November). *Code Red Asia Pacific's Time To Go Green*. https://www.pwc.com/asiapacific

Ravindra, S. (2019, September 17). *4 Applications of Big Data in HR (With Real-World Examples)*. The Kolabtree Blog. Retrieved October 21, 2021, from https://www.kolabtree.com/blog/4-applications-of-big-data-in-hr-with-real-world-examples/

Recruitment, C. (n.d.). *How Will the Fourth Industrial Revolution Impact the Future of Work? - Change Recruitment*. Https://Www.Changerecruitmentgroup.Com/Knowledge-Centre/How-Will-the-Fourth-Industrial-Revolution-Impact-the-Future-of-Work

Robles, M. M. (2012). Executive perceptions of the top 10 soft skills needed in today's workplace. *Business Communication Quarterly*, *75*(4), 453–465. doi:10.1177/1080569912460400

Rodriguez, E. G. (2021, August 17). *The Impact of AI on the Workforce*. Conversational AI Platform for Enterprise - Teneo | Artificial Solutions. Retrieved October 26, 2021, from https://www.artificial-solutions.com/blog/impact-of-ai-in-the-workforce

Roemer, K. (2021, May 25). *What the Internet of Things means for the future of work*. Best Practices for Professional Communities and Networking. Retrieved October 11, 2021, from https://guild.co/blog/what-iot-means-for-the-future-of-work/

Rüßmann, M., Lorenz, M., Gerbert, P., Waldner, M., Engel, P., Harnisch, M., & Justus, J. (2021, April 12). *Industry 4.0: The Future of Productivity and Growth in Manufacturing Industries*. BCG Global. Retrieved October 15, 2021, from https://www.bcg.com/publications/2015/engineered_products_project_business_industry_4_future_productivity_growth_manufacturing_industries

Simpson, S. (2021, September 9). *Stress Tolerance & Resiliency: Tough As Titanium*. PAIRIN. Retrieved October 26, 2021, from https://www.pairin.com/stress-tolerance-resiliency-tough-titanium/

Smith, E. (2010). Apprenticeships. In P. Peterson, B. McGaw, & E. Baker (Eds.), *International Encyclopedia of Education* (3rd ed., pp. 312–319). Elsevier.

Söderholm, P. (2020). The green economy transition: The challenges of technological change for sustainability. *Sustainable Earth*, *3*(1), 1–11.

Soon, C. C., & Salamzadeh, Y. (2021). The Impact of Digital Leadership Competencies on Virtual Team Effectiveness in MNC Companies in Penang, Malaysia. Journal of Entrepreneurship. *Business Economics (Cleveland, Ohio)*, *8*(2), 219–253.

Sulich, A., Rutkowska, M., & Poplawski, L. (2020). Green jobs, definitional issues, and the employment of young people: An analysis of three European Union countries. *Journal of Environmental Management*, *262*, 110314. https://doi.org/10.1016/j.jenvman.2020.110314

UNCTAD. (2014a). *Trade Remedies Targeting the Renewable Energy Sector*. UNCTAD.

United Nations. (2021, April). *Climate Change, Green Recovery And Trade*. United Nations Conference on Trade and Development.

Urciuoli, B. (2008). Skills and selves in the new workplace. *American Ethnologist*, *35*(2), 211–228.

Wahl, E. (n.d.). *The Importance of Creativity in the Workplace*. Https://Www.Allbusiness.Com/the-Importance-of-Creativity-in-the-Workplace-24566-1.Html

What is Industry 4.0 and how does it work? (n.d.b). Https://Www.Ibm.Com/My-En/Topics/Industry-4-0

Wilkins, J. (2018, August 15). *How Industry 4.0 Is Improving Peoples' Work-Life Balance*. https://www.impomag.com/home/article/13245182/how-industry-40-is-improving-peoples-worklife-balance

Woodman, R. W., Sawyer, J. E., & Griffin, R. W. (1993). Toward a theory of organisational creativity. *Academy of Management Review*, *18*(2), 293–321.

Wu, M., & Salzman, J. (2013). The next generation of trade and environment conflicts: The rise of green industrial policy. *Nw. UL Rev.*, *108*, 401.

Compilation of References

Aaker, J. L. (1997). Dimensions of brand personality. *JMR, Journal of Marketing Research, 34*(3), 347–356. doi:10.1177/002224379703400304

Aaker, J., & Fournier, S. (1995). A brand as a character, a partner and a person: Three perspectives on the question of brand personality. *Advances in Consumer Research. Association for Consumer Research (U. S.), 22*, 391–395.

AAOIFI. (2015). The accounting and auditing organization for islamic financial institutions shari'ah standards. Manama: Accounting and Auditing Organization for Islamic Financial Institutions (AAOIFI).

Abbasi, G. A., Tiew, L. Y., Tang, J., Goh, Y. N., & Thurasamy, R. (2021). The adoption of cryptocurrency as a disruptive force: Deep learning-based dual-stage structural equation modelling and artificial neural network analysis. *PLoS One, 16*(3), 1–26. doi:10.1371/journal.pone.0247582 PMID:33684120

Abe, N., Laumond, J.-P., Salaris, P., & Levillain, F. (2017). On the use of dance notation systems to generate movements in humanoid robots: The utility of Laban notation in robotics. *Social Sciences Information. Information Sur les Sciences Sociales, 56*(2), 328–344. doi:10.1177/0539018417694773

Abrigo, M. R., & Love, I. (2016). Estimation of panel vector autoregression in Stata. *The Stata Journal, 16*(3), 778–804. doi:10.1177/1536867X1601600314

Abugre, J. B. (2018). Cross-cultural communication imperatives: Critical lessons for western expatriates in multinational organizations (MNCs) in Sub-Saharan Africa. *Critical Perspectives on International Business, 14*(2/3), 170–187. doi:10.1108/cpoib-01-2017-0005

Abugre, J. B., & Debrah, Y. A. (2019). Assessing the impact of cross-cultural communication competence on expatriate business operations in multinational corporations of a Sub-Saharan African context. *International Journal of Cross Cultural Management, 19*(1), 85–104. doi:10.1177/1470595819839739

Accenture. (2014). *2013 skills and employment trends survey: Perspectives on training.* Available from https://www.accenture.com/us-en/Pages/insight-accenture-2013-skills-employmenttrends-survey-perspectives-on-training.aspx

Achi, A., Adeola, O., & Achi, F. C. (2022). CSR and green process innovation as antecedents of micro, small, and medium enterprise performance: Moderating role of perceived environmental volatility. *Journal of Business Research, 139*, 771–781. doi:10.1016/j.jbusres.2021.10.016

ACMF. (2018). *ASEAN green bond standards.* ASEAN Capital Markets Forum (ACMF).

Afonasova, M.A., Panfilova, E.E., & Galichkina, M.A. (2018). *Social and economic background of digital economy: Conditions for transition.* Academic Press.

Agarwal, R., & Prasad, J. (1998). A Conceptual and Operational Definition of Personal Innovativeness in the Domain of Information Technology. *Information Systems Research*, *9*(2), 204–215. doi:10.1287/isre.9.2.204

Aguirre-Rodriguez, A. (2014). Cultural factors that impact brand personification strategy effectiveness. *Psychology and Marketing*, *31*(1), 70–83. doi:10.1002/mar.20676

AH&LA. (2021). *American Hotel Lodging Association*. Available online at www.ahla.com/faq

Ahmed, M. M., & Shimada, K. (2019). The effect of renewable energy consumption on sustainable economic development: Evidence from emerging and developing economies. *Energies*, *12*(15), 2954. doi:10.3390/en12152954

Aiginger, K. (2014). *Industrial Policy for a Sustainable Growth Path. Policy Paper No.13*. Welfare Wealth Work for Europe.

Alabdullah, J. H., Van Lunen, B. L., Claiborne, D. M., Daniel, S. J., Yen, C. J., & Gustin, T. S. (2020). Application of the unified theory of acceptance and use of technology model to predict dental students' behavioral intention to use teledentistry. *Journal of Dental Education*, *84*(11), 1262–1269. doi:10.1002/jdd.12304 PMID:32705688

Alalwan, A. A., Baabdullah, A. M., Rana, N. P., Dwivedi, Y. K., & Kizgin, H. (2019). Examining the Influence of Mobile Store Features on User E-Satisfaction: Extending UTAUT2 with Personalization, Responsiveness, and Perceived Security and Privacy. In *Conference on e-Business, e-Services and e-Society* (pp. 50-61). Springer. 10.1007/978-3-030-29374-1_5

Alam, N., Duygun, M., & Ariss, R. T. (2016). Green sukuk: An innovation in Islamic capital markets. In A. B. Dorsman, Ö. Arslan-Ayaydin, & M. B. Karan (Eds.), *Energy and finance* (pp. 167–186). Springer International Publishing. doi:10.1007/978-3-319-32268-1_10

Albashrawi, M. A., Turner, L., & Balasubramanian, S. (2020). Adoption of Mobile ERP in Educational Environment. *International Journal of Enterprise Information Systems*, *16*(4), 184–200. doi:10.4018/IJEIS.2020100109

Albort-Morant, G., Henseler, J., Cepeda-Carrión, G., & Leal-Rodríguez, A. L. (2018). Potential and realized absorptive capacity as complementary drivers of green product and process innovation performance. *Sustainability*, *10*(2), 381.

Al-Duaij, A. (2019). The digitization of refinery data collection at KNPC Process. *KNPC-Tech*, (4).

Al-Khouri, A.M. (2012). eGovernment strategies the case of the United Arab Emirates (UAE). *European Journal of ePractice*, *17*(September), 126-150.

Allen, C., Reid, M., Thwaites, J., Glover, R., & Kestin, T. (2020). Assessing national progress and priorities for the Sustainable Development Goals (SDGs): Experience from Australia. *Sustainability Science*, *15*(2), 521–538. doi:10.100711625-019-00711-x

Al-Qudsi. (2021). *The 2020 Coronavirus Outbreak and Global Growth and Trade Collapse: Impact on Kuwait's overall Economy and Society, its Sectors and Business Firms and Vital Fiscal Recovery Plan*. Kuwait Institute for Scientific Research.

Al-Qudsi, S., & Hussain, A. (2022). *Abdullah Al-Salem University (ASU) and Digital Transformation*. Kuwait Institute for Scientific Research.

Al-Saedi, K., Al-Emran, M., Ramayah, T., & Abusham, E. (2020). Developing a general extended UTAUT model for M-payment adoption. *Technology in Society*, *62*, 101293. doi:10.1016/j.techsoc.2020.101293

Al-Sumait, F., Helsper, E. J., Navarro, C., Al-Saif, N., & Raut, N. (2022). *Kuwait's Digital Inequalities Report. from Digital Skills to Tangible Outcomes Project Report. From Digital Skills to Tangible Outcomes Project Report*. LSE.

Ameen, N., Tarhini, A., Reppel, A., & Anand, A. (2021). Customer experiences in the age of artificial intelligence. *Computers in Human Behavior*, *114*, 106548. Advance online publication. doi:10.1016/j.chb.2020.106548 PMID:32905175

Amidzic, G., Massara, A., & Mialou, A. (2014). *Assessing Countries Financial Inclusion Standing- A New Composite Index*. IMF Working Paper WP/14/36, International Monetary Fund.

Amin, M., Yahya, Z., Ismayatim, W., Nasharuddin, S., & Kassim, E. (2013). Service Quality Dimension and Customer Satisfaction: An Empirical Study in the Malaysian Hotel Industry. *Services Marketing Quarterly, 34*(2), 115–125.

Amit, R., & Zott, C. (2001). Value creation in e-business. *Strategic Management Journal, 22*(6-7), 493–520. doi:10.1002mj.187

Anand, P. K. K. (2014). Cross cultural diversity in today's globalized era. *Journal of Human Resource Management, 2*(6-1), 12-16.

Anbumozhi, V., & Kim, J. (Eds.). (2016). Towards a circular economy: Corporate management and policy pathways. Jakarta: Economic Research Institute for ASEAN and East Asia (ERIA).

Anbumozhi, V., & Kimura, F. (Eds.). (2018). Industry 4.0: Empowering ASEAN for the circular economy. Jakarta: Economic Research Institute for ASEAN and East Asia (ERIA).

Anciaes, P. R., Jones, P., & Mindell, J. S. (2014). *The value of the barrier effects of roads and railways: A literature review*. Street Mobility and Network Accessibility Series, Working Paper 03. University College London.

Andersén, J. (2021). A relational natural-resource-based view on product innovation: The influence of green product innovation and green suppliers on differentiation advantage in small manufacturing firms. *Technovation, 104*, 102254. doi:10.1016/j.technovation.2021.102254

Andersén, J., Jansson, C., & Ljungkvist, T. (2020). Can environmentally oriented CEOs and environmentally friendly suppliers boost the growth of small firms? *Business Strategy and the Environment, 29*(2), 325–334. doi:10.1002/bse.2366

André, E., Rist, T., & Müller, J. (1998). WebPersona: A lifelike presentation agent for the World-Wide Web. *Knowledge-Based Systems, 11*(1), 25–36. doi:10.1016/S0950-7051(98)00057-4

Anggreni, N., Ariyanto, D., Suprasto, H., & Dwirandra, A. A. N. B. (2020). Successful adoption of the village's financial system. *Accounting, 6*(6), 1129–1138. doi:10.5267/j.ac.2020.7.005

Anonymous. (2015). Digital Financial Inclusion. *Journal of Payment Strategy and System, 9*(3), 212–214.

Antonacopoulos, N. M.-D., & Pychyl, T. A. (2008). An examination of the relations between social support, anthropomorphism and stress among dog owners. *Anthrozoos, 21*(2), 139–152. doi:10.2752/175303708X305783

Anzolin, G., & Lebdioui, A. (2021). Three Dimensions of Green Industrial Policy in the Context of Climate Change and Sustainable Development. *European Journal of Development Research, 33*(2), 371–405. doi:10.105741287-021-00365-5

Appel, M., Izydorczyk, D., Weber, S., Mara, M., & Lischetzke, T. (2020). The uncanny of mind in a machine: Humanoid robots as tools, agents, and experiencers. *Computers in Human Behavior, 102*, 274–286. doi:10.1016/j.chb.2019.07.031

Araujo, T. (2018). Living up to the chatbot hype: The influence of anthropomorphic design cues and communicative agency framing on conversational agent and company perceptions. *Computers in Human Behavior, 85*, 183–189. doi:10.1016/j.chb.2018.03.051

Arcadis. (2018). *Sustainable Finance in the UAE*. Author.

Aria, M., & Cuccurullo, C. (2017). bibliometrix: An R-tool for comprehensive science mapping analysis. *Journal of Informetrics, 11*(4), 959–975. doi:10.1016/j.joi.2017.08.007

Armand, M., Grugeon, S., Vezin, H., Laruelle, S., Ribiere, P., Poizot, P., & Tarascon, J.-M. (2009). Conjugated dicarboxylate anodes for Li-ion batteries. *Nature Materials, 8*(2), 120–125. doi:10.1038/nmat2372 PMID:19151701

ARTEMIS (Assessment and Reliability of Transport Emission Models and Inventory Systems). (2007). Emission factor modelling and database for light vehicles. Deliverable 3, Report No: LTE0523. Funded by EU's 5th Framework Programme. INRETS.

ASEAN Secretariat & ERIA. (2021). *Framework for circular economy for the ASEAN economic community.* Jakarta: The ASEAN Secretariat & the Economic Research Institute for ASEAN and East Asia (ERIA).

ASEAN Secretariat, . (2015). *ASEAN 2025: Forging ahead together.* ASEAN Secretariat.

ASEAN Secretariat. (2021a, October 21). *ASEAN adopts framework for circular economy.* ASEAN. retrieved from https://asean.org/asean-adopts-framework-for-circular-economy/

ASEAN Secretariat, . (2021b). *ASEAN statistical yearbook 2021.* ASEAN Secretariat.

ASEAN Taxonomy Board. (2021). *ASEAN taxonomy for sustainable finance.* The ASEAN Secretariat.

Askari, H., Iqbal, Z., & Mirakhor, A. (2009). New issues in Islamic finance & economics, progress & challenges. Singapore: John Wiley & Sons (Asia).

Askari, H., Iqbal, Z., & Mirakhor, A. (2015). Introduction to islamic economics: Theory and application. Singapore: John Wiley & Sons (Asia).

Aslam, M., & Jaafar, R. (2020). Budget deficit and the federal government debt in Malaysia. In R. M. Yonk & V. Bobek (Eds.), *Perspectives on economic development: public policy, culture, and economic development.* IntechOpen. doi:10.5772/intechopen.91457

Asonitou, S., & Hassall, T. (2019, October 15). Which skills and competencies to develop in accountants in a country in crisis? *International Journal of Management Education, 17*(3), 100308. doi:10.1016/j.ijme.2019.100308

Atkinson, R. D. (2019, October 15). *Robotics and the Future of Production and Work.* https://itif.org/publications/2019/10/15/robotics-and-future-production-and-work

Atteridge, A., Axberg, G. N., Goel, N., Kumar, A., Lazarus, M., Ostwald, M., Polycarp, C., Tollefsen, P., Tovanger, A., Upadhyaya, Balogun, D. M., Sharma, R., Shekhar., Balmes, Meheng, D., Arshad, A., & Salehi, P. (2020). Assessing the Potentials of Digitalization as a tool for Climate Change Adaptation and Sustainable Development in Urban Centers. *Sustainable Cities and Society, 53.*

Avtar, R., Tripathi, S., Aggarwal, A. K., & Kumar, P. (2019). Population–urbanization–energy Nexus: A review. *Resources, 8*(3), 136. doi:10.3390/resources8030136

Awan, U., Arnold, M. G., & Gölgeci, I. (2021). Enhancing green product and process innovation: Towards an integrative framework of knowledge acquisition and environmental investment. *Business Strategy and the Environment, 30*(2), 1283–1295. doi:10.1002/bse.2684

Awan, U., Nauman, S., & Sroufe, R. (2021). Exploring the effect of buyer engagement on green product innovation: Empirical evidence from manufacturers. *Business Strategy and the Environment, 30*(1), 463–477. doi:10.1002/bse.2631

Baabdullah, A. M. (2020). Factors influencing adoption of mobile social network games (M-SNGs): The role of awareness. *Information Systems Frontiers, 2*(2), 411–427. doi:10.100710796-018-9868-1

Baarsma, B. E., & Lambooy, J. G. (2005). Valuation of externalities through neo-classical methods by including institutional variables. *Transportation Research Part D, Transport and Environment, 10*(6), 459–475. doi:10.1016/j.trd.2005.06.001

Badot, O., Bree, J., Damay, C., Guichard, N., Lemoine, J. F., & Poulain, M. (2016). The representation of shopping in children's books. *International Journal of Retail & Distribution Management, 44*(10), 976–995. doi:10.1108/IJRDM-08-2015-0134

Baig, A., Hall, B., Jenkins, P., Lamarre, E., & McCarthy, B. (2020). The COVID-19 recovery will be digital: A plan for the first 90 days. *McKinsey Digital, 14.*

Bairrada, C. M., Coelho, A., & Lizanets, V. (2019). The impact of brand personality on consumer behavior: The role of brand love. *Journal of Fashion Marketing and Management, 23*(1), 30–47. doi:10.1108/JFMM-07-2018-0091

Balan, F. (2016). Environmental quality and its human health effects: A causal analysis for the EU- 25. *International Journal of Applied Economics, 13*(1), 57–71.

Bandura, A. & Walters, R.H. (1977). *Social learning theory.* Prentice-Hall.

Barath, L., & Ferto, I. (2015). Heterogeneous technology, scale of land use and technical efficiency: The case of Hungarian crop farms. *Land Use Policy, 42,* 141–150. doi:10.1016/j.landusepol.2014.07.015

Barbuto, J., & Scholl, R. (1998). Motivation Sources Inventory: Development and Validation of New Scales to Measure an Integrative Taxonomy of Motivation. *Psychological Reports, 82,* 1011–1022.

Barcelos, R. H., Dantas, D. C., & Sénécal, S. (2019). The tone of voice of tourism brands on social media: Does it matter? *Tourism Management, 74,* 173–189. doi:10.1016/j.tourman.2019.03.008

Barker, K., Day, C. R., Day, D. L., Kujava, E. R., Otwori, J., Ruscitto, R. A., Smith, A., & Xu, T. (2017). Global Communication and Cross-Cultural Competence: Twenty-First Century Micro-Case Studies. *Global Advances in Business Communication, 6*(1), 5.

Barner-Rasmussen, W., Ehrnrooth, M., Koveshnikov, A., & Mäkelä, K. (2014). Cultural and language skills as resources for boundary spanning within the MNC. *Journal of International Business Studies, 45*(7), 886–905. doi:10.1057/jibs.2014.7

Başfirinci, Ç., & Çilingir, Z. (2015). Anthropomorphism and advertising effectiveness: Moderating roles of product involvement and the type of consumer need. *Journal of Social and Administrative Sciences, 2*(3), 108–131.

Bauman, A. A., & Shcherbina, N. V. (2018). Millennials, technology, and cross-cultural communication. *Journal of Higher Education Theory and Practice, 18*(3), 75–85.

Baum, R., & Bienkowski, J. (2020). Eco-efficiency in measuring the sustainable production of agricultural crops. *Sustainability, 12*(4), 1418. doi:10.3390u12041418

BBC. (2022). *The influence of digital communication on business activity.* Retrieved from https://www.bbc.co.uk/bitesize/guides/zjdwd6f/revision/3

Beaudoin, J., Farzin, H. Y., & Lin Lawell, C. C.-Y. (2015). Public transit investment and sustainable transportation: A review of studies of transit's impact on traffic congestion and air quality. *Research in Transportation Economics, 52,* 15–22. doi:10.1016/j.retrec.2015.10.004

Beck, T., Flynn, B., & Homanen, M. (2020). Covid-19 in emerging markets: Firmsurvey evidence. *Covid Economics,* (38).

Begum, S., Ashfaq, M., Xia, E., & Awan, U. (2022). Does green transformational leadership lead to green innovation? The role of green thinking and creative process engagement. *Business Strategy and the Environment, 31*(1), 580–597. doi:10.1002/bse.2911

Bekhet, H. A., Matar, A., & Yasmin, T. (2017). CO2 emissions, energy consumption, economic growth, and financial development in GCC countries: Dynamic simultaneous equation models. *Renewable & Sustainable Energy Reviews, 70*, 117–132. doi:10.1016/j.rser.2016.11.089

Belanche, D., Casaló, L. V., Flavián, C., & Schepers, J. (2020). Service robot implementation: A theoretical framework and research agenda. *Service Industries Journal, 20*(3-4), 203–225. doi:10.1080/02642069.2019.1672666

Bel, G., & Holst, M. (2018). Evaluation of the impact of Bus Rapid Transit on air pollution in Mexico city. *Transport Policy, 63*, 209–220. doi:10.1016/j.tranpol.2018.01.001

Bélisle, J.-F., & Bodur, H. O. (2010). Avatars as information: Perception of consumers based on their avatars in virtual worlds. *Psychology and Marketing, 27*(8), 741–765. doi:10.1002/mar.20354

Belitski, M., Kalyuzhnova, Y., & Khlystova, O. (2021). The Impact of the COVID-19 Pandemic on the Creative Industries: A Literature Review and Future Research Agenda. *Journal of Business Research.*

Belk, R. (2016). Understanding the robot: Comments on Goudey and Bonnin (2016). [English Edition]. *Recherche et Applications en Marketing, 31*(4), 83–90. doi:10.1177/2051570716658467

Benlian, A., Klumpe, J., & Hinz, O. (2020). Mitigating the intrusive effects of smart home assistants by using anthropomorphic design features: A multi-method investigation. *Information Systems Journal, 30*(6), 1010–1042. doi:10.1111/isj.12243

Bennett, D. E., & Thompson, P. (2016). Use of anthropomorphic brand mascots for student motivation and engagement: A promotional case study with Pablo the Penguin at the University of Portsmouth Library. *New Review of Academic Librarianship, 22*(2-3), 225–237. doi:10.1080/13614533.2016.1162179

Bensirri. (2020). *COVID-19 Kuwait Business Impact Survey.* Academic Press.

Bervell, B., Umar, I. N., & Kamilin, M. H. (2020). Towards a model for online learning satisfaction (MOLS): Reconsidering non-linear relationships among personal innovativeness and modes of online interaction. *Open Learning, 35*(3), 236–259. doi:10.1080/02680513.2019.1662776

Besson, P., & Rowe, F. (2012). Strategizing information systems-enabled organizational transformation: A transdisciplinary review and new directions. *The Journal of Strategic Information Systems, 21*(2), 103–124. doi:10.1016/j.jsis.2012.05.001

Beuthe, M., Degrandsart, F., Greerts, J.-F., & Jourquin, B. (2002). External costs of the Belgian interurban freight traffic: A network analysis of their internalization. *Transportation Research, 7*(4), 285–301.

Bhandari, D., & Garg, R. K. (2016). *Effects of Industrialization on Environment (Indian Scenario).* Academic Press.

Bharucha, J. (2018). Cutting through the clutter: Mascots in Indian marketing. *International Journal of Economics and Business Research, 16*(4), 534–545. doi:10.1504/IJEBR.2018.095351

Bhat, T. P. (2020). *India and Industry 4.0.* Working Paper. Institute for Studies in Industrial Development.

Bhattacharjee, S., Ghosh, B., & Chakraborty, N. (2008). Renewable Energy Assessment of Tripura for Power Generation. *Journal of Resources, Energy and Development, 5*(2).

Bible, M. (2013). The impacts of Côte d'Ivoire's urbanization on its economy and populace. *Global Majority E-Journal, 4*(2), 94–105.

Bikfalvi, A. (2011). Teamwork in production: Implementation, its determinants, and estimates for German manufacturing. *Human Factors and Ergonomics in Manufacturing & Service Industries, 21*(3), 244–259. doi:10.1002/hfm.20230

Bilan, Y., Streimikiene, D., Vasylieva, T., Lyulyov, O., Pimonenko, T., & Pavlyk, A. (2019). Linking between renewable energy, CO2 emissions, and economic growth: Challenges for candidates and potential candidates for the EU membership. *Sustainability, 11*(6), 1528. doi:10.3390u11061528

Bilgili, F., Koçak, E., & Bulut, Ü. (2016). The dynamic impact of renewable energy consumption on CO2 emissions: A revisited Environmental Kuznets Curve approach. *Renewable & Sustainable Energy Reviews, 54*, 838–845. doi:10.1016/j.rser.2015.10.080

Biswas, T., Genesan, K., & Ghosh, A. (2019). Sustainable Manufacturing for India's Low-carbon Transition. Four Bets for Hard-to-abate Sectors. Issue Brief. Council of Energy, Environment and Water.

BKF. (2021, November 10). ASEAN taxonomy for sustainable finance sebagai komitmen ASEAN dalam menghadapi dampak perubahan iklim. *The Fiscal Policy Agency (BKF)*. Retrieved from https://fiskal.kemenkeu.go.id/baca/2021/11/10/4319-asean-taxonomy-for-sustainable-finance-sebagai-komitmen-asean-dalam-menghadapi-dampak-perubahan-iklim

Blodgett, J. G., Wakefield, K. L., & Barnes, J. H. (1995). The effects of customer service on consumer complaining behavior. *Journal of Services Marketing, 9*(4), 31–42.

Bohsali, S., Abdel Samad, R., Papazian, S., Eid, O., Schroeder, B., & Hatz, K. (2016). *Preparing for the Digital Era: The State of Digitalization in GCC Businesses*. PWC.

Bojanic, D. (2009). Hospitality marketing mix and service marketing principles. In *Handbook of Hospitality Marketing Management* (pp. 81–106). Routledge. Retrieved from https://www.routledgehandbooks.com/doi/10.4324/9780080569437.ch3

Bonfiglio, A., Arzeni, A., & Bodini, A. (2017). Assessing eco-efficiency of arable farms in rural areas. *Agricultural Systems, 151*, 114–125. doi:10.1016/j.agsy.2016.11.008

Boons, F., & Lüdeke-Freund, F. (2013). Business models for sustainable innovation: State-of-the-art and steps towards a research agenda. *Journal of Cleaner Production, 45*, 9–19. doi:10.1016/j.jclepro.2012.07.007

Boothe, V. L., & Shendell, D. G. (2008). Potential health effects associated with residential proximity to freeways and primary roads: Review of scientific literature 1999-2006. *Journal of Environmental Health, 70*(8), 33–41. PMID:18468221

Bora, N. M. (2020). Financial Inclusion in India: A Case Study of North Eastern States. *International Journal of Scientific and Technology Research, 9*(2), 1319–1323.

Bos-Brouwers, B., & Hilke, J. (2010). Corporate sustainability and innovation in SMEs: Evidence of themes and activities in practice. *Business Strategy and the Environment, 19*(7), 417–435.

Bostock, H. C., & Lowe, D. J. (2018). Update on the formalisation of the Anthropocene. *Quaternary Australasia, 35*(1), 14–16.

Boundreaux, D. J., & Meiners, R. (2019). Externality: Origins and classifications. *Natural Resources Journal, 59*(1), 1–33.

Bouteraa, M. (2019). Conceptual study: Barriers of Islamic estate planning. *IBMRD's. Journal of Management Research, 8*(1), 28–34. doi:10.17697/ibmrd/2019/v8i1/142673

Bouteraa, M. (2020). Descriptive Approach of Green Banking in the United Arab Emirates (UAE). *IBMRD's. Journal of Management Research, 9*(1), 1–9. doi:10.17697/ibmrd/2020/v9i1/152324

Bouteraa, M., & Al-Aidaros, A. (2020). The Role of Attitude as Mediator in the Intention to Have Islamic Will. *International Journal of Advanced Research in Economics and Finance, 2*(1), 22–37.

Bouteraa, M., Hisham, R. R. I. R., & Zainol, Z. (2020). Green banking practices from Islamic and Western perspectives. *International Journal of Business. Economics and Law*, *21*(5), 1–11.

Bouteraa, M., Hisham, R. R. I. R., & Zainol, Z. (2021). Exploring Determinants of Customers' Intention to Adopt Green Banking: Qualitative Investigation. *Journal of Sustainability Science and Management*, *16*(3), 187–203. doi:10.46754/jssm.2021.04.014

Bouteraa, M., Raja Hisham, R. R. I., & Zainol, Z. (2020). Islamic Banks Customers' Intention to Adopt Green Banking: Extension of UTAUT Model. *International Journal of Business and Technology Management*, *2*(1), 121–136.

Brabant, S., & Mooney, L. A. (1989). When "critters" act like people: Anthropomorphism in greeting cards. *Sociological Spectrum*, *9*(4), 477–494. doi:10.1080/02732173.1989.9981906

Braccini, A. M., & Margherita, E. G. (2018). Exploring organizational sustainability of industry 4.0 under the triple bottom line: The case of a manufacturing company. *Sustainability*, *11*(1), 36. doi:10.3390u11010036

Braungart, M., McDonough, M., & Bollinger, A. (2007). Cradle to cradle design: Creating health emissions-a strategy for eco-effective product and system design. *Journal of Cleaner Production*, *15*(13-14), 1337–1348. doi:10.1016/j.jclepro.2006.08.003

Braun, V., & Clarke, V. (2006). Using thematic analysis in psychology. *Qualitative Research in Psychology*, *3*(2), 77–101. doi:10.1191/1478088706qp063oa

Bravo, M., Briceno, L., Cominetti, R., Cortes, E. C., & Martinez, F. (2010). An integrated behavioural model of the land-use and transport systems with network congestion and location externalities. *Transportation Research Part B: Methodological*, *44*(4), 584–596. doi:10.1016/j.trb.2009.08.002

Bravo-Moncayo, L., Naranjo, J. L., Garcia, I. P., & Mosquera, R. (2017). Neural based contingent valuation of road traffic noise. *Transportation Research Part D, Transport and Environment*, *50*, 26–39. doi:10.1016/j.trd.2016.10.020

Bribian, Z., Capilla, V., & Uson, A. (2011). Life cycle assessment of building materials: Comparative analysis of energy and environmental impacts and evaluation of the eco-efficiency improvement potential. *Building and Environment*, *46*(5), 1133–1140. doi:10.1016/j.buildenv.2010.12.002

Bristow, A. L., Wardman, M., & Chintakayala, V. P. K. (2015). International meta-analysis of stated preference studies of transportation noise nuisance. *Transportation*, *42*(1), 71–100. doi:10.100711116-014-9527-4

Brodsky, S. (2020, March 4). What are green sukuk? *Impactivate*. Retrieved from https://www.theimpactivate.com/what-are-green-sukuk/

Brow, M. (2019, May 28). *How industry 4.0 is affecting jobs*. Retrieved October 10, 2021, from https://industryeurope.com/how-industry-4-0-is-affecting-jobs/

Brown, K. (2019 December 19). *How 2020 can be a springboard year for the sustainable development goals*. https://unfoundation.org/blog/post/how-2020-can-be-a-springboard-year-for-the-sustainable-development-goals/

Brown, S. (2011). It's alive inside! A note on the prevalence of personification. *Irish Marketing Review*, *21*(1-2), 3–11.

Brundtland, G. H. (1987). Our common future—Call for action. *Environmental Conservation*, *14*(4), 291–294. doi:10.1017/S0376892900016805

Buana, G. K., & Musari, K. (2020). *A new sphere of sukuk: linking pandemic to Paris agreement. The World Financial Review.*

Buetow, S. (2010). Thematic analysis and its reconceptualization as 'saliency analysis'. *Journal of Health Services Research & Policy, 15*(2), 123–125. doi:10.1258/jhsrp.2009.009081 PMID:19762883

Bukhari, S.A.A., Hashim, F. & Amran, A. (2022). Pathways towards Green Banking adoption: moderating role of top management commitment. *International Journal of Ethics and Systems*. . doi:10.1108/IJOES-05-2021-0110

Bukhari, S. A. A., Hashim, F., & Amran, A. (2019). Determinants of Green Banking Adoption: A Theoretical Framework. *KnE Social Sciences, 3*(22), 1–14. doi:10.18502/kss.v3i22.5041

Bukhari, S. A. A., Hashim, F., & Amran, A. (2020). Green Banking: A road map for adoption. *International Journal of Ethics and Systems, 36*(3), 371–385. doi:10.1108/IJOES-11-2019-0177

Bukhari, S. A. A., Hashim, F., & Amran, A. (2021). Green banking: A conceptual framework. *International Journal of Green Economics, 15*(1), 59–74. doi:10.1504/IJGE.2021.117682

Bukhari, S. A. A., Hashim, F., Amran, A. B., & Hyder, K. (2020). Green Banking and Islam: Two sides of the same coin. *Journal of Islamic Marketing, 11*(4), 977–1000. Advance online publication. doi:10.1108/JIMA-09-2018-0154

Bukht, R., & Heeks, R. (2017). *Defining, conceptualising and measuring the digital economy*. Development Informatics Working Paper (68).

Burnley, S., Wagland, S., & Longhurst, P. (2019). Using life cycle assessment in environmental engineering education. *Higher Education Pedagogies, 4*(1), 64–79. doi:10.1080/23752696.2019.1627672

Burton, M., & Wong, J. (2021). *Australian teens lead class action against Whitehaven's coal mine expansion*. Thompson Reuters Foundation News. https://news.trust.org/item/20210301061639-sel6u

Buzzelli, M., & Jerrett, M. (2003). Comparing proximity measures of exposure to geostatistical estimates in environmental justice research. *Global Environment Change B, 5*(1), 13–21. doi:10.1016/j.hazards.2003.11.001

Byrne, J., & Lund, P. D. (2019). Sustaining our common future: Transformative, timely, commons-based change is needed. *Wiley Interdisciplinary Reviews. Energy and Environment, 8*(1), 1–6. doi:10.1002/wene.334

Caiado, R., Dias, R., Mattos, L., Quelhas, L., & Filho, W. (2017). Towards sustainable development through the perspective of eco-efficiency- a systematic literature review. *Journal of Cleaner Production, 165*, 890–904. doi:10.1016/j.jclepro.2017.07.166

California State University. (2020, December 15). *Academic publishing guide for faculty and researchers*. Retrieved March 25, 2021, from California State University: https://csus.libguides.com/publishing/choosing-a-publisher

Canbek, N. G., & Mutlu, M. E. (2016). On the track of Artificial Intelligence: Learning with Intelligent Personal Assistants. *International Journal of Human Sciences, 13*(1), 592–601. doi:10.14687/ijhs.v13i1.3549

Cao, J., Shang, Y., Mok, Q., & Lai, I. K. W. (2019). The impact of personal innovativeness on the intention to use cloud classroom: an empirical study in China. In *International conference on technology in education* (pp. 179-188). Springer. 10.1007/978-981-13-9895-7_16

Carbon, D. (2018). *State of Green Economy Report 2018*. World Green Economy Summit.

Carrier, M., Apparicio, P., Seguin, A.-M., & Crouse, D. (2014). The application of three methods to measure the statistical association between different social groups and the concentration of air pollutants in Montreal: A case of environmental equity. *Transportation Research Part D, Transport and Environment, 30*, 38–52. doi:10.1016/j.trd.2014.05.001

Carrillo-Hermosilla, J., Del Río, P., & Könnölä, T. (2010). Diversity of eco-innovations: Reflections from selected case studies. *Journal of Cleaner Production, 18*(10-11), 1073–1083. doi:10.1016/j.jclepro.2010.02.014

Caruso, G., Colantonio, E., & Gattone, S. A. (2020). Relationships between renewable energy consumption, social factors, and health: A panel vector auto regression analysis of a cluster of 12 EU countries. *Sustainability*, *12*(7), 2915. doi:10.3390u12072915

Carvalho, N., Chaim, O., Cazarini, E., & Gerolamo, M. (2018). Manufacturing in the fourth industrial revolution: A positive prospect in sustainable manufacturing. *Procedia Manufacturing*, *21*, 671–678. doi:10.1016/j.promfg.2018.02.170

Cavallaro, F. (2018). Policy implications from the economic valuation of freight transport externalities along the Brenner corridor. *Case Studies on Transport Policy*, *6*(1), 133–146. doi:10.1016/j.cstp.2017.11.008

Cayla, J. (2013). Brand mascots as organisational totems. *Journal of Marketing Management*, *29*(1-2), 86–104. doi:10.1080/0267257X.2012.759991

CE Delft. (2018). *Health impacts and costs of diesel emissions in the EU*. CE Delft. https://epha.org/wp-content/uploads/2018/11/embargoed-until-27-november-00-01-am-cet-time-ce-delft-4r30-health-impacts-costs-diesel-emissions-eu-def.pdf

Ceipek, R., Hautz, J., & Petruzzelli, A. M., Massis, D. A., & Marzler, K. (2020). A Motivation and Ability Perspective on Engagement in Emerging Digital Technologies: The Case of Internet of Things Solutions. *Long Range Planning*.

Cenni, I., & Goethals, P. (2017). Negative hotel reviews on TripAdvisor: A cross-linguistic analysis, *Discourse. Context & Media*, *16*, 22–30.

Ch'ng, P. C., Cheah, J., & Amran, A. (2021). Eco-innovation practices and sustainable business performance: The moderating effect of market turbulence in the Malaysian technology industry. *Journal of Cleaner Production*, *283*, 124556.

Chadha, A. (2011). Overcoming competence lock-in for the development of radical eco-innovations: The case of bio-polymer technology. *Industry and Innovation*, *18*(3), 335–350.

Chae, S. W., Lee, K. C., & Seo, Y. W. (2016). Exploring the effect of avatar trust on learners' perceived participation intentions in an e-learning environment. *International Journal of Human-Computer Interaction*, *32*(5), 373–393. doi:10.1080/10447318.2016.1150643

Chaim, O., Muschard, B., Cazarini, E., & Rozenfeld, H. (2018). Insertion of sustainability performance indicators in an industry 4.0 virtual learning environment. *Procedia Manufacturing*, *21*, 446–453. doi:10.1016/j.promfg.2018.02.143

Chang, Y., Ku, C., & Chen, C. (2017) Social media analytics: Extracting and visualizing Hilton hotel ratings and reviews from TripAdvisor. *International Journal of Information Management*, 14. doi:10.1016/j.ijinfomgt.2017.11.001

Chang, C. H. (2011). The influence of corporate environmental ethics on competitive advantage: The mediation role of green innovation. *Journal of Business Ethics*, *104*(3), 361–370. doi:10.100710551-011-0914-x

Chang, C. H. (2016). The determinants of green product innovation performance. *Corporate Social Responsibility and Environmental Management*, *23*(2), 65–76. doi:10.1002/csr.1361

Chan, H. K., Yee, R. W., Dai, J., & Lim, M. K. (2016). The moderating effect of environmental dynamism on green product innovation and performance. *International Journal of Production Economics*, *181*, 384–391. doi:10.1016/j.ijpe.2015.12.006

Chapra, M. U., & Khan, T. (2008). *Regulation and supervision for sharia bank*. Bumi Aksara.

Chartrand, T. L., Fitzsimons, G. M., & Fitzsimons, G. J. (2008). Automatic effects of anthropomorphized objects on behavior. *Social Cognition*, *26*(2), 198–209. doi:10.1521oco.2008.26.2.198

Chatterjee, S. (2020). Factors Impacting Behavioral Intention of Users to Adopt IoT in India. *International Journal of Information Security and Privacy*, *14*(4), 92–112. doi:10.4018/IJISP.2020100106

Chaturvedi, S., James, T. C., Saha, S., & Shaw, P. (2019). *2030 agenda and India: moving from quantity to quality.* Springer Singapore. doi:10.1007/978-981-32-9091-4

Chaudhary, R. (2019). Green human resource management and job pursuit intention: Examining the underlying processes. *Corporate Social Responsibility and Environmental Management*, *26*(4), 929–937. doi:10.1002/csr.1732

Chaurasia, S. S., Verma, S., & Singh, V. (2019). Exploring the intention to use M-payment in India: Role of extrinsic motivation, intrinsic motivation and perceived demonetization regulation. *Transforming Government: People. Process and Policy*, *13*(3/4), 276–305. doi:10.1108/TG-09-2018-0060

Chen, S., Severt, K., Shin, Y., Knowlden, A., & Hilliard, T. (2018). How'd you sleep? measuring business travelers' sleep quality and satisfaction in hotels. *Journal of Hospitality and Tourism Insights*, *1*(3), 188-202.

Chen, F., Chen, R. P., & Yan, L. (2020). When sadness comes alive, will it be less painful? The effects of anthropomorphic thinking on sadness regulation and consumption. *Journal of Consumer Psychology*, *30*(2), 277–295. doi:10.1002/jcpy.1137

Cheng, C.-C., Huang, K.-H., & Huang, S.-M. (2017). Exploring young children's images on robots. *Advances in Mechanical Engineering*, *9*(4), 1–7. doi:10.1177/1687814017698663

Cheng, Y., & Jiang, H. (2021). Customer–brand relationship in the era of artificial intelligence: Understanding the role of chatbot marketing efforts. *Journal of Product and Brand Management*. Advance online publication. doi:10.1108/JPBM-05-2020-2907

Chen, J.-S., Le, T.-T.-Y., & Florence, D. (2021). Usability and responsiveness of artificial intelligence chatbot on online customer experience in e-retailing. *International Journal of Retail & Distribution Management*, *49*(11), 1512–1531. doi:10.1108/IJRDM-08-2020-0312

Chen, K.-J. (2017). Humanizing brands: An examination of the psychological process of anthropomorphism and its effects on consumer responses. *Journal of Marketing Management*, *5*(2), 75–87. doi:10.15640/jmm.v5n2a7

Chen, K.-J., Lin, J.-S., Choi, J. H., & Hahm, J. M. (2015). Would you be my friend? An examination of global marketers' brand personiðcation strategies in social media. *Journal of Interactive Advertising*, *15*(2), 1–14. doi:10.1080/1525 2019.2015.1079508

Chen, R. P., Wan, E. W., & Levy, E. (2017). The effect of social exclusion on consumer preference for anthropomorphized brands. *Journal of Consumer Psychology*, *27*(1), 23–34. doi:10.1016/j.jcps.2016.05.004

Chen, Y. S., Lai, S. B., & Wen, C. T. (2006). The influence of green innovation performance on corporate advantage in Taiwan. *Journal of Business Ethics*, *67*(4), 331–339. doi:10.100710551-006-9025-5

Chen, Y., Chang, C., & Wu, F. (2012). Origins of green innovations: The differences between proactive and reactive green innovations. *Management Decision*, *50*(3), 368–398. doi:10.1108/00251741211216197

Chérif, E., & Lemoine, J.-F. (2019). Anthropomorphic virtual assistants and the reactions of Internet users: An experiment on the assistant's voice. *Recherche et Applications en Marketing*, *34*(1), 28–47. doi:10.1177/2051570719829432

Chien, C. C., & Peng, C. W. (2012). Does going green pay off in the long run? *Journal of Business Research*, *65*(11), 1636–1642.

Chiou, T. Y., Chan, H. K., Lettice, F., & Chung, S. H. (2011). The influence of greening the suppliers and green innovation on environmental performance and competitive advantage in Taiwan. *Transportation Research Part E, Logistics and Transportation Review*, *47*(6), 822–836. doi:10.1016/j.tre.2011.05.016

Choi, Y. K. (2019). Characters' persuasion effects in advergaming: Role of brand trust, product involvement, and trust propensity. *Internet Research*, *29*(2), 367–380. doi:10.1108/IntR-01-2018-0021

Choi, Y. K., Miracle, G. E., & Biocca, F. (2001). The effects of anthropomorphic agents on advertising effectiveness and the mediating role of presence. *Journal of Interactive Advertising*, *2*(1), 19–32. doi:10.1080/15252019.2001.10722055

Chopra, R. (2016). Environmental Degradation in India: Causes and Consequences. *International Journal of Applied Environmental Sciences, 11*(6), 1593–1601.

Choy, Y. K. (2015). 28 years into "Our Common Future": Sustainable development in the post-Brundtland world. *WIT Transactions on the Built Environment, 168*, 1197–1211. doi:10.2495/SD151032

Chusmir, L. (1989). Behavior: A measure of motivation needs. *Psychology: A Journal of Human Behavior, 26*(2-3), 1–10.

Çizakça, M. (2013). Proposal for innovation in the capital markets: Esham. *Global Islamic Finance Report,* 91-93.

Çizakça, M. (2014). *Can there be innovation in Islamic finance? Case study: Esham.* Paper was presented at the 11th IFSB Summit, Knowledge Sharing Partner Session: "New Markets and Frontiers for Islamic Finance: Innovation and the Regulatory Perimeter".

Çizakça, M. (2018). Modernizing a historical instrument (esham) for growth and financial inclusion. In Z. Iqbal, A. Omar, T. A. A. Manap, & A. A. Alawode (Eds.), Islamic finance: A catalyst for shared prosperity? (pp. 236-246) Jeddah: Islamic Development Bank (IsDB).

Çizakça, M. (2011). *Islamic capitalism and finance: Origins, evolution, and the future.* Edward Elgar Publishing. doi:10.4337/9780857931481

Coelho, F. J.-F., Bairrada, C. M., & de Matos Coelho, A. F. (2020). Functional brand qualities and perceived value: The mediating role of brand experience and brand personality. *Psychology and Marketing, 37*(1), 41–55. doi:10.1002/mar.21279

Cohen, J. (1988). *Statistical power analysis for the behavioral sciences.* Lawrence Erlbaum Associates.

Cohen, J. (1992). A power Primer. *Psychological Bulletin, 112*(1), 155–159. doi:10.1037/0033-2909.112.1.155 PMID:19565683

Colbert, A., Yee, N., & George, G. (2016). The digital workforce and the workplace of the future. *Academy of Management Journal, 59*(3), 731–739. doi:10.5465/amj.2016.4003

Commission of the European Communities. (1990). *Green paper on the urban environment.* European Commission.

Cravioto, J., Yamasue, E., Okumura, H., & Ishihara, K. N. (2013). Road transport externalities in Mexico: Estimates and international comparisons. *Transport Policy, 30*, 63–76. doi:10.1016/j.tranpol.2013.08.004

Creswell, J. W., & Poth, C. N. (2018). *Qualitative Inquiry & Research Design Choosing Among Five Approaches* (4th ed.). SAGE Publications, Inc.

Creswell, J., & Creswell, J. D. (2018). *Research Design: Qualitative, Quantitative, and Mixed Methods Approaches* (5th ed.). Sage publications, Inc.

Cricelli, L., & Strazzullo, S. (2021). The Economic Aspect of Digital Sustainability: A Systematic Review. Systematic Review. *Sustainability, 13*(8241), 1–15. doi:10.3390u13158241

Croci, E. (2016). Urban road pricing: A comparative study on the experiences of London, Stockholm and Milan. *Transportation Research Procedia*, *14*, 253–262. doi:10.1016/j.trpro.2016.05.062

Czaplicka-Kolarz, K., Kruczek, M., & Burchart-Korol, D. (2013). The concept of eco-efficiency in sustainable production management. *Zesz. Naukowe Ser. Organ. Zarz.*, *63*, 59–71.

Czyzewski, B., & Matuszczak, A. (2018). Towards measuring political rents in agriculture: Case studies of different agrarian structures in the EU. *Agricultural Economics*, *64*, 101–114.

Dąbrowska, J., Almpanopoulou, A., Brem, A., Chesbrough, H., Cucino, V., Di Minin, A., Giones, F., Hakala, H., Marullo, C., Mention, A.-L., Mortara, L., Nørskov, S., Nylund, P. A., Oddo, C. M., Radziwon, A., & Ritala, P. (2022). Digital transformation, for better or worse: A critical multi-level research agenda. *R & D Management*, radm.12531. doi:10.1111/radm.12531

Dahlman, C., Mealy, S., & Wermelinger, M. (2016). *Harnessing the digital economy for developing countries*. Academic Press.

Dangelico, R. M. (2016). Green product innovation: Where we are and where we are going. *Business Strategy and the Environment*, *25*(8), 560–576. doi:10.1002/bse.1886

Dangelico, R. M., & Pujari, D. (2010). Mainstreaming green product innovation: Why and how companies integrate environmental sustainability. *Journal of Business Ethics*, *95*(3), 471–486. doi:10.100710551-010-0434-0

Dangelico, R. M., Pujari, D., & Pontrandolfo, P. (2017). Green product innovation in manufacturing firms: A sustainability-oriented dynamic capability perspective. *Business Strategy and the Environment*, *26*(4), 490–506. doi:10.1002/bse.1932

Dario, P., Guglielmelli, E., & Laschi, C. (2001). Humanoids and personal robots: Design and experiments. *Journal of Robotic Systems*, *18*(12), 673–690. doi:10.1002/rob.8106

Dartnell, L. (2019). *Origins : how Earth's history shaped human history*. Basic Books.

Dauvergne, P. (2020). Is artificial intelligence greening global supply chains? Exposing the political economy of environmental costs. *Review of International Political Economy*. Advance online publication. doi:10.1080/09692290.2020.1814381

David-West, O. (2015). The Path to Digital Financial Inclusion in Nigeria: Experience of Firstmonie. *Journal of Payment Strategy and Systems*, *9*, 256–273.

De Bondt, C., Van Kerckhove, A., & Geuens, M. (2018). Look at that body! How anthropomorphic package shapes systematically appeal to consumers. *International Journal of Advertising*, *37*(5), 698–717. doi:10.1080/02650487.2018.1470919

De Dios Ortuzar, J., Bascunan, R., Rizzi, L. I., & Salata, A. (2021). Assessing the potential acceptability of road pricing in Santiago. *Transportation Research Part A, Policy and Practice*, *144*, 153–169. doi:10.1016/j.tra.2020.12.007

De Gauquier, L., Brengman, M., Willems, K., & Kerrebroeck, H. V. (2019). Leveraging advertising to a higher dimension: Experimental research on the impact of virtual reality on brand personality impressions. *Virtual Reality (Waltham Cross)*, *23*(3), 235–253. doi:10.100710055-018-0344-5

De Palma, A., & Lindsey, R. (2011). Traffic congestion pricing methodologies and technologies. *Transportation Research Part C, Emerging Technologies*, *19*(6), 1377–1399. doi:10.1016/j.trc.2011.02.010

Deal, J. J., Altman, D. G., & Rogelberg, S. G. (2010). Millennials at work: What we know and what we need to do (if anything). *Journal of Business and Psychology, 25*(2), 191–199. doi:10.100710869-010-9177-2

Deb, S. K., Deb, N., & Roy, S. (2019). Investigation of Factors Influencing the Choice of Smartphone Banking in Bangladesh. *Evergreen, 6*(3), 230–239. doi:10.5109/2349299

Deemer, R. B., Harrison, A. D., Siyue, I., Beaulieu, J. J., Delsontro, T., & Barrows, N. (2016). Greenhouse Gas Emission from Reservoir Water Surface: A New Global Synthesis. *Bioscience, 66*, 1–16.

DEFRA. (2014). *Environmental noise: valuing impacts on: sleep disturbance, annoyance, hypertension, productivity and quite*. DEFRA.

Dekkers, J. E. C., & van der Straaten, W. (2009). Monetary valuation of aircraft noise: A hedonic analysis around Amsterdam airport. *Ecological Economics, 68*(11), 2850–2858. doi:10.1016/j.ecolecon.2009.06.002

Delbaere, M., McQuarrie, E. F., & Phillips, B. J. (2011). Personification in advertising using a visual metaphor to trigger anthropomorphism. *Journal of Advertising, 40*(1), 121–130. doi:10.2753/JOA0091-3367400108

Delft, C. E. INFRAS & Fraunhofer ISI. (2011). External costs of transport in Europe. CE Delft.

Delft, C. E. (2008). *Health impacts of costs of diesel emissions in the EU*.

Delgado-Ballester, E., Palazón, M., & Pelaez-Muñoz, J. (2017). This anthropomorphised brand is so loveable: The role of self-brand integration. *Spanish Journal of Marketing - ESIC, 21*(2), 89-101. doi:10.1016/j.sjme.2017.04.002

DeLone, W. H., & McLean, E. R. (1992). Information systems success: The quest for the dependent variable. *Information Systems Research, 3*(1), 60–95. doi:10.1287/isre.3.1.60

Delone, W. H., & McLean, E. R. (2003). The DeLone and McLean Model of Information Systems Success: A Ten-Year Update. *Journal of Management Information Systems, 19*(4), 9–30. doi:10.1080/07421222.2003.11045748

Dementyeva, M., Koster, P. R., & Verhoef, E. T. (2015). Regulation of road accident externalities when insurance companies have market power. *Journal of Urban Economics, 86*, 1–8. doi:10.1016/j.jue.2014.11.001

Deng, X. (2006). Economic costs of motor vehicle emissions in China: A case study. *Transportation Research Part D, Transport and Environment, 11*(3), 216–226. doi:10.1016/j.trd.2006.02.004

Derwall, J., Guenster, N., Bauer, R., & Koedijk, K. (2005). The eco-efficiency premium puzzle. *Financial Analysts Journal, 61*(2), 51–63. doi:10.2469/faj.v61.n2.2716

DesJardins, J. (2016). Is it time to jump off the sustainability bandwagon? *Business Ethics Quarterly, 26*(1), 117–135. doi:10.1017/beq.2016.12

Dev, N. K., Shankar, R., & Qaiser, F. H. (2020). Industry 4.0 and Circular Economy: Operational Excellence for Sustainable Reverse Supply Chain Performance. *Resources, Conservation and Recycling, 153.*

Dickinger, A., & Lalicic, L. (2016). An analysis of destination brand personality and emotions: A comparison study. *Information Technology & Tourism, 15*(4), 317–340. doi:10.100740558-015-0044-x

Dienes, R., Abat, M., & Haddd, J. (2021). *GCC Digital Trends for 2021*. Oliver Wyman.

Dimitrov, A. (2018). The digital age leadership: A transhumanistic perspective. *The Journal of Leadership Studies, 12*(3), 79–81.

Dinard Standard. (2020). *State of the global islamic economy report 2020/2021*. Dinar Standard, Dubai Islamic Economic Development Center, and Salam Gateway.

Dirican, C. (2015). The impacts of robotics, artificial intelligence on business and economics. *Procedia: Social and Behavioral Sciences*, *195*, 564–573. doi:10.1016/j.sbspro.2015.06.134

Dixon, J., Belnap, C., Albrecht, C., & Lee, K. (2010). The importance of soft skills. *Corporate Finance Review*, *14*(6), 35–38.

Dogaru, L. (2020). The main goals of the fourth industrial revolution. renewable energy perspectives. *Procedia Manufacturing*, *46*, 397–401. doi:10.1016/j.promfg.2020.03.058

Doh, J. P., Tashman, P., & Benischke, M. H. (2019). Adapting to grand environmental challenges through collective entrepreneurship. *The Academy of Management Perspectives*, *33*(4), 450–468. doi:10.5465/amp.2017.0056

Do, N., Tham, J., Azam, S., & Khatibia, A. (2020). Analysis of customer behavioral intentions towards mobile payment: Cambodian consumer's perspective. *Accounting*, *6*(7), 1391–1402. doi:10.5267/j.ac.2020.8.010

Doyle, A. (2021, September 15). *Important Technical Skills With Examples*. https://www.thebalancecareers.com/technical-skills-list-2063775

Duffy, P., Black, K., O'Brian, P., Hyde, B., Ryan, A. M., Ponzi, J., & Alam, M. S. (2017). *National inventory report 2017*. EPA.

Du, L., Zhang, Z., & Feng, T. (2018). Linking green customer and supplier integration with green innovation performance: The role of internal integration. *Business Strategy and the Environment*, *27*(8), 1583–1595. doi:10.1002/bse.2223

Dumbravă, G. (2010). The concept of framing in cross-cultural business communication. *Annals of the University of Petrosani. Economics*, *10*(Part I), 83–90.

Dumbravă, G., & Koronka, A. (2009). "Actions Speak Louder than Words" – Body Language in Business Communication. *Annals of the University of Petrosani. Economics*, *9*(3), 249–254.

Dutta, G., Kumar, R., Sindhwani, R., & Singh, R. (2020). Digital Transformation Priorities of India's Discrete Manufacturing SMEs – A Conceptual Study in Perspective of Industry 4.0. *Competitiveness Review. An International Business Journal Incorporating Journal of Global Competitiveness*.

Duverge, G. (2021, August 20). *The Manager's Guide to Fostering Creativity in the Workplace*. Touro University World-Wide. Retrieved October 21, 2021, from https://www.tuw.edu/business/creativity-in-the-workplace/

Dyr, T., Misiurski, P., & Ziolkowska, K. (2019). Costs and benefits of using busses fuelled by natural gas in public transport. *Journal of Cleaner Production*, *225*, 1134–1146. doi:10.1016/j.jclepro.2019.03.317

EC. (2019). *Handbook on the external costs of transport*. Publications Office of the European Union.

Ece, M., Tosun, I., Ekinci, K., & Yalçındağ, N. S. (2018). Modeling of road traffic noise and traffic flow measures to reduce noise exposure in Antalya metropolitan municipality. *Journal of Environmental Health Science & Engineering*, *16*(1), 1–10. doi:10.100740201-018-0288-4 PMID:30258637

ECMT (European Conference of Ministers of Transport). (1998). *Efficient transport for Europe*. OECD.

Economic Times (ET). (2021). *Economic Survey flags high T & D Losses in Power Sector*. Retrieved on 25th February, 2022 from: https://m.economictimes.com/industry/energy/power/economic-survey-flags-high-td-losses-in-power-sector/articleshow/80585965.cms

Edlin, A. S., & Karaca-Mandic, P. (2006). The accident externality from driving. *Journal of Political Economy*, *114*(5), 931–955. doi:10.1086/508030

Edwards, B. I., & Cheok, A. D. (2018). Why not robot teachers: Artificial intelligence for addressing teacher shortage. *Applied Artificial Intelligence, 32*(4), 345–360. doi:10.1080/08839514.2018.1464286

Edwards, C., Edwards, A., Stoll, B., Lin, X., & Massey, N. (2019). Evaluations of an artificial intelligence instructor's voice: Social Identity Theory in human-robot interactions. *Computers in Human Behavior, 90*, 357–362. doi:10.1016/j.chb.2018.08.027

EEA. (2014). *Air pollution fact sheet 2014 Turkey.* EEA.

EEA. (2019). *EMEP/EEA Air pollutant emission inventory guidebook 2019.* EEA.

EEA. (2020). *Environmental noise in Europe-2020.* EEA.

Efefiong, A. E., & Sunday, E. (2017). Environmental degradation, North-South debate and sustainable development. *Socialscientia: Journal of Social Sciences and Humanities, 2*(4), 12–17.

Eisend, M., & Stokburger-Sauer, N. E. (2013). Brand personality: A meta-analytic review of antecedents and consequences. *Marketing Letters, 24*(3), 205–216. doi:10.100711002-013-9232-7

Eisner, R. (1989, Spring). Budget deficits: Rhetoric and reality. *The Journal of Economic Perspectives, 3*(2), 73–93. doi:10.1257/jep.3.2.73

El-Darwiche. (2022). *Energizing the Digital Economy in the Gulf Countries.* Strategy.

Eliasson, J., Hultkrantz, L., Nerhagen, L., & Smidfelt Rosqvist, L. (2009). The Stockholm congestion-charging trial 2006: Overview of effects. *Transportation Research Part A, Policy and Practice, 43*(3), 240–250. doi:10.1016/j.tra.2008.09.007

Ellen MacArthur Foundation. (2012). *Towards the circular economy vol. 1: An economic and business rationale for an accelerated transition.* Retrieved from https://www.ellenmacarthurfoundation.org/publications/towards-the-circular-economy-vol-1-an-economic-and-business-rationale-for-an-accelerated-transition

Ellen MacArthur Foundation. (2013). *Towards the circular economy vol. 1: Opportunities for the consumer goods sector.* Retrieved from https://www.ellenmacarthurfoundation.org/assets/ downloads/publications/TCE_Report-2013.pdf

Ellen MacArthur Foundation. (2019). *Completing the picture how the circular economy tackles climate change.* Retrieved from https://circulareconomy.europa.eu/platform/sites/default/files/emf_completing_the_picture.pdf

Ellen MacArthur Foundation. (2020). *Financing the circular economy, capturing the opportunity.* Retrieved from https://ellenmacarthurfoundation.org/financing-the-circular-economy-capturing-the-opportunity

Ellen MacArthur Foundation. (2021). *Completing the picture: How the circular economy tackles climate change.* Retrieved from https://ellenmacarthurfoundation.org/completing-the-picture

Ellingrud, K., Gupta, R., & Salguero, J. (2021, February 26). *Building the vital skills for the future of work in operations.* McKinsey & Company. Retrieved September 22, 2021, from https://www.mckinsey.com/business-functions/operations/our-insights/building-the-vital-skills-for-the-future-of-work-in-operations

El-Masri, M., & Tarhini, A. (2017). Factors affecting the adoption of e-learning systems in Qatar and USA: Extending the Unified Theory of Acceptance and Use of Technology 2 (UTAUT2). *Educational Technology Research and Development, 65*(3), 743–763. doi:10.100711423-016-9508-8

El-Saharty, S., Kheyfets, I., Herbst, C. H., & Ajwad, M. I. (2020). *The GCC countries' responses to COVID-19.* Anonymous. doi:10.1596/978-1-4648-1582-9_ch4

Emas, R. (2015). The concept of sustainable development: Definition and defining principles. *Brief for GSDR, 2015*, 1–3.

Emery, C. R., & Tian, R. G. (2003). The effect of cultural differences on the effectiveness of advertising appeals: A comparison between China and the US. *Transformations in Business & Economics*, *2*(3), 48–59.

Emmerink, R. H. M., Nijkamp, P., & Rietveld, P. (1995). Is congestion pricing a first-best strategy in transport policy? A critical review of arguments. *Environment & Planning B*, *22*(4), 581–602. doi:10.1068/b220581

Englund, M., & André, K. (2021, October 29). *A circular economy: a tool to bridge climate mitigation and adaptation?* Stockholm Environment Institute (SEI). Retrieved from https://www.sei.org/featured/circular-economy-mitigation-and-adaptation/

Epley, N., Waytz, A., Akalis, S., & Cacioppo, J. T. (2008). When we need a human: Motivational determinants of anthropomorphism. *Social Cognition*, *26*(2), 143–155. doi:10.1521oco.2008.26.2.143

Epley, N., Waytz, A., & Cacioppo, J. T. (2007). On seeing human: A three-factor theory of anthropomorphism. *Psychological Review*, *114*(4), 864–886. doi:10.1037/0033-295X.114.4.864 PMID:17907867

Erez, M. (1992). Interpersonal communication systems in organisations, and their relationships to cultural values, productivity and innovation: The case of Japanese corporations. *Applied Psychology*, *41*(1), 43–64. doi:10.1111/j.1464-0597.1992.tb00685.x

ERIA. (2021). *Framework for circular economy for the ASEAN economic community*. Brochure, The Economic Research Institute for ASEAN and East Asia (ERIA).

Ertz, M., & Leblanc-Proulx, S. (2018). Sustainability in the collaborative economy: A bibliometric analysis reveals emerging interest. *Journal of Cleaner Production*, *196*, 1073–1085. doi:10.1016/j.jclepro.2018.06.095

Eskine, K. J., & Locander, W. H. (2014). A name you can trust? Personiðcation effects are inñuenced by beliefs about company values. *Psychology and Marketing*, *31*(1), 48–53. doi:10.1002/mar.20674

Euchi, J., & Kallel, A. (2021). Internalization of external congestion and CO_2 emissions costs related to road transport: The case of Tunisia. *Renewable & Sustainable Energy Reviews*, *142*, 110858. doi:10.1016/j.rser.2021.110858

EUROSTAT. (2015). *Urban-rural typology update*. https://ec.europa.eu/eurostat/statisticsexplained/index.php?title=Archive:Urbanrural_typology_update&oldid=262364

EU-RTR. (2012). *Technical assistance for improving emissions control*. Final Report-Part II: Main Technical Results. PM Project number: 300424. Project co-financed by European Union and Republic of Turkey.

Evangelinos, C., & Tscharaktschiew, S. (2021). The valuation of aesthetic preferences and consequences for urban transport infrastructures. *Sustainability*, *13*(9), 4977. doi:10.3390u13094977

Extern, E. (2005). Externalities of Energy: Methodology 2005 update. EC.

Fan, A., Wu, L., & Mattila, A. S. (2016). Does anthropomorphism influence customers' switching intentions in the self-service technology failure context? *Journal of Services Marketing*, *30*(7), 713–723. doi:10.1108/JSM-07-2015-0225

Fan, A., Wu, L., Miao, L., & Mattila, A. S. (2020). When does technology anthropomorphism help alleviate customer dissatisfaction after a service failure? – The moderating role of consumer technology self-efficacy and interdependent self-construal. *Journal of Hospitality Marketing & Management*, *29*(3), 269–290. doi:10.1080/19368623.2019.1639095

Fatemi, A. M., & Fooladi, I. J. (2013). Sustainable finance: A new paradigm. *Global Finance Journal*, *24*(2), 101–113. doi:10.1016/j.gfj.2013.07.006

Fauzia, I. Y., & Musari, K. (2021). Waqf crowdfunding for financing the MSMEs: Evidence from ASEAN-3. In P. Ordoñez de Pablos, X. Zhang, & M. N. Almunawar (Eds.), *Handbook of research on disruptive innovation and digital transformation in Asia* (pp. 37–49). IGI Global., doi:10.4018/978-1-7998-6477-6.ch003

Ferraro, G. P. (2021). *The cultural dimension of international business*. Prentice-Hall.

Figge, F., & Hahn, T. (2004). Sustainable value added-measuring corporate contributions to sustainability beyond eco-efficiency. *Ecological Economics, 48*(2), 173–187. doi:10.1016/j.ecolecon.2003.08.005

Finger, M., Gavious, I., & Manos, R. (2018). Environmental risk management and financial performance in the banking industry: A cross-country comparison. *Journal of International Financial Markets, Institutions and Money, 52*(C), 240–261. doi:10.1016/j.intfin.2017.09.019

Fink, A. (2010). *Conducting research literature reviews*. Sage.

Fiske, A., Henningsen, P., & Buyx, A. (2019). Your robot therapist will see you now: Ethical implications of embodied artificial intelligence in psychiatry, psychology, and psychotherapy. *Journal of Medical Internet Research, 21*(5), e13216. Advance online publication. doi:10.2196/13216 PMID:31094356

Flanagin, A. J. (2000). Social pressures on organizational website adoption. *Human Communication Research, 26*(4), 618–646. doi:10.1111/j.1468-2958.2000.tb00771.x

Flavián, C. & Guinalíu, M. (2006). Consumer trust, perceived security and privacy policy. *Industrial Management & Data Systems, 106*(5), 601–620. . doi:10.1108/02635570610666403

Flavian, C., Guinaliu, M., & Lu, Y. (2020). Mobile payments adoption – introducing mindfulness to better understand consumer behavior. *International Journal of Bank Marketing, 38*(7), 1575–1599. doi:10.1108/IJBM-01-2020-0039

Fletcher, R. (2015). Focus On Festivals: Contemporary European case studies and perspectives. Goodfellow.

Fombrun, C. J. (1996). *Reputation: Realizing Value from the Corporate Image*. Harvard University Press.

Fonseca, R., Michaud, P. C., Galama, T., & Kapteyn, A. (2021). Accounting for the rise of health spending and longevity. *Journal of the European Economic Association, 19*(1), 536–579. doi:10.1093/jeea/jvaa003 PMID:33679266

Foreman, S. (1997). IC and the healthy organization. In E. Scholes (Ed.), *Gower Handbook of Internal Communication*. Gower.

Forrester Consulting. (2014, August). *The creative dividend: How creativity impacts business results*. https://landing.adobe.com/dam/downloads/whitepapers/55563.en.creative-dividends.pdf

Frecè, J. T., & Harder, D. L. (2018). Organisations beyond Brundtland: A definition of corporate sustainability based on corporate values. *Journal of Sustainable Development, 11*(5), 184–193. doi:10.5539/jsd.v11n5p184

Friesz, T., Kwon, C., & Bernstein, D. (2008). Analytical dynamic traffic assignment models. In D. A. Hensher & K. J. Button (Eds.), *Handbook of transport modelling* (Vol. 1). Elsevier Science.

Fukey, L., Issac, S., Balasubramanian, K., & Jaykumar, V. (2014). Service Delivery Quality Improvement Models: A Review. *Procedia. Social and Behavioral Sciences, 144*, 343–359.

Gadre, M., & Deoskar, A. (2020). Industry 4.0 – Digital Transformation, Challenges and Benefits. *International Journal of Future Generation Communication and Networking., 13*(2), 139–149.

Galea-Pace, S. (2020, July 6). *What is a Digital Workforce?* Manufacturing Global. Retrieved September 30, 2021, from https://manufacturingglobal.com/technology/what-digital-workforce

Ganesan, K., Choudhury, P., Palakshappa, R., Jain, R., & Raje, S. (2014). *Assessing Green Industrial Policy: The India Experience*. Academic Press.

Gao, Y., Tsai, S. B., Xue, X., Ren, T., Du, X., Chen, Q., & Wang, J. (2018). An empirical study on green innovation efficiency in the green institutional environment. *Sustainability, 10*(3), 724. doi:10.3390u10030724

Garanti & PwC. (2017). Capital projects and infrastructure spending in Turkey. Garanti BBVA Group and PwC.

García Vaquero, M., Sánchez-Bayón, A., & Lominchar, J. (2021). European Green Deal and Recovery Plan: Green Jobs, Skills and Wellbeing Economics in Spain. *Energies, 14*(14), 4145. doi:10.3390/en14144145

Garnier, M., & Poncin, I. (2013). The avatar in marketing: Synthesis, integrative framework and perspectives. *Recherche et Applications en Marketing, 28*(1), 85–115. doi:10.1177/2051570713478335

Geerdts, M., Van De Walle, G., & LoBue, V. (2016). Using animals to teach children biology: Exploring the use of biological explanations in children's anthropomorphic storybooks. *Early Education and Development, 27*(8), 1237–1249. doi:10.1080/10409289.2016.1174052

General Electric (GE). (2009). *Co Jen – GE Energy - Jenbacher Gas Engines*. https://www.gepower.com/prod_serv/products/recip_engines/en/cojen_issue_2009_en/GE_CoJen.pdf

General Electric (GE). (2010). *Now You Can Have It All – More Innovation, Power & Efficiency – J920*. Author.

Geng, Y., & Doberstein, B. (2008). Developing the circular economy in China: Challenges and opportunities for achieving leapfrog development. *International Journal of Sustainable Development and World Ecology, 15*(3), 231–239. doi:10.3843/SusDev.15.3:6

Geng, Y., Fu, J., Sarkis, J., & Xue, B. (2012). Towards a national circular economy indicator system in China: An evaluation and critical analysis. *Journal of Cleaner Production, 23*(1), 216–224. doi:10.1016/j.jclepro.2011.07.005

Geng, Y., Xue, Z., Dong, H., Fujita, T., & Chiu, A. (2014). Emergy-based assessment on industrial symbiosis: A case of Shenyang economic and technological development zone. *Environmental Science and Pollution Research International, 21*(23), 13572–13587. doi:10.100711356-014-3287-8 PMID:25023655

Geng, Y., Zhang, P., Cote, P., & Qi, Y. (2008). Evaluating the applicability of the Chinese eco-industrial park standard in two industrial zones. *International Journal of Sustainable Development and World Ecology, 15*(6), 543–552. doi:10.1080/13504500809469850

Ghalandari, K. (2012). The Effect of Performance Expectancy, Effort Expectancy, Social Influence and Facilitating Conditions on Acceptance of E-Banking Services in Iran: The Moderating Role of Age and Gender. *Middle East Journal of Scientific Research, 12*(6), 801–807. doi:10.5829/idosi.mejsr.2012.12.6.2536

Gheorghiu, G. (2020, May 15). *How will the Fourth Industrial Revolution Impact Remote Work?* https://www.g2.com/articles/fourth-industrial-revolution-impact-on-remote-work

Giachanou, A., & Crestani, F. (2016). Like it or not: A survey of twitter sentiment analysis methods. *ACM Computing Surveys, 49*(28), 21–41.

Giger, J.-C., Piçarra, N., Alves-Oliveira, P., Oliveira, R., & Arriaga, P. (2019). Humanization of robots: Is it really such a good idea? *Human Behavior and Emerging Technologies, 1*(2), 111–123. doi:10.1002/hbe2.147

Glanemann, N., Willner, S. N., & Levermann, A. (2020). Paris Climate Agreement passes the cost-benefit test. *Nature Communications, 11*(1), 1–11. doi:10.103841467-019-13961-1 PMID:31988294

Glover, J., & Friedman, H. L. (2015). *Transcultural competence: Navigating cultural differences in the global community.* American Psychological Association. doi:10.1037/14596-000

Gogoi, L. (2013). Degradation of Natural Resources and its Impact on Environment: A Study in Guwahati City, Assam, India. International Journal of Scientific and Research Publications, 3(12).

Gohlke, J. M., Thomas, R., Woodward, A., Campbell-Lendrum, D., Prüss-Üstün, A., Hales, S., & Portier, C. J. (2011). Estimating the global public health implications of electricity and coal consumption. *Environmental Health Perspectives, 119*(6), 821–826. doi:10.1289/ehp.1002241 PMID:21339091

Gölzer, P., & Fritzsche, A. (2017). Data-driven operations management: Organisational implications of the digital transformation in industrial practice. *Production Planning and Control, 28*(16), 1332–1343. doi:10.1080/09537287.2017.1375148

Goman, C. K. (1994). *Managing in a global organization: Keys to success in a changing world.* Thomson Crisp Learning.

Gomez, T., Gemar, G., Molinos-Senante, M., Sala-Garrido, R., & Caballero, R. (2018). Measuring the eco-efficiency of wastewater treatment plants under data uncertainty. *Journal of Environmental Management, 226,* 484–492. doi:10.1016/j.jenvman.2018.08.067 PMID:30145504

Gomez, V., Maria, A., & Gonzalez-Perez, M. A. (2021). *Digital Transformation as a Strategy to Reach Sustainability.* Smart and Sustainable Built Environment.

Gopinath, D. (2016). Why a Clearer Green Industrial Policy Matters for India: t Reconciling Growth, Climate Change and Inequality. *Local Economy: The Journal of the Local Economy Policy Unit, 31*(8), 830-835.

Górka, K., & Łuszczyk, M. (2014). "Green economy" and the knowledge-based economy and sustainable development. *Optimum. Economic Studies, 3*(69), 22–31.

Gorla, N. (2011). An assessment of information systems service quality using SERVQUAL+. *ACM SIGMIS Database: the DATABASE for Advances in Information Systems, 42*(3), 46–70. doi:10.1145/2038056.2038060

Goudey, A., & Bonnin, G. (2016). Must smart objects look human? Study of the impact of anthropomorphism on the acceptance of companion robots. *Recherche et Applications en Marketing, 31*(2), 1–20. doi:10.1177/2051570716643961

Government of India (GoI). (2015). *India's Trillion Dollar Digital Opportunity.* Ministry of Electronic and Information Technology. Retrieved on 25th November, 2021 from: https://www.digitalindia.gov.in/ebook/MeitY_TrillionDollarDigitalEconomy.pdf

Government of India. (2015). *Green Growth and Sustainable Development in India. Towards the 2030 Development Agenda. Summary for Policymakers.* The Energy and Resource Institute & Global Green Growth Institute.

Govindaraju, C. (2020). Measuring and benchmarking of policy factors influencing I4R: A reality check for ASEAN. In V. Anbumozhi, K. Ramanathan, & H. Wyes (Eds.), Assessing the readiness for industry 4.0 and the circular economy (pp. 108-147). Jakarta: Economic Research Institute for ASEAN and East Asia (ERIA).

Grant Thorton (GT). (2020). *Financial Inclusion in Rural India: Banking and ATM Sector in India.* Retrieved on 11th March, 2022 from: https://www.grantthorton.in/insights/articles

Greene, J. C., Caracelli, V. J., & Graham, W. F. (1989). Toward a Conceptual Framework for Mixed-Method Evaluation Designs. *Educational Evaluation and Policy Analysis, 11*(3), 255–274. doi:10.3102/01623737011003255

Greenpeace. (2005). *Recycling of Electronic Wastes in China & India: Workplace & Environmental Contamination.* Greenpeace International.

Gretzel, U., Yoo, K. H., & Purifoy, M. (2007). Online travel reviews study: Role and impact of online travel reviews. *A&M University, Texas: Laboratory for Intelligent Systems in Tourism.* Retrieved April 2, 2015 from http://195.130.87.21:8080/dspace/bitstream/123456789/877/1/Online%20travel%20review%20study%20role%20and%20impact%20of%20online%20.pdf

Griffith, D. A. (1998). Cultural meaning of retail institutions: A tradition-based culture examination. *Journal of Global Marketing, 12*(1), 47–59. doi:10.1300/J042v12n01_04

Griffiths, M. A., Perera, B. Y., & Albinsson, P. A. (2019). Contrived surplus and negative externalities in the sharing economy. *Journal of Marketing Theory and Practice, 27*(4), 445–463. doi:10.1080/10696679.2019.1644957

Griol, D., & Callejas, Z. (2013). An architecture to develop multimodal educative applications with Chatbots. *International Journal of Advanced Robotic Systems, 10*(3), 1–15. doi:10.5772/55791

Grohmann, B., Giese, J. L., & Parkman, I. D. (2013). Using type font characteristics to communicate brand personality of new brands. *Journal of Brand Management, 20*(5), 389–403. doi:10.1057/bm.2012.23

Gronroos, C. (1983). *The internal marketing function, strategic management and marketing in the service sector.* Marketing Science Institutes, Cambridge Report, 83-104.

Gronroos, C. (1987). Developing the service offering: a source of competitive advantage. In C. Susprenant (Ed.), *Add Value to Your Services* (p. 83). American Marketing Association.

Gronroos, C. (2011). Value Co-creation in Service Logic: A Critical Analysis. *Marketing Theory, 11*(3), 279–301.

GSMA. (2019). *Data Privacy Frameworks in MENA: Emerging Approaches and Common Principles.* GSMA.

Gu, Z., Liu, Z., Cheng, Q., & Saberi, M. (n.d.). Congestion pricing practices and public acceptance: a review of evidence. *Case Studies on Transport Policy, 6*(1), 94-101.

Guang, T., & Trotter, D. (2012). Key issues in cross-cultural business communication: Anthropological approaches to international business. *African Journal of Business Management, 6*(22), 6456–6464.

Guido, G., & Peluso, A. M. (2015). Brand anthropomorphism: Conceptualization, measurement, and impact on brand personality and loyalty. *Journal of Brand Management, 22*(1), 1–19. doi:10.1057/bm.2014.40

Guiltinand, J.P. & Donnelly, J.H. (1983). The use of product portfolio analysis in bank marketing planning. *Management Issues for Financial Institutions*, 50.

GulatiM. (2009). Industrial Pollution, Environmental Degradation and Disasters – Leveraging the Industry – Community. SSRN. doi:10.2139/ssrn.1531591

Gulz, A., & Haake, M. (2006). Design of animated pedagogical agents - A look at their look. *International Journal of Human-Computer Studies, 64*(4), 322–339. doi:10.1016/j.ijhcs.2005.08.006

Guoyou, Q., Saixing, Z., Chiming, T., Haitao, Y., & Hailiang, Z. (2013). Stakeholders' influences on corporate green innovation strategy: A case study of manufacturing firms in China. *Corporate Social Responsibility and Environmental Management, 20*(1), 1–14. doi:10.1002/csr.283

Gupta, K. K., Aneja, K. R., & Rana, D. (2016). Current Status of Cow Dung as a Bioresource for Sustainable Development. *Bioresources and Bioprocessing, 3*(1), 1–12. doi:10.118640643-016-0105-9

Gupta, K., & Arora, N. (2019). Investigating consumer intention to accept mobile payment systems through unified theory of acceptance model. *South Asian Journal of Business Studies, 9*(1), 88–114. doi:10.1108/SAJBS-03-2019-0037

Gupta, R., & Jain, K. (2019). The impact of anthropomorphism on purchase intention of smartphones: A study of young Indian consumers. *Indian Journal of Marketing*, *49*(5), 7–20. doi:10.17010/ijom/2019/v49/i5/144021

Gupta, V., & Thomas, A. (2019). Fostering tacit knowledge sharing and innovative work behaviour: An integrated theoretical view. *International Journal of Managerial and Financial Accounting*, *11*(3-4), 320–346. doi:10.1504/IJMFA.2019.104134

Gürses, D., Sarıoglu-Buke, A., Baskan, M., & Kılıc, I. (2003). Cost factors in pediatric trauma. *Canadian Journal of Surgery*, *46*(6), 441–445. PMID:14680351

Gursoy, D., Chi, O. H., Lu, L., & Nunkoo, R. (2019). Consumers acceptance of artificially intelligent (AI) device use in service delivery. *International Journal of Information Management*, *49*, 157–169. doi:10.1016/j.ijinfomgt.2019.03.008

Habibullah, M. S., Cheah, C. K., & Baharom, A. H. (2011). Budget deficits and inflation in thirteen asian developing countries. *International Journal of Business and Social Science*, *2*(9), 192-204.

Haeffner, M., & Panuwatwanich, K. (2017). Perceived impacts of industry 4.0 on manufacturing industry and its workforce: the case of Germany. In *International Conference on Engineering, Project, and Product Management*. Springer International Publishing. 10.1007/978-3-319-74123-9_21

Hagedorn, T., & Sieg, G. (2019). Emissions and external environmental costs from the perspective of differing travel purposes. *Sustainability*, *11*(24), 7233. doi:10.3390u11247233

Hair, J. F. Jr, Hult, G. T. M., Ringle, C. M., & Sarstedt, M. (2021). *A primer on partial least squares structural equation modeling (PLS-SEM)* (3rd ed.). SAGE Publications, Inc. doi:10.1007/978-3-030-80519-7

Hair, J. F. Jr, Sarstedt, M., Ringle, C. M., & Gudergan, S. P. (2018). *Advanced Issues in Partial Least Squares Structural Equation Modeling*. SAGE Publications, Inc.

Hair, J. F., Ringle, C. M., & Sarstedt, M. (2011). PLS-SEM: Indeed a Silver Bullet. *Journal of Marketing Theory and Practice*, *19*(2), 139–152. doi:10.2753/MTP1069-6679190202

Hair, J. F., Risher, J. J., Sarstedt, M., & Ringle, C. M. (2019). When to use and how to report the results of PLS-SEM. *European Business Review*, *31*(1), 2–24. doi:10.1108/EBR-11-2018-0203

Hair, J. F., Sarstedt, M., Ringle, C. M., & Mena, J. A. (2012). An assessment of the use of partial least squares structural equation modeling in marketing research. *Journal of the Academy of Marketing Science*, *40*(3), 414–433. doi:10.100711747-011-0261-6

Haleem, A., Khan, M. I., & Khan, S. (2019). Halal certification, the inadequacy of its adoption, modelling and strategising the efforts. *Journal of Islamic Marketing*, *11*(2), 384–404. doi:10.1108/JIMA-05-2017-0062

Hallsworth, M. (2012). How Complexity Economic Can Improve Government: Rethinking Policy Actors, Institutions and Structures. In *Complex New World: Translating New Economic Thinking into Public Policy* (pp. 39–49). Institute for Public Policy Research.

Hammer, M. S., Swinburn, T. K., & Neitzel, R. L. (2014). Environmental noise pollution in the United States: Developing an effective public health response. *Environmental Health Perspectives*, *122*(2), 115–119. doi:10.1289/ehp.1307272 PMID:24311120

Handarkho, Y. D. (2020). Impact of social experience on customer purchase decision in the social commerce context. *Journal of Systems and Information Technology*, *22*(1), 47–71. doi:10.1108/JSIT-05-2019-0088

Hand, D. (1998). Footix: The history behind a modern mascot. *French Cultural Studies*, *9*(26), 239–247. doi:10.1177/095715589800902607

Han, N. R., Baek, T. H., Yoon, S., & Kim, T. (2019). Is that coffee mug smiling at me? How anthropomorphism impacts the effectiveness of desirability vs. feasibility appeals in sustainability advertising. *Journal of Retailing and Consumer, 51*, 352–361. doi:10.1016/j.jretconser.2019.06.020

Harari, Y. N. (2014). *Sapiens : a brief history of humankind*. Random House.

Harari, Y. N. (2016). *Homo Deus: A brief history of tomorrow*. Random House.

Hariyanto, E. (2020). Potensi dan strategi penerbitan blue sukuk. *Indonesian Treasury Review: Jurnal Perbendaharaan, Keuangan Negara dan Kebijakan Publik, 5*(2), 151-170.

Hart, P. M., & Jha, S. (2015). The variation of consumer anthropomorphism across cultures. *Indian Journal of Marketing, 45*(11), 7–16. doi:10.17010/ijom/2015/v45/i11/81873

Hart, P. M., Jones, S. R., & Royne, M. B. (2013). The human lens: How anthropomorphic reasoning varies by product complexity and enhances personal value. *Journal of Marketing Management, 29*(1-2), 105–121. doi:10.1080/0267257X.2012.759993

Hart, P., & Royne, M. B. (2017). Being human: How anthropomorphic presentations can enhance advertising effectiveness. *Journal of Current Issues and Research in Advertising, 38*(2), 129–145. doi:10.1080/10641734.2017.1291381

Hart, S. L., & Ahuja, G. (1996). Does it pay to be green? An empirical examination of the relationship between emission reduction and firm performance. *Business Strategy and the Environment, 5*(1), 30–37. doi:10.1002/(SICI)1099-0836(199603)5:1<30::AID-BSE38>3.0.CO;2-Q

Harzing, A. W., & Feely, A. J. (2008). The language barrier and its implications for HQ-subsidiary relationships. *Cross Cultural Management, 15*(1), 49–61. doi:10.1108/13527600810848827

Hauschild, M. Z. (2015). Better–but is it good enough? On the need to consider both eco-efficiency and eco-effectiveness to gauge industrial sustainability. *Procedia CIRP, 29*, 1–7. doi:10.1016/j.procir.2015.02.126

Hausman, J. (2012). Contingent valuation: From dubious to hopeless. *The Journal of Economic Perspectives, 26*(4), 43–56. doi:10.1257/jep.26.4.43

Hau, T. D. (1995). A conceptual framework for pricing congestion and road damage. In B. Johansson & L. G. Mattsson (Eds.), *Road pricing: Theory, empirical assessment and policy. Transportation research, economics and policy*. Springer. doi:10.1007/978-94-011-0980-2_4

Hayden, D., & Dills, B. (2015). Smokey the bear should come to the beach: Using mascot to promote marine conservation. *Social Marketing Quarterly, 21*(1), 3–13. doi:10.1177/1524500414558126 PMID:26877714

He, R., & Liu, J. (2010). Barriers of cross cultural communication in multinational organizations: A case study of Swedish company and its subsidiary in China. Halmstad School of Business and Engineering, 1-32.

Healy, M. J., & Beverland, M. B. (2013). Unleashing the animal within: Exploring consumers' zoomorphic identity motives. *Journal of Marketing Management, 29*(1-2), 225–248. doi:10.1080/0267257X.2013.766233

HEATCO (Developing Harmonised European Approaches for Transport Costing and Project Assessment). (2004-2006). *Deliverable 5*. Funded by 6th Framework Programme IER. Available from: http://heatco.ier.uni-stuttgart.de/

Hebden, L., King, L., Kelly, B., Chapman, K., & Innes-Hughes, C. (2011). A menagerie of promotional characters: Promoting food to children through food packaging. *Journal of Nutrition Education and Behavior, 43*(5), 349–355. doi:10.1016/j.jneb.2010.11.006 PMID:21906547

Hellén, K., & Sääksjärvi, M. (2013). Development of a scale measuring childlike anthropomorphism in products. *Journal of Marketing Management, 29*(1-2), 141–157. doi:10.1080/0267257X.2012.759989

Helm, S., Eggert, A., & Garnefeld, I. (2010). Modeling the Impact of Corporate Reputation on Customer Satisfaction and Loyalty Using Partial Least Squares. In *Handbook of Partial Least Squares* (pp. 515–534). Springer Berlin Heidelberg. doi:10.1007/978-3-540-32827-8_23

Henseler, J., Ringle, C. M., & Sarstedt, M. (2015). A new criterion for assessing discriminant validity in variance-based structural equation modelling. *Journal of the Academy of Marketing Science, 43*(1), 115–135. doi:10.100711747-014-0403-8

Hensellek, S. (2020). Digital Leadership: A Framework for Successful Leadership in the Digital Age. *Journal of Media Management and Entrepreneurship, 2*(1), 55–69. doi:10.4018/JMME.2020010104

Herath, H. M. A. K., & Herath, H. M. S. P. (2019). Impact of Green Banking Initiatives on Customer Satisfaction: A Conceptual Model of Customer Satisfaction on Green Banking Impact of Green Banking Initiatives on Customer Satisfaction: A Conceptual Model of Customer Satisfaction on Green Banking. *IOSR Journal of Business and Management, 21*(1), 24–35. doi:10.9790/487X-2101032435

Hertwich, E. (2005). Consumption and the rebound effect-An industrial ecology perspective. *Journal of Industrial Ecology, 9*(1-2), 85–98. doi:10.1162/1088198054084635

Hess, T., Matt, C., Benlian, A., & Wiesböck, F. (2020). Options for formulating a digital transformation strategy. In *Strategic Information Management* (pp. 151–173). Routledge. doi:10.4324/9780429286797-7

Hidayat, S. E., & Musari, K. (2022). ASEAN towards a global halal logistics through the digitally-enabled community. *International Journal of Asian Business and Information Management, 13*(2), 1–15. doi:10.4018/IJABIM.20220701.oa1

Hill, J., Ford, W. R., & Farreras, I. G. (2015). Real conversations with artificial intelligence: A comparison between human–human online conversations and human–chatbot conversations. *Computers in Human Behavior, 49*, 245–250. doi:10.1016/j.chb.2015.02.026

Hlee, S., Lee, J., Yang, S. B., & Koo, C. (2016). An Empirical Examination of Online Restaurant Reviews (Yelp. com): Moderating Roles of Restaurant Type and Self-image Disclosure. In *Information and Communication Technologies in Tourism* (pp. 339–353). Springer.

Hoffmann, E. (2007). Consumer integration in sustainable product development. *Journal of Production Innovation Management, 16*(5), 332-338.

Hofstede, G., Hofstede, G. J., & Minkov, M. (2010). *Cultures and organizations: Software of the mind. Revised and Expanded* (3rd ed.). McGraw-Hill.

Hogarty, S. (2021, September 7). *What is flexibility in the workplace?* Ideas. Retrieved October 25, 2021, from https://www.wework.com/ideas/professional-development/management-leadership/flexibility-in-the-workplace

Hohenberger, C., & Grohs, R. (2020). Old and exciting? Sport sponsorship effects on brand age and brand personality. *Sport Management Review, 23*(3), 469–481. doi:10.1016/j.smr.2019.05.002

Holliday, C. (2016). 'I'm not a real boy, I'm a puppet': Computer-animated films and anthropomorphic subjectivity. *Animation, 11*(3), 246–262. doi:10.1177/1746847716661456

Holtbrügge, D., Weldon, A., & Rogers, H. (2013). Cultural determinants of email communication styles. *International Journal of Cross Cultural Management, 13*(1), 89–110. doi:10.1177/1470595812452638

Hood, C. (2017). *Input to the high-level commission on carbon prices. Background paper for the Commission.* EC.

Hornsey, R. (2018). "The penguins are coming": Brand mascots and utopian mass consumption in interwar Britain. *The Journal of British Studies, 57*(4), 812–839. doi:10.1017/jbr.2018.116

Hosany, S., Prayag, G., Martin, D., & Lee, W.-Y. (2013). Theory and strategies of anthropomorphic brand characters from Peter Rabbit, Mickey Mouse, and Ronald McDonald, to Hello Kitty. *Journal of Marketing Management, 29*(1-2), 48–68. doi:10.1080/0267257X.2013.764346

Huang, S. Y., Ting, C. W., & Li, M. W. (2021). The effects of green transformational leadership on adoption of environmentally proactive strategies: The mediating role of green engagement. *Sustainability, 13*(6), 3366. doi:10.3390u13063366

Hudek, H., Zganec, K., & Pusch, M. T. (2020). A Review of Hydro-power Dams in South-East Europe- Distribution, Trends and Availability of Monitoring Data using the example of a Multinational Danube Catchment Subarea. *Renewable & Sustainable Energy Reviews, 117*, 1–11. doi:10.1016/j.rser.2019.109434

Hudson, S., Huang, L., Roth, M. S., & Madden, T. J. (2016). The influence of social media interactions on consumer–brand relationships: A three-country study of brand perceptions and marketing behaviors. *International Journal of Research in Marketing, 33*(1), 27–41. doi:10.1016/j.ijresmar.2015.06.004

Hultén, B. (2015). *Sensory Marketing: Theoretical and Empirical Grounds*. Routledge. doi:10.4324/9781315690681

Hu, Z., Ding, S., Li, S., Chen, L., & Yang, S. (2019). Adoption Intention of Fintech Services for Bank Users: An Empirical Examination with an Extended Technology Acceptance Model. *Symmetry, 11*(3), 340. doi:10.3390ym11030340

IAMAI. (2017). *Index of Internet Readiness of Indian States*. Retrieved from: https://cms.iamai.in/Content/ResearchPapers/59923bed-ad4f-439b-b6d9-487fbbc16103.pdf

Iansiti, M., & Lakhani, K. R. (2014). Digital ubiquity: How connections, sensors, and data are revolutionizing business. *Harvard Business Review, 92*(11), 19.

IBB. (2011). *İstanbul Metropoliten Alanı kentsel ulaşım ana planı (IUAP) (Istanbul Metropolitan Region urban transportation plan)*. IBB Ulaşım Daire Başkanlığı-Ulaşım Planlama Mudurlugu.

IBB-Istanbul Buyuksehir Belediyesi. (2016). *İstanbul ulaşım ver hareketlilik raporu (Istanbul transporation and mobility report)*. IBB Ulaşım Daire Başkanlığı.

Ibe-enwo, G., Igbudu, N., Garanti, Z., & Popoola, T. (2019). Assessing the Relevance of Green Banking Practice on Bank Loyalty: The Mediating Effect of Green Image and Bank Trust. *Sustainability, 11*(17), 4651. doi:10.3390u11174651

IBM 2010 Global CEO Study: Creativity Selected as Most Crucial Factor for Future Success. (2010, May 18). *IBM Newsroom*. Retrieved October 21, 2021, from https://newsroom.ibm.com/2010-05-18-IBM-2010-Global-CEO-Study-Creativity-Selected-as-Most-Crucial-Factor-for-Future-Success

IEA. (2012). *Energy technology perspectives 2012 (ETP 2012)*. Available at: http://www.iea.org/etp/publications/etp2012/

Ikhsan, R. B., & Simarmata, J. (2021). SST-Servqual and customer outcomes in service industry: Mediating the rule of corporate reputation. *Management Science Letters, 11*, 561–576. doi:10.5267/j.msl.2020.9.010

Ilg, P. (2019). How to foster green product innovation in an inert sector. *Journal of Innovation & Knowledge, 4*(2), 129–138. doi:10.1016/j.jik.2017.12.009

IMPACT. (2008). *Handbook on estimation of external costs in the transport sector-Produced within the study Internalisation Measures and Policies for all external Cost of Transport*. IMPACT.

India Voluntary National Review. (2020). *Sustainable Development Goals Knowledge Platform*. Retrieved April 14, 2022, from https://sustainabledevelopment.un.org/memberstates/india

Industry 4.0 and Green Economy: Solutions. (2021b, December 21). *Industry 4.0 and Green Economy: Solutions*. Retrieved July 18, 2022, from https://www.esa-automation.com/en/industry-4-0-and-green-economy-solutions/

Industry Europe. (2019, May 28). *How industry 4.0 is affecting jobs*. Retrieved October 10, 2021, from https://industry-europe.com/how-industry-4-0-is-affecting-jobs/

INFRAS/IWW. (2004). *External costs of transport: Accident, environmental and congestion costs of transport in Western Europe*. INFRAS and IWW.

International Labour Organization (ILO). (n.d.). *What Is a Green Job?* Available online: https://www.ilo.org/global/topics/greenjobs/news/WCMS_220248/lang--en/index.htm

Iqbal, Z., & Mirakhor, A. (2011). An introduction to Islamic finance: Theory and practice (2nd ed.). Singapore: John Wiley & Sons (Asia). doi:10.1002/9781118390474

Iqbal, M., Nisha, N., & Raza, S. A. (2019). Customers' Perceptions of Green Banking: Examining Service Quality Dimensions in Bangladesh. In *Green business: Concepts, methodologies, tools, and applications*. IGI Global. doi:10.4018/978-1-5225-7915-1.ch053

Iqbal, M., Nisha, N., Rifat, A., & Panda, P. (2018). Exploring Client Perceptions and Intentions in Emerging Economies: The Case of Green Banking Technology. *International Journal of Asian Business and Information Management*, 9(3), 14–34. doi:10.4018/IJABIM.2018070102

Iqbal, M., Rifat, A., & Nisha, N. (2021). Evaluating Attractiveness and Perceived Risks. *International Journal of Asian Business and Information Management*, 12(1), 1–23. doi:10.4018/IJABIM.20210101.oa1

IRENA & ACE. (2016). Renewable energy outlook for ASEAN: a REmap analysis. International Renewable Energy Agency (IRENA) Dhabi and ASEAN Centre for Energy (ACE).

Isaksson, R., & Rosvall, M. (2020). Understanding building sustainability–the case of Sweden. *Total Quality Management & Business Excellence*, 1–15. doi:10.1080/14783363.2020.1853520

i-SCOOP. (2021, November 5). *Industry 4.0 and the fourth industrial revolution explained*. Retrieved November 6, 2021, from https://www.i-scoop.eu/industry-4-0/

IsDB. (2021). *Common principles for climate mitigation finance tracking*. Islamic Development Bank (IsDB).

Islam, M.A., Hossain, K.F., Siddiqui, M.H., & Yousuf, S. (2014). Green-Banking Practices in Bangladesh-A Scope to Make Banking Green. *International Finance and Banking*, 1(1), 1-38. . doi:10.5296/ifb.v1i1.5161

Islam, T., Islam, R., Pitafi, A. H., Xiaobei, L., Rehmani, M., Irfan, M., & Mubarak, M. S. (2021). The impact of corporate social responsibility on customer loyalty: The mediating role of corporate reputation, customer satisfaction, and trust. *Sustainable Production and Consumption*, 25, 123–135. doi:10.1016/j.spc.2020.07.019

ISRA. (2010). ISRA conpendium: For islamic finance terms, arabic-english. Kuala Lumpur: International Shari'ah Research Academy for Islamic Finance (ISRA).

ISRA. (2015). *Sistem keuangan Islam: Prinsip & operasi*. Rajawali Pers.

Istanbul'un Oto Ritmi. (2017). *Online report*. https://www.aa.com.tr/tr/ sirkethaberleri/egitim/istanbul-trafik-otoritmi-raporu-aciklandi/660063

Izuagbe, R., Ifijeh, G., Izuagbe-Roland, E. I., Olawoyin, O. R., & Ogiamien, L. O. (2019). Determinants of perceived usefulness of social media in university libraries: Subjective norm, image and voluntariness as indicators. *Journal of Academic Librarianship*, 45(4), 394–405. doi:10.1016/j.acalib.2019.03.006

Jahanshahi, D., Tabibi, Z., & van Wee, B. (2020). Factors influencing the acceptance and use of a bicycle sharing system: Applying an extended Unified Theory of Acceptance and Use of Technology (UTAUT). *Case Studies on Transport Policy, 8*(4), 1212–1223. doi:10.1016/j.cstp.2020.08.002

Jain, N., Thomas, A., Gupta, V., Ossorio, M., & Porcheddu, D. (2022). Stimulating CSR learning collaboration by the mentor universities with digital tools and technologies – An empirical study during the COVID-19 pandemic. *Management Decision*. doi:10.1108/MD-12-2021-1679

Jain, T., & Pareek, C. (2019). Managing Cross-Cultural Diversity: Issues and Challenges. *Global Management Review, 13*(2), 23–32.

Jakob, A., Craig, J. L., & Fisher, G. (2006). Transport cost analysis: A case study of the total costs of private and public transport in Auckland. *Environmental Science & Policy, 9*(1), 55–66. doi:10.1016/j.envsci.2005.09.001

Javaid, M., Haleem, A., Vaishya, R., Bahl, S., Suman, R., & Vaish, A. (2020). Industry 4.0 technologies and their applications in fighting COVID-19 pandemic. *Diabetes & Metabolic Syndrome, 14*(4), 419–422.

Javeria, A., Siddiqui, S. H., Rasheed, R., & Nawaz, M. S. (2019). An Investigation into Role of Leadership Commitment on Implementation of Green Banking: Moderating Influence of Responsible Leadership Characteristics. *Review of Economics and Development Studies, 5*(2), 245–252. doi:10.26710/reads.v5i2.561

Jeacle, I., & Carter, C. (2011). In TripAdvisor we trust: Rankings, calculative regimes and abstract systems. *Accounting, Organizations and Society, 36*(4), 293–309.

Jeyaraj, A., Rottman, J. W., & Lacity, M. C. (2006). A Review of the Predictors, Linkages, and Biases in IT Innovation Adoption Research. *Journal of Information Technology, 21*(1), 1–23. doi:10.1057/palgrave.jit.2000056

Jiang, L., & Kang, J. (2016). Combined acoustical and visual performance of noise barriers in mitigating the environmental impact of motorways. *The Science of the Total Environment, 543*, 52–60. doi:10.1016/j.scitotenv.2015.11.010 PMID:26584069

Ji, D. (2013). Evaluation on China's regional eco-efficiency-based on ecological footprint methodology. *Contemporary Economics and Management, 35*, 57–62.

Jin, S.-A. A. (2010). The effects of incorporating a virtual agent in a computer-aided test designed for stress management education: The mediating role of enjoyment. *Computers in Human Behavior, 26*(3), 443–451. doi:10.1016/j.chb.2009.12.003

Jin, S.-A. A., & Bolebruch, J. (2009). Avatar-based advertising in Second Life - The role of presence and attractiveness of virtual spokespersons. *Journal of Interactive Advertising, 10*(1), 51–60. doi:10.1080/15252019.2009.10722162

Jin, S.-A. A., & Sung, Y. (2010). The roles of spokes-avatars' personalities in brand communication in 3D virtual environments. *Journal of Brand Management, 17*(5), 317–327. doi:10.1057/bm.2009.18

Jochem, P., Doll, C., & Fichtner, W. (2016). External costs of electric vehicles. *Transportation Research Part D, Transport and Environment, 42*, 60–76. doi:10.1016/j.trd.2015.09.022

Jones, R. A. (2017). What makes a robot 'social'? *Social Studies of Science, 47*(4), 556–579. doi:10.1177/0306312717704722 PMID:28466752

Juaidi, A., Montoya, F. G., Gázquez, J. A., & Manzano-Agugliaro, F. (2016). An overview of energy balance compared to sustainable energy in United Arab Emirates. *Renewable & Sustainable Energy Reviews, 55*, 1195–1209. doi:10.1016/j.rser.2015.07.024

Julia, T., & Kassim, S. (2019). Exploring green banking performance of Islamic banks vs conventional banks in Bangladesh based on Maqasid Shariah framework. *Journal of Islamic Marketing*, *11*(3), 729–744. doi:10.1108/JIMA-10-2017-0105

Julia, T., & Kassim, S. (2020). Green Banking. In *Banking and Finance*. IntechOpen. doi:10.5772/intechopen.93294

Kaartemo, V., & Helkkula, A. (2018). A systematic review of artificial intelligence and robots in value co-creation: Current status and future research avenues. *Journal of Creating Values*, *4*(2), 211–228. doi:10.1177/2394964318805625

Kalita, P. (2018). *North East States lag behind in internet and mobile connectivity*. Retrieved from: https://timesofindia. indiatimes.com/city/guwahati/northeast-states-lag-behind-in-internet-mobile-connectivity/articleshow/67168080.cms

Kammerer, D. (2009). The effects of customer benefit and regulation on environmental product innovation.: Empirical evidence from appliance manufacturers in Germany. *Ecological Economics*, *68*(8-9), 2285–2295. doi:10.1016/j.ecolecon.2009.02.016

Kang, S.-H., & Gratch, J. (2014). Exploring users' social responses to computer counseling interviewers' behavior. *Computers in Human Behavior*, *34*, 120–130. doi:10.1016/j.chb.2014.01.006

Kang, S.-K., & Watt, J. H. (2013). The impact of avatar realism and anonymity on effective communication via mobile devices. *Computers in Human Behavior*, *29*(3), 1169–1181. doi:10.1016/j.chb.2012.10.010

Kaplan, A., & Haenlein, M. (2019). Siri, Siri, in my hand: Who's the fairest in the land? On the interpretations, illustrations, and implications of artificial intelligence. *Business Horizons*, *62*(1), 15–25. doi:10.1016/j.bushor.2018.08.004

Kapoor, A., Teo, E. Q., Azhgaliyeva, D., & Liu, Y. (2020). *The viability of green bonds as a financing mechanism for green buildings in ASEAN*. Asian Development Bank Institute (ADBI) Working Paper Series No. 1186.

Kapper, T. (2004). Bringing beauty to account in the environmental impact statement: The contingent valuation of landscape aesthetics. *Environmental Practice*, *6*(4), 296–305. doi:10.1017/S146604660400047X

Karadana, A. G., Metin Aksu, N., Akkaş, M., Akman, C., Üzümcügül, A., & Özmen, M. M. (2013). The epidemiology and costs analysis of patients presented to Emergency Department following traffic accidents. *Medical Science Monitor*, *19*, 1125–1130. doi:10.12659/MSM.889539 PMID:24316815

Karanika, K., & Hogg, M. K. (2020). Self–object relationships in consumers' spontaneous metaphors of anthropomorphism, zoomorphism, and dehumanization. *Journal of Business Research*, *109*, 15–25. doi:10.1016/j.jbusres.2019.10.005

Karimi, J., & Walter, Z. (2015). The role of dynamic capabilities in responding to digital disruption: A factor-based study of the newspaper industry. *Journal of Management Information Systems*, *32*(1), 39–81. doi:10.1080/07421222.2015.1029380

Karimova, G. Z., & Goby, V. P. (2021). The adaptation of anthropomorphism and archetypes for marketing artificial intelligence. *Journal of Consumer Marketing*, *38*(2), 229–238. doi:10.1108/JCM-04-2020-3785

Karim, Z. A., Asri, N. M., & Abdullah, A. H., Antoni, & Yusoff, Z. Z. M. (2006). The relationship between federal government revenue and spending: Empirical evidence from ASEAN-5 countries. *Jurnal Ekonomi Pembangunan*, *11*(2), 91–113.

Karjaluoto, H., Shaikh, A. A., Leppäniemi, M., & Luomala, R. (2019). Examining consumers' usage intention of contactless payment systems. *International Journal of Bank Marketing*, *38*(2), 332–351. doi:10.1108/IJBM-04-2019-0155

Kassarjian, H. H. (1977). Content analysis in consumer research. *The Journal of Consumer Research*, *4*(1), 8–18. doi:10.1086/208674

Kaye, L. (2021, December 6). The circular economy has a critical role in driving climate action. *Triple Pundit*. retrieved from https://www.triplepundit.com/story/2021/circular-economy-climate-action/732521

Keeble, B. R. (1988). The Brundtland report: 'Our common future'. *Medicine and War, 4*(1), 17–25. doi:10.1080/07488008808408783

Keller, W. (2000). Do trade patterns and technology flows affect productivity growth? *The World Bank Economic Review, 14*(1), 17–47. doi:10.1093/wber/14.1.17

Kelman, H.C. (1974). Further Thoughts on the processes of compliance, identification, and internalization. *Perspectives on Social Power*, 125-171.

Kemp, R., & Never, B. (2017). Green Transition, Industrial Policy and Economic Development. *Oxford Review of Economic Policy, 33*(1), 66–84. doi:10.1093/oxrep/grw037

Kenrick, D., Griskevicius, V., Neuberg, S., & Schaller, M. (2010). Renovating the pyramid of needs: Contemporary extensions built upon ancient foundations. *Perspectives on Psychological Science, 5*(3), 292–314. doi:10.1177/1745691610369469

Kesari, B., Soni, R., & Khanuja, R. S. (2014). A review on the need of cross cultural management in multinational corporations. *International Journal of Advanced Research in Management and Social Sciences, 3*(8), 120–127.

Ketron, S., & Naletelich, K. (2019). Victim or beggar? Anthropomorphic messengers and the savior effect in consumer sustainability behavior. *Journal of Business Research, 96*, 73–84. doi:10.1016/j.jbusres.2018.11.004

KFAS. (2021). *Kuwait Corporate Readiness for 4th Industrial Revolution*. Kuwait Foundation for the Advancement of Sciences.

Khan, I. S., Ahmed, M O., & Majava, J. (2021). *Industry 4.0 and Sustainable Development: A Systematic Mapping of Triple Bottom Line, Circular Economy and Sustainable Business Models Perspectives*. Academic Press.

Khan, A., Masrek, M. N., & Mahmood, K. (2019). The relationship of personal innovativeness, quality of digital resources and generic usability with users' satisfaction. *Digital Library Perspectives, 35*(1), 15–30. doi:10.1108/DLP-12-2017-0046

Khan, M. A. (2007). *Islamic economics and finance: A glossary*. Routledge International Studies in Money and Banking.

Khan, M., & Tarique. M. (2015). Industrial Pollution in Indian Industries: A Post Reform Scenario. *Journal of Energy Research and Environmental Technology, 2*(2), 182–187.

Khan, N., Khan, S., Tan, B. C., & Loon, C. H. (2021, February). Driving Digital Competency Model Towards IR 4.0 In Malaysia. *Journal of Physics: Conference Series, 1793*(1), 012049.

Khanna, M. (2020). *Growing Green Business Investments in Asia and the Pacific. Trends and Opportunities*. ADB Sustainable Development Working Paper Series. No.72. Asian Development Bank.

Khan, S. J., Kaur, P., Jabeen, F., & Dhir, A. (2021). Green process innovation: Where we are and where we are going. *Business Strategy and the Environment, 30*(7), 3273–3296. doi:10.1002/bse.2802

Khan, T. (2019). Venture waqf in a circular economy. *ISRA International Journal of Islamic Finance, 11*(2), 187–205. doi:10.1108/IJIF-12-2018-0138

Kiesler, S., Powers, A., Fussell, S. R., & Torrey, C. (2008). Anthropomorphic interactions with a robot and robot-like agent. *Social Cognition, 26*(2), 169–181. doi:10.1521oco.2008.26.2.169

Kim, H.-Y., & McGill, A. L. (2018). Minions for the rich? Financial status changes how consumers see products with anthropomorphic features. *The Journal of Consumer Research, 45*(2), 429–450. doi:10.1093/jcr/ucy006

Kim, S., & Dale, B. (2005). Life cycle assessment of various cropping systems utilized for producing biofuels: Bioethanol and biodiesel. *Biomass and Bioenergy, 29*(6), 426–439. doi:10.1016/j.biombioe.2005.06.004

Kirkpatrick, M. G., Cruz, T. B., Unger, J. B., Herrera, J., Schiff, S., & Allem, J.-P. (2019). Cartoon-based e-cigarette marketing: Associations with susceptibility to use and perceived expectations of use. *Drug and Alcohol Dependence, 201*, 109–114. doi:10.1016/j.drugalcdep.2019.04.018 PMID:31207451

Kivimaa, P. (2007). The determinants of environmental innovation: The impacts of environmental policies on the Nordic pulp, paper and packaging industries. *European Environment, 17*(2), 92–105. doi:10.1002/eet.442

Klassen, R. D., & Whybark, D. C. (1999). The impact of environmental technologies on manufacturing performance. *Academy of Management Journal, 42*(6), 599–615.

Kline, R. (2016). *Mean structures and latent growth models. Principles and Practice of Structural Equation Modeling* (4th ed.). The Guildford Press.

Kloepffer, W. (2008). Life cycles sustainability assessment of products. *The International Journal of Life Cycle Assessment, 13*(2), 89–94. doi:10.1065/lca2008.02.376

Knight, P., Freeman, I., Stuart, S., Griggs, G., & O'Reilly, N. (2014). Semiotic representations of Olympic mascots revisited: Virtual mascots of the games 2006-2012. *International Journal of Event and Festival Management, 5*(1), 74–92. doi:10.1108/IJEFM-03-2012-0010

Ko, H. J., Il Chang, S., & Lee, B. C. (2011). Noise impact assessment by utilising noise map and GIS: A case study in the city of Chungju, Republic of Korea. *Applied Acoustics, 72*(8), 544–550. doi:10.1016/j.apacoust.2010.09.002

Komikado, H., Morikawa, S., Bhatt, A., & Kato, H. (2021). High-speed rail, inter-regional accessibility, and regional innovation: Evidence from Japan. *Technological Forecasting and Social Change, 167*, 120697. doi:10.1016/j.techfore.2021.120697

Korhonen, J., Honkasalo, A., & Seppala, J. (2018). Circular economy: The concepts and limitations. *Ecological Economics, 143*, 37–46. doi:10.1016/j.ecolecon.2017.06.041

Korhonen, P., & Luptacik, M. (2004). Eco-efficiency analysis of power plants: An extension of data envelopment analysis. *European Journal of Operational Research, 154*(2), 437–446. doi:10.1016/S0377-2217(03)00180-2

Koskela, M., & Vehmas, J. (2012). Defining eco-efficiency: A case study on the Finnish forest industry. *Business Strategy and the Environment, 21*(8), 546–566. doi:10.1002/bse.741

Kostav, P., Arun, T., & Annim, S. (2015). Access to Financial Services: The Case of the Mzansi Account of South Africa. *Review of Development Finance, 5*(1), 34–42. doi:10.1016/j.rdf.2015.04.001

Kotler, P., & Armstrong, G. (2018). *Principles of Marketing* (17th ed.). Pearson.

KPMG. (2020). *UAE Banking Perspectives 2020: Adapting for new technologies, regulations and culture*. KPMG.

Kraak, V. I., & Story, M. (2015a). Influence of food companies' brand mascots and entertainment companies' cartoon media characters on children's diet and health: A systematic review and research needs. *Obesity Reviews, 16*(2), 107–126. doi:10.1111/obr.12237 PMID:25516352

Kraak, V. I., & Story, M. (2015b). An accountability evaluation for the industry's responsible use of brand mascots and licensed media characters to market a healthy diet to American children. *Obesity Reviews, 16*(6), 433–453. doi:10.1111/obr.12279 PMID:25875469

Krishna, A. (2012). An integrative review of sensory marketing: Engaging the senses to affect perception, judgment and behavior. *Journal of Consumer Psychology, 22*(3), 332–351. doi:10.1016/j.jcps.2011.08.003

Kumari, R., Jeong, J. Y., Lee, B.-H., Choi, K.-N., & Choi, K. (2019). Topic modelling and social network analysis of publications and patents in humanoid robot technology. *Journal of Information Science*. Advance online publication. doi:10.1177/0165551519887878

Kumar, J. C. R., & Majid, M. A. (2020). Renewable Energy for Sustainable Development in India: Current Status, Future Prospects, Challenges, Employment and Investment Opportunities. *Energy, Sustainability and Society*, *10*(2), 1–36. doi:10.118613705-019-0232-1

Kumar, K. A., Pinto, P., Hawaldar, I. T., & Kumar, B. R. P. (2016). Biogas from Cattle Dung as a Source of Sustainable Energy: A Feasibility Study. *International Journal of Energy Economics and Policy*, *10*(6), 370–375. doi:10.32479/ijeep.10135

Kuosmanen, T., & Kortelainen, M. (2005). Measuring eco-efficiency of production with data envelopment analysis. *Journal of Industrial Ecology*, *9*(4), 59–72. doi:10.1162/108819805775247846

Kwak, H., Puzakova, M., & Rocereto, J. F. (2017). When brand anthropomorphism alters perceptions of justice: The moderating role of self-construal. *International Journal of Research in Marketing*, *34*(4), 851–871. doi:10.1016/j.ijresmar.2017.04.002

Laker, D.R., & Powell, J.L. (2011). The differences between hard and soft skills and their relative impact on training transfer. *Human Resource Development Quarterly*, *22*(1), 111-122. doi:10.1002/hrdq.20063

Laksmidewi, D., & Soelasih, Y. (2019). Anthropomorphic green advertising: How to enhance consumers' environmental concern. *DLSU Business & Economics Review*, *29*(1), 72–84.

Laksmidewi, D., Susianto, H., & Afiff, A. Z. (2017). Anthropomorphism in advertising: The effect of anthropomorphic product demonstration on consumer purchase intention. *Asian Academy of Management Journal*, *22*(1), 1–25. doi:10.21315/aamj2017.22.1.1

Lal, T. (2018). Impact of Financial Inclusion on Poverty Alleviation through Cooperative Banks. *International Journal of Social Economics*, *45*(5), 808–828. doi:10.1108/IJSE-05-2017-0194

Landwehr, J. R., McGill, A. L., & Herrmann, A. (2011). It's got the look: The effect of friendly and aggressive "facial" expressions on product liking and sales. *Journal of Marketing*, *75*(3), 132–146. doi:10.1509/jmkg.75.3.132

Lanier, C. D. Jr, Rader, C. S., & Fowler, A. R. III. (2013). Anthropomorphism, marketing relationships, and consumption worth in the Toy Story trilogy. *Journal of Marketing Management*, *29*(1-2), 26–47. doi:10.1080/0267257X.2013.769020

LaPierre, J. (2019, November 14). *Augmented Reality in the Workplace*. Filament Games. Retrieved October 11, 2021, from https://www.filamentgames.com/blog/augmented-reality-in-the-workplace/

Lara-Rodríguez, J. S., Rojas-Contreras, C., & Oliva, E. J.-D. (2019). Discovering emerging research topics for brand personality: A bibliometric analysis. *Australasian Marketing Journal*, *27*(4), 261–272. doi:10.1016/j.ausmj.2019.06.002

Lau, Y. (2021, January 19). Soft Skills Are Essential To The Future Of Work. *Forbes*. Retrieved October 19, 2021, from https://www.forbes.com/sites/forbeshumanresourcescouncil/2021/01/20/soft-skills-are-essential-to-the-future-of-work/?sh=b19567e13416

Lauring, J., & Klitmøller, A. (2015). Corporate language-based communication avoidance in MNCs: A multi-sited ethnography approach. *Journal of World Business*, *50*(1), 46–55. doi:10.1016/j.jwb.2014.01.005

Lau, W. Y., & Yip, T. M. (2019). The nexus between fiscal deficits and economic growth in ASEAN. *Journal of Southeast Asian Economies*, *36*(1). *Special Issue: ASEAN: Towards Economic Convergence*, *36*(April), 25–36. doi:10.1355/ae36-1d

Leal Filho, W., Manolas, E., & Pace, P. (2015). The future we want. *International Journal of Sustainability in Higher Education, 16*(1), 112–129. doi:10.1108/IJSHE-03-2014-0036

Lee, K. H., & Kim, J. W. (2011). Integrating suppliers into green product innovation development: An empirical case study in the semiconductor industry. *Business Strategy and the Environment, 20*(8), 527–538. doi:10.1002/bse.714

Lee, M. S. (2019). Effects of personal innovativeness on mobile device adoption by older adults in South Korea: The moderation effect of mobile device use experience. *International Journal of Mobile Communications, 17*(6), 682. doi:10.1504/IJMC.2019.102719

Lee, N. R., & Kotler, P. (2020). *Social Marketing: Behavior Change for Social Good.* SAGE.

Lee, S., & Oh, H. (2021). Anthropomorphism and its implications for advertising hotel brands. *Journal of Business Research, 129*, 455–464. doi:10.1016/j.jbusres.2019.09.053

Lee, W. I., Shih, B., & Chung, Y. (2008). The exploration of consumers' behavior in choosing hospital by the application of neural network. *Expert Systems with Applications, 34*(2), 806–816.

Leighty, K. A., Valuska, A. J., Grand, A. P., Bettinger, T. L., Mellen, J. D., Ross, S. R., Boyle, P., & Ogden, J. J. (2015). Impact of visual context on public perceptions of non-human primate performers. *PLoS One, 10*(2), 1–6. doi:10.1371/journal.pone.0118487 PMID:25714101

Lemon, K. N., & Verhoef, P. C. (2016). Understanding customer experience throughout the customer journey. *Journal of Marketing, 80*(6), 69–96. doi:10.1509/jm.15.0420

Letheren, K., Martin, B. A., & Jin, H. S. (2017). Effects of personification and anthropomorphic tendency on destination attitude and travel intentions. *Tourism Management, 62*, 65–75. doi:10.1016/j.tourman.2017.03.020

Levinson, D. (2010). Equity effects of road pricing: A review. *Transport Reviews, 30*(1), 33–57. doi:10.1080/01441640903189304

Lewis, R. (2014). How different cultures understand time. *Business Insider, 1.*

Lieberman, A. (2004). The effect of enforcement of the master settlement agreement on youth exposure to print advertising. *Health Promotion Practice, 5*(3), 66S–74S. doi:10.1177/1524839904265427 PMID:15231099

Lifintsev, D. S., & Canhavilhas, J. (2017). Cross-cultural management: Obstacles to effective cooperation in a multicultural environment. *Scientific Bulletin of Polissya, 2*(2 (10)), 195–202. doi:10.25140/2410-9576-2017-2-2(10)-195-202

Lifintsev, D., & Wellbrock, W. (2019). Cross-cultural communication in the digital age. *Estudos em Comunicação, 1*(28), 93–104.

Li, J., Cai, C., & Zhang, F. (2020). Assessment of ecological efficiency and environmental sustainability of the Minjiang source in China. *Sustainability, 12*(11), 4783. doi:10.3390u12114783

Li, L., Su, F., Zhang, W., & Mao, J. Y. (2018). Digital transformation by SME entrepreneurs: A capability perspective. *Information Systems Journal, 28*(6), 1129–1157. doi:10.1111/isj.12153

Lillie, M., Kark, K., Mossburg, E., & Tweardy, J. (2020). *COVID-19: shaping the future through digital business.* Deloitte Global.

Lillis, M., & Tian, R. (2010). Cultural issues in the business world: An anthropological perspective. *Journal of Social Sciences, 6*(1), 99–112. doi:10.3844/jssp.2010.99.112

Lin, C.-H., & Huang, Y. (2018). How self-construals affect responses to anthropomorphic brands, with a focus on the three-factor relationship between the brand, the gift-giver and the recipient. *Frontiers in Psychology*, *9*(2070), 1–17. doi:10.3389/fpsyg.2018.02070 PMID:30455652

Lindhjem, H., Navrud, S., & Braathen, N. A. (2010). *Valuing lives saved from environmental, transport and health policies: A meta-analysis of stated preference studies*. OECD.

Linguistic Inquiry Word Count. (2022). Available online at https://www.liwc.app/

Link, H., Nash, C., Ricci, A., & Shires, J. (2016). A generalised approach for measuring the marginal social costs of road transport in Europe. *International Journal of Sustainable Transportation*, *10*(2), 105–119. doi:10.1080/15568318.2013.861044

Lin, R. J., Tan, K. H., & Geng, Y. (2013). Market demand, green product innovation, and firm performance: Evidence from Vietnam motorcycle industry. *Journal of Cleaner Production*, *40*, 101–107. doi:10.1016/j.jclepro.2012.01.001

Liu, Y., & Noor, R. (2020). *Energy efficiency in ASEAN: Trends and financing schemes*. Asian Development Bank Institute (ADBI) Working Paper Series No. 1196.

Liu, Y., Sheng, Z., & Azhgaliyeva, D. (2019). *Toward energy security in ASEAN: Impacts of regional integration, renewables, and energy efficiency*. Asian Development Bank Institute (ADBI) Working Paper Series No. 1041.

Liu, C., Henderson, B. H., Wang, D., Yang, X., & Peng, Z.-R. (2016). A land use regression application into assessing spatial variation of intra-urban fine particulate matter ($PM_{2.5}$) and nitrogen dioxide (NO_2) concentrations in city of Shanghai, China. *The Science of the Total Environment*, *565*, 607–615. doi:10.1016/j.scitotenv.2016.03.189 PMID:27203521

Liu, D. Y., Chen, S. W., & Chou, T. C. (2011). Resource fit in digital transformation: Lessons learned from the CBC Bank global e-banking project. *Management Decision*, *49*(10), 1728–1742. doi:10.1108/00251741111183852

Liu, J., Zhao, M., & Wang, Y. (2020). Impacts of government subsidies and environmental regulations on green process innovation: A nonlinear approach. *Technology in Society*, *63*, 101417. doi:10.1016/j.techsoc.2020.101417

Liu, S., Xing, J., Wang, S., Ding, D., Chen, L., & Hao, J. (2020). Revealing the impacts of transboundary pollution on $PM_{2.5}$-related deaths in China. *Environment International*, *134*, 105323. doi:10.1016/j.envint.2019.105323 PMID:31759275

Li, W., Winter, M., Kara, S., & Herrmann, C. (2012). Eco-efficiency of manufacturing processes: A grinding case. *CIRP Annals Manufacturing Technology*, *61*(1), 59–62. doi:10.1016/j.cirp.2012.03.029

Li, W., & Zhao, Y. (2015). Bibliometric analysis of global environmental assessment research in a 20-year period. *Environmental Impact Assessment Review*, *50*, 158–166. doi:10.1016/j.eiar.2014.09.012

Lloyd, S., & Woodside, A. G. (2013). Animals, archetypes, and advertising (A3): The theory and the practice of customer brand symbolism. *Journal of Marketing Management*, *29*(1-2), 5–25. doi:10.1080/0267257X.2013.765498

Loewen, P., & Lee-Whiting, B. (2021). *Automation, AI and COVID-19*. Public Policy Forum, Ottawa, Ontario.

Longacre, M. R., Roback, J., Langeloh, G., Drake, K., & Dalton, M. A. (2015). An entertainment-based approach to promote fruits and vegetables to young children. *Journal of Nutrition Education and Behavior*, *47*(5), 480–483. doi:10.1016/j.jneb.2015.06.007 PMID:26363938

Loo, P., & Leung, R. (2016). A service failure framework of hotels in Taiwan: Adaptation of 7Ps marketing mix elements. *Journal of Vacation Marketing*, *24*(1), 79–100. https://doi.org/10.1177/1356766716682555

Lousley, C. (2015). Narrating a global future: Our common future and the public hearings of the World Commission on Environment and Development. In *Global Ecologies and the Environmental Humanities* (pp. 263–285). Routledge.

Love, I., & Zicchino, L. (2006). Financial development and dynamic investment behavior: Evidence from panel VAR. *The Quarterly Review of Economics and Finance, 46*(2), 190–210. doi:10.1016/j.qref.2005.11.007

Luffarelli, J., Stamatogiannakis, A., & Yang, H. (2019). The visual asymmetry effect: An interplay of logo design and brand personality on brand equity. *JMR, Journal of Marketing Research, 56*(1), 89–103. doi:10.1177/0022243718820548

Lu, J.-L., & Siao, P.-Y. (2019). Determining the antecedents and consequences of the airline brand personality. *Journal of Airline and Airport Management, 9*(1), 1–13. doi:10.3926/jairm.121

Lujja, S., Mohammed, M. O., & Hassan, R. (2018). Islamic banking: An exploratory study of public perception in Uganda. *Journal of Islamic Accounting and Business Research, 9*(3), 336–352. doi:10.1108/JIABR-01-2015-0001

Lu, L., Cai, R., & Gursoy, D. (2019). Developing and validating a service robot integration willingness scale. *International Journal of Hospitality Management, 80*, 36–51. doi:10.1016/j.ijhm.2019.01.005

Luo, X., Tong, S., Fang, Z., & Qu, Z. (2019). Frontiers: Machines vs. humans: The impact of artificial intelligence chatbot disclosure on customer purchases. *Marketing Science, 38*(6), 913–1084. doi:10.1287/mksc.2019.1192

Lutkenhorst, W., Altenburg, T., Pegels, A., & Georgeta, V. (2014). *Green Industrial Policy Managing Transformation under Uncertainty.* Discussion Paper.

MacInnis, D. J., & Folkes, V. S. (2017). Humanizing brands: When brands seem to be like me, part of me, and in a relationship with me. *Journal of Consumer Psychology, 27*(3), 355–374. doi:10.1016/j.jcps.2016.12.003

Mahapatra, R. N., Swain, R., & Pradhan, R. R. (2014). A Synergetic Effect of Vegetative Waste and Cow Dung on Biogas Production. *International Journal of Emerging Technology and Advanced Engineering, 4*(11), 184–190.

Mahyar, H. (2016). Economic growth and life expectancy: The case of Iran. *Studies in Business and Economics, 11*(1), 80–87. doi:10.1515be-2016-0007

Majumdar, S. K., & Marcus, A. A. (2001). Rules versus discretion: The productivity consequences of flexible regulation. *Academy of Management Journal, 44*(1), 170–179.

Malik, G., & Singh, D. (2022). Personality matters: Does an individual's personality affect adoption and continued use of green banking channels? *International Journal of Bank Marketing, 40*(4), 746–772. doi:10.1108/IJBM-04-2021-0133

Manyika, J., Lund, S., Chui, M., Bughin, J., Woetzel, J., Batra, P., Ko, R., & Sanghvi, S. (2021, July 2). *Jobs lost, jobs gained: What the future of work will mean for jobs, skills, and wages.* McKinsey & Company. Retrieved October 10, 2021, from https://www.mckinsey.com/featured-insights/future-of-work/jobs-lost-jobs-gained-what-the-future-of-work-will-mean-for-jobs-skills-and-wages

Marakarkandy, B., Yajnik, N., & Dasgupta, C. (2017). Enabling internet banking adoption. *Journal of Enterprise Information Management, 30*(2), 263–294. doi:10.1108/JEIM-10-2015-0094

Marcus, A., Weinelt, B., & Goutrobe, A. (2015). *Expanding Participation and Boosting Growth: The Infrastructure Needs of the Digital Economy.* Academic Press.

Mardani, A., Streimikiene, D., Balezentis, T., Saman, M., Nor, K., & Khoshnava, M. (2018). Data envelopment analysis in energy and environmental economics; an overview of the state-of-the-art and recent development trends. *Energies, 11*(8), 1–21. doi:10.3390/en11082002

Maresova, P., Soukal, I., Svobodova, L., Hedvicakova, M., Javanmardi, E., Selamat, A., & Krejcar, O. (2018). Consequences of industry 4.0 in business and economics. *Economies, 6*(3), 46.

Marimuthu, M., Khan, H., & Bangash, R. (2021). Is the fiscal deficit of ASEAN alarming? Evidence from fiscal deficit consequences and contribution towards sustainable economic growth. *Sustainability, 13*(18), 10045. doi:10.3390u131810045

Marinaş, M. C., Dinu, M., Socol, A. G., & Socol, C. (2018). Renewable energy consumption and economic growth. Causality relationship in Central and Eastern European countries. *PLoS One, 13*(10), e0202951. doi:10.1371/journal.pone.0202951 PMID:30296307

Marr, B. (2019, April 29). The 10 Vital Skills You Will Need For The Future Of Work. *Forbes.* Retrieved October 20, 2021, from https://www.forbes.com/sites/bernardmarr/2019/04/29/the-10-vital-skills-you-will-need-for-the-future-of-work/?sh=38d50aa33f5b

Marr, B. (2020, December 21). What's Been The Impact Of Covid-19 On The 4th Industrial Revolution? *Forbes.* Retrieved October 21, 2021, from https://www.forbes.com/sites/bernardmarr/2020/12/21/whats-been-the-impact-of-covid-19-on-the-4th-industrial-revolution/?sh=5870b60e5c0d

Martin, B. A.-S., Jin, H. S., Wang, D., Nguyen, H., Zhan, K., & Wang, Y. X. (2020). The influence of consumer anthropomorphism on attitudes towards artificial intelligence trip advisors. *Journal of Hospitality and Tourism Management, 44*, 108–111. doi:10.1016/j.jhtm.2020.06.004

Martins, F., Felgueiras, C., Smitkova, M., & Caetano, N. (2019). Analysis of fossil fuel energy consumption and environmental impacts in European countries. *Energies, 12*(6), 964. doi:10.3390/en12060964

Maruthuvellu, S. G., Salamzadeh, Y., & Richardson, C. (2022). Digital Leadership Competencies in the Malaysian Context: A Study in Manager Levels. In P. Ordóñez de Pablos (Ed.), *Handbook of Research on Developing Circular, Digital, and Green Economies in Asia* (pp. 13–41). IGI Global. doi:10.4018/978-1-7998-8678-5.ch002

Maryam, S. Z., Mehmood, M. S., & Khaliq, C. A. (2019). Factors influencing the community behavioral intention for adoption of Islamic banking. *International Journal of Islamic and Middle Eastern Finance and Management, 12*(4), 586–600. doi:10.1108/IMEFM-07-2017-0179

Maslow, A. H. (1954). *Motivation and Personality.* Harper and Row.

Masukujjaman, M., & Aktar, S. (2014). Green Banking in Bangladesh: A Commitment towards the Global Initiatives. *Journal of Business and Technology (Dhaka), 8*(1–2), 17–40. doi:10.3329/jbt.v8i1-2.18284

Mayeres, I., Ochelen, S., & Proost, S. (1996). The marginal external costs of urban transport. *Transportation Research Part D, Transport and Environment, 1*(2), 111–130. doi:10.1016/S1361-9209(96)00006-5

Mazmanian, M. (2013). Avoiding the trap of constant connectivity: When congruent frames allow for heterogeneous practices. *Academy of Management Journal, 56*(5), 1225–1250.

McClelland, D. (1985). *Human Motivation.* Scott, Foresman and Company.

McGoldrick, P. J., Keeling, K. A., & Beatty, S. F. (2008). A typology of roles for avatars in online retailing. *Journal of Marketing Management, 23*(3-4), 433–461. doi:10.1362/026725708X306176

Mehedi, S., & Kuddus, M. A. (2017). Green Banking: A Case Study on Dutch-bangla Bank Ltd. *Academy of Accounting and Financial Studies Journal, 21*(2), 1–20.

Meitei, M.H. & Singh, H.B. (2020). Coverage and Correlates of Health Insurance in the North Eastern States of India. *Journal of Health Research.* . doi:10.1108/JHR-07-2020-0282

Melander, L. (2018). Customer and supplier collaboration in green product innovation: External and internal capabilities. *Business Strategy and the Environment, 27*(6), 677–693. doi:10.1002/bse.2024

Melo, P. C., & Graham, D. J. (2018). Transport-induced agglomeration effects: Evidence for US metropolitan areas. *Regional Science Policy & Practice*, *10*(1), 37–47. doi:10.1111/rsp3.12116

Mensah, I. K. (2020). Impact of Performance Expectancy, Effort Expectancy, and Citizen Trust on the Adoption of Electronic Voting System in Ghana. *International Journal of Electronic Government Research*, *16*(2), 19–32. doi:10.4018/IJEGR.2020040102

Merhi, M., Hone, K., & Tarhini, A. (2019). A cross-cultural study of the intention to use mobile banking between Lebanese and British consumers: Extending UTAUT2 with security, privacy and trust. *Technology in Society*, *59*, 101151. doi:10.1016/j.techsoc.2019.101151

Mesquita, A., Oliveira, L., & Sequeira, A. (2019, April). The future of the digital workforce: current and future challenges for executive and administrative assistants. In *World Conference on Information Systems and Technologies* (pp. 25-38). Springer.

Mhlanga, D. (2020). Industry 4.0 in Finance: The Impact of Artificial Intelligence (AI) on Digital Financial Inclusion. *International Journal of Financial Studies*, *8*(3), 1–14. doi:10.3390/ijfs8030045

Michanowicz, D. R., Shmool, J. L. C., Tunno, B. J., Tripathy, S., Gillooly, S., Kinnee, E., & Clougherty, J. (2016). A hybrid land use regression/AERMOD model for predicting intra-urban variation in $PM_{2.5}$. *Atmospheric Environment*, *131*, 307–315. doi:10.1016/j.atmosenv.2016.01.045

Miesler, L. (2012). Product choice and anthropomorphic designs: Do consumption goals shape innate preferences for human-like forms? *The Design Journal*, *15*(3), 373–392. doi:10.2752/175630612X13330186684231

Miesler, L., Leder, H., & Herrmann, A. (2011). Isn't it cute: An evolutionary perspective of baby-schema effects in visual product designs. *International Journal of Design*, *5*(3), 17–30.

Mijoska, B. M., Trpkova-Nestorovska, M., & Trenevska, B. K. (2020). Predicting Consumer Intention to Use Mobile Banking Services in North Macedonia. *International Journal of Multidisciplinary in Business and Science*, *6*(10), 5–12.

Miladinov, G. (2020). Socioeconomic development and life expectancy relationship: Evidence from the EU accession candidate countries. *Genus*, *76*(1), 1–20. doi:10.118641118-019-0071-0

Milano, M. (2019). *The digital skills gap is widening fast. Here's how to bridge it.* Https://Www.Weforum.Org/Agenda/2019/03/the-Digital-Skills-Gap-Is-Widening-Fast-Hereshow-to-Bridge-It/

Miles, C., & Ibrahim, Y. (2013). Deconstructing the meerkat: Fabular anthropomorphism, popular culture, and the market. *Journal of Marketing Management*, *29*(15-16), 1862–1880. doi:10.1080/0267257X.2013.803142

Miles, P., Miles, G., & Cannon, A. (2012). Linking servicescape to customer satisfaction: Exploring the role of competitive strategy. *International Journal of Operations & Production Management*, *32*(7), 772–795.

Mimoun, M. S.-B., Poncin, I., & Garnier, M. (2012). Case study—Embodied virtual agents: An analysis on reasons for failure. *Journal of Retailing and Consumer Services*, *19*(6), 605–612. doi:10.1016/j.jretconser.2012.07.006

Minkov, M. (2018). A revision of Hofstede's model of national culture: Old evidence and new data from 56 countries. *Cross Cultural & Strategic Management*, *25*(2), 231–256. doi:10.1108/CCSM-03-2017-0033

Mithas, S., Khuntia, J., & Agarwal, R. (2009). Information technology and life expectancy: A country- level analysis. *ICIS 2009 Proceedings*, 146.

Mizutani, F., Suzuki, Y., & Sakai, H. (2011). Estimation of social costs of transport in Japan. *Urban Studies (Edinburgh, Scotland)*, *48*(16), 3537–3559. doi:10.1177/0042098011399597

Mohamed, E., & Lashine, S. (2003). Accounting knowledge and skills and challenges in a global business environment. *Managerial Finance, 29*(6), 3–16.

Mohanty, A., Misra, M., & Drzal, L. (2002). Sustainable bio-composites from renewable resources: Opportunities and challenges in the green materials world. *Journal of Polymers and the Environment, 10*(1-2), 19–26. doi:10.1023/A:1021013921916

Mohsin, M. I. A. (2012). Waqf-shares: New product to finance old waqf properties. *Banks and Bank Systems, 7*(2), 72–78.

Mondejar, M. E., Avtar, R., Diaz, H. L. B., Dubey, R. K., Esteban, J., Morales, A.G., Hallam, B., Mbungu, N. T., Okolo, C. C., Prasad, A. K., She, Q., & Segura, S. G. (2021). Digitalization to achieve Sustainable Development Goals: Steps towards a Smart Green Planet. *Science of the Total Environment, 794*(10).

Mondini, G. (2019). Sustainability assessment: From brundtland report to sustainable development goals. *Valori e Valutazioni*, (23).

Moon, J. H., Kim, E., Choi, S. M., & Sung, Y. (2013). Keep the social in social media: The role of social interaction in avatar-based virtual shopping. *Journal of Interactive Advertising, 13*(1), 14–26. doi:10.1080/15252019.2013.768051

Moore, L. J. (2003). 'Billy, the sad sperm with no tail': Representations of sperm in children's books. *Sexualities, 6*(3-4), 277–300. doi:10.1177/136346070363002

Moremoholo, T. P., & de Lange, R. W. (2018). Anthropomorphic graphics: How useful are they as an instructional aid to facilitate learning? *The Independent Journal of Teaching and Learning, 13*(2), 67-81.

Mourey, J. A., Olson, J. G., & Yoon, C. (2017). Products as pals: Engaging with anthropomorphic products mitigates the effects of social exclusion. *The Journal of Consumer Research, 44*(2), 414–431. doi:10.1093/jcr/ucx038

Mousas, C., Anastasiou, D., & Spantidi, O. (2018). The effects of appearance and motion of virtual characters on emotional reactivity. *Computers in Human Behavior, 86*, 99–108. doi:10.1016/j.chb.2018.04.036

Mouter, N. (Ed.). (2020). *Standard transport appraisal methods*. Elsevier.

Muehlenbachs, L., Staubli, S., & Chu, Z. (2021). The accident externality from trucking: Evidence from shale gas development. *Regional Science and Urban Economics, 88*, 103630. doi:10.1016/j.regsciurbeco.2020.103630

Mugny, G., Butera, F., Sanchez-Mazas, M. & Pérez, J.A. (1995). Judgements in conflict: The conflict elaboration theory of social influence. *Perception-Evaluation-Interpretation*, 160-168.

Mull, I., Wyss, J., Moon, E., & Lee, S.-E. (2015). An exploratory study of using 3D avatars as online salespeople: The effect of avatar type on credibility, homophily, attractiveness and intention to interact. *Journal of Fashion Marketing and Management, 19*(2), 154–168. doi:10.1108/JFMM-05-2014-0033

Murphy, J., Gretzel, U., & Pesonen, J. (2019). Marketing robot services in hospitality and tourism: The role of anthropomorphism. *Journal of Travel & Tourism Marketing, 36*(7), 784–795. doi:10.1080/10548408.2019.1571983

Murray, H. A. (1938). *Explorations in Personality*. Oxford University Press.

Musari, K. (2020a, January 7). Measuring the opportunities of white sukuk for SDGs. *Bisnis Indonesia*, 2.

Musari, K. (2020b, April 14). Pandemic and catastrophe sukuk. *Bisnis Indonesia*, 2.

Musari, K. (2020c). *Cash waqf linked sukuk, a new blended finance of fiscal instrument for sustainable socio-economic development: Lesson learned from Indonesia*. A paper was presented at 12th International Conference on Islamic Economics and Finance (ICIEF) "Sustainable Development for Real Economy" with hosted by Istanbul Sabahattin Zaim University (IZU) and jointly organized by Islamic Research and Training Institute (IRTI) - Islamic Development Bank (IDB) and International Association of Islamic Economics (IAIE) with the collaboration of Statistical, Economic and Social Research and Training Centre for Islamic Countries (SESRIC) and Hamad Bin Khalifa University, Istanbul, Turkey.

Musari, K. (2021d). *Between esham and cash waqf linked sukuk to fiscal and development sustainability: Comparative analysis*. A paper was presented at Research Center for Islamic Economics (IKAM)'s 9th Islamic Economics Workshop under the theme "Economic Growth and Development in Low Income Countries" in collaboration with Scientific Studies Association (ILEM), Turkish Entrepreneurship and Business Ethics Association (IGIAD), and Istanbul Commerce University.

Musari, K. (2021e). Mencari skema pembiayaan syariah inovatif untuk pembangunan. *Kempalan News*. Retrieved from https://kempalan.com/2021/11/27/mencari-skema-pembiayaan-syariah-inovatif-untuk-pembangunan/

Musari, K. (2021f). *The journey of research to find the taxonomy of domestic/public borrowing in history of Islamic public finance: From sakk, esham, to sukuk*. A presentation material in Sharing Session for Capacity Building of Employee in the Environment of Directorate of Islamic Financing (DPS) Directorate General of Budget Financing and Risk Management (DJPPR) Ministry of Finance (MoF) Republic of Indonesia, Jember-Jakarta. doi:10.13140/RG.2.2.25530.31683

Musari, K. (2022b). *Integrating green sukuk and cash waqf linked sukuk, the blended islamic finance of fiscal instrument in Indonesia: A proposed model for fighting climate change*. International Journal of Islamic Khazanah, 12(2), 133-144. doi: 10.15575/ijik.v12i2.1775010.15575/ijik.v12i2.17750

Musari, K., & Hidayat, S. E. (2021). *The role of green sukuk in maqasid al-shari'a and SDGs: Evidence from Indonesia*. A paper was presented at International Conference on Islamic Finance 2021 – "Sustainability & The Fourth Industrial Revolution, Implications for Islamic Finance and Economy in Post Pandemic Era" held by the Center for Islamic Economics and Finance (CIEF) in the College of Islamic Studies (CIS) at Hamad Bin Khalifa University with the support of the Qatar Financial Centre (QFC) Authority.

Musari, K., & Sayah, F. (2021). *Green financing through green sukuk in the fight against climate change: Lessons from Indonesia*. A paper was presented at the 1st Virtual International Scientific Forum "The Green Economy as A New Development Model to Support the Dimensions of Sustainable Development in Algeria - A Study of Experiences" organized by Université Lounici Ali de Blida 2.

Musari, K., & Zaroni. (2021). Reverse logistics in the age of digital transformation for circular economy and halal logistics through the leadership of Asia. In *Handbook of research on disruptive innovation and digital transformation in Asia* (pp. 83-103). Hershey, PA: IGI Global. . doi:10.4018/978-1-7998-6477-6.ch006

Musari, K. (2021a). Esham, the origin of sukuk for facing the crisis: Historical experience. *Iqtishoduna: Jurnal Ekonomi Islam, 10*(1), 45–58. doi:10.36835/iqtishoduna.v10i1.945

Musari, K. (2021b). Green sukuk, Islamic green financing: A lesson learned from Indonesia. In O. M. Olarewaju & I. O. Ganiyu (Eds.), *Climate change and the sustainable financial sector* (pp. 1–16). IGI Global. doi:10.4018/978-1-7998-7967-1.ch001

Musari, K. (2021c). Circular economy for plastics and digitally-enabled community towards ASEAN halal hub in Asia. In P. Ordóñez de Pablos (Ed.), *Handbook of research on developing circular, digital, and green economies in Asia* (pp. 1–12). IGI Global. doi:10.4018/978-1-7998-8678-5.ch001

Musari, K. (2022a). A comparative study of Islamic fiscal instrument securitization in history to modern ages: Esham, sukuk, cash waqf linked sukuk (CWLS). In Ş. Akkaya & B. Ergüder (Eds.), *Handbook of research on challenges in public economics in the era of globalization* (pp. 397–418). IGI Global. doi:10.4018/978-1-7998-9083-6.ch021

Muzumdar, J. M., Schommer, J. C., Hadsall, R. S., & Huh, J. (2013). Effects of anthropomorphic images and narration styles in promotional messages for generic prescription drugs. *Research in Social & Administrative Pharmacy, 9*(1), 60–79. doi:10.1016/j.sapharm.2012.04.001 PMID:22695216

N. I. T. I. Aayog. (2018). *SDG India Index, Baseline Report, 2018.* Author.

N. I. T. I. Aayog. (2019). *Localising SDG's Early Lessons from India 2019.* Author.

N. I. T. I. Aayog. (2020a). *SDG India index & dashboard 2019-20.* Author.

N. I. T. I. Aayog. (2020b). *India VNR 2020 Decade of Action taking SDGs from Global to Local of NITI Aayog.* Author.

N. I. T. I. Aayog. (2021). *SDG India index and dashboard 2020-21 partnerships in the decade of action. NITI Aayog, GoI, 1-202. OHCHR, Voluntary National Reviews, OHCHR and the 2030 Agenda for Sustainable Development.* Retrieved April 13, 2022, from https://www.ohchr.org/en/sdgs/voluntary-national-reviews

Naci, H., & Baker, T. D. (2008). Productivity losses from road traffic deaths in Turkey. *International Journal of Injury Control and Safety Promotion, 15*(1), 19–24. doi:10.1080/17457300701847648 PMID:18344092

Nair, R., Viswanathan, P. K., & Bastian, B. L. (2021). Reprioritising Sustainable Development Goals in the Post-COVID-19 Global Context: Will a Mandatory Corporate Social Responsibility Regime Help? *Administrative Sciences, 11*(4), 150. doi:10.3390/admsci11040150

Namdeo, A., Goodman, P., Mitchell, G., Hargreaves, A., & Echenique, M. (2019). Land-use, transport and vehicle technology futures: Air pollution assessment of policy combinations for the Cambridge Sub-Region of the UK. *Cities (London, England), 89*, 296–307. doi:10.1016/j.cities.2019.03.004

Nam, H., & Kannan, P. K. (2020). Digital environment in global markets: Cross-cultural implications for evolving customer journeys. *Journal of International Marketing, 28*(1), 28–47. doi:10.1177/1069031X19898767

Nanay, B. (2021). Zoomorphism. *Erkenntnis, 86*(1), 171–186. doi:10.100710670-018-0099-0

Nan, X., Anghelcev, G., Myers, J. R., Sar, S., & Faber, R. (2006). What if a web site can talk? Exploring the persuasive effects of web-based anthropomorphic agents. *Journalism & Mass Communication Quarterly, 83*(3), 615–631. doi:10.1177/107769900608300309

Nash, C. (1997). Transport externalities: Does monetary valuation make sense? In G. de Rus & C. Nash (Eds.), *Recent developments in transport economics.* Asgate Press.

Nash, C. (Ed.). (2015). *Handbook on research methods and applications in transport economics and policy.* Edward Elgar Publishing. doi:10.4337/9780857937933

Nautiyal, T., & Ismail, S. (2019). Financial Inclusion and Economic Growth in India: An Empirical Analysis of Feedback Mechanism. *International Journal of Social Science and Economic Research, 4*(6), 4078–4093.

Naveenan, R. V., Madeswaran, A., & Arun, K. R. (2021). Green Banking Practices In India-The Customer's Perspective. *Academy of Entrepreneurship Journal, 27*(4), 1–19.

Neal, A. G. (1985). Animism and totemism in popular culture. *Journal of Popular Culture, 19*(2), 15–24. doi:10.1111/j.0022-3840.1985.00015.x

NEEDS. (2006). New Energy Externalities Development for Sustainability (NEEDS). Deliverable D4.2: Assessment of biodiversity losses: Econcept AG and ESU-services Zurich.

Nelliyat, P. (2007). *Industrial Growth and Environmental Degradation: A Case Study of Tirupur Textile Cluster*. Development Economics Working Papers. No.22507. East Asian Bureau of Economic Research.

Newbery, D. (1994). The case for a public road authority. *Journal of Transport Economics and Policy, 28*(3), 235–253.

Newton, F. J., Newton, J. D., & Wong, J. (2017). This is your stomach speaking: Anthropomorphized health messages reduce portion size preferences among the powerless. *Journal of Business Research, 75*, 229–239. doi:10.1016/j.jbusres.2016.07.020

Ngoc Duy, P. (2018). Repurchase Intention: The Effect of Service Quality, System Quality, Information Quality, and Customer Satisfaction as Mediating Role: A PLS Approach of M-Commerce Ride Hailing Service in Vietnam. *Marketing and Branding Research, 5*(2), 78–91. doi:10.33844/mbr.2018.60463

Nguyen, N., & Leblanc, G. (2001). Corporate image and corporate reputation in customers' retention decisions in services. *Journal of Retailing and Consumer Services, 8*(4), 227–236. doi:10.1016/S0969-6989(00)00029-1

Nigam, A. K., & Pant, M. K. (2020). *Weighted Sustainable Development Goal Index*. Academic Press.

Nisha, N., Iqbal, M., & Rifat, A. (2020). Green Banking Adoption. *International Journal of Technology and Human Interaction, 16*(2), 69–89. doi:10.4018/IJTHI.2020040106

Nishimura, H. (2019). *Challenges and good practices for the 3R and circular economy in ASEAN and East Asia region*. A material presentation at the 9th Regional 3R Forum on Asia and the Pacific 2019.

Noble, C. H., Bing, M. N., & Bogoviyeva, E. (2013). The effects of brand metaphors as design innovation: A test of congruency hypotheses. *Journal of Product Innovation Management, 30*(S1), 126–141. doi:10.1111/jpim.12067

Nyika, J., Mwema, F., Mahamood, R., Akinlabi, E. & Jen, T. (2021). A five-year scientometric analysis of the environmental effects of 3D printing. *Advances in Materials and Processing Technologies*, 1-10.

Nyika, J. (2020). Climate change situation in Kenya and measures towards adaptive management in the water sector. *International Journal of Environmental Sustainability and Green Technologies, 11*(2), 34–47. doi:10.4018/IJESGT.2020070103

Nyika, J., & Dinka, M. (2022). A scientometric study on quantitative microbial risk assessment in water quality analysis across 6 years (2016-2021). *Journal of Water and Health, 20*(2), 329–343. doi:10.2166/wh.2022.228

O'Connor, B., Balasubramanyan, R., Routledge, B., & Smith, N. (2010). From tweets to polls: Linking text sentiment to public opinion time series. *Fourth international AAAI conference on weblogs and social media*, 122-129.

O'Kane, P., Hargie, O., & Tourish, D. (2004). Communication without frontiers: The impact of technology upon organizations. In D. Tourish & O. Hargie (Eds.), *Key Issues in Organizational Communication* (pp. 74–95). Routledge.

O'Reilly, T. (2005). *What is Web 2.0: Design patterns and business models for the next generation of software*. Retrieved from http://www. oreillynet. com/pub/a/oreilly/tim/news/2005/09/3 0/what-is-web-20. html

Obaidullah, M., & Khan, T. (2008). Islamic microfinance development: Challenges and initiatives. Policy Dialogue Paper No. 2. Jeddah: Islamic Research and Training Institute (IRTI) Islamic Development Bank (IDB).

OECD. (2012). *Mortality risk valuation in environment, health and transport policies*. OECD.

OECD. (2013). *The port and its environment: Methodological approach for economic appraisal*. OECD Publishing.

OECD. (2014). *The costs of air pollution: Health impact of road transport*. OECD.

OECD. (2016). *OECD economic surveys: Turkey 2016*. OECD.

OECD. (2018). *OECD economic surveys: Turkey*. OECD.

OECD. (2019). *OECD environmental performance reviews: Turkey 2019*. OECD.

OECD. (2020). Air and climate: Greenhouse gas emissions from source. OECD Environment Statistics Database.

Oklevik, O., Supphellen, M., & Maehle, N. (2020). Time to retire the concept of brand personality? Extending the critique and introducing a new framework. *Journal of Consumer Behaviour, 19*(3), 211–218. doi:10.1002/cb.1805

Okoro, E. (2013). International Organizations and Operations: An Analysis of Cross-Cultural Communication Effectiveness and Management Orientation. *Journal of Business and Management, 1*(1), 1–13.

Olaleye, S. A., Ukpabi, D., Karjaluoto, H., & Rizomyliotis, I. (2019). Understanding technology diffusion in emerging markets: The case of Chinese mobile devices in Nigeria. *International Journal of Emerging Markets, 14*(5), 731–751. doi:10.1108/IJOEM-01-2018-0055

Onyusheva, I., Thammashote, L., & Thongaim, J. (2020). Urban Business Environment: Managing Cross-Cultural Problems. *The EUrASEANs: Journal on Global Socio-Economic Dynamics, 1*(20), 30–43. doi:10.35678/2539-5645.1(20).2020.30-43

Osabohien, R., Aderemi, T., Akindele, D. B., & Okoh, J. I. (2020). *Carbon Emissions and Life Expectancy in Nigeria*. Academic Press.

Osinski, B. L., Getson, J. M., Bentlage, B., Avery, G., Glas, Z., Esman, L. A., Williams, R. N., & Prokopy, L. S. (2019). What's the draw? Illustrating the impacts of cartoons versus photographs on attitudes and behavioral intentions for wildlife conservation. *Human Dimensions of Wildlife, 24*(3), 231–249. doi:10.1080/10871209.2019.1587649

Özen, E., Genç, E., & Kaya, Z. (2014). Estimation of the costs of traffic accidents in Turkey: An evaluation in terms of the insurance and financial system. *Journal of Yaşar University, 9*(33), 5649–5673. doi:10.19168/jyu.94397

Özgenel, M., & Günay, G. (2017). Congestion pricing implementation in Taksim zone: A stated preference study. *Transportation Research Procedia, 27*, 905–912. doi:10.1016/j.trpro.2017.12.065

Ozili, P. K., & Opene, F. (2021). (Preprint). The role of banks in the circular economy," SSRN. *The Electricity Journal*. Advance online publication. doi:10.2139srn.3778196

Pai, R. R., & Alathur, S. (2019). Determinants of individuals' intention to use mobile health: insights from India. *Transforming Government: People, Process and Policy, 13*(3/4), 306–326. doi:10.1108/TG-04-2019-0027

Parasuraman, A., Zeithaml, V., & Berry, L. (1988). SERVQUAL: A Multiple-Item Scale for Measuring Consumer Perceptions of Service Quality. *Journal of Retailing, 64*(Spring), 12–40.

Parasuraman, A., Zeithaml, V., & Berry, L. (1991, Winter). Refinement and reassessment of the SERVQUAL scale. *Journal of Retailing, 67*(4), 420–450.

Park, N., Jang, K., Cho, S., & Choi, J. (2021). Use of offensive language in human-artificial intelligence chatbot interaction: The effects of ethical ideology, social competence, and perceived humanlikeness. *Computers in Human Behavior, 121*, 106795. Advance online publication. doi:10.1016/j.chb.2021.106795

Park, S. H. (1998). *Industrial Development and Environmental Degradation. A Source Book on the Origins of Global Pollution*. Edward Elgar Publishing.

Patnaik, S., Sen, S., & Mahmoud, M. S. (Eds.). (2020). Smart Village Technology: Concepts and Developments. Springer. doi:10.1007/978-3-030-37794-6

Patsiaouras, G., Fitchett, J., & Saren, M. (2014). Boris Artzybasheff and the art of anthropomorphic marketing in early American consumer culture. *Journal of Marketing Management, 30*(1-2), 117–137. doi:10.1080/0267257X.2013.803141

Patterson, A., Khogeer, Y., & Hodgson, J. (2013). How to create an influential anthropomorphic mascot: Literary musings on marketing, make-believe, and meerkats. *Journal of Marketing Management, 29*(1-2), 69–85. doi:10.1080/0267257X.2012.759992

Pearce, D., Atkinson, G., & Maurato, S. (2006). *Cost-benefit Analysis and the environment: Recent developments*. OECD.

Pelau, C., Dabija, D.-C., & Ene, I. (2021). What makes an AI device human-like? The role of interaction quality, empathy and perceived psychological anthropomorphic characteristics in the acceptance of artificial intelligence in the service industry. *Computers in Human Behavior, 122*, 106855. Advance online publication. doi:10.1016/j.chb.2021.106855

Pereira, R. H. M., Schwanen, T., & Banister, D. (2016). Distributive justice and equity in transportation. *Transport Reviews, 37*(2), 170–191. doi:10.1080/01441647.2016.1257660

Peric, K. (2015). Editorial: Digital Financial Inclusion. *Journal of Payment Strategy and Systems, 9*(3), 212–214.

Perreault, H. (2004). Business educators can take a leadership role in character education. *Business Education Forum, 59*(1), 23–24.

Pesaran, M. H. (2007). A simple panel unit root test in the presence of cross-section dependence. *Journal of Applied Econometrics, 22*(2), 265–312. doi:10.1002/jae.951

Peters, K., & Buijs, P. (2022). Strategic ambidexterity in green product innovation: Obstacles and implications. *Business Strategy and the Environment, 31*(1), 173–193. doi:10.1002/bse.2881

Petropoulos, G. (2021). *Automation, COVID-19, and Labor Markets. ADBI Working Paper 1229.* Asian Development Bank Institute. Available https://www.adb.org/publications/automation-covid-19-and-labor-markets

Petty, R. D., & D'Rozario, D. (2009). The use of dead celebrities in advertising and marketing: Balancing interests in the right of publicity. *Journal of Advertising, 38*(4), 37–49. doi:10.2753/JOA0091-3367380403

Phillips, B. J., Sedgewick, J. R., & Slobodzian, A. D. (2019). Spokes-characters in print advertising: An update and extension. *Journal of Current Issues and Research in Advertising, 40*(2), 214–228. doi:10.1080/10641734.2018.1503110

Picoto, W. N., & Pinto, I. (2021). Cultural impact on mobile banking use – A multi-method approach. *Journal of Business Research, 124*, 620–628. doi:10.1016/j.jbusres.2020.10.024

Pigou, A. C. (1920). *The economics of welfare*. MacMillan and Co.

Pikkarainen, T., Pikkarainen, K., Karjaluoto, H., & Pahnila, S. (2004). Consumer acceptance of online banking: An extension of the technology acceptance model. *Internet Research, 14*(3), 224–235. doi:10.1108/10662240410542652

Pilicherla, K. K., Adapa, V., Ghosh, M., & Ingla, P. (2021). Current Efforts on Sustainable Green Growth in the Manufacturing Sector to Complement "Make in India" for Making "Self-Reliant India. *Environmental Research*. PMID:34695432

Pizzi, S. (2006). Recent developments in eco-efficient bio-based adhesives for wood bonding: Opportunities and issues. *Journal of Adhesion Science and Technology, 20*(8), 829–846. doi:10.1163/156856106777638635

Podsakoff, P. M., MacKenzie, S. B., Lee, J.-Y., & Podsakoff, N. P. (2003). Common method biases in behavioral research: A critical review of the literature and recommended remedies. *The Journal of Applied Psychology, 88*(5), 879–903. doi:10.1037/0021-9010.88.5.879 PMID:14516251

Porter, M. E., & Van der Linde, C. (1995). Toward a new conception of the environment-competitiveness relationship. *The Journal of Economic Perspectives, 9*(4), 97–118. doi:10.1257/jep.9.4.97

Prabhat & Zetterberg. (2009). *Reducing Greenhouse Gas Emission in India. Financial Mechanism and Opportunities for EU-India Collaboration.* Report for Swedish, Mistry of Environment. Stockholm Environment Institute. Project Report.

PricewaterhouseCoopers. (2021, November). *Code Red Asia Pacific's Time To Go Green.* https://www.pwc.com/asiapacific

Prud'homme, R., Koning, M., Lenormand, L., & Fehr, A. (2012). Public transport congestion costs: The case of the Paris subway. *Transport Policy, 21,* 101–109. doi:10.1016/j.tranpol.2011.11.002

Pryn, M. R., Cornet, Y., & Salling, K. B. (2015). Applying sustainability theory to transport infrastructure assessment using a multiplicative AHP decision support model. *Transport, 30*(3), 330–341. doi:10.3846/16484142.2015.1081281

Purcarea, V., Gheorghe, I., & Petrescu, C. (2013). The Assessment of Perceived Service Quality of Public Health Care Services in Romania Using the SERVQUAL Scale. *Procedia Economics and Finance, 6*(2), 573–585.

Purwanto, E., & Loisa, J. (2020). The Intention and Use Behaviour of the Mobile Banking System in Indonesia: UTAUT Model. *Technology Reports of Kansai University, 62*(6), 2757–2767.

Puzakova, M., Kwak, H., & Rocereto, J. (2009). Pushing the envelope of brand and personality: Antecedents and moderators of anthropomorphized brands. *Advances in Consumer Research. Association for Consumer Research (U. S.), 36,* 413–420.

Puzakova, M., Rocereto, J. F., & Kwak, H. (2013). Ads are watching me - A view from the interplay between anthropomorphism and customisation. *International Journal of Advertising, 32*(4), 513–538. doi:10.2501/IJA-32-4-513-538

PwC. (2019). *Data Privacy Landscape.* Author.

Pyrkov, T. V., Avchaciov, K., Tarkhov, A. E., Menshikov, L. I., Gudkov, A. V., & Fedichev, P. O. (2019). Longitudinal analysis of blood markers reveals progressive loss of resilience and predicts ultimate limit of human lifespan. *bioRxiv, 618876.* Advance online publication. doi:10.1101/618876

Qingyu, L., Zhicai, J., Baofeng, S., & Hongfei, J. (2007). Method research on measuring the external costs of urban traffic congestion. *Journal of Transportation Systems Engineering and Information Technology, 7*(5), 9–12. doi:10.1016/S1570-6672(07)60035-X

Qi, T., Zhang, X., & Karplus, V. J. (2014). The energy and CO2 emissions impact of renewable energy development in China. *Energy Policy, 68,* 60–69. doi:10.1016/j.enpol.2013.12.035

Qiu, L., & Benbasat, I. (2009). Evaluating anthropomorphic product recommendation agents: A social relationship perspective to designing information systems. *Journal of Management Information Systems, 25*(4), 145–182. doi:10.2753/MIS0742-1222250405

Qiu, L., & Benbasat, I. (2010). A study of demographic embodiments of product recommendation agents in electronic commerce. *International Journal of Human-Computer Studies, 68*(10), 669–688. doi:10.1016/j.ijhcs.2010.05.005

Qiu, L., Jie, X., Wang, Y., & Zhao, M. (2020). Green product innovation, green dynamic capability, and competitive advantage: Evidence from Chinese manufacturing enterprises. *Corporate Social Responsibility and Environmental Management, 27*(1), 146–165. doi:10.1002/csr.1780

Radler, V. M. (2018). 20 Years of brand personality: A bibliometric review and research agenda. *Journal of Brand Management, 25*(4), 370–383. doi:10.105741262-017-0083-z

Rado, G., & Filkova, M. (2019). *ASEAN green financial instruments guide.* Climate Bonds Initiative, ClimateWorks Foundation.

Ranalder, L., Busch, H., Hansen, T., Brommer, M., Couture, T., Gibb, D., & Sverrisson, F. (2020). *Renewables in Cities 2021 Global Status Report.* Academic Press.

Rao, M. S., Podile, V., & Navvula, D. (2020). Financial Inclusion Index: An Indian Experience. *High Technology Letters, 26*(9), 816–825.

Rasoulinezhad, E., Taghizadeh-Hesary, F., & Taghizadeh-Hesary, F. (2020). How is mortality affected by fossil fuel consumption, CO2 emissions and economic factors in CIS region? *Energies, 13*(9), 2255. doi:10.3390/en13092255

Ratanya, F. C. (2017). Institutional repository: Access and use by academic staff at Egerton University, Kenya. *Library Management, 38*(4/5), 276–284. doi:10.1108/LM-02-2017-0018

Rauschnabel, P. A., & Ahuvia, A. C. (2014). You're so lovable: Anthropomorphism and brand love. *Journal of Brand Management, 21*(5), 372–395. doi:10.1057/bm.2014.14

Ravindra, S. (2019, September 17). *4 Applications of Big Data in HR (With Real-World Examples).* The Kolabtree Blog. Retrieved October 21, 2021, from https://www.kolabtree.com/blog/4-applications-of-big-data-in-hr-with-real-world-examples/

Raza, S. A., Shah, N., & Ali, M. (2019). Acceptance of mobile banking in Islamic banks: Evidence from modified UTAUT model. *Journal of Islamic Marketing, 10*(1), 357–376. doi:10.1108/JIMA-04-2017-0038

RBI. (2014). *Financial Inclusion in India-An Assessment.* Retrieved on 25th November, 2021 from: https://rbidocs.rbi.org.in/rdocs/Speeches/PDFs/MFI101213FS.pdf

Reavey, B., Puzakova, M., Andras, T. L., & Kwak, H. (2018). The multidimensionality of anthropomorphism in advertising: The moderating roles of cognitive busyness and assertive language. *International Journal of Advertising, 37*(3), 440–462. doi:10.1080/02650487.2018.1438054

Recruitment, C. (n.d.). *How Will the Fourth Industrial Revolution Impact the Future of Work? - Change Recruitment.* Https://Www.Changerecruitmentgroup.Com/Knowledge-Centre/How-Will-the-Fourth-Industrial-Revolution-Impact-the-Future-of-Work

Reese, S. (1998). Culture Shock. *Marketing Tools.,* (May), 44–49.

Rehman, A., Ullah, I., Afridi, F. E. A., Ullah, Z., Zeeshan, M., Hussain, A., & Rahman, H. U. (2021). Adoption of green banking practices and environmental performance in Pakistan: A demonstration of structural equation modelling. *Environment, Development and Sustainability, 23*(9), 13200–13220. doi:10.100710668-020-01206-x

Reinhardt, F.L. (1998). Environmental product differentiation: implications for corporate strategy. *California Management Review, 40*(4), 43-73.

Republic of Turkey. (2015). *Intended Nationally Determined Contribution (INDC).* https://www4.unfccc.int/sites/submissions/INDC/Published%20Documents/Turkey/1/The_INDC_of_TURKEY_v.15.19.30.pdf

Resca, A., Za, S., & Spagnoletti, P. (2013). Digital platforms as sources for organizational and strategic transformation: A case study of the Midblue project. *Journal of Theoretical and Applied Electronic Commerce Research, 8*(2), 71–84. doi:10.4067/S0718-18762013000200006

Reserve Bank of India. (2021). *Green Finance in India: Progress and Challenges.* RBI Bulletin.

Rhee, H. T., Yang, S.-B., & Kim, K. (2016). Exploring the comparative salience of restaurant attributes: A conjoint analysis approach. *International Journal of Information Management, 36*, 1360–1370.

Rifat, A., Nisha, N., Iqbal, M., & Suviitawat, A. (2016). The role of commercial banks in green banking adoption: A Bangladesh perspective. *International Journal of Green Economics, 10*(3/4), 226. doi:10.1504/IJGE.2016.081906

Riikkinen, M., Saarijärvi, H., Sarlin, P., & Lähteenmäki, I. (2018). Using artificial intelligence to create value in insurance. *International Journal of Bank Marketing, 36*(6), 1145–1168. doi:10.1108/IJBM-01-2017-0015

Rincon, J. A., Costa, A., Novais, P., Julian, V., & Carrascosa, C. (2018). A new emotional robot assistant that facilitates human interaction and persuasion. *Knowledge and Information Systems, 60*(1), 363–383. doi:10.100710115-018-1231-9

Rizzi, I. L., & De La Maza, C. (2017). The external costs of private versus public road transport in the Metropolitan Area of Santiago, Chile. *Transportation Research Part A, Policy and Practice, 98*, 123–140. doi:10.1016/j.tra.2017.02.002

Robertson, V.-L. D. (2014). Of ponies and men: My little pony: Friendship is magic and the brony fandom. *International Journal of Cultural Studies, 17*(1), 21–27. doi:10.1177/1367877912464368

Robles, M. M. (2012). Executive perceptions of the top 10 soft skills needed in today's workplace. *Business Communication Quarterly, 75*(4), 453–465. doi:10.1177/1080569912460400

Rodriguez, E. G. (2021, August 17). *The Impact of AI on the Workforce.* Conversational AI Platform for Enterprise - Teneo | Artificial Solutions. Retrieved October 26, 2021, from https://www.artificial-solutions.com/blog/impact-of-ai-in-the-workforce

Roemer, K. (2021, May 25). *What the Internet of Things means for the future of work.* Best Practices for Professional Communities and Networking. Retrieved October 11, 2021, from https://guild.co/blog/what-iot-means-for-the-future-of-work/

Rogers, M. (1983). *Diffusion of Innovation* (3rd ed.). The Free Press.

Rogers, M. (1995). *Diffusion of Innovations* (4th ed.). The Free Press.

Roser, M., Ortiz-Ospina, E., & Ritchie, H. (2013). *Life Expectancy.* Retrieved from: https://ourworldindata.org/life-expectancy

Roy, T. (2017). The Origins of Import Substituting Industrialization in India. *Journal of Economic History of Developing Regions, 32*(1), 71–95. doi:10.1080/20780389.2017.1292460

Rüßmann, M., Lorenz, M., Gerbert, P., Waldner, M., Engel, P., Harnisch, M., & Justus, J. (2021, April 12). *Industry 4.0: The Future of Productivity and Growth in Manufacturing Industries.* BCG Global. Retrieved October 15, 2021, from https://www.bcg.com/publications/2015/engineered_products_project_business_industry_4_future_productivity_growth_manufacturing_industries

Saeed, M. R., Burki, U., Ali, R., Dahlstrom, R., & Zameer, H. (2021). The antecedents and consequences of brand personality: A systematic review. *EuroMed Journal of Business.* Advance online publication. doi:10.1108/EMJB-12-2020-0136

Safina, M. S., & Valeev, A. A. (2015). Study of humanitarian high school student's readiness for intercultural communication formation. *Review of European Studies, 7*(5), 52–60. doi:10.5539/res.v7n5p52

Sahoo, B., Singh, A. & Jain, N. (2016). Green Banking In India: Problems And Prospects. *International Journal of Research -Granthaalayah, 4*(8), 92–99. doi:10.5281/zenodo.61169

Saito, K., Kato, T., & Shimane, T. (2010). Traffic congestion and accident externality: A Japan-US comparison. *The B.E. Journal of Economic Analysis & Policy, 10*(1), 1–31. doi:10.2202/1935-1682.2057

Salem, M., Tsurusaki, N., Divigalpitiya, P., Osman, T., Hamdy, O., & Kenawy, E. (2020). Assessing progress towards sustainable development in the urban periphery: A case of greater Cairo, Egypt. *International Journal of Sustainable Development and Planning, 15*(7), 971–982. doi:10.18280/ijsdp.150701

Salih, S., Arman, H., & Al-Qudsi, S. (2018). *An Action Plan for Improving Kuwait's Global Competitiveness Path: An Engine for Transformation into Knowledge Innovation Economy.* Kuwait Institute for Scientific Research.

Sánchez-Torres, J. A., Sandoval, A. V., & Alzate, J.-A. S. (2018). E-banking in Colombia: Factors favouring its acceptance, online trust and government support. *International Journal of Bank Marketing, 36*(1), 170–183. doi:10.1108/IJBM-10-2016-0145

Santos, G. (2017). Road fuel taxes in Europe: Do they internalize road transport externalities? *Transport Policy, 53,* 120–134. doi:10.1016/j.tranpol.2016.09.009

Sarabhai, K. V. (2015). ESD for sustainable development goals (SDGs). *Journal of Education for Sustainable Development, 9*(2), 121–123. doi:10.1177/0973408215600601

Sashittal, H., & Jassawalla, A. (2019). Brand entification as a post-anthropomorphic attribution among Twitter-using Millennials. *Marketing Intelligence & Planning, 37*(7), 741–753. doi:10.1108/MIP-10-2018-0446

Savacool, B. K., Kim, J., & Yang, M. (2021). The hidden costs of energy and mobility: A global meta-analysis and research synthesis of electricity and transport externalities. *Energy Research & Social Science, 72,* 101885. doi:10.1016/j.erss.2020.101885

Sayed, M. N., & Shusha, A. (2019). Determinants of Financial Inclusion in Egypt. *Asian Economic and Financial Review, 9*(12), 1383–1404. doi:10.18488/journal.aefr.2019.912.1383.1404

Schaltegger, S., & Synnestvedt, T. (2002). The link between green and economic success: Environmental management as the crucial trigger between environmental and economic performance. *Journal of Environmental Management, 65*(4), 339–346. PMID:12369398

Scheffran, J., & Battaglini, A. (2010). Climate and conflicts: The security risks of global warming. *Regional Environmental Change, 11*(S1), 27–39. doi:10.100710113-010-0175-8

Schwarzer, J. (2013). *Industrial Policy for a Green Economy. International Institute for Sustainable Development Report.* Trade Investment & Climate Change.

Sebastian, I. M., Ross, J. W., Beath, C., Mocker, M., Moloney, K. G., & Fonstad, N. O. (2020). How big old companies navigate digital transformation. In *Strategic information management* (pp. 133–150). Routledge. doi:10.4324/9780429286797-6

Sekaran, U., & Bougie, R. J. (2019). *Research methods for business: A skill building approach* (8th ed.). Wiley and Sons.

Selvaraj, P., & Ragesh, T. V. (2019). Innovative Approach of Regional Rural Bank in Adopting Technology Banking and Improving Service Quality Leading to Better Digital Banking. *Vinimaya, 39*(1), 22–32.

Şener, İ., Varoğlu, A., & Karapolatgil, A. A. (2016). Sustainability reports disclosures: Who are the most salient stakeholders? *Procedia: Social and Behavioral Sciences, 235,* 84–92. doi:10.1016/j.sbspro.2016.11.028

Sen, K. A., Tiwari, G., & Upadhyay, V. (2010). Estimating marginal external costs of transport in Delhi. *Transport Policy, 17*(1), 27–37. doi:10.1016/j.tranpol.2009.09.003

Sensuse, D. I., Rochman, H. N., Al Hakim, S., & Winarni, W. (2021). Knowledge management system design method with joint application design (JAD) adoption. *VINE Journal of Information and Knowledge Management Systems, 51*(1), 27–46. doi:10.1108/VJIKMS-10-2018-0083

Serrano-García, J., Bikfalvi, A., Llach, J., & Arbeláez-Toro, J. J. (2021). Orchestrating capabilities, organizational dimensions and determinants in the pursuit of green product innovation. *Journal of Cleaner Production, 313*, 127873. doi:10.1016/j.jclepro.2021.127873

Severson, R. L., & Lemm, K. M. (2016). Kids see human too: Adapting an individual differences measure of anthropomorphism for a child sample. *Journal of Cognition and Development, 17*(1), 122–141. doi:10.1080/15248372.2014.989445

Shaari, H., Salleh, S. M., Yong, P. L., Perumal, S., & Zainol, F. A. (2019). Assessing the effect of university brand personality and attitude towards donation on alumni donor behavioural intention: Malaysian perspective. *International Journal of Management Education, 13*(4), 377–396. doi:10.1504/IJMIE.2019.102595

Shachak, A., Kuziemsky, C., & Petersen, C. (2019). Beyond TAM and UTAUT: Future directions for HIT implementation research. *Journal of Biomedical Informatics, 100*, 103315. doi:10.1016/j.jbi.2019.103315 PMID:31629923

Shahbaz, M., Raghutla, C., Chittedi, K. R., Jiao, Z., & Vo, X. V. (2020). The effect of renewable energy consumption on economic growth: Evidence from the renewable energy country attractive index. *Energy, 207*, 118162. doi:10.1016/j.energy.2020.118162

Shah, P., & Dubhashi, M. (2015). Review Paper on Financial Inclusion- The Means of Inclusive Growth. *Chanakya International Journal of Business Research, 1*(1), 37–48. doi:10.15410/cijbr/2015/v1i1/61403

Shahzad, M., Qu, Y., Javed, S. A., Zafar, A. U., & Rehman, S. U. (2020). Relation of environment sustainability to CSR and green innovation: A case of Pakistani manufacturing industry. *Journal of Cleaner Production, 253*, 119938. doi:10.1016/j.jclepro.2019.119938

Shamseer, L., Moher, D., Clarke, M., Ghersi, D., Liberati, A., Petticrew, M., Shekelle, P., & Stewart, L. A. (2015). Preferred reporting items for systematic review and meta-analysis protocols (PRISMA-P) 2015: Elaboration and explanation. *BMJ, 349*. doi:10.1136/bmj.g7647

Shanker, R. (2002). *Services Marketing, The Indian Perspective*. Excel Books.

Sharma, M. (2008). *Index of Financial Inclusion*. Indian Council for Research on International Relations, Working Paper No. 2015. Retrieved on 25th February, 2022 from: http://icrier.org/pdf/Working_Paper_215.pdf

Sharma, G. D., Thomas, A., & Paul, J. (2021). Reviving tourism industry post-COVID-19: A resilience-based framework. *Tourism Management Perspectives, 37*, 100786. doi:10.1016/j.tmp.2020.100786 PMID:33391988

Sharma, N. K. (2015). Industry Initiatives for Green Marketing in India. *Business and Economics Journal, 7*(1). doi:10.4172/2151-6219.1000192

Sharma, S., & Henriques, I. (2005). Stakeholder influences on sustainability practices in the Canadian forest products industry. *Strategic Management Journal, 26*(2), 159–180. doi:10.1002mj.439

Shaumya, S., & Arulrajah, A. (2017). The Impact of Green Banking Practices on Banks Environmental Performance: Evidence from Sri Lanka. *Journal of Finance and Bank Management, 5*(1), 77–90. doi:10.15640/jfbm.v5n1a7

Shea, M. (2014). User-friendly: Anthropomorphic devices and mechanical behaviour in Japan. *Advances in Anthropology, 4*(1), 41–49. doi:10.4236/aa.2014.41006

Shekarrizfard, M., Faghih-Imani, A., Crouse, D. L., Goldberg, M., Ross, N., Eluru, N., & Hatzopoulou, M. (2016). Individual exposure to traffic related air pollution across land-use clusters. *Transportation Research Part D, Transport and Environment, 46*, 339–350. doi:10.1016/j.trd.2016.04.010

Sheldon, R. (2017). The E factor 25 years on: The rise of green chemistry and sustainability. *Green Chemistry, 19*(1), 18–43. doi:10.1039/C6GC02157C

Shen, L., & Zhou, J. (2014). Examining the effectiveness of indicators for guiding sustainable urbanization in China. *Habitat International, 44*, 111–120. doi:10.1016/j.habitatint.2014.05.009

Sherman, G. D., & Haidt, J. (2011). Cuteness and disgust: The humanizing and dehumanizing effects of emotion. *Emotion Review, 3*(3), 245–251. doi:10.1177/1754073911402396

Shmueli, G., Ray, S., Estrada, J. M. V., & Chatla, S. B. (2016). The elephant in the room: Predictive performance of PLS models. *Journal of Business Research, 69*(10), 4552–4564. doi:10.1016/j.jbusres.2016.03.049

Shmueli, G., Sarstedt, M., Hair, J. F., Cheah, J. H., Ting, H., Vaithilingam, S., & Ringle, C. M. (2019). Predictive model assessment in PLS-SEM: Guidelines for using PLSpredict. *European Journal of Marketing, 53*(11), 2322–2347. doi:10.1108/EJM-02-2019-0189

Shofa, J. N. (2021, October 14). ASEAN on a mission towards a sustainable energy future. *Jakarta Globe*. Retrieved from https://jakartaglobe.id/news/asean-on-a-mission-towards-a-sustainable-energy-future

Shulka, P. R., & Dhar, S. (2016). *India's GHG Emission Reduction and Sustainable Development. Enabling Asia Stabilize the Climate.* Springer.

Shylaja, H. N. (2020). Financial Inclusion with reference to Access to Banking Services. *International Journal of Scientific and Technology Research, 9*(1), 3749–3755.

Silva, S., Soares, I., & Pinho, C. (2012). *The impact of renewable energy sources on economic growth and CO2 emissions: A SVAR approach.* Academic Press.

Simpson, S. (2021, September 9). *Stress Tolerance & Resiliency: Tough As Titanium.* PAIRIN. Retrieved October 26, 2021, from https://www.pairin.com/stress-tolerance-resiliency-tough-titanium/

Singh, A., & Hess, T. (2020). How chief digital officers promote the digital transformation of their companies. In *Strategic Information Management* (pp. 202–220). Routledge. doi:10.4324/9780429286797-9

Singh, A., & Tandon, P. (2013). Financial Inclusion in India: An Analysis. *International Journal of Marketing. Financial Services and Management Research, 1*(6), 41–54.

Singh, C., Mittal, A., Goenka, A., Goud, C. R. P., Ram, K., Suresh, R. V., Chandrakar, R., Garg, R., & Kumar, U. (2014). Financial Inclusion in India: Select Issues. *IIMB-WP*, (474), 1–43.

Singh, M. (2018). Study of CRISIL-INCLUSIX as an Index of Financial Inclusion. *International Journal of Management Humanities and Social Science, 3*(1), 36–49.

Singh, N., & Sinha, N. (2020). How perceived trust mediates merchant's intention to use a mobile wallet technology. *Journal of Retailing and Consumer Services, 52*, 101894. doi:10.1016/j.jretconser.2019.101894

Singh, S. K., Giudice, M. D., Chierici, R., & Graziano, D. (2020). Green innovation and environmental performance: The role of green transformational leadership and green human resource management. *Technological Forecasting and Social Change, 150*, 119762. doi:10.1016/j.techfore.2019.119762

Singh, S., Sapre, A., & Kewlani, S. (2016). Differential priming of gender and coupling of affect and cognition in anthropomorphic stimulation. *Metamorphosis, 15*(2), 91–101. doi:10.1177/0972622516675949

Sivaramakrishnan, S., Wan, F., & Intera, Z. T. (2007). Giving an "e-human touch" to e-tailing: The moderating roles of static information quantity and consumption motive in the effectiveness of an anthropomorphic information agent. *Journal of Interactive Marketing, 21*(1), 60–75. doi:10.1002/dir.20075

Skordoulis, M., Kyriakopoulos, G., Ntanos, S., Galatsidas, S., Arabatzis, G., Chalikias, M., & Kalantonis, P. (2022). The Mediating Role of Firm Strategy in the Relationship between Green Entrepreneurship, Green Innovation, and Competitive Advantage: The Case of Medium and Large-Sized Firms in Greece. *Sustainability, 14*(6), 3286. doi:10.3390u14063286

Small, K. A., & Verhoef, E. T. (2007). *The economics of urban transportation.* Routledge. doi:10.4324/9780203642306

Small, K. A., Winston, C., & Yan, J. (2006). Differentiated road pricing, express lanes, and carpools: Exploiting heterogeneous preferences in policy design. *Brookings-Wharton Papers for Urban Affairs, 53,* 96.

Smith, E. (2010). Apprenticeships. In P. Peterson, B. McGaw, & E. Baker (Eds.), *International Encyclopedia of Education* (3rd ed., pp. 312–319). Elsevier.

Smith, K. R., Frumkin, H., Balakrishnan, K., Butler, C. D., Chafe, Z. A., Fairlie, I., ... Schneider, M. (2013). Energy and human health. *Annual Review of Public Health, 34.* PMID:23330697

Smith, S., Newhouse, J. P., & Freeland, M. S. (2009). Income, insurance, and technology: Why does health spending outpace economic growth? *Health Affairs, 28*(5), 1276–1284. doi:10.1377/hlthaff.28.5.1276 PMID:19738242

Söderholm, P. (2020). The green economy transition: The challenges of technological change for sustainability. *Sustainable Earth, 3*(1), 1–11.

Song, M., Wang, S., & Zhang, H. (2020). Could environmental regulation and R&D tax incentives affect green product innovation? *Journal of Cleaner Production, 258,* 120849. doi:10.1016/j.jclepro.2020.120849

Song, W., Wang, G. Z., & Ma, X. (2020). Environmental innovation practices and green product innovation performance: A perspective from organizational climate. *Sustainable Development, 28*(1), 224–234. doi:10.1002d.1990

Song, W., & Yu, H. (2018). Green innovation strategy and green innovation: The roles of green creativity and green organizational identity. *Corporate Social Responsibility and Environmental Management, 25*(2), 135–150. doi:10.1002/csr.1445

Soni, S., & Jain, S. (2017). Building anthropomorphic brands: Big success of Chhota Bheem. *FIIB Business Review, 6*(2), 58–66. doi:10.1177/2455265820170209

Soni, V. D. (2020). Information technologies: Shaping the World under the pandemic COVID-19. *Journal of Engineering Sciences, 11*(6).

Soon, C. C., & Salamzadeh, Y. (2021). The Impact of Digital Leadership Competencies on Virtual Team Effectiveness in MNC Companies in Penang, Malaysia. Journal of Entrepreneurship. *Business Economics (Cleveland, Ohio), 8*(2), 219–253.

Souiden, N., Ladhari, R., & Chaouali, W. (2020). Mobile banking adoption: A systematic review. *International Journal of Bank Marketing, 39*(2), 214–241. doi:10.1108/IJBM-04-2020-0182

Sparks, B., & Browning, V. (2011). The impact of online reviews on hotel booking intentions and perception of trust. *Tourism Management, 32*(6), 1310–1323.

Spears, N. E., Mowen, J. C., & Chakraborty, G. (1996). Symbolic role of animals in print advertising: Content analysis and conceptual development. *Journal of Business Research, 37*(2), 87–95. doi:10.1016/0148-2963(96)00060-4

Sridhar, M., & Mehta, A. (2018). The Moderating and Mediating Role of Corporate Reputation in the Link Between Service Innovation and Cross-Buying Intention. *Corporate Reputation Review, 21*(2), 50–70. doi:10.105741299-018-0044-9

Srouji, J. (2020). Digital Payments, Cashless Economy and Financial Inclusion in the United Arab Emirates: Why is everyone still transacting in Cash? *Journal of Risk and Financial Management*, *13*(11), 2–10. doi:10.3390/jrfm13110260

Steinberger, J. K., Roberts, J. T., Peters, G. P., & Baiocchi, G. (2016). Pathways of Human Development and Carbon Emissions Embodied in Trade (2012). *The Globalization and Environment Reader*, 396.

Steinberger, J. K., Lamb, W. F., & Sakai, M. (2020). Your money or your life? The carbon-development paradox. *Environmental Research Letters*, *15*(4), 044016. doi:10.1088/1748-9326/ab7461

Steinberg, M. (2010). A vinyl platform for dissent: Designer toys and character merchandising. *Journal of Visual Culture*, *9*(2), 209–228. doi:10.1177/1470412910372760

Stevens, L., Kearney, M., & Maclaran, P. (2013). Uddering the other: Androcentrism, ecofeminism, and the dark side of anthropomorphic marketing. *Journal of Marketing Management*, *29*(1-2), 158–174. doi:10.1080/0267257X.2013.764348

Stewart, F., & Mok, R. (2022, January 6). Striking the right note: Key performance indicators for sovereign sustainability-linked bonds. *World Bank Blogs*. Retrieved from https://blogs.worldbank.org/psd/striking-right-note-key-performance-indicators-sovereign-sustainability-linked-bonds

Stiftung, B. (2019). *BTI 2018 | United Arab Emirates Country Report, Sustainability*. Available at: https://www.bti-project.org/en/reports/country-reports/detail/itc/ARE/

Stockholm Environment Institute. (2013). *Annual Report 2013*. Stockholm Environment Institute. Available online: https://www.sei.org/wp-content/uploads/2017/12/sei-us-annualreport-2013.pdf

Stopher, P. R. (2004). Reducing road congestion: A reality check. *Transport Policy*, *11*(2), 117–131. doi:10.1016/j.tranpol.2003.09.002

Storti, C. (2011a). Figuring foreigners out: A practical guide. Academic Press.

Storti, C. (2011b). The Art of Crossing Cultures. Academic Press.

Stravinskienė, J., Matulevičienė, M., & Hopenienė, R. (2021). Impact of Corporate Reputation Dimensions on Consumer Trust. *The Engineering Economist*, *32*(2), 177–192. doi:10.5755/j01.ee.32.2.27548

Sudharsanan, N., & Ho, J. Y. (2020). Rural–Urban Differences in Adult Life Expectancy in Indonesia: A Parametric g-formula–based Decomposition Approach. *Epidemiology (Cambridge, Mass.)*, *31*(3), 393–401. doi:10.1097/EDE.0000000000001172 PMID:32267655

Sulich, A., Rutkowska, M., & Poplawski, L. (2020). Green jobs, definitional issues, and the employment of young people: An analysis of three European Union countries. *Journal of Environmental Management*, *262*, 110314. https://doi.org/10.1016/j.jenvman.2020.110314

Sumner Thomas. (2015). *Carbon dioxide levels rise fast and high*. Science News for Students. https://www.sciencenewsforstudents.org/article/carbon-dioxide-levels-rise-fast-and-high

Sun, Y., & Sun, H. (2021). Green innovation strategy and ambidextrous green innovation: The mediating effects of green supply chain integration. *Sustainability*, *13*(9), 4876. doi:10.3390u13094876

SWEROAD. (2001). *Methods and values for appraisal of traffic safety improvements. Traffic safety project*. General Directorate of Highways.

Tabachnick, B. G., & Fidell, L. S. (2013). *Using multivariate statistics* (6th ed.). Pearson/Allyn & Bacon.

Tam, K.-P., Lee, S.-L., & Chao, M. M. (2013). Saving Mr. Nature: Anthropomorphism enhances connectedness to and protectiveness toward nature. *Journal of Experimental Social Psychology, 49*(3), 514–521. doi:10.1016/j.jesp.2013.02.001

Tang, M., Walsh, G., Lerner, D., Fitza, M. A., & Li, Q. (2018). Green innovation, managerial concern and firm performance: An empirical study. *Business Strategy and the Environment, 27*(1), 39–51. doi:10.1002/bse.1981

Tang, R., Tian, L., Thach, T.-Q., Tsui, T. H., Brauer, M., Lee, M., Allen, R., Yuchi, W., Lai, P.-C., Wong, P., & Barratt, B. (2018). Integrating travel behavior with land use regression to estimate dynamic air pollution exposure in Hong Kong. *Environment International, 113*, 100–108. doi:10.1016/j.envint.2018.01.009 PMID:29421398

Taoketao, E., Feng, T., Song, Y., & Nie, Y. (2018). Does sustainability marketing strategy achieve payback profits? A signaling theory perspective. *Corporate Social Responsibility and Environmental Management, 25*(6), 1039–1049. doi:10.1002/csr.1518

Tarhini, A., Alalwan, A. A., Shammout, A. B., & Al-Badi, A. (2019). An analysis of the factors affecting mobile commerce adoption in developing countries. *Review of International Business and Strategy, 29*(3), 157–179. doi:10.1108/RIBS-10-2018-0092

Tarhini, A., El-Masri, M., Ali, M., & Serrano, A. (2016). Extending the UTAUT model to understand the customers' acceptance and use of internet banking in Lebanon. *Information Technology & People, 29*(4), 830–849. doi:10.1108/ITP-02-2014-0034

Tay, B. T.-C., Low, S. C., Ko, K. H., & Park, T. (2016). Types of humor that robots can play. *Computers in Human Behavior, 60*, 19–28. doi:10.1016/j.chb.2016.01.042

Thakur, R., Angriawan, A., & Summey, J. H. (2016). Technological opinion leadership: The role of personal innovativeness, gadget love, and technological innovativeness. *Journal of Business Research, 69*(8), 2764–2773. doi:10.1016/j.jbusres.2015.11.012

The Heritage Foundation. (2020). *United Arab Emirates, economic freedom index 2020.* Available at: https://www.heritage.org/index/country/unitedarabemirates

The World Counts. (2021). *How Does Pollution Affect Humans?* https://www.theworldcounts.com/stories/how-does-pollution-affect-humans

The World-Wide Fund for Nature. (2010). *UAE has the world's largest environmental footprint, The nation.* Available at: https://www.thenational.ae/uae/environment/uae-has-world-s-largest-environmental-footprint-1.525694

Thirlwall, A. P. (1989). *Growth and development: with special reference to developing economies.* Springer. doi:10.1007/978-1-349-19837-5

Thomas, A. & Gupta, V. (2021a). Tacit knowledge in organizations: bibliometrics and a framework-based systematic review of antecedents, outcomes, theories, methods and future directions. *Journal of Knowledge Management.* doi:10.1108/JKM-01-2021-0026

Thomas, A. (2021). Business Beyond COVID-19: Towards Open Innovation. In Globalization, Deglobalization, and New Paradigms in Business (pp. 189-212). Palgrave Macmillan.

Thomas, A., & Chopra, M. (2020). On how big data revolutionizes knowledge management. In *Digital transformation in business and society* (pp. 39–60). Palgrave Macmillan. doi:10.1007/978-3-030-08277-2_3

Thomas, A., Cillo, V., Caggiano, V., & Vrontis, D. (2020). Drivers of social capital in enhancing team knowledge sharing and team performance: Moderator role of manager's cultural intelligence. *International Journal of Managerial and Financial Accounting, 12*(3-4), 284–303. doi:10.1504/IJMFA.2020.112358

Thomas, A., & Gupta, V. (2021b). Social capital theory, social exchange theory, social cognitive theory, financial literacy, and the role of knowledge sharing as a moderator in enhancing financial well-being: From bibliometric analysis to a conceptual framework model. *Frontiers in Psychology*, *12*, 12. doi:10.3389/fpsyg.2021.664638 PMID:34093360

Thomas, A., & Gupta, V. (2022). The role of motivation theories in knowledge sharing: An integrative theoretical reviews and future research agenda. *Kybernetes*, *51*(1), 116–140. doi:10.1108/K-07-2020-0465

Thomas, A., Gupta, V., Riso, T., Briamonte, M. F., Usai, A., & Fiano, F. (2021, November). Enhancing Innovative Behavior at the Workplace: the Moderating Role of Entrepreneurial Orientation and Web 2.0. In *2021 IEEE International Conference on Technology Management, Operations and Decisions (ICTMOD)* (pp. 1-8). IEEE. 10.1109/ICTMOD52902.2021.9739415

Thomas, A., & Paul, J. (2019). Knowledge transfer and innovation through university-industry partnership: An integrated theoretical view. *Knowledge Management Research and Practice*, *17*(4), 436–448. doi:10.1080/14778238.2018.1552485

Thompson, A., Peteraf, M., Gamble, J., Strickland, A. J. III, & Jain, A. K. (2013). *Crafting & executing strategy 19/e: The quest for competitive advantage: Concepts and cases*. McGraw-Hill Education.

Tian, R. G. (2000). The implications of rights to culture in trans-national marketing: An anthropological perspective. *High Plains Applied Anthropologist*, *20*(2), 135–145.

Tol, R. S. J., & Lyons, S. (2008). *Incorporating GHG emission costs in the economic appraisal of projects supported by state development agencies*. Working Paper 247. ESRI.

Tol, R. (2009). The economic effects of climate change. *The Journal of Economic Perspectives*, *23*(2), 29–51. doi:10.1257/jep.23.2.29

Tol, R. S. J. (2005). The marginal damage costs of carbon dioxide emissions: An assessment of the uncertainties. *Energy Policy*, *33*(16), 2064–2074. doi:10.1016/j.enpol.2004.04.002

Tondu, B. (2012). Anthropomorphism and service humanoid robots: An ambiguous relationship. *The Industrial Robot*, *39*(6), 609–618. doi:10.1108/01439911211268840

Torres, C., Canudas-Romo, V., & Oeppen, J. (2019). The contribution of urbanization to changes in life expectancy in Scotland, 1861–1910. *Population Studies*, *73*(3), 387–404. doi:10.1080/00324728.2018.1549746 PMID:30702026

Touré-Tillery, M., & McGill, A. L. (2015). Who or what to believe: Trust and the differential persuasiveness of human and anthropomorphized messengers. *Journal of Marketing*, *79*(4), 94–110. doi:10.1509/jm.12.0166

Tran, X., Nguyen, B., & Nguyen, M. (2015). *Effects of the Big Five Personality Traits on Recreation Types – The Case of Vietnam Tourism*. University of Massachusetts Amherst, Travel of Tourism Research Association: Advancing Tourism Research Globally.

Tran, X. V., & Ralston, L. (2006). Travel Preferences: The Influence of Unconscious Motives. *Annals of Tourism Research*, *33*(2), 424–441. doi:10.1016/j.annals.2005.10.014

Tran, X. V., Tran, H., & Tran, T. (2018). Information Communications Technology (ICT) and Tourism Experience: Can Serotonin become a measurement for tourism experience? *Ereview of Tourism Research*, *9*, 20–24.

Tran, X. V., Williams, J., Carter, K., Joosten, V., & Mitre, B. (2017). Learning Styles, Motivation, and Career Choice: Insights for International Business students from Linguistic Inquiry. *Journal of Teaching in International Business*, *28*(3-4), 142–156.

Tran, X., Dewi, N., Jenkins, Z., Tran, D., & Vo, N. (2016). Applying game theory and time series in Smith Travel Accommodation Resort (STAR). *Advances in Hospitality and Tourism Research, 4*(2), 140–161.

Triantos, A., Plakoyiannaki, E., Outra, E., & Petridis, N. (2016). Anthropomorphic packaging: Is there life on "Mars"? *European Journal of Marketing, 50*(1/2), 260–275. doi:10.1108/EJM-12-2012-0692

Tripathi, S. N., & Reddy, C. S. (2020). IIPA Inputs to the 19th Session of the Committee of Experts on Public Administration (CEPA). *The Indian Journal of Public Administration, 66*(3), 404–417. doi:10.1177/0019556120963319

Trivedi, A. S. (2016). Reality of Financial Inclusion: India. *International Journal of Research and Analytical Reviews, 3*(3), 87–92.

Trivedi, J. (2018). Measuring the comparative efficacy of endorsements by celebrities vis-à-vis animated mascots. *Journal of Creative Communications, 13*(2), 117–132. doi:10.1177/0973258618761407

Tseng, M. L., Wang, R., Chiu, A. S., Geng, Y., & Lin, Y. H. (2013). Improving performance of green innovation practices under uncertainty. *Journal of Cleaner Production, 40*, 71–82. doi:10.1016/j.jclepro.2011.10.009

Tukker, A., & Tischner, U. (2006). Product services as a research field: Past, present and future. Reflections from a decade of research. *Journal of Cleaner Production, 14*(17), 1552–1556. doi:10.1016/j.jclepro.2006.01.022

Tung, F.-W. (2016). Child perception of humanoid robot appearance and behavior. *International Journal of Human-Computer Interaction, 32*(6), 493–502. doi:10.1080/10447318.2016.1172808

Tung, R. L. (2008). The cross-cultural research imperative: The need to balance cross-national and intra-national diversity. *Journal of International Business Studies, 39*(1), 41–46. doi:10.1057/palgrave.jibs.8400331

Turkstat. (2019). *Economic statistics.* https://www.tuik.gov.tr/

TurkStat. (2020). *Road vehicle statistics.* https://www.tuik.gov.tr/

Tuškej, U., & Podnar, K. (2018). Consumers' identification with corporate brands: Brand prestige, anthropomorphism and engagement in social media. *Journal of Product and Brand Management, 27*(1), 3–17. doi:10.1108/JPBM-05-2016-1199

Tuydes Yaman, H., & Dalkıç, G. (2019). Evaluation of the pricing preferences and value of time for High Speed Rail (HSR) users in Turkey. *Journal of the Faculty of Engineering and Architecture of Gazi University, 34*(1), 255–273.

U.S. Travel Association. (2020). Accessed from https://www.ustravel.org

UAE Ministry of Climate Change and Environment (MOCCAE). (2017). *UAE State of Green Economy report 2017.* Author.

UAE Ministry of Environment and Water (MoEW). (2017a). *State of Green Finance in the UAE The first national survey on contributions of financial institutions to Green Economy.* Author.

UAE Ministry of Environment and Water (MoEW). (2017b). *United Arab Emirates State of Green Economy Report.* Author.

Unal, S., Dalgic, T., & Akar, E. (2018). How avatars help enhancing self-image congruence. *International Journal of Internet Marketing and Advertising, 12*(4), 374–395. doi:10.1504/IJIMA.2018.095400

UNCTAD. (2014a). *Trade Remedies Targeting the Renewable Energy Sector.* UNCTAD.

Union of Concerned Scientists. (2017). *Benefits of Renewable Energy Use.* https://www.ucsusa.org/resources/benefits-renewable-energy-use

UNITE. (2003). *Unification of accounts and marginal costs for transport efficiency: Final report for publication.* University of Leeds.

United Nations Framework Convention on Climate Change (UNFCCC). (2021). *The Paris Agreement, What is the Paris Agreement?* Available at: https://unfccc.int/process-and-meetings/the-paris-agreement/the-paris-agreement

United Nations Industrial Development Organization. (2010). A Greener Footprint for Industry: Opportunities and Challenges of Sustainable Industrial Development. Author.

United Nations. (2020). *E-Government Survey 2020. Digital Government in the decade of action for Sustainable Development. With addendum on COVID-19 Response.* Author.

United Nations. (2021, April). *Climate Change, Green Recovery And Trade.* United Nations Conference on Trade and Development.

University of Leeds. (2020, March 26). Longer lives not dependent on increased energy use. *ScienceDaily.* Retrieved May 21, 2021 from www.sciencedaily.com/releases/2020/03/200326193906.htm

Urciuoli, B. (2008). Skills and selves in the new workplace. *American Ethnologist, 35*(2), 211–228.

Ustaoglu, E., & Aydınoglu, A. C. (2019). Regional variations of land-use development and land-use/cover change dynamics: A case study of Turkey. *Remote Sensing, 11*(7), 885. doi:10.3390/rs11070885

Van Eck, N., & Waltman, L. (2010). Software survey: VOSviewer, a computer program for bibliometric mapping. *Scientometrics, 84*(2), 532–538. doi:10.100711192-009-0146-3 PMID:20585380

Van Fan, Y., Perry, S., Klemes, J. J., & Lee, C. T. (2018). A review on air emissions assessment: Transportation. *Journal of Cleaner Production, 194,* 673–684. doi:10.1016/j.jclepro.2018.05.151

Van Hemel, C., & Cramer, J. (2002). Barriers and stimuli for ecodesign in SMEs. *Journal of Cleaner Production, 10*(5), 439–453. doi:10.1016/S0959-6526(02)00013-6

van Pinxteren, M. M.-E., Wetzels, R. W.-H., Rüger, J., Pluymaekers, M., & Wetzels, M. (2019). Trust in humanoid robots: Implications for services marketing. *Journal of Services Marketing, 33*(4), 507–518. doi:10.1108/JSM-01-2018-0045

van Rooij, M. (2019). Carefully constructed yet curiously real: How major American animation studios generate empathy through a shared style of character design. *Animation, 14*(3), 191–206. doi:10.1177/1746847719875071

Van Veldhoven, S., & Schmidt, C. (2021, November 5). How the circular economy can help nations achieve their climate goals. *World Resources Institute.* Retrieved from https://www.wri.org/insights/how-circular-economy-can-help-nations-achieve-their-climate-goals

Vandana, & Kumar, V. (2018). Mom I want it: Impact of anthropomorphism on pester power among children. *International Journal of Business Innovation and Research, 16*(2), 168-185. doi:10.1504/IJBIR.2018.091912

Vasquez, C. (2011). Complaints online: The case of TripAdvisor. *Journal of Pragmatics, Postcolonial Pragmatics, 43*(6), 1707–1717.

Veer, E. (2013). Made with real crocodiles: The use of anthropomorphism to promote product kinship in our youngest consumers. *Journal of Marketing Management, 29*(1-2), 195–206. doi:10.1080/0267257X.2012.759990

Venkatesh, G. (2021). Sustainable Development Goals–Quo Vadis, Cities of the World? *Problemy Ekorozwoju, 16*(1).

Venkatesh, V., Brown, S. A., & Bala, H. (2013). Bridging the Qualitative-Quantitative Divide: Guidelines for Conducting Mixed Methods Research in Information Systems. *Management Information Systems Quarterly, 37*(1), 21–54. doi:10.25300/MISQ/2013/37.1.02

Venkatesh, V., Brown, S. A., Maruping, L. M., & Bala, H. (2008). Predicting Different Conceptualizations of System Use: The Competing Roles of Behavioral Intention, Facilitating Conditions, and Behavioral Expectation. *Management Information Systems Quarterly*, *32*(3), 483–502. doi:10.2307/25148853

Venkatesh, V., Brown, S., & Sullivan, Y. (2016). Guidelines for Conducting Mixed-methods Research: An Extension and Illustration. *Journal of the Association for Information Systems*, *17*(7), 435–494. doi:10.17705/1jais.00433

Venkatesh, V., & Davis, F. D. (2000). A Theoretical Extension of the Technology Acceptance Model: Four Longitudinal Field Studies. *Management Science*, *46*(2), 186–204. doi:10.1287/mnsc.46.2.186.11926

Venkatesh, V., Morris, M. G., Davis, G. B., & Davis, F. D. (2003). User Acceptance of Information Technology: Toward a Unified View. *Management Information Systems Quarterly*, *27*(3), 425–478. doi:10.2307/30036540

Venkatesh, V., Thong, J. Y. L., & Xu, X. (2012). Consumer Acceptance and Use of Information Technology: Extending the Unified Theory of Acceptance and Use of Technology. *MIS Quarter*, *36*(1), 157–178. doi:10.2307/41410412

Venkatesh, V., & Zhang, X. (2010). Unified Theory of Acceptance and Use of Technology: U.S. Vs. China. *Journal of Global Information Technology Management*, *13*(1), 5–27. doi:10.1080/1097198X.2010.10856507

Verganti, R., Vendraminelli, L., & Iansiti, M. (2020). Innovation and design in the age of artificial intelligence. *Journal of Product Innovation Management*, *37*(3), 212–227. doi:10.1111/jpim.12523

Verhoef, E. (1994). External effects and social costs of road transport. *Transportation Research Part A, Policy and Practice*, *28*(4), 273–287. doi:10.1016/0965-8564(94)90003-5

Verma, R., Sah, N. K., Sharma, D. K., & Bisen, P. S. (2017). Journal of Energy, Environment & Carbon Credits. Strategies for Reduction of Carbon Emission in India. *Policy Review*.

Vial, G. (2019). Understanding digital transformation: A review and a research agenda. *The Journal of Strategic Information Systems*, *28*(2), 118–144. doi:10.1016/j.jsis.2019.01.003

Vinyals-Mirabent, S., Kavaratzis, M., & Fernández-Cavia, J. (2019). The role of functional associations in building destination brand personality: When official websites do the talking. *Tourism Management*, *75*, 148–155. doi:10.1016/j.tourman.2019.04.022

Vitaliano, D. F., & Held, J. (1990). Marginal cost road damage user charges. *The Quarterly Review of Economics and Business*, *30*(2), 32.

Wagner, M. (2008). Empirical influence of environmental management on innovation: Evidence from Europe. *Ecological Economics*, *66*(2-3), 392–402. doi:10.1016/j.ecolecon.2007.10.001

Wahl, E. (n.d.). *The Importance of Creativity in the Workplace*. Https://Www.Allbusiness.Com/the-Importance-of-Creativity-in-the-Workplace-24566-1.Html

Wang, B., & Wang, Z. (2018). Imported technology and CO2 emission in China: Collecting evidence through bound testing and VECM approach. *Renewable & Sustainable Energy Reviews*, *82*, 4204–4214. doi:10.1016/j.rser.2017.11.002

Wang, H., Tao, D., Yu, N., & Qu, X. (2020). Understanding consumer acceptance of healthcare wearable devices: An integrated model of UTAUT and TTF. *International Journal of Medical Informatics*, *139*, 104156. doi:10.1016/j.ijmedinf.2020.104156 PMID:32387819

Wang, M., Li, Y., Li, J., & Wang, Z. (2021). Green process innovation, green product innovation and its economic performance improvement paths: A survey and structural model. *Journal of Environmental Management*, *297*, 113282. doi:10.1016/j.jenvman.2021.113282 PMID:34314965

Wang, Z., Asghar, M. M., Zaidi, S. A. H., Nawaz, K., Wang, B., Zhao, W., & Xu, F. (2020). The dynamic relationship between economic growth and life expectancy: Contradictory role of energy consumption and financial development in Pakistan. *Structural Change and Economic Dynamics*, *53*, 257–266. doi:10.1016/j.strueco.2020.03.004

Wang, Z., Asghar, M. M., Zaidi, S. A. H., & Wang, B. (2019). Dynamic linkages among CO2 emissions, health expenditures, and economic growth: Empirical evidence from Pakistan. *Environmental Science and Pollution Research International*, *26*(15), 15285–15299. doi:10.100711356-019-04876-x PMID:30929174

Wang, Z., Zhao, Y., & Wang, B. (2018). A bibliometric analysis of climate change adaptation based on massive research literature data. *Journal of Cleaner Production*, *199*, 1072–1082. doi:10.1016/j.jclepro.2018.06.183

Wardman, M., Chintakayala, P., de Jong, G., & Ferrer, D. (2012). *European wide meta-analysis of values of travel time: Final report to the European Investment Bank*. University of Leeds.

Watson, D. (2019). The rhetoric and reality of anthropomorphism in artificial intelligence. *Minds and Machines*, *29*(3), 417–440. doi:10.100711023-019-09506-6

Waytz, A., Cacioppo, J., & Epley, N. (2010). Who sees human?: The stability and importance of individual differences in anthropomorphism. *Perspectives on Psychological Science*, *5*(3), 219–232. doi:10.1177/1745691610369336 PMID:24839457

WDI. (2021). *World development indicators*. The World Bank. https://databank.worldbank.org/source/world-development-indicators

Weber, J. (2005). Helpless machines and true loving care givers: A feminist critique of recent trends in human-robot interaction. *Journal of Information. Communication and Ethics in Society*, *3*(4), 209–218. doi:10.1108/14779960580000274

WEF. (2022). *More than A Third of the World's Population is Still Offline*. Available at: https://www.weforum.org/videos/more-than-a-third-of-the-world-s-population-is-still-offline

Wei, Z., & Sun, L. (2021). How to leverage manufacturing digitalization for green process innovation: An information processing perspective. *Industrial Management & Data Systems*, *121*(5), 1026–1044. doi:10.1108/IMDS-08-2020-0459

What is Industry 4.0 and how does it work? (n.d.b). Https://Www.Ibm.Com/My-En/Topics/Industry-4-0

Whitehead, R. (2021, April 27). Planned ASEAN taxonomy for sustainable finance would benefit from Islamic input, say international experts. *Salaam Gateway*. Retrieved from https://www.salaamgateway.com/story/planned-asean-taxonomy-for-sustainable-finance-would-benefit-from-islamic-input-say-international-ex

WHO. (1999). *Guidelines for community noise*. WHO.

WHO. (2009). *Night noise guidelines for Europe*. WHO Regional Office for Europe.

Wiafe, I., Koranteng, F. N., Tettey, T., Kastriku, F. A., & Abdulai, J. D. (2019). Factors that affect acceptance and use of information systems within the Maritime industry in developing countries. *Journal of Systems and Information Technology*, *22*(1), 21–45. doi:10.1108/JSIT-06-2018-0091

Wijnen, W., Weijermars, W., & van den Berghe, W. (2017). *Crash cost estimates for European countries: Deliverable 3.2 of the H2020 project SafetyCube*. Loughborough University.

Wilkins, J. (2018, August 15). *How Industry 4.0 Is Improving Peoples' Work-Life Balance*. https://www.impomag.com/home/article/13245182/how-industry-40-is-improving-peoples-worklife-balance

Winter, D. G. (1993). Power, affiliation and war: Three tests of a motivational model. *Journal of Personality and Social Psychology*, *65*, 532–545.

Wirtz, J., Patterson, P. G., Kunz, W. H., Gruber, T., Lu, V. N., Paluch, S., & Martins, A. (2018). Brave new world: Service robots in the frontline. *Journal of Service Management*, *29*(5), 907–931. doi:10.1108/JOSM-04-2018-0119

Wood, M. (2019). The potential for anthropomorphism in communicating science: Inspiration from Japan. *Cultura e Scuola*, *2*(1), 23–34. doi:10.1177/209660831900200103

Woodman, R. W., Sawyer, J. E., & Griffin, R. W. (1993). Toward a theory of organisational creativity. *Academy of Management Review*, *18*(2), 293–321.

World Bank (WB). (2014). *Digital Financial Inclusion*. Retrieved on 25th November, 2021 from: https://www.worldbank.org/en/topic/financialinclusion/publication/digital-financial-inclusion

World Bank Group. (2018). *CO2 emissions (kt), World Bank group*. Available at: https://data.worldbank.org/indicator/EN.ATM.CO2E.KT?locations=AE

World Bank. (2017). *Report of the high-level commission of carbon prices*. The World Bank.

World Bank. (2020). *Pioneering the green sukuk: Three years on. Knowledge & Research The Malaysia Development Experience Series*. International Bank for Reconstruction and Development/The World Bank.

Worldatlas. (2019). *Countries with The Largest Ecological Footprints, world Atlas*. Available at: https://www.worldatlas.com/articles/countries-with-the-largest-ecological-footprints.html

Wu, M., & Salzman, J. (2013). The next generation of trade and environment conflicts: The rise of green industrial policy. *Nw. UL Rev.*, *108*, 401.

Wursthon, S., Poganietz, W., & Schebek, L. (2011). Economic -environmental monitoring indicators for European countries: A disaggregated sector-based approach for monitoring eco-efficiency. *Ecological Economics*, *70*(3), 487–496. doi:10.1016/j.ecolecon.2010.09.033

Xie, X., Hoang, T. T., & Zhu, Q. (2022). Green process innovation and financial performance: The role of green social capital and customers' tacit green needs. *Journal of Innovation & Knowledge*, *7*(1), 100165. doi:10.1016/j.jik.2022.100165

Xie, X., Huo, J., Qi, G., & Zhu, K. X. (2015). Green process innovation and financial performance in emerging economies: Moderating effects of absorptive capacity and green subsidies. *IEEE Transactions on Engineering Management*, *63*(1), 101–112. doi:10.1109/TEM.2015.2507585

Xu, K. (2019). First encounter with robot Alpha: How individual differences interact with vocal and kinetic cues in users' social responses. *New Media & Society*, *21*(11-12), 2522–2547. doi:10.1177/1461444819851479

Xu, T., You, J., Li, H., & Shao, L. (2020). Energy efficiency evaluation based on data envelopment analysis: A literature review. *Energies*, *12*(14), 3548. doi:10.3390/en13143548

Yang, J. Y., & Roh, T. (2019). Open for green innovation: From the perspective of green process and green consumer innovation. *Sustainability*, *11*(12), 3234. doi:10.3390u11123234

Yang, K. C.-C. (2006). The influence of humanlike navigation interface on users' responses to Internet advertising. *Telematics and Informatics*, *23*(1), 38–55. doi:10.1016/j.tele.2005.03.001

Yang, L. W., Aggarwal, P., & McGill, A. L. (2020). The 3 C's of anthropomorphism: Connection, comprehension, and competition. *Counselling Psychology Review*, *3*(1), 3–19. doi:10.1002/arcp.1054

Yang, Y., Liu, Y., Lv, X., Ai, J., & Li, Y. (2021). Anthropomorphism and customers' willingness to use artificial intelligence service agents. *Journal of Hospitality Marketing & Management*. Advance online publication. doi:10.1080/19368623.2021.1926037

Yeow, A., Soh, C., & Hansen, R. (2018). Aligning with new digital strategy: A dynamic capabilities approach. *The Journal of Strategic Information Systems*, *27*(1), 43–58. doi:10.1016/j.jsis.2017.09.001

Yin, J., Gong, L., & Wang, S. (2018). Large-scale assessment of global green innovation research trends from 1981 to 2016: A bibliometric study. *Journal of Cleaner Production*, *197*, 827–841. doi:10.1016/j.jclepro.2018.06.169

Yin, K., Wang, R., An, Q., Yao, L., & Liang, J. (2014). Using eco-efficiency as an indicator for sustainable urban development: A case study of Chinese provincial capital cities. *Ecological Indicators*, *36*, 665–671. doi:10.1016/j.ecolind.2013.09.003

Yin, R. K. (2017). *Case study research and applications: Design and methods* (6th ed.). SAGE Publications, Inc.

Yoon, J., Vonortas, N. S., & Han, S. (2020). Do-It-Yourself laboratories and attitude toward use: The effects of self-efficacy and the perception of security and privacy. *Technological Forecasting and Social Change*, *159*, 120192. doi:10.1016/j.techfore.2020.120192

You, X., & Okunade, A. A. (2017). Income and technology as drivers of Australian healthcare expenditures. *Health Economics*, *26*(7), 853–862. doi:10.1002/hec.3403 PMID:27683015

Yu, C.-E. (2020). Humanlike robots as employees in the hotel industry: Thematic content analysis of online reviews. *Journal of Hospitality Marketing & Management*, *29*(1), 22-38. doi:10.1080/19368623.2019.1592733

Yu, C.-E., & Ngan, H. F. (2019). The power of head tilts: Gender and cultural differences of perceived human vs humanlike robot smile in service. *Tourism Review*, *74*(3), 428–442. doi:10.1108/TR-07-2018-0097

Zaidi, S., & Saidi, K. (2018). Environmental pollution, health expenditure and economic growth in the Sub-Saharan Africa countries: Panel ARDL approach. *Sustainable Cities and Society*, *41*, 833–840. doi:10.1016/j.scs.2018.04.034

Zailani, S., Govindan, K., Iranmanesh, M., Shaharudin, M. R., & Chong, Y. S. (2015). Green innovation adoption in automotive supply chain: The Malaysian case. *Journal of Cleaner Production*, *108*, 1115–1122. doi:10.1016/j.jclepro.2015.06.039

Zakaria, M., & Bibi, S. (2019). Financial development and environment in South Asia: The role of institutional quality. *Environmental Science and Pollution Research International*, *26*(8), 7926–7937. doi:10.100711356-019-04284-1 PMID:30684185

Zaman, M., Botti, L., & Thanh, T. (2016). Does managerial efficiency relate to customer satisfaction? The case of Parisian boutique hotels. *International Journal of Culture, Tourism and Hospitality Research*, *10*(4), 455–470. https://doi.org/10.1108/IJCTHR-08-2015-0095

Zameer, H., Wang, Y., Vasbieva, D. G., & Abbas, Q. (2021). Exploring a pathway to carbon neutrality via reinforcing environmental performance through green process innovation, environmental orientation and green competitive advantage. *Journal of Environmental Management*, *296*, 113383. doi:10.1016/j.jenvman.2021.113383 PMID:34328865

Zannin, P. H. T., Calixto, A., Diniz, F. B., & Ferreira, J. A. C. (2003). A survey of urban noise annoyance in a large Brazilian city: The importance of a subjective analysis in conjunction with an objective analysis. *Environmental Impact Assessment Review*, *23*(2), 245–255. doi:10.1016/S0195-9255(02)00092-6

Zeithaml, V., Bitner, M., & Gremle. (2018). *Services Marketing: Integrating Customer Focus Across the Firm* (7th ed.). McGraw-Hill Education.

Zhang, B., Bi, J., Fan, Z., Yuan, Z., & Ge, J. (2008). Eco-efficiency analysis of industrial system in China: A data envelopment analysis approach. *Ecological Economics*, *68*(1-2), 306–316. doi:10.1016/j.ecolecon.2008.03.009

Zhang, D., Zhang, Z., & Managi, S. (2019). A bibliometric analysis on green finance: Current status, development, and future directions. *Finance Research Letters*, *29*, 425–430. doi:10.1016/j.frl.2019.02.003

Zhang, F., Chen, J., & Zhu, L. (2021). How Does Environmental Dynamism Impact Green Process Innovation? A Supply Chain Cooperation Perspective. *IEEE Transactions on Engineering Management*.

Zhang, Y., Huang, K., Yajuan, Y., & Yang, B. (2017). Mapping of water footprint research: A bibliometric analysis during 2006-2015. *Journal of Cleaner Production*, *149*, 70–79. doi:10.1016/j.jclepro.2017.02.067

Zhang, Z., Cao, T., Shu, J., & Liu, H. (2020). Identifying key factors affecting college students' adoption of the e-learning system in mandatory blended learning environments. *Interactive Learning Environments*, 1–14. doi:10.1080/1049482 0.2020.1723113

Zhao, D., Ye, Q., & Zhu, K. (2016). The influence of consumers' information search behavior on purchase decisions for experience goods: Empirical evidence from hotel industry. *WHICEB 2016 Proceedings*, 297–302.

Zhao, S. (2006). Humanoid social robots as a medium of communication. *New Media & Society*, *8*(3), 401–419. doi:10.1177/1461444806061951

Zha, X. F. (2005). Artificial intelligence and integrated intelligent systems in product design and development. In C. T. Leondes (Ed.), *Intelligent Knowledge-Based Systems* (pp. 1067–1123). Springer. doi:10.1007/978-1-4020-7829-3_32

Zhong, S., Geng, Y., Liu, W., Gao, C., & Chen, W. (2016). A bibliometric review on natural resource accounting during 1995-2014. *Journal of Cleaner Production*, *139*, 122–132. doi:10.1016/j.jclepro.2016.08.039

Zhu, H., Wong, N., & Huang, M. (2019). Does relationship matter? How social distance influences perceptions of responsibility on anthropomorphized environmental objects and conservation intentions. *Journal of Business Research*, *95*, 62–70. doi:10.1016/j.jbusres.2018.10.008

Zhu, Q., Sarkis, J., & Geng, Y. (2005). Green supply chain management in China: Pressures, practices and performance. *International Journal of Operations & Production Management*, *25*(5), 449–468. doi:10.1108/01443570510593148

Zhu, Y., Nel, P., & Bhat, R. (2006). A cross-cultural study of communication strategies for building business relationships. *International Journal of Cross Cultural Management*, *6*(3), 319–341. doi:10.1177/1470595806070638

Zielinska-Chmielewska, A., Olszanska, A., Kazmierczyk, J., & Andrianova, E. (2021). Advantages and constraints of eco-efficiency measures: The case of the Polish food industry. *Agronomy (Basel)*, *11*(2), 299. doi:10.3390/agronomy11020299

About the Contributors

Patricia Ordóñez de Pablos is a professor in the Department of Business Administration in the Faculty of Business and Economics at The University of Oviedo, Spain. She completed her education in The London School of Economics, UK. Her teaching and research interests focus on the areas of strategic management, knowledge management, organizational learning, human resource management, intellectual capital, information technologies, with special interest in Asia (Bhutan, China, Laos, Myanmar). She is Editor-in-Chief of the International Journal of Learning and Intellectual Capital (IJLIC) and International Journal of Asian Business and Information Management (IJABIM), respectively. She has edited books for IGI Global, Routledge, and Springer. In 2021, she earned placement on Stanford University's "Ranking of the World Scientists: World's Top 2% Scientists" list, which can be found here: https://econo.uniovi.es/noticias/-/asset_publisher/XiGH/content/enhorabuena-a-la-profesora-patricia-ordonez-de-pablos;jsessionid=7DECA9C6930CC81559878BD6A43B8483?redirect=%2F.

* * *

Noor Fareen Abdul Rahim is a Senior Lecturer with Graduate School of Business, Universiti Sains Malaysia (USM) since 2017. Before her career in USM, she was a banker with RHB Bank Berhad for 16 years before joining Universiti Utara Malaysia from 2015 to 2016. She has published her work in various SCOPUS and ISI journals. Her area of interest includes Organisational Behavior, Human Resource Management, Occupational Safety and Health, Internal Control System, Enterprise Risk Management, Operational Risk Management, and Technology Management. She is also involved with Executive Development Programs as a facilitator for government and private institution.

Shaikha Al-Fulaij holds B.Sc. degree in computer engineering from Kuwait University in the year 1992 with First Class Honor. Area of specialization and interest includes database management, object-oriented design, and software development. Joined KISR in January 1992 and participated in numerous projects in the area of data analysis and modeling, and in the area of Information Technology.

Subhanil Banerjee is a doctorate in Economics. His research interest areas include Econometrics, Indian Economics, Digitalization, and Entrepreneurship.

Mohamed Bouteraa currently is a PhD Researcher at the Islamic Business School (IBS), Universiti Utara Malaysia (UUM). Bouteraa does research in Green Banking, Business Sustainability, Islamic banking, Islamic finance, consumer behaviour.

Maria Teresa D'Agostino is a Junior Research Fellow at Department of Economics and Law, University of Cassino and Southern Lazio. Her research fields include knowledge management, sustainability, and circular economy. She regularly attends seminars and conferences on these issues.

Megersa Olumana Dinka is a graduate with PhD from University of Natural Resources and Applied Life Science (Vienna) in 2010. He has expert knowledge in water resource engineering discipline specific to hydrology, hydraulics and water management. He has about 16 years of experience as academician and 20 years of experience as a researcher. He has taught various courses and modules at undergraduate and postgraduate levels successfully. Most of the courses he taught are related to hydrology, hydraulics and watershed (water) management aspects. Currently he is teaching Hydrology, Hydraulics and Water Treatment Technology Modules at University of Johannesburg. Moreover, he also supervised a number of postgraduate students (28 MSc and 4 PhD) successfully and still supervising a number of undergraduate and postgraduate students at University of Johannesburg. He has published a number of peer reviewed scientific articles (>50) and book chapters in accredited international journals and book publishers. He has reviewed a number of articles for various international journals.

Adem Gök is currently employed in Department of Economics at Kırklareli University, Turkey as an associate professor. He received his bachelor degree in economics from Boğaziçi University in 2008 and master degree in economics (English) from Marmara University in 2012. He holds a Ph.D in economics (English) from Marmara University since 2016. His research area includes foreign direct investment, economics of governance, environmental economics, economics of education and financial economics.

Shilpi Gupta is an ICWA and MBA (Finance). Her research interests areas include Behavioral finance, Entrepreneurship, Digitalization and stock market behavior.

Raja Rizal Iskandar bin Raja Hisham is currently a Senior Lecturer at Othman Yeop Abdullah Graduate School of Business (OYAGSB), Universiti Utara Malaysia (UUM). He successfully completed his doctorate of philosophy study from Universiti Kebangsaan Malaysia (UKM) in 2017. His PhD thesis title is "Kepimpinan dan Tadbir Urus Pengendali Takaful di Malaysia". His thesis awarded as "Anugerah Tesis Cemerlang" by UKM. He obtained Master of Business Administration (MBA), specializing in Islamic Banking and Finance from UKM in 2011 while his first degree is Bachelor of Business Administration (BBA) in Finance (Hons.) from UiTM in 2007. Presently, Dr. Raja Rizal Iskandar is appointed as a Research Fellow of Institute of Shariah Governance & Islamic Finance (ISGaIF) and as an Associate Research Fellow of Institute of Sustainable Growth & Urban Development (ISGUD). Professionally, Dr. Raja Rizal Iskandar is a qualified Islamic Financial Planning (IFP) trainer and Certified Qualification of Islamic Finance (Wealth Management) by Financial Planning of Association Malaysia (FPAM) since 2020. In addition, he is also a Certified Innermetrix Consultant (CIC) specializing in psychometric assessments. He actively involved in consultancy works such as providing academic workshops i.e. data analysis, research etc. as well as being a resource person for statistical data analysis for postgraduate students. He was appointed as the Panel of Evaluators for Undergraduate Research for Management & Science University (MSU) consecutively in 2017 and 2018.

Sivasubramanian K. has completed Ph.D. He has published more than 30 research papers in national and international journals. He received two best paper awards. He is also reviewer for various international Scopus-indexed journals.

Namita Kapoor has over 22 years of experience in academia teaching and policy research . Her area of interest includes Sustainability and Market Research. She has published various research papers in international journals of high repute. She has also conducted training , workshops and FDPs on Research Methodology, Long Run Capital Budgeting and Data Analysis using MS excel and SPSS. She is reviewer of prestigious journals indexed in Scopus, Web of Science and listed in ABDC.

Nirmala M. M. is currently working as Assistant Professor in Kristu Jayanti College, Bangalore. She is pursing Ph.D on food security. Her area of interest is on international trade and development. She has published research papers in various national and international journals.

Khairunnisa Musari is an Assistant Professor at the Department of Islamic Economics, Postgraduate Program and the Faculty of Islamic Economics and Business, Kiai Haji Achmad Siddiq State Islamic University (UIN KHAS), Jember, Indonesia. She is a member of the Indonesian Association of Islamic Economist (IAEI). She has experience as a Senior Specialist for Islamic Finance of United Nations Development Programme (UNDP) Indonesia. She was listed as the Top 150 Most Influential Women in Islamic Business & Finance 2020 and Top 50 Most Influential Women in Islamic Business & Finance 2021 by Cambridge-IFA. She has a great interest in sukuk, waqf, esham, fiscal & monetary policies, circular economy, halal logistics, and Islamic microfinance and nanofinance.

Chiara Nespoli is a Research Fellow at the University of Bologna "Alma Mater Studiorum". She pursued her Ph.D. at the "Seconda Università degli Studi di Napoli", investigating on the importance of the emotional ownership for enterprises' economic success. Her research interests are focused on, but not limited to, Knowledge Management concerning the rising phenomenon of Cooperate Universities, and Innovation and Knowledge for encouraging enterprise competitiveness.

Bình Nghiêm-Phú is an Associate Professor at the School of Economics and Management, University of Hyōgo, Japan. The majority of his research aims at understanding consumers' perceptions and evaluations of the characteristics and images of products, services, organizations, and places. He adopts the approaches of applied psychology theories to the implementation of marketing and management activities.

Joan Nyika is a PhD graduate of the University of South Africa in 2021. She specializes in hydro-biogeochemistry and has more than 7 years of teaching and research in the university. She is currently serving as a post doctoral research fellow at the University of Johannesburg, South Africa and a lecturer at the Technical University of Kenya in Nairobi, Kenya. She is involved in teaching and supervision of undergraduate and postgraduate students and has published and reviewed several article journals and book chapters that are internationally accredited.

Rosa Palladino is a Research fellow at Department of Economics, Quantitative Methods and Business Strategies, at University of Milan Bicocca. She obtained her Ph.D. in Law and socio-economic institutions: normative, organizational and historical-evolutionary profiles at Parthenope University. Her research fields include Knowledge management, Innovation and Technology Management, Corporate Governance, Non-financial Information, Sustainable Accounting and Reporting. She regularly attends seminars and conferences on these issues. Her research has been published in international books and journals (e.g., Journal of Business Research (3*), Technological Forecasting and Social Change (3*), International Marketing Review (3*), Journal of Intellectual Capital (2*), Journal of Cleaner Production (2*), Meditari Accountancy Research (1*) and Sustainability). She is a reviewer for Journal of Business Research (Elsevier), Journal of Knowledge Management (Emerald), Journal of Intellectual Capital (Emerald), Sustainability and "Environment, Development, and Sustainability (ENVI)" edited by Springer. Recently, she attended to IAME Conference on the digitalization issues in the ports and shipping industry in Hong Kong (Asia) and to IEEE International Conference on "Technology Management, Operations and Decisions. Disruptive Technologies and Social Impacts" in Marrakech, Morocco (Africa).

Chandra Sekhar Patro is currently serving as Assistant Professor at Gayatri Vidya Parishad College of Engineering (Autonomous), Visakhapatnam, India. He has PhD in Faculty of Commerce and Management Studies from Andhra University, India. He has a post-graduate degree in Management (MBA) from JNT University, Commerce (M.Com.) from Andhra University, and Financial Management (MFM) from Pondicherry University. Dr. Patro has more than 12 years of experience in teaching and research in the area of Commerce and Management Studies. His teaching interests include marketing management, financial management, and human resource management. His research interests include marketing especially e-marketing, consumer behavior and HR management. Dr. Patro has published articles and chapters in reputed national and international journals. He has participated and presented various papers in national, international seminars and conferences. He has been associated with various social bodies as a member and life member of these associations.

Giuseppe Russo, Ph.D., is currently Associate Professor of Business Management at the Department of Economics and Law at the University of Cassino and Southern Lazio, where he teaches Public Management, Strategic Management and Innovation Management. He is coordinator of several Masters and President of the Master's Degree Course in Economics and Business Law. He earned the Italian National qualification as Full Professor in 2018. He was Visiting Professor at the Masaryk University of Brno (Czech Republic), Autonomous University of Madrid (Spain), University of Zaragoza (Spain) and Polytechnic Institute of Setubal (Portugal). He is scientific director and member of several research projects funded by the Italian Ministry of Economic Development and author of four books and of more than one hundred papers and book chapters in the research areas of business management, knowledge economy, intellectual capital, planning and control. He won the "2019 Emerald highly commended award for Excellence in research" and the "Administrative Sciences 2021 Best Paper Award". He is engaged as editorial board member for the Journal of Risk and Financial Management, International Business Research, and Journal Business and Management Horizons.

Yashar Salamzadeh is a PhD scholar in Human Resources Management and currently works as a lecturer in digital business at University of Sunderland, school of business and management. He previously has worked as a Senior Lecturer in Graduate School of Business at Universiti Sains Malaysia, the head of "global strategy and OB" research cluster and the head of micro-credential program. He had published more than 100 research articles in international and national journals and conferences. He has the experience of twelve years teaching in MBA and Master of management courses in five different universities in middle east, south-east Asia and Europe. He has supervised more than 70 MBA and master students and currently supervising 10 PhD/DBA students. He has led the lunch of a new specialization for MBA courses at GSB, USM on "Digital Leadership". He has worked as a project management in more than ten national and international research projects. He has the experience of six years management consultancy for different organizations in Iran and Malaysia. He also has cooperated in more than 25 international journals as an editorial board member and review board member. His fields of interest include Entrepreneurship, Entrepreneurial Universities, Leadership and Digital Leadership, Digital HRM, Digital transformation, Business Models, Strategic Management, Green Business and CSR, HRM (HCM) and Networked Organizations.

Nausheen Sodhi is a Senior Research Fellow, pursuing her Ph.D. at Panjab University, India and has over 7 years of experience in research and teaching. She is researching on the economic impact of governance in Indian states by constructing a comprehensive index of governance performance using 75 variables identified under various dimensions of good governance. Her areas of research include good governance and public policy, environmental governance, institutional economics and development economics.

Jillian Rae Suter is currently an Assistant Professor at the Faculty of Informatics, Shizuoka University, Japan. Her research is directed by the social marketing theories. She is implementing research on consumer culture, notably the impact of the rise and fall in popularity of "Cool Japan" on both the national economy and society, and the global market.

Asha Thomas is an Assistant Professor at Wroclaw University of Science and Technology (WUST), Poland. Her PhD is in knowledge management. Her areas of research interest include knowledge management, open innovation, big data, grass-root innovation, and SMEs. She has about 12 years of experience in teaching and over three years of experience in the IT and Telecom industries. She has several research papers published in top journals, including the 'Tourism Management Perspectives, 'Journal of Knowledge Management',' Knowledge Management Research and Practices', 'Frontiers in Psychology',' Sustainability', Kybernetes'. She has published 15 books at a national level and book chapters with publishers like 'Palgrave Macmillan', 'Springer'. She is a reviewer of many leading journals. She has also contributed a policy draft in G20 (T20) summit 2021 which was held in Rome, Italy.

Zairani Zainol is currently a Senior Lecturer at the College of Business, Universiti Utara Malaysia. She obtained her Ph.D(Islamic Banking) from the University of Edinburgh, Scotland in 2007. Prior to that, she graduated with a Master of Business Administration (MBA) in 1999 and a Bachelor in Business Administration (BBA (Hons)) in 1992 from the Universiti Utara Malaysia (UUM). She also holds a Diploma in Business Studies (1989) from the Universiti Teknologi Mara (UiTM). She has six years (1992-1998) working experience in Bank Islam (M) Berhad (BIMB). She started her career with BIMB in 1992 as an officer class one and her last post was assistant branch manager before she left the bank in 1998 to join UUM as a tutor. She is also involved in research, consultancy and academic textbooks writing, funded either by UUM, Ministry of Higher Education (MOHE) or other institutions, such as International Shariah Research Academy for Islamic Finance (ISRA), Open Universiti of Malaysia (OUM) She has written numerous articles in Islamic finance and banking and her works have been published in International journals and proceedings. In her teaching tasks, she has taught several subjects in the area of finance, banking and Islamic finance and banking at undergraduate and postgraduate levels. She also a panel of Auditor for Malaysian Qualification Assurance (MQA) in the area of Islamic Banking and Finance.

Index

55-60, 65-68, 74, 87, 89, 96-98, 101, 106, 121-123, 125-127, 129-131, 138-139, 144-145, 152-153, 155-156, 159-160, 166, 169, 171, 175, 186, 188, 190, 192-193, 209, 215, 226, 228, 232-233, 243, 250-252, 256, 259, 274-278, 280-283, 287, 289, 297-300, 302-304, 307-309, 315, 319, 321, 323

F

Facilitating Conditions 68, 77, 92, 98, 101
Future of Jobs 306, 313

G

GB Technology Services 67, 73-76, 78, 80, 87-88, 101-102
Globalization 3-4, 6, 55, 61, 121-125, 127, 129, 135, 140, 155, 228
Government Support 64, 72, 74, 79-80, 83-84, 86-87, 97, 101
Green Banking 64-65, 67, 90, 93-97, 100
Green Cwls 220, 222
Green Economy 12-13, 24-25, 41, 91, 98, 229, 308, 320, 322
Green Esham 210, 222
Green Innovation 43-45, 57-58, 60-62
Green Jobs 306, 308-309, 320, 322
Green Process Innovation 43-45, 52, 56, 59, 61-63
Green Product Innovation 43-44, 50, 56-61
Green Sukuk 210, 218, 220, 222, 224-225, 228-229
Green Technology 2, 6, 64-65
Growth 1-6, 9-12, 41, 52, 57, 65, 88, 94, 104-105, 110, 112, 117-119, 122, 142-143, 145, 152-156, 159, 161-162, 165, 169, 171-173, 177-178, 186, 192, 201, 203, 209, 213-216, 219, 222, 225, 227-228, 235, 240, 242, 245-248, 251-252, 266, 297-298, 301-303, 305, 308, 312, 322

H

HDVs 254, 257-258, 268-271, 274-275

I

Inclusix 231, 233-235, 242, 244-246
Indicator-Based Assessment 195, 209
Industry 1-3, 5, 7, 9-12, 33, 37, 40, 51, 57, 59-60, 65, 68, 72-73, 87, 92-93, 99-100, 104-105, 111, 117, 138, 170, 190-191, 202, 205, 210, 212, 223-224, 226, 247, 253, 260, 285, 292-294, 296, 301, 306-309, 312, 314, 317-323

Innovation 36, 39, 43-45, 50-63, 74, 76-79, 88, 94, 96-97, 103, 106, 110-112, 115-117, 119, 132, 137, 145, 153, 170, 188, 205, 214, 220, 223-226, 228, 280, 285, 293
Intention to Adopt GB Technology Services 73, 75-76, 80, 101
Internet Connectivity 231
IR4.0 306, 318
Islamic Finance 210, 212, 219-220, 224-229

J

Joint-Venture 210, 220-221, 223
Journal 10-12, 16-17, 25-41, 45, 47-48, 56-62, 89-100, 118-120, 136-139, 153-156, 161, 170-171, 173, 175-176, 179-180, 188-191, 209, 225-229, 247-248, 276-283, 294-296, 304, 319-322

L

LCVs 249, 257-258, 268-271, 275
Life Expectancy 141-156
Location 133, 135, 166, 254-255, 273, 276, 285-289, 291-292

M

Marginal External Costs 249, 252, 260, 267, 273-274, 280, 282
Marketing 12-18, 21, 23-42, 60, 68, 88, 90, 92-97, 100, 116, 122, 124, 129-130, 134, 137-139, 248, 278, 286, 289, 294-296
Mixed Methods 64, 69, 91, 98
Motorcycles 249, 254, 257-258, 268-271, 275

N

Nazhir 222, 230
Noise 249-254, 261-264, 267, 271, 274, 276-280, 283-284

O

Organizational Culture 121, 140
Organizations 43, 50-56, 61, 104, 121-125, 128-132, 134-138, 172-173, 187, 202, 295
Our Common Future 297-298, 302-304

P

Panel VAR 141, 146-148, 150, 154

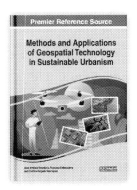
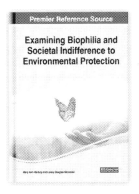

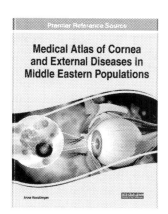

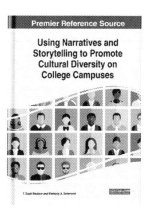

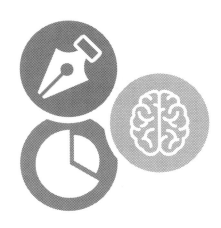

 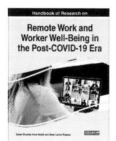 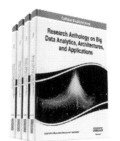 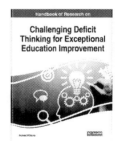

Printed in the United States
by Baker & Taylor Publisher Services